Lecture Notes in Artificial Intelligence 13250

Subseries of Lecture Notes in Computer Science

Series Editors

Randy Goebel
University of Alberta, Edmonton, Canada

Wolfgang Wahlster
DFKI, Berlin, Germany

Zhi-Hua Zhou
Nanjing University, Nanjing, China

Founding Editor

Jörg Siekmann
DFKI and Saarland University, Saarbrücken, Germany

More information about this subseries at https://link.springer.com/bookseries/1244

Minghui Dong · Yanhui Gu · Jia-Fei Hong (Eds.)

Chinese Lexical Semantics

22nd Workshop, CLSW 2021
Nanjing, China, May 15–16, 2021
Revised Selected Papers, Part II

 Springer

Editors
Minghui Dong (iD)
Institute for Infocomm Research
Singapore, Singapore

Yanhui Gu
Nanjing Normal University
Nanjing, China

Jia-Fei Hong
National Taiwan Normal University
Taipei, Taiwan

ISSN 0302-9743   ISSN 1611-3349 (electronic)
Lecture Notes in Artificial Intelligence
ISBN 978-3-031-06546-0   ISBN 978-3-031-06547-7 (eBook)
https://doi.org/10.1007/978-3-031-06547-7

LNCS Sublibrary: SL7 – Artificial Intelligence

This Springer imprint is published by the registered company Springer Nature Switzerland AG
The registered company address is: Gewerbestrasse 11, 6330 Cham, Switzerland

Preface

The 2021 Chinese Lexical Semantics Workshop (CLSW 2021) was the 22nd event since the establishment of this series in 2000. CLSW has been held in different Asian cities including Beijing, Hong Kong, Taipei, Singapore, Xiamen, Hsin Chu, Yantai, Suzhou, Wuhan, Zhengzhou, Macao, Leshan, and Chia-Yi. Over the years, CLSW has become one of the most important venues for scholars to report and discuss the latest progress in Chinese lexical semantics and related fields, including theoretical linguistics, applied linguistics, computational linguistics, information processing, and computational lexicography. CLSW has significantly impacted and promoted academic research and application development in the related fields.

CLSW 2021 was hosted by Nanjing Normal University, China. This year, 261 papers were submitted to the workshop, setting the highest record ever. All submissions went through a double-blind review process, with at least two independent reviewers assigned to each paper. Of all the paper submissions, 91 (34.8%) were accepted as oral presentations and 85 (32.6%) as poster presentations. Among the accepted papers, the top-rated English papers were further selected to be included in the proceedings. They are organized in topical sections covering all major topics of lexical semantics, semantic resources, corpus linguistics, and natural language processing. We are pleased that these shortlisted papers are published by Springer as part of their Lecture Notes in Artificial Intelligence (LNAI) series and are to be submitted for indexing by Ei and Scopus.

The Organizing Committee would like to express our gratitude to the conference chairs: Ting Liu (Harbin University of Technology) and Jie Xu (Macao University), the honorary members of the Advisory Committee: Shiwen Yu (Peking University), Chin-Chuan Cheng (University of Illinois), Chu-Ren Huang (Hong Kong Polytechnic University), and Xinchun Su (Xiamen University), and the other members of the Advisory Committee for their guidance in promoting and running the workshop. We sincerely appreciate the invited speakers for their outstanding keynote talks: Yiming Yang (Jiangsu Normal University), Chu-Ren Huang (Hong Kong Polytechnic University), Qun Liu (Huawei Noah's Ark Lab), and Ge Xu (Minjiang University). Also, we would like to acknowledge the members of the Organizing Committee, Nanjing Normal University, and the student volunteers for their tremendous contribution to this event.

Our gratitude also goes to the Program Committee members and reviewers for their time and efforts in the paper review work. Last but not least, we thank all the authors and attendees for their scientific contribution and participation, which made CLSW 2021 a great success.

April 2022

Weiguang Qu
Minghui Dong
Jia-Fei Hong
Yanhui Gu

Organization

Conference Chairs

Jie Xu   University of Macau, Macao SAR, China
Ting Liu   Harbin Institute of Technology, China

Academic Committee Chairs

Shiwen Yu   Peking University, China
Chin-Chuan Cheng   Taiwan Normal University, Taiwan
Ka Yin Benjamin T'sou   The Education University of Hong Kong,
                                 Hong Kong SAR, China

Academic Committee

Yanbin Diao   Beijing Normal University, China
Jia-Fei Hong   Taiwan Normal University, Taiwan
Chu-Ren Huang   The Hong Kong Polytechnic University,
                                 Hong Kong SAR, China
Donghong Ji   Wuhan University, China
Peng Jin   Leshan Normal University, China
Zhuo Jing-Schmidt   University of Oregon, USA
Kim Teng Lua   Chinese and Oriental Languages Information
                                 Processing Society, Singapore
Meichun Liu   City University of Hong Kong, Hong Kong SAR,
                                 China
Qin Lu   The Hong Kong Polytechnic University,
                                 Hong Kong SAR, China
Xinchun Su   Xiamen University, China
Zhifang Sui   Peking University, China
Shu-Kai Hsieh   Taiwan University, Taiwan
Jie Xu   University of Macau, Macao SAR, China
Hongying Zan   Zhengzhou University, China
Yangsen Zhang   Beijing Information Science and Technology
                                 University, China
Sung Lin Chen   Cheng Kung University, Taiwan

Program Committee Chairs

Minghui Dong	Agency for Science, Technology and Research, Singapore
Jia-Fei Hong	Taiwan Normal University, Taiwan
Yanhui Gu	Nanjing Normal University, China

Program Committee

Kathleen Ahrens	The Hong Kong Polytechnic University, Hong Kong SAR, China
Xiaojing Bai	Tsinghua University, China
Dabhur Bayar	Inner Mongolia University, China
Shu Cai	Google, USA
Cairangjia	Qinghai Normal University, China
Siaw Fong Chung	Chengchi University, Taiwan
Ren-Feng Duann	Taitung University, Taiwan
Minxuan Feng	Nanjing Normal University, China
Wenhe Feng	Wuhan University, China
Helena Gao	Nanyang Technological University, Singapore
Shu-Ping Gong	Chiayi University, Taiwan
Shulun Guo	Shanghai Jiao Tong University, China
Chunjie Guo	Nanjing University of Aeronautics and Astronautics, China
Yingjie Han	Zhengzhou University, China
Lin He	Wuhan University, China
Chan-Chia Hsu	Taipei University of Business, Taiwan
Yuxiang Jia	Zhengzhou University, China
Yuru Jiang	Beijing Information and Science Technology University, China
Shengyi Jiang	Guangdong University of Foreign Studies, China
Peng Jin	Leshan Normal University, China
Yonghong Ke	Beijing Normal University, China
Huei-Ling Lai	Chengchi University, Taiwan
Lung-Hao Lee	Central University, Taiwan
Baoli Li	Bozhi Technology, China
Bin Li	Nanjing Normal University, China
Chihkai Lin	Tatung University, Taiwan
Jingxia Lin	Nanyang Technological University, Singapore
Maofu Liu	Wuhan University of Science and Technology, China
Yao Liu	Institute of Scientific and Technical Information of China, China

Pengyuan Liu	Beijing Language and Culture University, China
Meichun Liu	City University of Hong Kong, Hong Kong SAR, China
Zhifu Liu	China Three Gorges University, China
Donghong Liu	Central China Normal University, China
Yunfei Long	University of Nottingham, UK
Chiarung Lu	Taiwan Normal University, Taiwan
Wei-Yun Ma	Columbia University, USA
Mengxiang Wang	Beijing Union University, China
Lingling Mu	Zhengzhou University, China
Weiming Peng	Beijing Normal University, China
Likun Qiu	Alibaba, China
Weiguang Qu	Nanjing Normal University, China
Gaoqi Rao	Beijing Language and Culture University, China
Yanqiu Shao	Beijing Language and Culture University, China
Yangyang Shi	Meta, USA
Jihua Song	Beijing Normal University, China
Chunyang Song	Shanghai Jiao Tong University, China
Zuoyan Song	Peking University, China
Qi Su	Peking University, China
Xuri Tang	Huazhong University of Science and Technology, China
I-Ni Tsai	Taiwan University, Taiwan
Jin Wang	Yunnan University, China
Shan Wang	University of Macau, Macao SAR, China
Meng Wang	Jiangnan University, China
Lei Wang	Peking University, China
Yunwang Wu	Peking University, China
Jiun-Shiung Wu	Chung Cheng University, Taiwan
Hongbing Xing	Beijing Language and Culture University, China
Jiajuan Xiong	The University of Hong Kong, Hong Kong SAR, China
Jie Xu	University of Macau, Macao SAR, China
Dengfeng Yao	Beijing Union University, China
Shuangyun Yao	Huazhong Normal University, China
Dong Yu	Beijing Language and Culture University, China
Hongying Zan	Zhengzhou University, China
Weidong Zhan	Peking University, China
Junping Zhang	Beijing Language and Culture University, China
Keliang Zhang	Information Engineering University, Luoyang, China
Lei Zhang	Northeast Normal University, China

Kunli Zhang	Zhengzhou University, China
Qingqing Zhao	Institute of Linguistics, Chinese Academy of Social Sciences, China
Zezhi Zheng	Xiamen University, China
Hua Zhong	Fujian Normal University, China
Yu-Yun Chang	Chengchi University, Taiwan
Zhimin Wang	Beijing Language and Culture University, China
Shih-Wen Chyu	Taiwan Normal University, Taiwan

Organizing Committee Chairs

Weiguang Qu	Nanjing Normal University, China
Junsheng Zhou	Nanjing Normal University, China
Shehui Liang	Nanjing Normal University, China
Dongbo Wang	Nanjing Agricultural University, China
Bin Li	Nanjing Normal University, China
Minxuan Feng	Nanjing Normal University, China

Publication Committee Chairs

Qi Su	Peking University, China
Pengyuan Liu	Beijing Language and Culture University, China
Xuri Tang	Huazhong University of Science and Technology, China

Contents – Part II

Contents – Part I

Natural Language Processing and Language Computing

Cognitive Science and Experimental Studies

Human Body Metaphor in News Headlines

Bingbing Yang and Zhimin Wang[✉]

Research Institute of International Chinese Language Education,
Beijing Language and Culture University, Beijing, China
wangzm000@qq.com

Abstract. This paper extracts the human body metaphors from 38,458 news headlines and makes a statistical analysis of the classification. Our exploration shows that the frequency of metaphors in each part is affected by its functional characteristics and movement flexibility. Metaphors with "eyes, lower limbs, hands" as the source domain occupy a large proportion. Meanwhile, the typical features and actions of the body parts are mapped to the target domain of news headlines through metaphor. In addition, many metaphors in news headlines have a positive or negative emotional tendency, which can reflect the attitude of news content to a certain extent.

Keywords: Human body metaphor · News headline · Distribution characteristics · Cognitive subject

1 Introduction

Metaphors exist widely in our language. Metaphor is not only a rhetorical device but also a way of thinking. News headlines frequently use short and profound language to attract readers' interest. A lot of metaphors are contained in news headlines in order to obtain a communication effect. For instance:

(1) Zhèngfǔ wǎngzhàn dà shòushēn, fúwù zěnyàng bù suōshuǐ.
    government website big slimming, services how not shrink.
    How does the government website slimming and its services will not shrink.
(2) Jǐngtì huì biànliǎn de jīnróng fúwù fèi.
    alert can change face Prc[1] financial service fee
    Be wary of 'financial services fees' that will 'change faces'.
(3) Pǔxiě gāo zhìliàng fāzhǎn piānzhāng, yōngbào xīn shídài de chūntiān.
    compose high quality develop chapter embrace new era Prc spring

Compose a chapter of high-quality development and embrace the spring of a new era.

---

[1] The abbreviations used in this paper include: Prc for a sentence-final particle, F for the frequency of each entry.

© Springer Nature Switzerland AG 2022
M. Dong et al. (Eds.): CLSW 2021, LNAI 13250, pp. 3–17, 2022.
https://doi.org/10.1007/978-3-031-06547-7_1

In (1), 'shòushēn (slimming)' taking the human body as the source domain, metaphorically reduces the layout of government websites. Face-changing was originally a performance skill of Sichuan Opera, the source domain is the 'face' in (2), the metaphor of 'financial services fees' is inconsistent with the original, 'biànliǎn (face changing)' adds negative emotional meaning. In (3), 'pǔxiě (compose)' and 'yōngbào (embrace)' are hand movements, which imply positive emotions.

News headlines exert the first visual impact on the readers, and it plays a vital role in the spread of the article. There are many metaphorical phenomena with the human body as the source domain in news headlines. 'Nearly taken from the body, far from the objects' is a primitive thinking feature of mankind. The typical thinking characteristic of early humans was to take people themselves as the standard for measuring things around them. Abstract projection from the body as the origin domain produces a large number of metaphorical phenomena.

As for metaphor, there are in-depth studies in relative research [1–4]. The research on the human body metaphor mainly focuses on the comparative analysis of Chinese and other foreign languages [5–7], as well as the metaphor of a certain body part [8–10]. Metaphors widely exist in news headlines. Metaphors can accelerate the interpretation of news headlines, effectively convey information and help us simplify the cognitive process [11–13]. Unfortunately, the current research on human body metaphors is lacking in news headlines. This paper extracts the news headlines of *People's Daily*. We provide quantitative data through the classified analysis of the human body metaphor. Moreover, this paper explores the characteristics of news headlines and probe into the deep cognitive reasons of metaphor. The results indicated that it can help Chinese learners to understand Chinese news better.

The layout of this paper is as follows. In Sect. 2 we present human body metaphors under the perspective of metaphorical inheritance. The distribution of metaphors in various parts of the human body is analyzed in Sect. 3; Sect. 4 summarizes the metaphorical of different body parts. The cognitive analysis of human metaphor is explained in Sect. 5; Sect. 6 investigates the emotional embodiment of metaphor in news. Finally, the conclusion of this paper and the future improvements will be discussed in Sect. 7.

2   Human Body Metaphor from the Perspective of Metaphorical Inheritance

News headlines are the concentration of news content, which usually utilize easy-to-understand and attractive expressions. Many complex and abstract things would be replaced by metaphors when it is difficult to describe clearly. Hence, familiar and vivid things can be used as metaphors, which are indicated as the source domain. Metaphorical expressions frequently appear in news headlines.

Each part of the human body has the most typical and vivid characteristics. Using various parts of the body as source domains is also the earliest way for people to recognize the world. The human body is often used as the source domain of metaphorical projection.

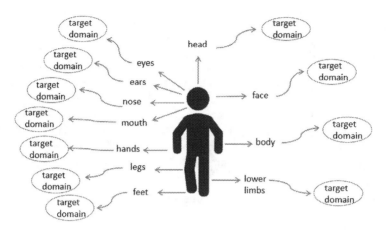

Fig. 1. Metaphorical mapping of various parts of the human body.

As shown in Fig. 1, each part of the body is mapped to different target domains when projecting metaphorical mapping. A metaphorical mapping network is formed from this, which takes each part of the human body as the source domain and mapped to the target domain in a wider field. Due to the different activities undertaken by each part and the distinct degree of features, the metaphorical mapping ability of each part is unequal. For example, the eyes are the windows for people to recognize the world and the most active parts of the face. Therefore, there are rich metaphors with eyes as the source domain. The eyes are often mapped to target domains such as cognitive ability through metaphors. The activity of the 'nose' is weak and its function is relatively single, so the number and richness of metaphors are less.

The source domain of each part includes not only the body part itself, but also several typical traits. A feature or function of the source domain is activated to fulfill the mapping from the body part to the target domain during projecting metaphorical mapping. Metaphor is a mapping from a source domain to a target domain, which is always a mapping of a concrete domain to an abstract domain [14]. The premise of metaphor is that the source domain and target domain share a certain similarity. The goal is to let the target domain inherit the typical attributes of the source domain [15]. For example, the 'head' is the top and most important part of the human body, which coordinates all the activities. Metaphors with 'head' as the source domain often inherit the typical characteristic the head represents 'the first' as a result. Metaphorical expressions such as 'shǒunǎo/lóngtóu (leader)' frequently appear in the headlines. These metaphors arise because the typical trait of the leader and the 'head' are similar to the meaning of 'important/the first', and they inherit the typical feature of the 'head' through cross-domain metaphor mapping. To fulfill the richness and popularity of expression in news headlines, the typical characteristics of various parts are served as metaphors generally, and they are mapped to the fields of politics and diplomacy.

3   Distribution of Metaphors in Various Parts

3.1   Corpus Description

The source of the corpus for this research is from *People's Daily* corpus, the most important media in China. The news headlines dated from 2018 to May 12, 2019, with a total of 38458 news headlines. This research applies a combination of quantitative and qualitative analysis to explore the metaphorical features of news headlines. Due to the particularity of the corpus, we mainly discuss the metaphorical mapping with the human cognitive as the source domain and the news content as the target domain.

3.2   Classification and Statistics of Human Body Metaphors

According to the statistics of *People's Daily* headlines metaphors, this paper summarizes 9 metaphor source domains, namely 'body, head, face, eyes, nose, mouth, ears, hands, lower limbs'. The metaphors which take 'heart/blood' etc. as the source domain, we classified them into other categories. The statistics of the number of entries and the total word frequencies are as shown in Fig. 2 and Fig. 3, respectively.

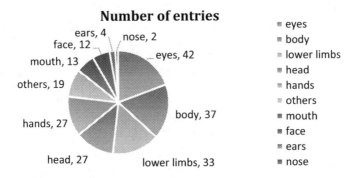

Fig. 2. The number of metaphorical entries in different parts of the human body.

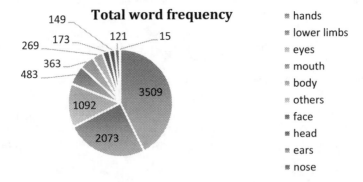

Fig. 3. The frequency of metaphorical words in different parts of the human body.

As Fig. 2 displays, the metaphor entries in descending order are 'eyes, body, lower limbs, hands, and heads, others, mouth, face, ears, nose'.

It can be seen from Fig. 3 that the number of human body metaphors is abundant, with a total of 8,207 items, accounting for 21.34% of the total news headlines. The total frequency of metaphorical words in descending order are 'hands, lower limbs, eyes, mouth, body, others, face, head, ears, nose'. The order is different from which of the metaphorical entries.

4 Metaphor Classification of Various Parts of the Human Body

Metaphors in various parts of the human body are unevenly distributed from the aforementioned details. This section will analyze the metaphorical distribution of each part according to the word frequency.

4.1 Metaphor with 'Hand' as the Source Domain

'Hand' is the most flexible part of the human body. In the news headlines of *People's Daily* corpus, the following metaphorical terms are common:

(4) Tuījìn zhùfáng zūlìn shìchǎng guīfànhuà.
    promote housing lease market standardization
    Promote the standardization of the housing rental market.

'Tuījìn (promote)' in (4) is posed by hand, expressing new meanings in news headlines. Through the statistical analysis, the high-frequency entries[2] of 'hand' metaphors and their quantities are given in Table 1.

Table 1. Metaphors with 'hands' as the source domain.

Entry	F	Entry	F	Entry	F
tuījìn (promote)	764	fú (support)	712	tuīdòng (push forward)	704
xiě (write)	436	zhuā (grasp)	203	diǎnzàn (like)	89
ná (take)	84	dǎkāi (open)	82	tóurù (put into)	79
jǔ (lift)	72	zhāi (pick)	51	yōngbào (embrace)	49
tiāo (pick)	38	mō (touch)	34	cā (wipe)	30
huà (draw)	21	nǐng (twist)	18	bàotuán (hold together)	11
pěng (hold)	10				

From Table 1 we can see that the metaphors composed of 'hands' are mostly verbs, among which the most relevant metaphor is 'tuījìn', which projecting the metaphors of implementation in various policies and measures; the second is 'fú', which means

---

[2] The frequency of the entries listed in the table in this paper is more than 10.

'help, poverty alleviation', it can reflect the importance China has attached to poverty alleviation work in recent years.

4.2   Metaphor with 'Lower Limbs' as the Source Domain

The composition of 'lower limbs' is mainly 'legs and feet', which are the main parts of human body displacement, as is followed by obvious movements and large amplitude. Therefore, the metaphors of the composition are used frequently.

(5) Gēnshàng shídài qiánjìn bùfá.
     keep up era forward pace
     Keep up the pace with the progress of the times.

In (5), 'qiánjìn (go forward)' is the action of the lower limbs, 'bùfá (pace)' is a noun related to the lower limbs, which is used as a metaphor in the news headline. The following Table 2 gives statistical data of the metaphors composed of the actions of the 'lower limbs'.

Table 2. Metaphors with 'lower limbs' as the source domain.

Entry	F	Entry	F	Entry	F
zǒu (go)	1109	mài (stride)	218	jìnrù (enter)	133
jiǎo (foot)	69	qiánxíng (go forward)	65	kuàyuè (step over)	58
tà (tread)	47	mànbù (stroll)	43	qiánjìn (go ahead)	40
lìzú (stand on)	38	bùfá (pace)	36	zhǐbù (stop)	24
pǎotuǐ (run errands)	19	jiǎobù (pace)	18	zhàn (stand)	14
pǎolù (run off)	11	qǐbù (get started)	11	tiào (jump)	11

From Table 2, we can see that the metaphoric terms with the 'lower limbs' action as the source domain are rich. The largest number is 'zǒu' with 1,109 times, accounting for 2.88% of the total number of news headlines, followed by 'mài'. These metaphors are generally used to describe the process.

4.3   Metaphor with 'Eyes' as the Source Domain

The eyes are the most important organs and agility parts of the five sense organs. They are responsible for receiving information. Therefore, the number of entries and the word frequency of eyes is the most abundant. Usage is shown as below:

(6) Gěi shìguāng xūqiúzhě zēngtiān yìshuāng 'huìyǎn'.
     give sight requester add a pair wisdom eyes.
     Add a pair of 'wisdom eyes' to those who need vision

In (6), the 'huìyǎn (wisdom eyes)' are not real eyes. Due to the abundant terms of 'eye' metaphors, the following will be divided into two categories for statistical analysis, namely the metaphors with 'yǎn (eye)' as the word-formation component (Table 3), metaphors with the 'eyes' movement and function as the source domain (Table 4).

Table 3. Metaphors with 'yǎn' as word formation components.

Structure	Entry and the frequency
Attributive-centred	rénmínyǎn (people's eyes) (55)/qīngyǎn (blue eyes) (34)/jiàoyùyǎn (educational eyes) (29)/cáijīngyǎn (financial eyes) (12)
Verb-object	liàngyǎn (dazzling) (13)/fàngyǎn (look at) (11)
Verb-supplement	yǎnzhōng (in the eyes) (21)

Table 3 presents the high-frequency words of the 'eyes' metaphor. According to the structure, the metaphors with 'yǎn' as the word-formation component can be divided into five types with a total of 24 items, and a total frequency of 237 times. Among the five structures, the most numerous is the fixed-center structure.

Table 4. Metaphors with 'eyes' movements and function as the source domain.

Entry	F	Entry	F	Entry	F
shìyě (vision)	263	shìdiǎn (viewpoint)	150	tòushì (perspective)	122
shìjiǎo (perspective)	121	shìxiàn (sight)	66	dīng (stare)	32
huítóukàn (look back)	30	shìjué (visual)	21	zhǔwàng (look forward to)	12

It can be seen from Table 4 that the eyes metaphors are frequently applied in the news headlines. In addition, the word-formation component of 'shì (vision)' constantly appears in the high-frequency metaphorical words.

4.4   Metaphor with 'Mouth' as the Source Domain

As an important vocal and eating organ in the human body, 'mouth' has strong flexibility, so it has rich metaphors and emerges frequently in news metaphors, as in the sentence below.

(7) Xīn zhēngchéng hūhuàn gōngrén jiējí xīn zuòwéi.
     new journey call worker class new conduct
     The new journey calls new work of the working class.

In the sentences above, 'hūhuàn (call)' is a metaphor for 'hope'. There are richer metaphors in news headlines that consist of the actions of the 'mouth', as shown in Table 5.

Table 5. Metaphors with the 'mouth' action as the source domain.

Entry	F	Entry	F	Entry	F
shuō (say)	362	hūhuàn (call)	135	chī (eat)	28
jiào (shout)	21	jiǎng (speak)	12		

The metaphors with 'mouth' action as the source domain have 10 entries, with a total frequency of 574 times. In addition to the metaphors in which the 'mouth' action is the source domain, there are also some metaphors related to 'kǒu (mouth)': kǒuqì (tone)/kǒuwèi (taste)/kǒutóu (oral), all of which are word-building components for 'mouth' metaphor, but the number of entries is small, and the words also showed low-frequency.

4.5   Metaphor with 'Body' as the Source Domain

Unlike other parts, the body is not an organ, but a whole. The quantity of metaphorical entries is abundant, with 37 items. The metaphor headlines are as follows:

(8)   Zhìliàng xīng nóng, xiàng nóngyè qiángguó zhuǎnshēn.
quality prosper agriculture, towards agriculture power turn around
Prospering agriculture by quality, turning to an agricultural power.

In (8) 'zhuǎnshēn (turn around)' means direction's change. The metaphor of 'body' reflects that people perceive others as a whole. In the headlines of *People's Daily*, The entries in Table 6 shows the high-frequency metaphoric of 'body'.

Table 6. Metaphors with 'body' as the source domain.

Entry	F	Entry	F	Entry	F
shēnbiān (by one's side)	117	shēnfèn (identity)	47	zìshēn (self)	28
biànshēn (transform)	26	zhōngshēn (lifelong)	20	tóushēn (devote into)	14
shòushēn (slimming)	10	zhuǎnshēn (turn around)	10		

There are abundant metaphoric entries with 'body' as the source domain, but most of the entries are not frequent, so they are not displayed in Table 6. The word 'shēn (body)' is most often used as the root morpheme, as the head word or the subject.

4.6   Metaphor with 'Face' as the Source Domain

This paper separates the 'face' from the 'five senses', where the 'face' is used as a whole to project metaphors. The example metaphor headlines in (9):

(9)   Lǐ'an xiǎozhèn zhǎnlù xīnyán.
Li'an town reveal new face
The small town of Li'an reveals its new face.

The 'face' in (9) does not refer to a human face, but a metaphorical new meaning that is projected into the field of architecture. According to the statistics of this paper, there are 12 metaphoric entries with 'face' as the source domain, the word frequency is 173 times. The high frequency words are: miànduìmiàn (face to face) (76)/xīnyán (new face) (40)/miànkǒng (face) (33)/miànmào (appearance) (11). The word 'miàn (face)' is often used as the root morpheme.

4.7   Metaphor with 'Head' as the Source Domain

The metaphors of "head" in Chinese are very rich, but the number of metaphors which express the news content is less than that of the above-mentioned human parts. We divide the metaphors composed of 'head' as the source domain into 10 categories according to the metaphorical meaning. Examples of metaphorical categories and entries are below: ① Metaphorical first: tóutiáo (headline)/dàitóu (take the lead)/ lóngtóu (leader) etc.; ② Metaphorical aspect: duōtóu (multi-start)/qítóubìngjìn (advance together); ③ Metaphorical devotion: máitóu (immerse oneself in); ④ Metaphorical thoughts: tóunǎo (brains)/qiāntóuwànxù (a multitude of things); ⑤ Metaphorical responsibility: tóuxián (title)/tóushang (head); ⑥ Metaphorical winners: tóujiǎo (top corners); ⑦ Metaphorical failure and suppression: dītóu (yield); ⑧ Metaphorical the suppressed thing gets stretched: táitóu (head up); ⑨ Metaphorical appear: lòutóu (emerge); ⑩Metaphorical appearance: gǎitóuhuànmiàn (makeover).

The total number of metaphorical entries with "head" as the source domain is 27, the total word frequency is 149 in the corpus. 'Head' in news headlines is the most commonly used metaphor for the meaning of 'the first'. For example, 'tóutiáo (headline)' is the most frequent word that indicates the most important item in the news. The word 'dàitóu (take the lead)' with the second-highest word frequency is metaphorizing itself first acts first to lead others, which can also reflect the characteristics of political life to a certain extent. For example:

(10)   Dǎngyuán dàitóu jiě nántí.
        party member take the lead solve problem.
        Party members take the lead in solving problems.

4.8   Metaphor with 'Ears/Nose' as the Source Domain

Although the ear is highly functional, this part lacks mobility and cannot actively perform its functions. It can only listen passively. Therefore, there are fewer metaphors and only the following entries: 'qīngtīng (hearken)' 'tīngfēng (listening to the wind)' 'língtīng (listen)' 'shùnfēng'ěr (clairaudience)'. The morpheme 'tīng' is mainly used as a word-formation of metaphor among them.

The nose is the center of the face and also a key organ of the face. Similar to the ears, the nose has poor mobility and flexibility, and its function is not very obvious compared to other organs. Therefore, there are fewer metaphors containing nose. There are only two cases: 'niú bízi (ox nose)' and 'bízi (nose)', which means a key part of metaphorical things.

4.9   Metaphor with Other Parts of the Human Body as the Source Domain

There are some other metaphors except the above nine categories of metaphors. Their parts are difficult to distinguish, too small or the number of entries is single, we group them into 'other categories', such as 'lìdù (strength)', 'shénjīng (nerves)', etc., with the following headlines:

(11)   Wǒ guó jiādà lúnzuòxiūgēng lìdù.
I nation increase crop rotation and fallow strength
China has increased the strength of crop rotation and fallow.

'lìdù (strength)' belong to the human body, but they are used here as a metaphor and do not mean the human body. Table 7 shows the other metaphors in the news headlines.

Table 7. Metaphors with 'others' as the source domain.

Entry	F	Entry	F	Entry	F
lìdù (strength)	69	bèihòu (behind)	43	shēngmìnglì (vitality)	25
zàoxuè (hematopoietic)	18	rèxuè (righteous ardour)	16	shēngzhǎng (grow)	14
shénjīng (nerves)	13	shūxuè (blood transfusion)	12	xuèmài (bloodline)	11
tiěwàn (iron hand)	10				

As shown in Table 7, among the metaphors of 'others' of the human body, 'lìdù' has the largest quantity, followed by 'bèihòu'. In addition, there are a certain number of metaphors related to blood and heart.

5   Cognitive Analysis of Human Metaphor

5.1   Metaphorical Mapping of the Human Body Under the Concept of Metaphorical Inheritance

Metaphor is the modification of language through the compilation and processing of language forms, so as to strengthen the power of language performance [16]. Editors often use the characteristics of human body parts to describe the characteristics of things in another field, so that the abstract and complex target field has a more specific and clear expression. Each part of the human body has different characteristics and functions. The typical features and the characteristics of the actions can be mapped to the target domain. The metaphorical mapping process shows in Fig. 4:

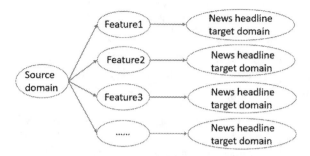

Fig. 4. Metaphor mapping diagram under the concept of metaphor inheritance.

Figure 4 indicates that some typical features of the 'source domain' are metaphorically mapped to the news headline target domain. For example, the 'nose' is located in the center of the face and has the typical characteristics of 'central and critical'. This typical feature of the nose is often applied in language expression. This typical feature of the nose is often mapped to the target object to make the target domain obtain this feature. 'Kuàyuè (step over)' is a leg movement. It has the characteristics of 'great power and surpassing', which are mapped to the target domain of politics. These characteristics are correspondingly inherited, indicating that great difficulties have been overcome and great progress has been made.

5.2   Cognitive Rules of the Human Body Metaphor

The metaphors of various parts of the human body in the news headlines are unequal. From the perspective of human body composition, the head, torso, and limbs are the main components of the human body, the hands and lower limbs constitute the main activities of the human body. Hands are the most flexible parts of the body with the most labor force and creativity. Policy developments and problem-solving require human manipulation in the political field. 'Hands' indicate the carry out of the action of various tasks such as 'promote the development of something, grasp the problems', etc. The lower limbs are responsible for the main movements of the human body, verbs such as 'zǒu (walk)/mài (step)' always express the process of affairs. From the rules of human movement and space, people usually rely on the lower limbs when entering a space, which is related to spatial metaphors. 'Jìnrù (enter) /bùrù (step into)' bring the meaning of reaching a certain abstract field.

'Eyes' have the most metaphorical terms among the five sense organs. The eyes are the main organs through which people receive information. 'Eyes' constantly project metaphors in the reception of various phenomena. Although the nose is also significant, its function is relatively single, and it lacks mobility. The metaphor composed of 'nose' is relatively few. Only two metaphoric terms appeared, acting as metaphors for the key parts.

5.3   The Source Domain Does not Appear in the News Headline

Some human body cognitive domains do not present in the corpus in contrast to the above. In the human facial features, there is no 'eyebrow' as the origin domain in the corpus. The role of 'eyebrow' in the face is weaker than 'eyes/mouth', its projection ability in abstract domains such as news is also the same, no metaphor with 'eyebrow' as the source domain in the corpus of this research. In the fields related to human viscera, only 'heart', 'liver', 'kidney' etc. appeared, other internal organs did not emerge. The viscera cannot be clearly felt because they are inside, and the viscus lacks empirical cognition. Therefore, the number of metaphors with internal organs as the source domain is relatively small. Owing to the special function of some internal organs, there is a lack of similar concepts in the news.

In addition, the subordinate concepts of head, trunk, and limbs, such as hair, scalp, chest, abdomen, fingers, nails, knees, etc., do not appear as metaphors. It can be seen that the smaller the body part, the more obvious its personalized characteristics, and the more difficult it is to find relevant projection concepts in the news target domain.

6   The Emotional Embodiment of Metaphor in News

Human body vocabulary itself generally does not have an emotional tendency, but it regularly indicates positive or negative emotion in news headlines. The metaphorical cognitive theory believes that metaphor plays an important role in the conceptualization of emotions [14]. News headlines convey the overall emotional orientation of the news. This paper counts the proportion of emotional tendency expressed by metaphors through the annotation of the corpus (see Fig. 5).

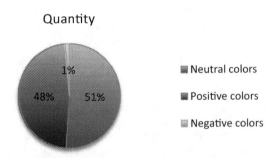

Fig. 5. Metaphorical emotional tendency proportion map.

As Fig. 5 illustrates, the metaphorical expressions of the human body in the news headlines contain more emotional expressions with neutral tendency, which stands for 51%. Meanwhile, 48% contain the positive implication, but there are not many usages of negative tendency which stand for 1% from the whole corpus. It shows that news headlines tend to adopt positive expressions. Section 6.1 and 6.2 analyze the usage of positive and negative emotional embodiment in headlines.

6.1   Human Body Metaphors Have a Positive Emotional Tendency

Positive descriptions or comments on facts are common in news, the metaphors convey news attitudes. See some examples below.

(12)   Chàngxiǎng Zhōng Jiǎn yǒuhǎo zhǔ xuánlǜ.
       sing China Cambodia friendly main melody
       Singing the main theme of China-Cambodia friendship.

(13)   Cóng gǎnshang shídài dào yǐnlǐng shídài de wěidà kuàyuè.
       from catch up era to lead era Prc great span
       A great leap from catching up with the times to leading the times.

(14)   Jīngjì qióng shì biànshēn jiàoyù dà shì.
       economy poor city turn into education big city
       The economically poor city turns into a big education city.

In (12), 'chàngxiǎng' is a mouth metaphor and expresses positive emotional meaning. The word 'chàngxiǎng/gēchàng (sing)' is usually used for metaphors to refer to active policies or a good life. The emotions of people are mostly high and vigorous when singing. As a result, the word 'chàng' has positive emotional meaning. In (13), 'kuàyuè' implies overcoming and getting rid of difficulties, delivers historical and political progress in the news. 'Biànshēn' usually refers to the development of things for the better. In (14), 'biànshēn' shows a metaphor that the city has undergone major changes and is developing in a good direction, which implies positive meaning.

6.2   Human Body Metaphors Have a Negative Emotional Tendency

News has the effect of pinpointing current malpractices. Human body metaphors also have negative emotional expressions in the news headlines.

(15)   Qīntūn sǐzhě fúzhùjīn, yánchěng!
       embezzle deceased assistance fund, severe punishment
       Severe punishment for embezzling the deceased's aid!

(16)   Bàn wán huìyuánkǎ, lǎobǎn pǎolù le.
       Manage finish membership card, boss ran away Prc
       after finishing the membership card, the boss ran away.

(17)   Jǐngtì huì biànliǎn de 'jīnróng fúwù fèi'.
       alert can change face Prc financial service fee
       Be wary of 'financial services fees' that will 'change faces'.

In (15), the action of 'qīntūn' in Chinese usually refers to swallowing the food intact, which is indelicate. The metaphor is negative, it metaphors corruption and bribery in the field of political life. In (16), 'Pǎolù' signifies running away and shirking responsibility. The metaphorical meaning of 'biànliǎn' in (17) means that the attitude toward others changes to deteriorate. The metaphor here implies the problem of 'financial services fees' where the situation is when applying for loans, it is not in line with the original plan. The use of metaphors here shows the editor's attitude and adds to the interest of the news.

7   Conclusion

Human body metaphors are extensively distributed in news headlines. In this paper, we investigate the types of human body metaphors and explore the emotional tendency of metaphors based on the 38,458 news headlines from *People's Daily* corpus.

Our research shows that the quantity of metaphors is distributed unevenly in the news headlines. Metaphors with 'eyes, lower limbs, hands' as the source domain occupy a larger number in the headlines, while metaphors with 'ears, nose' as the source domain are less numerous. Secondly, the metaphor makes the target domain of news headlines inherit the typical characteristics of the source domain through mapping. The stronger the function and flexibility of body parts, the more metaphorical phenomena. In addition to the metaphorical types mentioned in this paper, there are some human body parts that have no metaphorical expression in the corpus. The parts are implicit, and their personalized characteristics are too obvious, it is difficult to find relevant mapping concepts in the news target domain. Thirdly, we found out that many human body metaphors in news headlines have a positive or negative emotional tendency, which can reflect the news attitudes to a certain extent.

The plan for further study includes a more in-depth comparison between English and Chinese body metaphors. We will explore the linguistic cognitive reasons behind the metaphor. This will be done by cross-language comparison, applying the method of linguistic metrology.

Acknowledgments. The work was supported by Major Program of National Social Science Foundation of China (18ZDA295); Funding Project of Education Ministry for Development of Liberal Arts and Social Sciences (16YJA740036); Top-ranking Discipline Team Support Program of Beijing Language and Culture University (JC201902); the Fundamental Research Funds for the Central Universities (18YBT03); BLCU Supported Project for Young Researchers Program (supported by the Fundamental Research Funds for the Central Universities) (19YCX047).

References

1. Shu, D.: Yǐnyùxué yánjiū [Metaphor Research]. Foreign Language Education Publishing, Shanghai (2008)
2. Hu, Z.: Rènzhī yǐnyùxué [Cognitive Metaphor]. Peking University Publishing, Beijing (2004)
3. Wang, Z.: Hànyǔ míngcí yǐnyù de yǔyì yìngshè fēnxī [Semantic mapping analysis of Chinese noun metaphors]. Yǔyán jiàoxué yǔ yánjiū [Lang. Teaching Res.] **03**, 89–96 (2009)
4. Xu, S.: Yǐnyù yùtǐ de jiàngòu—fēnxínglùn shìyù xià yǐnyù yánjiū zhīyī [The construction of metaphors—one of the metaphor studies from the perspective of fractal theory]. Wàiyǔjiàoxué [Foreign Lang. Teach.] **41**(01), 6–11 (2020)
5. Chen, J.: Yīnghànyǔ réntǐ yǐnyùhuà rènzhī duìbǐ [Comparison of metaphorical cognition of human body in English and Chinese]. Liáochéng dàxué xuébào zhéxué shèhuì kēxué bǎn [J. Liaocheng Univ. Soc. Sci. Ed.) **01**, 89–91 (2005)
6. Liu, Z.: Yīnghàn réntǐ yǐnyù rènzhī duìbǐ yánjiū [A cognitive contrastive study of human metaphors in English and Chinese]. Chángchūn shīfàn xuéyuàn xuébào [J. Changchun Normal Univ.] **31**(04), 68–70 (2012)

7. Lin, R.: Hànyǔ hé Xībānyá réntǐ yǐnyù duìbǐ [Comparison of human body metaphors in Chinese and Spanish]. Pǔ' ěr xuéyuàn xuébào [J. Pu'er Univ.] **35**(01), 96–97 (2019)
8. Zhang, J.: Jīyú tǐyàn zhéxué de réntǐ yǐnyù rènzhī yánjiū [Research on metaphorical cognition of human body based on embodied philosophy]. Xī' ān wénlǐ xuéyuàn xuébào [J. Xi'an Univ. Arts Sci.] **14**(03), 105–109 (2011)
9. Sun, Y.: Réntǐ yǐnyù de duōyì lùxiàng tuīyǎn—cóng 'tóu(head)' shuōqǐ [Deduction of the polysemous path of human metaphor—starting from 'head']. Dōngběi shīdà xuébào zhéxué shèhuì kēxué bǎn [J. Northeastern Normal Univ. Philos. Soc. Sci. Ed.] **05**, 121–124 (2013)
10. Li, H., Li, X.: Cóng rènzhī jiǎodù kàn yīnghàn réntǐcí 'yǎn' de yǐnyù tèdiǎn jí wénhuà chāyì [The metaphorical characteristics and cultural differences of the human body word 'eye' in English and Chinese from a cognitive perspective]. Yīngyǔ guǎngchǎng [English Square] **03**, 13–14 (2019)
11. Bai, H.: Xīnwén biāotí de yǐnyù fēnxī [Metaphor analysis of news headlines]. Dōngnán dàxué xuébào zhéxué shèhuì kēxué bǎn [J. Southeast Univ. Philos. Soc. Sci. Ed.] (S2), 177–178+181 (2006)
12. Liu, C.: Xīnwén biāotí zhōng de yǐnyù jíqí yǔyòng gōngnéng [Metaphors and pragmatic functions in news headlines]. Huáběi zhíyè jìshù xuéyuàn xuébào [J. Huaibei Vocation. Tech. College] **02**, 84–86 (2007)
13. Deng, Y.: Cóng rènzhī jiǎodù qiǎnxī xīnwén biāotí zhōng de yǐnyù [A cognitive analysis of metaphors in news headlines]. Fùyáng shīfàn xuéyuàn xuébào shèhuì kēxué bǎn [J. Fuyang Normal Univ. Soc. Sci. Ed.] **04**, 49–52 (2012)
14. Lakoff, G., Johnson, M.: Metaphors We Live By. The University of Chicago Press, Chicago, London (1980)
15. Wang, Z., Zhao, H.: Yǐnyù jìchéng lǐniàn xià de 'xiàng X yīyàng A' de xiànzhì yánjiū [Research on the limitation of 'xiàng X yīyàng A' under the concept of metaphorical inheritance]. Dāngdài xiūcíxué [Contemporary Rhetoric] **02**, 15–25 (2021)
16. Feng, X.: Yǐnyù—sīwéi de jīchǔ piānzhāng de kuàngjià [Metaphor—The Framework of the Basic Chapter of Thinking]. University of International Business and Economics Publishing, Beijing (2004)

Human Cognitive Constraints
on the Separation Frequency and Limit
of Separable Words

Xiaoming Han[(✉)] and Haifeng Wang[(✉)]

School of Chinese as a Second Language, Peking University, Beijing, China
{hanxiaoming, china}@pku.edu.cn

Abstract. Based on the CCL corpus, the paper employs Java to statistically analyze the Chinese characters and words inserted between the AB morphemes of the separable words. The conclusion is as follows: (1) In terms of average value, considering frequency, the top five average values of inserted Chinese characters and words are about 4 ± 2, and regardless of frequency, the top five average values of inserted Chinese characters and words are about 8 ± 3; (2) In terms of frequency distribution, about 2 ± 1 Chinese characters or words can be inserted, and the maximum capacity of Chinese characters and words can be inserted is about 7 ± 2. The separated form of separable words can be regarded as gestalt, closely related to human working memory and information processing ability. It has psychological reality: the limit of human processing information is about 'seven', and about 'four' is the sensitive point of information easier to process.

Keyword: Separable word · Separation frequency · Separation limit · Cognition · Working memory

1 Introduction

Separable word is a unique linguistic phenomenon in modern Chinese, which refers to compound words that are integral and single in meaning but can have other components inserted into their structure [1], such as 洗澡 *xǐzǎo* 'bathe', 见面 *jiànmiàn* 'meet'. Compared with words, separable words can be extended; compared with phrases, their meanings are frozen, so they have become key points and difficulties in ontology studies and Chinese teaching. Studies on separable words are currently abundant, and those on separation of separable words mainly focus on the generalization and summary of different separations [2–9]. Meanwhile, academia has also paid attention to the separation motivation of separable words. Some of the more representative ones were from the synchronic aspect: the formal perspective of 'noun group incorporation' [10], 'light verb movement' [11, 12], 'haplology' [13], 'cognate object' [14, 15]; the functional perspective of 'rhyme promotion' [2, 16, 17], 'formal metonymy' [9], 'analogous function' [18–21], 'pragmatic drive'[6, 20, 22, 23], etc. The diachronic aspect: lexicalization [24–27]; de-lexicalization [17], etc. However, as regards the

M. Dong et al. (Eds.): CLSW 2021, LNAI 13250, pp. 18–41, 2022.
https://doi.org/10.1007/978-3-031-06547-7_2

existing studies, attention to the frequency[1] and limits[2] of separation of separable words is far from sufficient. Almost no frequency statistics have been conducted, while studies in this area are directly related to human comprehension and processing of separable words, and can, to a certain extent, provide a 'quantitative' account of the motivation of separation of separable words. Hence it is necessary to start some discussions from this point.

This paper will examine the separations of separable words from both the average value and frequency distributions, obtain the frequency and limits of different separations, and interpret them from the perspective of human cognition to provide 'quantitative' evidence for explaining the motivation of separation of separable words.

2 Research Subjects

The current understanding of the nature of separable words is inconsistent, and it is first necessary to establish the criteria for identifying separable words, and on this basis, to determine the object of the study.

2.1 Identification Criteria

The property that separable words can be 'combined' or 'separated' results in a blurred boundary between them and phrases, making it difficult to define and identify the separable words. However, to ensure the research is scientific, the criteria for identifying and distinguishing separable words should be clearly defined when determining the scope of the study. In previous studies, Wang [8] had a more precise scientific criterion for identifying separable words and considered that the condensed predicate-object separate structure is a separable word. The condensed predicate-object separate structure refers to a kind of AB bisyllabic structure in Chinese, which cannot be divided in meaning. However, it can be inserted in the middle form, and A and B can be separated or combined. The following categories are mainly included.

(1) The separable bisyllabic structure AB is condensed if the meaning entries of both are identified as morphemes in the Modern Chinese Dictionary. For example, 理发 *lǐfà* 'get a haircut', 道歉 *dàoqiàn* 'apologize'.

---

[1] Wang [8] has proposed a formula to calculate the separation frequency: the separation frequency of separable word (F) = the number of separated examples/the total number of valid examples. The number of separated examples is the number of examples containing the separated form of the separable words that we obtained from the corpus. The total number of valid examples is the sum of the number of valid examples in which the separable word and its separated form occur. The separation frequency discussed in this paper differs from this in that it refers to the frequency of the components that can be inserted between the two morphemes AB of the separable word. We, therefore, term the former as separation rate and the latter as separation frequency.

[2] The separation limit is the maximum allowed insertion of components between the two morphemes AB of separable words.

(2) The separable bisyllabic structure AB is also condensed if one of the meaning entries in the Modern Chinese Dictionary is identified as a morpheme. For example, 洗澡*xǐzǎo* 'bathe', 冒险*màoxiǎn* 'adventure'.

(3) The separable bisyllabic structure AB is also condensed if the meaning entries of A and B are identified as words in the Modern Chinese Dictionary, but the meaning is abstract and not an addition of the meanings of A and B. For example, 拐弯 *guǎiwān* 'pursue a new course'.

Except for the above forms, all other bisyllabic structures will not be considered as separable words.

2.2   Range of Subjects

Based on the above criteria, this paper examines the only four learners' dictionaries of separable words available: *Dictionary of Modern Chinese Separable Word Usage (DSWU)* [28], *Dictionary of Modern Chinese Separable Word Learning (DSWL)* [29], *Dictionary of Commonly Used Chinese Separable Words (DCSW)* [30], *Dictionary of Listening and Remembering HSK Separable Word (DHSW)* [31], find that the four dictionaries vary greatly in word inclusion (Table 1), which is mainly due to the different references and bases of the four dictionaries. *DSWU* was based on the Modern Chinese Dictionary, refers to recent books, newspapers and TV broadcasts. 4066 entries were counted, and 1738 commonly used of them were selected as the entries. *DSWL* and *DCSW* were based on *The Syllabus of Graded Words and Characters for Chinese Proficiency* [32]. 210 and 268 common words were identified as dictionary entries, respectively. *DHSW* was based on the Outline of Graded Vocabulary of HSK, and 188 separable words required to be mastered were included (Table 1).

Table 1. Statistics of words entries in four learners' dictionaries of separable word

Learners' dictionaries of separable word	Word entries (个)[3]
Dictionary of Modern Chinese Separable Word Usage	1738
Dictionary of Modern Chinese Separable Word Learning	210
Dictionary of Commonly Used Chinese Separable Words	268
Dictionary of Listening and Remembering HSK Separable Word	188

The four dictionaries also show significant differences in the specific collection of words. According to the statistics of the four dictionaries, only 80 separable words are included in all four dictionaries, and 123 separable words are included in three dictionaries. These 203 separable words can be considered as the separable words with high acceptance at present. Since this paper focuses on the separated forms of separable words, and according to the examination, not all separable words have richer forms of separation. Hu and Fan [33] conducted a statistical survey on the dominated compound

---

[3] '个(gè)' is a measure word in Chinese, which is in brackets, same as below.

words without object[4] in the Modern Chinese Dictionary: the amount of dominated compound words without objects was 3,674, of which 2,450 can be separated, accounting for 67% of the total. Shi [34] also made similar statistics on the predicate-object compound verbs in *The Contemporary Chinese Dictionary* [35], which showed that among 4908 verbs, 2889 (about 58.86%) could be separated, accounting for 92.86% of all separable words in the dictionary. Therefore, to make the study more reliable and scientific, we mainly select the separable words with separated forms and higher separating rates as the objects of this paper.

Wang [8] has made a more detailed statistical analysis of 207 separable words and identified the top 60 separable words as the key separable words. We match 203 separable words of high acceptance in the dictionary with 60 key separable words, and finally, identify 51 separable words with high acceptance and separating rates as the subjects of this study (Table 2).

Table 2. Word list of the separable words studied in this paper

Audio sequence	Separable words
B	拜年(bàinián, 'pay a New Year call'), 帮忙(bāngmáng, 'help')
C	操心(cāoxīn, 'worry'), 插嘴(chāzuǐ, 'interrupt, get a word in'), 吵架(chǎojià, 'quarrel'), 吃惊(chījīng, 'be startled'),吃苦(chīkǔ, 'bear hardships'),出名 (chūmíng, 'become famous')
D	打架(dǎjià, 'come to blows'), 打针(dǎzhēn, 'give an injection'), 当面 (dāngmiàn, 'face to face'), 倒霉(dǎoméi, 'have bad luck'), 丢人(diūrén, 'lose face')
F	翻身(fānshēn, 'free oneself, improve fundamentally by reducing poverty'), 放假(fàngjià, 'have a holiday')
G	干杯(gānbēi, 'drink a toast'), 搞鬼(gǎoguǐ, 'play tricks'), 告状(gàozhuàng, 'lodge a complaint against sb.'), 鼓掌(gǔzhǎng, 'applaud'), 挂钩(guàgōu, 'link up with'), 拐弯(guǎiwān, 'pursue a new course')
H	狠心(hěnxīn, 'harden one's heart'), 化妆(huàzhuāng, 'make up')
J	见面(jiànmiàn, 'meet'), 接班(jiēbān, 'take one's turn on duty'), 结婚(jiéhūn, 'marry'), 敬礼(jìnglǐ, 'salute'), 鞠躬(jūgōng, 'bow')
K	开课(kāikè, 'give a course')
L	劳驾(láojià, 'excuse me'), 理发(lǐfà, 'get a haircut'), 留神(liúshén, 'take care')
P	排队(páiduì, 'queue up')
Q	请假(qǐngjià, 'ask for leave')
S	伤心(shāngxīn, 'feel heartbroken'), 上当(shàngdàng, 'be fooled'), 生气 (shēngqì, 'take offence'), 睡觉(shuìjiào, 'sleep')

(continued)

---

[4] i.e., verb-object compounds.

Table 2. (*continued*)

Audio sequence	Separable words
T	叹气(*tànqì*, 'sigh'), 听话(*tīnghuà*, 'heed what an elder or superior says'), 跳舞(*tiàowǔ*, 'dance')
W	问好(*wènhǎo*, 'say hello')
X	洗澡(*xǐzǎo*, 'bathe'), 下台(*xiàtái*, 'get out of a predicament or an embarrassing situation'), 泄气(*xièqì*, 'feel discouraged')
Z	遭殃(*zāoyāng*, 'suffer a disaster or calamity'), 沾光(*zhānguāng*, 'benefit from association with sb. or sth.'), 照相(*zhàoxiàng*, 'take a photo'), 争气(*zhēngqì*, 'try to make a good showing'), 做主(*zuòzhǔ*, 'take the responsibility for a decision'), 站岗(*zhàngǎng*, 'stand guard')

3 Research Procedure

The separation frequency and limit are obtained by calculating the inserted components between the two AB morphemes of the separable words. The research process mainly includes the following procedures.

1. The 51 separable words selected above are retrieved in the CCL corpus of peking university with the formula 'A$20B'[5] to obtain the original linguistic data.
2. A script written in Java is used to extract the part of the original linguistic data from morpheme 'A' to morpheme 'B'[6], which is then manually filtered to exclude irrelevant usages based on the criteria for identifying separable words.
3. The secondary corpus obtained through the above filtering process is placed in a java program written for frequency calculation, and two main aspects of statistics are done.
(1) Calculate the number of inserted Chinese characters between the two morphemes A and B of the separable words, including statistics on the frequency of inserted characters, statistics on the average number of inserted characters, and statistics on the frequency of the maximum number of inserted characters allowed.
(2) The inserted components between the two morphemes A and B of the separable words are divided using Java's word segmentation program, manually proofread, and then the statistical work in (1) is repeated.
4. Conclude and explain the reasons.

---

[5] 'A$20B' refers to the insertion of 20 Chinese characters between the two morphemes A and B of separable words. The number of 20 Chinese characters was chosen as the retrieval number in consideration of the fact that it should be as exhaustive as possible, so a larger value was chosen for the retrieval process. This avoids excluding some separated forms with a large number of inserted Chinese characters.

[6] This step speeds up the filtering of irrelevant usages, but it also brings some uncertainty, with parts of the corpus requiring secondary confirmation in the original corpus. Thanks to Dr. Wang of Beihang University for his help.

4 Results

Among the 51 separable words, 8 words, including '听话*tīnghuà*, 当面*dāngmiàn*, 见面*jiànmiàn*, 上当*shàngdàng*, 跳舞*tiàowǔ*, 帮忙*bāngmáng*, 开课*kāikè*, 沾光*zhānguāng*', have more complicated separated forms, which can be known to a certain extent from the inserted Chinese characters between them. The number of Chinese characters inserted into these separable words exceeds 15, ranking in the top 8 (Table 3). For example:

(1) 在此之前，他曾上过盟军伏号为 "警卫员" 的秘密战役的当: 一个伪战争计划，巧妙地泄露给了最高统帅部。（《从乞丐到元首》）

   *Zài cǐ zhīqián, tā céng **shàng** guò méngjūn fúhào wéi 'jǐngwèiyuán' de mìmì zhànyì de **dàng**: yī gè wěi zhànzhēng jìhuà, qiǎomiào de xièlòu gěi le zuìgāo tǒngshuài-bù.*

   'Before that, he had **been fooled** by the secret battle of the Allied volt called 'Guard': a pseudo war plan was cleverly leaked to the supreme command.'

(2) 广东的高尔夫球爱好者，只要是品性诚实的，都有机会花很少的钱，沾上美国高尔夫协会让杆评分系统的光。（《新华社》）

   *Guǎngdōng de gāoěrfū-qiú àihào-zhě, zhǐyào shì pǐnxìng chéngshí de, dōu yǒu jīhuì huā hěnshǎo de qián, **zhān** shàng měiguó gāoěrfū xiéhuì rànggǎn píngfēn xìtǒng de **guāng**.*

   'Golf lovers in Guangdong, as long as they are honest, have the opportunity to spend very little money and **get the light of** the USGA handicap scoring system.'

Table 3. Statistics on the inserted Chinese characters between AB morphemes of separable words

Ranking	Separable words	Number of Chinese characters between AB (个)
1	听话	20
2	当面	19
3	见面	17
4	上当	16
5	跳舞	16
6	帮忙	15
7	开课	15
8	沾光	15

Based on the work of 'corpus collection → corpus extraction → corpus filtering → corpus statistics', the results will be explained and further discussed.

Whether the inserted components between AB morphemes of separable words pose difficulties for comprehension and whether information receivers adopt word processing or lexical processing for separable words are not yet uniformly answered and still deserve attention, and therefore will be explained below from both word and lexical aspects.

4.1   Inserted Chinese Characters Between AB of Separable Word

The inserted Chinese characters among the AB morphemes of 51 separable words selected in this paper is complicated and is illustrated below mainly in terms of the average value and frequency distribution[7] of the number of inserted characters.

The Average Number of Inserted Characters

Total Average

The total average of the number of inserted characters between the two morphemes of the separable words is the ratio of the total number of inserted characters to the total number of occurrences. Statistically, it is found that the results widely vary whether consider the frequency of inserted words or not. Considering the frequency of inserted characters can reflect the full spectrum of native speakers' use of separable words, but the drawback is that the size of the corpus limits it. Disregarding the frequency of inserted characters gives a clearer view of the number of inserted characters allowed in separable words. Therefore, the total average is calculated separately from the consideration of frequency and the disregard of frequency. The calculation is as follows[8]:

$$Total\ average_{(Considering\ frequency)} = \frac{(NIC \times FO)sw1 + (NIC \times FO)sw2 + \ldots + (NIC \times FO)swn}{FOsw1 + FOsw2 + \ldots + FOswn} \quad (1)$$

$$Total\ average_{(Disregarding\ frequency)} = \frac{NICsw1 + NICsw2 + \ldots + NICswn}{Wordtype} \quad (2)$$

The total average of 51 separable words inserted with Chinese characters is as follows: if the frequency of inserted Chinese characters is considered, the total average of 51 separable words inserted with Chinese characters is 2.27 Chinese characters, and if the frequency of Chinese characters is not considered, but only the possible occurrence of inserted Chinese characters is concerned, the total average is 4.90 Chinese characters, which has a large gap between the two (Table 4).

Table 4. Total average of Chinese characters inserted in 51 separable words

Statistics	Total average (个)
Considering frequency	2.27
Disregarding frequency	4.90

Average of Each Word

Specifically, the average number of inserted characters for each separable word is shown below. Similarly, if we consider the frequency of the separable words, the

---

[7] The frequency is primarily the proportion of the various occurrences of a Chinese character or word's separated insertion to all circumstances.

[8] 'NIC' means Number of Inserted Characters, 'FO' means Frequency of Occurrence, 'sw' means separable word.

highest average number of inserted Chinese characters is 当面*dāngmiàn*, with an average of 4.91 characters, and the top five are '当面*dāngmiàn*, 开课*kāikè*, 接班*jiēbān*, 沾光*zhānguāng*, 听话*tīnghuà*', with a concentration of 4 ± 1 characters (Table 5). The least number of inserted Chinese characters on average is 出名*chūmíng*, with only 1.06 characters, and the next five are '出名*chūmíng*, 泄气*xièqì*, 结婚*jiéhūn*, 问好*wènhǎo*, 挂钩*guàgōu*', with a concentration of about 1 character (Table 6).

Table 5. The first five places of the average Chinese characters inserted in separable word (considering frequency)

Ranking	Separable words	Average (个)
1	当面	4.91
2	开课	4.42
3	接班	4.18
4	沾光	4.05
5	听话	3.79

Table 6. The last five places of the average Chinese characters inserted in separable word (considering frequency)

Ranking	Separable words	Average (个)
47	挂钩	1.23
48	问好	1.17
49	结婚	1.17
50	泄气	1.15
51	出名	1.06

If the frequency of inserted Chinese characters in each case is not considered, the average of inserted Chinese characters differs significantly from that in the case of considering the frequency, in which the average of inserted Chinese words for '听话*tīnghuà*' is the highest, at 10.50 Chinese characters, while '下台*xiatai*' is the lowest, at 1.50 Chinese characters. The top five separable words are '听话*tīnghuà*, 当面*dāngmiàn*, 见面*jiànmiàn*, 开课*kāikè*, 上当*shàngdàng*', with 9 ± 2 characters, and the bottom five separable words are '留神*liúshén*, 搞鬼*gǎoguǐ*, 翻身*fānshēn*, 插嘴*chāzuǐ*, 下台*xiàtái*', with 1 ± 1 characters.

Table 7. The first five places of the average Chinese characters inserted in separable word (disregarding frequency)

Ranking	Separable words	Average (个)
1	听话	10.50
2	当面	10.11
3	见面	9.29
4	开课	8.67
5	上当	8.63

Table 8. The last five places of the average Chinese characters inserted in separable word (disregarding frequency)

Ranking	Separable words	Average (个)
47	留神	2.00
48	搞鬼	2.00
49	翻身	2.00
50	插嘴	2.00
51	下台	1.50

Frequency of use can reflect the use of insertion types. However, as far as the average is concerned, if the frequency of each insertion case is considered, it can give a more objective picture of the overall Chinese character insertion of each separable word, but it also brings a problem that the difference in the frequency of use can lead to a more extensive base of certain Chinese character insertion cases, which also has a certain effect on the presentation of the insertion of Chinese characters in separable words. Therefore, we separately count the average of the cases without considering the frequency of use of each case, that is, only starting from the type of insertion cases. As can be seen from Tables 5, 6, 7 and 8, considering frequency or not has a certain difference on the presentation of the results. Differences exist between the top five and bottom five separable words, both in terms of the average and the specificity of each word. Without considering frequency, we can see that the top five clitic words are more frequently used in daily communication and have more types of inserted characters. In comparison, the bottom five are significantly less commonly used in daily communication and have fewer types of inserted characters. The relationship between the frequency of separable words and the inserted Chinese characters needs further correlation testing.

Frequency Distribution of Inserted Characters

Among the 51 separable words, the top three with the highest frequency of inserted characters are concentrated in inserting 1 to 5 Chinese characters, accounting for 87.56% of the total. 42 of the separable words rank in the top three in terms of frequency of inserted characters are inserted with 1 to 3 Chinese characters, accounting for 82.35%, with the most cases of inserting 1 Chinese character, with an average of 49.06%, nearly half. The remaining five words that rank in the top three in terms of the number of inserted characters show the insertion of 4 and 5 characters (Table 9). Thus, we believe that, although the meaning of each separable word is different and the syntactic distribution is not the same, it is relatively consistent in terms of the number of inserted characters, mainly concentrated between the insertion of 1 and 3 characters. In connection with the separating characteristics of separable words, we can find that this may be related to human information processing. The fewer the Chinese characters inserted between the two AB morphemes, the easier it may be to understand and process them.

Table 9. Statistics on the top three Chinese characters inserted between the AB of 51 separable words

Separable words	Number of inserted characters					Total percentage
	1	2	3	4	5	
插嘴	23.26%	64.34%	12.40%			100.00%
翻身	55.77%	36.54%	7.69%			100.00%
搞鬼	33.77%	59.74%	6.49%			100.00%
留神	67.69%	30.77%	1.54%			100.00%
问好	85.00%	13.33%	1.67%			100.00%
下台	20.13%	79.87%				100.00%
吃惊	56.36%	43.43%	0.16%			99.95%
出名	94.97%	4.03%	0.88%			99.87%
挂钩	78.64%	20.74%	0.31%			99.69%
结婚	90.10%	4.04%	5.45%			99.59%
拜年	61.59%	35.37%	2.44%			99.39%
叹气	24.55%	53.49%	20.88%			98.93%
泄气	93.37%	1.10%	4.42%			98.90%
鼓掌	79.52%	13.86%	5.42%			98.80%
争气	54.58%	35.86%	7.57%			98.01%
打架	69.06%	22.48%	6.19%			97.72%
狠心	67.23%	27.31%	2.94%			97.48%
鞠躬	20.95%	63.51%	11.62%			96.08%
干杯	64.22%	24.60%	7.03%			95.85%
吵架	53.42%	35.71%	6.52%			95.65%
照相	62.40%	17.44%	15.12%			94.96%
做主	20.34%	69.49%	0.00%	5.08%		94.92%
放假	70.43%	16.14%	7.71%			94.29%
理发	71.26%	13.79%	8.05%			93.10%
拐弯	60.64%	19.15%	12.77%			92.55%
睡觉	44.08%	42.68%	5.70%			92.46%
遭殃	79.75%	6.33%	6.33%			92.41%
洗澡	57.84%	21.19%	12.36%			91.39%
操心	19.00%	48.55%	23.48%			91.03%
化妆	60.37%	24.88%		4.15%		89.40%
倒霉	58.88%	23.36%	7.01%			89.25%
生气	41.94%	32.96%	12.30%			87.20%
见面	49.68%	25.18%	12.05%			86.91%
打针	34.56%	39.30%	11.75%			85.61%
劳驾	47.58%	29.84%		7.26%		84.68%
请假	43.27%	21.63%	18.76%			83.66%
告状	33.56%	31.21%	15.44%			80.20%
敬礼	36.67%	26.67%	16.06%			79.39%

(*continued*)

Table 9. (*continued*)

Separable words	Number of inserted characters					Total percentage
	1	2	3	4	5	
吃苦	32.16%	21.78%	25.43%			79.36%
排队	36.52%	25.54%	15.77%			77.83%
丢人	32.17%	26.96%		18.26%		77.39%
帮忙	29.08%	27.98%	17.53%			74.59%
跳舞	28.79%	28.57%	15.10%			72.46%
听话		34.03%	22.59%	14.30%		70.91%
站岗	35.56%	12.59%			22.22%	70.37%
伤心		24.25%	24.62%	18.61%		67.48%
上当	26.57%	21.05%	18.49%			66.11%
当面			19.29%	31.33%	14.57%	65.19%
接班	18.48%	22.28%	20.11%			60.87%
开课	13.89%	23.89%	14.44%			52.22%
沾光	15.41%		18.77%	17.09%		51.26%
Average	49.06%	29.57%	11.06%	14.51%	18.40%	87.56%

The 51 separable words we selected have a separating frequency, and the top positions of the 51 separable words inserted between AB are also more concentrated. However, there is a significant difference in the maximum number of Chinese characters inserted between AB for each separable word. 37 separable words can be inserted between 6 and 9 Chinese characters, accounting for 72.55%, with an average proportion of 1.60%. Some of the separable words can be inserted into more than 10 Chinese characters (including 10), which are less common, with an average of 0.44%, and mainly include 19 separable words, such as 帮忙*bāngmáng*, 吵架*chǎojià*, 吃苦 *chīkǔ*, 打针*dǎzhēn*, 当面*dāngmiàn*, accounting for 37.25% (Table 10), and generally concentrate between 10 and 13 Chinese characters (Table 11).

Table 10. Statistics on the Chinese characters inserted between the AB of 51 separable words

Separable words	The proportion of 6–9 inserted Chinese characters	The proportion of more than 10 inserted Chinese characters
帮忙	1.16%	0.09%
操心	0.53%	
吵架	0.46%	0.31%
吃苦	1.34%	0.29%
打架	0.49%	
打针	0.48%	0.29%
当面	5.99%	0.47%
倒霉	0.93%	
丢人	1.74%	

(*continued*)

Table 10. (*continued*)

Separable words	The proportion of 6–9 inserted Chinese characters	The proportion of more than 10 inserted Chinese characters
放假	0.38%	
告状	0.78%	
拐弯	2.13%	
化妆	1.23%	
见面	0.69%	0.06%
接班	3.26%	1.96%
结婚	0.06%	
敬礼	1.89%	0.76%
鞠躬	0.47%	
开课	5.37%	1.35%
劳驾	2.42%	
理发	2.30%	
排队	2.36%	0.25%
请假	0.98%	
伤心	1.79%	0.19%
上当	2.02%	0.29%
生气	0.28%	
睡觉	0.40%	0.05%
叹气	0.05%	0.02%
跳舞	3.18%	0.33%
听话	3.25%	0.38%
洗澡	0.36%	0.11%
泄气	0.55%	
遭殃	1.27%	
沾光	4.90%	0.47%
站岗	2.59%	0.74%
照相	0.58%	
争气	0.40%	
Average	1.60%	0.44%

Table 11. Statistics on the insertion of more than 10 (including 10) Chinese characters between the AB of 51 separable words

Separable words	The proportion of 10–13 inserted Chinese characters	The proportion of more than 10 inserted Chinese characters	10 –13 inserted Chinese characters account for more than 10 inserted Chinese characters
帮忙	0.38%	0.51%	73.33%
吵架	0.31%	0.31%	100.00%
吃苦	0.57%	0.57%	100.00%

(*continued*)

Table 11. (*continued*)

Separable words	The proportion of 10–13 inserted Chinese characters	The proportion of more than 10 inserted Chinese characters	10 –13 inserted Chinese characters account for more than 10 inserted Chinese characters
打针	0.88%	0.88%	100.00%
当面	2.89%	4.72%	61.25%
见面	0.19%	0.45%	42.86%
接班	2.17%	9.78%	22.22%
敬礼	1.52%	1.52%	100.00%
开课	3.33%	9.44%	35.29%
排队	0.67%	0.74%	90.91%
伤心	0.38%	0.75%	50.00%
上当	1.41%	2.05%	68.75%
睡觉	0.15%	0.26%	57.14%
叹气	0.02%	0.02%	100.00%
跳舞	1.62%	2.28%	70.97%
听话	2.79%	4.13%	67.72%
洗澡	0.11%	0.11%	100.00%
沾光	1.68%	2.80%	60.00%
站岗	0.74%	0.74%	100.00%
average	1.15%	2.21%	73.71%

From the 51 separable words with inserted Chinese characters between AB, there are significant differences among the words, mainly in two aspects: (1) the average of inserted Chinese characters differs greatly among the words, and considering the frequency or not also affects our understanding of the separable words' separating situation; (2) the frequency of inserted Chinese characters differs greatly among the words, and most separable words focus on inserting 1–3 Chinese characters, but some can insert more than 10 Chinese characters, which is related to the nature of separable words themselves, and may also be associated with the capacity of human information processing and the way of processing.

4.2   Inserted Words Between AB of Separable Word

The inserted Chinese characters between the AB of separable words have been analyzed, but since the way the information receiver processes the separation of the separable words is not known, whether the insertion is processed in the form of Chinese characters or words, even chunks or constructions need to be further examined. The following will be examined and analyzed from the perspective of words, while the interpretation of chunks and constructions will be discussed in another article.

For the separable words, the inserted components are first divided into words by Java's word segmentation program and then supplemented by manual proofreading.

The final statistical results show that the inserted words are also more diverse, still illustrated in terms of the average and frequency distribution of the inserted words.

The Average Number of Inserted Words

Examining the average of inserted words gives a complete picture of the 51 separable words, mainly in terms of the total average and the average of each word.

Total Average

If the frequency of various cases of inserted words is considered, the total average of 51 separable words inserted into words is 1.8. In contrast, if only different types of inserted words are considered, the number of inserted words is improved and is 3.4 (Table 12). Inserted words are different from that of Chinese characters in that words are composed of morphemes, which in Chinese correspond to Chinese characters, so the number of words is smaller than the number of Chinese characters.

Table 12. Total average of inserted words of 51 separable words

Statistics	Total average (个)
Considering frequency	1.80
Disregarding frequency	3.40

Average of Each Word

Considering the frequency distribution of the inserted words, the top five words in the average of inserted words for each separable word are '当面*dāngmiàn*, 沾光 *zhānguāng*, 听话*tīnghuà*, 接班*jiēbān*, 开课*kāikè*', with a concentration of 3 ± 1 words, and the most inserted word is '*dangmian*' with an average of 3.5 words (Table 13); the bottom five are '泄气*xièqì*, 留神*liúshén*, 结婚*jiéhūn*, 出名*chūmíng*, 问好*wènhǎo*', with a concentration of about 1, and the least inserted word is '*chuming*', with only 1.05 words. By comparing with the average of inserted Chinese characters, the top five separable words remain unchanged. However, the order of each word is different.'留神*liúshén*' appear in the bottom five of inserted words and '挂钩*guàgōu*' is in the bottom five of inserted characters, while the remaining four words are the same. As can be seen from Table 14, these separable words are used less frequently.

Table 13. The first five places of average words inserted in separable words (considering frequency)

Ranking	Separable words	Average (个)
1	当面	3.50
2	沾光	2.79
3	听话	2.72
4	接班	2.66
5	开课	2.57

Table 14. The last five places of average words inserted in separable words (considering frequency)

Ranking	Separable words	Average (个)
47	泄气	1.08
48	留神	1.08
49	结婚	1.07
50	出名	1.05
51	问好	1.03

Without considering the frequency, the average number of inserted words has increased significantly, with the most being 听话*tīnghuà* at 7.00 words, and the top five words including 听话*tīnghuà,* 当面*dāngmiàn,* 见面*jiànmiàn,* 跳舞*tiàowǔ,* 沾光*zhānguāng* at 6 ± 1 words. At the same time, the bottom five included 下台*xiàtái,* 问好 *wènhǎo,* 留神*liúshén,* 翻身*fānshēn,* 插嘴*chāzuǐ,* all of which is 1.5. Whether or not the frequency is considered has a great influence on the statistical results, and compared with the situation where can Chinese characters, added four words including '跳舞 *tiàowǔ,* 沾光*zhānguāng,* 睡觉*shuìjiào,* 排队*páiduì*' are added to the top five, and the bottom five words are changed from '搞鬼*gǎoguǐ*' to '问好*wènhǎo*' (Tables 15 and 16).

Table 15. The first five places of average words inserted in separable words (disregarding frequency)

Ranking	Separable words	Average(个)
1	听话	7.00
2	当面	6.50
3	见面	6.18
4	跳舞	6.00
5	沾光	5.50
5	睡觉	5.50
5	上当	5.50
5	排队	5.50
5	开课	5.50

Table 16. The last five places of average words inserted in separable words (disregarding frequency)

Ranking	Separable words	Average (个)
47	下台	1.50
48	问好	1.50
49	留神	1.50
50	翻身	1.50
51	插嘴	1.50

As it can be seen above, the averages of the inserted words of separable words are illustrated. Some differences are found with the inserted Chinese characters: when the frequency is considered, the top five inserted Chinese characters and words are concentrated in 4 ± 1 and 3 ± 1, while the bottom five are all concentrated in about 1; when the frequency is not considered, the top five inserted Chinese characters and words are focus on 9 ± 2 and 6 ± 1, while the bottom five are all concentrated in 1 ± 1. In summary, it can be found that the top five of the average of inserted Chinese characters and words are concentrated around 4 ± 2 when the frequency is considered, whereas the top five of the average of inserted Chinese characters and words are concentrated around 8 ± 3 when the frequency is not considered.

Frequency Distribution of Inserted Words

Examining the frequency distribution of inserted words provides a more comprehensive understanding of the use of separated forms of separable words. It enables indirect observation of the processing of information receivers. Statistically, in contrast to the top three frequencies of inserted Chinese characters, mainly concentrated in inserting 1–5 Chinese characters, the top three higher frequencies of inserted words for each separable word are primarily focused between 1–4 words. The top three frequencies of inserted words among 47 separable words (>92.16%) are 1–3, and the percentage of all inserted words is more than 75%, with an average of 95.03%, and the highest in the insertion of 1 word, accounting for 62.35% (Table 17). It can be seen that the most frequently used separate way of separable words is the insertion of 1 word in the middle, while the insertion of 1 ± 1 words is more common.

Table 17. Statistics on the top three frequencies of inserted words among 51 separable words

Separable words	Inserted words				Total percentage
	1	2	3	4	
拜年	62.80%	35.98%	1.22%		100.00%
插嘴	79.84%	20.16%			100.00%
吃惊	56.53%	43.42%	0.05%		100.00%
倒霉	66.82%	25.70%	7.48%		100.00%
翻身	87.82%	12.18%			100.00%
搞鬼	90.91%	8.44%	0.65%		100.00%
鼓掌	84.94%	12.35%	2.71%		100.00%
挂钩	79.88%	19.81%		0.31%	100.00%
留神	92.31%	7.69%			100.00%
问好	96.67%	3.33%			100.00%
下台	72.08%	27.92%			100.00%
泄气	93.92%	4.97%		1.10%	100.00%
争气	87.25%	11.16%	1.59%		100.00%
做主	83.05%	10.17%	6.78%		100.00%
出名	95.72%	3.90%	0.25%		99.87%
结婚	94.08%	4.98%	0.76%		99.82%

(continued)

Table 17. (*continued*)

Separable words	Inserted words				Total percentage
	1	2	3	4	
叹气	30.51%	68.45%	0.87%		99.82%
照相	75.19%	20.93%	3.49%		99.61%
狠心	79.41%	18.49%	1.68%		99.58%
打架	74.92%	21.50%	2.61%		99.02%
吵架	59.44%	34.98%	4.33%		98.76%
洗澡	72.30%	21.30%	4.86%		98.45%
生气	45.77%	42.44%	10.08%		98.29%
睡觉	55.63%	37.17%	5.40%		98.20%
干杯	67.73%	24.60%	5.75%		98.08%
放假	79.29%	16.43%	2.29%		98.00%
鞠躬	24.59%	70.00%	3.38%		97.97%
拐弯	70.21%	21.28%	6.38%		97.87%
理发	80.46%	11.49%	5.75%		97.70%
操心	48.55%	41.16%	7.92%		97.63%
打针	56.84%	31.93%	8.60%		97.37%
遭殃	81.01%	11.39%	3.80%		96.20%
见面	55.00%	30.70%	10.46%		96.17%
告状	35.57%	41.28%	17.79%		94.63%
化妆	67.74%	21.66%	5.07%		94.47%
劳驾	53.23%	29.03%	12.10%		94.35%
丢人	42.61%	39.13%	11.30%		93.04%
请假	57.19%	27.84%	7.87%		92.89%
吃苦	47.66%	32.16%	12.77%		92.59%
帮忙	41.47%	32.16%	16.85%		90.48%
敬礼	40.00%	35.45%	14.55%		90.00%
排队	51.08%	17.45%	21.16%		89.69%
站岗	45.19%	13.33%	30.37%		88.89%
上当	31.58%	31.07%	24.78%		87.42%
跳舞	58.62%	17.45%	8.69%		84.76%
伤心	16.92%	33.83%	32.14%		82.89%
当面		7.79%	56.34%	18.70%	82.83%
接班	25.00%	36.41%	20.65%		82.07%
听话		55.40%	17.52%	8.62%	81.53%
开课	39.44%	22.78%	16.67%		78.89%
沾光	20.17%	27.17%	29.13%		76.47%
average	62.35%	25.45%	10.57%	7.18%	95.03%

Combining Tables 17 and 18, we can see that, unlike the statistical results for inserted Chinese characters, the inserted words are more concentrated, with fewer cases where 5 to 9 words can be inserted, accounting for an average of only 1.06%, and only 11 separable words where more than 10 words (including 10) can be inserted, accounting for 21.57% of the total number of separable words. The maximum number of words that can be accommodated between AB of separable words is 11 ± 2, but there are fewer such separable words. The details are shown in Table 18.

Table 18. Statistics on the inserted words between AB of 51 separable words

Separable words	The proportion of 5–9 inserted words	The proportion of more than 10 inserted words
帮忙	0.40%	
操心	0.26%	
吵架	0.31%	
吃苦	0.76%	0.11%
打架	0.33%	
打针	0.35%	
当面	2.84%	0.18%
丢人	0.87%	
放假	0.36%	
拐弯	2.13%	
化妆	1.38%	
见面	0.31%	0.03%
接班	2.61%	
结婚	0.06%	
敬礼	2.12%	
鞠躬	0.27%	
开课	2.78%	0.56%
劳驾	0.81%	
排队	1.16%	0.07%
请假	0.61%	
伤心	1.07%	0.19%
上当	0.90%	0.13%
生气	0.50%	
睡觉	0.20%	0.04%
叹气	0.03%	
跳舞	1.62%	0.07%
听话	2.09%	0.12%
洗澡	0.17%	
遭殃	1.27%	
沾光	2.18%	0.56%
站岗	2.22%	
average	1.06%	0.19%

Thus, the inserted words between separable words are different from the inserted Chinese characters. The former is more concentrated than the latter, and in comparison, fewer separable words can be inserted with more than 10 words. However, they have certain commonalities, which can be summarized as follows: the cases with the higher frequency distribution of inserted Chinese characters and words are concentrated in inserting 1–3 Chinese characters or words, and the maximum capacity of inserted Chinese characters and words is about 7 ± 2.

In summary, we have done statistics and analysis of the inserted Chinese characters and words between AB of the separable words separately and find some differences in the inserted Chinese characters and words. However, due to the relationship between Chinese characters and words, the two can be somewhat integrated, which leads us to the following conclusions: First, as far as the average is concerned, the top five of the average of inserted Chinese characters and words is about 4 ± 2 when the frequency is considered, and the top five of the average of inserted Chinese characters and words is about 8 ± 3 when the frequency is not considered. Second, in terms of frequency distribution, the cases where the frequency distribution of inserted Chinese characters and words is more intensive are concentrated in inserting 2 ± 1 Chinese characters or words. The maximum capacity of inserted Chinese characters and words is about 7 ± 2.

5   Discussion

The statistical analysis of the inserted Chinese characters and words between the AB morphemes of 51 separable words with a high separation frequency gives us a clearer insight into the use of separated forms of separable words. The key to distinguishing between separable words and phrases is that the meaning of separable words is still integral and singular even when they are separated, but it is observed that the boundaries are not clear. The solidity of the meaning is crucial for users to correctly use and understand the meaning of separable words. For example:

(3) 那本书在京城未能买到, 来到这家旧书店仅花了3角钱便如愿以偿。小书店还
     帮了一些没有地方藏书的"困难户"的大忙。（《市场报》）
     *Nà běn shū zài jīngchéng wèinéng mǎi dào, láidào zhè jiā jiù shūdiàn jǐn huā le sānjiǎo qián biàn rúyuàn-yǐcháng.Xiǎo shūdiàn hái **bang** le yìxiē méiyǒu dìfāng cángshū de 'kùnnán-hù'de dà **máng**.*
     'The book was not available in Beijing, but I could get it for only 30 cents at this used bookstore. The small bookstores also **helped** some 'poor households' who had no place to collect books.'

(4) 拍卖市场开张那天, 他用出10倍于规定的价格, 当着那些曾将他抓进大牢的公
     安人员的面将那注销的户口又买了回来, 还得意洋洋地说: "我胡汉山又回来
     了!（《1994年报刊精选》）
     *Pāimài shìchǎng kāizhāng nàtiān, tā shuǎi chū 10 bèi yú guiding de jiàgé, **dāng** zhe nàxiē céng jiāng tā zhuā jìn dàláo de gōng'ān-rényuán de **miàn** jiāng nà zhùxiāo de hukou yòu mǎi le huílái, hái déyì-yángyáng de shuō: 'Wǒ Hú-hànshān yòu huílái le!'*

'On the opening day of the auction market, he threw out 10 times the stipulated price, bought back the canceled account **in front of** the public security men who had put him in jail, and said proudly, 'I, Hu Hanshan, am back again!'

From the above two examples, we chose the words '帮忙 *bāngmáng*' and '当面 *dāngmiàn*'. The former '忙 *máng*' is still a morpheme and cannot be a separate word, inserting '... *le yìxiē méiyǒu dìfāng cángshū de kùnnán-hù de dà...*', the latter's '面 *miàn*' can become a word, inserting '...*zhe nàxiē céng jiāng tā zhuā jìn dàláo de gōng'ān-rényuán de...*'. The insertion of these two words is more complicated, but the reader can still understand, which shows the singularity and wholeness of the meaning of the separable words. Nevertheless, why does the insertion of such a large number of constituents between the AB of the separable words not affect the understanding of the information receiver, and how does this singularity and wholeness of meaning arise? We suspect that this is related to the concept of gestalt in human cognition. The psychologist's view of gestalt perception can be traced to the 'gestalt law of perceptual organization' or gestalt principles, usually illustrated by line diagrams and dot patterns. The most important of these principles are the principles of adjacency, similarity, closure, and continuity. The more the construction of an individual component conforms to these rules, the more likely it is to be a clear and uncontested organization (called Prägnanz by gestalt psychologists), and the more suitable it is for gestalt perception [36]. Although the separated form of the separable word, as an abstract linguistic symbol system, is less intuitive than the pattern, it largely conforms to the gestalt principle and therefore can be regarded as an abstract whole.

On the other hand, the information receivers tend to perceive the information as a gestalt when visually received to obtain its overall meaning despite the more complex insertion of components between the two AB morphemes. Note that this is only a speculation, and the influencing factors are far from simple: the frequency of joint use of the AB morpheme of the separable words, the mutual information of the two, and the information receiver's prior knowledge all affect comprehension and processing. This part still needs to be examined or verified using experimental means.

Then what are the frequencies and limits of the components that can be inserted between the two morphemes of the separable words? The statistics related to the 51 separable words with high separated frequencies have been described above. Most of the statistics performed in terms of both average and frequency distributions focus on such numbers as 4 ± 2, 8 ± 3, 2 ± 1, and 7 ± 2. These numbers can be understood as the frequency and limits of human use or processing of separation of separable words.

Studies in cognitive psychology have shown that the process of human linguistic information processing is chunking, i.e., the formation of smaller units into larger and larger structural units according to a certain structural pattern [37]. Miller [38] pointed out that the limit of human information processing capability is 'seven chunks or so (7 ± 2)'. Miller [39] made a series of judgment experiments based on information theory to illustrate the importance of '7 ± 2' in human information processing. Lu [40] also stated that the number of discrete chunks remembered in mind at any given moment during the dynamic process of chunking in understanding sentences does not exceed about seven chunks. Lu and Ying [41] pointed out that a sentence consists of no more than seven or so structural components, a number that is exactly in line with the seven or so proposed by Miller [37]. This is by no means accidental but reflects the most fundamental commonality of human language as an information carrier, namely, that the syntactic structure of human language takes full advantage of, and is also limited by, the general information processing capacity of humans. This human ability to process information is highly related to the working memory of human beings. Humans process information instantaneously, using the capacity of short-term memory. It is generally believed that the limit of short-term memory of about seven (7 ± 2) is only the limit of memory. In essence, it is the limit of the human ability to process information, i.e., the limit of the functioning of the mind [41].

Research results in cognitive psychology have been conducted to illustrate the limits of human information processing capacity using terms such as chunks, information chunks, and structural components of sentences. Although not exactly equivalent to concepts such as chunk, the insertions of separable words explored in this paper can be considered units of human information processing. Upon examination, the top five of the average inserted Chinese characters and words for the 51 separable words is about 8 ± 3, and the maximum capacity of inserted Chinese characters and words is about 7 ± 2. Therefore, it is psychologically realistic that the maximum number of Chinese characters or words inserted into the separable words is around the number 'seven', which provides evidence that the maximum capacity of human information processing is 7 ± 2. However, the number of components that can be inserted into some of the separable words exceeds seven, or even reaches more than ten, which is very rare. It is observed that in such cases, most of the B morpheme of the separable words have been transformed into words or have become independently usable words, so the speed and capacity of information processing should be increased, and therefore the comprehensible capacity will be increased.

Why is it that the frequency of inserted Chinese characters and words between AB is higher at $4 \pm 2/2 \pm 1$? Baddeley, Thomson and Buchanan [42] noted that 'Immediate memory performance is directly influenced by the spoken length of memory items. Ordered serial recall of lists of one-syllable words was considerably better than recall of lists containing five-syllable items'. Current psychological research has also demonstrated that the four or so (4 ± 1) is a sensitive point [43]: when more than four discrete chunks are memorized in mind, the difficulty in processing the subsequent material increases sharply. Lu and Cai [44] demonstrated the limitation of the 'four' on the linguistic structure by calculating the combination of sentence components and analyzing other linguistic phenomena related to four: When the number of instantaneous chunks exceeds 4, listeners tend to combine to reduce the rapidly increasing memory load. In explaining the causes of the four chunk format in Chinese, Shen [45] also believed that it is related to human memory or span of attention: the capacity limit of short-term memory is generally 7 ± 2, the span of attention is generally 4 ± 1, and 7 ± 2 can be roughly regarded as a double of 4 ± 1. Meanwhile, he also pointed out that this is a general law of people's cognitive psychology. The fact that the 51 separable words we observed, with a high frequency of inserted characters and words, are mainly around 'four' also confirms the psychological realism of the information capacity that humans can process more easily. However, the specificity of the separable words requires further verification.

6 Summary

The property that separable words could be either separated or combined makes them a unique phenomenon in Chinese. At present, there are more discussions on the types of separation but less on the nature and quantity of inserted components. This paper, based on the CCL corpus and programmed by Java, examines the inserted Chinese characters and words between the AB morphemes of separable words and makes a detailed statistical analysis: in terms of the average value, the top five of the average value of inserted Chinese characters and words is about 4 ± 2 when the frequency is considered, and the top five of the average value of inserted Chinese characters and words is about 8 ± 3 when the frequency is not considered; in terms of the frequency distribution, the higher frequency of inserted Chinese characters and words is about 2 ± 1 Chinese characters or words, and the maximum capacity of inserted Chinese characters and words is about 7 ± 2. These are closely related to human's working memory and information processing ability and are psychologically realistic: the limit of human beings to process information is about 'seven', and about 'four' is the sensitive point where information is easier to process. In addition, the separated form of the word can be regarded as a gestalt, and the receiver of information tends to use the concept of gestalt to process the separable word.

There are still many shortcomings in this paper. The processing of statistical results is not refined enough, and many discussions are still at the speculative stage which needs to be verified by experimental means. Future research will have to take these questions into consideration.

References

1. Tang, Z.F.: Dictionary of Chinese Linguistics. Encyclopedia of China Publishing House, Beijing (2007).(in Chinese)
2. Zhao, Y.R.: A Grammar of Spoken Chinese. The Commercial Press, Beijing (1979)
3. Li, Q.H.: Discussion on the characteristics and usage of clutch words. Lang. Teach. Linguist. Stud. **2**, 91–100 (1983)
4. Duan, Y.H.: On separable word. J. Nanjing Normal Univ. (Soc. Sci. Ed.) **2**, 112–115 (1994)
5. Rao, Q.: Structural characteristics and pragmatic analysis of separable words–a concurrent discussion on the teaching of separable words in intermediate and advanced Chinese for foreigners. Chin. Lang. Learn. **1**, 32–35 (1997)
6. Wang, T.L.: The Study on Separable Words of Modern Chinese. Master's Thesis, Chinese Academy of Social Sciences (2001)
7. Ma, C.X.: Analysis of separation and reunion vocabulary of verb object type. J. Inner Mongolia Normal Univ. (Philos. Soc. Sci. Ed.) **6**, 118–121 (2005)
8. Wang, H.F.: The Study on the Separable Words' Separated Form Function of Mandarin Chinese. Peking University Press, Beijing (2011)
9. Yuan, Y.L.: Syntactic features of separable words used in separation: from a perspective of formal metonymy. Contemp. Linguist. **20**(4), 587–604 (2018)
10. Tang, T.C.: Incorporation in Chinese grammar. In: Fengfu, C., Makoto, K.N. (eds.) An Anthology of Chinese Studies by Taiwanese Scholars - Grammatical Part, pp. 215–336. Tianjin People's Publishing House, Tianjin (1991)

11. James Huang, C.-T.: On Ta de laoshi dang-de hao (他的老师当得好) and related problems. Linguist. Sci. **3**, 225–241 (2008)
12. Wang, G.S., Wang, J.: Modern Chinese separable words from the perspective of light verbs. J. Central China Normal Univ. (Human. Soc. Sci.) **50**(2), 101–105 (2011)
13. Guo, R.: The mechanism for the formation of separable words and incompleted words: and the mechanism for the formation of pseudo-attributives. Linguist. Sci. **16**(3), 225–249 (2017)
14. Pan, H.H., Ye, K.: Separable words and cognate objects in mandarin Chinese. Contemp. Linguist. **17**(3), 304–319+376–377 (2015)
15. Ye, K., Pan, H.H.: Revisiting the syntax of separable words: a reply to Yuan (2018) and others. Contemp. Linguist. **20**(4), 605–615 (2018)
16. Feng, S.L.: Prosodically determined word-formation in mandarin Chinese. Soc. Sci. China **18**(4), 120–137+194 (1997)
17. Li, Z.J.: Delexicality: from a word back to a phrase Jiehun(结婚) and Xizao(洗澡). Stud. Lang. Linguist. **4**, 101–106 (2006)
18. Lv, S.X.: Language Miscellany. Shanghai Education Publishing House, Shanghai (1984)
19. Cui, S.X.: Ionization and nucleus stress. Chin. Lang. Learn. **5**, 62–68 (2008)
20. Zhao, H.: Tentative discussion on the nature and causes of separable words. J. Southwest Univ. Sci. Technol. (Philos. Soc. Sci. Ed.) **26**(5), 32–35 (2009)
21. Wang, J.: The causes of separable words from the derivation of verbal complement structure in ancient Chinese. Chin. Linguist. **4**, 75–82 (2015)
22. Wang, H.F.: Ruminations on the separated motives of modern chinese separable words. Linguist. Res. **3**, 29–34 (2002)
23. Diao, Y.B.: a comparative study of separable verbs usage across the strait. Overseas Chin. Educ. **4**, 435–446 (2016)
24. Dong, X.F.: On the lexicalization of syntactic structure. Stud. Lang. Linguist. **3**, 56–65 (2002)
25. Hua, S.: Noun-incorporation and Chinese V-O detachable-words. J. PLA Univ. Foreign Lang. **4**, 36–39 (2003)
26. Liu, S.X.: Chinese Descriptive Lexicography (rearranged version). The Commercial Press, Beijing (2005)
27. Cao, X.W.: A study on the nestification of Chinese V-O verbs and the related construction patterns. Linguist. Sci. **15**(2), 140–149 (2016)
28. Yang, Q.H.: Dictionary of Modern Chinese Separable Word Usage. Beijing Normal University Publishing House, Beijing (2002)
29. Wang, H.F.: Dictionary of Modern Chinese Separable Word Learning. Peking University Press, Beijing (2013)
30. Zhou, S.Z.: Dictionary of Commonly Used Chinese Separable Words. Beijing Language and Culture University Press, Beijing (2016)
31. Gao, Y.A.: Dictionary of Listening and remembering HSK Separable Word. Beijing Language and Culture University Press, Beijing (2009)
32. Chinese Proficiency Test Department of the National Office for Teaching Chinese as a Foreign Language: The Syllabus of Graded Words and Characters for Chinese Proficiency. Beijing Language and Culture University Press, Beijing (1992)
33. Hu, Y.S., Fan, X.: Verb Studies. Henan University Press, Kaifeng (1995)
34. Shi, M.Z.: Grammatical features of the predicate-object compound. Lang. Teach. Linguist. Stud. **1**, 123–134 (1999)
35. The Dictionary Department of the Institute of Linguistics of the Chinese Academy of Social Sciences.: The Modern Chinese Dictionary Contemporary Chinese Dictionary (Revised edition). The Commercial Press, Beijing (1996)

36. Ungerer, F., Schmid, H.-J.: An Introduction to Cognitive Linguistics, 2nd edn. Pearson Education Limited, Harlow (2006)
37. George, A.M.: Human memory and the storage of information. I.R.E. Trans. Inf. Theory **2**(3), 129–137 (1956)
38. Miller, G.A.: The magical number seven, plus or minus two: some limits on our capacity for processing information. Psychol. Rev. **63**(2), 81–97 (1956)
39. Miller, G.A.: The magical number seven, plus or minus two: some limits on our capacity for processing information. Psychol. Rev. **101**(2), 343–352 (1994)
40. Lu, B.F.: Synchronous chunking process and its quantity description for utterance comprehension. Stud. Chin. Lang. **2**, 106–112 (1986)
41. Lu, B.F., Ying, X.F.: The basic restriction of human information processing capability on language structure. Lang. Teach. Linguist. Stud. **3**, 14–24 (2019)
42. Baddley, A.D., Thomson, N., Buchanan, M.: Word length and the structure of short-term memory. J. Verbal Learn. Verbal Behav. **14**, 575–589 (1975)
43. Cowan, N.: The magical number 4 in short-term memory: Are consideration of mental storage capacity. Behav. Brain Sci. **24**(1), 87–185 (2001)
44. Lu, B.F., Cai, Z.G.: Chunking and structural complexity of linguistic units. Chin. Teach. World **23**(1), 3–16 (2009)
45. Shen, J.X.: On four chunk format in Chinese. Chin. Teach. World **33**(3), 300–317 (2019)

A Quantitative Research on the Spatial Imageries for *Among Flowers*

Ning Cheng(⊠)

Department of Chinese Language and Literature, Tsinghua University,
Beijing 100084, China
chengn20@mails.tsinghua.edu.cn

Abstract. Both creation and appreciation of poems need imagery as an important element. The imagery in classical poems is a unique artistic image produced by the creators pouring their thoughts and feelings into external objects. *Among Flowers* is the earliest collection of CI, and the works it contains are quite distinctive in the use of imagery, especially the description of space is richer, forming many spatial imageries. This paper uses the digital humanistic method to analyze the spatial imageries in *Among Flowers* and constructs a semantic network with nouns of locality, and finds the distribution characteristics of the spatial imageries mostly used by poets. In addition, this paper also takes the text vectorization algorithm to achieve clustering and further analyzes the different levels of spatial imageries clusters in *Among Flowers*. Finally, this paper compares and analyzes the stylistic differences for authors in using spatial imageries of different levels.

Keywords: *Among Flowers* · Spatial imageries · Semantic network · word2vec

1 Introduction

The concept of "意象" has been mentioned in the pre-Qin literature. Such as "书不尽言, 言不尽意…圣人立象以尽意" in *Zhou Yi*, which shows the relationship between "意" and "象". The combination of "意" and "象" can be seen in "夫畫布爲熊麋之象, 名布爲侯, 禮貴意象, 示義取名也" mentioned in *Lun Heng* and "廣不謝大將軍而起行, 意象慍怒而就部, 引兵與右將軍食其合軍出東道" mentioned in *Han Shu*. However, the "意象" mentioned in this period is different from the concept of imagery in the aesthetic category. The imagery used in Chinese poetry and literary theory starts from "獨照之匠, 闚意象而運斤。此蓋馭文之首術, 謀篇之大端" mentioned in *Wen Xin Diao Long*.

Nowadays, the theory of poetic imagery has completed and matured, but there is no uniform standard in the field of specific definition of imagery. Based on the definition given by the scholars on the imagery, we can summarize the two basic characteristics, namely, "objective image" and "subjective sentiment" [1]. Spatial imagery refers to external objects that can trigger readers' spatial perception. This kind of imagery either has some spatial attribute characteristics, or can be combined with other words to construct compound spatial imageries. For example, by using the language knowledge

M. Dong et al. (Eds.): CLSW 2021, LNAI 13250, pp. 42–55, 2022.
https://doi.org/10.1007/978-3-031-06547-7_3

base HowNet [2] to search "帘" (curtain), which appears more often in *Among Flowers*, we find that its semantic origin contains the feature of "covering", which means that this word has the attribute of space blocking, so it can be regarded as a member of spatial imagery.

Chen [3] pointed out that imagery is the basic symbol of poetry art with words as the carrier. *Zhou Yi* mentioned that "夫象者, 出意者也; 言者, 明象者也。盡意莫若象, 盡象莫若言". "言" means language here, and "意" and "象" opposed to "言" are, for poetry, the imagery of poetry with language as its material shell. "The inner emotions expressed by the poet through "帘" (curtain) are produced by attaching to the word symbol "帘", which enables the spatial imagery to be measured, so that the imagery in the poem can be explored and studied at a macro level in a quantitative manner. At present, many academic achievements have used quantitative methods to study the imagery of poetry. For example, Spurgeon [5] first used quantitative methods to analyze the imagery in Shakespeare's *Sonnets*, and finally found that garden imagery occupies a very important position in Shakespeare's works by comparing the works of others. In addition, Chen [3] discovered in his works the distribution laws of special and general imageries, simple images and compound imageries in poetry. In the study of imagery measurement of CI, Sun [6] analyzed the seasonal imagery in the works concerning the subject of traveling and military service conducted by "柳永" (Liu Yong), one of the great poets of Song Dynasty.

Among Flowers, compiled by "赵崇祚" (Zhao Chongzuo) in the third year of "广政" (Guang Zheng) of post Shu (940 AD), is the first anthology of literati CI in China. Its editing marks the formation of a new concept of CI style, and its dissemination promotes the establishment of new creation and evaluation standards [7]. The anthology contains a total of 500 classic works by 18 poets, most of which have great characteristics in the use of imageries, and the description of space is very rich, forming multi-level spatial images. This paper analyzes these works based on semantic network and text vectorization, so as to explore the spatial perception category and creative style of poets in *Among Flowers*.

2 Semantic Network Analysis of Spatial Imagery

Among Flowers has distinctive features in the selection and description of imageries and most of the objects in the collection can be used as imagery for analysis. The top 50 words with the highest frequency are listed in descending order as shown in Table 1.

Table 1. High-frequency word count of *Among Flowers*

Frequency Rank 1–10		Frequency Rank 11–20		Frequency Rank 21–30		Frequency Rank 31–40		Frequency Rank 31–40	
花	273	月	135	一	103	画	91	思	81
春	216	相	134	来	100	小	91	归	81
香	204	云	113	时	100	山	89	日	81
金	175	烟	113	帘	99	轻	88	何	79
红	163	翠	113	水	99	处	87	恨	78
风	161	梦	112	深	97	天	87	长	76
不	158	愁	112	柳	97	满	85	残	76
人	158	上	109	罗	95	心	85	双	74
无	146	雨	107	屏	94	断	82	暗	74
玉	141	情	107	语	94	绣	82	莺	73

From Table 1, it can be seen that the most appearing in *Among Flowers* is "花" (flowers), and the imagery of flowers and birds is very characteristic in *Among Flowers*, only the types of flowers involve apricot, pear, peach, plum, cherry, lotus, peony and dozens of other species. In addition, the words "帘" (curtain) and "屏" (screen), which have spatial properties, are among the high-frequency words, which are closely related to the portrayal of female characters in boudoir. In order to prove the specificity of the spatial imagery of "帘" (curtain) and "屏" (screen) in *Among Flowers*, the proportion of these two words appearing in other poetry anthologies[1] (*The Complete Tang Poems*, *The Complete Tang and Five Dynasties CI*, and *The Complete Song CI*) was calculated for comparison, and the results are shown in Fig. 1.

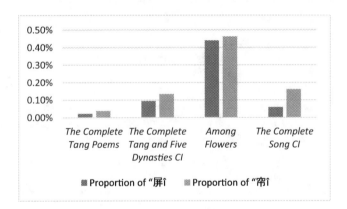

Fig. 1. Percentage of occurrences of the words "屏" and "帘" in each anthology

---

[1] These anthologies were collected via the Web, and although there may be biases between editions, the effect on the statistical results is negligible.

Figure 1 shows that the two words "屏" and "帘" have the highest percentage of occurrence in *Among Flowers*, both of which exceed 0.4%, followed by *The Complete Tang and Five Dynasties CI*, which covers *Among Flowers*, then *The Complete Song CI*, and finally *The Complete Tang Poems*. The result proves that the use of the words "屏" and "帘" in *Among Flowers* is unique. In addition, the use of the word "帘" exceeds that of "屏" in all data sets, which shows that the word "帘" can carry a richer range of emotions for the poets.

In their literary creation, writers would consciously use spatial terms, geographical terms, and spatial symbols to indicate the existence of space, but symbols are not just symbols; they are often rich in the poet's own sentiments [8]. There are a great number of nouns indicating spatial orientation, such as "上" (up), "下" (down), "中" (middle) "外" (outside) in *Among Flowers*. The combination of these nouns and prefixes often forms a composite spatial imagery, such as "门外" (outside the door) and "窗外" (outside the window), and this pattern is notably reflected in *Among Flowers*. Table 2 shows several examples as follows.

Table 2. Examples of "orientation words + prefixes" patterns in *Among Flowers*

Sample 1	玉楼明月长相忆, 柳丝袅娜春无力。门外草萋萋, 送君闻马嘶。画罗金翡翠, 香烛消成泪。花落子规啼, 绿窗残梦迷。(温庭筠《菩萨蛮·玉楼明月长相忆》)
Sample 2	凤凰相对盘金缕, 牡丹一夜经微雨。明镜照新妆, 鬓轻双脸长。画楼相望久, 栏外垂丝柳。音信不归来, 社前双燕回。(温庭筠《菩萨蛮·凤凰相对盘金缕》)
Sample 3	星斗稀, 钟鼓歇, 帘外晓莺残月。兰露重, 柳风斜, 满庭堆落花。虚阁上, 倚栏望, 还似去年惆怅。春欲暮, 思无穷, 旧欢如梦中。(温庭筠《更漏子·星斗稀》)
Sample 4	红粉楼前月照, 碧纱窗外莺啼。梦断辽阳音信, 那堪独守空闺。恨对百花时节, 王孙绿草萋萋。(毛文锡《何满子·红粉楼前月照》)

"门外" (outside the door), "栏外" (outside the bar), "帘外" (outside the curtain), "窗外" (outside the window) all reflect the beauty of space separation, creating a sense of distance and hierarchy between inside and outside world. In addition to "外" (outside), there are other composite imageries of "spatial orientation + conjugate prefix" in *Among Flowers*, and the distribution probabilities of these patterns are variable. By extracting these patterns, we can construct the co-occurrence matrix and further develop the semantic network analysis to calculate the mediation centrality of different nodes. For example, Qiu [9] explored the spatial perception of poets in the Middle Tang Dynasty by counting the conjugated prefixes of orientation words, and illustrated the rich spatial perception of poets in the Paradise in the Middle Tang Dynasty. This paper adopts such an approach to discover the core spatial imagery in *Among Flowers*.

The extraction of orientation words is the first task to conduct spatial imagery analysis. By matching the text of *Among Flowers* with the common orientation word list, the orientation word list applicable to *Among Flowers* was finally extracted, and the words with the frequency of occurrence more than 2 were taken for subsequent analysis, and the statistical results are shown in Table 3.

Table 3. Commonly used orientation words in *Among Flowers*

Frequency Rank 1–8		Frequency Rank 9–15	
上	109	下	27
里	65	间	27
前	49	西	23
中	43	畔	7
外	37	北	6
南	36	底	5
边	29	旁	2
东	29	–	–

The conjugated prefix words were further extracted based on the counted orientation words, and then the data were manually proofread and cleaned to screen out noisy data such as "思前" in "无言斜倚小书楼, 暗思前事不胜愁" and "花前" in "照花前后镜, 花面交相映", etc., and retain only the phrases with spatial attributes. It should be noted that most of the conjugated prefixes of orientation words are in the form of one-character words, such as "宫" (palace) in "宫外" (outside the palace), but there are cases where the conjugated prefixes are multi-character words, and most of

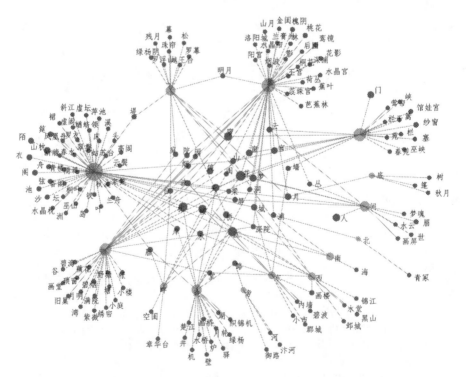

Fig. 2. Semantic network visualization of "orientation words + prefixes" patterns

them are special nouns, such as The prefix "馆娃宫 + 外", "织锦机 + 边", and so on. If only the front single character is extracted, "宫 + 外" satisfies the condition, while "机 + 边" becomes noisy data. Therefore, this situation was taken into account when cleaning the data, instead of taking only the prefix ingle character for the study. Based on the final proofreading of the completed composite spatial imagery results, semantic network analysis was performed, and the visualization results are shown in Fig. 2.

In Fig. 2, orientation words are shown with light gray nodes, and prefix words conjugated with orientation words are shown with dark gray nodes. The lines between nodes represent conjugation relationships, and the size of the circle represents the number of conjugations of the nodes, which can reflect the common perspective of the wordsmith in observing things and the objects most perceived in terms of spatial orientation. The diagram shows the overall spatial perception dimension of the human subject in *Among Flowers*, involving both wide and deep spatial imagery, wide in the vastness of space and deep in the narrowness and depth of space.

Further analysis reveals that the main focus of the poets in *Among Flowers* is not limited to the "炉边,枕上,床上,帘中…" in the boudoir, but also to natural spaces outside the house, and mostly refers to water, such as "岛上,洲上,隋堤上,岸边,湖边, 江南,浦北,碧波东,汴河旁,碧湾中,烟波里…". This is closely related to the geographical environment in which the poets lived. During the Five Dynasties period, the northern region was constantly at war, while the southern region was relatively far away, and there was a big river blocking it, so the literati went south to stay in Xi Shu and other places, which was rich in land, surrounded by mountains and river, and had a superior waterway environment. Therefore, there are more spatial imageries such as "江上、河旁、湖边".

It can also be observed in Fig. 2 that the number of prefixes for different orientation words varies, with "X + 上" having the largest number of patterns, appearing 80 times, followed by "X + 里", appearing 29 times, and "X + 中" in the third place, appearing 22 times. The "里" and "中" here can be the same concept, indicating the internal space, as opposed to the "外". The pattern of "X + 外" appears only 17 times, ranking fifth, which is one-third of the total of "X + 里" and "X + 中", and this difference between inside and outside reflects the beauty of hierarchy of space. we can find that the writers tend to focus on the inside of objects when activating the hierarchy of space.

The following analysis is made from the perspective of prefix words. The nodes of prefix words in the middle part of Fig. 2 are connected to several nodes of orientation words, which indicates that the subject of creation can often perceive these objects directly, such as "花,楼,帘,窗". By extracting the objects with the most spatial orientation words, we can further explore the most commonly used and core composite spatial imagery in *Among Flowers*. Table 4 shows the extraction results, which are arranged in descending order according to the degree of the nodes in Fig. 2, and the results with the degree greater than 2 are shown.

Table 4. Distribution of the most conjugated prefix words connected by orientation words

Conjugated prefix words	Output degree	Orientation words	Conjugated prefix words	Output degree	Orientation words
花	6	间, 里, 畔, 中, 下, 外	天	3	上, 外, 边
楼	5	上, 东, 中, 西, 畔	屏	2	上, 间
江	5	南, 畔, 边, 上, 西	岸	2	边, 上
山	4	下, 外, 西, 上	庭	2	中, 下
波	4	中, 里, 上, 东	烟	2	中, 里
帘	4	中, 外, 里, 下	院	2	中, 里
城	4	上, 东, 西, 里	枕	2	上, 边
梦	3	中, 里, 间	梁	2	上, 间
脸	3	畔, 上, 边	丛	2	间, 里
浦	3	北, 里, 南	洞	2	里, 边
路	3	东, 旁, 边	水	2	西, 上
窗	3	外, 中, 里	园	2	里, 中
月	3	里, 下, 底	堂	2	西, 中
云	3	外, 间, 里	堤	2	下, 上
台	3	下, 畔, 上	墙	2	外, 东
桥	3	南, 边, 下	闺	2	畔, 里

Table 4 shows the object spaces frequently referred to by poets. Among them, the output degree of "花,楼,江,山,波,帘,城" are all more than three. Comparing this statistic with the poems of the Middle Tang Dynasty analyzed by Qiu [9], we find the same thing, that is, "江,山,城" are also more prominent in the poems of the Middle Tang Dynasty, but the difference lies in the fact that "花,楼,波,帘" are not prominent in the poems of the Middle Tang Dynasty. Other items such as "屏上", "屏间", "枕上", "枕边", "浦北", "浦南", etc. also reflect the characteristic spatial imagery of *Among Flowers*.

In addition to the spatial imagery of the "orientation words + prefixes" patterns analyzed above, this paper also finds some unique verbs that are used more frequently in *Among Flowers*, such as "倚" (lean) and "掩" (cover), which appears 58 times and 46 times respectively. They are mostly combined with words with the semantic feature of "cover" (such as "帘", etc.) to form dynamic spatial imagery with a blocking nature. Take the verb "掩" as an example, its spatial imagery is shown in Fig. 3. Wei [10] point out that the use of this kind of blocking composite imagery in *Among Flowers* reflects a unique aesthetic tendency in Chinese literature, namely the "beauty of separation", which is mainly expressed in the sense of hierarchy, haziness and distance.

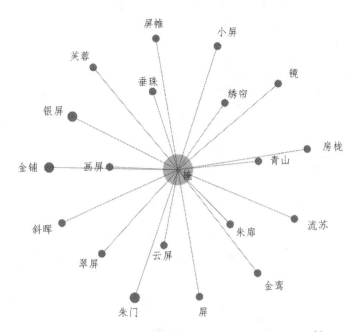

Fig. 3. The dynamic spatial imagery formed by the word "掩"

3　Spatial Imagery Clustering Based on Word2vec Model

The second section of this paper explores the spatial imagery that frequently appears in *Among Flowers*. From the perspective of the Container Schema [11], the middle part of Fig. 2 is rich in objects, covering not only natural scenery, but also pavilions, as well as the intimate space in the boudoir. The spatial imagery involved in *Among Flowers* has a highly hierarchical sense from far to near relative to the human body, and Fig. 4 illustrates this spatial span.

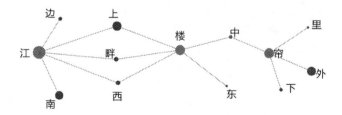

Fig. 4. The spatial span in *Among Flowers*

In order to more clearly explore the different categories of spatial imagery clusters and each sub-element under the different categories in *Among Flowers*, this paper traines high-dimensional word vectors based on the word2vec model, mapping them on

Among Flowers text dataset for cluster clustering analysis, and calculates the semantic relevance of each sub-element under different levels of space.

The Word2vec model was proposed by Mikolov [12], which is essentially a 3-layer neural network containing an input layer, a hidden layer, and an output layer. The number of neurons in the input layer is consistent with the size of the trained vocabulary table, and the number of neural units in the hidden layer is the dimensional size of the final word vector obtained. The number of neural units in the output layer is the same as the number of neural units in the input layer. Suppose the vocabulary size is V, and the set vector length is N, then the weight matrix from the input layer to the hidden layer is $Wi = V \times N$, and each row represents a word in the vocabulary. The weight matrix from the hidden layer to the output layer is $Wo = N \times V$. The goal of this model is to obtain the results of the probability distribution of the words in the output layer, which reflects the degree of correlation between the words and the input context words, so it is necessary to connect the *softmax* function to the output layer and convert the calculated values in the output layer into the form of probabilities. After the predicted probability vector is calculated, the prediction error is obtained by subtracting the predicted probability vector from the target vector, and then the back propagation algorithm is used to update the weights Wi and Wo, and continuously iteratively learn the binary word pair relationship between the context words and the target words in the corpus to generate a word vector representation with fixed dimensions of the target words.

The model is based on the distributional hypothesis, which assumes that the semantics of words are determined by their contexts, and words with similar contexts have similar semantics. Therefore, it can find out the semantic relationship between words, which is represented by the distance between spatial vectors, and the semantic relationship is proportional to the spatial distance. For ancient texts, single- character words are dominant, and the trained character vectors can better reflect the semantic relationships among words. Since the data volume of *Among Flowers* is relatively limited, the trained model is not sufficient to better represent the semantic relationships between words. This study trained the word vectors based on a large-scale raw corpus of ancient Chinese, and then mapped the text of *Among Flowers* with the trained word vectors, and finally visualized the mapped high-dimensional word vectors by dimensionality reduction to discover the class clustering effect of words in *Among Flowers*. The effect of word vector dimensionality reduction visualization is shown in Fig. 5.

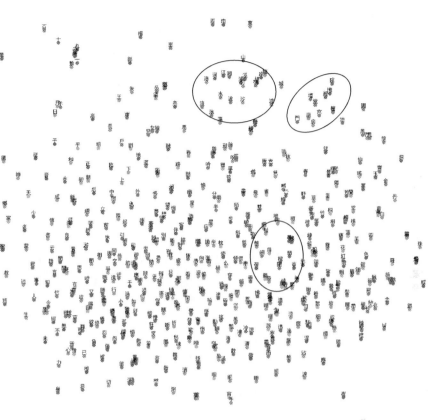

Fig. 5. Visualization of the vector of the top 550 words of the frequency

In Fig. 5, the closer the words are to each other, the stronger the semantic correlation is, and it is easy to find that the figure contains many clusters. For example, "袖,带,群,纱,衣,衫" for women's clothing, "钟,鼓,笛,筝,弦,声" for musical instruments, and "金,丹,青,黄,白" for colors, and "霜,露,雨,雪,霏" for weather, "凄,凉,愁,泠,寒" for the state of mind, and so on.

In addition to the above-mentioned clusters, the main focus of this paper is on the clusters that can represent spatial imagery. In Fig. 5, it is easy to find three such clusters, namely, "江" as the representative of "江,河,海,湖,沙…", "楼" as the representative of "宫,殿,楼,阁,堂…" and "帘" as the representative of "窗,帷,枕,帐,幕…". These three categories of spatial imagery hierarchically reflect the different visual environments and spatial scopes of writers. The "江" category reflects the natural scenery, with a wide field of view; the "帘" category reflects the environment in the boudoir, with a closed field of view; the "楼" category connects the two, with a narrower field of view than "江" and a wider field of view than "帘". In the following, the semantic correlation between the word vectors is calculated to extract the sub-elements under each spatial cluster. The cosine distance is calculated by the following formula.

$$\cos \theta = \frac{\sum_{1}^{n}(Ai \times Bi)}{\sqrt{\sum_{i=1}^{n}(Ai)^2} \times \sqrt{\sum_{i=1}^{n}(Bi)^2}} \qquad (1)$$

In the formula, i denotes the dimension of the vector. The results of the semantic relevance calculation are shown in Table 5.

Table 5. Calculated results of semantic relevance of three types of spatial imagery (in descending order of semantic relevance)

Most relevant to imagery "帘" (boudoir space)	Most relevant to imagery "楼" (architectural space)	Most relevant to imagery "江" (Water space)
窗 0.7058882117271423	台 0.5978765487670898	湘 0.6180854439735413
帷 0.6168897151947021	栏 0.59778928756671387	河 0.603803277015686
栊 0.5252200961112976	阁 0.508845329284668	溪 0.5360757112503052
槛 0.5209416747093201	窗 0.5080914497375488	浦 0.5209130048751831
纱 0.5147920250892639	桥 0.5031951665878296	海 0.5002914667129517
帐 0.5136486291885376	槛 0.48219576478004456	水 0.45215854048728943
篁 0.4807305335998535	堂 0.47944408655166626	岸 0.4085049629211426
...	...	...

4   A Comparative Analysis of the Differences in the Use of Spatial Imagery in the Poets' Works

In the third section of this paper, three different levels of spatial imagery are obtained by clustering, namely, boudoir space, architectural space and water space, and three sets of spatial imagery are formed by extracting the sub-elements under each type of imagery cluster. Based on these three kinds of spatial imagery, this section quantifies the statistics of different poets' works and examines the differences in the use of different spatial imagery by each poet.

Firstly, the distribution of the number of works in *Among Flowers* was counted, and the results are shown in Fig. 6.

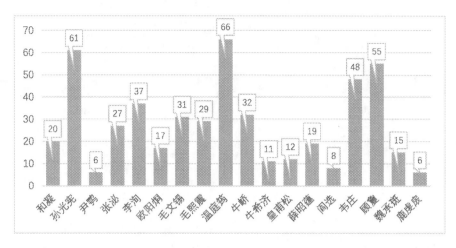

Fig. 6. The distribution of the number of works by each poet in *Among Flowers*

By observing the results in Fig. 6, it can be found that the number of collected works of the 18 poets varies, with the most collected poet being "温庭筠" (Wen Tingyun) with 66 pieces and the least collected being "尹鹗" (Yin E) and "鹿虔扆" (Lu Qianyi) with only 6 pieces. In order to discover the tendency characteristics of different poets to use a certain type of spatial imagery in their compositions, the boudoir space, the architectural space and the water space are set as set A, set B and set C respectively, and if an element i in the set exists in a certain work, the tendency value q of that spatial imagery is added by 1. Finally, the tendency value q and the total number of works m are averaged to obtain the average probability of a certain type of spatial imagery appearing in each poet's work. The results are shown in Table 6.

Table 6. Average spatial imagery distribution of each writer (unit: %)

Serial number	Poet	The boudoir space	The architectural space	The water space
1	和凝	25.00%	20.00%	45.00%
2	孙光宪	36.07%	52.46%	47.54%
3	尹鹗	66.67%	**83.33%**	16.67%
4	张泌	66.67%	40.74%	40.74%
5	李洵	43.24%	27.03%	64.86%
6	欧阳烔	29.41%	35.29%	52.94%
7	毛文锡	32.26%	45.16%	58.06%
8	毛熙震	62.07%	41.38%	13.79%
9	温庭筠	48.48%	54.55%	39.39%
10	牛峤	46.88%	59.38%	28.13%
11	牛希济	36.36%	54.55%	27.27%
12	皇甫松	16.67%	25.00%	**75.00%**

(continued)

Table 6. (*continued*)

Serial number	Poet	The boudoir space	The architectural space	The water space
13	薛昭蕴	26.32%	52.63%	47.37%
14	阎选	62.50%	50.00%	25.00%
15	韦庄	39.58%	43.75%	37.50%
16	顾夐	**69.09%**	50.91%	20.00%
17	魏承斑	60.00%	33.33%	20.00%
18	鹿虔扆	66.67%	50.00%	16.67%

From Table 6, we can find that among the three types of spatial imagery, the most inclined to depict the boudoir space is "顾夐" (Gu Xiong), accounting for 69.09% of his works, and the least is "皇甫松" (Huang Fusong), accounting for 16.67% of his works; the most inclined to depict the architectural space is "尹鹗" (Yin E), accounting for 83.33% of his works, and the least is "和凝" (He Ning), accounting for 20% of his works; the most inclined to depict the water space is "皇甫松" (Huang Fusong), accounting for accounting for 75% of his works, and the least is "毛熙震" (Mao Xizhen), accounting for 13.79% of his works.

5　Conclusion

This study adopts a quantitative approach to explore the spatial imagery in *Among Flowers*, firstly, we analyzed the spatial attributes of "帘" and "屏" through word frequency statistics. Then, we used semantic network analysis to discover the most frequently referred composite spaces in "花,楼,江,山,波,帘,城", and we conducted semantic clustering analysis through word2vec model to discover three types of spatial imagery in *Among Flowers*: "the boudoir space", "the architectural space" and "the water space". Finally we calculated the semantic correlation and extracted the spatial sub-elements in different spatial clusters, and then analyzed the stylistic differences in the use of spatial imagery by different poets.

Acknowledgements. This research is supported by the Major Project of Chinese National Social Science Foundation (No. 18ZDA238).

References

1. Hao, X., Ge, S., Zhang, Y., et al.: The construction and analysis of annotated imagery corpus of three hundred tang poems. Workshop on Chinese Lexical Semantics, pp. 517–524. Springer, Cham (2019). https://doi.org/10.1007/978-3-030-38189-9_53
2. Dong, Z.: HowNet. HowNet's Home Page. http://www.keenage.com. (in Chinese)
3. Chen, Z.: Theory of Poetic Imagery. China Social Science Press (1990). (in Chinese)
4. Xie, Q.: A Study of the Imagery of "Mountain" in Five Dynasties' CI. Hua Mulan Culture Press (2012). (in Chinese)

5. Spurgeon, C.F.E.: Shakespeare's Imagery and what it Tells Us. Cambridge University Press (1935)
6. Xiaomei, S.: Autumn is the most favorite imagery of the four seasons–statistics and analysis of autumn imagery in Liuyong's poems on travels and journeys. Shanxi Normal Univ. J. (Soc. Sci. Ed.) **01**, 104–107 (2011). (in Chinese)
7. Feiyue, L.: Editorial dissemination and construction of a new lyrical style in *Among Flowers*. Zhongzhou J. **03**, 169–174 (2012). (in Chinese)
8. Huang, X.: Studies in the Poetics of Genre and Space. Guangdong Higher Education Publishing Company (2019)
9. Weiyun, Q., Cheng, Y.: Heart in paradise, gazing at earth: a digital humanities study of the spatial orientation of Chinese tang poetry. J. Southwest Univ. National. (Human. Soc. Sci. Ed.) **41**(08), 161–171 (2020). (in Chinese)
10. Wei, W., Fengtao, L.: The theory of imagery characteristics of *Among Flowers*. J. Qilu Stud. **02**, 115–118 (2012). (in Chinese)
11. Lakoff, G., Johnson, M.: Metaphors We Live By. University of Chicago Press (2008)
12. Mikolov, T., Chen, K., Corrado, G., et al.: Efficient estimation of word representations in vector space. arXiv preprint arXiv:1301.3781 (2013)

Study on the Order of Double-Syllable Double Attributives and Selection Restrictions—Take the Structures of $a_1 + a_2 + De + n$ and $a_1' + De + a_2' + n'$ as Examples

Rui Song[1], Wenjie Zhao[2], and Zhimin Wang[1(✉)]

[1] Research Institute of International Chinese Language Education,
Beijing Language and Culture University, Beijing, China
songrui1990@126.com
[2] School of Information Science, Beijing Language and Culture University,
Beijing, China

Abstract. This paper analyzes differences between Structure A: "$a_1 + a_2 + de + n$" and structure B: "$a_1' + de + a_2' + n'$", which are extracted from the corpus of *People's Daily* from 2019 to 2020. Influential factors and constraints from semantics, syntax, word order, rhythm, etc. are proposed in the paper. Our study shows that semantic similarity of double-syllable double attributive adjectives in structure A is higher than that of structure B. The character *de* in two structures serves as a "segmentation mark" to maintain stability of structures and cannot be shifted freely. Moreover, we examine that factors influencing word order of double attributives are the result of the combination of semantics, cognition, habit, rhythm, etc. Among them, the dominant factor of structure A is cognition, while that of the structure B is semantics. Besides, we argue that high-frequency nouns of the two structures are mostly abstract nouns and are poor in semantic self-containedness. In addition, words at the nuclear stress location in the two structures mainly end with a falling tone. The paper is further analyzed from the perspective of prosodic structure and highlighting effect. This study provides new insights to account for the combination mechanisms of multiple attributives, as well as contributing to the construction of knowledge database with a novel method.

Keywords: Double-syllable double attributives · Semantic features · Word order constraints

1 Introduction

Double-syllable double attributive is a characteristic structure in Chinese, as in:
Structure A: "$a_1 + a_2 + de + n$".

(1) a. Xǔ Zhìlǐ yòng jījí lèguān de tàidù miànduì shēnghuó.

Xu Zhili use positive optimism de attitude face life
'Xu Zhili faces life with positive and optimistic attitude.'
b. Xǔ Zhìlǐ yòng lèguān jījí de tàidù miànduì shēnghuó.

Xu Zhili use optimism positive de attitude face life
'Xu Zhili faces life with optimistic and positive attitude.'

(2) a. Zhèzhǒng huòqǔ fāngshì cúnzài jiǎndān piànmiàn de wèntí.

this kind obtain way exist simple one-sided de problem
'There is a simple and one-sided problem with this method of acquisition.'
*b. Zhèzhǒng huòqǔ fāngshì cúnzài piànmiàn jiǎndān de wèntí.

this kind obtain way exist simple one-sided de problem
'There is a one-sided simple problem with this method of acquisition.'

Structure B: "a₁' + *de* + a₂' + n'".

(3) a. Wèi rénmín chuàngzào xìngfú de měihǎo shēnghuó.

for people create happy de beautiful life
'Create a happy and beautiful life for people.'
b. Wèi rénmín chuàngzào měihǎo de xìngfú shēnghuó.

for people create beautiful de happy life
'Create a beautiful and happy life for people.'

(4) a. Bìngdú sùyuán shì yánjǐn de kēxué wèntí.

virus traceability is rigorous de scientific issue
'Virus traceability is a rigorous scientific issue.'
*b. Bìngdú sùyuán shì kēxué de yánjǐn wèntí.

virus traceability is scientific de rigorous issue
'Virus traceability is a scientific rigorous issue.'

In structure A, as shown in (1a), *jījí lèguān de tàidù* 'positive and optimistic attitude' can also be referred as *lèguān jījí de tàidù* 'optimistic and positive attitude'. Meanwhile, in (1b), *jiǎndān piànmiàn de wèntí* 'simple and one-sided problem' is not identical to *piànmiàn jiǎndān de wèntí 'one-sided simple problem'* semantically. In structure B, as shown in (2a), *xìngfú de měihǎo shēnghuó* 'happy and beautiful life' can also be referred as *měihǎo de xìngfú shēnghuó 'beautiful and happy life'. However, in (2b), yánjǐn de kēxué wèntí* 'rigorous scientific issue' generally cannot be uttered as *kēxué de yánjǐn wèntí* 'scientific rigorous issue'. We examine that there exist distinct features in the two structures. How are the two structures used in corpus? What are the features and differences of the two structures in semantics and syntax? What are the rules and restrictions in terms of the order of internal adjectives? What are the characteristics of the nouns in the two structures? These are the issues to be discussed in this paper.

Scholars have conducted many researches on structures and categories of adjectives, semantic features of adjectives, rules in the use of adjectives as attributives and the rules of combination [1–6]. However, few scholars have made a distinction of multiple attributives between monosyllable and double-syllable attributive adjectives. Besides, comparative analysis of double-syllable double attributives from newspaper corpus is under-researched. The expressions in newspaper corpus is more formal and tends to be in written language, which conform to the expressive characteristics of double attributive adjectives.

This paper uses data from *People's Daily* in the past two years as the corpus, and extracts all the collocations of the two structures based on the combination of "co-occurrence + dependence". It investigates the semantic and syntactic differences of different structures of double-syllable double attributives, and explores the restraints of the order of adjectives. It summarizes the regular characteristics of high-frequency nouns in the two structures, and analyzes the selection restrictions of syntactic collocation from the perspective of prosody. It provides case support for international Chinese education and teaching. Meanwhile, it can also provide important data for multiple attributive combination research as well as for the construction of knowledge database of multiple attributives.

The layout of this paper is as follows. In Sect. 2 screening and processing of the corpus is presented. Function of *de* and semantic characteristics of the two structures are introduced in Sect. 3. In Sect. 4 we analyze the order of adjectives in the two structures and their restrictive factors. The characteristics of nouns in the two structures are specified in Sect. 5. Effects of prosody on the two structures are discussed in Sect. 6. Finally, a summary and future research directions are presented in Sect. 7.

2   Corpus Screening and Processing

The process of refining the corpus is: collecting samples → manual labeling → establishing standard collection → testing and adjusting the extraction procedure → extracting the corpus from *People's Daily* → cleaning and duplication eliminating + manual proofreading.

"The Beijing Language and Culture University Corpus (BCC)" [7] is taken as a standard collection to verify the accuracy of the extraction procedure. "$a_1 + a_2 + de + n$" and "$a_1' + de + a_2' + n'$" structures are searched in the corpus. 10,000 pieces in the fields of newspapers, literature, technology and Sina Weibo are downloaded and manually marked. Several types of combinations not including in the scope of this paper's research are removed, such as:

Overlapping adjectives:

" yīn   lěng   yīn   lěng   de   tiān,   rè   hū   rè   hū   de   mántou."
cloudy cold cloudy cold   de   weather, warm hu   warm hu   de   steamed bun
'cloudy and cold weather, warm steamed bun'

Nouns: names of persons or objects:

" kěài   měilì   de   Wáng Hóng"
  cute   beautiful de   Wang Hong
'cute and beautiful Wang Hong'

Adverbs modify adjectives:

" kōngqián   qiángdà de   bīnglì,   wánquán   de   héfǎ   dìwèi."
unprecedentedly powerful de troops, completely de legitimate   status
'unprecedentedly powerful troops, completely legitimate status'

Noun NP structure[1]:

"dānchún jiǎndān de xiàoyuán àiqíng, gāojí   de   yōumò   értóng wénxué."
innocent simple de campus   love, advanced de humorous children literature
'innocent and simple campus love, advanced and humorous children's literature

After establishing a standard collection based on the two structures, extraction procedure is tested and verified. The extraction procedure is designed under the principle of "co-occurrence first and dependency second". Based on the python development environment, automatic word segmentation tools (nlpir, pkuseg [8], Harbin Institute of Technology ltp [9], Baidu participle) are employed for automatic segmentation and part-of-speech tagging. On such basis, the word *de* is set as the center, and two characters preceding and following *de* are selected as the extraction window. Strings that are in line with Structure A ($a_1 + a_2 + de + n$) and Structure B ($a_1' + de + a_2' + n'$) are extracted. The dependency syntax analysis tools of Baidu and ltp are used to analyze the corpus, and the adjective complement structure such as *ruǎnyìng shìzhōng de dǎoguǎn 'neither too hard nor too soft catheter'* is removed. After several rounds of debugging and verifications, both the recognition rate and accuracy rate of the two standard collections are above 95%.

The application extraction procedure is used to extract corpus from *People's Daily* from 2019 to 2020[2]. *People's Daily* is a national key news website, which includes important news, reviews, observations, international, economic, political, cultural, social news and advertisements, etc. Its language style includes the characteristics of written, objective, concise, neat and others. Therefore, the corpus is suitable for the current study. NP structure in the noun collection from Yu Shiwen's "A Dictionary of Modern Chinese Information" is set as the standard for duplication elimination and

---

[1] The research scope of this article only considers the case where the nouns in the structure are bare nouns, so the corpus of NP structure of nouns is removed.

[2] The corpus of "People's Daily" in this article comes from "People's Daily" Graphic Database http://data.people.com.cn/".

cleaning. Manual proofreading is performed to remove structural combinations that do not conform to grammatical norms such as *chéngshí shǒuxìn de tóngshí* 'honest and faithful meanwhile', *míngxiǎn de lèisì huā* 'evident similar flower'. Finally, extraction results are shown as follows: the number of tokens in structure A is 3089. The number of types is 1910. There are 575 types of a_1, 641 types of a_2 and 987 types of nouns in structure A. The number of tokens in structure B is 2492. The number of types is 1537. There are 457 types of a_1', 314 types of a_2' and 553 types of nouns in structure B.

3   Analysis of Semantic and Syntactic Features

Double-syllable double attributives defined in this paper indicate that each of the two attributives can form an attribute-centre structure with the central noun. In addition, the two attribute-centre structures are in a parallel relationship. For example: *fùzá yánjùn de xíngshì* 'complex and severe situation' can be divided into *fùzá de xíngshì* 'complex situation' + *yánjùn de xíngshì* 'severe situation'; *zhòngyào de xiànshí yìyì* 'vital and practical significance' can be divided into *zhòngyào de yìyì* 'vital significance' + *xiànshí de yìyì* 'practical significance'. In other words, adjectives in the two structures aim to describe the central noun from the perspective of semantics.

It can be concluded from the data that there are hundreds of adjectives that can be functional in their respective structures. Through comparative analysis we can observe that the semantic similarity of adjectives within the two structures is different, for example:

(5) a. Structure A: gōngzhèng   hélǐ   de   fāngxiàng.

                    fair   reasonable   de   direction

                    'fair and reasonable direction'

     b. Structure B: jùtǐ   de   mínzhǔ   zhìdù.

                    concrete de   democratic system

                    'concrete democratic system'

(6) a. Structure A: ānníng   tiánjìng   de   fēnwéi.

                    quiet   tranquil   de   atmosphere

                    'quiet and tranquil atmosphere'

     b. Structure B: bìyào   de   jiànkāng   zhèngmíng.

                    necessary de   health   certificate

                    'necessary health certificate'

According to the semantic category of "Harbin Institute of Technology Synonyms Cilin Extended Edition" (hereinafter referred to as "Cilin"), in example (5), the structure A *gōngzhèng* 'fair' and *hélǐ* 'reasonable' are in (E feature) category. *Jùtǐ* 'concrete' in structure B is in (E feature) category, while *mínzhǔ* 'democratic' is in (D abstract) category. By comparison, words in the same semantic category demonstrate higher semantic similarity. Adjectives can be in the same semantic category, but the semantic similarity between the two structures can still be very different. In example (6), all of adjectives are in (E feature) category. In (6)a, the meaning of *ānníng* 'quiet' is *āndìng, níngjìng* 'settled and quiet'[3], and *tiánjìng* 'tranquil' means *ānjìng, níngjìng* 'quiet and tranquil'. The two expression are similar semantically, and can be used as synonyms in some contexts. While in structure B the meaning of *bìyào* 'necessity' is *bùkě quēshǎo de* 'indispensable', and the meaning of *jiànkāng* 'health' is *fāyù liánghǎo de, qíngkuàng zhèngcháng de* 'well-developed, in a normal situation'. They are distinctly set apart with low semantic similarity.

From syntactic category, *de* is used as an attributive marker (Shuxiang Lv [5]), and its main function is to form a phrase of *de to* modify nouns. It plays a descriptive or restrictive role. This paper claims that in the two types of double-syllable double attributive structures, *de* not only plays a role of modification and connection, but also a role of "segmentation" and "stabilization". First of all, the position of *de* cannot be shifted freely. Except in special circumstances, *de* in structure A cannot be moved forward, such as *kāifàng bāoróng de zītài* 'open and inclusive position'. We generally do not claim *kāifàng de bāoróng zītài* 'open inclusive position' because in terms of structure, *kāifàng bāoróng* 'open and inclusive' as a semantic whole is indivisible, and almost no "segmentation mark" like *de* can be inserted. Similarly, *de* in structure B cannot be shifted backward. For example, *chéngshú de zhòngyào biāozhì* 'important signal of maturity' is generally not mentioned as *chéngshú zhòngyào de biāozhì* 'maturity important signal', because zhòngyào biāozhì 'important signal' as a semantic whole cannot be segmented freely. Nevertheless, there are a few cases where *de* can be shifted between the two structures. Among all the extracted corpus in this paper, there are only 18 cases, accounting for 0.52% of all extracted cases. For example, *jiǎndān shíyòng de jìshù* 'simple and practical technology' can also be referred as *jiǎndān de shíyòng jìshù* 'simple practical technology'.

In addition, as one kind of "segmentation mark", the character *de* can also play a role in maintaining structural stability, as shown in Fig. 1.

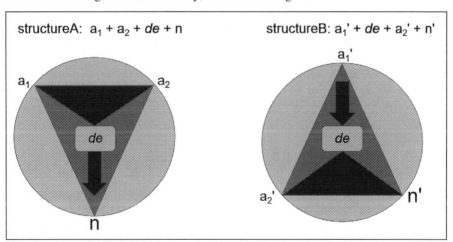

Fig. 1. Schematic diagram of the stability of the two structures

---

[3] The definitions of the relevant words in this article are all from the "Modern Chinese Dictionary" (7th edition).

Assuming that the both of the two structures can form a stable structure with a tangent triangle inside the circle, the character *de* occupies the center of the circle. As mentioned above, "a_1 and a_2" in structure A are close in semantic relationship with high semantic similarity. They are used as a whole to modify nouns. For example, *gānjìng wèishēng de huánjìng* 'clean and sanitary environment' is composed of *gānjìng* 'clean' + *wèishēng* 'sanitary'. Acting on *de* + *huánjìng* 'de + environment' to form a stable structure of an inverted triangle. If *de* is removed, it will become *gānjìng wèishēng huánjìng* 'clean, sanitary environment', which is not a common expression. *De* cannot be moved forward into *gānjìng de wèishēng huánjìng* 'clean sanitary environment'. Weights of "a_1 and a_2" before *de* are the same, which suggests d*e* is at the segmentation point before the noun. Semantics can be balanced and the overall structure can be kept steady.

In structure B, the semantic closeness between "a_2' + n'" is higher. "a_1'" acts on *de* first, and then forms a stable equilateral triangle structure with "a_2' + n'". For example: in *wēixiǎn de guānjiàn shíkè* 'dangerous critical moment', *guānjiàn shíkè* 'critical moment' as a semantic whole is modified by *wēixiǎn* + *de* 'dangerous + de'. The word *de* is at the segmentation of the semantic balance of the whole sentence, which can neither be shifted backward nor removed. The sentence can neither be mentioned as *wēixiǎn guān jiàn de shíkè* 'danger, critical moment' nor "*wēixiǎn guānjiàn shíkè* 'danger criticality moment'. The former causes semantic separation and the latter causes semantic imbalance. Both are not in line with the feature of the language. Therefore, the position of *de* is extremely critical as an important "segmentation mark" that maintains semantic balance and structural stability.

4   Restrictive Factors of Adjective Order

As pointed out above, most of "a_1" and "a_2" in structure A are in the same semantic category, and the semantic similarity is high. Even the segmentation mark *de* cannot be inserted. Whether the order between "a_1" and "a_2" can be changed is worth studying. Based on the existing corpus, we have counted the number and proportion of types where adjective order in the two structures can be interchangeable, as demonstrated in Table 1.

Table 1. Examples of compound words in interchangeable adjective order

Combination of interchangeable adjective order	Number	Percentage	Examples
$a_1 + a_2 + n = a_2 + a_1 + n$	74	3.87%	gānjìng zhěngjié de jiēdào ≈ zhěngjié gānjìng de jiēdào
$a_1' + a_2' + n' = a_2' + a_1' + n'$	18	1.17%	xìngfú de měihǎo shēnghuó ≈ měihǎo de xìngfú shēnghuó

Although adjectives in structure A are in the same semantic category and are relatively high in semantic similarity, only 3.87% combinations' order are interchangeable. It implies that in most cases, the adjective order in structure A is not interchangeable. In structure B, there are 1.17% interchangeable combinations. We find that a very small number of interchangeable word examples require different restriction conditions. The adjectives "a_1 and a_2" in structure A are highly similar, and the overall semantic difference of the structure preceding and following the exchange is not significant. The semantic relevance of "a_2'" and "n'" in structure B is high. Even if "a_2'" and "n'" can be changed, the semantics of the structure as a whole will change, such as the difference between *měihǎo shēnghuó* 'beautiful life' and *xìngfú shēnghuó* 'happy life'.

In the vast majority of combinations that cannot be interchanged, what are the constraints? Previous scholars have conducted many researches on the order rules of multiple attributives ([6, 10], etc.), such as semantic principles, economic principles, cognitive motivation, habitual conventions, prosodic combination, etc. All of them can be reflected in the corpus of this paper. However, the paper argues that the restrictive factors affecting the word order of the double-syllable double attributives are multiple. For example:

(7) a."chéngshí shǒuxìn de jīngshén."

honest faithful de spirit
'honest and faithful spirit'
b. "tōngsú yìdǒng de yǔyán."

popular understandable de language
'popular and understandable language'
c. "kuānchǎng míngliàng de xīn jū."

spacious bright de new home
'spacious and bright new home'
d. "guǎngmào měilì de tǔdì."

vast beautiful de land
'vast and beautiful land'

Chéngshí shǒuxìn 'honest and faithful' and *tōngsú yìdǒng* 'popular and understandable' in example (7) are influenced not only by customary conventions but also by rhythmic combination (2 + 2 right-handed steps). They work together to form a stable structure. In daily life, we generally do not use expressions like *shǒuxìn chéngshí de jīngshén* 'faithful and honest spirit' or *yìdǒng tōngsú de yǔyán* 'understandable and popular language'.

However, when multiple factors work together, a dominant factor will also be highlighted. This paper argues that in structure A, the dominant factor is the cognitive one, such as *kuānchǎng míngliàng de xīnjū* 'spacious and bright new home'. From the perspective of modification, the semantic similarity between "a_1 and a_2" is high, and the semantic difference is not evident. However, from a cognitive point of view, *kuānchǎng* 'spacious' is the overall description of the house, and *míngliàng* 'bright' is the description of the lighting effect of the house. It reflects the Chinese thinking of "integrity" and "overall view". In the process of modification and description, it follows the cognitive habit of "first overall-second details". The knowledge structure is stored in brains, and a stable structure of collocation is gradually formed in the process of retrieval and usage. Similarly, in the following examples:

"kuānkuò   gānjìng   de   mǎlù."

wide   clean   de   road

'wide and clean road'

"gāodà   cūzhuàng   de   qiáodūn"

tall   stout   de   piers

'tall and stout piers'

"liáokuò   zhuàngměi   de   cǎoyuán"

vast   magnificent   de   grassland

'vast and magnificent grassland'

The overall situation of the objects is described before the details or other features. Therefore, this paper argues that cognitive order and thinking habits are the dominant factors affecting the order of adjectives in Structure A.

Moreover, in structure A, due to the semantic similarity of "a_1 and a_2" and the combined effect of multiple factors, the word order of some double attributives has formed a fixed form. It can reflect the historical accumulation and cultural traditions of political language in our country and it has continued through times. For example, in *jiānqiáng yǒulì de dǎng zǔzhī* 'strong and powerful party organization', *jiānqiáng yǒulì* 'strong and powerful' first appeared in *People's Daily* in the second edition on June 14, 1947 from *yóujī zhànzhēng yě yīn mínbīng de xùnsù jiànlì yǔ fāzhǎn ér gèngjiā jiānqiáng yǒulì* 'Guerrilla warfare becomes stronger and more powerful because of the rapid establishment and development of the militia'. Since then, it has been carried forward and used, forming a fixed form of collocation and word order. A similar situation: *pínqióng luòhòu de guójiā* 'poor and left-behind country' was first published in the first edition in November 1946; *yīngyǒng wánqiáng de zuòfēng* 'brave and tenacious style' was first published in the third edition on January 4, 1964.

The word order of structure B is influenced by multiple factors, but the dominant factor is the semantic factor. For example:

(8) a. "yōuxiù de chuántǒng wénhuà."

excellent de traditional culture
'excellent traditional culture'
b. "wěidà de gǔlǎo wénmíng."

great de ancient civilization
'great ancient civilization'
c. "yánjǐn de kēxué jīngshén."

rigorous de scientific spirit
'rigorous scientific spirit'

d. "tūchū de xiānjìn jítǐ."

outstanding de advanced collective
'outstanding advanced collective'

Yōuxiù de chuántǒng wénhuà 'excellent traditional culture' and *wěidà de gǔlǎo wénmíng* 'great ancient civilization' in example (8) are influenced by both the highlighting principle and the economic principle. The highlighting principle suggests that the most important thing in the sentence should be highlighted which indicates highlighting "a_1'" before *de*. In (8)a, *yōuxiù* 'excellent' is highlighted. The economic principle argues that it is necessary to omit the meaningless part, that is, *de* between "a_2'" and "n'". *Wěidà de gǔlǎo wénmíng* 'great ancient civilization' is derived from the combination of *wěidà de* 'great de' and *gǔlǎo de wénmíng* 'ancient civilization' after omitting *de*.

We believe that the word order of structure B is also a stable structure formed under the combination of many factors. However, the prerequisite for a stable structure is the closeness of the semantic relationship and collocation between "a_2'" and "n'". In example (8), if the word order is changed, it will cause semantic contradictions or structural instability between "a_2'" and "n'". We generally don't utter *kēxué de yánjǐn jīngshén* 'scientific rigorous spirit', or *xiānjìn de tūchū jítǐ* 'advanced outstanding collective'. This is also the phenomenon and issue raised at the beginning of this paper.

5 The Collection of Nouns and Their Characteristics

The semantic characteristics of the two structures and influential factors of adjective order are discussed above. What are the specific high-frequency nouns that can be used in the two structures, and what are the characteristics of them? The paper counts 897 types of nouns in structure A, 553 types of nouns in structure B, 258 types of the intersection of the two common nouns. The results are given as follows in Table 2.

Table 2. The number of nouns and their intersections in the two structures

Sort	Nouns in structure A: 897 types	Frequency	Intersection of nouns 258 types	Frequency	Nouns in structure B: 553 types	Frequency
1	shì jiè 'world'	140	shì jiè 'world'	165	jiē duàn 'stage'	111
2	fāng xiàng 'direction'	84	huán jìng 'environment'	114	yì yì 'meaning'	77
3	huán jìng 'environment'	84	fāng xiàng 'direction'	88	wèn tí 'problem'	61
4	yǔ yán 'language'	63	yì yì 'meaning'	84	lì liàng 'strength'	46
5	tài dù 'attitude'	63	tài dù 'attitude'	76	jú miàn 'situation'	44
6	cuò shī 'measure'	58	wèn tí 'problem'	74	yuán yīn 'reason'	37
7	xíng shì 'circumstances'	44	cuò shī 'measure'	69	yīn sù 'factor'	37
8	jī chǔ 'basis'	39	yǔ yán 'language'	64	zuò yòng 'effect'	34
9	xīn tài 'mentality'	38	xíng shì 'situation'	60	qíng huái 'feelings'	33
10	fāng shì 'mode'	37	fēn wéi 'atmosphere'	56	jué xīn 'determination'	30

The central noun is the object modified by double attributives. From the distribution, many nouns in the overlapping area can be used by both structures. We extract the top ten word tokens in the two structures in order of frequency and top ten word tokens in the intersection of nouns. The words are shown in Table 3.

Table 3. The top ten word tokens

Sort	Structure A: $a_1 + a_2 + de + n$	Frequency	Intersection of nouns	Structure B: $a_1' + de + a_2' + n'$	Frequency
1	qīngjié měilì de shìjiè	91	shì jiè	chījìn de guānjiàn jiēduàn	109
2	gōngzhèng hélǐ de fāngxiàng	69	huán jìng	zhòngyào de xiànshí yìyì	42
3	fánróng měihǎo de shìjiè	28	fāng xiàng	ānquán de zhòngyào zǔchéngbùfèn	22
4	yánjùn fùzá de xíngshì	21	yì yì	liánghǎo de wèishēng xíguàn	19
5	kāifàng bāoróng de zītài	20	tài dù	yǒuxiào de jiànkāng cèlüè	16
6	jījí lèguān de tàidù	19	wèn tí	wēixiǎn de guānjiàn shíkè	13
7	jiānqiáng yǒulì de dǎngzǔzhī	18	cuò shī	ānquán de wēixiǎn wùpǐn	13
8	fùzá yánjùn de xíngshì	18	yǔ yán	gōngkāi de mìmì bùfèn	13
9	pínqióng luòhòu de shāncūn	16	xíng shì	xiànhuó de xiànshí míngzhèng	13
10	tōngsú yìdǒng de yǔyán	16	fēn wéi	jìnzé de shíjì chéngxiào	12

According to the semantic category of "Ci Lin", the top ten nouns in the intersection are in D-abstract category. In addition, nine out of the ten high-frequency nouns in structure A are in D-abstract except for *shāncūn* 'village' which is in the C-space-time category. W*ùpǐn* 'item' in structure B is in B-objects; *shíkè* 'moment', C-space-time; *bùfèn* 'part' and *zǔchéng bùfèn* 'component', E-characteristics, and the other six are in D-abstract.

Most of high-frequency nouns in the two structures are abstract nouns. Abstract nouns are the generalizations of abstract things. Compared with concrete nouns, abstract nouns are weak in semantic self-containedness and require more modifiers to form a stable structure, which is reflected in our corpus. Without the modification of double attributive, it is difficult for abstract nouns to achieve semantic self-containedness. For example:

(9)   "zhèlǐ yuánmíng gǔdǐngzi cūn, yīn dāngdì yīzuò gūlì
      here original name Gudingzi Village, because local one isolated
      tūchū de shānfēng ér dé míng."
      prominent de mountain er get name
      'This place was originally called Gudingzi Village, named after an isolated and prominent mountain peak in the area.'

(10) "bìjiāng bùduàn wèi jiànshè qīngjié měilì de shìjiè zuòchū xīn gòngxiàn."
      will certainly continue for build clean beautiful de world make new contribution
      'will certainly continue to make new contributions to building a clean and
      beautiful world.'

In Structure A, comparing *gūlì tūchū de shānfēng* 'isolated and prominent mountain peak' and *qīngjié měilì de shìjiè* 'clean and beautiful world', *shānfēng* 'mountain
peak' is in B-objects, which is also a low-frequency concrete term, while *shìjiè* 'world'
is in D-abstract. If attributive modifications are removed at the same time, *yīzuò
shānfēng* 'one mountain' can still be semantically self-contained. Understanding
Jiànshè shìjiè 'build a world' is difficult, which suggests it cannot be semantically self-
contained.

(11) "tā zǒng néng yǐ tèyǒu de cíxìng sǎngyīn hé wěiwěidàolái de huàyǔ,
      he always can use unique de magnetic voice and pleasant de utterances
      dài rénmen zǒurù wénwù de shìjiè."
      take people into cultural relics de world
      'He can always take people into the world of cultural relics with his unique
      magnetic voice and pleasant utterances.'
(12) "yìqíng fángkòng gōngzuò dào le zuì chījìn de guānjiàn jiēduàn,
      epidemic prevention work arrive le most strenuous de critical stage
      yào háobù fàngsōng zuòhǎo yìqíng fángkòng zhòngdiǎn gōngzuò."
      want none relax do a good job epidemic prevention key tasks
      'The epidemic prevention and control has reached the most strenuous critical
      stage, and we must not relax the key tasks of epidemic prevention and control.

In structure B, *sǎngyīn* 'voice' is in B-object category, *jiēduàn* 'stage' is in D-
abstract. After modifiers are removed, *yǐ sǎngyīn hé huàyǔ, dài rénmen zǒurù*... 'lead
people into…by voice and utterances' can still express the basic meaning of the sentence, but the meaning of *gōngzuò dàole zuì jiēduàn, yào* 'work has reached the most
stage, we must…' is incomplete.

In the nouns intersection of the two structures, there are many nouns ending with a
falling tone, such as *shìjiè* 'world', *huánjìng* 'environment', *fāngxiàng* 'direction', etc.
The ratio of tones of the intersection of nouns is calculated and presented in Fig. 2.

Nearly half of the nouns in the intersection end with a falling tone as demonstrated
in Fig. 2. In addition, the ratios of nouns ending with a falling tone in structure A and B
are 45.48% and 55.46% respectively, which indicates falling tone occupies the largest
proportion in their respective structures. Both of the two structures appear at the end of
the sentences in the corpus. Therefore, we examine that the high-frequency nouns that
can enter the two structures mainly end with a falling tone, which is in line with the
phenomenon that the stress of ordinary rhythm appears at the end in Chinese language
[11].

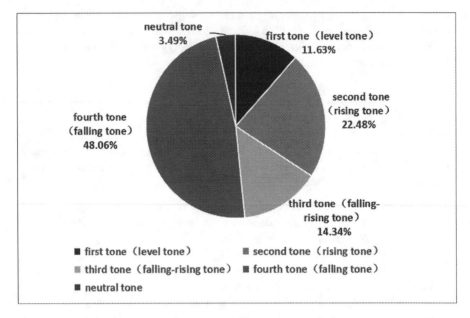

Fig. 2. Tone ratio in the intersection of nouns

6   The Restriction of Prosodic Structure of Double Attributive Adjectives on Syntax

As pointed out above, nouns ending in a falling tone in the two structures account for the majority. Which is the major tone of every adjective in the two structures? The result is displayed in Table 4.

Table 4. The proportion of tones of adjectives in the two structures

Structure A: Tone Ratio of Adjectives		Structure B: Tone Ratio of Adjectives	
a_1	a_2	a_1'	a_2'
Second tone (rising tone)	Fourth tone (falling tone)	Fourth tone (falling tone)	Fourth tone (falling tone)
41.92%	54.06%	49.08%	49.48%

The falling tone is used the most except for a_1. What is the role of tones on prosodic combination of adjectives?

Foot is the most basic unit of rhythm in language [12]. In Chinese, two syllables are a natural foot. Different prosodic syntactic interface units: prosodic clitic group[4] are formed in the two structures. Restriction of prosody on syntax is operated and realized through the principle of nuclear stress [13]. Nuclear stress is also known as normal stress, which describes the stress structure without the influence of special context in a sentence [13].

The common rhythms of seven syllables include [4 + 3] such as *qīngjié měilì de shìjiè* 'clean and beautiful world', and [3 + 4] such as the "*chījìn de guānjiàn jiēduàn* 'strenous critical stage'. The rhythmic form of structure A is [4 + 3]. *Qīngjié měilì* 'clean and beautiful' forms a rhythmic adhesion group, and the expression forms a syntactic pattern with *shìjiè* 'world'. Structure B is in the form of [3 + 4]. *Guānjiàn jiēduàn* 'critical stage' as a rhythmic adhesion group constitutes the form of *chījìn de* 'strenous' + *guānjiàn jiēduàn* 'critical stage'. [14] specified the nuclear stress of Chinese as "government-based NSR", that is, given two nodes Ci and Cj, if Ci and Cj are in the order of selection and batch jurisdiction, Cj is more prominent. For example, *shì jiè* 'world' in *qīngjié měilì de shìjiè* 'clean and beautiful world' is more prominent. *guān jiàn* 'critical' in *chījìn de guānjiàn jiēduàn* 'strenous critical stage' is more prominent.

High-frequency collocations in the corpus suggest that words at the nuclear stress location in different structures are different, but a falling tone dominates the high-frequency words at the location. We observe that words ending with a falling tone are more prominent when they are at nuclear stress location. The falling tones are short and powerful, and the tones can change significantly from high to low, increasing the highlighting effect in the sentences. Syntactic merge and movement are restrained and cannot be shifted freely because of these restrictions on the prosodic structure.

7 Conclusion

A comparative analysis between structure A: "$a_1 + a_2 + de + n$" and structure B: "$a_1' + de + a_2' + n'$" is conducted after extracting them from *People's Daily*. We discuss influential factors and constraints from semantics, syntax, word order, rhythm, etc. Semantic similarities of adjectives in two structures are studied and syntactic functions of *de* are analyzed. In addition, we summarize the categorical characteristics of high-frequency nouns, restrictions of prosody on syntax and the choice of collocation. *De* in the two structures cannot be shifted or deleted freely, and as a "segmentation mark", *de* can play a role in maintaining structural stability. By contrast, the semantic similarity of "a_1 and a_2" in structure A is higher. The influential factors of the order of double-syllable double attributives include semantics, cognition, habit, and rhythm, etc. Among them, the dominant factor of structure A is cognition. While the dominant factor for structure B is semantics. Besides, in the noun intersection of the

---

[4] The prosodic adhesion group is between prosodic words and prosodic phrases. It is a first-level unit composed of the combination of prosodic words and adhesion words. This kind of prosodic adhesion group has only one stress as a whole, and most of the stress fall on the attached component "host" [13].

two structures, abstract nouns ending with a falling tone is most frequent. From the perspective of the combination of prosodic structures, words ending with a falling tone at the nuclear stress location are more prominent.

The research further clarifies the important role of *de* in the combination of multiple attributives, and enriches knowledge resources of collocations of double-syllable double attributives. Moreover, it can provide rich case support for international Chinese education and teaching, and provide data reference for the establishment of multiple attributives database. In the future, we will continue to expand the size of the corpus, optimize the extraction mode, establish case database, and carry out further research on the recognition of collocations, text error correction and automatic output of multiple attributives.

Acknowledgments. The work was supported by Major Program of National Social Science Foundation of China (18ZDA295); Funding Project of Education Ministry for Development of Liberal Arts and Social Sciences (16YJA740036); Top-ranking Discipline Team Support Program of Beijing Language and Culture University (JC201902); the Fundamental Research Funds for the Central Universities (18YBT03) ; BLCU Supported Project for Young Researchers Program (supported by the Fundamental Research Funds for the Central Universities) (19YCX047).

References

1. Shen, J.: Bù Duìchèn Hé Biāojìlùn [Asymmetry and Marking Theory], pp. 288–310. Jiangxi Education Publishing House, Jiangxi (1999)
2. Shi, Y.: Cognitive and Semantic Foundations of Grammar, pp. 46–63. Jiangxi Education Publishing House, Jiangxi (2000)
3. Zhang, G.: Xiàndài Hànyǔ Xíngróngcí Gōngnéng Yǔ Rènzhī Yánjiū[Research on the Function and Cognition of Modern Chinese Adjectives], pp. 19–94. The Commercial Press, Beijing (2006)
4. Chen, Q.: Xiàndài Hànyǔ Xíngróngcí Yǔ Míngcí Niánhé Jiégòu[Adjective and Noun Adhesive Structure in Modern Chinese], pp. 17–154. China Social Sciences Press, Beijing (2012)
5. Lǚ, S., et al.: Xiàndài Hànyǔ BābǎiCí Zēngdìngběn[800 Words in Modern Chinese. Extended version]. The Commercial Press, Beijing (1999)
6. Zhao, C.: Xiàndài Hànyǔ Xíngmíng Zǔhé Yánjiū[Study on the Combination of Adjectives and Nouns in Modern Chinese], pp. 18–57. Jinan University Press, Guangzhou (2012)
7. Xun, E., Rao, G., Xiao, X., Zang, J.: The construction of the BCC corpus in the age of big data. Corpus Linguist. **1**, 93–109 (2016)
8. Luo, R., Xu, J., Zhang, Y., Ren, X., Sun, X.: PKUSEG: A Toolkit for Multi-Domain Chinese Word Segmentation. Arxiv (2019)
9. Che, W., Li, Z., Liu, T.: LTP: a chinese language technology platform. In: Proceedings of the Coling 2010:Demonstrations, pp. 13–16 (2010)
10. Zhang, M.: Rènzhī Yǔyánxué Yǔ Hànyǔ Míngcí Duǎn yǔ[Cognitive Linguistics and Chinese Noun Phrases], pp. 217–309. China Social Sciences Press, Beijing (1998)
11. Feng, S.: On the prosodic structure of Chinese and its restriction on syntactic 12. Structure. Stud. Lang. Linguist. **1**, 108–122 (1996)

12. Feng, S.: On Chinese "Natural Foot." Stud. Chin. Lang. **1**, 40–47 (1998)
13. Feng, S.: Hànyǔ Yùnlǜ Yǔfǎ Jiàochéng[Chinese Prosody Grammar Course], pp. 33–102. Peking University Press, Beijing (2018)
14. Feng, S.: Prosodically constrained postverbal PPs in mandarin Chinese. Linguistics **6**, 1–10 (2003)

Embodied Grounding of Concreteness/Abstractness: A Sensory-Perceptual Account of Concrete and Abstract Concepts in Mandarin Chinese

Yin Zhong[1]([⊠]), Chu-Ren Huang[2], and Kathleen Ahrens[1]

[1] Department of English and Communication, The Hong Kong Polytechnic University, Kowloon, Hong Kong
beth.zhong@connect.polyu.hk,
kathleen.ahrens@polyu.edu.hk
[2] Department of Chinese and Bilingual Studies, The Hong Kong Polytechnic University, Kowloon, Hong Kong
churen.huang@polyu.edu.hk

Abstract. Most previous research has investigated how embodied cognition captures concrete notions (e.g. *money*), but the role sensory modalities play in more abstract concepts (e.g. *time*) lacks empirical research—in particular, how abstractness is grounded in perceptual experiences. In this paper, a sensorimotor strength rating study (also known as modality exclusivity norms) is conducted, to ascertain the sensory-perceptual information encoded in both concrete and abstract nouns in Mandarin Chinese. The preliminary results suggest that a sensation denoting one's internal bodily feelings—interoception—captures more abstract information than the five basic human senses, and that the abstract concepts perceived predominantly by interoception mainly comprise OBJECT EVALUATION, MENTAL, THINKING, TIME, and SPACE as their ontological domains. This study affirms the embodied grounding of the concrete and abstract concepts, and further sheds light on the grounded account of mind-body-interactions.

Keywords: Concreteness/abstractness · Perceptual strength · Sensory modalities · Interoception · Modality exclusivity

1 Introduction

It has increasingly been evidenced in recent literature that the interaction between our bodily experiences and representations of the outside world grounds cognitive processes. This interaction, known as 'embodied cognition', posits that perceptual, motor, and emotional experiences are the fundamental foundation for semantic representations and conceptual structures of the external world [1–4]. Yet this claim is still debated when referring to abstract concepts. If we adopt the dichotomy of concreteness and abstractness, concrete concepts are 'single, bounded, identifiable referents that can be experienced via at least one of our five senses', whereas abstract notions are those that 'lack bounded and clearly perceivable referents and cannot be experienced directly

© Springer Nature Switzerland AG 2022
M. Dong et al. (Eds.): CLSW 2021, LNAI 13250, pp. 72–83, 2022.
https://doi.org/10.1007/978-3-031-06547-7_5

through our senses' [5, 6]. For example, the concept of *cat* is easily projected as a kind of carnivorous mammal with soft fur, a short snout, and retractable claws; and the meaning of such a concept can be acquired through our sensorimotor experiences when we see, hear, touch, or even smell it. Alternatively, consider the concept of *life*; it does not have a clearly identifiable referent and is therefore difficult to be perceived by any sensory modalities. Namely, we cannot see, hear, taste, smell, or touch *life*, unless it is expressed figuratively.

The representation of abstract concepts in cognitive processes challenges the idea of embodied cognition, and has been discussed widely from the perspective of competing theories (see [6] for a summary). Recent behavioural and fMRI evidence has proposed that concreteness and abstractness should recruit all of the sensorimotor, affective (i.e., emotional), linguistic, and social experiences in order to account for the heterogeneous nature of abstract concepts. These dimensions weigh differently in abstract concepts, as well as in different types of abstract concepts [7–9]. This proposal highlights the importance of both sensorimotor and linguistically conveyed information, and, at the same time, calls for a more fine-grained investigation into the role that different dimensions play in the representations of concrete and abstract concepts.

The dichotomy of concreteness and abstractness was previously approached by the use of concreteness rating studies. Primarily, these studies identified concrete words as words that can be perceived through our sensory input, whereas abstract words are those that cannot be experienced directly by the human senses but are defined through linguistic input [5, 10]. Such a distinction between concreteness and abstractness presupposed that concrete concepts are grounded in our sensorimotor experiences, and abstract words are only conceptualised via linguistic information. Moreover, sometimes concreteness has even been treated no differently from imageability. For example, one of the most influential theories in explaining concreteness effects in word processing performance[1]—Dual-coding Theory—suggests that concrete concepts directly activate verbal and imagistic representations (i.e., perceptual and modality-specific information), while abstract words only connect to images via other verbal codes [11]. However, abstractness is not equivalent to low imageability, even though the two concepts are highly correlated [12]. It was not until recently that more importance has been given to the role modality-specific information plays in the distinction of concreteness and abstractness. For example, concreteness and abstractness were operationalised in terms of 'the extent to which a word evokes a sensory and/or perceptual experience' [13], and Connell and Lynott [14] further showed that the concreteness effect was better explained by the perceptual strength of the five senses, rather than by concreteness or imageability ratings.

Even though the correlation between perceptual grounding and concrete words is considerably robust, abstract lacks such validation. In light of the embodied account, Connell et al. [15] proposed that interoception, a physiologically distinct category of perceptual experience related to the awareness of the signals coming from the body, is particularly crucial for abstract concepts and emotional experiences. Interoception, or

---

[1] Concreteness effects refer to the advantage of concrete over abstract concepts in processing, recognition, and recall [11].

interoceptive sensation/perception, mainly detects signals from the visceral system (e.g. cardiovascular, respiratory, gastrointestinal, bladder) and inner bodily states (e.g. hunger, thirst, temperature, itch, tickle, sensual touch, painful sensations) [16–18]. A recent behavioural study studied the interaction between concreteness and abstractness and interoception. In this study, participants were asked to rate the difficulty and pleasantness of concrete and abstract words while performing a concurrent task related to interoceptive experiences, i.e., determining how good the participants were at counting their heartbeats. Their finding showed that interoceptive experiences were found to have a stronger influence on abstract concepts, and particularly on emotionally abstract concepts [9]. Taken together, it is essential to consider interoception when approaching concreteness and abstractness through sensory-perceptual experiences, because this inner bodily sensation could possibly be a 'mediator' that associates physical senses with mental states. More importantly, the linguistic representations of interoceptive sensation are still, to a certain extent, obscure.

This study grounds on the sensory-perceptual account to examine concreteness and abstractness in nouns in Mandarin Chinese. Only two-syllable nouns were considered as they contain rich linguistic information, despite having no contextual background; nouns straddle both concrete and abstract concepts to a comparably significant amount.

Three main research questions are as follows:

RQ1. How is concreteness/abstractness operationalised through sensory-perceptual strengths?

RQ2. What is the relationship between concreteness and abstractness and sensory-perceptual strengths?

RQ3. Which is the best predictor of concreteness effects among the sensory-perceptual strengths?

From the results of related studies [15, 19], we hypothesize that:

Hypothesis 1. Visual strength is the most robust in detecting concrete concepts, while the strength of interoception favours abstract concepts.

Hypothesis 2. The five traditional sensory modalities, vision, hearing, taste, smell, and touch, will be more pertinent to concrete concepts, while interoception will show a more positive correlation with abstract concepts.

Hypothesis 3. The model that includes interoception will be the best predictor of concreteness effects in cognitive processing.

In addition, the uniqueness of the Chinese language and culture might lead to a different understanding of interoception and its represented concepts. We would like to summarize the ontological domains that represent this mysterious concept, and to make further clarifications about the linguistic representations of interoception in Mandarin Chinese.

2 Method

2.1 Stimuli

Stimuli in this study were first extracted from a Chinese online corpus, *Chinese Web 2011 (zhTenTen11)* in the *Sketch Engine* [20].[2] They were found as frequently co-occurring with perceptual verbs in perceptual events—看 *kàn* 'to look; to see', 聽 *tīng* 'to listen; to hear', 嘗 *cháng* 'to taste', 聞 *wén* 'to smell', 嗅 *xiù* 'to smell; to sniff',[3] 摸 *mō* 'to touch', and 感覺 *gǎnjué* 'to feel'.[4] This yielded a total of 757 lexical items across five sensory modalities [cf. 22]. These words were further mapped to Xu and Li [10]'s concreteness and abstractness ratings for two-character Chinese words and Tsang et al.'s [23] word list in a lexical decision study. Altogether, 332 perceptual nouns were identified in the above-mentioned two word lists, and were tagged as 'concrete' in the dataset ($M_{concreteness}$ = 2.24, $SD_{concreteness}$ = 0.64, $range_{concreteness}$ = 1.08–3.63).[5] To compile a balanced word list containing both concrete and abstract nouns, we extracted another 332 disyllabic nouns from Xu and Li [10] according to their abstract ratings, ranked from high to low, tagged as 'abstract' ($M_{concreteness}$ = 3.88, $SD_{concreteness}$ = 0.18, $range_{concreteness}$ = 3.67–4.5). A Mann-Whitney test indicated that a statistically significant difference between the 'concrete' group (mean rank = 167.50) and the 'abstract' group (mean rank = 499.50), $U(N_{concrete}$ = 332, $N_{abstract}$ = 332) = .000, $z = -22.299$, p = .000 exists. Altogether, the stimuli used in this study contained 664 disyllabic nouns in Mandarin Chinese, with concreteness and abstractness ratings collected from Xu and Li [10], reaction time, error rates, number of strokes, word frequency, and other related dimensions provided in Tsang et al. [23].

2.2 Procedure

This study followed the design in sensorimotor norms and other modality exclusivity norms studies [24, 25]. Participants were asked to rate how much they experienced each concept (664 disyllabic nouns) based on their six perceptual senses (*vision, hearing, taste, smell, touch,* and *interoception*)[6] and the five action effectors from different parts of the body (*foot/leg, hand/arm, head excluding mouth, mouth/throat,* and *torso*), from 0 = no feelings at all, to 5 = very strong feelings.[7]

---

[2] Accessed at https://the.sketchengine.co.uk/auth/corpora/.

[3] Two olfactory verbs were chosen because the instances related to olfactory perception are assumed to be scarce in the corpus; this was to ensure that the study contained the largest possible number of results from the two different constructions in the corpus.

[4] Although 感覺 *gǎnjué* 'to feel' is not normally considered a tactile verb, it is defined as 'to perceive and distinguish external stimuli via bodily sensations' in the *Chinese WordNet 2.0* [21]. Therefore, it is highly tactile-related and is believed to trigger bodily feelings, such as temperature-related sensations.

[5] The concreteness/abstractness rating is on a scale from 1 = very concrete, 5 = very abstract.

[6] Interoception was translated as '身體內部感覺 *shēntǐ-nèibù-gǎnjué* bodily-internal-feelings' according to the term used in psychological studies. Examples such as 'feeling hungry, exhausted, disgusting' were provided in the instructions.

[7] Strengths of the action effectors will not be discussed in this paper due to the page limit.

After the ratings were collected, we examined the norms by assigning a dominant modality for each word. Specifically, the sensory modality that was most associated with each word (the maximum perceptual strength across the senses) was assigned, as well as a modality exclusivity score, which is the extent to which the word is associated with a single perceptual modality. The modality exclusivity score is calculated by the range of mean strength ratings divided by their sum.

The questionnaire was designed, distributed, and collected using an online survey platform named 问卷星 (Sojump),[8] with all of the words written in Simplified Chinese. Self-reported questions were asked before the survey to collect the language background and demographic information of the participants. Participants also needed to disclose cognitive disorders, such as an impaired ability to perceive stimuli through sensory organs. Basic Chinese knowledge questions, including translating pinyin to Chinese characters, identifying radicals, and selecting word meanings, were also asked to confirm comprehension of Chinese. These questions were later used as the criteria to control the quality of the results.

2.3   Participants

The 664 words were randomly divided into 22 lists, with 30 or 31 words per list. Each list was distributed among 25 participants. Beyond the quality control questions mentioned above, if a participant gave a low rating (below 2) for a word that was clearly related to a sensory modality (e.g. 味道 *wèidào* 'taste; smell' should be strongly perceived by either the gustatory or olfactory modality), their answers were also removed from the results. After eliminating all of the problematic results, a total of 438 participants remained (female = 284; male = 154). Their average age was 26 years old (SD_{age} = 8.58, range = 18–60 years old). All participants identified Chinese as their first language (inclusive of Chinese dialects). Each participant was rewarded with RMB10 Yuan in exchange for their participation. They spent an average of 15.7 min on each list.

3   Results

3.1   Operationalization of Concreteness/Abstractness Through Sensory-Perceptual Strengths

A chi-square test of independence was first performed to examine the relation between concreteness and abstractness and dominant modality groups. The relation between the two categories suggests significant correlation, χ^2 (7, N = 660) = 442.70, $p < .001$. Namely, dominant modalities were not symmetrically distributed in concreteness and abstractness dichotomy. Table 1 presents the distribution of each dominant modality in abstract and concrete concepts:

---

[8] Accessed at https://www.wjx.cn/.

Table 1. Distributions of dominant modalities in abstract and concrete groups.

Dominant modality	Abstract	Concrete	Total
Vision	45 (13.6%)	165 (50.0%)	210 (31.8%)
Hearing	6 (1.8%)	115 (34.9%)	121 (18.3%)
Taste	1 (0.3%)	18 (5.5%)	19 (2.9%)
Smell	0 (0.0%)	8 (2.4%)	8 (1.2%)
Taste/Smell[a]	0 (0.0%)	3 (0.9%)	3 (0.5%)
Touch	0 (0.0%)	8 (2.4%)	8 (1.2%)
Interoception	274 (83.0%)	13 (3.9%)	287 (43.5%)
Vision/Interoception	4 (1.2%)	0 (0.0%)	4 (0.6%)

Note. The percentage in the parentheses is the percentage each dominant modality holds in abstract and concrete groups
[a]The slash indicates that a maximum perceptual strength was found in both sensory modalities, i.e., three words received their highest rating in both the gustatory and olfactory senses. It is the same for the Visual/Interoception category.

These results confirmed our first hypothesis that visual strength dominates concreteness, and auditory perception follows. This is because concrete nouns are extracted from perceptual events in the corpus, and they primarily co-occurred with visual and auditory perceptual events. Interestingly, nouns that were retrieved from tactile events were considerable in the corpus, however only a limited number were identified with touch as the dominant modality; this suggests that tactile sense might be overshadowed by visual sense in terms of its perceptual strength, especially when it is related to an object. This finding is also corroborated by the dominance of vision in human perceptual systems—the visual sensation takes up the largest region in the brain [26], and the visual modality can influence the perceptual contents of other sensory modalities [27].

In regard to the abstract concepts, interoception seems to have occupied the leading position, with visual perception accounting for only a small portion. In general, it is found that concrete concepts distribute across all the dominant sensory modalities, to varying degrees. Abstract concepts, however, have very vague relations with gustatory, olfactory, and tactile dominant groups.

3.2 Relationship Between Concreteness/Abstractness and Sensory-Perceptual Strengths

Inter-correlations of perceptual strength ratings, presented in Table 2, showed that interoception is the only dimension that demonstrates a moderate positive correlation with the abstract concepts ($r = 0.43$). The other five traditional sensory modalities showed statistically negative correlations with the abstract concepts, in which visual strength is the strongest ($r = -0.60$), followed by tactile sense ($r = -0.42$). This verified our second hypothesis that the five traditional sensory modalities are more pertinent to concrete concepts, while interoception favours abstractness.

In addition, interoceptive strength was negatively correlated to visual ($r = -0.24$) and tactile ($r = -0.11$) senses, but positively related to auditory ($r = 0.02$), gustatory

($r = 0.07$), and olfactory ($r = 0.05$) perceptions. This finding is surprisingly in line with Connell et al. [15], implying that concepts that can be perceived inside our body tend not to be visible or touchable, but can sometimes be heard, tasted, or smelled. Yet none of the above relationships was particularly strong.

Another finding is that modality exclusivity is negatively correlated to concreteness at the statistically significant level of 0.05 ($r = -0.11$). In other words, if a concept tends to be more multimodal (can be perceived by multiple sensory modalities), it could be more abstract; when it is a unimodal concept (can be perceived by sole sense or a minimal number of senses), it is inclined to be more concrete.

Table 2. Correlation matrix between modalities based on mean ratings of perceptual strength

	1	2	3	4	5	6	7
1. Vision		.12**	.14***	.18***	.52***	−.24***	−.60***
2. Hearing			−.11**	−.11**	−.08*	.02	−.28***
3. Taste				.92***	.44***	.07	−.12**
4. Smell					.46***	.05	−.16***
5. Touch						−.11**	−.42***
6. Interoception							.43***
7. Concreteness							

Note. * Correlation is significant at 0.05. ** Correlation is significant at 0.01. *** Correlation is significant at 0.001

3.3   Predictor of Concreteness Effects Through Maximum Sensory-Perceptual Strength

Concreteness effects refer to the observations that concrete nouns are processed relatively faster and more accurately than abstract nouns in cognitive tasks [28]. It is shown that the maximum perceptual strength without interoception [14], and that with interoception [15], could be a predictor of concreteness effects in predicting semantic facilitation in word recognition. Therefore, we replicated the method used in Connell et al. [15] to examine the effect of maximum perceptual strength on lexical processing performance.

The lexical decision data was retrieved from MELD-SCH [23], with the focus of two measures—standardized reaction times with individual variance removed (zRT) and error rates (ERR). Other lexical characteristics, including word length in the number of characters, the total number of strokes, word frequency, and contextual diversity based on SUBTLEX-CH [29], were extracted as lexical predictors.

Bayesian linear regression was conducted in JASP [30]. A null model was started, inclusive of the predictors. Then, one model with the five modalities and another with the six modalities were added to form two alternative models. Comparatively, the second model, including interoception (log BF_{20}), outperformed the first model with the maximum perceptual strength across the five traditional modalities (log BF_{10}), in both the reaction times (zRT) and accuracy (ERR) performance in the lexical decision task. As presented in Table 3, the outcome was logged 10–12 times when the maximum perceptual strength incorporated interoception versus when interoception was excluded. This finding further suggests that interoceptive perception is also essential to cognitive processing.

Table 3. Log Bayes factors (BF) for regression model comparisons of each maximum perceptual strength predictor against the null model (other lexical predictors), and for the inclusion of interoception against its exclusion.

Maximum perceptual strength	Model comparison	zRT	ERR
Five Traditional Modalities	BF_{10}	20.739	16.634
Six Modalities including interoception	BF_{20}	31.337	28.669
Benefit of interoception	BF_{21}	10.598	12.035

4   Discussion

The results presented above have demonstrated that concreteness and abstractness are closely correlated to sensory-perceptual strengths, and that interoception pertains more to abstract notions. Nevertheless, what still remains to be understood is how people understand the concept of interoception, and how interoception is lexicalized in the Chinese language. Table 4 summarises ontological domains of the concepts with interoception as their dominant modality. The classification of each concept was consulted in *E-HowNet* (an ontological knowledge network that links different ontologies, including *HowNet* sememes and *WordNet* synsets) [31] and *SUMO* (Suggested Upper Merged Ontology, an upper-level formal ontology that underlies a hierarchy of classes and related relationships of the knowledge system) [32].

Table 4. Ontological domains of the concepts with interoception as their dominant modality

Ontological domains			Example words
Event (58)	Act (22)	Alter Mental (9)	悲嘆*bēitàn* 'sigh mournfully'
		Alter Physical (5)	呼吸*hūxī* 'breath'
	State (36)	Object Evaluation (14)	苦海*kǔhǎi* (literally translated as sea of bitterness) 'abyss of misery'
		Mental Act (10)	體驗*tǐyàn* 'experience'
		Mental State (6)	刺激*cìjī* 'stimuli'
Object (203)	Abstract (40)	Fact (17)	因果*yīnguǒ* 'cause and effect; karma'
		Mental (23)	胸懷*xiōnghuái* 'heart; mind'
	Attribute (91)	Object Evaluation (65)	膽識*dǎnshì* 'courage and insight'
		Property (13)	阻力*zǔlì* 'resistance'
		Situation (13)	情況*qíngkuàng* 'situation'
	Space (4)		餘地*yúdì* 'room (figuratively)'
	Thing (51)	Information (8)	內情*nèiqíng* 'inside story'
		Mental (9)	情感*qínggǎn* 'emotion; feeling'
		Thinking (24)	心思*xīnsī* 'thought'
		Humanized (6)	靈魂*línghún* 'soul'
	Time (17)		歲月*suìyuè* 'time and tide'

Note. Only domains containing a certain number of words are presented (≥ 4). The number in the parentheses indicates the number of words under that category

As demonstrated in the table above, the ontological domains are comprised of a large number of concepts that denote inner state and emotional feelings, which suggests that people might have a vague understanding of interoception as a physiological perception but that they treat it as a unified whole along with other mental related concepts. This is partly true as interoceptive awareness and emotional experience share overlapping information processing mechanisms [33, 34], thus facilitating aggregated information of internal bodily feelings, such as time perception [33, 34]. Moreover, the insular cortex, a neural system related to interoception, has also been implicated in emotional experiences and decision making [35]. Given the intertwined relations between interoception, emotion, and inner bodily state, research suggests that interoception is possibly the most readily accessible sense that associates physical sensations with mental representations, thus scaffolding the grounds for abstract concepts.

The research also indicates that lexemes and radicals can reflect the interaction between physical and mental feelings via interoception in the Chinese language. For instance, words with interoception as their dominant modality mostly embrace internal organs, such as 心 *xīn* 'heart', 胸 *xiōng* 'chest', and 膽 *dǎn* 'gall', as well as carry the radicals 心/忄 'heart', 力 'power; strength', and 疒 'sickness'. This association is because the Chinese language primarily resorts to internal body organs to conceptualize emotions. Specifically, idioms in Chinese associate liver, heart, lungs, intestines, and stomach to the emotions of anger, sadness, and anxiety [36, 37]. For example, 大動肝火 *dà-dòng-gānhuǒ* (literally translated as big-move liver-fire) 'get angry', 撕心裂肺 *sīxīn-lièfèi* (literally translated as tear-heart split-lungs) 'be extremely grieved', 牽腸掛肚 *qiāncháng-guàdù* (literally translated as pull-intestines and hang-stomach) 'feel deep anxiety'. Furthermore, Chinese culture attaches particular weight to the gall-bladder, and the gallbladder can be further mapped to courage (e.g. 有膽 *yǒu-dǎn* (literally translated as 'have-gallbladder') 'courageous' and 大膽 *dàdǎn* (literally translated as 'big-gallbladder') 'bold' [cf. 38]); therefore, Chinese people believe that the absence of a gallbladder is equivalent to a lack of courage and decision-making ability.[9] Considering that metaphors are one way that people abstract [40] and are grounded in both our physical and cultural experiences [41–43], we can further affirm that internal states (i.e., interoceptive awareness) can be captured and re-enacted in a way similar to how external experiences are captured by our traditional five senses; however, inner bodily feelings might be lexicalized and represented distinctively across languages as driven by particular social and cultural experiences.

5   Conclusion

Abstract reasoning is one of the hallmarks of the human cognition system and thus distinguishes humans from animals. Nonetheless, researchers have a more advanced understanding of how concrete entities develop from and link up with the embodied and grounded cognition as compared with how abstract thoughts do so. One example is

---

[9] Note that the importance of gallbladder and its connotation to courage can be traced to traditional Chinese medicine, in which gallbladder is suggested to be responsible for making judgements and decision-making [39].

that people have a much more fine-grained categorization of concrete concepts (e.g. natural objects, artefacts, living and not living beings); however, abstract concepts, have mostly been treated as a whole [7]. Thus, further investigation as to how abstractness and different kinds of abstract concepts are grounded in our bodily experiences, especially given that previous approaches in examining concreteness and abstractness dichotomy were found insufficient in capturing a full picture of abstractness, is needed.

The present study exploits sensory-perceptual strengths to reveal their relations with concrete and abstract concepts in Mandarin Chinese. In line with the assumptions made by proponents of embodied cognition, concrete concepts were found to be more represented by the five traditional sensory modalities, in which the perceptual strength of vision is found to be critical to the determination of conceptual concreteness. Conversely, interoception, a sensation from the inside body, is more prevalent in abstract notions, and serves as a better predictor in lexical decision tasks. Moreover, modality exclusivity can also reflect the distinction between concreteness and abstractness—the more multimodal a concept is, the more abstract a concept is, and vice versa.

In general, this research supports the idea that abstractness is grounded to a larger extent in inner bodily feelings as compared with the traditional sensory modality system. The dichotomy of concreteness and abstractness requires scrutinizing to aggregate both the sensorimotor and linguistic information, along with inner bodily experiences. Nevertheless, it is noted that understanding interoceptive perception is not as straightforward as the other basic senses, and the scaffolding role it plays between physical and mental feelings still requires further investigation.

Acknowledgement. This research was funded in part by a grant (1-ZVTL) from The Hong Kong Polytechnic University.

Ethics Statement. This study was conducted in accordance with the Human Subjects Ethics Sub-committee (HSESC) (or its Delegate) of The Hong Kong Polytechnic University (HSESC Reference Number: HSEARS20200810001). Consent was acquired from the participants prior to the experiment in the form of online surveys; participants were informed that their confidentiality and anonymity would be assured, and they could terminate the experiment at any time without providing any reason.

References

1. Barsalou, L.W.: Grounded cognition. Annu. Rev. Psychol. **59**, 617–645 (2008)
2. Gibbs, R.W.: Embodiment and Cognitive Science. Cambridge University Press, Cambridge, New York (2006)
3. Gallese, V., Lakoff, G.: The brain's concepts: the role of the sensory-motor system in conceptual knowledge. Cogn. Neuropsychol. **22**, 455–479 (2005)
4. Pecher, D., Zwaan, R.A.: Grounding Cognition: The Role of Perception and Action in Memory, Language, and Thinking. Cambridge University Press, Cambridge (2005)

5. Brysbaert, M., Warriner, A.B., Kuperman, V.: Concreteness ratings for 40 thousand generally known English word lemmas. Behav. Res. Methods **46**(3), 904–911 (2013). https://doi.org/10.3758/s13428-013-0403-5

6. Borghi, A.M., Binkofski, F., Castelfranchi, C., Cimatti, F., Scorolli, C., Tummolini, L.: The challenge of abstract concepts. Psychol. Bull. **143**, 263–292 (2017)

7. Borghi, A.M.: A future of words: Language and the challenge of abstract concepts. J. Cogn. **3**, 42 (2020)

8. Villani, C., Lugli, L., Liuzza, M.T., Borghi, A.M.: Varieties of abstract concepts and their multiple dimensions. Lang. Cogn. **11**, 403–430 (2019)

9. Villani, C., Lugli, L., Liuzza, M.T., Nicoletti, R., Borghi, A.M.: Sensorimotor and interoceptive dimensions in concrete and abstract concepts. J. Mem. Lang. **116**, 104173 (2021)

10. Xu, X., Li, J.: Concreteness/abstractness ratings for two-character Chinese words in MELD-SCH. PloS one **15**, e0232133 (2020)

11. Paivio, A.: Mental Representations: A Dual Coding Approach. Oxford University Press, New York, New York (1990)

12. Kousta, S.-T., Vigliocco, G., Vinson, D.P., Andrews, M., Del Campo, E.: The representation of abstract words: why emotion matters. J. Exp. Psychol. Gen. **140**, 14–34 (2011)

13. Juhasz, B.J., Yap, M.J.: Sensory experience ratings for over 5,000 mono- and disyllabic words. Behav. Res. Methods **45**(1), 160–168 (2012). https://doi.org/10.3758/s13428-012-0242-9

14. Connell, L., Lynott, D.: Strength of perceptual experience predicts word processing performance better than concreteness or imageability. Cognition **125**, 452–465 (2012)

15. Connell, L., Lynott, D., Banks, B.: Interoception: the forgotten modality in perceptual grounding of abstract and concrete concepts. Philosophic. Trans. Biol. Sci. **373**, 20170143 (2018)

16. Cameron, O.G.: Visceral Sensory Neuroscience: Interoception. Oxford University Press, New York (2002)

17. Craig, A.D.: How do you feel? Interoception: the sense of the physiological condition of the body. Nat. Rev. Neurosci. **3**, 655–666 (2002)

18. Craig, A.D.: Interoception: the sense of the physiological condition of the body. Curr. Opin. Neurobiol. **13**, 500–505 (2003)

19. Lynott, D., Connell, L., Brysbaert, M., Brand, J., Carney, J.: The Lancaster Sensorimotor Norms: multidimensional measures of perceptual and action strength for 40,000 English words. Behav. Res. Methods **52**, 1271–1291 (2019)

20. Kilgarriff, A., et al.: The sketch engine: ten years on. Lexicography **1**, 7–36 (2014)

21. Huang, C.-R., et al.: Chinese Wordnet: design, implementation, and application of an infrastructure for cross-lingual knowledge processing. J. Chin. Inf. Process. **24**, 14–23 (2010)

22. Zhong, Y.: Sensory lexicon, sensory modalities and lexical categories in Mandarin Chinese (Unpublished doctoral dissertation). Faculty of Humanities. The Hong Kong Polytechnic University, Hong Kong (2020)

23. Tsang, Y.-K., et al.: MELD-SCH: a megastudy of lexical decision in simplified Chinese. Behav. Res. Methods **50**(5), 1763–1777 (2017). https://doi.org/10.3758/s13428-017-0944-0

24. Chen, I.-H., Zhao, Q., Long, Y., Lu, Q., Huang, C.-R.: Mandarin Chinese modality exclusivity norms. PLoS ONE **14**, e0211336 (2019)

25. Lynott, D., Connell, L., Brysbaert, M., Brand, J., Carney, J.: The Lancaster Sensorimotor Norms: multidimensional measures of perceptual and action strength for 40,000 English words. Behav. Res. Methods **52**, 1271–1291 (2020)

26. Drury, H.A., Van Essen, D.C., Anderson, C.H., Lee, C.W., Coogan, T.A., Lewis, J.W.: Computerized mappings of the cerebral cortex: a multiresolution flattening method and a surface-based coordinate system. J. Cogn. Neurosci. **8**, 1–28 (1996)
27. Stokes, D., Biggs, S.: The dominance of the visual. In: Stokes, D., Matthen, M., Biggs, S. (eds.) Perception and Its Modalities, pp. 350–378. Oxford University Press, Oxford (2015)
28. Jessen, F., et al.: The concreteness effect: evidence for dual coding and context availability. Brain Lang. **74**, 103–112 (2000)
29. Cai, Q., Brysbaert, M.: SUBTLEX-CH: Chinese word and character frequencies based on film subtitles. PLoS ONE **5**, e10729–e10729 (2010)
30. JASP Team: JASP (Version 0.14.1) [Computer software] (2020)
31. Ma, W.-Y., Shih, Y.-Y.: Extended HowNet 2.0 - an entity-relation common-sense representation model. In: 11th International Conference on Language Resources and Evaluation (LREC-11) European Language Resource Association (2018)
32. Niles, I., Pease, A.: Towards a standard upper ontology. In: International Conference on Formal Ontology in Information Systems, pp. 2–9 (2001)
33. Craig, A.D.: Emotional moments across time: a possible neural basis for time perception in the anterior insula. Philosophic. Trans. Biologic. Sci. **364**, 1933–1942 (2009)
34. Wittmann, M.: The inner experience of time. Philosop. Trans. Biol. Sci. **364**, 1955–1967 (2009)
35. Dunn, B., et al.: Listening to your heart: How interoception shapes emotion experience and intuitive decision making. Psychol. Sci. **21** 1835–1844 (2010)
36. Yu, N.: Metaphor from body and culture. In: Gibbs, R.W. (ed.) The Cambridge Handbook of Metaphor and Thought, pp. 247–261. Cambridge University Press, New York (2008)
37. Yu, N.: From Body to Meaning in Culture: Papers on Cognitive Semantic Studies of Chinese. John Benjamins Pub. Co., Amsterdam (2009)
38. Yu, N.: Metaphor, body, and culture: the Chinese understanding of gallbladder and courage. Metaphor. Symb. **18**, 13–31 (2003)
39. Zhu, X., Liu, J., Wang, F., Zhao, Q., Zhang, X., Gu, J.: Influence of traditional Chinese culture on the choice of patients concerning the technique for treatment of cholelithiasis: cultural background and historical origins of gallbladder-preserving surgery. Surgery **167**, 279–282 (2020)
40. Jamrozik, A., et al.: Metaphor: bridging embodiment to abstraction. Psychon. Bull. Rev. **23**, 1080–1089 (2016)
41. Kövecses, Z.: Metaphor in Culture: Universality and Variation. Cambridge University Press, Cambridge, UK (2005)
42. Lakoff, G., Johnson, M.: Metaphors We Live By. University of Chicago Press, Chicago (1980)
43. Lakoff, G., Johnson, M.: Philosophy in the Flesh: The Embodied Mind and Its Challenge to Western Thought. Basic Books, New York (1999)

A Diachronic Study on Linguistic Synesthesia in Chinese

Qingqing Zhao[1(✉)] and Yunfei Long[2]

[1] Chinese Academy of Social Sciences, Beijing 100732, China
zhaoqq@cass.org.cn
[2] University of Essex, Colchester Essex CO4 3SQ, UK
yl20051@essex.ac.uk

Abstract. This paper focuses on linguistic synesthesia in Chinese from a diachronic perspective. Based on the commonly and frequently-used sensory adjectives whose contemporary predominant sensory usages are different from their original sensory meanings in Chinese, this study finds that diachronic transfers of linguistic synesthesia largely obey the tendencies of the synchronic transfers of Mandarin synesthesia. In addition, this study shows that the diachronic transfers of linguistic synesthesia in Chinese are grounded in the perceived similarity, the sensory association, and onomatopoeia. Furthermore, given the similarities and differences between diachronic and synchronic transfers of linguistic synesthesia in Chinese, this paper highlights the important research value of diachronic examination of linguistic synesthesia.

Keywords: Linguistic synesthesia · Chinese · Diachronic · Synchronic pattern

1 Introduction

Linguistic expressions, such as *sweet voice* in English and 暖黄 *nuan3 huang2* 'warm yellow' in Mandarin Chinese, employ lexical items commonly considered to be in one sensory modality to describe perceptions in another. These expressions are referred to as linguistic synesthesia or synesthetic metaphor in the literature [1–4].

Research on linguistic synesthesia mainly focuses on the transfer directionality of lexical items between five sensory modalities (i.e., touch, taste, smell, vison, and hearing) from a synchronic perspective. For instance, [3] employed a corpus-based approach to generalize frequency-based directionalities of linguistic synesthesia in Modern English and Italian, as shown in Fig. 1. However, based on the corpus data from Modern Chinese (i.e., Mandarin), [4] proposed another transfer pattern of linguistic synesthesia. In [4]'s model, linguistic synesthesia exhibits three different types of transfer directionalities, including the unidirectional, bidirectional, and biased-directional transfers, as shown in Fig. 2. In addition, theoretical models accounting for the directionality of linguistic synesthesia are mostly based on the synchronic data of synesthetic usages in the language. For example, in accordance with synesthetic expressions in Modern Hebrew, English, and Indonesian, Shen and colleagues suggested that synesthetic transfers followed the embodiment principle mapping from more embodied modalities to less embodied ones [5–9]. Similarly, [10–12] utilized the

M. Dong et al. (Eds.): CLSW 2021, LNAI 13250, pp. 84–94, 2022.
https://doi.org/10.1007/978-3-031-06547-7_6

synesthetic patterns of Mandarin Chinese to demonstrate that linguistic synesthesia is grounded in both the embodiment and neural bases.

Touch > Taste > Smell > Hearing > Sight

Fig. 1. Directionality of synesthetic transfers in Modern English and Italian ([3], p. 79)

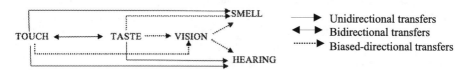

Fig. 2. Transfer directionalities of linguistic synesthesia in Modern Chinese ([4], p. 9).

Compared with extensive studies on linguistic synesthesia from a synchronic perspective, less attention has been paid to examining the phenomenon from a diachronic perspective. Exceptions can only be found in [2] and [13]. Specifically, [2] generalized a transfer hierarchy of linguistic synesthesia based on the semantic change of sensory adjectives in English. [13] found that the diachronic semantic shifts in linguistic synesthesia conformed to the synchronic transfer patterns of the phenomenon in Italian. However, there has been no study on linguistic synesthesia in Chinese from a diachronic perspective so far. This paper aims to explore linguistic synesthesia in Chinese from a diachronic perspective, i.e., the semantic shifts between sensory modalities occurring over time. This paper will examine whether the diachronic transfers of linguistic synesthesia in Chinese are consistent with the synchronic pattern of Mandarin synesthesia generalized by [4]. In addition, this study will also investigate whether the theoretical accounts proposed based on the synchronic transfers of linguistic synesthesia could explain the diachronic transfers of linguistic synesthesia in Chinese.

In what follows, Sect. 2 will present the methodology for data collection and analysis. This study adopts a combinative method relying on both the experimental ratings and the philological information. Section 3 will figure out the transfers of linguistic synesthesia in Chinese and their underlying mechanisms from a diachronic perspective. The last section is the conclusion.

2   Data Collection

Based on the ratings from 0 to 5 given by native Mandarin speakers, [14] collected the perceptual strength in five sensory modalities for 171 Mandarin adjectives. That is, [14] examined the extent to which the concept described by each of the 171 commonly-used sensory adjectives in contemporary Chinese can be perceived via touch, taste, smell, vision, and hearing. For instance, the mean ratings for the adjective 亮 *liang4* 'bright' are around 0.20 in touch, 0.02 in taste, 0.03 in smell, 4.92 in vision, and 0.90 in hearing given by native Mandarin speakers. In addition, based on the highest rating score that each of the adjectives received, [14] assigned the dominant sensory modalities to the adjectives. For example, the dominant sense for the adjective 亮 *liang4* 'bright' is vision, as the adjective obtained the highest rating score in the visual modality. As the dominant sensory modalities of the adjectives assigned by [14] reflect the most accessible sensory meanings of the adjectives for native Mandarin speakers, this study takes them as the contemporary predominant sensory usages of the adjectives in Modern Chinese. Therefore, for example, the contemporary predominant sensory usages of the adjectives 脆 *cui4* 'crisp', 涩 *se4* 'astringent', 腥 *xing1* 'of fishy smell', 肥 *fei2* 'fat', and 朗朗 *lang3-lang3* 'loud' are tactile, gustatory, olfactory, visual, and auditory properties respectively (see [14]).

This current study focuses on the diachronic transfers of linguistic synesthesia in Chinese, hence relying on the original sensory domains of lexical items as the sources of linguistic synesthetic transfers. Specifically, this study follows [4] and [12] to utilize the philological information to determine the original sensory domains for the adjectives included in [14]. For instance, the adjective 涩 *se4* was paraphrased as "not smooth" in 说文解字 *Shuo1wen2 Jie3zi4* 'Explaining Graphs and Analyzing Characters' [15] and 说文解字注 *Shuo1wen2 Jie3zi4 Zhu4* 'Annotation on *Shuowen Jiezi*' [16]. Besides, the radical of the character 涩 *se4* is 氵 referring to water, which indicates a surface with the unsmooth property due to the lack of water. Thus, the original sensory modality of the adjective 涩 *se4* is touch. Therefore, the contemporary predominant gustatory usage of the adjective 涩 *se4* referring to "astringent" (see [14]) was derived from a diachronic transfer of linguistic synesthesia from the tactile modality to the gustatory modality.

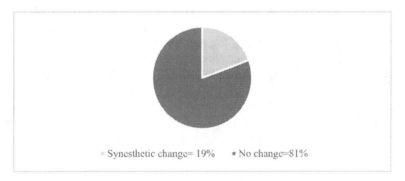

Fig. 3. Percentages of the adjectives with and without synesthetic changes over time in Chinese.

By carefully examining each adjective included in [14] for its original sensory domain, this study finds 33 adjectives whose contemporary predominant sensory domains are different from their original sensory domains. As shown in Fig. 3, the adjectives exhibiting synesthetic changes over time take up around 19% of all adjectives included in [14]. It is important to note that the adjectives included by [14] are all commonly and frequently used in Modern Chinese. Thus, it can be presumed that linguistic synesthesia is one of important types of semantic change for lexical items in Chinese, which has not received enough attention in existing research. The following section will examine the 33 adjectives that show diachronic transfers of linguistic synesthesia in Chinese for their transfer directionalities and underlying mechanisms.

3 Diachronic Transfers of Linguistic Synesthesia in Chinese

In accordance with [4]'s synchronic transfer pattern of Mandarin synesthesia, this study finds that among the 33 adjectives undergoing the semantic shift of linguistic synesthesia diachronically, there are 17 adjectives consistent with the synchronic pattern, as shown in Table 1. However, there are 16 adjectives, which do not follow the synchronic pattern generalized by [4], as shown in Table 2. In terms of the transfer types between sensory modalities, there are more types for the adjectives consistent with the synchronic pattern than those of adjectives inconsistent with the pattern, i.e., five vs. three as illustrated in Tables 1 and 2. Therefore, the numbers of both the adjectives and the transfer types that follow the synchronic pattern of linguistic synesthesia are larger than those that do not follow the synchronic pattern, despite without showing sharp differences.

Table 1. Diachronic transfers consistent with the synchronic pattern in Chinese.

Transfer types	Adjectives (17)
VISON→HEARING (8)	朗朗 *lang3-lang3* 'loud', 滔滔 *tao1-tao1* 'surging', 静 *jing4* 'quiet', 隐隐 *yin3-yin3* 'faint', 盈盈 *ying2-ying2* 'clear', 杂 *za2* 'mixed', 汪汪 *wang1-wang1* 'barking', 潇潇 *xiao1-xiao1* 'whistling'
TOUCH→TASTE (3)	烂 *lan4* 'tender', 酥 *su1* 'crisp', 燥 *zao4* 'dry'
TOUCH→VISION (3)	笨 *ben4* 'clumsy', 烈 *lie4* 'scorching', 灼灼 *zhuo2-zhuo2* 'shining'
TOUCH→HEARING (2)	强 *qiang2* 'strong', 轻 *qing1* 'light'
VISON→SMELL (1)	纯 *chun2* 'pure'

Table 2. Diachronic transfers inconsistent with the synchronic pattern in Chinese.

Transfer types	Adjectives (16)
VISION→TOUCH (13)	沉 *chen2* 'heavy', 微微 *wei1-wei1* 'slight', 稠 *chou2* 'dense', 厚 *hou4* 'thick', 绵绵 *mian2-mian2* 'continuous', 薄 *bao2* 'thin', 木 *mu4* 'numb', 嫩 *nen4* 'tender', 深 *shen1* 'deep', 松 *song1* 'shaggy', 凸 *tu1* 'protruding', 弯 *wan1* 'bent', 纤纤 *xian1-xian1* 'slender'
VISION→TASTE (2)	焦 *jiao1* 'charred', 稀 *xi1* 'sparse'
SMELL→TASTE (1)	膻 *shan1* 'of mutton's smell'

It is important to note that all the three diachronic transfers that do not obey the synchronic pattern (i.e., from vision to touch, vision to taste, and smell to taste) were also attested by [4] for Mandarin synesthesia. In other words, these diachronic transfers are not contrary to the biased-directional patterns between touch and vision, taste and vision, and taste and smell suggested by [4] (see Fig. 2). Thus, our study generally supports the finding by [13] on the diachronic transfers of linguistic synesthesia in Italian. That is, semantic shifts of linguistic synesthesia diachronically prefer to follow the patterns of linguistic synesthesia synchronically. However, as the diachronic transfers inconsistent with the synchronic pattern are also found, it is the most likely that diachronic transfers of linguistic synesthesia would also show frequency-based rather than absolute directional tendencies, similar to the synchronic transfers of linguistic synesthesia as found by various studies, such as [3, 4] and [11]. This study focuses on the diachronic synesthetic transfers for the commonly and frequently-used 33 Chinese sensory adjectives, and leaves the general diachronic transfer pattern of linguistic synesthesia in Chinese for further study.

3.1   Diachronic Transfers Consistent with the Synchronic Pattern

As shown in Table 1, among the diachronic transfers consistent with the synchronic pattern, there are the most adjectives showing the transfer from vison to hearing. Some of the adjectives mapping from vision to hearing preserved their polarities on the perceptual intensity over time, including 朗朗 *lang3-lang3* 'loud' and 滔滔 *tao1-tao1* 'surging' for a relatively high perceptual intensity, and 静 *jing4* 'quiet' and 隐隐 *yin3-yin3* 'faint' for a relatively low perceptual intensity. For example, 滔滔 *tao1-tao1* 'surging' was originally used to describe the torrential and vast visual property of rivers, as shown in (1a). However, the dominant sensory usage of 滔滔 *tao1-tao1* 'surging' in Modern Chinese is to conceptualize the surging auditory perception of powerful speeches, as shown in (1b). Thus, the perceptual intensity was retained for the adjective 滔滔 *tao1-tao1* 'surging' when transferring from vision to hearing. The adjective 盈盈 *ying2-ying2* 'clear' and 杂 *za2* 'mixed' retained their subjective evaluations in linguistic synesthesia diachronically, where the former focused on the positive evaluation, while the latter on the negative evaluation. As illustrated in example (2), the unpleasant evaluation on perceptions was preserved for the adjective 杂 *za2* 'mixed' when mapping from vision to hearing. Thus, the diachronic transfers of Chinese linguistic synesthesia from vision to hearing are analogous to the synchronic mappings between the two modalities in Mandarin. That is, the perceived similarity on the perceptual intensity or subjective evaluation provides a cognitive basis for linguistic synesthesia, as argued by [11, 12].

（1）a. 滔滔   江汉（《诗经》）
     tao1-tao1   *jiang1-han4 (Shi1jing1)*
     surging-surging   Yangtze River-Han River (The Book of
Songs)

     'surging and torrential Yangtze River and Han River'
   b. 滔滔   雄辩
     tao1-tao1   *xiong2-bian4*
     surging-surging   powerful-argument
     'surging powerful argument'

（2）a. 中   无   杂   树（《桃花源记》）
     zhong1   *wu2*   *za3*   *shu4 (Tao2hua1yuan2ji4)*
     middle   without   mixed   tree (An Idyllic Land of Peach-Blossom
Spring)

     'with no other sundry trees'
   b. 杂   音
     za2   *yin1*
     mixed   sound
     'noise'

Interesting cases for diachronic transfers from vision to hearing in Chinese synesthesia are 汪汪 *wang1-wang1* 'barking' and 潇潇 *xiao1-xiao1* 'whistling'. In these two cases, onomatopoeia functioned in synesthetic transfers. Specifically, 汪汪 *wang1-wang1* 'barking' and 潇潇 *xiao1-xiao1* 'whistling' originally conceptualized the visual perceptions of liquid (mostly water) and rain respectively. However, in contemporary Chinese, they are predominantly used to mimic the sound made by the dog and wind respectively. Thus, the transfers from vision to hearing of linguistic synesthesia diachronically in Chinese are grounded in both the perceptual similarity and onomatopoeia.

The diachronic transfers in Chinese from touch to taste consistent with the synchronic pattern are all grounded in the sensory association, as argued by [12] for synchronic transfers of linguistic synesthesia in Modern Chinese (e.g., 冷 *leng3* 'cold' and 暖 *nuan3* 'warm' used for color). That is, the recurring concurrency of tactile and gustatory perceptions provides the cognitive basis for the adjectives 烂 *lan4* 'tender', 酥 *su1* 'crisp', and 燥 *zao4* 'dry' mapping from touch to taste diachronically, as shown in Table 1. For example, 燥 *zao4* 'dry' originally referred to the tactile property of dryness in Classic Chinese, as shown in (3a). However, as the adjective can be frequently used to describe the dry food that is considered to make people feel dry and hot by traditional Chinese medicine, 燥 *zao4* 'dry' underwent the transfer from touch to taste, as shown in (3b). In addition, the sensory association between touch and taste has also been attested by various experimental studies such as [17, 18] on English and [14] on Mandarin Chinese. That is, based on the perceptual strength in sensory modalities, these experimental studies have found that there are significant correlations between the ratings in the tactile and gustatory modalities.

（3）a. 水　　　　流　　　湿，　火　　　就　　　燥（《易经》）

        shui3　　*liu2*　　*shi1,*　*huo3*　*jiu4*　*zao4 (Yi4jing1)*

        water　　flow　　damp　fire　approachdry (The Book of Changes)

        'Wherever the water flows, it is damp, while the fire approaches, it is dry.'

    b. 燥性　　　　　　　　食物

       zao4-xing1　　　　*shi2-wu4*

       dry-property　　　　food-object

       'food that can make people feel dry and hot' (in the context of traditional Chinese medicine)

The diachronic transfers from touch to vision, from touch to hearing, and from vision to smell all show the perceived similarity underlying linguistic synesthesia diachronically. Specifically, the adjectives 烈 *lie4* 'scorching', 灼灼 *zhuo2-zhuo2* 'shining', 强 *qiang2* 'strong', and 纯 *chun2* 'pure' preserved their high perceptual intensities, while 轻 *qing1* 'light' retained its low perceptual intensity in diachronic transfers of linguistic synesthesia. Similarly, the negative evaluation on perceptions was preserved in the transfer of the adjective 笨 *ben4* 'clumsy' from touch to vision.

In sum, the diachronic transfers of linguistic synesthesia in Chinese consistent with the synchronic pattern are similar to Mandarin synesthesia that are grounded in the perceived similarity and the sensory association as suggested by [12]. However, onomatopoeia is found to work in the diachronic transfers of linguistic synesthesia in Chinese, which has not been reported for Mandarin synesthesia.

3.2   Diachronic Transfers Inconsistent with the Synchronic Pattern

Among the diachronic transfers inconsistent with the synchronic pattern, there are the most adjectives showing the transfer from vision to touch, as shown in Table 2. The adjectives 沉 *chen2* 'heavy' originally referring to 'deep' in Classic Chinese and 微微 *wei1-wei1* 'slight' preserved their perceptual intensities when mapping diachronically from vision to touch. Specifically, 沉 *chen2* 'heavy' retained the high perceptual intensity, while 微微 *wei1-wei1* 'slight' preserved the low perceptual intensity, as shown in examples (4) and (5).

(4) a. 沉   泉（《吁嗟篇》）
      chen2   *quan2 (Yu4jie1 Pian1)*
      deep   pool (Yu4jie1 Pian1)
      'abyss'

   b. 包   太   沉   了
      bao1   *tai4*   *chen2*   *le*
      bag   too   heavy   le
      'The bag is too heavy.'

(5) a. 积翠   远   微微（《留真人东山还》）
      ji2-cui4   *yuan2* *wei1-wei1* (Liu2zhen1ren2 Dong1shan1
Huan2)

      accumulate-green   far   slight-slight (Liu2zhen1ren2 Dong1shan1
Huan2)

      'The accumulating green color is far and slight.'

   b. 微微   振动
      wei1-wei1   *zhen4-dong4*
      slight-slight   vibration-move
      'slight vibration'

For the transfers from vision to touch, all other adjectives are grounded in the sensory association when mapping diachronically in Chinese, including 稠 *chou2* 'dense', 厚 *hou4* 'thick', 绵绵 *mian2-mian2* 'continuous', 薄 *bao2* 'thin', 木 *mu4* 'numb', 嫩 *nen4* 'tender', 深 *shen1* 'deep', 松 *song1* 'shaggy', 凸 *tu1* 'protruding', 弯 *wan1* 'bent', and 纤纤 *xian1-xian1* 'slender'. That is, the visual perceptions conceptualized by these adjectives are recurrently concurrent with specific tactile perceptions, which might motivate the adjectives to map from vison to touch. Examples in (6a-b) illustrate the visual usage in Classic Chinese and the tactile usage in Modern Chinese for the adjective 松 *song1* 'shaggy'. In addition, the significant connection between vision and touch has also been attested by experimental studies including [14] and [17, 18], based on the perceptual ratings in the visual and tactile modalities.

(6) a. 柳   浅   梅   深   鬓影   松
      （《采桑子》
      liu3   *qian3*   *mei2*   *shen1* *bin4-ying3*   *song1*
      (Cai3sang1zi)
      willow   shallow   plum blossom   deep   temples-shadow shaggy
      'The willow is shallow, the plum blossom is deep, and the shadow of hair on the temples is shaggy.'

   b. 土质   松   软
      tu3-zhi4   *song1* *ruan3*
      soil-property   shaggy   soft
      'The soil is soft.'

Although the connection between vision and taste has not been shown by experimental studies such as [14] and [17, 18], the diachronic transfers of the adjectives 焦 *jiao1* 'charred' and 稀 *xi1* 'sparse' from vision to taste could also be considered to be grounded in the sensory association. That is, edible objects with the charred or sparse visual properties usually have specific gustatory properties. For instance, a piece of charred candy normally induces a special pleasant taste, and a bowl of porridge with the sparse visual property is usually of a mild taste. Thus, when 焦 *jiao1* 'charred' and 稀 *xi1* 'sparse' used for edible objects, they are usually utilized for specific food, as illustrated in (7) and (8).

（7）a. 焦   糖
      jiao1   *tang2*
      charred   candy
      'caramel'

（8）a. 稀   饭
      xi1   *fan4*
      sparse   rice
      'porridge'

In terms of the diachronic transfer from smell to taste, there is only one adjective, i.e., 膻 *shan1* 'of mutton's smell' used for the gustatory perception when tasting the mutton. Thus, the case is also grounded in the sensory association. In addition, the significant correlation between taste and smell has also been demonstrated in the perceptual ratings by [14] and [17, 18].

To summarize, although there are diachronic transfers of linguistic synesthesia in Chinese that do not follow the synchronic pattern of Mandarin synesthesia, these transfers do show similar underlying mechanisms to Mandarin synesthesia. That is, these diachronic transfers are grounded in the perceived similarity and the sensory association, analogous to linguistic synesthesia in Modern Chinese as suggested by [12]. In addition, it is important to note that except for 沉 *chen2* 'heavy' and 微微 *wei1-wei1* 'slight', most adjectives that do not follow the synchronic pattern are grounded in the sensory association when mapping diachronically. Thus, for diachronic transfers of linguistic synesthesia inconsistent with the synchronic pattern, the sensory association is the dominant mechanism for transfers between sensory modalities. It is different than synchronic transfers of linguistic synesthesia in Modern Chinese, whose dominant underlying mechanism is the perceived similarity based on [12]'s study.

3.3   Summary

Diachronic transfers of linguistic synesthesia in Chinese show two types of transfers: one is the transfer consistent with the synchronic pattern of linguistic synesthesia in Modern Chinese, and the other is the transfer inconsistent with the synchronic pattern. This study has shown above that the transfers consistent with the synchronic pattern have more adjectives and mapping types than the transfers inconsistent with the synchronic pattern. In addition, there are differences in the mechanisms underlying the two types of diachronic transfers. For the diachronic transfers consistent with the synchronic pattern, linguistic synesthesia is found to be grounded in the perceived similarity, the sensory association, and onomatopoeia, and the perceived similarity is the dominant underlying mechanism which provides the cognitive basis for the most of the sensory adjectives in linguistic synesthesia diachronically. However, in terms of the diachronic transfers inconsistent with the synchronic pattern, linguistic synesthesia is found to be motivated by the perceived similarity and the sensory association, and the sensory association is the dominant underlying mechanism.

Despite the differences between the two types of diachronic transfers of linguistic synesthesia in Chinese, it is essential to note that the mechanisms underlying diachronic transfers are analogous to the mechanisms underlying synchronic mappings of linguistic synesthesia in Modern Chinese. That is, except for the function of onomatopoeia found in two adjectives (i.e., 汪汪 *wang1-wang1* 'barking' and 潇潇 *xiao1-xiao1* 'whistling'), all other adjectives that transferred diachronically behave similarly to the adjectives that map synchronically in linguistic synesthesia.

4 Conclusion

This study examines linguistic synesthesia in Chinese from a diachronic perspective. Based on the adjectives whose contemporary predominant sensory usages are different from their original sensory meanings, this paper finds that over half of the diachronic transfers of the adjectives follow the synchronic transfer pattern of linguistic synesthesia in Modern Chinese generalized by [4]. In addition, except for two of the diachronic transfers that are grounded in onomatopoeia, all other transfers are similar to the synchronic transfers of Mandarin synesthesia, where the perceived similarity and the sensory association are underlying mechanisms. Thus, this study confirms the finding by [13] that semantic shifts of linguistic synesthesia diachronically largely obey the directionalities of linguistic synesthesia synchronically.

There are two research issues that need further study. One is the detailed transfer route of each adjective when they mapped their sensory meanings from one modality to another modality over time. The other issue is concerned with onomatopoeia. [19]'s recent study has found that onomatopoeia plays an important role in linguistic synesthesia in the composition of Mandarin state adjectives. Thus, a closer examination on the function of onomatopoeia in linguistic synesthesia is needed.

Acknowledgments. We would like to acknowledge the financial support from the National Social Science Fund of China for project (No. 19CYY006).

References

1. Ullmann, S.: The Principles of Semantics. Basil Blackwell, Oxford (1957)
2. Williams, J.M.: Synaesthetic adjectives: a possible law of semantic change. Language **52**(2), 461–478 (1976)
3. Strik Lievers, F.: Synaesthesia: a corpus-based study of cross-modal directionality. Funct. Lang. **22**(1), 69–95 (2015)
4. Zhao, Q., Huang, C.-R., Ahrens, K.: Directionality of linguistic synesthesia in Mandarin: a corpus-based study. Lingua **232**, 1–15 (2019)
5. Shen, Y.: Cognitive constraints on poetic figures. Cognitive Linguist. **8**(1), 33–71 (1997)

6. Shen, Y., Cohen, M.: How come silence is sweet but sweetness is not silent: a cognitive account of directionality in poetic synaesthesia. Lang. Lit. **7**(2), 123–140 (1998)
7. Shen, Y., Eisenman, R.: "Heard melodies are sweet, but those unheard are sweeter": synaesthetic metaphors and cognition. Lang. Lit. **17**(2), 107–121 (2008)
8. Shen, Y., Gil, D.: Sweet fragrances from Indonesia: a universal principle governing directionality in synaesthetic metaphors. In: Auracher, J., Peer, W.V. (Eds.), New Beginnings in Literary Studies, pp. 49–71. Cambridge Scholars Publishing, Newcastle (2008)
9. Shen, Y., Gadir, O.: How to interpret the music of caressing: target and source assignment in synaesthetic genitive constructions. J. Pragmat. **41**(2), 357–371 (2009)
10. Zhao, Q., Huang, C.-R.: Mapping models and underlying mechanisms of synaesthetic metaphors in Mandarin [Xiandai Hanyu Tonggan Yinyu de Yingshe Moxing yu Zhiyue Jizhi]. Lang. Teach. Ling. Stud. **1**, 44–55 (2018)
11. Zhao, Q., Huang, C.-R., Long, Y.: Synaesthesia in Chinese: a corpus-based study on gustatory adjectives in Mandarin. Linguistics **56**(5), 1167–1194 (2018)
12. Zhao, Q.: Embodied Conceptualization or Neural Realization: A Corpus-Driven Study of Mandarin Synaesthetic Adjectives. Springer, Singapore (2020)
13. Strik Lievers, F., De Felice, I.: Metaphors and perception in the lexicon. In: Speed, L.J., O'Meara, C., San Roque, L., Majid, A. (eds.) Perception Metaphors, pp. 85–104. John Benjamins, Amsterdam (2019)
14. Chen, I., Zhao, Q., Long, Y., Lu, Q., Huang, C.-R.: Mandarin Chinese modality exclusivity norms. PLoS ONE **14**(2), e0211336 (2019)
15. Xu, S.: Explaining Graphs and Analyzing Characters [Shuowen Jiezi]. Zhonghua Book Company, Beijing (121/1963)
16. Duan, Y.: Commentary on explaining graphs and analyzing characters [Shuowen Jiezi Zhu]. Phoenix Press, Nanjing (1815/2007)
17. Lynott, D., Connell, L.: Modality exclusivity norms for 423 object properties. Behav. Res. Methods **41**(2), 558–564 (2009)
18. Lynott, D., Connell, L.: Modality exclusivity norms for 400 nouns: the relationship between perceptual experience and surface word form. Behav. Res. Methods **45**(2), 516–526 (2012)
19. Zhao, Q.: ABB-pattern state adjectives in Mandarin: a study from the perspective of synaesthetic metaphor [Tonggan Yinyu Shijiao de Xiandai Hanyu ABB Shi Zhuangtai Xingrongci]. Chin. Teach. World **2**, 206–219 (2021)

The Relationship Between Lexical Richness and the Quality of CSL Learners' Oral Narratives

Qing Ma and Xingsan Chai[(✉)]

Beijing Language and Culture University, Beijing, China
cxs66@blcu.edu.cn

Abstract. The framework of lexical richness proposed by Read (2000) is an important tool for measuring the quality of writing, but this framework has been rarely applied into the metrics of oral narrative quality. Based on the measured data of HSK (Advanced) oral tests, this research selects four dimensions of lexical richness: lexical diversity, lexical sophistication, lexical density and lexical errors and 16 measurement indexes to explore the correlation between lexical richness and the quality of oral narratives. Furthermore, we examine the predictive validity of each index for oral achievements, pick out the key indexes which can reflect the quality of CSL learners' oral narratives and conduct a regression model. The research results show that Guiraud index, the ratio of lexical errors, the ratio of level C vocabularies and lexical density III can effectively test the quality of oral narratives.

Keywords: Lexical richness · Lexical diversity · Lexical sophistication · Lexical density · Lexical errors

1 Introduction

In the field of second language (L2) teaching and researches, lexical richness refers to the size and the range of a L2 writer's productive vocabulary [1]. Lexical richness consists of four interrelated aspects: lexical diversity (or lexical variation), lexical sophistication, lexical density, and lexical errors [2], to some extent, which can reflect the quality of oral or written language of L2 learners. Through sorting out the previous literature, the studies on lexical richness of second language can mainly divided into four aspects.

The first aspect involves the exploring for the measurement indicators and their respective validity of lexical richness. [3] analyzed the pros and cons of measurement indicators in his previous studies, and ultimately selected lexical diversity, lexical errors, and lexical sophistication to measure lexical richness. [4] creatively chose Lexical Frequency Profile as another effective measurement indicator of lexical richness.

The second respect is to examine the relationship between lexical richness and the quality of language production. [5] extracted 25 measurement indicators from lexical diversity, lexical sophistication and lexical density, and investigated the relationship

M. Dong et al. (Eds.): CLSW 2021, LNAI 13250, pp. 95–105, 2022.
https://doi.org/10.1007/978-3-031-06547-7_7

between the lexical richness and the quality of oral narrative of ESL (English as a second language) learners. [6] took Read's lexical richness framework like lexical diversity, lexical sophistication, lexical frequency profile and lexical error as the observation dimension, based on which extended the measurement indicators to 27. She also explored the relationship between the lexical richness and writing scores of CSL (Chinese as a second language) learners and constructed the regression equation of predicting writing achievements. Her empirical results showed that the proportion of lexical errors, the number of both word types and common words can be used as the effective parameters to predict writing achievements and explain 92.8% of total variation.

Thirdly, the researchers mainly pay attention to the comparative studies of productive vocabulary richness between L2 learners and native language learners. [7] collected the writing samples of 130 college freshmen, including 56 native English speakers and 74 ESL learners. Through comparing the two groups, they concluded that although these native speakers and second-language speakers had no differences in syntactic complexity, lexical density (the ratio between lexical words and function words) and lexical sophistication, they had significant differences in lexical variation, especially verb variation.

The last angle refers to the studies on dynamic development of lexical richness. [8] analyzed the development characteristics of vocabulary richness of English beginners' writings by looking at the following dimensions: lexical sophistication, lexical variation and the rate of lexical error. He found a weaker ability of beginners to comprehensively make use of vocabulary and a lower vocabulary richness, but as the grade rises, lexical richness became higher and higher, while the specific development varied from dimension to dimension. [9] explored the diachronic development changes of vocabulary richness in English writing through a longitudinal research. The results agreed that the lexical variation in English writing showed a non-linear trend, appearing the phenomenon of vocabulary plateau among the college seniors. The lexical density generally displayed an upward trend, and the level of lexical sophistication increased with a higher grade.

At present, both home and abroad researchers regard the second and fourth angle as the focus of lexical richness, and the second type is more inclined to explore the relationship between learners' lexical richness and writing quality [6, 10–13]. At the same time, the fewer studies focus on the relationship between lexical richness and oral narrative quality and most of the previous researches from this angle are carried out under the background of English as a second language. Considering the increasing number of worldwide CSL learners, it may become a new research direction to explore the correlation between lexical richness and oral narrative quality in the perspective of Chinese as a second language. In view of the current research status, this study will examine the relationship between the CSL learners' lexical richness and oral narrative quality from lexical diversity, lexical sophistication, lexical density and lexical errors according to Read's lexical richness analysis framework, and on this basis we will also present effective parameters to measure oral narrative quality (oral scores).

2 Lexical Richness Measures

2.1 Lexical Diversity

Lexical diversity, also known as lexical variation, means that language learners use various vocabularies to express the same meaning, thus avoiding the reuse of certain words. According to [2] lexical richness analysis framework, lexical variation is measured by the type-token ratio (TTR). However, this method has certain defects. In details, it is susceptible to the length of the language material. In other words, it means the longer the material is, the more the repeated words will be used, while the smaller the TTR will become. So some scholars have improved the TTR so as to reduce the effects of the length of language material on the measurement results. For example, [14] proposed Root TT (also known as Guiraud index), [15] put forward Uber index, and [16] brought up D and so on. Although the measure index has been constantly optimized, the effectiveness of these indicators remains to be further studied. Therefore, [5] demonstrated that the word type (the number of not repeated words in the language material) and Guiraud index are most closely related to the writing quality of the subjects by exploring the relationship between the 20 measurement indicators representing lexical diversity and the writing quality. On account of the validity discussion above on measurement indicators and their own operability of these indicators, this research will adopt total words (tokens), word types, TTR, Guiraud index, Uber index to measure lexical richness. These five indicators are calculated as following:

(1) Tokens = the total number of words in the text
(2) Word types = the total number of words not repeated in the text
(3) TTR = types/tokens
(4) Guiraud index = types/$\sqrt{\text{tokens}}$
(5) Uber index = logtokens^2/(logtokens − logtypes)

2.2 Lexical Sophistication

Lexical sophistication refers to the proportion of low-frequency words or advanced vocabularies used by second language speakers under expression. When conducting the ESL researches, lexical sophistication is usually tested by working out the proportion of sophisticated word families in total word families [2, 3]. However, due to the lack of morphological changes in Chinese, it is not suitable to use word family as a unit for statistics. After taking into account a variety of factors, we finally choose words and word types as statistical units, and choose the proportion of sophisticated words, sophisticated word types and the vocabularies at each level as the measurement indicators of lexical sophistication. The sophistication words are aimed at the above C-level (including C-level) vocabularies from Outline of HSK Vocabulary Level Grade. The mentioned indexes are calculated as following:

(1) Ratio of sophisticated words = total number of sophisticated words/total number of words
(2) Ratio of sophisticated word types = total number of sophisticated word types/the total word types

(3) Ratio of vocabularies at each level = the total number of words in a certain level/total number of words

2.3 Lexical Density

Lexical density refers to the proportion of the number of lexical (or content) words in the language material in the total words [17]. It is an important characteristic that distinguishes the written from spoken language [2]. When involved with measuring lexical density, there exist two methods. One is the formula proposed by [17]: total number of lexical words/ total number of words in the composition; and the other is from [18]: the number of lexical items as a ration of the number of clauses. In addition, some researchers have adjusted the above two formulas in accordance with their own research needs. [19] defined the lexical density as "the lexical words/error-free words". [13] redefined the lexical words from the formula in [17] into tokens and types of lexical words and achieved the lexical density based on the number of types and tokens of lexical words. Our research adopts [13] definition to the lexical words and the formula mode of [17] to calculate lexical density (lexical density I, lexical density II). In addition, we take the proportion of content word types (lexical density III) as another index for lexical density. The above indicators are calculated as following:

(1) Lexical density I = total number of lexical words/tokens
(2) Lexical density II = total number of lexical word types/tokens
(3) Lexical density III = total number of lexical word types/total number of types

2.4 Lexical Density

[2] pointed out that the lexical errors in most studies are measured by the number of lexical errors or the proportion of lexical errors in the texts, but in this situation, we will not know how to judge vocabulary errors and distinguish vocabulary errors from non-lexical ones. To better address this problem, some researchers have given a more detailed list of the typical lexical errors. [3] explained lexical errors as minor spelling mistakes, major spelling mistakes, derivation mistakes, faux-aims (deceptive cognates), lexical errors due to interference from another language on the curriculum and confusion between two lexemes; [20] classified lexical errors into lexical choice errors and lexical form errors, with grammar and syntactic errors not included. The authors believe that [20] has a reasonable definition on lexical errors, so this study will be carried out on the basis of it.

According to the framework of lexical errors in [20], form errors are mainly manifested in derivational errors, verb forms, phonetically similar-semantically unrelated errors and major spelling errors. While form errors in Chinese are more reflected as wrong written characters and homonym characters. Considering these two errors are not included by vocabulary application abilities, this study only considers errors in meaning or lexical choice when identifying vocabulary errors. Meaning or lexical choice errors mainly refers to the fact that the intended meaning goes a wrong way due to the learners' failure to choose the appropriate vocabularies. They mainly conclude vocabulary redundancy or absence, vocabulary collocation errors, synonym distinction errors, coining words, word misuse and so on. After identifying the types of vocabulary errors, we measure the lexical errors by the error proportion, which is the ratio of incorrect words to total words.

3 Methods

3.1 Research Questions

This research focuses on the relationship between lexical richness and CSL Learners' oral narrative quality (defined as oral test scores). To be specific, we intend to deal with the following two research questions:

(1) How does the lexical richness relate to the quality of test takers' oral narratives?
(2) What is the ratio of measurement indicators of the lexical richness to oral test scores? What are the main indicators that can best reflect the quality of CSL Learners' oral narratives?

3.2 The Subjects

This study first selected 2,339 Korean CSL learners from the 4784 candidates who took the HSK (Advanced) oral test held in April 2010, among which 90 Korean were randomly selected as the subjects, including 44 boys and 46 girls. CSL learners from different mother tongue backgrounds will differ in the performance of oral abilities due to the distinctions in learning strategies and personality characteristics, so our study selected the test objects from the same mother tongue background.

3.3 The Measurement

The HSK (Advanced) oral test is the language material source of this research. The HSK (Advanced) oral test is a standardized Chinese proficiency test developed by the Chinese Test Center of Beijing Language University, which composes of two parts. The first part required the candidates to read a short passage of about 250 words, and the second part was two propositional speeches. In view of the research purpose of this study, we chose the answers of the first topic "Please introduce the health keeping methods for the middle-aged and the old to keep fit and live longer-in the propositional statement" as the test material.

3.4 Data Processing

Transcription. To be first, iFLYTEK's transcription software "Short Form ASR" was used to transcribe the selected language material. Then, a group of linguistic-majored postgraduates and doctoral students checked the machine-generated transcription carefully. In the end, a speech corpus of about 40,000 words was obtained.

Word Segmentation and POS Tagging. Corpus Word Parser[1] is employed to segment the obtained corpus and POS (part-of-speech) tagging. On the basis of *Chinese Proficiency Vocabulary and Grade Outline of Chinese Characters* [21] and *Modern Chinese Dictionary* [22], We also conducted a further artificial check aimed at reducing any possible ambiguity and errors from machine-generated word segmentation.

4   Results of Pearson Correlation Analysis

4.1   Correlation Between Lexical Variation and Oral Narrative Quality

To understand the relationship between lexical variation and the quality of oral narratives, we performed a Pearson correlation analysis between each measurement index of lexical variation and oral scores. The results are presented in the table below.

Table 1. Correlation between lexical variation and oral scores.

	Tokens	Word types	TTR	Guiraud index	Uber index
Oral scores	0.705^{**}	0.760^{**}	$-.534^{**}$	0.738^{**}	-0.025

As Table 1 shows, lexical variation has a significant positive correlation with tokens, word types and Guiraud index; while TTR has a negative correlation with oral scores; no significant correlation is found between Uber Index and oral scores. The involved indicators in Table 1 range from large to small: word types, Guiraud index, tokens and TTR. This suggests that word types and Guiraud index can be used as the effective indicators to measure lexical variation.

4.2   Correlation Between Lexical Sophistication and Oral Narrative Quality

We made a Pearson-related analysis to observe how oral scores are related to lexical sophistication. The results are shown in the table below (index 1 = Ratio of sophisticated words; index 2 = Ratio of sophisticated word types; index 3 = Ratio of level A vocabularies; index 4 = Ratio of level B vocabularies; index 5 = Ratio of level C vocabularies; index 6 = Ratio of level D vocabularies; index 7 = Ratio of words beyond the vocabulary):

Table 2. Correlation between lexical sophistication and oral scores.

	Index 1	Index 2	Index 3	Index 4	Index 5	Index 6	Index 7
Oral scores	0.353^{**}	0.553^{**}	-0.348^{**}	0.161	0.387^{**}	-0.071	0.253^{*}

---

[1] Corpus Word Parser is from WWW.CNCORPUS.ORG.

The results in Table 2 shows that ratio of sophisticated words, ratio of sophisticated words types, ratio of level C vocabularies and ratio of words beyond the vocabulary have a significant positive correlation with oral scores; Ratio of level A vocabularies has a signification negative correlation with oral scores; No significant correlation is found between ratio of level B vocabularies and oral scores, neither is ratio of level D vocabularies and oral scores. The involved indicators in Table 2 from large to small is: ratio of sophisticated word types, ratio of level C vocabularies, ratio of sophisticated words, ratio of level A vocabularies and ratio of words beyond the vocabulary. This indicates that ratio of level C vocabularies and ratio of sophisticated words are more effective indicators that can reflect the relationship between lexical sophistication and oral scores than others.

4.3   Correlation Between Lexical Density and Oral Narrative Quality

Through Pearson's related analysis, we explore the relationship between lexical density and oral score. The results are as following:

Table 3. Correlation between lexical density and oral scores.

	Lexical density I	Lexical density II	Lexical density III
Oral scores	−0.133	−0.107	−0.523**

From the results in Table 3, we can see that lexical density I and Lexical density II have no signification correlation with oral scores, but Lexical density III does. The results here are different from previous studies on the relationship between lexical density and writing quality. For example, [6, 13] have proved that lexical density does not reflect the quality of writing. This table also supports Read's view that lexical density is better suited to measure the quality of spoken language than writing.

4.4   Correlation Between Lexical Errors and Oral Narrative Quality

Using Pearson-related analysis, we explored the relationship between lexical errors and oral scores. The result is shown in Table 4:

Table 4. Correlation between lexical errors and oral scores.

	Ratio of lexical errors
Oral scores	−0.688**

The result in the Table 4 has shown a significant negative correlation between ratio of lexical errors and oral scores.

5   The Results of Multiple Regression Analysis

5.1   Multiple Regression Analysis Between Lexical Richness and Oral Scores

Lexical richness has always been regarded as an important tool for measuring the quality of writing. [10] examined the influence of vocabulary, content, language use, etc., on the quality of writing. It was found that vocabulary factors could explain 83.75% of total variation. When exploring the relationship between lexical richness and writing quality, [6] found that word types, lexical errors and the number of everyday words can explain the 92.8% variation of writing scores. However, there has existed little research on the effect of lexical richness on the quality of oral narratives so far. Therefore, we take 16 measurement indicators of lexical richness from four dimensions as independent variables and the oral scores as dependent variables to conduct regression analysis and establish a regression model to investigate the proportion of lexical richness in the measurement of oral narrative quality. The details are shown in Table 5, Table 6 and Table 7:

Table 5. Model summary.

Model	R	R^2	Adjusted R^2	Std. error of the estimate	R^2 change	Sig. F change
1	.748[a]	.559	.552	10.430	.559	.000
2	.819[b]	.671	.661	9.075	.112	.000
3	.860[c]	.740	.728	8.130	.069	.000
4	.883[d]	.780	.767	7.531	.040	.001

d. Predictive variable: (Constant) Guiraud index, ratio of lexical errors, ratio of level C vocabularies, lexical density III

The results in Table 5 show that the model 4 has the best imitative effect with a $R = 0.883$, $R^2 = 0.780$, adjusted $R^2 = 0.767$, $p < 0.05$. This shows that the regression equation is meaningful. In this model, Guiraud index, lexical errors, ratio of level C vocabularies and lexical density III can explain 76.7% of total variation. Comparing this conclusion with [6] (decide 92.8% of total variation), it can be seen that the influence of lexical richness on writing scores is stronger than on oral scores. Therefore, for the evaluation of oral quality, more factors besides lexical richness should be taken into account.

Table 6. ANOVA.

Model		Sum of squares	df	Mean square	F	Sig.
4	Regression	12900.152	4	3225.038	56.856	.000
	Residual	3630.283	64	56.723		
	Total	16530.435	68			

Table 6 gives the results of ANOVA analysis, and it demonstrates that model 4 has statistical difference ($F(4,64) = 56.856$, $p < 0.01$), which means Guiraud index, ratio of lexical errors, ratio of level C vocabularies and lexical density III there exists a linear correlation with the oral scores of the subjects.

Table 7. Multiple linear regression coefficient.

Model 4	Unstandardized coefficients		Standardized coefficients	t	p
	B	Standard error	Beta		
(intercept)	60.104	11.358		5.292	.000
Guiraud index	4.655	1.155	.323	4.030	.000
Ratio of lexical errors	−1.853	.320	−.397	−5.784	.000
Ratio of level C vocabularies	1.774	.357	.314	4.966	.000
Lexical density III	−0.395	.115	−.235	−3.427	.001

Table 7 lists out the regression coefficients of the model 4. In Model 4, Guiraud index ($p < 0.01$), ratio of lexical errors ($p < 0.01$), ratio of level C vocabularies ($p < 0.01$) and lexical density III ($p < 0.01$) are effective predictor variables. Based on the data in Table 7, the regression equation of Model 4 could be written as:

$Y = 60.104 + 6.655 \times Guiraud\ index -1.853 \times ratio\ of\ lexical\ errors + 1.774 \times ratio\ of\ level\ C\ vocabularies -0.395 \times lexical\ density\ III.$

The standardized regression coefficients of the four indicators in Table 7 range from large to small $|-0.397| > 0.323 > 0.314 > |-0.235|$. It can be seen that ratio of lexical errors has the greatest impact on the oral scores. The results also make it clear that lexical density can also be thought as an effective indicator to predict oral scores. However, both [6, 13] hold that lexical density had no significant effect on writing quality. So what is believed is that lexical density is more appropriate to measure oral quality.

5.2 Validity Test of Regression Equation

In order to test the validity of the regression equation, we randomly sampled the corresponding data of the remaining 21 subjects into the above-mentioned regression equation, figured out their predicted oral results, and then connected them with their actual oral scores. The results are shown in Table 8:

Table 8. Correlation between actual scores and predicted scores.

	Predicted scores	Actual scores
Predicted scores	1	.803[**]
Actual scores	.803[**]	1

**.Correlation is significant at the 0.01 level (2-tailed)

As can be seen from Table 8, the correlation coefficient between the actual scores and predicted scores is 0.803, and there is a very significant positive correlation between the actual oral scores and predicted scores at the significance 0.01 level ($p < 0.01$), so the prediction effect of this model is relatively good, and the system of these indicators has a satisfied predictive value.

6   Conclusion

Based on the HSK (Advanced) oral test data, this research explores the correlation between lexical richness and the quality of oral narratives, and conducts a regression analysis on 16 indicators of lexical richness from four dimensions. The study indicates that the oral scores of CSL learners have a significant correlation with token, word types, Guiraud index, TTR, ratio of sophisticated words, ratio of sophisticated word types, ratio of level C vocabularies, ratio of words beyond the vocabulary, ratio of level A vocabularies, lexical density III and the ratio of lexical errors. Meanwhile, Guiraud index, ratio of lexical errors, ratio of level C vocabularies and lexical density III are effective indicators to predict the oral scores, and can explain 76.7% of total variation.

There are also some limitations in our research, which are specifically shown in the following aspects: (1) The lexical richness of oral narratives may be influenced by the familiarity of the topic, the individual differences and other factors; (2) Read's lexical richness framework is mainly applied to ESL writing researches, but we have applied this framework to CSL oral narratives research, so in future research we need to explore a more suitable framework to measure the lexical richness of CSL learners.

Acknowledgments. This project was supported by the Key Projects of National Social Science Fund of China (Award Number 17AYY011). The content is solely the responsibility of the authors and does not necessarily represent the official views of National Social Science Fund of China. We would like to thank the examines and test centers who helped us gather the data.

References

1. Wolfe-Quintero, K., Inagaki, S., Kim, H.: Second Language Development in Writing: Measures of Fluency, Accuracy, and Complexity. University of Hawaii, National Foreign Language Resource Center (1998)
2. Read, J.: Assessing Vocabulary. Cambridge University Press, Cambridge (2000)
3. Arnaud, P.: The lexical richness of L2 written productions and the validity of vocabulary tests. In: Culhane, T., Klein-Braley, C., Stevenson, D.K. (eds.) Practice and Problems in Language Testing, pp. 14–28. University of Essex, Colchester (1984)
4. Laufer, B., Nation, P.: Vocabulary size and use: lexical richness in l2 written production. Appl. Linguis. **3**, 307–322 (1995)
5. Lu, X.-F.: Relationship of lexical richness to the quality of ESL learners' oral narratives. Mod. Lang. J. **96**(2), 190–208 (2012)
6. Wang, Y.: The correlation between lexical richness and writing score of CSL learner—the multivariable linear regression model and equation of writing quality. Appl. Linguis. **2**, 93–101 (2017). (in Chinese)

7. Eckstein, G., Ferris, D.: Comparing L1 and L2 texts and writers in first-year composition. TESOL Quar. **52**(1), 137–162 (2018)
8. Zhang, H.-P.: On developmental features of lexical richness in EFL writings by Chinese beginner learners of English. Mod. Foreign Lang. **43**(4), 529–540 (2020). (in Chinese)
9. Zhu, H.-M., Wang, J.-J.: Developmental features of lexical richness in English writing: a self-built corpus-based longitudinal study. Foreign Lang. World **6**, 77–86 (2013). (in Chinese)
10. Astika, G.G.: Analytical assessments of foreign students' writing. RELC J. **24**(1), 61–70 (1993)
11. Liu, D.-H.: The influence of vocabulary size on EFL writing. Mod. Foreign Lang. **2**, 180–187 (2003). (in Chinese)
12. Tan, X.-C.: A study of Chinese English learners' productive vocabulary development. Foreign Lang. Teach. Res. **3**, 202–207+241 (2006). (in Chinese)
13. Wu, J.-F.: Research on lexical richness development in CSL writing by English native speakers. Chin. Teach. World **2**, 129–142 (2016). (in Chinese)
14. Guiraud, H.: Les Caractères Statistiques du Vocabulaire. Presses Universitaires de France, Paris (1954)
15. Dugast, D.: Sur Quoi Se Fonde La Notion D'étendue Théoretique Du Vocabulaire. Le Francais Moderne **46**(1), 25–32 (1978)
16. Malvern, D.D., Richards, B.J., Chipere, N., Durán, P.: Lexical Diversity and Language Development: Quantification and Assessment. Palgrave Macmillan, Houndmills (2004)
17. Ure, J.: Lexical density and register differentiation. In: Perren, G., Trim, J.: Applications of Linguistics: Selected Papers of the Second International Congress of Applied Linguistics. Cambridge University Press, Cambridge (1971)
18. Halliday, M.A.K.: Spoken and Written Language. Deakin University Press, Victoria (1985)
19. Huang, L, Qian, X.-J.: An inquiry into Chinese learners' knowledge of productive vocabulary: a quantitative study. Chin. Lang. Learn. **1**, 56–61 (2003). (in Chinese)
20. Engber, C.A.: The relationship of lexical proficiency to the quality of ESL composition. J. Second. Lang. Writ. **4**(2), 139–155 (1995)
21. National Chinese Proficiency Test Committee Office Test Center: Chinese Proficiency Vocabulary and Grade Outline of Chinese Characters. Economic Science Press, Beijing (2001). (in Chinese)
22. Institute of Linguistics.: Modern Chinese Dictionary. Commercial Press, Beijing (2016). (in Chinese)

Interpreting Accomplishments by Script Knowledge: A Comparison Study Between Chinese and French

Yingyi Luo and Xiaoqian Zhang[(✉)]

Institute of Linguistics, Chinese Academy of Social Sciences, Beijing, China
{luoyingyi,yyszhangxq}@cass.org.cn

Abstract. In this study, a recent model of "event-script homomorphism" which highlights the representation of script knowledge is empirically examined as a mechanism to identify accomplishment events in comparison with another `acknowledged model of "event-argument homomorphism". We tested Chinese and French native speakers' interpretations of perfective sentences with incremental theme accomplishment predicates. Results showed that the representation of an accomplishment usually implies the incremental theme being mostly affected, as claimed by the "event-argument homomorphism" model. Similarly, and importantly, the representation also implies the completion of the script, with the marking stages having happened. This suggests that the "event-script homomorphism" model can be applied to explain the identification of accomplishment events, on a par with the "event-argument homomorphism" model. A difference of interpretation between Chinese and French was observed in incremental theme involvement but was reduced in script completion, and manifested mainly by verbs of destruction.

Keywords: "Event-argument homomorphism" model · "Event-script homomorphism" model · Accomplishment · Incremental theme · Event · Script knowledge

1 Introduction

Events are often treated as entities [1]. One question subsequently arises as to how events can be segmented as individuals so as to be counted like objects. In this study, a model of "event-script homomorphism" as a mechanism to identify accomplishments is suggested and empirically examined. Our aim is to understand how adequately this model, *vis-à-vis* another model – i.e., the "event-argument homomorphism", can be applied to a specific type of accomplishments: that is, *incremental theme accomplishments*.

In the eyes of semanticists, the theme of an accomplishment verb sometimes plays an important role in the identification of an accomplishment event ([2–13] among others). As they propose, there is a "homomorphism from the denotation of the theme to the extent of the event in which the theme is a participant" [12, p. 94]: as the event described by the incremental verb progresses, the theme also undergoes some changes;

© Springer Nature Switzerland AG 2022
M. Dong et al. (Eds.): CLSW 2021, LNAI 13250, pp. 106–115, 2022.
https://doi.org/10.1007/978-3-031-06547-7_8

in fact, the event is "accomplished" when the theme is also completely affected. For instance, in the event of *building a house*, the direct object *a house* "is used up 'bit by bit'" as the event of *building* progresses [12, p. 92]. An accomplishment of *building a house* cannot be identified as an event of *building a house* if the house is merely half built (see [3] for a similar example); it can only be identified as an individual event of *building a house* when the house is completely built. Verbs such as *build* are called *incremental verbs* and their objects *incremental themes* (henceforth IT).

Alternatively, there exists another approach, which is mainly adopted by researchers of event perception and cognition. It considers the event schemas or scripts – i.e., a type of semantic knowledge about the commonalities across a set of events [14] – to be critical in event identification. In line with this, Zhang et al. [15] proposed an "event-script homomorphism" model to explain how accomplishments can be identified: the progression of an accomplishment event corresponds to the unfolding of the stages composing the accomplishment script, which establishes a homomorphism between the accomplishment and the script. For instance, the event of *frying a plate of raw chicken legs* is commonly considered to have a script composed by a number of sequential stages: marinate the chicken legs, coat the chicken legs with flour, place the chicken legs in hot oil for a while and take them out of the oil. When the chicken legs have been taken out of the oil after being there for a period of time – that is, when the final stage of the script is finished, the event of *frying a plate of raw chicken legs* reaches its ending. Therefore, the event script acts as a criterion to segment one individual event since the completion of the last stage of the event script marks the completion of the accomplishment (see Table 1 for another example). Script knowledge can be concisely encoded in the main verb phrase of a sentence and retrieved when the verb phrase is accessed during comprehension.

This study investigated the adequacy of this hypothesized "event-script homomorphism" model in explaining the mental representations of accomplishments during sentence reading. Specifically, we selected a typical type of accomplishments, i.e., *incremental theme accomplishments*, as a target to test for these events' general conformity with the "event-argument homomorphism" model. As exemplified above, the "event-argument homomorphism" model predicts that the extent to which an IT is affected determines the progression of an IT accomplishment. Evidence [16] has shown that such an accomplishment verb phrase is interpreted to entail that, when the event is completed, the whole IT – or a major part of it – is affected. Analogously, as stated by the "event-script homomorphism" model, these IT verb phrases would activate a reading according to which "when the event is completed, the script is considered finished", leading to a representation in which the critical stages of the script have all been settled.

To this end, we conducted an experiment where native speakers were asked to read perfective sentences with verb phrases describing accomplishments, and to report their interpretations in terms of the degree of object involvement and the degree of script completion. These two measurements correspond to the two models, respectively, and can be compared from an experimental perspective. They are predicted to be highly correlated if the "event-script homomorphism" model functions as well as the "event-argument homomorphism" model.

We also compared interpretation patterns between Chinese and French native speakers to examine the universality of accomplishment event cognition. Because of the considerable typological differences between the two languages [16–20], one might expect that diverging interpretation patterns for the two groups of speakers would emerge. However, we are more prone to argue in favor of a general cognition mechanism underlying humans, which would result in more commonalities than differences across languages.

Table 1. Exemplar trial of accomplishment *wipe the classroom floor* in Chinese and French.

Target Predicate	Chinese Predicate → 擦教室的地板		
	French Predicate → nettoyer le sol de la salle de classe		
	English Translation → to wipe the classroom floor		
Critical Sentence	Chinese Critical Sentence → 小明擦了教室的地板。		
	French Critical Sentence → Julien a nettoyé le sol de la salle de classe.		
	English Translation → Xiaoming wiped the classroom floor.		
IT Judgment	**Chinese**	**French**	**English Translation**
	请问地板被擦了多少? (可多选) (a) 小部分 (b) 一半 (c) 大部分 (d) 全部	Jugez quelle partie du sol Julien a probablement nettoyé. (choix multiple possible) (a) Une petite partie du sol de la salle de classe (b) Une moitié du sol de la salle de classe (c) Une grande partie du sol de la salle de classe (d) Tout le sol de la salle de classe	How much of the floor has been wiped? (multiple choice allowed) (a) a small part (b) half of it (c) a large part (d) all of it
Script Judgment	**Chinese**	**French**	**English Translation**
	请判断下列哪些场景与"小明擦了教室的地板。"的描述相符? (可多选) (a) 打一桶清水 (b) 打一桶清水 → 用清水洗拖布并拖地板 (c) 打一桶清水 → 用清水洗拖布并拖地板 → 用干拖布拖地板	Quelles sont les situations/quelle est la situation qui correspond(ent) à la description de la phrase "Julien a nettoyé le sol de la salle de classe"? (choix multiple possible) (a) remplir un seau d'eau (b) remplir un seau d'eau → mouiller une serpillière dans l'eau et laver le sol de la salle de classe avec la serpillière mouillée (c) remplir un seau d'eau → mouiller une serpillière dans l'eau et laver le sol de la salle de classe avec la serpillière mouillée → sécher le sol avec une serpillière sèche	Please judge which of the following scenario(s) is/are consistent with the sentence "Xiaoming wiped the classroom floor". (multiple choice allowed) (a) fill a bucket with water (b) fill a bucket with water → wet a mop and wipe the classroom floor with it (c) fill a bucket with water → wet a mop and wipe the classroom floor with it → dry the floor with a dry mop

2   Methods

2.1   Participants

Thirty native Mandarin speakers, aged from 18 to 22 years old (24 females), were recruited from Chinese universities to attend the Chinese experiment. Thirty-three native French speakers attended the French experiment, with 3 being excluded from further data analysis due to their misunderstanding of the task. The remaining thirty French participants were aged from 21 to 75 years old (13 females). One reported that she was also a native speaker of Cantonese. All participants received a monetary reward.

2.2   Design and Materials

Eleven verb phrases of IT accomplishments were targeted (see Table 2). These verbs in their English form were discussed in [6, 7, 12, 21, 22]. We translated them into Chinese and French, and put them in sentences framed like "Subject + Verb-le$_{\text{perfective marker}}$ + Object" in Chinese and "Subject + Verb$_{\text{passé composé form}}$ + Object" in French. Thus, target sentences were created – 11 for Chinese and 11 for French.

We also developed scripts for the accomplishment events described by the target predicates, preparing prototypical sequences of stages based on encyclopedic research. Web-sourced encyclopedia such as *wikiHow.com* and *zhihu.com* were consulted, where questions regarding "how" an activity/event takes place are asked and answered with the typical procedure of the event. The drafted scripts were subsequently confirmed by two linguists. Among 11 target accomplishments, two described an event with a 2-stage script, three with a 3-stage script, and six with a 4-stage script (Table 2).

Each sentence was presented twice to each participant, either followed by an *IT judgment task* or by a *script judgment task* (not necessarily in this order). In the IT task, participants had to judge to what extent one physical property (surface, size, volume, etc.) of the IT was affected. As illustrated in Table 1, option A, B, C, and D referred to different degrees of affectedness/involvement, from a small proportion to the full proportion. Participants were allowed to choose any option – as well as any combination – from the provided four as long as the indicated extent of object involvement was considered to be a feasible reading derived from the sentence. Thus, there were theoretically up to fifteen possible response patterns since this could consist of one up to all four options.

In the script judgment task, participants read the target sentence and chose from optional combinations of stages according to the sentence interpretation. The combinations of stages were structured in an increasingly compositional manner, analogously to the logic of option setup in the IT judgment task: A described the first stage of the schema script, B described the second stage joining the first, C (if there was) described the third stage joining the first and the second, and so on. When participants chose the last option, it meant that they inferred from the target sentence that all N stages of the script had been completed; when they chose the penultimate option, it meant that the last stage was considered unnecessary to happen in the target event; when they chose more than one option, it meant that more than one stage sequence was considered a possible reading.

2.3   Procedure

For both languages, the eleven target predicates were assigned to three lists, each list having in total 44 trials (one sentence and one judgment task) for different research purposes. Identical target sentences with different tasks were assigned to the same list to minimize individual differences between tasks. Each list adopted a pseudo-randomized sequence such that consecutive trials would not share one target sentence. Each list was then administered to ten Chinese and ten French participants.

Each participant was randomly assigned to one version and received the test via the *Wènjuàn Xīng* (www.wjx.cn), a crowdsourcing website for questionnaire research. They were required to read the instructions and make judgments trial by trial. Only one trial at a time was shown on screen, i.e., the target sentence and its corresponding judgment task. Participants were not allowed to go back to the preceding trials once they made a choice. Additionally, for each trial, participants were given the option to leave a comment if they had any concern. Only three trials (one in Chinese and two in French) were commented, and they were all settled in the post-test interview.

2.4   Data Categorization

Both tasks allowed participants to choose either single or multiple options. For the IT judgment task, a response involving the combination of C and D, or the single options C or D was classified as "Salient Consequence", meaning that the event representation activated by the sentence included a marking consequence of over 50% of IT being affected; instead, the selection of all options (ABCD) indicated "No Salient Consequence" meaning that any level of involvement was possible according to the sentence interpretation.

Similarly, for the script judgment task, choosing a script with N or/and N-1 step was classified as "Salient Consequence" showing that the event representation included the consequence of most stages of the script being completed; on the contrary, a response consisting of all options was classified as "No Salient Consequence" of script in the accomplishment event representation. For the two accomplishments described with a 2-stage script, choosing both options was also classified as "No Salient Consequence".

3   Results

IT Judgment Task. 54 trials (49.1%) for Chinese and 76 trials (69.1%) for French out of 110 were interpreted to imply that the IT was 100% affected. Interpretations that refer to "over half of the IT being affected" made up 19.1% for Chinese and 14.5% for French, resulting in the total proportion of "Salient Consequence" responses taking 68.2% for Chinese and 83.6% for French. On the other hand, 29.1% trials in Chinese and 11.8% trials in French were read in a way that the IT could be affected to any degree. Particularly, most Chinese speakers responded to sentences with *dismantle* and *destroy* as "No Salient Consequence" (see Table 2). Chinese speakers made more "No Salient Consequence" as well as fewer "Salient Consequence responses" than French speakers, as reflected by the significant result of the Chi-square test (p-value < .008, which is the criterion according to Bonferroni correction).

Table 2. Distribution of response types for each verb phrase. CHN: Chinese; FR: French.

	IT judgment				Script judgment			
	>50%		No Salient Consequence		N-1 & N		No Salient Consequence	
	CHN	FR	CHN	FR	CHN	FR	CHN	FR
2-stage script								
Examine a/that paper copy	8	7	2	3	7	10	3	
Burn a pile of leaves	7	6	3	1	7	7	3	3
3-stage script								
Wipe the floor of the classroom	7	10	1		10	9		
Paint a wall	7	8	3	2	10	10		
Fry a plate of raw chicken legs	8	8	2	1	10	10		
4-stage script								
Dismantle a plane model	1	8	9	1	2	8	8	2
Build a house	10	9		1	3	2		1
Draw a picture	10	9		1	6	8	1	
Destroy a car	1	9	9		1	6	8	3
Dye a piece of cloth	9	7	1	3	9	9		
Iron a sheet	7	10	2		10	10		

Script Judgment Task. Chinese and French participants considered the option with all stages as the only appropriate script consistent with their interpretation of the target sentence in 63 (57.3%) and 69 trials (62.7%) out of the total 110 trials, respectively. Adding the number of trials that were answered with the selection of "N-1 or/and N stage(s)", the total proportion of "Salient Consequence" reached up to 72.7% for Chinese and 80% for French. By contrast, a relatively small number of trials, 20.9% for Chinese and 8.1% for French, were answered with all options being selected, suggesting that the interpretation of these accomplishment events did not indicate a clear ending stage. Most of these trials involved the predicates *dismantle* and *destroy* especially for Chinese speakers, similarly to the findings in the IT judgement task. It should be noted that for trials with a 3-stage script none was considered "No Salient Consequence". Interestingly, the Chi-square test failed to show significant distinction of responses between the languages (p-value > .016) although the pattern was numerically similar to that of IT judgment.

Cross-task Analysis. First, the distribution of "Salient Consequence" responses and "No Salient Consequence" responses between the two tasks was compared with a Chi-square test in Chinese and French, respectively. No significant result was found (ps > .05), meaning that there was not enough evidence to argue that interpretation patterns differ across tasks as reflected by the present data; rather, they appeared to be similar.

Moreover, for the sentences in which the object was judged as being completely affected (CHN:54, FR:76), a large percentage (CHN:45 trials, 83.3%; FR:64 trials, 84.2%) was also considered as the script being completed and approaching the "Salient

Consequence", whereas only 2 trials of Chinese and 2 of French had a "No Salient Consequence" response in the script judgment task (see Table 3). However, for sentences interpreted as all stages of the given script being completed (CHN:63, FR:69), a numerically smaller proportion of trials (CHN:51 trials, 80.9%; FR:54 trials, 78.3%) was considered approaching "Salient Consequence" for IT while an increased number (CHN:11 trials, 17.5%; FR:11 trials, 15.9%) was answered with "No Salient Consequence" – the IT could be affected to any extent. The asymmetry of two types of maximum levels was captured by Chi-square tests for both Chinese and French speakers ($ps < .008$).

Table 3. Proportion of response types by the script judgment and the IT judgment tasks among the 110 trials for either language. CHN: Chinese; FR: French.

		Script judgment					
		N stage only		N-1 or/and N stage		Any stage	
		CHN	FR	CHN	FR	CHN	FR
	100%	34.5%	45.5%	6.4%	12.7%	1.8%	1.8%
IT judgment	>50%	11.8%	3.6%	4.5%	4.5%	3.6%	4.5%
	Any degree	10.0%	10.0%	2.7%	0.9%	15.5%	0.9%

4   Discussion and Conclusion

To examine two models functioning as mechanisms by which accomplishments are identified in language use, we investigated the readers' interpretation of IT accomplishments in terms of both the degree of object involvement and the degree of script completion. As the "event-argument homomorphism" model predicts, both Chinese and French participants considered the event described by the perfective accomplishment sentence as implying a major part of the object being affected.

Moreover, participants were also inclined to believe that the critical stage of the event's script had to be included in the accomplishment event representation, with a similar tendency to interpret the IT as being affected. This finding is central to our concerns because it suggests that the "event-script homomorphism" model explains the mental representations of IT accomplishments as adequately as the "event-argument homomorphism" model. Provided that the change of the IT is assumed to be vital for the incremental accomplishment event identification, we believe that the proceeding of the script also underlies whether an event can be individualized as an accomplishment.

In fact, in view of the "maximum consequence" of the two measurements, the full object involvement strongly associates with the completion of the critical stage in the representation of an accomplishment event but not vice versa; the completion of the script's final stage seems to have a *weaker* association with the IT being affected to a major extent. We thus speculate that the IT involvement is more likely to be conditional on the script completion for segmenting an incremental theme accomplishment. More evidence is needed to address this hypothesis.

The finding of reduced language difference in the script judgment task further suggests that Chinese and French may have great commonalities in interpreting accomplishment events, particularly by script knowledge, despite showing some distinctions in judging IT involvement as observed in the present and previous studies. The implication of this finding is twofold. First, as we predicted, the "event-script homomorphism" model shows improved adequacy in uncovering and depicting the universality of interpreting accomplishments across languages because it approaches the general mechanism of event cognition underlying humans. Second, the tendency that Chinese speakers favor a reading of "No Salient Consequence" in IT judgment tasks compared to French speakers must be reconciled by noting that the reading of "No Salient Consequence" is uncommon for most predicates both in Chinese and in French. Instead, it emerged more frequently for Chinese accomplishment verbs of destruction, like *dismantle* or *destroy,* as reflected by our data. In other words, Chinese and French speakers may share interpretations of most IT accomplishments, yet they diverge in their semantic representation of verbs of destruction.

With reference to the IT involvement quantification on a scale of proportions, one may wonder whether the script judgment task is sufficiently "standardized". The sequential stages may differ across people if they are asked to verbally develop their own scripts, due to individual differences of experiences, world knowledge, as well as strategies in individuating sub-events. However, scholars also have the consensus that there is presumably a high degree of uniformity across people in the way events are perceived [23] in which key aspects of our mental representations of events such as times, locations, entities, and relations among them lay the foundation. The script judgment task was thus designed to preserve and present the uniformed perceptual structure of an event in terms of stages, i.e., the "greatest common divisor". For this sake, the scripts of events were first drafted based on the web-sourced encyclopedia of "how to do something" that introduces the typical procedure of an event, and their validity was further evaluated by two linguists. Feedbacks from participants confirmed that the scripts we developed were well agreed by both Chinese and French native speakers, as they did not report any difficulties in understanding the stage sequences and succeeded in completing the task.

In light of that, not only themes but more elements of events, which are all included under the broad concept of script, are considered to engage in event identification in the "event-script homomorphism" model; therefore, we expect this model to be more effective in explaining diverse event types, and in particular complex events in which more than one aspect/property of the themes changes along with the events' progression. In the follow-up study, we tested against this expectation with experiments and the primary result is promising.

In conclusion, this study showed that the representation of an accomplishment usually implies not only the IT being mostly affected, but also the script being completed with the marking stages having happened. This suggests that the "event-script homomorphism" model can be adequately applied to explain accomplishment events identification from the perspective of script knowledge on a par with the "event-argument homomorphism" model.

Acknowledgments. We thank the reviewers and audiences of the conference for their helpful comments on the earlier drafts of the manuscript. We thank Ludovica Onofri for proofreading and suggesting substantial improvements. This work is supported by the Young Scholar Program of National Social Science Fund of China (18CYY024), and the General Program of Institute of Linguistics, Chinese Academy of Social Sciences (YB21-08).

References

1. Davidson, D.: The logical form of action sentences. In: Rescher, N. (ed.) The Logic of Decision and Action, pp. 81–95. Pittsburgh University Press, Pittsburgh (1967)
2. Beavers, J.: Lexical aspect and multiple incremental themes. In: Demonte, V., McNally, L. (eds.) Telicity, Change, and State. A Cross-Categorial View of Event Structure, pp. 23–59. Oxford University Press (2012)
3. Bochnak, M.R.: Two sources of scalarity within the verb phrase. In: Arsenijevic, B., Gehrkem, B., Marin, R. (eds.) Studies in the Composition and Decomposition of Event Predicates, pp. 99–123. Springer, Dordrecht (2013)
4. Dowty, D.R.: Word Meaning and Montague Grammar. The Semantics of Verbs and Times in Generative Semantics and Montague's PTQ. D. Reidel Publishing Company, Dordrecht (1979)
5. Dowty, D.: Thematic proto-roles and argument selection. Language **67**(3), 547–619 (1991)
6. Filip, H., Rothstein, S.: Telicity as a semantic parameter. In: Formal Approaches to Slavic Linguistics vol. 14, pp. 39–56. Michigan Slavic Publications, Ann Arbor (2006)
7. Kratzer, A.: Telicity and the meaning of objective case. In: Guéron, J., Lacarme, J. (eds.) The Syntax of Time, pp. 388–423. MIT Press, Cambridge, Massachusetts (2004)
8. Krifka, M.: Nominal reference, temporal constitution and quantification in event semantics. In: Bartsch, R., van Benthem, J.F.A.K., van Emde Boas, P. (eds.) Semantics and Contextual Expression, vol. 11, pp. 75–115. Foris Publications, Dordrecht (1989)
9. Krifka, M.: Thematic relations as links between nominal reference and temporal constitution. In: Sag, I., Szabolcsi, A. (eds.) Lexical Matters, pp. 29–53. CSLI Publications, Chicago University Press, Chicago (1992)
10. Krifka, M.: The origins of telicity. In: Rothstein, S. (ed.) Events and Grammar, vol. 70, pp. 197–235. Kluwer Academic Publishers, Dordrecht (1998)
11. Ramchand, G.C.: Verb Meaning and the Lexicon: A First Phase Syntax. Cambridge University Press, Cambridge (2008)
12. Rothstein, S.: Structuring Events: A Study in the Semantics of Lexical Aspect. Blackwell Publishing, Oxford (2004)
13. Wechsler, S.: Resultatives under the 'event-argument homomorphism' model of telicity. In: Erteschik-Shir, N., Rapoport, T. (eds.) The Syntax of Aspect: Deriving Thematic and Aspectual Interpretation, pp. 255–273. Oxford University Press, Oxford (2005)
14. Radvansky, G.A., Zacks, J.M.: Event Cognition. Oxford University Press, Oxford (2014)
15. Zhang, X., Luo, Y., Hu, J.: Accomplishment predicates in Mandarin and their lexical semantics. In: Liu, M., Kit, C., Su, Q. (eds.) CLSW 2020. LNAI, vol.12278, pp. 303–319. Springer, Cham (2021)
16. Li, T.: Incomplete Perfectivity and Its Acquisition in Mandarin Chinese. M.A. thesis, The Chinese University of Hong Kong (2019)
17. Chu, C.C.: Some semantic aspects of action verbs. Lingua **40**, 43–54 (1976)
18. Sybesma, R.: Why Chinese verb-le is a resultative predicate. J. East Asian Linguis. **6**(3), 215–261 (1997)

19. Tai, J.H.Y., Chou, J.Y.: On the equivalent of "kill" in Mandarin Chinese. J. Chin. Lang. Teach. Assoc. **10**(2), 48–52 (1975)
20. Zhang, A.: On non-culminating accomplishments in Mandarin. Ph.D. thesis, The University of Chicago (2018)
21. Partee, B.: Nominal and temporal semantic structure: aspect and quantification. In: Hajičová, E., Červenka, M., Leška O., Sgall, P. (eds.) Prague Linguistic Circle Papers: Travaux du Cercle Linguistique de Prague Nouvelle Série vol. 3, pp. 91–108. John Benjamins Publishing (1999)
22. Tenny, C.: Core events and adverbial modification. In: Tenny, C., Pustejovsky, J. (eds.) Events as Grammatical Objects, pp. 285–334. Center for the Study of Language and Information, Stanford (2000)
23. Barwise, J., Perry, J.: Situations and Attitudes. UK: Bradford Book (1983)

Lexical Resources and Corpus Linguistics

Creation and Significance of Database
of *Dictionary of Cognate Words*

Shuyi Fang[(✉)] and Liangyue Xu

School of Chinese Language and Literature, Southwest Minzu University,
Chengdu, China
fsy904767647@163.com

Abstract. This paper introduces the procedure of creating a database of Wang Li's *Dictionary of Cognate Words*, including the conceptual data model design, the logical data model design, and the table structure design. Thus we can investigate information contained herein with the help of this database, and conducting quantitative researches on the *Dictionary of Cognate Words* in an efficient way. In detail, our main contributions can be summarized as follows: (i) It makes a comprehensive analysis of the *Dictionary of Cognate Words* and refutes some previous claims with wrong views. (ii) It demonstrates a distribution of Chinese cognate words and their relations. (iii) It provides samples for the subsequent digitization of dictionaries and further shows how to analyze large-scale corpus with database approaches.

Keywords: *Dictionary of Cognate Words* · Database · Wang Li · Cognate words · Quantitative

1 Introduction

Since the 1980s, quantitative research on specialized types of literature has been flourishing for decades. Initially, it was always conducted manually. Su claims that database software can deal with more corpus analysis due to its variant data processing functions (2010) [1]. Accordingly, such software has become the primary tool for data processing and quantitative studies, expanding the study scope and object types in related research fields at present.

Influenced by Structuralism, more and more scholars have realized that dictionaries can be regard as a śystem composed of different elements. At the same time, dictionaries are often characterized by their length and complexity. It's never wise to do quantitative studies only relying on manual approaches. Consequently, using a database to extract and analyze information has become a mainstream direction for dictionary research in recent years.

The *Dictionary of Cognate Words* was written by Wang Li, and its first version was published in 1982. It is the earliest dictionary of Chinese cognate words ever written under the guidance of scientific methodology. Due to its authority and convenience, subsequent studies on Chinese cognate words always refer to the entries herein as references. For example, Yuan has conducted an analysis on the relations among those glyphs in the *Dictionary of Cognate Words* (2009) [2]. Wei has analyzed the

© Springer Nature Switzerland AG 2022
M. Dong et al. (Eds.): CLSW 2021, LNAI 13250, pp. 119–129, 2022.
https://doi.org/10.1007/978-3-031-06547-7_9

pronunciation relations mentioned in this book (2011) [3] after Yuan. Coincidentally, Ni has also done research on comparing sound correspondences between the *Dictionary of Cognate Words* and the *Chinese Glottogonic Dictionary* (2012) [4]. Nevertheless, no scholar has attempted to establish or design a database that contains all essential information in the *Dictionary of Cognate Words*, let alone make a comprehensive analysis of it. From our point of view, the construction of this database will contain three values as follows.

1.1   Need for Quantitative Research in Specific Books

It's hard to make qualitative criticism on the *Dictionary of Cognate Words* for its inclusion of more than 4,000 items and intricate relations between them. What's more, to confirm those relations among Chinese cognate words, Wang has collected amounts of ancient literature. These exegetical materials are often representative and typical, but they were not valued enough in the past. Just as Su points out, researchers without the help of quantitative analysis will definitely require a more profound insight and a grasp of language features to compensate, but not any researcher can meet such requirements (2010) [1]. This statement reveals the significance of conducting quantitative researches. However, due to the complexity of the *Dictionary of Cognate Words* in terms of style and content, it is still difficult to ensure the objectivity and precision of manual statistical results. In this regard, using a database shows its advantages over those traditional quantitative researching methods.

1.2   Need for Information Extraction

The transformation from written text to an electronic form that can be recognized by computers will help us gain a more profound understanding of the inner system of the *Dictionary of Cognate Words*. After sorting, we find that information contained in this book is complex. Unfortunately, there isn't any full-text database of the *Dictionary of Cognate Words*, so studying focuses are simply limited. This research aims to construct a database that covers all necessary information of this book and make use of it, so as to help us understand its inner system more deeply than ever before.

1.3   Need for Digitization of Literature

This database should have the following advantages except assisting quantitative researches: firstly, it will meet popular demand with its query functions, which allows users to freely find what they need in a short time; secondly, data information can be updated timely thus it will absorb the latest research results on revising this book; thirdly, this database only takes up little space, and all data can be conveniently and safely stored. Using a database to do studies exactly promotes the development of related research methods. Meanwhile, it also caters to the demand for digitization of literature, especially dictionaries, in recent years.

2 Design of the Full-Text Database

After an exhaustive search of the existing versions, we find that Wang's *Dictionary of Cognate Words* has been published respectively by The Commercial Press (1982) [5], Shandong Education Press (1992) [6], and China Publishing House (2014) [7]. Due to some unreasonable tampering to the text in later versions, most scholars still prefer the earliest version published by The Commercial Press.

Consequently, we excerpt all the text from the 1982 version for constructing the database, and all the page numbers mentioned below would refer to the corresponding pages in this version as well. We have chosen to establish this database based on Microsoft Access 2019, which is the mainstream relational database currently. The database modeling process is summarized as follows.

2.1 Conceptual Data Model

As the first step of the DBAS (Database Application System) life cycle model, the design of the conceptual data model aims to abstract the data structures, the internal relations between entities, and data constraints from the real world. The E-R model of the *Dictionary of Cognate Words* is now obtained by analysis as Fig. 1.

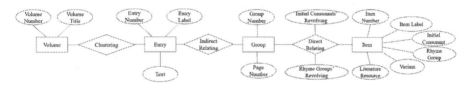

Fig. 1. The conceptual data model of the *Dictionary of Cognate Words*

Four entities and their attributes are explained in the following.

The entity of 'volume' has two attributes: 'volume number' is the serial number for a certain volume; 'volume title' refers to the title of each volume. For example, '之部' is the 'volume title' of the first volume in the *Dictionary of Cognate Words*.

As 'entry' is exactly a controversial term, it is necessary to state our definition of so-called 'entry' here: an 'entry' means a 'word family' composed of several entries for cognate words based on specific rules. For example, on page 115 of the *Dictionary of Cognate Words*, '是', '寔' and '實' are placed in the same cognate word entry from our point of view. The entity of 'entry' has three attributes: 'entry number' is the serial number for a certain entry; 'entry label' is determined by the first word listed in this entry, as a form of shorthand for the related entry name. For example, in the entry '是, 寔, 實', we consider '是' as the 'entry label' thus we can name this entry '是' for convenience; 'text' refers to Wang's own commentary below each entry, usually quoting the exegetical materials or literature illustration of its use.

A 'group' is the most miniature set of cognate words matched and listed by phonetic relations. For example, the group '是, 寔, 實' consists of two cognate word groups: the one is 'zjie 是: zjiek寔' and the other is 'zjiek寔: djiet實'. The entity of 'group' has only two attributes: 'group number' is the serial number for a certain entry; 'page number' means the corresponding page number in the *Dictionary of Cognate Words* (1982 version).

An 'item' is a character or a word that forms a heading and brings out an explaination in a dictionary. It can be similar to a headword, but sometimes it will be hard to tell words from Chinese characters in this book, so we use 'item' to generalize about both. This entity has six attributes: 'item number' is the serial number for a certain item; 'item label' refers to the concrete form of each item, including any variant listed in the bracket, which will be marked out in 'variant' field; 'initial consonant' and 'rhyme group' can be identified based on Wang's reconstruction of the old Chinese; 'literature resource' refers to the resource of a certain item. Then 'variant' should identify all those items listed in brackets due to the disputable definition of so-called variants of Chinese characters. To ensure the objectivity and uniqueness of statistical results, we only have to resort to this seemingly unscrupulous solution.

Three relationships and their attributes are explained in the following.

'Clustering': It connects two entities, 'volume' and 'entry'. A volume always contains several entrys.

'Indirect relating': It connects two entities, 'entry' and 'group'. A cognate word entry often consists of several groups. One or more identical characters will exist in each group to concatenate these groups for most cases, but there are also some exceptions, such as the entry of '苞, 茂, 楸, 葆, 菽, 茆' on page 243.

'Direct relating': It connects two entities, 'group' and 'character'. Wang matches those characters with certain phonetic and semantic relations into pairs. There are two attributes of this relationship: 'initial consonants' revolving' and 'rhyme groups' revolving', demonstrating pronunciation relations between characters in a certain group.

2.2   Logical Data Model

The design of logical structure transforms the E-R model into a logical data model, which will adapt to the specific database management system and become the basis of subsequent physical structure design.

There are four entities as mentioned above: 'volume', 'entry', 'group', and 'item'. And there are three relationships: 'clustering', 'indirect relating' and 'direct relating'. Since any of the relationship connects two entities, and should be a one-to-many relationship, we have obtained the following four relational schemas (with primary keys underlined).

Volume (volume number, volume title)

Entry (entry number, entry label, text)

Group (group number, page number, initial consonants' revolving, rhyme groups' revolving)

Item (item number, item label, initial consonant, rhyme group, variant, literature resource)

2.3   Analysis of Normal Forms

There are four relational schemas, namely 'volume', 'entry', 'group', and 'item'. We confirm that all attributes of any relational schema can no longer be decomposed, which demonstates these relational schemes are in 1NF. Next, we find each of them conforms to a full functional dependency of 'primary key field → other fields'. And there is no partial function dependency, nor transfer function dependency. Thus we can conclude that all relational schemas are also in BCNF.

It is theoretically possible to create a database without redundancy. However, to improve the retrieval efficiency, denormalization will be necessary. Firstly we merge the relational schemas of 'volume', 'entry', and 'group' into one, thus generating a table named 'dic_groups'. Meanwhile, other data is stored in the table of 'dic_items' separately. As a consequence, the number of database joins is reduced, and the retrieval efficiency is improved.

2.4   Design of Table Structure

This database contains two tables, 'dic_groups' and 'dic_items'. Since the primary key of table 'dic_groups' is 'gID', a foreign key for table 'dic_items'. Therefore, 'dic_-groups' should be regarded as the main table, joined to the table of 'dic_items' by 'iID'. Now we will describe the structure of each table (Tables 1 and 2).

Table 1. Structure of Table 'dic_groups'

Field name	Title	Data type	Length	Value range	Primary key	Foreign key
gID	Group number	Number	Integer	The serial number of the group	Y	N
gtiaohao	Entry number	Number	Integer	The serial number of the entry	N	N
gtiaomu	Entry label	Text	2	The first item label of an entry	N	N
gshengzhuan	Initial consonants' revolving	Text	5	'雙聲'; '準雙聲'; '旁紐'; '準旁紐'; '鄰紐'	N	N
gyunzhuan	Rhyme groups' revolving	Text	5	'疊韻'; '對轉'; '旁轉'; '旁對轉'; '通轉'	N	N
gjuanhao	Volume number	Number	Integer	The serial number of the volume	N	N
gjuanmu	Volume title	Text	4	The title of the volume	N	N
gyema	Page number	Number	Integer	/	N	N
gyuanwen	Text	Memo	/	/	N	N

Table 2. Structure of Table 'dic_characters'

Field name	Title	Data type	Length	Value range	Primary key	Foreign key
iID	Item number	Number	Integer	The serial number of the item	Y	N
ibiaomu	Item label	Text	2	All item labels, including those variants	N	N
gID	Group number	Number	Integer	The serial number of the group	N	Y
ishengniu	Initial consonant	Text	5	The initial consonant of the related item	N	N
iyunbu	Rhyme group	Text	5	The rhyme group of the related item	N	N
iyiti	Variant	Yes/No	1	True; False	N	N
ilaiyuan	Literature resource	Text	10	'《說文》字'; '徐鉉新附字'; Null	N	N

3 Research on the *Dictionary of Cognate Words* with Database

Based on Microsoft Access 2019, we have already created a full-text database of Wang's *Dictionary of Cognate Words* as Fig. 2 and Fig. 3, thus proving the feasibility of our table structure design.

Fig. 2. Part of Table 'dic_groups'

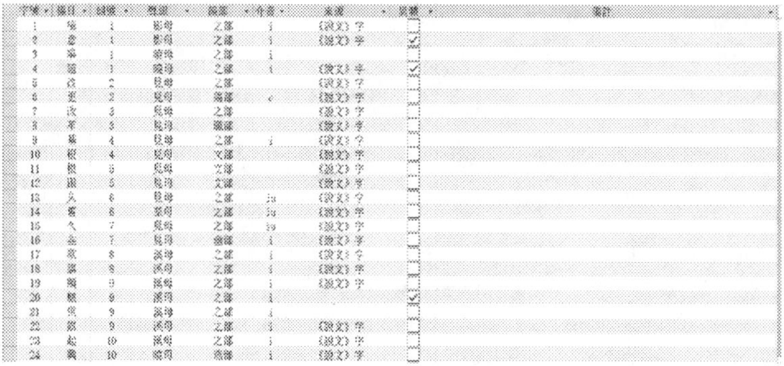

Fig. 3. Part of Table 'dic_items'

With the help of this database, we have conducted a series of quantitative studies on the *Dictionary of Cognate Words*. Our findings are set out below.

3.1 Overview of the *Dictionary of Cognate Words*

By extracting the fields of 'eID' and 'gID' from the database, we confirm that the *Dictionary of Cognate Words* exactly contains 1,026 cognate word entries and 1,605 cognate word groups. It is different from previous viewpoints of scholars. For example, Yin has pointed out that the *Dictionary of Cognate Words* contained 1,031 cognate word entries (2000) [8]. Shao and Du have also counted, and they get 1029 entries (2005) [9], while Ni has revised the result to 1,026 (2012) [4]. Now our counting results can prove that Ni was right. In addition, Yuan has found that there are 1,586 cognate word groups instead of 1,605 (2009) [2]. After checking, we insist on our results.

With the cross-tabulation, we can count the number of items in each volume. Items in each volume are not evenly distributed, as Table 3.

Table 3. Distribution of items in the *Dictionary of Cognate Words*

Number of items in each volume	Title of eligible volumes	Proportion (%)
0–100	'屋部', '沃部', '覺部', '蒸部', '盍部'	17.2
101–200	'支部', '職部', '錫部', '鐸部', '東部', '歌部', '物部', '質部', '真部', '緝部', '談部'	37.9
201–300	'之部', '侯部', '幽部', '耕部', '微部', '脂部', '月部', '文部', '侵部'	31.0
301–400	'宵部', '陽部'	6.9
401–500	'元部'	3.4
More than 500	'魚部'	3.4

It can be seen that '魚部' contains much more items than any other volume. There are two possible explanations for this: firstly, words with /a/ as the main vowel are common in Chinese according to scholars, and for the second, '魚部' is always closely related to other rhyme groups in the old Chinese thus it's more likely to form the relations among cognate words. In addition, even Wang has claimed that there are 33 initial consonants in the old Chinese, including '俟母', but there is no example for this initial consonant in the text of the *Dictionary of Cognate Words*.

Then we count the number of cognate word groups and the number of items contained in each entry. We conclude that most entries only contain one or two groups, and nearly 93% of the entries contain less than ten items. It demonstrates that Wang has strictly limited the number of cognate words in a certain entry, which is necessary for guaranteeing the scientific nature of research (Tables 4 and 5).

Table 4. Number of groups contained in an entry

Number of groups in an entry	Number of eligible entrys	Proportion (%)
1	722	70.4
2	163	15.9
3	72	7.0
4	34	3.3
5	20	1.9
6	6	0.6
7	8	0.8
13	1	0.1

Table 5. Number of items contained in an entry

Number of items in an entry	Number of eligible entries	Proportion (%)
2	308	30.0
3–5	461	44.9
6–10	180	17.5
11–15	50	4.9
16–20	19	1.9
21–30	7	0.7
34	1	0.1

We have also noticed an entry on page 341 which contains as many as 34 items. It contradicts Wang's statement that 'the number of items included in any entry will be no more than 20' [5]. It shows that Wang was not blindly reducing the number of cognate words for the purpose to avoid errors, as some scholars suspect [8]. Wang would include all those cognate words verified in the *Dictionary of Cognate Words*, rather than being bound by prejudice.

3.2   Items in the *Dictionary of Cognate Words*

By extracting the fields of 'iID', 'ibiaomu', and 'iyiti' from the database, we find 4,850 items listed in the *Dictionary of Cognate Words* (including repeat items and all those in brackets). After de-duplication, there are 3,429 items left. 972 items among them are listed in brackets, and this number will go down to 734 after de-duplication. Meanwhile, not all words listed in the *Dictionary of Cognate Words* are monosyllabic, but there are also 12 disyllabic words (after de-duplication): '髑髏', '扶搖', '丁寧', '魁瘣', '虺尵', '二十', '蒺藜', '疾黎', '蒺黎', '蒺蔾', '什麼', '三十'.

Many scholars have also counted the number of items listed in the *Dictionary of Cognate Words*, but there is still no agreement. Qiu was the first to point out that the number of non-repeating items in this book was 3,059 (1992) [10]. Yin initially concludes that the *Dictionary of Cognate Words* collected 3,174 items (1994) [11], but then revised his result to 3,164 (2000) [8]. Shao and Du maintain that there were 3,342 items and 977 variants (2005) [9], while Yuan's result is '4118 single items, including 947 variants' (2009) [2]. Besides, Ni counted out 3329 items in total (2012) [4]. The disagreement among different scholars on the number of items contained herein is interesting. Some of their results are not far from ours, which might be due to carelessness. But some of them must be explained for different statistical principles, different implementation of de-duplication, different definitions of Chinese character varients, and so on.

By extracting the fields of 'iID' and 'ilaiyuan', we agree that there are 3,350 items which also exist in *Shuo Wen Jie Zi*, accounting for 69.1% of the total number of items in the *Dictionary of Cognate Words*. It proves that Wang did use *Shuo Wen Jie Zi* for reference in his writing process. However, he was never confined to the items in *Shuo Wen Jie Zi*. Wang has also listed a number of items generated in later dynasties. This approach has indeed played an important role in dispelling the misconception that characters not existing in *Shuo Wen Jie Zi* should have been created much later. However, it is still questionable whether those words (or characters) that only exist in middle Chinese can be related to other items according to the same rules of relations.

3.3   Other Information in the *Dictionary of Cognate Words*

By extracting the fields of 'gshengzhuan' and 'gyunzhuan' from the database, we can analyze the pronunciation relations of each cognate word group statistically. The results are as follows.

Table 6. Situation of initial consonants' revolving

Relations between initial consonants	Counting result	Proportion (%)
'疊韻'	1032	64.3
'對轉'	199	12.4
'通轉'	132	8.2
'旁轉'	210	13.1
'旁對轉'	32	2.0

Table 7. Situation of Rhyme groups' revolving

Relations between Rhyme groups	Counting result	Proportion (%)
'雙聲'	1082	67.4
'準雙聲'	53	3.3
'旁紐'	343	21.4
'鄰紐'	123	7.7
'準旁紐'	4	0.2

According to Wang's opinion, '疊韻' should be the most common pronunciation relation among all, a bit more than '對轉'. As for '旁轉', '通轉', '旁對轉', they are relatively rare. This hypothesis is quite different from the distribution in reality. As Table 6 demonstrates, '疊韻' is undoubtedly the most common relation, while '旁轉' is the second most frequent, slightly more frequent than '對轉'. And the proportion of '通轉' can not be considered to be much lower compared to them.

However, as Table 7 shows, '雙聲' is the most frequent, followed by '旁紐'. The rest of the various types are relatively rare. It accords with Wang's initial hypothesis.

Likewise, Wei has also conducted similar research on pronunciation relations in the *Dictionary of Cognate Words* before us (2011) [3], but we do not entirely agree with his research. Wei indicates that there are 1,027 times of '疊韻', 194 times of '對轉', 200 times of '旁轉', and only 29 times of '通轉'. His statistical results are too far from ours. Moreover, Wei seems to have ignored the situation of '旁對轉', which is absolutely a kind of pronunciation relation that appears in this book. His other statistics listed for demonstrating the situation of initial consonants' revolving also differed from us. After checking the text, we think Wei's results are suspective.

4   Conclusion

This paper is not only discussing the design and creation of a database of the *Dictionary of Cognate words*, but also offering some of our related research findings with this database. Database approaches will provide new perspectives for studying traditional literature and improve our researching efficiency. However, we must realize that no matter what kind of software we use, qualitative analysis is still crucial when we need to explain those quantitative results. A database is only a tool for the convenience of storing or extracting data. Only by further qualitative analyzing and summarizing those rules, can we solve a problem thoroughly.

References

1. Su, X.-C.: Vocabulary Measurement and its Implementation. The Commercial Press, Beijing (2010). (in Chinese)
2. Yuan, J.-H.: Enlightenment of *Dictionary of Cognate Words* on studying cognate words from the character perspective. J. Ningxia Univ. (Human. Soc. Sci. Ed.) **31**(5), 11–16 (2009). (in Chinese)

3. Wei, Q.-Y.: Relations of paronyms on initials and rhyme group. J. Henan Univ. (Soc. Sci.) **51**(5), 150–153 (2011). (in Chinese)
4. Ni, Y.: The Research of Comparing the Law of Sound Correspondences of The Cognate Words between 'Cognate Words Dictionary' and 'Chinese Glottogonic Dictionary.' Capital Normal University, Beijing, China (2012). (in Chinese)
5. Wang, L.: Dictionary of Cognate Words. The Commercial Press, Beijing (1982). (in Chinese)
6. Wang, L.: Dictionary of Cognate Words. Shandong Education Press, Jinan (1992). (in Chinese)
7. Wang, L.: Dictionary of Cognate Words. China Publishing House, Beijing (2014). (in Chinese)
8. Yin, J.-M.: An Introduction to Chinese Etymology. Shanghai Education Press, Shanghai (2000). (in Chinese)
9. Shao, W.-L., Du, L.-R.: Questions to classification and markings of pronunciation relations in a dictionary of paronyms. Chin. Lang. **2**, 177–179 (2005). (in Chinese)
10. Qiu, X.-G.: A New Study of Ancient Literature and History. Jiangsu Classics Publishing House, Nanjing (1992). (in Chinese)
11. Yin, J.-M.: Notes on the *Dictionary of Cognate Words*. Res. Ancient Chin. Lang. **1**, 35–39 (1994). (in Chinese)

Chinese Predicate Chunk Knowledge Base Construction and Internal Boundary Recognition

Chengwen Wang[1], Xiang Liu[2], Gaoqi Rao[2], Endong Xun[2],
and Zhifang Sui[1(✉)]

[1] The MOE Key Laboratory of Computational Linguistics, Peking University,
Beijing, China
{wangcw, szf}@pku.edu.cn
[2] Institute of Big Data and Language Education,
Beijing Language and Culture University, Beijing, China

Abstract. Under current researches on Chinese language, sentences are usually chunked into the components of the same level. However, in actual Chinese environment, the predicate block in a sentence and the subject and object component blocks before and after it constitute the skeleton of the event representation, and the subblocks inside the predicate block modify the core predicates from different perspectives and serve as the related components of the event. Therefore, it is necessary to treat the predicate block and the component inside the predicate block as different levels of block components. Dividing into primary and secondary components plays an important role in understanding the main semantics of a sentence by abstracting the outline and facilitating the event reasoning and calculation. Therefore, this paper first defines predicate as the core of the predicate block and further defines the sub-block inside the predicate block. The predicate-centered predicate blocks are annotated with encyclopedia corpus with relatively high sentence complexity. At the same time, the components inside the predicate block are divided based on the subblock types defined in this paper. As of now, the knowledge base includes 36,360 predicate blocks. Based on this knowledge base, this paper creates an internal boundary recognition task for predicate blocks, and tests it with a sequential labeling model, which provides a baseline for the subsequent researches in the future.

Keywords: Predicate chunk · Boundary recognition · Chunks

1 Introduction

Chunk parsing, as a shallow analysis technique of natural language processing, has a good performance in tasks such as named-entity recognition and information extraction. Abney first proposed a grammar-based chunk parsing theory in the early 1990s [1]. The CONLL-2000 proposed the chunking shared task and defined 11 basic chunks in English such as NP, VP, PP, ADJP, ADVP and CONJP [2]. Afterwards, related work at home and abroad has also been carried out on a large scale.

© Springer Nature Switzerland AG 2022
M. Dong et al. (Eds.): CLSW 2021, LNAI 13250, pp. 130–144, 2022.
https://doi.org/10.1007/978-3-031-06547-7_10

For the definition of chunk, it is divided into two types depending on whether it is based on grammatical nature and function: one is the definition of chunks based on grammatical nature or function represented by Abney, and the chunk and phrase structure from this perspective have good isomorphism. The other one is based on the actual language, and the chunk defined by statistical characteristics is called multiword expression in the system of some scholars. This type of chunk is more of a language unit with a relatively solid form and meaning, which appears in high frequency and steady state in big data.

Regardless of whether the definition of chunk is based on grammar or not, the above-mentioned chunk parsing technique performs better when facing simple parsing tasks. However, for in-depth semantic parsing, shallow chunking cannot meet its needs. The main reasons are as follows:

(1) Division of chunks should pay attention to the distinction between primary and secondary

For sentence comprehension, the core is to grasp the predicate the component that expresses the core semantics of the sentence and parse the subject and object components of the event. Correspondingly, chunks such as subject, object and predicate are the core components of an event, which play an important role in understanding the semantics of a sentence. Furthermore, going deep into the predicate chunk, parsing the relationship between the core predicate and other modifier chunks, can further parse the related elements of an event, such as non-core arguments, modality, tense, voice and other information.

(2) The chunk based on the nature or function of a unit lacks core predicate information

Taking the syntactic function of the Chinese unit as the starting point, dividing sentences into subject chunks, object chunks, and concurrent chunks is a method that many scholars often choose when defining chunks. However, the relationship between the core predicate and its dominating components is essential for deep semantic understanding. The chunk system that can be constructed entirely based on syntactic function lacks the information that highlights the core predicate and its semantic relationship with the dominated chunks. The predicate-centered chunk is the core of the semantic understanding of a sentence, and its internal modifiers mostly serve as modality, tense and voice.

Based on the above analysis, this article believes that from the perspective of in-depth syntactic and semantic analysis of Chinese language, the existing chunk system fails to effectively reflect the primary and secondary components of the chunk. That is to say, parsing the predicate chunk and its sub-chunks which carrying event-related information into different levels cannot effectively reflect the dependent relationship between the core predicate and the subordinate chunk.

Therefore, this article adopts a "big to small" knowledge base building strategy: first, mark the predicate chunk with continuous modifiers centered on the core predicate; secondly, divide the adverbial component before the core predicate in the predicate chunk into sub-chunks. The definite division of predicate and sub-chunk boundary provides the basic unit for the construction of the dependency relationship between the predicate and the dominated chunks, which provides data support for further semantic relationship parsing (argument relationship and modal relationship). At the same time, based on the knowledge base, the sequence labeling model is used to recognize the sub-chunk boundary within the predicate chunk.

The rest of the article is organized as follows: Sect. 1 summarizes the previous related research work; Sect. 2 clarifies the meaning of predicate chunk and establishes the types of sub-chunks; Sect. 3 introduces the construction of knowledge base, including corpus selection, labeling process and statistical analysis, etc.; Sect. 4 introduces the boundary recognition experiment; the last part is the summary of this article.

2   Related Studies

2.1   Researches on the Chunk Definitions and Classifications

Chunk parsing theory was proposed by Abney in the early 1990s. The CONLL-2000 proposed chunk parsing as Shared Task, which made the theory popularized and applied.

In China, Zhou Qiang of Peking University started relevant research at an early stage [3]. Follow-up scholars [4–7] have done continuous work on the definition of Chinese chunk types and the recognition of chunk boundaries. The definition of the chunks of existing work is mostly based on the grammatical system of Chinese: on the one hand, it lacks the coverage of some constructional component chunks; on the other hand, the chunk representation based on the grammatical system lacks the disclosure of core predicate components.

Parsing of multiword expressions and chunking have many similarities in nature and in function. At present, there is no unified definition of Multiword Expression. Sag [8] once defined multiword expression as a combination of multiple words that cross word boundaries (or spaces), and these combinations have special meanings. Researchers often used Choueka's [9] definition of collocation as the definition of multiword expressions: a sequence of two or more consecutive words that has characteristics of a syntactic and semantic unit whose exact and unambiguous meaning or connotation cannot be derived directly from the meaning or connotation of its components. Multiword expression is more consistent with the chunk unit of high frequency co-occurrence based on big data defined from a statistical point of view. In Chinese complex adverbials, some fixed multiword expressions and some phrases such as prepositions are used to modify the core predicate behind.

2.2   Research on Recognition of Chunk Boundaries

Chunk recognition usually adopts rule-based methods and statistical methods, and of course there are methods that combine both techniques.

In the study of foreign languages, Church [10] regarded the problem of simple noun phrase recognition as a process of tagging each word, using the N-ary co-occurrence method based on part-of-speech tagging and the Viterbi method to solve it. Zhang et al.

[11] took the lead in adopting a transformation-based error-driven learning method to solve the problem of simple noun phrase recognition, and the recall rate reached 88%. Taku Kudo [12] used SVM as the classifier, and adopted the method of classifier ensemble to identify simple noun phrases. The base classifier is constructed in a variety of ways, such as using different marker sets, different analysis directions, and different voting methods. Some subsequent work is also based on feature engineering, using corresponding machine learning models for chunk recognition [13, 14].

In the work of Chinese chunk recognition, Liu Fang, Zhao Tiejun et al. [15] adopted the enhanced Markov model and transformation-based error-driven methods to identify Chinese chunks based on 8 custom chunk types. Li Sujian defined 12 types of chunks, and adopted a combination of maximum entropy model, finite state automaton, and transformation-based error-driven method for chunking, and achieved good results. Huang Degen [16] proposed a distributed strategy based on CRFs and a transformation-based error-driven strategy, the F value of the open test reached 92.91%.

In summary, the current chunking technique is mainly based on supervised learning methods, relying on the support of high-quality large-scale training corpus. Compared with semi-supervised or unsupervised chunk recognition methods, although they rely less on high-quality tagged corpus, their performance is relatively poor compared to supervised learning.

3 Definition of Predicate Chunk and Establishment of Sub-chunk Types

3.1 Definition of Predicate Chunk

This article adopts a "big to small" knowledge base building strategy: first, mark the predicate chunk with continuity modifiers centered on the core predicate; secondly, further divide the modifiers before the core predicate in the predicate chunk into sub-chunks. Therefore, the definition of predicate chunk needs to be given first.

Predicate chunk refers to a chunk unit centered on the core predicate with continuous modifiers before and after. In this definition, verbs or adjectives can function as core predicates, which are mainly the core components of the syntax and semantics of a sentence, representing actions, behaviors, states or relationships, etc. The continuous modifiers surrounding the core predicate that do not include the subject and object are mainly adverbial components and complements, which are collectively referred to as modifiers in this definition.

According to the presence or absence of front or back modifiers, its formal definition is as follows:

Predicate chunk = modifier (front) + core predicate
Predicate chunk = core predicate + modifier (back)
Predicate chunk = modifier (front) + core predicate + modifier (back)

Specific examples are as follows:

(1) 这种程序包(一般都(有))6个程序模块。(This program (usually (has)) six modules.)
(2) 专家系统((嵌入)到CACSD软件包中)。(Expert system ((is embedded in) the CACSD package).)
(3) 这类仪表(通过杠杆或钢丝绳等机构将浮标位移(传递)出去)。(This instrument ((delivers) the displacement of the buoy through tools such as levers or wire ropes).)

In the above examples, the outer brackets represent the entire predicate chunk, while the inner brackets represent the core predicate components, and the front and back modifiers are underlined.

Through the annotation and observation of the corpus, in the actual corpus, the predicate chunks of Type 1 and Type 3 are widely distributed. At the same time, the modality or argument components of Chinese are mainly contained in the premodifier of the core predicate. Therefore, this article takes Type 1 and Type 3 as the research objects of predicate chunk.

3.2   Determination of Sub-chunk Type

Chinese is a language rich in prepositions. Prepositions can often form a frame structure with some postpositions, particles and abstract nouns to modify the core predicates behind them as a whole. The components in front of these frame structures can also be modified by emphasized components. At the same time, there are many adverbs used in conjunction in Chinese [17]. The adverbs used will be integrated in semantic function, and they will modify the core predicate behind them as a whole. There is a significant difference in the semantics when using adverbs separately to modify the core predicate.

Many solidified multiword expressions and framed expressions serve as adverbials for predicates. These components often have the characteristics of integration of form and meaning, which are difficult to describe with effective grammatical rules, but they have certain characteristics in form, which are convenient for cognition and recognition of multiword expression units from the form.

In summary, such language form exist in Chinese, and its main manifestations are: first, the modifiers before the core verb in the predicate chunk are more complicated, and the character length and structural components are more complex than the modifiers after the core predicate. Secondly, many units modify its following predicates as a whole in the form of chunks. Finally, many Chinese components that express modality and argument information are mainly distributed in the premodifiers. Therefore, based on the analysis and observation of the premodifier components in this article, different sub-chunk types characterized by typical marker words are established, and sub-chunk types that express fixed semantics are incorporated, such as component chunks that indicate time and location. The details are as follows:

[1] Framed chunks
Framed chunks mainly refer to framed structural chunks formed by prepositions and corresponding postpositions, particles and proper nouns. Under normal circumstances, it modifies the core predicate behind as a whole.

(4) [在某种动力的作用下][能](下降)[1] (It [can] (decrease) [under the function of certain power][1])

(5)   [在火药发明以后][为适应军事和娱乐需要而](出现)([After the advent of gunpowder], [in order to satisfy military and entertainment needs], it (appeared))

(6) [按照双方协商同意的办法](处理) (It (will be handled) [in accordance with the approach agreed upon by both parties])

Note: "在…下", "为…而" and "按照…方法" are framed structures.

[2] Multiword expression chunks

Multiword expression chunks mainly refer to the overall multiword components that are relatively solid in structure and whose internal levels cannot or do not need to be strictly divided.

(7) [常常][不得不](采用) ([often] [have to] (use))

(8) [后果和影响上][越来越](深远) ([more and more] (profound) [consequences and impacts])

Note: For components such as "不得不" and "越来越", it is enough to clearly express the meaning of "no alternative" and "emphasis", and there is no need to further divide them.

[3] Preposition chunk

Preposition chunk mainly refers to the prepositional phrase chunk composed of preposition and prepositional phrase. Usually, the preposition chunk is modified by adverbs or other modifiers.

(9) [为中国海洋渔业, 海洋运输, 港口建设, 海洋环境保护, 海洋石油开发等部门和科研单位](提供) ((provide) [departments and research institutes regarding China's marine fishery sector, maritime transportation, port construction, marine environmental protection, offshore oil exploration, etc.])

(10) [不按原定步骤][根据说明书](完成) ([not follow the original steps] [but the instruction manual] (to complete))

(11) [特别是在空调器上][广泛](采用) (be [widely] (applied) [to air conditioners especially])

Note: The prepositional phrase in eg2 is negated by "不", and the prepositional phrase in eg3 is emphasized by "特别是". Prepositions are modified by modifiers, and they are widely present in front of predicates'premodifiers. They need to be treated as a whole with prepositional phrases.

[4] Locality chunk

Locality chunk refers to a chunk composed of typical nouns of locality attached to corresponding components. Noun of locality can be single word, such as "上, 下, 左 and 右". It can also be a compound location word such as "之前, 之后, 以前 and 以后". With the increase in the usage oflocality, its semantics have been extended from the original single meaning of location to the meanings such as time, scope and condition.

---

[1] Use "[]" to identify the internal chunk boundaries of the modifiers, and "()" to identify the core predicate.

(12)   [1916年][英国皇家空军的SE5型飞机的仪表板上][已](装有) ([In 1916,] [the instrument panels of Royal Aircraft Factory S.E.5] [were already] (equipped with))

(13)   [采用随动控制时在实施控制以前][不](知道) ([While adopting the servo control system, before the control is implemented], you [don't] [know])

(14)   [新常态下][要坚定不移地](走) ([Under the new normal], [we should firmly] (follow)).

Note: Only eg1 represents a place, and the meanings in other examples are further extended.

[5] Particle chunk

Particle chunk mainly refers to the chunk formed by particle attached to the corresponding components. Among the premodifiers of predicates, particles are mainly metaphor particles.

(15)   [削足适履似的][去](应用) ([make] (the application) [in a Procrustean way])

[6] Time chunk

Time chunks are the chunks formulated from a semantic point of view, generally composed of time adverbs, time nouns, and some time phrases.

(16)   [1975年][在布加勒斯特召开的第三届国际控制论与系统大会上][以控制论与经济系统](作为) ([In 1975], [at the third International Conference on Control Theory and Systems held in Bucharest], [with control theory and economic systems] (as))

(17)   [在中国][只不过][刚刚](拉开) ([In China], [only] [just] (open))

[7] Location chunk

Location chunk is also a chunk made from a semantic point of view, which generally includes location nouns and place names. These components usually appear together with prepositions, but when a considerable part of them acts as a modifier, they do not co-occur with the preposition.

(18)   [冕上面](有) [On the crown] (there is)

(19)   [南方诸大陆(南美，南非和南澳大利亚)和印度][广泛](分布着) ([be widely] (distributed) [throughout southern continents, including (South America, South Africa and South Australia) and India])

[8] Chunk of adverbs used in conjunction

Adverbs can modify not only predicates but also adverbs. When adverbs are used in conjunction, their semantics will merge, which is significantly different from the semantics of using adverbs to modify core predicates alone.

(20)   [着实很](有效)([really] (effective).

(21)   [不妨也](实施)([might as well] (do it))

Note: When adverbs are used together, they generally have the effect of semantic strengthening, semantic highlighting and semantic addition, and it needs to be taken as an object to build a dependency relationship with the core predicate.

In summary, for the complex premodifiers of the core predicate, further segmentation and the characteristics of the internal chunks of the modified components need to be further segmented. This article focused on typical form tags (small words), and at the same time, formulated 8 chunk types combining semantic features. Later in this article, the premodifiers of core predicates will be marked with chunk boundaries according to the 8 types.

4 Knowledge Base Construction

According to the definition of the predicate chunk and the 8 chunk (sub-chunk) types, we have constructed a predicate chunk knowledge base, which stores predicate chunks and core predicate information, while retaining the chunk boundary information of the premodifiers of the core predicate. The specific construction steps are as follows: (1) corpus selection; (2) specific labeling; (3) statistical analysis.

4.1 Corpus Selection

The knowledge base mainly selects encyclopedia corpus as the labeling object, mainly because encyclopedia corpus contains content that introduces things in detail from all sides, and its language complexity is relatively high. Through our analysis on encyclopedia, patents and elementary school students' composition corpus, we find that the average word length of a single sentence in the encyclopedia corpus is longer than the latter two, which enables us to select more complex predicate chunks, so as to facilitate the analysis of the chunk complexity of premodifiers of the core predicate. The encyclopedia corpus selected in this article contains 43,727 sentences.

4.2 Labeling Process

The labeling process is mainly divided into two steps. First, for the input sentence, the predicate chunk is marked with "()", and then the core predicate is marked with "()". Secondly, on the basis of the predicate chunk identification, for the premodifiers of core predicate, according to the above 8 sub-chunk types, the specific boundaries are marked with "[]". For example:

Sentence = "穆藕初逐渐转向政界活动，　1943年9月16日在重庆病故," ("Mu Ouchu gradually turned his focus to political activities, and died from a disease in Chongqing on September 16, 1943.")
Predicate chunk = {(逐渐(转向)), (1943年9月16日在重庆(病故))} ({{(gradually (turned his focus to)), ((died from a disease) in Chongqing on September 16, 1943)})
Chunk labeling within predicate chunk = {[逐渐] (转向), [1943年9月16日][在重庆](病故)} ([gradually] (turned his focus to), (died from a disease) [in Chongqing] [on September 16, 1943]})

When the specific work was carried out, two graduates in linguistics made pairwise annotations. First, the predicate chunk was labeled, and then the sub-chunks within the predicate chunk were labeled. Finally, the consistent labeling results were saved, and the inconsistencies were directly discarded. The schematic diagram of specific data processing is shown in Fig. 1.

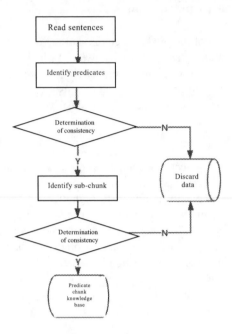

Fig. 1. Labeling process

4.3   Statistical Analysis

After the completion of the labeling work, we conducted a statistical analysis of the labeled data from several perspectives such as the number of predicate chunks, the length distribution of predicate chunks, and the number of sub-chunks within the predicate chunk.

Up to now, out of 43,727 encyclopedia sentences, 36,360 predicate chunks which meet the research objects of this article have been labeled.

When counting the length of the predicate chunk, only the length of the core predicate and the premodifiers were counted. Table 1 shows the length distribution of the predicate chunk.

Table 1. Length distribution of the predicate chunk

Range of length	Number of chunks
2–20	34,984
21–40	1,242
41–60	115
61–80	13
Above 80	6

By analysing the chunks we noticed that the length of the predicate chunks in the encyclopedia style is widely distributed, ranging from 2 to 140, and concentrated in the range of 2–20. The predicate chunks in the range 2–20 are further counted and sorted in descending order by the number of sub-chunks. The results are shown in Fig. 2:

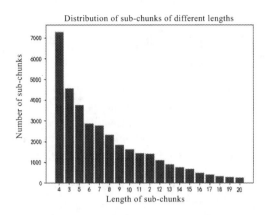

Fig. 2. Distribution of sub-chunks of different lengths (within 20)

It can be seen from Fig. 2 that the number of chunks with a length of 2 is ranked tenth, and the length of the chunks with a rank higher than that is greater than 2, from which we can see that theencyclopedia style is indeed more complex and can provide rich internal information. It is necessary to divide the internal structure of the predicate chunk into sub-chunks.

After chunking the premodifiers of core predicate in the predicate chunk into sub-chunks, a sequence of chunks can be formed (the core predicate is also recognized as a predicate chunk). Table 2 shows the distribution of predicate chunks with different numbers of sub-chunks.

Table 2. Distribution of predicate chunks (containing different numbers of sub-chunks)

Number of sub-chunks	Number of predicate chunks
2	26,482
3	8,716
4	1,102
5	60

It can be seen from Table 2 that most of the internal structures of the predicate chunk have 2 levels, and the number of chunks with 3&4 levels also occupies a considerable proportion. From the perspective of level alone, the level of predicate chunks is relatively simple. However, the statistical analysis of the predicate chunk at level 2 shows that its length ranges from 2 to 102. Many predicate chunks at level 2 have lengths ranging from 4 to 14, mainly because of the frequent occurrence of preposition chunks and framed expressions. Such data also give proofs from another perspective that it is crucial to divide and identify the chunk boundary within the predicate chunk of the encyclopedia style.

5   Automatic Recognition of the Internal Boundary of Predicate Chunk

The task of recognizing the internal boundary of predicate chunk is mainly to give a predicate chunk, and identify the boundary of the premodifier, the core predicate, and the internal chunk boundary of the modifier within the predicate chunk. Its formal description is as follows: for a predicate chunk, it can be recognized as a continuous chunk sequence of [modifier chunk $_1$] [modifier chunk $_2$] [modifier chunk $_i$] [core predicate]. This article defines the task as a sequence labeling task, using conditional random field (CRF) model and deep learning-based BERT + CRF to conduct experiments, the details are as follows.

5.1   Task Modeling and Data

Given a predicate chunk $X = \{x_1, x_2, ...,x_n\}$ of length n, select the most likely labeling sequence $Y = \{y_1, y_2, ...,y_n\}$ from all possible labeling sequences, and finally, the position of the internal boundary of the predicate chunk is restored from the obtained labeling sequence.

There are four ways to label a character in a sentence, namely "BMES". B represents the beginning of a chunk; M represents the middle character of a chunk; E represents the last character of a chunk; S represents that the character corresponds to a chunk alone. An example of sequence labeling for the recognition of the internal structure boundary of a predicate chunk is shown in Table 3.

Table 3.   Example of sequence labeling

Sentence	在	冰	水	中	比	热	水	中	易	溶	解
Label	B	M	M	E	B	M	M	E	S	B	E
Result	在冰水中				比热水中				易	溶解	

The knowledge base currently contains 36,360 pieces of data. We process the chunks in the form of "modifier + core predicate + modifier", and only retain the core predicates and premodifiers, while adding a predicate chunk of the form "modifier + core predicate" to form our experimental data. According to the labeling system of "BMES", we exported the predicate chunks in the knowledge base as a sequence labeling format file, and randomly divided the training set and the test set at a ratio of 7:3. The specific data set statistics are shown in Table 4:

Table 4. Division of experimental data

Data set	Number of predicate chunks
Training set	25,452
Test set	10,908

5.2 Experimental Model

Conditional random field (CRF) is a conditional probability distribution model of a set of input random variables given a set of conditions for another set of output random variables; its characteristic is that it assumes that the output random variables constitute a Markov random field. This article used a linear conditional random field to directly process the input data to obtain the globally optimal labeling sequence.

When directly using the CRF model for sequence labeling tasks, it is necessary to specify a feature template in advance, and the conditional random field usually uses a text window to define features. This article uses 12 types of character feature templates, including unary character feature templates C_0 (current character), C_{-1} (the first character after current character), C_1 (the first character behind current character), C_{-2} (the second character before current character), C_2 (the second character after current character), the binary character feature template $C_{-2}C_{-1}$, $C_{-1}C_0$, C_0C_1, C_1C_2 and the ternary character template $C_{-2}C_{-1}C_0$, $C_{-1}C_0C_1$, $C_0C_1C_2$.

BERT has powerful two-way encoding capabilities. In our experiments, we used deep learning-based BERT + CRF as a comparison experiment. The model experiment

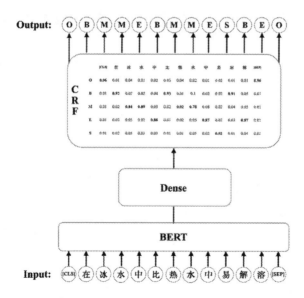

Fig. 3. The BERT + CRF model of the boundary recognition within predicate chunk

used the pre-trained language model BERT-Base[2], which includes 12 layers of Transformer Encoder Block, the output dimension is 768 [18]. The input is the sum of token embedding, position embedding and segment embedding. After outputting through BERT, we use Dense to transform the dimensions into a divergence matrix that can be used for CRF. Finally, the optimal path is obtained through CRF. The specific model is shown in Fig. 3.

5.3   Experimental Results

In this study, the precision rate, recall rate and F value in chunks are used as the evaluation indicators of the experimental results. The specific experimental results are shown in Table 5:

Table 5. Experimental results

Methods	P(%)	R(%)	F(%)
CRF	91.9	90.5	91.2
BERT + CRF	93.7	93.5	93.6

It can be seen from Table 5 that compared with the CRF model that relies on the characteristics of the character template, the BERT + CRF model that relies on the deep learning method has an improvement of 2% to 3% in various indicators. This comparison result shows to a certain extent that BERT can effectively represent the contextual knowledge within the predicate chunk, thereby providing support for label prediction.

In the result statistics, it is found that the number of sub-chunks within the predicate chunk is not uniform, and then the internal boundaries of the predicate chunk containing different numbers of sub-chunks are identified, and the specific results are shown in Table 6.

Table 6. Experimental results of different sub-chunks

Methods	2/(%)			3/(%)			4/(%)			5/(%)		
	P	R	F	P	R	F	P	R	F	P	R	F
CRF	94.1	95.3	94.7	89.0	84.8	86.8	80.0	68.4	73.8	76.4	68.8	72.4
BERT + CRF	95.2	96.7	96.0	92.2	90.1	91.1	84.6	76.1	80.1	80.0	70.0	74.7

---

[2] https://github.com/google-research/bert.

It can be seen from Table 6 that as the number of sub-chunks increases, the performance of both CRF model and BERT + CRF model on this task has a certain decline. However, BERT + CRF has a better performance than CRF model.

5.4 Experimental Outlooks

On the one hand, predicate chunks with a large number of sub-blocks are relatively sparse in the corpus, resulting in poor evaluation results. It is difficult to truly reflect the model's ability in dealing with multi-level chunks. In future work, data will be labeled for multi-level chunks, and the model performance will be retested when it reaches a certain scale.

On the other hand, through the analysis of incorrect cases, the model does not handle the preposition nesting well, such as "it is invalid for cases that do not fit the scenario." When dealing with this kind of occasions, the boundary is often incorrect, and it needs to be improved later.

6 Conclusion

The original intention of this research work is to provide a new chunking perspective, that is, to distinguish predicate chunks (event components) and sub-chunk (event correlation components) within predicate chunks at different levels. With a larger predicate chunk, it is convenient for it to build external dependencies and present the skeleton in a sentence. Internally, the predicate chunk is further divided into sub-chunks to facilitate the construction of the dependency relationship between the core predicate and the modifier chunk it dominates. At the same time, this article uses predicate chunk as a research perspective to construct a predicate chunk knowledge base labeled with internal chunk boundaries. This resource can bring data support to the research of semantic analysis centered on predicates, while facilitating the computational research based on the knowledge base.

Acknowledgement. This paper is supported by the National Key Research and Development Program of China 2020AAA0106700, NSFC project U19A2065 and NSFC project 62076038.

References

1. Steven, A.: Parsing by chunks. In: Berwick, R., Abney, S., Tenny, C. (eds.) Principle-Based Parsing, pp. 257–278. Kluwer Academic Publishers (1991)
2. Tjong Kim Sang, E.F., Buchholz, S.: Introduction to the CoNLL-2000 shared task: chunking. In: Proceedings of the 2nd Workshop on Learning Language in Logic and the 4th Conference on Computational Natural Language Learning, vol. 7. Association for Computational Linguistics, pp. 127–132 (2000)
3. Qiang, Z.: Automatically bracket and tag Chinese phrases. Doctoral dissertation, Peking University (1996). (in Chinese)
4. Su-Jian, L., Qun, L., Zhi-Feng, Y.: Chunk parsing with maximum entropy principle. Chin. J. Comput. **26**(12), 1722–1727 (2003). (in Chinese)

5. Li, H., Zhu, J.-B., Yao, T.-S.: SVM based Chinese text chunking. J. Chin. Inf. Process. **18** (2), 1–7 (2004). (in Chinese)
6. Li, H., Huang, C.N., Gao, J., et al.: Chinese chunking with another type of spec. In: The Third SIGHAN Workshop on Chinese Language Processing, pp. 24–26 (2004)
7. Chen, W., Zhang, Y., Isahara, H.: An empirical study of Chinese chunking. In: Proceedings of the COLING/ACL on Main Conference Poster Sessions, pp. 97–104. Association for Computational Linguistics (2002)
8. Sag, I.A., Baldwin, T.: Multiword expressions: a pain in the neck for NLR. In: Proceedings of CICLing, pp. 1–15 (2002)
9. Choueka, Y:. Looking for needles in a haystack or locating interesting collocation expressions in large textual databases. In: Proceedings of the RIAO Conf. User—Orient Content—Based Text and Image Hamdling (1988)
10. Church, K.W., Hanks, P.: Word association norms, mutual information and lexicography. Comput. Linguist. **15**, 22–29 (1990)
11. Zhang, T., Damerau, F., Johnson. D.: Text chunking based on a generalization of winnow. J. Mach. Learn. Res. **2**, 615–637 (2002)
12. Kudo, T., Matsumoto, Y.: Chunking with support vector machines. In: Meeting of the North American Chapter of the Association for Computational Linguistics on Language Technologies, vol. **9**, pp. 1–8 (2001)
13. Park, S.B., Zhang, B.T.: Text chunking by combining hand-crafted rules and memory-based learning. In: Erhard, W., Roth, D. (eds.) Proceedings of the 41st Annual Meeting of the Association for Computational Linguistics, Sapporo, Japan: Association for Computational Linguistics, pp. 497–504 (2004)
14. Taku, K., Yuji, M.: Use of support vector learning for chunk identification. In: Proceedings of the 2nd Workshop on Learning Language in Logic and the 4th Conference on Computational Natural Language Learning. Stroudsburg, PA, USA, pp. 142–144. Association for Computational Linguistics (2000)
15. Liu, F., Tiejun, Z., Hao, Y., Muyun, Y., Gaolin, F.: Chinese chunking analysis based on statistics. J. Chinese Inf. Process. **6**, 28–32+39 (2000). (in Chinese)
16. Degen, H., Jing, Y.: A Distributed strategy for CRFs based Chinese text chunking. J. Chin. Inf. Process. **23**(1), 16–22 (2009). (in Chinese)
17. Shao, T., Wang, C., Rao, G., Xun, E.: The semantic change and distribution of adjoining adverbs in modern Chinese. From minimal contrast to meaning construct. In: Frontiers in Chinese Linguistics, vol. 9. Springer, Singapore (2000), https://doi.org/10.1007/978-981-32-9240-6
18. Devlin, J., Chang, M.W., Lee, K., Toutanova, K.: BERT: pre-training of deep bidirectional transformers for language understanding (2018)

Translational Equivalents for Culture-Specific Words in Chinese-English Dictionaries

Qian Li[(✉)]

Guangdong University of Foreign Studies, Guangzhou, China
lqchristina@gdufs.edu.cn

Abstract. As an indispensable element of the language, Chinese culture is particularly attractive to learners, whereas it remains to be a challenge because of its profound history and complex background. The present study collects a group of typical Chinese culture-specific words (CSWs) and examines the adoption of translational equivalents for those CSWs in four Chinese-English dictionaries with different target reader groups. It shows that as compared to the dictionaries for general purposes, those dictionaries intended for Chinese as Foreign Language (CFL) learners prefer to provide a larger amount of encyclopedic explanation to meet user's needs. A combination of translational equivalents plus explanation is the major means adopted by those dictionaries. Furthermore, the inappropriateness of certain translational equivalents suggests the necessity for a close scrutiny of various aspects in the process of equivalent identification, including sense discrimination between different target language words, context information of the potential equivalents, and cultural connotation of each constituent part of an equivalent.

Keywords: Culture-specific words · Translational equivalents · Bilingual · Lexicography

1 Introduction

Culture-specific words (CSWs), also known as culture-bound words [1]; culture-specific terms [2]; and cultural words [3], have received the attention from different fields, e.g. translation, lexicography, cultural and literature studies. According to Florin [4], CSWs are "words and combinations of words denoting objects and concepts characteristic of the way of life, the culture, the social and historical development of one nation and alien to another". Newmark [3] categorizes CSWs into the following areas: 1) ecology 2) material culture 3) social culture 4) organizations, customs, ideas and 5) gestures and habits (pp. 94–103).

As far as Chinese CSWs are concerned, Chang [5] and Chen [6] defined them as "words with typical Chinese social and cultural meanings". Similar to what was done by Newmark [3], Cheng [7] proposed to classify the Chinese CSWs into four groups: 1) material cultural 2) institutional culture 3) behaviour culture and 4) psychological culture. While some general words with cultural connotations are considered as an important part of CSWs [8], most CSWs are pure cultural words which are particularly used to refer to Chinese culture-related objects, behaviours, and customs. Some researchers [9] explored

M. Dong et al. (Eds.): CLSW 2021, LNAI 13250, pp. 145–151, 2022.
https://doi.org/10.1007/978-3-031-06547-7_11

the contrasts between Chinese CSWs and their equivalents in other languages, and argued that there exists no equivalence in other languages to match Chinese CSWs. This study aims to explore whether the English equivalents provided in the Chinese-English dictionaries can match the Chinese CSWs and convey the cultural meaning of those words.

2 Lexicographic Equivalents

An important "given" in translation is that languages are an isomorphic: no two linguistic systems can be fully matched, regardless of their proximity [10]. This is most evident in CSWs as well as larger lexical units such as prefabricated chunks, idioms and proverbs. In the literature, lexicographic equivalents can be categorized into the following four types [11].

A. Cognitive equivalents: Cognitive equivalents, as lexicographers' first choice, possess "an explanatory potential to faithfully represent the meaning of the source language (SL) lexical items", and "tend to be reassuringly identical, no matter which bilingual dictionary for a given language pair one happens to consult" [11]. Take the examples of "hear" and "hand" in English. They are matched with the cognitive equivalents "心 xin" and "手 shou" respectively in Chinese in any English-Chinese dictionary or vice versa.

B. Translational equivalents: Since cognitive equivalents are not available in many cases, bilingual lexicographers have to resort to translational equivalents as "a substitute for SL item in a particular context or contexts" [11]. Given the variety of contexts, a number of translational equivalents for a single SL headword will be collected and presented in a bilingual dictionary. Take the case of 热情(re qing) in Chinese. A set of translational equivalents including "enthusiasm; ardour; devotion; warmth; zeal" will appear in a Chinese-English dictionary.

C. Explanatory equivalents: Explanatory equivalents occur as a supplementary choice in the absence of cognitive and proper translational equivalents. They are considered as "a TL paraphrase of a SL item, situated between a TL equivalent and a TL definition" and are mostly employed when culture-specific items are involved [11]. An example of an explanatory equivalent goes as follows in Chinese-English dictionaries:
E.g. 1. 粽子 zong zi traditional Chinese rice-pudding

D. Functional equivalence: Distinct from the above three types of equivalents, functional equivalence does not "require a lexical equivalent for the SL lemma itself" and it holds "between portions of text larger than individual lexical items" [11]. This type of lexicographic equivalence seems especially close to the concerns of translation theories. Given that functional equivalence usually appears at the level of units larger than a single lexical item, it will not be taken into account in the present study which focuses on lexical items only.

When CSWs are involved, cognitive equivalents are rare and explanatory equivalents are not suitable in length for most cases. As a result, translational equivalents are the most accessible and appropriate ones for cultural words translation.

3 The Present Study

Three typical Chinese cultural specific words are selected from the HSK (*Hanyu Shuipin Kaoshi* – Chinese Proficiency Test) vocabulary list. They are 相声 *xiang sheng,* 凤凰 *feng huang,* and 针灸 *zhen jiu* which are pure CSWs and can reflect the typical Chinese culture images. This study examines the different cases in which translational equivalents are provided for those CSWs among different Chinese-English dictionaries (for general purposes vs. intended for CFL learners). The Chinese-English dictionaries for general purposes refer to those which are intended mainly for Chinese native speakers, and from which CFL learners may find some help as well. In addition, three English dictionaries, when necessary, are cited.

Chinese-English Dictionaries for General Purposes
A Chinese-English Dictionary (CED)
A New-Century Chinese-English Dictionary (NCCED)

Chinese-English Dictionaries Intended for CFL Learners
A Chinese-English Basic Dictionaryfor Chinese Language Learning (BDCLL)
A Chinese-English Dictionaryfor Foreign Learners (CEDFL)

English Dictionaries
Oxford Advanced Learners' Dictionary (OALD)
Merriam- Webster Dictionary Online (Webster)
Oxford English Dictionary (OED)
    Take the case of 相声 (*xiang sheng*) in the four Chinese-English dictionaries.

> **E.g. 2相声(*xiang sheng*)** comic dialogue; cross-talk (CEDFL) (NCCED)(CED) comic dia-
> logue; cross-talk, a kind of Chinese folk art in which the performers tell jokes, utter humorous
> questions and answers, sing songs, and give exaggerated performance to make the audience
> laugh, often satirical or as tribute to new people and new things. It is usually performed by two
> persons, and also single or by more than two.
>
> (BDCLL)

    Distinct from the other three dictionaries just providing equivalent lexical items, BDCLL has further supplied an explanation, delivering detailed information about what *xiang sheng* is and how it is performed. From users' perspective, the combination of translational equivalents and encyclopedic explanation offered them with complete knowledge serving for both SL comprehension and TL production.
    Here it is worthwhile to examine the translational equivalents **"comic dialogue"** and **"cross-talk"** unanimously provided in the four dictionaries. In the entries, the two equivalents are separated by a semi-colon which indicates either of them can be selected to translate *xiang sheng* into English. The question is whether both equivalents convey the same (or at least the similar) meaning of *xiang sheng* as a Chinese CSW.
    Take the case of "comic dialogue" first. It is a free combination, and it cannot be located as an entry headword in either of the following dictionaries, OALD, Webster, Collins English Dictionary and Oxford English Dictionary. When we consult the usage record in a corpus, the hit frequency of "comic dialogue" in COCA is 3 (out of one billion), which reveals its rare use and even weird collocation in English. The provision

of a rare TL item may further confuse language users either in language decoding or encoding activities.

The second equivalent "cross talk" is presented as an entry headword in English dictionaries as follows:

cross-talk n. a situation in which a communication system is picking up the wrong signals

(OALD)

cross talk 1 unwanted signals in a communication channel (as in a telephone, radio, or computer) caused by transference of energy from another circuit (as by leakage or coupling).

2 a: conversation that does not relate to the main topic being discussed b: conversation or repartee engaged in for an audience

(Webster)

cross-talk n. *Telephony (a)* see quot. 1887; in wider use, any unwanted transfer of signals from one circuit, channel, etc., to another; also, in *Radio*, a reproduced signal due to waves that are not of the frequency to which the receiver is tuned; *(b)* altercation, repartee, back- chat; conversation; also *attributive.*

(OED)

The only sense of "cross talk" in OALD shows its usage as a telephony term, which is completely irrelevant with the SL term *xiang sheng.* Similarly, both Webster and OED treat the telephony usage as the first sense. Webster provides a second sense concerning conversation, and its second sub-sense "conversation or repartee engaged in for an audience" matches the fundamental meaning of *xiang sheng.* OED offers a group of equivalents, i.e. "altercation, repartee, back-chat; conversation". When the senses of those words are compared and discriminated, it is revealed that only the word "repartee" conveys the sense of "quick and witty reply" similar to that of *xiang sheng,* whereas both "altercation" and "back-chat" contain the connotative sense of "rude remarks" which is opposed to the associative sense of *xiang sheng.*

Zgusta [12] argued that "one of the greatest dangers of the translational equivalent consists of the possibility or even necessity of using many different expressions of the target language to generate a really smooth translation in varying contexts. However, if such an equivalent has no explanatory power by itself, its value is limited to the context (s) or collocation(s) to which it applies." The analysis of "cross talk" echoed his statement to some extent– there are just limited contexts for "cross talk" to be interpreted as an equivalent to *xiang sheng.* When "cross talk" is used as the translational equivalent, there is a possibility that *xiang sheng* will not be understood as a public amusement performance at all.

The case analysis of *xiang sheng* reveals that firstly, certain translational equivalents provided in Chinese-English dictionaries cannot appropriately convey the cultural image of the word, and this may bring about a communication barrier between the two languages. Secondly lexicographers need to be cautious about equivalents with multiple senses. When a target language (TL) equivalent candidate (e.g. cross talk) consists of several senses, a strict sense discrimination is necessary on both the SL headword and the TL candidate. The more senses of a TL word overlap with those of its SL lemma, the more appropriate an TL equivalent will be.

In bilingual dictionaries, some established equivalents are adopted by lexicographers in C-E dictionaries. Whether the equivalents are appropriate is still a question. Take "*feng huang*" as the example.

E.g. 3 凤 凰 *feng huang* phoenix, lucky birds in ancient Chinese legend, "凤*feng*" referring to the male bird and "凰 *huang*", the female; usu. fig. outstanding talents (BDCLL) phoenix (a legendary bird in Chinese mythology) (NCCED) phoenix (凤 *feng* being the male and 凰 *huang* being the female) (CED) **phoenix** (in stories) a magic bird that lives for several hundred years before burning itself and then being born again from its ashes (OALD) a legendary bird which according to one account lived 500 years, burned itself to ashes on a pyre, and rose alive from the ashes to live another period (Webster).

A comparison between the Chinese-English dictionaries and the cited English dictionaries shows that the existence of the equivalents, in fact, does not ensure the concept matching between 凤 凰 (*feng huang*) and phoenix in Chinese and English culture respectively. In Chinese culture, *feng huang*, as a legendary bird, was recorded in the Chinese history about 4,000 years ago. Its meaning has undergone several changes during the 4,000 years. In the early history, there was a gender difference between *feng* and *huang*, and gradually the distinction became vague. Then, people use *long* (dragon) to stand for the ancient emperors, and *feng huang* (phoenix) to refer to the empresses. As such, *feng huang* signifies power, happiness and harmony in Chinese culture. In contrast, in English, phoenix, as a legendary bird as well, is a symbol of rebirth after disaster. To distinguish those cultural differences, the Chinese-English dictionaries offered a brief explanation as a supplement to the equivalent itself. Similarly, English dictionaries provided encyclopedic explanation about the word phoenix in English culture. Only a detailed explanation, in this case, can contribute to a clear discrimination of cultural meaning in both languages. When translators are consulting Chinese-English dictionaries for production activities, the provision of such an explanation is of crucial help to avoid the erroneous use of a CSW.

There is another case in which the mere provision of translational equivalents may not be sufficient to reflect the cultural feature of the SL lemma. Here is the example of *zhen jiu*.

E.g. 4 针 灸*zhenjiu* acupuncture and moxibustion, acupuncture puts filiform needles into the patients body according to certain acupoints, treating ailments by twisting and pulling the needles, while moxibustion puts burning moxa close to or on the skin according to certain acupoints, using simulation of the heat to treat ailments. (BDCLL)

The words "acupuncture" and "moxibustion" are adopted to match *zhen* and *jiu* respectively. Without background knowledge in Chinese medicine, readers cannot make a distinction between the medical terms "acupuncture" and "moxibustion". To simply offer two professional terms appears to be far from sufficient. In this entry, lexicographers provided detailed information concerning the medical procedures of the two terms, hoping that CFL learners will learn more from the explanation of an encyclopedic nature.

However, the length of an explanation needs to be treated with caution. In a Chinese-English learner's dictionary like BDCLL containing 1,386 pages, such an explanation consisting of 43 words may be oversized when space is highly valued in a paper dictionary, whereas it is feasible in an online dictionary. More importantly, the major drawback of using a lengthy explanation on its own is that it sacrifices the brevity of the target language. Fortunately in this case, translational equivalents are offered in combination with explanation. In this way, the CSW entry can provide both insertable equivalents for a TL production task and comprehensive information for a SL comprehension purpose.

4 Conclusion

Culture specific words, being unique and complex, have remained to be the focus of interests in bilingual lexicography for decades. To offer an equivalent to a CSW, in essence, does not only convey the meaning of a word itself, but transmit the feature of the source language culture. When dealing with the identification of equivalents, bilingual lexicographers adopted a variety of equivalents in Chinese-English dictionaries. Chinese-English bilingual lexicographers tend to adopt translational equivalents as their first choice. As an important element in producing a smooth target language text, translational equivalents are expected to reflect as many cultural elements as possible, and this will be achieved with the awareness of strict sense discrimination on target language candidates, especially when polysemous items are involved.

Users may, to some extent, be well informed of the Chinese culture via a single equivalent type or a combination of different equivalent varieties. The examples cited in this study, however, highlight some problems in equivalent identification in Chinese-English dictionaries, e.g. the inaccuracy of the target language equivalents. Whatever problems exist, the imperfectness can never surpass the significance of bilingual lexicographers' endeavor for better equivalents of CSWs. It is hoped that bilingual lexicographers may figure out effective solutions to those problems to further optimize the treatment of CSWs in Chinese-English dictionaries in the future.

References

1. Lefevere, A.: Translating Literature. The Modern Language Association of America, New York (1992)
2. Williams, J.: The Translation of culture-specific terms. Lebende Sprach, pp. 55–58 (1993)
3. Newmark, P.: A Textbook of Translation. Prentice Hall, Hertfordshire (1988)
4. Florin, S.: Realia in translation. In: Zlateva, P. (ed.) Translation as a Social Action: Russian and Bulgarian Perspectives, pp. 122–128. Routledge, London and New York (1993)
5. Chang, J.: Chinese Words and Culture. Beijing University Press, Beijing (1995)
6. Chen, J.: Chinese Language and Chinese Society. Guangdong Education Press, Guangzhou (1999)
7. Cheng, Y.: Chinese Culture. Foreign Language and Research Press, Beijing (2003)
8. Su, B.: Language, cultural meaning of words and lexicography. Lexicograph. Res. 46–53 (1996)
9. Mei, L.: Proverbs and Idioms in Chinese. World Chin. Educ. 25–32 (1993)
10. Gouws, R, H.: Equivalent Relations, context and cotext in bilingual dictionaries, hermes. J. Linguist. 195–210 (2002)
11. Adamska-Salaciak, A.: Between designer drugs and afterburners: a lexicographic semantic study of equivalence. Lexicos. 1–22 (2011)

12. Zgusta, L.: Translational Equivalence in the Bilingual Dictionary. In: Hartmann, R.R K. (eds.) LEXeter 1983 Proceedings, pp. 147–154. Max Niemeyer, Tubingen (1983)

(b) Dictionaries

13. CED =*A Chinese-English Dictionary.* Ed. by Wei Dongya. Foreign Language Teaching and Research Press, revised edn. 1995.
14. NCCED =*A New-Century Chinese-English Dictionary.* Ed. by Hui Yu. Foreign Language Teaching and Research Press. 2004.
15. BDCLL=*A Chinese-English Basic Dictionaryfor Chinese Language Learning.* Ed. by Qian Wangsi, Yao Naiqiang. Foreign Language Press. 2007.
16. CEDFL=*A Chinese-English Dictionaryfor Foreign Learners.* Ed. by ShanghaiTranslation Publishing House, 2008.
17. OALD = *OxfordAdvanced Learners'DictionaryOnline.*[<https://www.oxfordlearnersdictionaries.com/>; last access: Dec 12, 2020]
18. Webster =*Merriam- Webster Dictionary Online.*[<https://www.merriam-webster.com/dictionary/>; last access: Dec 10, 2020]
19. OED = *Oxford English Dictionary Online.*[<https://www.oed.com/>; last access: Dec 15, 2020]

Quantitative Analysis of Chinese and English Verb Valencies Based on Probabilistic Valency Pattern Theory

Jianwei Yan and Haitao Liu[(⊠)]

Department of Linguistics, Zhejiang University, Hangzhou, China
lhtzju@yeah.net

Abstract. This study examines the similarities and differences between Chinese and English verb valencies based on the Probabilistic Valency Pattern Theory (PVPT). We adopted the Parallel Universal Dependencies treebanks of Chinese and English to ensure that the comparison is under the same semantic meanings conveyed. The results show that (1) The verb valencies of both languages share similar distributions. One important difference is that Chinese has significantly more monovalent verbs (valency equals one) than English does; (2) For conveying similar meanings, Chinese adopts more verbs than English does, while the average combinatorial ability of Chinese verbs is relatively smaller; (3) The overall probabilistic valency pattern (PVP) of verbs in Chinese and English are similar; however, those of specific high-frequent verbs in Chinese and English demonstrate their own features. The findings may shed light on depicting the characteristics of Chinese and English verbs, thus facilitating studies in both linguistics and natural language processing.

Keywords: Chinese · English · Verb valency · Probabilistic Valency Pattern Theory (PVPT) · Distribution · Mean verb valency · Probabilistic Valency Pattern (PVP)

1 Introduction

As a syntactic-semantic theory of words, the valency theory has been widely used in theoretical linguistics, language teaching and natural language processing. The concept of valency, in effect, derived initially from the field of chemistry and was introduced into the field of linguistics by Tesnière [1]. Later, it became an indispensable part of modern dependency grammar. As stated in Tesnière [2: 239], the verb may "be compared to a sort of atom, susceptible to attracting a greater or lesser number of actants, according to the number of bonds the verb has available to keep them as dependents. The number of bonds a verb has constitutes what we call the verb's valency". Valency means the ability of words to combine with other words, and verbs play an essential role in the valency theory. Therefore, great attention has been paid to the word class of verbs. Different verbs may adopt special complement forms, resulting in different valency patterns [3].

In Fig. 1, we presented four tree representations of avalent, monovalent, divalent, and trivalent verbs in Chinese. As shown, the Chinese verb "下雨 (*it rains*)" is avalent,

© Springer Nature Switzerland AG 2022
M. Dong et al. (Eds.): CLSW 2021, LNAI 13250, pp. 152–162, 2022.
https://doi.org/10.1007/978-3-031-06547-7_12

"游泳 (*swims*)" in "她游泳 (*she swims*)" is monovalent, "吃 (*eats*)" in "他吃水果 (*he eats fruits*)" is divalent, and "给 (*gave*)" in "她给了他一本書 (*she gave him a book*)" is trivalent.

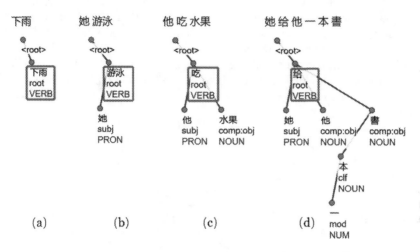

Fig. 1. Tree representations of avalent, monovalent, divalent, and trivalent verbs in Chinese.

Therefore, valency reflects the ability of the central word to combine with other words. The combination of these words leads to an abstract relationship, that is, dependency relation, such as the *subj* relation between 她 (*she*) and 游泳 (*swims*) in Fig. 1(b). The number of dependency relations of a verb reflects the size of its combining ability or valency, and this ability of verbs can be accurately and quantitatively described through treebanks or annotated corpora [5].

Valency is not only a theory but also a method of analyzing languages. It has been used in database construction, syntactic research, natural language processing, second language learning, etc. For instance, Götz-Votteler [6] proposed that a verb-specific description of participants can be regarded as an accurate way of describing semantic valency. Liu [7] found that the English verb valency is positively correlated with both the frequency of the verb and the number of polysemy of the verb. Gao et al. [8] analyzed the synergetic properties among valency, frequency, word length, polysemy and polytexuality, and presented a synergetic model of Chinese verb valency. More recently, Zhang and Liu [9] investigated the motifs of generalized valencies based on English and Chinese treebanks and found that valency motifs can function as a basic language entity and a diversification process. Moreover, the underlying framework of many studies is, in effect, the valency theory, though it has not been explicitly pointed out, e.g., [10, 11]. Meanwhile, the valency theory has also undergone some developments, such as the Full Valency Theory proposed by Čech et al. [12] and Čech et al. [13], and the Probabilistic Valency Pattern Theory (PVPT) advocated by Liu [4], Liu and Feng [5] and Liu [14].

Traditionally, the valency of a specific word can be found in a dictionary, which is called the static valency. Once the word is utilized in a sentence, its potential ability to combine with other words is realized, and the valency becomes a dynamic one, and a dependency relation is formed. Therefore, we can use dependency treebanks to study the combining power of words.

Liu [4] firstly introduced the concept of probability into the traditional valency model and proposed the theory of "Weighted Valency Pattern", which adopts quantitative methods to analyze the weight or probability of the dependency relations. This theory describes and defines every dependency relation between word classes to improve "the expressing and explaining capacity of the patterns" [4: 127]. Later, it was renamed "Probabilistic Valency Pattern Theory" to emphasize the role of probability in this theory [5, 14]. Figure 2 presents the probabilistic valency pattern (PVP) of a word (or a word class).

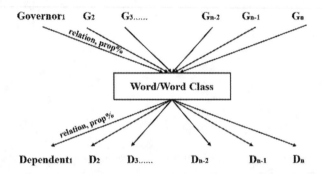

Fig. 2. Probabilistic valency pattern (PVP) diagram of a word (or word class).

The rectangle in Fig. 2 represents the word or word class under investigation. G_1, G_2, G_3,... G_{n-2}, G_{n-1}, G_n are words or word classes that govern the central word or word class. D_1, D_2, D_3,... D_{n-2}, D_{n-1}, D_n are words or word classes governed by the central word or word class; namely, they are dependents of the central word. The arrows indicate the dependency relations between the central word and its governors or between the central word and its dependents, accompanied by the probabilities of these relations. Therefore, the PVP can reflect language use more objectively and is conducive to reveal linguistic universals.

Based on 13 word classes and 34 dependency relations in Chinese, Liu and Feng [5] constructed PVP diagrams of several word classes and proposed a framework of natural language processing based on the PVPT. They are of great importance for the statistical understanding of the Chinese language from a probabilistic perspective. However, there still lacks comparative studies of different languages based on the theory of PVP.

This paper aims to examine the differences and similarities between Chinese and English based on the PVPT. Special attention would be paid to the word class of verbs. Moreover, following Zhang and Liu [9: 236–237], we would only focus on verbs' dependents. It means the lower part of the diagram in Fig. 2.

To be specific, we adopt the Parallel Universal Dependencies (PUD)[1] treebanks of Chinese and English to ensure that the comparison is under the premise of consistent

---

[1] For more information on PUD treebanks, see http://universaldependencies.org/conll17/.

semantics. Then we calculate the frequency of all dependents dominated by all verbs in both languages, respectively. Moreover, since the probabilities of a word class dominated by verbs are unbalanced, the probability of each dependency relation is also computed.

Three research questions are of our concern:

Question (1): Does the verb valency distribution of Chinese demonstrate differences from that of English?

Question (2): Does the mean verb valency of Chinese demonstrate differences from that of English?

Question (3): Does the probabilistic valency pattern of verbs in Chinese differ from that in English? What are the characteristics of the probabilistic valency patterns of the most frequent verbs in Chinese and English?

To recap, based on the PVPT and the parallel treebanks of Chinese and English, we aim to analyze the ability of verbs to combine with other related words in sentences, also the probability of each dependency relation dominated by verbs. Through comparative analysis, we attempt at depicting the characteristics of verb valency patterns of both languages and facilitating the field of linguistics and natural language processing.

2 Methods and Materials

2.1 Materials

The parallel PUD Chinese and English annotated corpora retrieved from the Surface-Syntactic Universal Dependencies (SUD)[2] database [15] are adopted as linguistic materials for the current study. The reason for using SUD treebanks is that the annotation scheme of the SUD treebanks emphasizes the syntactic relations between words within sentences [16], thus can better demonstrate how verbs in a language combine with other words. In addition, the adoption of the parallel treebanks can ensure that the comparison of the combining abilities of Chinese and English verbs is under the premise of semantic consistency. Moreover, the genre of these two treebanks is news or Wikipedia, a typical genre of written language, which can eliminate the influence of genre on the combing ability of verbs. Table 1 shows the basic information on the PUD Chinese and English treebanks.

Table 1. Information on the PUD Chinese and English treebanks.

	Chinese	English
Sentences	1,000	1,000
Tokens	21,415	21,176

---

[2] The SUD treebanks can be downloaded at https://surfacesyntacticud.github.io/data/.

As shown in Table 1, the number of sentences in both treebanks is 1,000, and all sentences are neatly aligned. Also, the number of tokens in both treebanks is very close. Hence, these two annotated corpora are comparable. Based on these materials, we aim to investigate whether there are differences in terms of the combing ability of Chinese and English verbs under the premise of similar semantic meanings conveyed.

2.2   Methods

Following the previous method [4, 5, 9, 14], we calculate the valencies of both Chinese and English verbs based on the Probabilistic Valency Pattern Theory (PVPT). Figure 3 presents the representations of two sample sentences in the PUD Chinese.

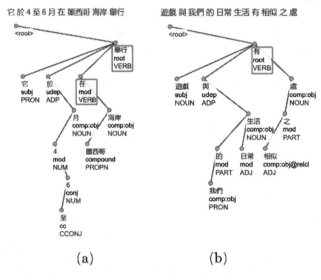

(a)   (b)

Fig. 3. Tree representations of two sample sentences in the PUD Chinese treebank: (a) 它於4至6月在墨西哥海岸舉行, which means *It was conducted just off the Mexican coast from April to June*; (b) 遊戲與我們的日常生活有相似之處, which means *There are parallels to draw here between games and our everyday lives.*[3]

As shown in Fig. 3(a), the verb 舉行 (*conduct*) is trivalent, forming three dependency relations with other words, namely, a *subj* relation with 它 (*it*), a *udep* relation with 於 (*from*), and a *mod* relation with 在 (*off*). Meanwhile, the other verb 在 (*on*) in Fig. 3(a) is monovalent, which dominates 海岸 (*beach*) to form a *comp:obj* relation. Hence, in this sentence, one trivalent verb and one monovalent verb are found, and their mean verb valency is $(3 + 1)/2 = 2$. The probabilistic valency pattern (PVP) of the verbs or the probability of dependency relations dominated by the verbs in the sentence is 25% *subj*, 25% *udep*, 25% *mod*, and finally 25% *comp:obj* (Note: we do not

---

[3] The diagrams were generated at https://universaldependencies.org/conllu_viewer.html.

take punctuation into our consideration when calculating the combining abilities of verbs in the current study).

Similarly, in Fig. 3(b), the only verb 有 (*there are*) is trivalent. It forms three dependency relations with other words in the sentence, i.e., 遊戲, 與, and 處. Thus, only one trivalent verb is found in this sentence, and the mean verb valency is 3. Moreover, the probabilistic valency pattern of the verb is 33.33% *subj*, 33.33% *udep*, and 33.33% *comp:obj*.

When we consider these two sentences together, the distribution of verb valency is one monovalent verb and two trivalent ones. Then, the mean verb valency is $(3 + 1 + 3)/3 = 2.33$. Finally, the probabilistic valency pattern of the verbs is $2/7 = 28.57\%$ *subj*, 28.57% *udep*, $1/7 = 14.29\%$ *mod*, 28.57% *comb:obj*.

Mathematically, we can formulate the mean verb valency of a sentence or treebank as follows:

$$\text{mean verb valency}(\text{sentence}/\text{treebank}) = \frac{1}{n}\sum_{i=1}^{n} |V_i| \qquad (1)$$

In this formula, n is the number of verbs in the sentence or treebank. V_i is the i-th verb's valency in the sentence or treebank.

Then, the probability of each dependency relation governed by verbs in a sentence or treebank can be formulated as:

$$\text{probability of each dependency relation governed by verbs (sentence/treebank)}$$
$$= \frac{\text{frequencies of each specific dependency relation}}{\text{total number of dependents of all verbs in a sentence or treebank}} * 100\% \qquad (2)$$

After we compute the probabilities of all dependency relations governed by verbs in the sentence or treebank according to formula (2), we can obtain the probabilistic valency pattern of the verbs in the sentence or treebank.

Based on formula (1) and formula (2), we can quantify the combining ability of all verbs in annotated corpora and investigate the similarities and differences of different languages in terms of verb valencies.

3   Results and Discussions

3.1   Verb Valency Distribution of Chinese and English

Firstly, we computed the valencies of all verbs in both PUD Chinese and English treebanks. In order to present the general distributions of verb valencies, we counted the numbers of avalent verbs, monovalent verbs, divalent verbs, trivalent verbs, etc. The result was shown in Fig. 4.

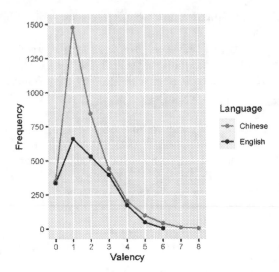

Fig. 4. Distribution of verb valencies in the PUD Chinese and English treebanks.

In Fig. 4, the *x*-axis represents the valency value, and the *y*-axis represents valency's corresponding frequency. The figure shows that the valencies of the two languages share a similar distribution. Specifically, both languages have certain amounts of avalent verbs, and the largest amounts of monovalent verbs; and then, as the valencies increase, the numbers of verbs with a specific valency decrease.

However, there are also some differences between Chinese and English verb valencies. First of all, the numbers of all Chinese verb valencies are always greater than those of English. More importantly, the number of monovalent verbs in Chinese accounts for 1476/3467 = 42.57%, while that in English is only 659/2150 = 30.65% (the total amounts of verbs in Chinese and English are 3,467 and 2,150, respectively). Moreover, the difference between Chinese and English in terms of the monovalent verb frequencies is statistically significant ($\chi 2$ (1, $N = 5617$) = 79.542, $p < 0.05$)), while those of other valency are similar and not statistically significant.

The result shows that under the premise of certain semantics, the Chinese language adopts more content verbs to realize their valency in sentences, and most of these verbs are low valency verbs.

3.2   Mean Verb Valency of Chinese and English

Another question then may arise: What are the mean values of Chinese and English verb valencies? Is there any significant difference between these two languages in terms of mean verb valency? We computed the means of all valencies and drew a boxplot, as shown in Fig. 5.

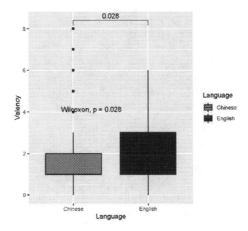

Fig. 5. Boxplot of mean verb valencies in the PUD Chinese and English treebanks.

The Wilcoxon test in Fig. 5 shows that the mean verb valency of Chinese (M = 1.770; SD = 1.301) is significantly smaller than that of English (M = 1.800; SD = 1.278) (p = 0.028 < 0.05). This result shows that although Chinese has more verbs than English does in the parallel treebanks (frequency: 3,467 > 2,150), the mean verb valency of Chinese is lower than that of English (mean verb valency: 1.770 < 1.800). This relationship between mean verb valency and the number of verbs is noteworthy and interesting. Hence, we reviewed the frequency information on content words and function words in these two treebanks in Table 2.

Table 2. Information on numbers of content words and function words in the PUD Chinese and English treebanks.

	Chinese	English
Function words[a]	6,036	8,361
Content words	12,171	10,306

[a]For more information on POS tags, see https://universaldependencies.org/u/pos/index.html

A Chi-square test based on Table 2 shows that there is a significant difference between the number of function words and the number of content words in Chinese and English ($\chi2$ (1, N = 36,874) = 524.07, p < 0.05). Also, the number of verbs in Chinese (3,467) is far more than in English (2,150). Combined with the result in Fig. 5 that the mean combining ability of Chinese verbs is smaller than or not as strong as that of English, it may suggest that under the premise of the same semantics, the more the number of content words, the weaker the valency's combining ability of the content words.

3.3 Probabilistic Valency Pattern of Chinese and English Verbs

Since the PVPT can not only quantitatively describe how the central word or word class form dependency relations with other words, but also demonstrate the weight or probability of these dependency relations [4, 5, 14], we extracted all dependency relations that are dominated by the verbs in Chinese and English and calculated the probabilities of these relations in both treebanks, as shown in Fig. 6.

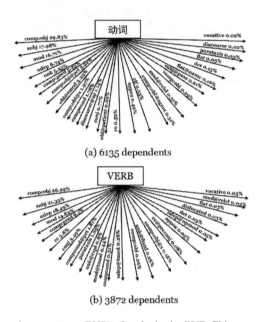

(a) 6135 dependents

(b) 3872 dependents

Fig. 6. Probabilistic valency pattern (PVP) of verbs in the PUD Chinese and English treebanks.

As shown in Fig. 6, the probability of each dependency relation is unbalanced. In other words, the likelihoods or probabilities of the word classes dominated by the verbs are different. Specifically, the dependency relations, *comp:obj*, *subj*, and *mod* are most likely to connect Chinese verbs and their dependents with a probability as high as 64.52% (29.83% + 17.98% + 16.71%). The result is very similar to that in Liu and Huang [17]. Meanwhile, the dependency relations dominated by English verbs are also *comp:obj*, *subj*, and *mod* with a probability of 66.11% (26.29% + 21.33% + 18.49%). The results show that the subordinated words that tend to be dominated by verbs share certain similarities in Chinese and English.

In addition, we also computed the PVP of each verb to demonstrate its realization of the combining ability with other words. For example, the top ten most frequent Chinese verbs in the PUD Chinese are: 在 (frequency = 109), 有 (78), 於 (60), 是 (40), 爲 (39), 來 (25), 說 (25), 用 (21), 作 (20), and 到 (20), while those in the PUD English are: *have* (46), *say* (35), *take* (26), *make* (24), *use* (24), *be* (17), *become* (16), *do* (16), *follow* (16), and *know* (16). So are these high-frequent verbs in Chinese and English also share a similar PVP?

We took the most frequent verb 在 in Chinese and *have* in English as examples. There are 153 dependents of 在 in PUD Chinese, and the PVP of 在 with these dependents is as follows: *comp:obj* 69.93%, *subj* 9.8%, *comp:obj@prt* 9.15%, *mod* 4.58%, *obl@tmod* 2.61%, *unk* 1.96%, *comp:obl@x* 0.65%, *comp:pred* 0.65%, and *compound* 0.65%. As for *have*, 141 dependents can be found in the PUD English treebank, and its PVP is: *comp:obj* 34.04%, *subj* 24.11%, *comp:pred* 11.35%, *mod* 11.35%, *cc* 7.09%, *conj* 4.96%, *udep* 3.55%, *parataxis* 2.84%, *unk@expl* 0.71%.

We can see that different verbs have different PVPs, and we can also draw the PVP diagram of each verb, similar to Fig. 6. By characterizing the PVP of each central verb, we can better grasp the main information of the text. As Liu and Feng [5] stated, the PVPT is of great significance for the acquisition of corpus knowledge and the application of natural language processing.

4 Conclusion

This study adopted the Probabilistic Valency Pattern Theory (PVPT) to investigate the similarities and differences between Chinese and English verb valencies. The parallel treebanks of Chinese and English were used to ensure that the comparison is under the premise of the same semantic meanings conveyed.

We found that the general distributions of verb valencies in Chinese and English are similar, though Chinese has more verbs with small valencies, especially monovalent ones. Moreover, the number of verbs and the mean verb valency is inversely proportional for expressing the same semantics. Specifically, Chinese uses more verbs than English does. Correspondingly, the Chinese verbs' ability to combine with other words is relatively smaller. Finally, the PVPs of Chinese and English verbs are generally similar, while those of specific verbs are distinctive to demonstrate their own characteristics.

Proposed in Liu [4] and developed in Liu and Feng [5] and Liu [14], the PVPT combines the probability and dependency relations into the valency theory. It is expected to better construct statistical models of natural language processing, facilitating data access, syntactic eligibility, ambiguity resolution, sentence interpretation, etc.

Meanwhile, based on the PVPT, we can also better explain some theoretical linguistic issues on specific structures, such as collocations, idioms, garden path sentences, etc. The current study is an exemplification of how PVPT can be used to describe the characteristics of Chinese and English lexical verbs, demonstrating their own features.

In all, as a linguistic theory that focuses on verbs or predicates, the PVPT can capture the characteristics of the verb class and function as a core to combine other lexical elements to realize syntactic and semantic meanings of sentences. Although the corpus sizes of the PUD treebanks adopted are not so large due to the availability of parallel treebanks, the findings in this study may still shed new light on depicting the characteristics of Chinese and English verbs and facilitating the fields of both linguistics and natural language processing.

References

1. Tesnière, L.: Eléments de la Syntaxe Structurale. Klincksieck, Paris (1959)
2. Tesnière, L.: Elements of Structural Syntax. John Benjamins Publishing Company, Amsterdam (2015). (in English, translated by Osborne, T., Kahane, S)
3. Köhler, R.: Quantitative Syntax Analysis. De Gruyter Mouton, Berlin (2015)
4. Liu, H.: Syntactic parsing based on dependency relations. grkg/Humankybernetik **47**(4), 124–135 (2006)
5. Liu, H., Feng, Z.: Probabilistic valency pattern theory for natural language processing. Linguistic Sci. **6**(3), 32–41 (2007). (in Chinese)
6. Götz-Votteler, K.: Describing semantic valency. In: Herbst, T., Götz-Votteler, K. (eds.) Valency: Theoretical, Descriptive and Cognitive Issues, pp. 37–50. De Gruyter, Berlin (2008)
7. Liu, H.: Quantitative properties of English verb valency. J. Quant. Linguist. **18**(3), 207–233 (2011). https://doi.org/10.1080/09296174.2011.581849
8. Gao, S., Zhang, H., Liu, H.: Synergetic properties of Chinese verb valency. J. Quant. Linguist. **21**(1), 1–21 (2014). https://doi.org/10.1080/09296174.2013.856132
9. Zhang, H., Liu, H.: Motifs of generalized valencies. In: Liu, H., Liang, J. (eds.) Motifs in Language and Text, pp. 231–260. De Gruyter, Berlin (2017)
10. Wang, E., Yuan, Y.: The meaning of polysemous adjective 'Hao(Good)'. In: Wu, Y., Hong, JF., Su, Q. (eds.) Chinese Lexical Semantics. CLSW 2017, LNCS, vol. 10709, pp. 180–189. Springer, Heidelberg (2018). https://doi.org/10.1007/978-3-319-73573-3_15
11. Wang, L.: Towards a lexical analysis on chinese middle constructions. In: Hong, J.-F., Su, Qi., Wu, J.-S. (eds.) CLSW 2018. LNCS (LNAI), vol. 11173, pp. 236–244. Springer, Cham (2018). https://doi.org/10.1007/978-3-030-04015-4_20
12. Čech, R., Pajas, P., Mačutek, J.: Full valency. verb valency without distinguishing complements and adjuncts. J. Quant. Linguist. **17**(4), 291–302 (2010). https://doi.org/10.1080/09296174.2010.512162
13. Čech, R., Kosek, P., Navrátilová, O., Mačutek, J.: Full valency and the position of enclitics in the Old Czech. In: Proceedings of the First Workshop on Quantitative Syntax (Quasy, SyntaxFest 2019), pp. 83–88. Association for Computational Linguistics, Paris (2019). https://doi.org/10.18653/v1/W19-7910
14. Liu, H.: Dependency Grammar: From Theory to Practice. Science Press, Beijing (2009).(in Chinese)
15. Gerdes, K., Guillaume, B., Kahane, S., Perrier, G.: SUD or surface-syntactic universal dependencies: an annotation scheme near-isomorphic to UD. In: Proceedings of the Second Workshop on Universal Dependencies (UDW 2018), pp. 66–74. Association for Computational Linguistics, Brussels (2018). https://doi.org/10.18653/v1/W18-6008
16. Yan, J., Liu, H.: Semantic roles or syntactic functions: the effects of annotation scheme on the results of dependency measures. Stud. Linguist. (2021). https://doi.org/10.1111/stul.12177
17. Liu, H., Huang, W.: A Chinese dependency syntax for treebanking. In: Proceedings of the 20th Pacific Asia Conference on Language, Information and Computation, pp. 126–133. Tsinghua University Press, Beijing (2006)

A Quantitative Approach to the Stylistic Assessment of the Middle Chinese Texts

Bing Qiu[(⊠)] and Wei Bian

Department of Chinese Language and Literature, School of Humanities and
Social Sciences, Tsinghua University, Beijing, China
qiubing@mail.tsinghua.edu.cn

Abstract. The stylistic assessment is an important research domain as a language is intrinsically a complex of different stylistic varieties. Aiming at a quantitative assessment of the colloquialization level of the Middle Chinese texts, the spoken and written words in the literature with a focus on some core words are examined. In our survey, each axis is composed of both written and spoken words corresponding to the same sense. Then a quantitative approach to stylistic assessment is proposed. Statistical survey on some typical texts of Chinese shows that there are complicated mixtures, both inside a certain text on different axes, and inside a certain category, either native texts or Chinese translated Buddhist scriptures, across different texts, which gives a glimpse of the dynamic language evolution in the Middle Ages.

Keywords: Stylistic assessment · Middle Chinese · Spoken words · Written words

1 Introduction

A language is a complex of different stylistic varieties, each of which is applicable to a certain type of situation. Stylistic classification is an important research domain and has substantial potential for wide applications ranging from stylistic device analysis, emotional coloring determination to authorship attribution, to name a few. Martin Joos in his book The Five Clocks [1] simplified the range of language variation by dividing it into five styles, i.e., frozen, formal, consultative, casual and intimate styles, to reflect different levels of formality.

Generally, stylistic assessment involves many perspectives, such as expressive means, aesthetic functions, stylistic devices, register and rhythm. In the paper, we will only focus on the spoken style (i.e., colloquial style) and the written style, which reflects the difference between speech and writing, in regards to the texts in Middle Chinese.

It is worth noting that Middle Chinese, which is commonly defined as the language variety of Chinese during the historical period ranging from about East Han dynasty (25–220 A.D.) to about Sui dynasty (581–618 A.D), is of great significance in the research on the evolution of the Chinese language. Middle Chinese constitutes the key transition from Ancient Chinese to Modern Chinese. A considerable part of the Chinese language elements underwent significant changes in the Middle Ages, which even

M. Dong et al. (Eds.): CLSW 2021, LNAI 13250, pp. 163–171, 2022.
https://doi.org/10.1007/978-3-031-06547-7_13

exerted a profound influence on Modern Chinese [2]. Furthermore, there occurred a large-scale indirect language contact during the Middle Ages, which was induced by sutra translation from the source languages, Sanskrit in most cases, into Chinese. It is another important topic to find out the stylistic difference between the native literature and the Chinese translation of Buddhist sutras. Many scholars have noticed that the colloquial level of the Chinese translation of Buddhist scriptures is relatively high. There are many more oral elements in the translation of Buddhist scriptures in the Eastern Han Dynasty compared to the non-religious documents of the same period [3]. Also, the Buddhist scriptures are close to spoken language [4, 5]. However, the Chinese-translated Buddhist scriptures in different periods and by different translators also differ greatly in their degree of colloquialization.

There have been many achievements in the stylistic classification of Indo-European languages as well as modern Chinese. It was reported that the written and spoken queries in English are compared in terms of length, duration, and part of speech to support qualitative and quantitative analyses [6]. A computationally tractable formulation of linguistically well-motivated features in stylistic text classification was proposed based on Systemic Functional Linguistics (SFL), which was mainly demonstrated in English [7]. The Random Walk Model (RWM) was introduced as a formal approach to text analysis for Russian texts [8]. The modern Chinese texts are classified into the formal written style, the colloquial style and the conversational style based on the sentence length, word length, part of speech (POS) and so forth [9].

However, it is difficult to determinate the style of the texts in the Middle Ages. The main barriers lie in two aspects. Firstly, there is no clear, feasible and objective standard to determinate the style of a given text in the Middle Ages. Even for a given word, it is difficult to judge whether it is a spoken word or a written word at that time [10]. Secondly, there is no quantitative index to measure the degree of colloquialization of a given text. The aforementioned conclusion that the Buddhist scriptures are close to spoken style was qualitative, mainly drawn from the scholars' subjective experience. To the best of our knowledge, few of the existing studies are focused on the stylistic classification of the Middle Chinese texts and no quantitative approach has been proposed yet.

Our contributions are mainly three-fold. First, we proposed a feasible method to count the alternative written and spoken forms for some entries from a glossary of the core vocabulary items in Middle Chinese [11]. Each of the entries was presented as an axis in this paper. Second, we further proposed mathematical formulation to score the degree of colloquialization on each axis and then accumulated the scores to be a quantitative index for the stylistic assessment in a comprehensive manner. Third, we visualized the style of the Middle Chinese texts and discussed the stylistic difference between the native Chinese literature and the Chinese translation of Buddhist scriptures.

2   Methodology of the Quantitative Stylistic Classification

In this section, we will first introduce the mathematical formulation of the proposed methodology and then take a study case to demonstrate how to evaluate the score of the colloquialization.

There are two related form sets, i.e., the written forms and the spoken ones for a given axis. For a given text, let $S(a)$ denote the count of spoken forms and $W(a)$ denote the count of spoken forms on a given axis, denoted by a. Furthermore, we define the raw score of the colloquialization on this axis as:

$$Q(a) = \frac{S(a)}{S(a) + W(a)}. \tag{1}$$

However, to avoid the situation that $S(a) + W(a) = 0$, we apply the Laplace smoothing, also called Additive Smoothing, to revise the score to

$$Q(a) = \frac{S(a) + 1}{S(a) + W(a) + 2}. \tag{2}$$

For a given axis, the greater the count of spoken words is, or the lesser the count of written words is, the closer the score of the colloquialization is to 1. As a special case, if the count of spoken words is the same as the count of written words, the score of the colloquialization is then exactly 1/2. Finally we take the average of all the scores as the quantitative index for the stylistic assessment in a comprehensive manner.

As the first epic poem (Kāvya) in the history of Indian Sanskrit literature, *Buddhacarita* was introduced into China in the Middle Ages and thereafter exerted a great influence on Chinese literature [12]. Therefore, we will take the Chinese translation of *Buddhacarita*, 佛所行贊 (*Fo Suo Xing Zan*, in pinyin, abbr. *FSXZ*) as a study case to discuss its degree of colloquialization.

Take the axis of "eye" as an example. There are two corresponding Chinese words, "眼" (*yan* in pinyin, literally, eye or eyeball) and "目" (*mu* in pinyin, literally, eye) to express such a sense. According to the existing work by Wang Weihui (2014), "眼" had replaced "目" in the spoken language by the end of the Han Dynasty, and later such replacement had also been completed in the literary language by the late Six Dynasties. Note that the replacement of commonly used words took place in a gradual process. In a specific text, the two words might co-occur. For example, the Chinese word "眼" appears 28 times and the "目" appears 40 times in the same text.

Thus, the score of the colloquialization on the axis "眼" versus "目" is (28 + 1)/(28 + 40 + 2) = 0.414. Therefore, if viewed in light of this axis, the colloquial degree of *FSXZ* is slightly lower than the medium level.

3   Quantitative Stylistic Analysis of Middle Chinese Texts

In this section, we will first introduce the texts and axes surveyed in the paper. Then, we will show the statistical data and assessment results and discuss the degree of colloquialization for typical texts in both categories.

We took three native Chinese texts, say, "世说新语" (Shi Shuo Xin Yu in pinyin), "齐民要术" (Qi Min Yao Shu in pinyin) and "颜氏家训" (Yan Shi Jia Xun in pinyin), and three Chinese translated Buddhist scriptures, say, "佛所行赞" (Fo Suo Xing Zan in pinyin), "百喻经" (Bai Yu Jing in pinyin) and "妙法莲花经" (Miao Fa Lian Hua Jing in pinyin), to perform the quantitative analysis for different kinds of texts. All the information of the texts is listed in Table 1.

Table 1. The texts to be surveyed for the quantitative stylistic analysis.

Title in Chinese	Pinyin and abbreviation	Category
世说新语	Shi Shuo Xin Yu, SSXY	Native Text
齐民要术	Qi Min Yao Shu, QMYS	Native Text
颜氏家训	Yan Shi Jia Xun, YSJX	Native Text
佛所行赞	Fo Suo Xing Zan, FSXZ	Translation
百喻经	Bai Yu Jing, BYJ	Translation
妙法莲花经	Miao Fa Lian Hua Jing, MFLHJ	Translation

In the following analysis, a total of 5 axes would be examined, which are listed in Table 2.

Table 2. The axes to support the analysis of the colloquialization degree

Symbol	Axis	Spoken word	Written word
a_1	Wing	翅(Chi in pinyin)	翼(Yi in pinyin)
a_2	Eye	眼(yan in pinyin)	目(mu in pinyin)
a_3	Ship, boat	船(Chuan in pinyin)	舟(Zhou in pinyin)
a_4	Foot	脚(Jiao in pinyin)	足(Zu in pinyin)
a_5	Look	看(Kan in pinyin)	视(Shi in pinyin)

Thereafter, based on the proposed methodology, we conducted statistical investigations on the usage of the spoken words and the written words on all the axes. The results are shown in Table 3.

Table 3. The count results and the scores for the stylistic classification.

Axis index	Statistic symbol	SSXY	QMYS	YSJX	FSXZ	BYJ	MFLHJ
1	S:W(wing)	2:4	3:3	0:2	2:0	0:0	0:0
	Q(wing)	0.375	0.500	0.250	0.750	0.500	0.500
2	S:W(eye)	14:16	16:31	3:22	28:40	19:8	15:9
	Q(eye)	0.469	0.347	0.148	0.414	0.690	0.615
3	S:W(ship)	31:3	4:1	1:4	7:10	4:0	1:1
	Q(ship)	0.889	0.714	0.286	0.421	0.833	0.500
4	S:W(foot)	7:6	35:32	0:3	3:50	4:3	1:24
	Q(foot)	0.533	0.522	0.200	0.073	0.556	0.074
5	S:W(look)	53:35	37:11	3:4	3:17	11:3	0:7
	Q(look)	0.600	0.760	0.444	0.182	0.750	0.111
Average	Q	0.573	0.569	0.266	0.368	0.666	0.360

In order to compare the similarities and differences of their styles more clearly, we illustrate the data in Fig. 1 in the form of a radar chart.

The polygons in Fig. 1 respectively indicate the axes of investigation. The points indicate the colloquialization degree of a given text on different axes. Furthermore, these points are connected to form a closed segmented line reflecting the spoken or written style of this text.

As illustrated in Fig. 1, the polygon corresponding to *BYJ* is the biggest in general, showing that spoken words are selected more commonly than written words on almost all axes. *BYJ*, literally, *Scripture of 100 parables*, is a representative work of Chinese translation of Buddhist scriptures and indeed shows an inclination towards spoken words. The degree of colloquialization is highest in *BYJ* among all the texts, which agrees with the conclusion by scholars' experience [3–5]. However, there is no strong inclination towards spoken words in another two texts of Chinese translation of Buddhist scriptures, *FSXZ* and *MFLHJ*, both of which show that there is a tendency towards spoken words only on some certain axes.

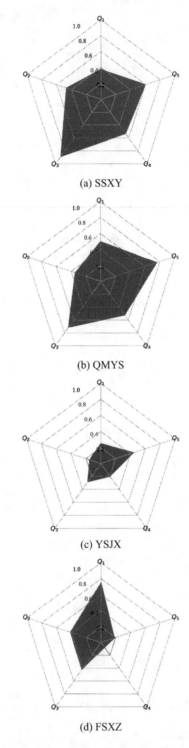

(a) SSXY

(b) QMYS

(c) YSJX

(d) FSXZ

Fig. 1. Radar charts of the degree of colloquialization for all the texts.

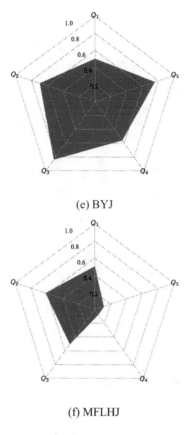

(e) BYJ

(f) MFLHJ

Fig. 1. (*continued*)

According to the statistical data, the spoken words are more likely to be chosen in the native Chinese texts, *SSXY* and *QMYS*. However, the polygon of *YSJX* is obviously small, indicating that it is of a strong "classical" style with heavy usage of written words.

Also depicted in Fig. 1, different texts demonstrate conspicuous individual characteristics on different axes. There have emerged complicated mixed situations. One mixture lies inside a certain text, as it may tend to use colloquial words on one axis, but written words on another axis. Another mixture lies inside a certain category of texts, either native Chinese texts or Chinese translated Buddhist scriptures as a whole, as there are obvious differences in the degree of colloquialization for different texts of the same category. Such complicated mixtures highlight the highly dynamic process of the language evolution in the Middle Ages.

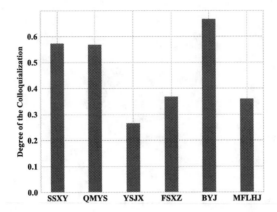

Fig. 2. The average degree of colloquialization of all the texts.

In a comprehensive manner, the quantitative assessment of the colloquialization degree of each text is shown in Fig. 2, in which each bar represents a certain text, and its height tells the average degree of colloquialization. According to their colloquialization degree, the texts are ranked as *BYJ, SSXY, QMYS, FSXZ, MFLHJ* and *YSJX* in descending order.

It is worth noting that the above conclusions are consistent with the existing research. However, based on the proposed quantitative methodology, not only the preference of spoken words or written words on a given axis can be demonstrated, but also the degree of colloquialization is quantitatively assessed.

4   Conclusion

The stylistic assessment of the texts in Middle Chinese, especially the quantitative determination of their degree of colloquialization, is an important but difficult issue.

In order to obtain the degree of colloquialization of the Middle Chinese texts, we first examined the spoken and written words in the literature. In fact, spoken words and written words were often used alternatively to express the same concept in a certain text, such as the Chinese words "眼" and "目", both of which had the sense of "eye". This indicates that the lexis of Middle Chinese is a transition from that of Ancient Chinese to that of Modern Chinese. It also reminds us that we can carry out a quantitative analysis from the perspective of commonly used words, that is, the set of the axis is composed of both spoken and written words corresponding to the same sense.

Second, we proposed a quantitative measurement for evaluating the degree of colloquialization and its related mathematical formulation. The statistical analysis shows that the texts in the Middle Ages all showed a mixture of spoken and written styles. We also noticed that different texts have significant individual characteristics in their degree of colloquialization, and meanwhile, the same text varies in its degree of colloquialization on different axes. Such mixtures show that Middle Chinese was in dynamic evolution. It can also be seen that the methodology presented in this paper is helpful to reveal the above-mentioned mixed situations and to better the study on Middle Chinese.

Acknowledgments. The work was supported by the Social Science Foundation of Beijing, China (Grant No. 17YYC019) and Tsinghua University Initiative Scientific Research Program (Grant No. 2019THZWLJ28). The author would also like to thank the national youth talent support plan in the Ten Thousand Talent Program.

References

1. Joos, M.: The Five Clocks: A Linguistic Excursion Into the Five Styles of English Usage, 5th edn. Harcourt, San Diego (1967)
2. Qiu, B., Li, J.: Reconstruction of uncertain historical evolution of the polysyllablization of Chinese lexis. J. Appl. Math. **2014**(123983), 1–9 (2014)
3. Erik, Z.: The Buddhist Conquest of China: The Spread and Adaptation of Buddhism in Early Medieval China. Leiden, Brill (1972)
4. Lyu, S.: 800 Words of Modern Chinese (*Xiandai Hanyu Babai Ci* in pinyin). Shangwu Press, Beijing (1980).(in Chinese)
5. Fang, Y., Wang, Y.: Reading "Buddhist Scriptures and the study of medieval Chinese vocabulary" (*Du "FoDian Yu Zhonggu Hanyu Cihui Yanjiu"* in pinyin). Res. Ancient Chin. (Gu Hanyu Yanjiu) **1**, 11–16 (1994). (in Chinese)
6. Crestani, F., Heather, D.: Written versus spoken queries: a qualitative and quantitative comparative analysis. J. Am. Soc. Inf. Sci. **57**(7), 881–890 (2006)
7. Whitelaw, C., Argamon, S.: Systemic functional features in stylistic text classification. In: Technical Report FS-04-07 AAAI Fall Symposim on Style & Meaning in Language. Art, Music & Design, pp. 74–83. AAAI Press, California (2004)
8. Kramarenko, A.A., Nekrasov, K.A., Filimonov, V.V., Zhivoderov, A.A., Amieva Kramarenko, A.A.: A stylistic classification of Russian-language texts based on the random walk model. In: AIP Conference Proceedings 1886 (020072), pp.1–7, American Institute of Physics (2017)
9. Hou, R., Yang, J., Jiang, M.: A study on chinese quantitative stylistic features and relation among different styles based on text clustering. J. Quant. Linguist. **21**(3), 246–280 (2014)
10. Hua, Z.: Spoken words in medieval written language from "Luoyang Jialan Ji." J. Central South Univ. (Soc. Sci. Edn.) **10**(2), 260–263 (2004). (in Chinese)
11. Wang, W.: History and Current Situation of Chinese Core Words. Shangwu Press, Beijing (2017).(in Chinese)
12. Qiu, B.: Two-fold linguistic evidences on the identification of Chinese translation of Buddhist sutras: taking *Buddhacarita* as a case. In: Hong, J.-F., Zhang, Y., Liu, P. (eds.) CLSW 2019. LNCS (LNAI), vol. 11831, pp. 853–858. Springer, Cham (2020). https://doi.org/10.1007/978-3-030-38189-9_85

Construction and Evaluation of Chinese Word Segmentation Datasets in Malay Archipelago

Shengyi Jiang[1,2], Yingwen Fu[1], and Nankai Lin[1(✉)]

[1] School of Information Science and Technology,
Guangdong University of Foreign Studies, Guangzhou, Guangdong, China
neakail@outlook.com
[2] Guangzhou Key Laboratory of Multilingual Intelligent Processing,
Guangdong University of Foreign Studies, Guangzhou, Guangdong, China

Abstract. In recent years, there has been numerous mature research on Chinese word segmentation (CWS). However, the existing research mainly focuses on mainland Mandarin word segmentation, and the research on CWS of other countries/regions is still far from satisfactory. Although Chinese in the Malay Archipelago countries and Mandarin in mainland China are homologous, there exist some differences between them during their respective development processes. Therefore, common CWS tools cannot accurately and effectively segment Chinese texts of different countries. This paper conducts research on the Chinese texts of five countries in Malay Archipelago (Indonesia, Malaysia, Brunei, Singapore, and the Philippines), builds five CWS datasets respectively for each country, and explores the performance of some advanced word segmentation tools and sequence labeling models on the constructed datasets. The experimental results show the effectiveness of BERT (Bidirectional Encoder Representations from Transformers) model in CWS task, providing a baseline for CWS in five Malay Archipelago countries. Furthermore, we explore the enhancement of two training strategies on CWS task, and the experimental results show that these two strategies cannot significantly improve the CWS performance of Malay Archipelago. Besides, in view of the different performances on CWS of different countries, we deeply analyze their objective and historical reasons. The reasons behind it mainly fall into the corpus size, the Chinese language policy and the language education norms on different Malay Archipelago countries.

Keywords: Malay Archipelago · Chinese word segmentation · Dataset · BERT

1 Introduction

Chinese word segmentation (CWS) is fundamental to Chinese natural language processing (NLP). Since word is the basic semantic unit of Chinese, the quality of word segmentation directly affects the performance of downstream tasks. In recent years, there has been numerous mature research (such as PKUSEG [1], Jieba[1], etc.) on CWS.

---

[1] https://github.com/fxsjy/jieba.

M. Dong et al. (Eds.): CLSW 2021, LNAI 13250, pp. 172–183, 2022.
https://doi.org/10.1007/978-3-031-06547-7_14

However, existing research mainly focuses on mainland Mandarin word segmentation, and the research on CWS of other countries/regions is still far from satisfactory.

With immigration and foreign dissemination, the Chinese language appeared and was used in various countries. The language life of the Chinese society is largely based on dialects, Mandarin and local ethnic languages, gradually forming a multilingual-used situation. Take the Philippines as an example, about nine out of ten Chinese Filipinos are native of Fujian and live relatively concentratedly, resulting in the Southern Fujian dialect has become the official Chinese language of the local Chinese community. Today, the Philippine Chinese commonly used by Chinese Filipinos is formed under the combined effects of Filipino, English, Hokkien and Cantonese. Due to the special historical background and social environment, Chinese societies in other countries have also formed distinctive Chinese language, such as Singapore Chinese, Indonesian Chinese, etc. This is the common Chinese language beyond dialects. However, due to the influence of dialects, these overseas Chinese languages have developed into extraterritorial variants of Mandarin with obvious local characteristics, which are significantly different from Mandarin Chinese in various aspects such as phonetics, vocabulary and even grammar. Even though Chinese communities in different countries have basically formed a common written language, there are still many dialect elements in it[2]. In the face of the above-mentioned differences in Chinese, general Chinese word segmentation tools cannot accurately and effectively segment Chinese texts of different countries. Therefore, in the research on CWS of other countries, it is completely necessary to build word segmentation datasets and train word segmentation models for Chinese texts of different countries.

This paper conducts research on Chinese texts of five countries in Malay Archipelago (Indonesia, Malaysia, Brunei, Singapore, and the Philippines), builds five CWS datasets respectively for each country, and explores the performance of some advanced word segmentation tools (PKUSeg [1], Jieba (see Footnote 1), LTP [22], NLPIR [23]) and sequence labeling models (Bi-LSTM-CRF, Bi-LSTM-LAN, BERT) on the constructed datasets. Experimental results show the excellent performance of the BERT model in CWS task, providing a baseline for CWS in five Malay Archipelago countries. Furthermore, we explore the enhancement of two training strategies on CWS task, and the experimental results show that these two strategies cannot significantly improve the CWS performance of Malay Archipelago. Besides, in view of the different performances on CWS of different countries, we deeply analyze their objective and historical reasons.

2 Related Work

At present, CWE research is mainly divided into two categories: general CWE and domain-specific CWE.

---

[2] http://qwgzyj.gqb.gov.cn/hwjy/127/382.shtml.

2.1   General CWS

Chen et al. [2] was the first to introduce deep learning model to CWS task and used word embeddings to represent the contextual semantic information of Chinese words. Based on deep learning model, Zhang et al. [3] used a windowing method in the input layer of the model to capture local feature information of words. This could significantly improve the performance of CWS models. Furthermore, Cai et al. [4] proposed a word-based method to explicitly inject word information to the existed CWS models. In terms of capturing character information, Shao et al. [5] introduced the radical information of characters to the joint task of part-of-speech (POS) tagging and CWS. In addition, Dai et al. [6] used a convolutional neural network (CNN) to extract the pixel information of characters and then integrated it into the CWS task. Besides, in order to alleviate data-hungry problem, Zhu et al. [7] tried to use automatically obtained weakly labeled data to improve word segmentation performance. In particular, he introduced a loss function for weakly labeled data to the Bi-LSTM-CRF model and proposed a simple but effective data filtering method to filter data with high confidence from massive weakly labeled data. Additionally, he also used external features to further improve word segmentation performance [8]. Later, Li [9] used FOFE coding method to integrate the sequence contextual information into the neural-based word segmentation model. He designed and implemented a general sequence labeling system that could be used for word segmentation, named entity recognition (NER) and terminology extraction.

2.2   Domain-Specific CWS

The existing CWS tools are mainly oriented to general domain, and they fail to work well when applied to a specific domain. Therefore, many researchers struggle to study CWS for a specific domain.

In terms of ancient CWS research, Yang [10] tried to apply deep learning method to automatically extract the long-distance context information of ancient Chinese, and proposed a general model framework for ancient CWS and POS tagging. This model achieved good results on both ancient CWS and POS tagging tasks. Besides, Li [11] used a new word discovery method based on mutual information and adjacent entropy of words to find unregistered words from the "Hanshu" and used NLPIR to segment "Hanshu". Experiments proved that the method of new word discovery combined with dictionary information could effectively improve the accuracy of ancient CWS. In terms of Buddhist CWS, Hua [12] discussed the specific characteristics of Buddhist documents in the Medieval Chinese corpus, and established a word segmentation standard for Medieval Buddhist documents.

As for legal domain, Yao et al. [13] proposed a word segmentation method for Chinese legal documents. The proposed method included two steps: (1) automatically generate some labeled data as a legal seed dictionary, and (2) apply a multi-layer neural network to segment the texts containing words in the legal dictionary.

In medical domain, Xiong et al. [14] constructed a Chinese clinical text corpus for CWS and POS tagging, and compared a variety of state-of-the-art methods on this corpus. In addition, Xing [15] proposed a multi-task learning method for medical CWS by transferring knowledge from high-resourced domains to assist the CWS task in low-resourced domains. Aiming at the research on CWS of TCM symptoms, Mao [16] designed a TCM symptom segmentation algorithm based on two-way conditional probability statistical model and relative position.

In addition, for multiple specific domains, Huang et al. [17] proposed a multi-standard joint model, which shared parameters between all layers and integrated different scoring standards into a single model. Besides, he used transfer learning methods to improve OOV (Out of Vocabulary) word segmentation performance. Recently, an advanced tool PKUSEG [1] has been build to support CWS in multiple domains. This toolkit is dedicated to providing specific pre-trained models for data in different domains (including news, Internet, medicine, tourism, and their combination). According to the domain characteristics of the text to be segmented, users can freely choose different models. Xu et al. [18] proposed a method based on transfer learning for multiple domains, using a high-resource corpus to improve the low-resource word segmentation model. First, a teacher model is trained on the high-resourced corpus which is then used to initialize the student model. Furthermore, a weighted data similarity method is proposed to train the student model on low-resourced domain.

3   Dataset

We obtain Chinese news articles from five countries in Malay Archipelago and then use Jieba (see Footnote 1) tool to pre-segment all articles. Later the pre-segmented datasets are manually audited and revised the wrong segmentation. The detailed statistics of the constructed datasets are shown in Table 1. We take sentences as the division unit, using (70%, 10%, 20%) of the datasets respectively as the (training, validation, test) set.

Table 1. Statistics of the datasets.

Country	Websites	#Num of sentences	#Num of tokens
Brunei	China-Embassy[a]	4371	153873
Indonesia	ShangbaoIndonesia[b], Guojiribao[c]	31211	885294
Singapore	Lianhezaobao[d]	8982	280607
Malaysia	Kwongwah[e], Seehua[f], Sinchew[g]	53872	3078532
Philippine	Unitednews[h]	2667	76733

[a]http://bn.china-embassy.org/chn/
[b]http://www.shangbaoindonesia.com/
[c]http://www.guojiribao.com
[d]http://www.zaobao.com/
[e]https://www.kwongwah.com.my/
[f]http://news.seehua.com/
[g]https://www.sinchew.com.my/
[h]http://www.unitednews.net.ph

4 Experiment

4.1 Baseline

We compare the performance of four commonly used word segmentation tools (PKUSeg [1], Jieba (see Footnote 1), LTP [22], NLPIR [23]) and three sequence labeling models on the constructed corpus datasets:

- Bi-LSTM-CRF [19]: Bi-LSTM-CRF uses the Bi-LSTM network to extract semantic features the words and then feeds the extracted features to the CRF layer. The label sequence with the highest score is used as the final prediction.
- Bi-LSTM-LAN [20]: Bi-LSTM-LAN (Hierarchically Refined Label Attention Network) uses label knowledge to better capture the long-term dependencies between labels, and solves the problem of labeling paranoia to a certain extent. Bi-LSTM-LAN has achieved great performance in multiple sequence labeling tasks such as POS tagging and NER in terms of accuracy and speed.
- BERT [21]: Google's BERT is pre-trained on large-scale unlabeled data to obtain text representations containing rich semantic information, which can be fine-tuned in specific downstream NLP tasks. BERT has achieved good results in multiple text classification tasks and sequence labeling tasks.

4.2 Experimental Setting

The hyperparameters of the three sequence labeling baselines are shown in Table 2.

Table 2. Experimental setting.

Model	Parameter	Value
Bi-LSTM-CRF	Hidden unit	150
	Layer	1
	Learning rate	0.01
	Optimizer	Adam
	Word embedding dimension	100
Bi-LSTM-LAN	CNN layer	4
	LAN layer	1
	Attention head	5
	Weight decay	1e−8
	Word embedding dimension	100
	Optimizer	SGD
	Learning rate	0.015
	Learning rate decay	0.05

(*continued*)

Table 2. (*continued*)

Model	Parameter	Value
BERT	Learning rate	5e−5
	Dropout	0.5
	Optimizer	Adam
	Weight decay	0.001
Common	Max sequence length	256
	Loss function	Cross entropy

4.3 Evaluation Metrics

We use precision (P), recall (R) and F-value as evaluation metrics based on an existing toolkit seqeval[3]. Given an input sequence with N words, the result of word segmentation is to output a series of word segmentations. Assuming that each segmentation can be recorded as an interval $[i,j]$ according to its start and end position in the sequence, where $0 \leq i \leq j \leq n$, all intervals of the ground truth segmentations form a set A, and the set of all intervals of the word segmentation results are set B, then

$$P = \frac{|A \cap B|}{|B|} \tag{1}$$

$$R = \frac{|A \cup B|}{|B|} \tag{2}$$

$$F = \frac{2 \cdot P \cdot R}{P + R} \tag{3}$$

4.4 Result and Analysis

The word segmentation results of the four commonly used word segmentation tools (PKUSeg, Jieba, LTP, and NLPIR) on the CWS datasets of five countries are shown in Table 3. It can be seen that NLPIR has the lowest average F-value of only 76.81%. PKUSeg and LTP achieve relatively similar performances, with an average F-value of 85.41% and 85.07%, respectively. PKUSeg has the highest average precision of 85.41%, while the average recall of LTP is the highest, reaching 85.66%. In terms of specific results of each country, PKUSeg's word segmentation performance is more stable, while LTP has certain fluctuations between the segmentation results of different

---

[3] https://github.com/chakki-works/seqeval.

Table 3. Main performance of commonly used word segmentation tools.

Country	Method	P	R	F
Brunei	PKUSeg	**85.51%**	**84.08%**	**84.79%**
	Jieba	79.28%	78.67%	78.98%
	LTP	84.20%	83.79%	84.00%
	NLPIR	74.05%	79.97%	76.90%
Indonesia	PKUSeg	**88.36%**	87.56%	87.96%
	Jieba	86.81%	84.86%	85.87%
	LTP	87.89%	**88.36%**	**88.13%**
	NLPIR	76.84%	78.13%	77.48%
Singapore	PKUSeg	85.22%	86.28%	**85.87%**
	Jieba	**85.99%**	85.10%	85.53%
	LTP	83.45%	**86.32%**	84.86%
	NLPIR	73.57%	83.24%	78.11%
Malaysia	PKUSeg	83.80%	84.59%	84.19%
	Jieba	**84.93%**	**84.64%**	**84.79%**
	LTP	82.14%	84.57%	83.34%
	NLPIR	65.57%	76.77%	70.73%
Philippine	PKUSeg	84.18%	84.33%	84.25%
	Jieba	83.71%	84.01%	83.86%
	LTP	**84.85%**	**85.24%**	**85.04%**
	NLPIR	80.00%	81.68%	80.83%
Average	PKUSeg	**85.41%**	85.37%	**85.41%**
	Jieba	84.14%	83.46%	83.81%
	LTP	84.51%	**85.66%**	85.07%
	NLPIR	74.01%	79.96%	76.81%

countries. On the whole, the segmentation effectiveness of all tools above is not satisfactory, with an average F-value of below 90%. This indicates that the existing CWS tools cannot meet the needs of CWS in other countries. Later we further explore the segmentation performances of three deep learning models on the constructed datasets.

The word segmentation results of Bi-LSTM-CRF, Bi-LSTM-LAN, and BERT on the constructed datasets are shown in Table 4. Among them, the Malaysian Chinese dataset with the largest corpus size achieves the best performance and the best result F-value reaches 96.48%. From the average results of five datasets, we can seen that the effectiveness of BERT is far superior to the other two models, achieving the best results.

Table 4. Main performance of three deep learning models.

Country	Method	P	R	F
Brunei	Bi-LSTM-CRF	90.64%	**90.77%**	90.70%
	Bi-LSTM-LAN	90.18%	88.25%	89.21%
	BERT	**91.95%**	90.61%	**91.28%**
Indonesia	Bi-LSTM-CRF	88.50%	89.58%	89.04%
	Bi-LSTM-LAN	91.49%	91.63%	91.56%
	BERT	**92.89%**	**92.65%**	**92.77%**
Singapore	Bi-LSTM-CRF	89.07%	90.42%	89.74%
	Bi-LSTM-LAN	89.09%	89.51%	89.30%
	BERT	**94.21%**	**94.17%**	**94.19%**
Malaysia	Bi-LSTM-CRF	89.03%	89.52%	89.27%
	Bi-LSTM-LAN	87.46%	87.19%	87.32%
	BERT	**92.85%**	**92.63%**	**92.74%**
Philippine	Bi-LSTM-CRF	91.66%	92.33%	91.99%
	Bi-LSTM-LAN	95.75%	95.88%	95.82%
	BERT	**96.49%**	**96.47%**	**96.48%**
Average	Bi-LSTM-CRF	89.78%	90.52%	90.15%
	Bi-LSTM-LAN	90.79%	90.49%	90.64%
	BERT	**93.68%**	**93.31%**	**93.49%**

We further experiment with two strategies to improve the performance of the BERT model on the constructed datasets: **Continual Language Model Pre-training** and **Language Model Post-training**. The experimental results are shown in Table 5. In the continual language model pre-training strategy, we use the Chinese dataset of each country to continual pre-train the pre-trained BERT model for domain adaption with an unsupervised masked language modeling (MLM) objective. The learned model is then leveraged to fine-tune for CWS task. In the language model post-training strategy, we first use the MSRA corpus of Microsoft Research Asia [24, 25] to post-train the pre-trained BERT model with a supervised CWS objective. With this strategy, the BERT model can learn more segmentation knowledge. After that, the constructed dataset of each country is utilized to further fine-tune the post-trained model. Different from the performance in other tasks, in the CWS task, the two strategies above do not significantly improve the performance of the model. After introducing two strategies, the CWS performance in some datasets even has declined. The performance of the continual pre-training strategy dropped by an average F-value of 0.35% and the post-training strategy dropped by an average F-value of 0.13%. The experimental results show that these two strategies can not significantly improve the CWS performance of Malay Archipelago.

Table 5. Performance of pre-training and post-training strategies.

Country	Method	P	R	F
Brunei	BERT + Pre-training	91.09%	**90.90%**	90.99%
	BERT + Post-training	91.71%	90.73%	91.22%
	BERT	**91.95%**	90.61%	**91.28%**
Indonesia	BERT + Pre-training	91.39%	90.85%	91.12%
	BERT + Post-training	92.88%	92.34%	92.61%
	BERT	**92.89%**	**92.65%**	**92.77%**
Singapore	BERT + Pre-training	**94.21%**	93.96%	94.09%
	BERT + Post-training	93.67%	93.56%	93.62%
	BERT	**94.21%**	**94.17%**	**94.19%**
Malaysia	BERT + Pre-training	93.20%	**92.80%**	**93.00%**
	BERT + Post-training	92.88%	**92.80%**	92.84%
	BERT	92.85%	92.63%	92.74%
Philippine	BERT + Pre-training	96.51%	96.47%	96.49%
	BERT + Post-training	**96.52%**	**96.50%**	**96.51%**
	BERT	96.49%	96.47%	96.48%
Average	BERT + Pre-training	93.28%	93.00%	93.14%
	BERT + Post-training	93.53%	93.19%	93.36%
	BERT	**93.68%**	**93.31%**	**93.49%**

We further analyze the experimental results longitudinally. The CWS performances of different countries are quite different. Malaysian CWS and Singapore CWS have relatively better results, reaching 96.51% and 94.19%, respectively, while the performances of other three countries (Brunei, Indonesia and the Philippines) are poor. The reasons behind it mainly fall into two aspects, one is the corpus size, and the other is the Chinese language policy on different Malay Archipelago countries. By comparing the corpus sizes of different countries, we can see that the main reason for the poor results of CWE in Brunei and the Philippines is the data-hungry problem. Secondly, the development of Chinese education in Brunei has experienced difficulties under the external restrictions of the Western colonial government and the Malay government's education policy of prioritizing English and Malay. In addition, Brunei Chinese schools, as the main front of Chinese education, also have encountered many difficulties in its own development. The restrictions on teaching materials and teachers also have had a relatively negative internal impact on the Chinese development in Brunei [26]. A notable feature of Brunei's language policy was the emphasis on standard Malay, English and support for Brunei Malay [27]. Therefore, Chinese has always been underestimated in Brunei, aggravating the slow Chinese development in Brunei, which therefore has affected the readability and difficulty of understanding Brunei Chinese materials. In the Philippines, Chinese education has experienced a period of germination, prosperity, stagnation, and recovery and prosperity after the war. However, the Philippine policy of Chinese education which implemented during the Marcos administration severely inhibited the development of Chinese education [28]. As a result, there was a shortage of resources for Chinese language education in the Philippines. The teaching mode was mainly based on a single grammar translation. The Chinese language teaching had no space for free development because of the church supervision. It followed the traditional model teaching method [29], which led to the Chinese language level in the Philippines gradually decreased. The reason for the poor effectiveness of the Indonesian CWS model is that the Chinese Indonesians are weak in using Chinese. Since Indonesia's coup in 1965, Indonesian authorities have closed overseas Chinese schools and banned the display of Chinese art and culture in public, as well as the use of Chinese. Existing studies have shown that in the comparison of the Chinese language ability of the Chinese people in Malaysia, Indonesia, and Thailand, Chinese Indonesians have the weakest Chinese language ability [30]. At the same time, due to being affected by multiple languages or dialects, there have been some mutations and errors in Indonesian Chinese compared with Mandarin [31]. In addition, language education norms are also a factor that leads to Chinese differences in five countries. In the process of the Malaysian government taking measures to promote and enhance the status of Malay as national language, the Malaysian Chinese community has made long-term unremitting efforts to inherit the native Chinese language. Now in Malaysia, Chinese education has a relatively complete system from elementary school, middle school to tertiary college [32]. In contrast, Indonesia does not have a complete Chinese teaching system which significantly increases the difficulty of understanding Indonesian Chinese texts. Therefore, the poor readability of Indonesian Chinese texts increases the difficulty of model training.

5 Conclusion

This paper conducts research on the Chinese texts of five countries in Malay Archipelago (Indonesia, Malaysia, Brunei, Singapore, and the Philippines), builds and open-sources five Chinese word segmentation (CWS) datasets respectively for each country. What is more, we provide a baseline based on BERT model for CWS task of different countries in Malay Archipelago. The experimental results show the effectiveness of BERT model in CWS task. Furthermore, we explore the enhancement of two training strategies on CWS task, and the experimental results show that these two strategies cannot significantly improve the CWS performance of Malay Archipelago. At the same time, we deeply analyze the objective and historical reasons that affect the performance of CWS in different Malay Archipelago countries. The reasons behind it mainly fall into the corpus size, the Chinese language policy and the language education norms on different Malay Archipelago countries. In the future, we will continue to expand the corpus size of five CWS datasets and improve the quality of them.

Acknowledgement. This work was supported by the National Natural Science Foundation of China (No. 61572145), the Major Projects of Guangdong Education Department for Foundation Research and Applied Research (No. 2017KZDXM031) and National Social Science Foundation of China (No. 17CTQ045). The authors would like to thank the anonymous reviewers for their valuable comments and suggestions.

References

1. Luo, R., Xu, J., Zhang, Y., Ren, X., Sun, X.: PKUSEG: A Toolkit for Multi-Domain Chinese Word Segmentation. CoRR (2019)
2. Chen, X., Qiu, X, Zhu, C., Liu, P., Huang, X.: Long short-term memory neural networks for Chinese word segmentation. In: Proceedings of the 2015 Conference on Empirical Methods in Natural Language Processing, pp. 1197–1206 (2015)
3. Zhang, M., Zhang, Y., Fu, G.: Transition-based neural word segmentation. In: Proceedings of the 54th Annual Meeting of the Association for Computational Linguistics, pp. 421–431 (2016)
4. Cai, D., Zhao, H.: Neural word segmentation learning for Chinese. In: Proceedings of the 54th Annual Meeting of the Association for Computational Linguistics, pp. 409–420 (2016)
5. Shao, Y., Hardmeier, C., Tiedemann, J., Nivre, J.: Character-based joint segmentation and POS tagging for Chinese using bidirectional RNN-CRF. In: Proceedings of the Conference on the Eighth International Joint Conference on Natural Language Processing, pp. 173–183 (2017)
6. Dai, F.Z., Cai, Z.: Glyph-aware embedding of Chinese characters. In: Proceedings of the First Workshop on Subword and Character Level Models in NLP, pp. 64–69 (2017)
7. Zhu, Y., Li, Z.H., Huang, D.P., Zhang, M.: Domain adaptation for Chinese word segmentation using partial annotations. J. Chinese Inf. Process. 33(09), 1–8 (2019)
8. Zhu, Y.: Research on Domain Adaptation of Chinese Word Segmentation with Multi-source Features and Data. Soochow University (2019)
9. Li, Z.X.: Research on Chinese Word Segmentation Methods Using Context Information. Beijing Jiaotong University (2018)
10. Yang, S.C.: Research on the Methods of Ancient Chinese Word Segmentation and Part-of-speech Tagging. North China University of Science and Technology (2018)
11. Li, X.Y.: Study on word segmentation in ancient texts based on neologism discovery and dictionary information. Softw. Guide 18(04), 60–63 (2019)
12. Hua, Z.H.: The word segmentation norms of Buddhist documents in the medieval Chinese corpus. J. Southeast Univ. (Philos. Soc. Sci.) 21(01), 135–142+145 (2019)
13. Yao, L., et al.: Word segmentation for chinese judicial documents. In: Cheng, X., Jing, W., Song, X., Lu, Z. (eds.) Data Science. CCIS, vol. 1058, pp. 466–478. Springer, Singapore (2019). https://doi.org/10.1007/978-981-15-0118-0_36
14. Xiong, Y., Wang, Z., Jiang, D., Qingcai, X., Hua, C.: A fine-grained Chinese word segmentation and part-of-speech tagging corpus for clinical text. BMC Med. Inform. Decis. Mak. 19(2), 179–184 (2019)
15. Xing, J., Zhu, K., Zhang, S.: Adaptive multi-task transfer learning for Chinese word segmentation in medical text. In: Proceedings of the 27th International Conference on Computational Linguistics, pp. 3619–3630 (2018)
16. Mao, Y.: Research of Chinese Word Segmentation and Sentence Similarity on Traditional Chinese Medecine Symptom. Zhejiang University (2017)
17. Huang, K., Huang, D., Liu, Z., Mo, F.: A joint multiple criteria model in transfer learning for cross-domain Chinese word segmentation. In: Proceedings of the 2020 Conference on Empirical Methods in Natural Language Processing, pp. 3873–3882 (2020)
18. Xu, J., Sun, X.: Transfer Deep Learning for Low-Resource Chinese Word Segmentation with a Novel Neural Network. CoRR (2017)
19. Huang, Z., Xu, W., Yu, K.: Bidirectional LSTM-CRF Models for Sequence Tagging. CoRR (2015)

20. Cui, L., Zhang, Y.: Hierarchically-refined label attention network for sequence labelling. In: Proceedings of the 2019 Conference on Empirical Methods in Natural Language Processing and the 9th International Joint Conference on Natural Language Processing, pp. 4115–4128 (2019)
21. Devlin, J., Chang, M.W., Chang Lee, K., Toutanova, K. BERT: Pre-training of Deep Bidirectional Transformers for Language Understanding. CoRR (2018)
22. Che, W., Feng, Y., Qin, L., Liu, T.: N-LTP: A Open-source Neural Chinese Language Technology Platform with Pretrained Models. CoRR (2020)
23. Zhang, H., Yu, H., Xiong, D., Liu, Q.: HHMM-based Chinese lexical analyzer ICTCLAS. In: Proceedings of the second SIGHAN workshop on Chinese language processing. Association for Computational Linguistics, pp. 184–187 (2013)
24. Thomas, E.: The second international Chinese word segmentation bakeoff. In: Proceedings of the Fourth SIGHAN Workshop on Chinese Language Processing, pp. 123–133 (2020)
25. Zhang, Y.N.: Research on Domain Adaptation Method for Chinese Segmentation Based on Instance Transfer Learning. Beijing Jiaotong University (2019)
26. Wen, A.D.: Investigation and Research on the Status Quo of Chinese Education in Brunei. Shaanxi Normal University (2015)
27. Zhang, Z.G., Guo, C.X.: Research on Brunei's language policy and its enlightenment to China. J. Xi'an Int. Stud. Univ. 24(03), 28–31 (2016)
28. Sui, R.S.: The Analysis of the Chinese Education in Philippines During the Marcos. Fujian Normal University (2016)
29. Fan, J. J.: A Study on the current situation of Chinese language Education in the Philippines. Xi'an Shiyou University (2020)
30. Zhou, W., An, D.: On code-switching in mandarin conversations of ethnic Chinese in Malaysia, Indonesia and Northern Thailand. J. Yibin Univ. 19(03), 88–94 (2019)
31. Zhang, L.C.: Analysis of the language situation in Indonesian Chinese newspapers and periodicals. Overseas Chinese Educ. 2010(01), 33–39 (2010)
32. Ke, Y.H.: The contrast of educational policies for Chinese language teaching in Malaysia and Singapore. Around Southeast Asia 2009(10), 48–52 (2009)

Social Changes Manifested in the Diachronic Changes of Reform-Related Chinese Near Synonyms

Longxing Li[1,2(✉)], Vincent Xian Wang[2], and Chu-Ren Huang[3]

[1] Faculty of Languages and Translation, Macao Polytechnic University, Macao, China
yb67707@um.edu.mo
[2] Faculty of Arts and Humanities, University of Macau, Macao, China
{yb67707,vxwang}@um.edu.mo
[3] Department of Chinese and Bilingual Studies, The Hong Kong Polytechnic University, Hong Kong, China
churen.huang@polyu.edu.hk

Abstract. This paper examines several reform-related Chinese near synonyms in the thousand-year long history of China, comparing them in both diachronic and synchronic dimensions. Through the enquiries of word frequency and usages in diachronic Chinese corpora and historical Chinese language databases, the results reveal the interplay between social realities and language use. This study is an initial effort to relating a number of socially and historically significant synonymous words to the thousand-year long history of China through corpus linguistic enquiry.

Keywords: Social change · Reform · *Gaige* · Near synonyms · Corpus linguistics

1 Introduction

Reform is an important social activity and an important way of improving the social system. Numerous reforms have been carried out in different regions and sectors in the long human history and have played a significant role in promoting social progress and improving livelihood of people. This is also the case in China where reforms have exerted tremendous impact on the development of the Chinese nation. Qi [1] claims in his work *A History of Reforms in China* that every single step in the development of (Chinese) history is accompanied by reforms. Qi and Jiang [2], in the preface of their edited 10-volume series *General History of Reforms in China*, classified reforms into two categories: one is reforms for *fundamental* social change which typically happened in the transitional period of social formation, such as Shang Yang's Reform (商鞅變法) in the Warring States Period (475 BC – 221 BC) and the Hundred Days' Reform (戊戌變法, 11 June–21 September 1898) in the late Qing Dynasty (1636–1912); the other is *partial* reforms of various sectors in the progressive development of the society. The majority of reforms belong to the second category. The most influential

---

The original version of this chapter was revised: an error in the affiliation of a co-author was corrected. The correction to this chapter is available at https://doi.org/10.1007/978-3-031-06547-7_32

M. Dong et al. (Eds.): CLSW 2021, LNAI 13250, pp. 184–193, 2022.
https://doi.org/10.1007/978-3-031-06547-7_15

reform in contemporary China is the Reform and Opening-up which started from 1978 till now and will most likely be carried forward.

Due to its significance, reform has been a heated and lasting research topic in social sciences, especially in economics, politics, public administration, law, and history. Most previous studies about reform from linguistic or cultural perspectives only regard certain significant reforms as the social or historical background. Linguistic studies of reform started to attract researchers' attention only recently. Keywords study is one perspective of linguistic studies on reform. *Reform* has been investigated as a keyword of culture and society in English by many scholars, e.g., [3, 4], and [5]. Its Chinese equivalent *gaige* is also gaining attention. Adopting a historical semantics approach, Li et al. [6] compared the Chinese keyword 改革 *gaige* and the English word *reform*, revealing their diachronic changes and current lexical behavior. Li and Wang [7] further compared *gaige* between the Chinese Mainland and Taiwan, finding the significance and impact of reforms in the two societies and revealing the social, cultural, and political factors behind. The two most recent studies are just a beginning of lexical research on the Chinese significant socio-cultural keyword *gaige,* addressing the interlingual comparison and the comparison between regional varieties.

Since *gaige* is not the only lexical instantiation of the concept of reform in Chinese, the word behavior and frequency change of *gaige* alone may not fully reflect the change of various reforms and the complex social reality. Hilpert [8] expressed similar concern in using vast diachronic database that corpus frequencies are not always equivalent to frequencies of entities and events in the real world. There are many other expressions of reform events that are not named *gaige* in Chinese history. Various reforms range from the milder ones like *gailiang*, *gaizhi*, *gexin*, *weixin*, *xinzheng*, and *bianfa* to the more radical and violent ones such as *geming* and *qiyi* can be found in examples of Shang Yang Bianfa (商鞅變法 Shang Yang Reform), Wang Mang Gaizhi (王莽改制 Wang Mang Restructuring), Wang Anshi Bianfa (王安石變法 Wang Anshi Reform), Wuxu Bianfa (戊戌變法 also named Bairi Weixin, Hundred Days of Reform), and Xinhai Geming (辛亥革命 the Revolution of 1911). Through consulting dictionaries and relying on native speaker's intuition, nine reform-related near synonyms in Chinese are selected as shown in Table 1. The scope is now expanded from the single word *gaige* to a list of Chinese 'reform' words in this study. Two research questions are proposed: 1. What are the diachronic changes of reform-related Chinese near synonyms and how do they interplay? 2. What are the reasons for such changes and interplay?

Following the brief introduction, the paper demonstrates the research methods in Section Two, presents major research findings in Section Three, and discusses the results and draws a conclusion in Section Four.

2   Method

Our methodology generally belongs to the field of corpus linguistics as an empirical and quantitative approach to studying language in real life [9]. In particular, we focus on identifying the widespread patterns of naturally occurring language that may be overlooked by a small-scale analysis [10]. Near synonym-driven research is one of the most productive fields in corpus linguistics, e.g., [11] and [12]. By minimizing the lexical contrast, the word frequency distribution in corpora lead to pinpointed linguistics accounts. Due to the constraint of each available ancient Chinese corpus, it is difficult to describe the changes with one single corpus or database. So, we made use of several complementary historical Chinese corpus resources.

The first resource used is the CCL corpus [13] developed by the Center for Chinese Linguistics at Peking University. It contains rich historical Chinese texts from the Zhou dynasty (1046 BC–256 BC) to the Republic of China (ROC, 1911–1949). Tagged with dynasty information, the corpus serves as a good resource to trace the etymology and enables a finer observation of the changes of occurrence of the words across time. However, to retrieve the trends throughout the thousand-year long Chinese history is too complicated and cannot be covered in such a limited space. Thus, after a brief picture is depicted across dynasties, the focus will be shifted to the use of 'reform' words in the most recent one and a half centuries during which the Chinese society has undergone radical changes, transforming from feudal to capitalist and further to socialist society. We will draw on two main resources to describe the trends of these words from the late Qing Dynasty to present. One is Quan Guo Bao Kan Suo Yin (CNBKSY, national index of journals and newspapers) which is used to describe the trends of this set of near synonyms from the late Qing dynasty to the mid-20th century. Another is the BCC corpus [14], which is used to track the change after the establishment of The People's Republic of China in 1949.

The CNBKSY, founded in 1955 by Shanghai Library, is currently a comprehensive knowledge service system that integrates an online service platform with printed versions. Covering a time span from 1833 to 1952, CNBKSY is a valuable collection of journals and newspapers published from the late Qing dynasty to the early years of People's Republic of China. The available data used for retrieving the words from the CNBKSY database include Volume 1 and Volume 2 of Chinese Periodical Full-text Database (1911–1949, 民國時期期刊全文數據庫), the North-China Daily News & Herald Newspapers and Hong Lists (1850–1951 字林洋行中英文報紙全文數據庫), and the Chinese Historical Journals of Guangdong-Hong Kong-Macao (粵港澳中文歷史期刊全文數據庫). In the trial searches of these words in the database, the occurrence of *gexin* was found a little unreasonably high compared with the previous findings in BCC and CCL. This is because every item published in the journals and newspapers with *gexin* in their names was counted in occurrence, e.g., *Gexin Hao* 革新號 and *Gexin* (*Guangdong*) (革新(廣東)). Therefore, the search of each word is confined to the article's title, abstract, or body of each entry.

Two sub-corpora in the BCC corpus are used. The BCC ancient Chinese subcorpus is used as an extra source of information in addition to CCL. The BCC diachronic sub-corpus with data from People's Daily published from 1946 to 2015 is to investigate the change of these words in recent decades. The CNBKSY and BCC diachronic sub-corpus data are both from print media and are complementary in time coverage.

3   Results

This section investigates the diachronic change of Chinese reform-related near syn-onyms. Table 1 lists the nine near synonyms with their times of occurrence in the ancient Chinese corpora of BCC and CCL. The ancient Chinese sub-corpus in BCC does not allow the retrieval of data by period, thus the numbers in the second column of Table 1 indicate times of occurrence of each word in the whole sub-corpus. The third column of Table 1 shows the occurrence of these words from Zhou dynasty to Qing dynasty in CCL ancient Chinese corpus. Although data from ROC period are included in the CCL ancient Chinese corpus, it is listed separately since the Chinese language during that period was not so 'ancient' and the nature of the social system was totally different. Different from normalized frequency, the number of occurrences cannot reveal the diachronic changes of frequency of each word, but it depicts roughly which words among this set of near synonyms were more commonly occurred in the corpus. Overall, *weixin*, *geming*, and *qiyi* are the top three most frequently occurred words among the nine in both BCC and CCL ancient Chinese corpora but with different order, i.e., *weixin*, *geming*, and *qiyi* in BCC and the other way around in CCL. The reason for *weixin* being ranked the first place in BCC is that many occurrences of *weixin* are found in names for persons and places. *Weixin* can be a good name because its two com-posing characters 維*wei* means to maintain/keep and 新*xin* means new/fresh, both having good connotations. However, *geming* (revolution) and *qiyi* (uprising) may not be a good choice for names according to their meaning and our native speakers' intuition. So, *geming* and *qiyi* are in fact the most frequently occurred words among the nine in ancient Chinese. *Gailiang* and *gexin* are the least ocurred. *Bianfa*, *gaizhi*, *gaige*, and *xinzheng* are ranked somewhere in the middle. These are general observations regarding the popularity of each single 'reform' word in ancient Chinese. More detailed diachronic changes of occurrence are observed through retrieving these words dynasty by dynasty in the CCL corpus.

Table 1. Occurrences of reform-related Chinese words in ancient Chinese corpora

Words	BCC-ancient	CCL-ancient		
		Zhou to Qing	ROC	Total
weixin 維新	7586 (1)[a]	186 (3)	132	318
geming 革命	7155 (2)	233 (2)	445	678
qiyi 起義	5550 (3)	342 (1)	220	562
bianfa 變法	5495 (4)	119 (4)	67	186
xinzheng 新政	3719 (5)	72 (7)	124	196
gaizhi 改制	2503 (6)	103 (5)	24	127
gaige 改革	2487 (7)	103 (5)	79	182
gailiang 改良	943 (8)	13 (8)	46	59
gexin 革新	309 (9)	2 (9)	13	15

[a]The number in the bracket indicates the rank of the word's occurrence in the corresponding corpus.

Taking advantage of the dynasty information provided by CCL ancient Chinese corpus, we carried out dynasty-by-dynasty retrieval of these words to trace their source and historical use. CCL's category of dynasties includes Zhou, Spring and Autumn Period, Warring States Period, Western Han, Eastern Han, Six Dynasties, Tang, Five Dynasties, Song, Yuan, Ming, Qing, and Republic of China (shortened in Table 2 as Z, SA, WS, WH, EH, SD, T, FD, S, Y, M, Q, and ROC respectively). Table 2 presents the occurrence of each word in CCL from Zhou dynasty to Qing dynasty except the short-lived Sui dynasty during which none of these words were retrieved. The earliest dynasty each word occurred was shaded grey. *Weixin* and *geming* recorded the earliest occurrence in Zhou dynasty as in 周雖舊邦, 其命維新 (Although Zhou is an old state, its mission lies in innovation) from *The Book of Songs* and 汤武革命 (Shang's and Tang's Revolutions) from *The Book of Changes* respectively. *Gailiang, bianfa*, and *gaizhi* also have a long history dating back to the Spring and Autumn Period and the Warring States Period. *Gexin* appeared the latest in Song dynasty and it also occurred the least of times in the corpus.

Table 2. Occurrences of reform-related Chinese synonyms in each dynasty in CCL

	Z 周	SA 春秋	WS 戰國	WH 西漢	EH 東漢	SD 六朝	T 唐	FD 五代	S 宋	Y 元	M 明	Q 清
weixin	2	1	3	1	0	14	5	0	80	0	13	67
geming	1	1	2	0	4	17	35	3	93	0	12	65
qiyi	0	0	0	0	0	13	6	2	181	4	50	86
bianfa	0	0	11	6	1	3	2	0	33	0	10	53
xinzheng	0	0	0	0	1	0	5	0	13	0	8	45
gaizhi	0	0	1	1	12	6	12	0	31	0	3	36
gaige	0	0	0	0	0	9	12	0	48	0	10	24
gailiang	0	1	0	0	0	0	0	0	0	0	0	12
gexin	0	0	0	0	0	0	0	0	1	0	0	1
total	3	3	17	8	18	**62**	**77**	5	**480**	4	**106**	**389**
cnf.	10	3	7	8	7	11	9	3	14	4	5	8

Taken this set of near synonyms as a whole, Song and Qing dynasties have the largest number of raw occurrences, followed by Ming, Tang, and the Six Dynasties. However, the raw number of occurrences are not comparable across dynasties as the data size of each dynasty is different. To enable comparison between dynasties, the cumulative normalized frequency (cnf) of these words in each dynasty taken as a whole is calculated. It is believed that the cumulative normalized frequency can reflect the social stability, dynamism, and innovation of each dynasty. If this set of words are more frequently used in a certain period, the society tends to be less stable, more dynamic, or more innovative. However, due to the limited size of data especially in the earlier dynasties, the calculated figures should be interpreted cautiously. Taken only the dynasties with at least 60 occurrences (**bolded** in Table 2) of these words into account, i.e., Song, Qing, Ming, Tang, and Six Dynasties, Song witnessed the highest cumulative normalized frequency, followed by Six Dynasties, Tang, Qing, and Ming. Song dynasty witnessed the highest cnf probably because Qingli Xinzheng (Qingli New Deal) and Wang Anshi Reform, two of the most well-know and influential reforms in ancient China, happened in this dynasty. The Six Dynasties recorded the second highest cnf because it is a period of fast regime substitution. Qing, with the second largest number of raw occurrences, is unexpectedly low in cnf. The well-known Hundred Days of Reform and the Late Qing reforms (1901–1911) are important historical events. Nevertheless, since the reforms occurred at the very end of the dynasty, literatures in that period were not able to cover the events as extensively or sufficiently as in Song dynasty and Six Dynasties.

In the following section, we focus more on the changes of these words in the most recent one and a half centuries during which China undergoes unprecedented social and political transformation. Figure 1 shows the diachronic changes of frequency of five Chinese reform-related near synonyms in the CNBKSY database, including *gexin, weixin, gaige, gailiang* and *geming*. To make the figure more reader-friendly, only the frequency change of these words from 1911 to 1949 are shown in Fig. 1, while the period before 1911 with few occurrences spotted are not presented.

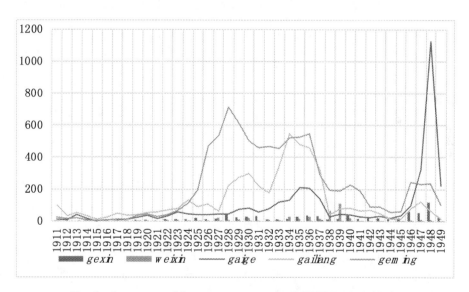

Fig. 1. Occurrence of five near synonyms in CNBKSY (1911–1949)

Overall, during the whole period from 1882 to 1949 covered by CNBKSY, *geming, gailiang,* and *gaige* have been recorded many more occurrences (8,685, 5,189, and 3,596 respectively) than the rest of the near synonyms. *Gexin, weixin, gaizhi, qiyi, xinzheng,* and *bianfa* have much fewer occurrences in the database. The least occurred four words are excluded from Fig. 1. Within the late Qing period (which is not shown in the figure), *gailiang, geming, weixin,* and *gaige* have relatively more occurrences.

However, the order of the top three most frequently occurred words changed to *geming*, *gailiang*, and *gaige* in the ROC period, which is different from what was found in CCL ROC sub-corpus, i.e., *geming*, *qiyi*, and *weixin* (see Table 1). The different distribution may be caused by the difference of source texts genre. The CCL ROC sub-corpus is made up of fictions, while the CNBKSY database is of journals and news-papers which are much more responsive to social reality and more reflective of the then social status quo. For example, *weixin* was not among the top three in the CNBKSY news database because it should be more likely a top word for the late Qing dynasty during which Bairi Weixin (Hundred Days of Reform) occurred.

The occurrence of *geming* raised significantly since 1921, peaked in 1928 with 715 times of occurrences, and maintained at a relatively high level until 1936. Then its occurrence reduced quickly from 547 times in 1936 to 61 times in 1945. *Gaige* raised steadily from 1921 to 1936 and then experienced a significant drop, keeping at a low level till 1946. Very abruptly, the occurrence of *gaige* surged from 97 times in 1946 to 1,126 times in 1948. There are two periods that witnessed the most frequent use of this group of near synonyms: one being 1924–1937 and the other being 1946–1949. The rise and fall of occurrences are a reflection of the social and historical background. The two periods are periods when China was in complicated domestic situations, under-going cooperation and conflicts between the Communist Party and Kuomintang, civil wars, competing of ideologies, and many other events and issues concerning the future of China. Between the two periods is a valley with a much smaller number of occurrences recorded (1938–1945). This is a period when China was facing the Japanese aggression and a period during which resisting the invaders was the main task for the nation. So, be it *gaige*, *gailiang*, or *geming*, reform/revolution is essentially an internal affair of a nation and it can give way to resisting external invading.

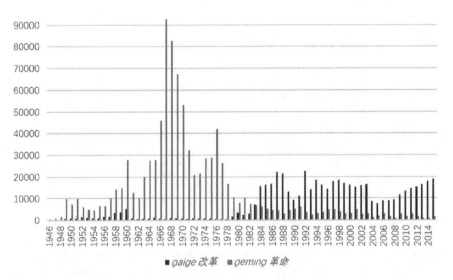

Fig. 2. The occurrence of *gaige* and *geming* in the BCC Diachronic corpus

The period after the establishment of the People's Republic of China in 1949 is a period with *geming* and *gaige* having the predominant number of occurrences. The cumulative occurrence for *geming* and *gaige* is 535,850 and 931,336 respectively, far exceeding that of the following words – *gailiang* at 20,301 and *xinzheng* at 15,965. Thus, the focus of this set of near synonyms is turned to *geming* and *gaige* as shown in Fig. 2. It can be observed that the frequency distribution of the two words illustrates an obvious shift. The year 1983 is the turning point when the frequency of *gaige* surpassed that of *geming* for the first time in the corpus. This is not simply a shift of word frequency, but an indicator of great transition of the Chinese society. Two significant historical movements brought about such changes. The first is the 10-year long Cultural Revolution from 1966 to 1976, which matches the peak of *geming* and bottom of *gaige* in occurrences. The second is the Reform and Opening-up initiated at the end of 1978 till now. Despite that the Cultural Revolution ended in 1976 and the Reform and Opening-up started in December 1978, it still took six years before *gaige* surpassed *geming* in terms of occurrence. The period after 1984 witnessed the relatively frequent and stable use of *gaige*, with only several years' (1990, 2004–2008) occurrence below 10,000 times. The drastic shift in the frequency of *geming* and *gaige* implies that the focus of the society has been shifted from ideological struggle to the improvement of social systems and economic development.

Looking at the trends of *geming* and *gaige* in both Fig. 1 and Fig. 2 together, the two words seem to have both a co-development and a competition relation. The two co-development periods are 1911 to 1923 and 1937 to 1945. The first co-development period from 1911 to 1923 falls into the first dozen years of the Republic of China and the Warlord Era during which the political situation was very unstable so that the government had no time to spare for reforms. This period features very few occurrences of both words during the first six years and followed by slow-paced increase till 1923. The second co-development period, the period for the War of Resistance against Japanese Aggression as mentioned above, witnessed similar downward trend in the use of both words. Also, there are two periods during which *gaige* and *geming* compete. One period situates in the ROC administration. When *geming* increased significantly and became predominant between 1924 and 1933, *gaige* remained at a low level of use, while, when *gaige* surged from 1946 to 1948, *geming* maintained a relatively low frequency. The other period of competition lies in the time of People's Republic of China. The year 1983 witnessed *gaige*'s surpassing of *geming* in occurrence and marked the replacement of the social keyword *geming* in the first half of the period by the keyword *gaige* in the later half. In this sense, *geming* and *gaige* are alternately two of the social keywords for China in the recent century, especially after 1949. Their interplay reflects the changes of ideology, social status quo and shifting themes of the society.

4 Conclusion

Started from looking at nine reform-related Chinese near synonyms, this paper narrows down its scope in words studied from the ancient dynasties to the recent century and further focuses on the lexical competition and co-development of *geming* and *gaige*. As is represented by *geming* and *gaige*, this group of near synonyms can be divided into two categories, one being the more sudden, radical and violent *geming* and *qiyi*, the other being the more progressive and milder *gaige*, *weixin*, and *gailiang*, etc. The first category usually takes the bottom-up approach, revolting against the government, while the second takes the top-down approach, led by the government. So, these two categories of words may alternate in position as the regimes or administrations undergo changes. It is never easy nor feasible to summarize a one-size-fits-all principle or co-relation between word use and history, but what we can confirm is that word changes are closely associated with social and political changes and rich historical information can be dug out through word changes. This study is an initial effort to relating a number of socially and historically significant synonyms to the thousand-year long history of China through corpus linguistic enquiry. It enriches previous studies on *gaige* as in [6] and [7] and studies on socially significant near synonyms as in [11, 12, 15]. In the future, more detailed and specific studies can be conducted with a closer examination of concordances which provides richer information and more contexts. The big data approach, digital humanities, philology, and history can also offer new insights.

Acknowledgments. The first and the second authors would like to acknowledge the research project RP/FLT-04/2022 supported by the Macao Polytechnic University.

References

1. Qi, X.: A History of Reforms in China. Hebei Education Press, Shijiazhuang (1997).(in Chinese)
2. Qi, X., Jiang, X.: Preface of general history of reforms in China. J. Hebei Univ. (Philos. Soc. Sci.) **04**, 38–40 (1998). (in Chinese)
3. Ryan, S.M.: Reform. In: Burgett, B., Hendler, G. (eds.), Keywords for American Cultural Studies. NYU Press, New York (2007)
4. Hindess, B.: Reform and revolution. In: Bennett, T., Grossberg, L., Morris, M. (eds.), New Keywords: A Revised Vocabulary of Culture and Society, pp. 300–304. Blackwell Publishing (2005)
5. Williams, R.: Keywords: A Vocabulary of Culture and Society. Oxford University Press. (1976, 1983, 2015)
6. Li, L., Dong, S., Wang, X.: Gaige and reform: a Chinese-English comparative keywords study. In: Su, Q., Zhan, W. (eds.) From Minimal Contrast to Meaning Construct: Corpus-based, Near Synonym Driven Approaches to Chinese Lexical Semantics, pp. 321–332. Springer, Singapore (2020). https://doi.org/10.1007/978-981-32-9240-6_22
7. Li, L., Wang, X.: Gaige (Reform) in Mandarin Chinese across the Taiwan Strait: a corpus-assisted comparative keywords study. In: Language and Culture Studies at Macao, pp. 104–113 (2019). (in Chinese)

8. Hilpert, M.: The great temptation: what diachronic corpora do and do not reveal about social change. In: Rautionaho, P., Nurmi, A., Klemola, J. (eds.), Corpora and the Changing Society: Studies in the evolution of English, pp. 3–27. John Benjamins (2020)
9. Teubert, W., Krishnamurthy, R.: Corpus Linguistics: Critical Concepts in Linguistics. Routledge, Milton Park (2007)
10. Baker, P., McEnery, T.: A corpus-based approach to discourses of refugees and asylum seekers in UN and newspaper texts. J. Lang. Politics. **4**(2), 197–226 (2005)
11. Li, L., Huang, C.-R., Gao, X.: A SkE-assisted comparison of three "prestige" near synonyms in Chinese. In: Hong, J.-F., Su, Q., Wu, J.-S. (eds.) Chinese Lexical. LNCS (LNAI), vol. 11173, pp. 256–266. Springer, Cham (2018). https://doi.org/10.1007/978-3-030-04015-4_22
12. Li, L., Huang, C.-R., Wang, X.: Lexical competition and change: a corpus-assisted investigation of gambling and gaming in the past centuries. SAGE Open **10**(3), 1–14 (2020)
13. Xun, E., Rao, G., Xiao, X., Zang, J.: The construction of the BCC corpus in the age of big data. Corpus Linguist. **3**(1), 93–109 (2016)
14. Zhan, W., Guo, R., Chang, B., Shen, Y., Chen, L.: The building of the CCL corpus: its design and implementation. Corpus Linguist. **6**(1), 71–86 (2019)
15. Wang, X., Huang, C.-R.: From near synonyms to power relation variations in communication: a cross-strait comparison of "Guli" and "Mianli." In: Hong, J.-F., Su, Q., Wu, J.-S. (eds.) Chinese Lexical Semantics. LNCS (LNAI), vol. 11173, pp. 155–166. Springer, Cham (2018). https://doi.org/10.1007/978-3-030-04015-4_13

Semantic Classification of Adverbial Adjectives Based on Chinese Chunkbank

Zhenzhen Qin, Tian Shao, Gaoqi Rao, and Endong Xun[✉]

Beijing Language and Culture University, Beijing, China
qyzybyzyjyzh@163.com

Abstract. The semantics and semantic classification of words play an important role in natural language processing. Existing adjective classification systems generally suffer from insufficient coverage and rough classification, and there are few classifications for adverbial adjectives. In this paper, we investigated adjectives in dictionaries and papers combined with automatically extracted context, fully considering the different semantic properties of adjectives in different contexts. In other words, adverbial adjectives were classified in this paper based on semantics combined with context. We finally segregated adverbial adjectives into 8 major categories, 19 middle categories, and 107 minor categories using semantic standards. This paper provides a reference for the semantic classification system of other parts of speech, and also helps the application of text sentiment analysis, retrieval, and man-machine conversation.

Keywords: Adjective classification · Adverbial adjective · Semantic classification · Chinese Chunkbank

1 Introduction

The words used to describe the characteristics of nouns are called adjectives [1]. Adjectives are often discussed separately from property-adjective and status-adjective[1] [2–4]. This paper doesn't analyze the validity of the definition, but refers to those parts of speech in the modern Chinese dictionary that are described as adjectives. Amongst adjectives, adverbial adjectives are used to modify predicates in the adverbial position, and mostly express the way or state of action. Previous research on adverbials mostly focused on adverbs, but there is less focus on adverbial adjectives in research. However, the frequency of adjectives used as adverbials in Chinese is second only to attributives and predicates, accounting for 19.1% of adjectives [5], and is therefore an important part of adverbial research. Previous studies on adverbial adjectives mostly revolved around their syntactic roles, that is, whether they can be used as adverbials, complements, and predicates [5–8]. Adverbial adjectives can modify sentences in terms of emotion, degree, frequency, state, etc., which makes language more accurate, and endows a unique value to adverbial adjectives (especially with respect to their semantic research).

---

[1] Property-adjective describes the attributes and inherent features of the object. Status-adjective describes the current status of the object.

M. Dong et al. (Eds.): CLSW 2021, LNAI 13250, pp. 194–206, 2022.
https://doi.org/10.1007/978-3-031-06547-7_16

The research on semantics is mostly based on semantic classification. From a theoretical point of view, semantic classification is more detailed than other forms of analyses and can be used in semantic research and semantic knowledge representation. From an application point of view, semantic classification provides reliable synonym clustering, and semantic support for retrieval systems, relationship extraction, emotional computing, and in automatic writing, which is indispensable in natural language understanding (NLU). However, existing semantic classifications generally suffer from insufficient coverage and inaccurate classification, and there are few studies on "adverbial adjectives". Yamada [6], He [8], and Liu [9] examined 1,115 and 666, and 918 adjectives, respectively. Zhu [2], Xing [10], Liu [11], Zhang [4] etc. divided adjectives into two kinds; Zhang [7] and Li [12] classified them into four kinds, and Wang [13], who provided the most detailed classification, divided them into 5 categories and 28 sub-categories.

In this study, adverbial adjectives are classified in detail. Starting from the semantic point of view, this study considers different semantic properties in different contexts, that is, it classifies adverbial adjectives by semantics and context. A total of 4,594 words in dictionaries and papers have been classified meticulously in this study into three-levels and a total of 107 categories.

2   Resource Construction

The data in this paper is divided into two parts: structure chunkbank data and adjective list.

2.1   Structure Chunkbank Data Resource Construction

Corpus-based research faithfully "reflects the use of language" [14]. The research data was obtained from the structure chunkbank created by Lu [15], which is large-scale, wide-ranging, high-quality, and well-labeled. As large as 2T, the corpus is constantly updated, covering news, encyclopedias, legal documents, patents, literature, etc. It emphasizes the predicate chunk and the boundary between the central predicate and the adverbial and complement. It ensures that the extracted structures are all "adjective + verb", which is highly pertinent, and thereby avoids interference from complex attributives, decreases the review work, and ensures extraction accuracy.

The structure chunkbank focuses on labeling predicate chunks. The extraction was carried out in the structured corpus, which looks like:

(ROOT (IP (VP-PRD (NULL-MOD 全面) (VP-PRD 推进)) (NP-OBJ 依法治国的

战略部署)))

The orange "VP-PRD" represents the predicate chunk, which contains the adverbial of "NULL-MOD". Automatic extraction is limited in the "VP-PRD" that contains "NULL-MOD", that is, in the orange brackets. The "NULL-MOD" before the predicate head is used as an adverbial to match the adjective table, and the following "VP-PRD" is extracted as the modified predicate head.

Language materials automatically obtained from a large-scale real-use corpus are authentic and wide-covered, but suffer from the sparseness, domain bias, and noise of the corpus. As for manual acquisition, it is more detailed, but is subjective and has limited coverage [16]. The two steps—word list construction and corpus extraction used involved automatic extraction and manual verification, wherein, human resources assisted and verified the extraction, therefore maximize strengths and avoid weaknesses of automatic extraction and manual acquisition.

2.2   Construction of Adverbial Adjective List

Constructing the adverbial adjective list requires a wide-covering adjective list extracted from the corpus. Subsequently, sentences need to be extracted, wherein adjectives are used as adverbials, and contextual judgments need to be artificially synthesized. Finally, adjectives that can be used as adverbials were put in the list.

Source of the Adjective List. The adjective list used in this study is composed from two word lists—4,898 words from dictionaries and 762 words from papers.

The dictionary word list includes all the adjectives extracted from the seventh edition of the "Modern Chinese Dictionary" [17], totaling 4,898 words. It contains polysemous words, which may not be adjectives when used as adverbials, and the list needed to be filtered according to word collocation. Word collocations play a role in displaying and stipulating the meanings of polysemous words. Therefore, the choice of meanings of polysemous words must be determined according to the collocation of words in information processing [18]. Hence, it is necessary to examine the sense of each adjective and each extracted sentence, and then filter them grammatically and semantically. For example, only taking collocation into consideration, can we tell that "快走" means "③{副}赶快: 赶快走(③ adv. as soon as possible: leave as soon as possible)" or "①{形} 速度高: 快速走(① adj. high-speed: high-speed walking)"? Limiting "adjective senses as adverbials" instead of words or entry can eliminate the interference of adverbs and other senses. At the same time, it is also conducive to associate parts of speech with syntactic components as much as possible, and explore the law of adjectives in adverbial positions.

The paper word list refers to adjectives and overlapping forms of adjectives listed in papers of Zhu [2], Hu [19], Yamada [6], Zhang [4], and Liu [9], and includes 362 overlapping words and 392 common adjectives. Overlapping words include repetitions (such as "凉凉"), affixations (such as "凉冰冰"), and constructional overlapping words (such as "凉凉快快,傻了吧唧").

The above two word lists were combined and preliminarily screened according to whether the words appear in the position of adverbials. Finally, a total of 4,594 adjectives were obtained.

Construction of Adverbial Adjective List. The construction of the adjective list is divided into two steps—structure chunkbank verification and manual inspection.

(1)   Structure Chunkbank Verification

Based on the adjective list, we extracted sentences using adverbial adjectives from the structure chunkbank. We used "|VP-PRD (~)V VP-PRD|" to search the structure chunkbank, wherein, "~" represents each adjective traversed in the list, and VP-PRD means that the part in "| |" is the predicate chunk, and V stands for the predicate head. In general, the entire search query means "the predicate chunk in which the adjective in the list modified the predicate head". The output was limited to 50 characters before and after the predicate chunk, to preserve the context for manual verification.

(2) Manual Inspection

The extracted results were manually filtered, and only sentences that have adjective senses as adverbials were retained. Manual inspection consisted of two steps: grammatical filtering and semantical filtering. For each adjective, the unit of investigation was the sense in the dictionary.

The first step was to screen example sentences according to grammatical standards. Since the extracted data may have noise or a little mislabeling, manual inspection and denoising were required to reduce the influence on the statistical results. Python codes were applied to extract all the entries of adverbial adjectives in sentences in the "Modern Chinese Dictionary". According to the membership measurement table of verb-adverbial structure as proposed by Yuan [20], the verb-adverbial structure was screened, and the nominal positive structures and parallel structures were deleted.

The second step was to screen sentences according to semantic standards. There are many polysemies in Chinese, so it is necessary to keep the sentences with adjective senses of words in the list as adverbials, and delete other senses as adverbials, to ensure the accuracy of the adverbial adjective. After manual screening, the sentences needed to be sampled to estimate the quality of manual screening. The sampling process is as follows:

Firstly, we designed a questionnaire with 50 example sentences that resulted from the filter step extracted using random selection. We recruited 20 participants from linguistic and non-linguistic backgrounds, including 10 males and 10 females. The format of the questionnaire is as follows:

(1) 以Allenblum为首的一些3Drealms前雇员在家里搞起了地下开发， Pitchford听到这个消息后还跑来参观他们的成果。

【地下】dìxià①{名}地面之下; 地层内部: ～ 水|～铁道|～商场。②{形}属性词。秘密活动的; 不公开的: ～ 党|～工作|转入 ～ 。

【地下】dìxia{名}地面上: 钢笔掉在 ～ |～一点灰尘都没有, 像洗过的一样。

Then, the study participants were required to choose the most suitable meaning from the given dictionary senses to explain the bold words. If none of the senses was suitable, they had to note their own understanding.

The result showed that 92% of the questions received consistent and correct answers, which indicates that manual screening is reliable. For the other 8% where there were differences, we used the part of speech subordination scale table proposed by Yuan [20] to evaluate, as is shown in the following.

(2) 顺手晒晒, 8 cm 的比天高。

【顺手】shùnshǒu(～儿)①{形}做事没有遇到阻碍; 顺利: 事情办得相当 ～ |开始试验不很 ～, 也是很自然的。②{副}很轻易地一伸手; 随手: 他 ～ 从水里捞上一颗菱角来。③{副}顺便; 捎带着: 院子扫完了, ～ 儿也把屋子扫一扫。

The subordination degree of "顺手" to adverb is 0.7, and to adjective is 0.9, which shows that it is a less typical adverb and a typical adjective. In the sentence, the word meets all the measurement standards of the adverb, such as "can be used as an adverbial to directly modify predicate components such as verbs or adjectives, but cannot be used as the predicate and head predicate". At the same time, "顺手" in sentence (2) is rarely used as the predicate or head predicate – which further confirms that it is an adverb-adverbial.

(3) 运行30分钟, 可选择标准洗。

【标准】biāozhǔn①{名}衡量事物的准则: 技术 ~ |实践是检验真理的唯一 ~ 。②{形}本身合于准则, 可供同类事物比较核对的: ~ 音|~时|她的发音很 ~ 。

The subordination degree of "标准" to nouns is 0.9, and that to adjectives is 1, which suggest that it is a typical noun and adjective. In the sentence, it is closer to being an adjective according to the measurement standard such as "can be modified by the degree adverb 很" and "can be used as the predicate head or predicate", hence it is identified as having the adverbial adjective structure.

After measuring the words with objections using the part of speech subordination scale table, we get relatively accurate sentences that have the adverbial adjective structure. Then, the code was used to extract the adverbials and predicate heads to get the adverbial adjective list and the list of verbs modified by each adjective.

Analysis of Screened Results

After screening the words, a total of 895 adjectives were obtained that can be used as adverbials, of which 819 were retrieved from the "Modern Chinese Dictionary" [17]. It is worth mentioning that most of the frequently discussed color words cannot be used as adverbials.

Simple statistics of the filtered results show that 80% of adjectives that can be used as adverbials were disyllabic words. In addition, the average frequency of disyllabic adjectives in the chunkbank is much higher than that of other adjectives. See Table 1 for details.

Table 1. Frequency and proportion of adjectives with different syllables.

Adjective syllables	Number of words	Percentage	Frequency in the chunkbank	Average frequency of each word
Monosyllable	110	12.29%	15,057	136.88
Bisyllable	724	80.89%	191,501	264.50
Trisyllable	18	2.01%	127	7.06
Four-syllable	24	2.68%	158	6.58

3   Standard of Classification

From the perspective of semantics, this paper fully considers the different semantic properties of adjectives in different contexts, that is, adverbial adjectives are classified in this paper based on semantics combined with context.

As mentioned above, natural language processing is inseparable from the study of semantics and semantic classification. To do a good job in semantic classification, we must first formulate clear standards, which is lacking in the academic circle as regards the classification of adjectives. There are four categories of classification standards in various grammatical works, namely, syntactic role standard, argument number standard, formal structure standard, and semantic feature standard, of which the last one is most used.

Semantic classification is one of the common means to describe semantic features [21]. Zhu [2] divided adjectives into qualifying adjectives and state adjectives. Zhang [7] classified reduplicated adjectives into color, situation, modality, and emotion. Li [12] divided adjectives into qualifying, form, state, and degree adjectives. Liu [11] classified them into actors-descriptive and action-descriptive according to the object described, and also divided them into positive and negative adjectives according to the emotions. Wang [13] divided adjectives into the following: event value, physical value (concentration, temperature, color, length, width, and height), human-related value (age, character, relationship, situation), spatial value (far and near, flat and oblique, neat and messy), and time value (early and late, long and short). Lu [22] proposed "attribute value" and "attribute domain" for verbs and predicable adjectives, including 36 categories, namely distance, color, time, psychology, etc.

A large part of adverbial adjectives are emotional words[2], and academic circles have a more detailed classification of emotional words for application. Due to the needs of text emotion computing, computational linguistics has paid much attention to the classification of emotion words in recent years, and semantic features are often used as the classification criteria of emotion words. Both, the National Taiwan University Semantic Dictionary and Jun Li of Tsinghua University[3], classified emotional words into negative and positive according to their emotion. HowNet is more detailed: it divided emotional words into propositions, positive emotions, positive evaluations, degree levels, negative emotions, and negative evaluations. Lin [24] made a secondary classification on this basis of 7 major categories and 21 middle categories. The 7 major categories were "happy, good, anger, sorrow, fear, evil, and surprise", and the 21 middle categories were mostly clusters of synonyms, such as "happy, relieved, respect, praise" etc. See the Table 2 below for details.

---

[2] Emotion is an attitude experience that people have about whether they meet their own needs [23]. The words expressing human emotions are called emotional words, including attitude, evaluation, emotion, or view.

[3] http://nlp.csai.tsinghua.edu.cn/site2/index.php/13-sms.

Table 2. Classification and comparison of emotional words.

Classification in this paper		Hongfei Lin
Positive emotions	Happy	Happy, Relieved
	Proud	
		Respect, Praise, Believe, Love, Wish
Negative emotions	Angry	Angry
	Sad	Sad, Disappoint, Guilty, Longing
		Panic, Fear, Shame
		Bored, Hate, Reprimand, Begrudge, Doubt
	Amazed	Amazed
	Anxious, Regretful, Downcast, Resigned	
Neutral emotion	Shy	
Degree	Extreme	Extreme
	Severe	Very
	Moderate	Relatively
	Slight	Slightly
		Insufficiently
	Excessive	Super
Perception	Style, Shape, Sound, Direction, Distance, Position	Perception
		Deem
Positive evaluation	Excellent, Vivid, Clear, Easy, Good-looking, Compliant, Close, Decent, Ingenious, Sublime, Successful, True, Magical, Cheap, Precise, Efficient	
Negative evaluation	Poor, Vague, False, Uncomfortable, Unjust, One-sided, Reverse, Difficult, Terrible, Abnormal	
Neutral evaluation	Normal, Equal, Common, Overt, Approximate, Subjective & objective, Amateur & professional, Pure, Direct & indirect, Paid & free, General & special, Natural & artificial, Cavalier	
Positive state	Firm, Solid, Comfortable, Calm, Casual, Hardworking, Proficient, Active, Healthy	
Negative state	Poor, Cold, Sloppy, Miserable, Ferocious, Confused, Tired	
Neutral state	Serious, Deadly, Secret, Innocent	
Positive character	Sharp, Brave, Smart, Practical, Careful, Enthusiastic, Sincere, Humorous	
Negative character	Stupid, Lazy, Wayward, Selfish, Pessimistic	
Frequency and quantity	Small amount, Large amount, All, Extra	
	Accidental, Often, Inevitable	
Time	Sooner & later, Permanent & temporary, Past & future, Fast & slow, Age	

The classification standards and category naming of adjectives and emotional words from the semantic point of view, and fully consider their different semantic properties in different contexts, that is, we combined context and used semantics as the classification standard.

The minor categories have been defined as per the following principles: share similar meanings and emotions, combine as much as possible, and lessen the number of sub-categories. To be compatible with other classification systems, the naming should be consistent with the predecessors, to the greatest extent possible.

4   Classification Results[4] and Analysis

4.1   Classification Results

After classification, a three-level semantic classification system is obtained, including 8 main categories, 19 medium categories and 107 subcategories, as is shown in Table 3, and the main and medium categories are as follows:

Table 3. Semantic classification results

Perception	Style	他手中的弹珠直直滚出，"啪"地撞上了地上的另一颗。
	Shape	"世界的眼睛"圆睁，"人类的良心"复苏。
	Sound	在 曹奎的带领下，树人小学合唱团的歌声悠扬响起。
	Direction	下午3点进园，沿着八一湖东岸顺时针走。
	Distance	站在楼前远远看去，402室阳台上晒有衣服。
	Position	相关负责人说，国庆的几天，展销会露天举行。
State	Positive state	数据显示，6月初楼市成交平稳上升。
	Neutral state	1971年，基辛格秘密来华。
	Negative state	由于当时双方年龄都偏大了，在父母的催促下草率结婚。
Emotions	Positive emotions	《芝麻开门》爆笑来袭，大王、肖骁两人欢乐搭档。
	Neutral emotion	女子依稀十四五岁光景，慢吟吟、羞答答唱着……
	Negative emotions	美国网友愤怒谴责："谁能告诉我这个白痴是谁?"
Character	Positive character	不久，女孩邀请程先生来安庆看她，程先生便爽快应约。
	Negative character	清风和黄濑任性抢球，把对方当作了得分游戏的道具。

(continued)

---

[4] The classification results of this article have been open source. Please refer to http://bcc.blcu.edu.cn for details.

Table 3. (*continued*)

Evaluation	Positive evaluation	另外, 农机类个股也出现不错上涨。
	Neutral evaluation	20日下午17时, 山阳县政府网站突然无法正常打开。
	Negative evaluation	华尔街时报对Castlight进行了负面报道。
Time		销售部的小张天天晚来早走, 也没见他拿回一个单子。
Frequency and Quantity	Quantity	德意志革命使得德国移民大量迁入。
	Frequency	北京某高校对98级新生调查表明, 8.77%的人经常失眠。
Degree		作为家人, 不要对他们过分苛求。

4.2   Result Analysis

Compared with the classification of adverbs, we found that the three categories of adverbial adjectives "degree, frequency, and time", which accounted for 37.24% of the frequency of all adjectives, are highly similar to the "adverbs of degree, time adverbs, frequency order adverbs, and range adverbs" [25].

The semantics provided by other categories are unique to adjectives, such as "emotion, characteristic, perception" and so on. He [8] proposed that the adjectives that can be used directly as adverbs are basically adjectives of quantity, time, frequency, scope, condition, or manner. Although the classification results of this study are somewhat different from their viewpoints, the general semantic categories obtained are similar.

After extracting the attributive clauses from the corpus, we found that all adjectives except for "决死" can be directly used as attributives. The total frequency is as high as 113,522,677 times, which is 553 times the frequency of adverbials (205,247 times). This shows that although adjectives are often used as adverbials, their main function is still attributive.

The frequency of each intermediate classification in the corpus is shown in Fig. 1:

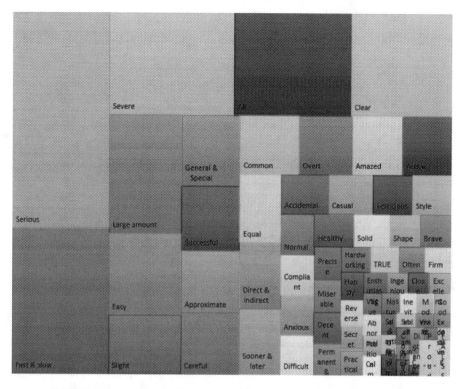

Fig. 1. The frequency of each intermediate classification in the corpus.

The category with the highest frequency and the highest average frequency of words is "Serious", which includes 14 words, namely, "严, 严密, 严肃, 庄严, 严正, 庄重, 俨然, 正经, 恭敬, 严格, 严酷, 威严, 正式, 隆重", with average frequency of 1,875.86 times, followed by the three categories of "all (1,243.42 times), successful (1,183.00 times), direct & indirect (1,135.00 times)".

Statistics on the classified adjectives show that the number of positive adjectives is significantly higher than negative adjectives, and the frequency of positive evaluation, state and character is significantly higher than the corresponding negative words; however, the opposite trend can be seen with respect to terms of "emotion" (Table 4).

Table 4. Frequency and number of positive/negative emotion words

	Total frequency	Number of adjectives	Average frequency	Illustrative sentence
Positive evaluation	34,379	174	197.58↑	1903年44岁的柯南·道尔在《空屋》中安排福尔摩斯巧妙归来。
Negative evaluation	4,211	54	77.98↓	如果某些个人或群体消极对待, CMR项目的价值将无法体现。
Positive state	11,167	72	155.10↑	铜陵等市积极跟进, 2015年前全省地级市均加入发布行列。
Negative state	3,546	40	88.65↓	记者1日获悉, 被马蜂叮咬的5人中3人不幸死亡, 2人受伤。
Positive character	7,277	72	101.07↑	踏踏实实耕耘, 熬才有出路, 没有什么捷径可走。
Negative character	121	11	11.00↓	一位银行人士悲观判断, 5年内香港甲组控股银行或消失殆尽。
Positive emotions	969	31	31.26↓	新丰的鸡犬看到我好像认识我一样, 欣然相迎。
Negative emotions	5,724	54	106.00↑	第二天在英德, 阿斯责备杉菜爽约, 杉菜愤怒离开。

5   Conclusion

In this paper, we covered adjectives in dictionaries and papers, and performed manual verification based on structured data extraction. Adjectives were divided into three levels based on semantics, and their context and senses were taken into consideration. Then, the clustering of synonyms with similar meanings and similar motions was obtained to improve the accuracy and comprehensiveness of information retrieval, machine translation, and question answering systems. This is also greatly beneficial to the advancement of emotional computing.

Compared with previous studies, this study enjoys the following characteristics:

1. Research on adjectives in adverbial position reveals the rules of adjectives as adverbials. Previous studies on adjectives rarely focused on grammatical roles, which was not conducive to exploring the characteristics of a certain grammatical position. The research on adverbial adjectives fills the gap and provides reference for research on other parts of speech and other grammatical roles.
2. The classification is systematic and detailed. The major categories are highly generalized, and the middle categories are classified according to emotional color and more detailed semantics, which lays the foundation for text sentiment analysis. The minor categories are mostly synonyms, which provide support for applications such as retelling, retrieval, and question answering.
3. The selection and classification are based upon examples from the corpus, and the different grammatical and semantic properties of adjectives in different contexts are fully considered, that is, the categories are divided in combination with specific contexts.

4. The automatic extraction of corpus is combined with manual verification, and both breadth and fineness are taken into account.

However, the semantic classification of adjectives was done manually, so it is inevitable that subjectivity may affect the classification results, although a large number of real example sentences in the corpus have been referenced. In addition, due to the limitation of the size of the corpus, there are omissions or field biases in language phenomena. This problem can only be solved by the continuous supplementing and improvement of the corpus.

Appendix

Take a query for example:

Condition("$1 = [AABB];mid($2)! = [起来 上去 下去 上来 不起 得 出去 进来 进去 出去 不好 不定 个不停];len($2) = 2")

Handle0=GetAS("$VP-PRD","","","","","","","","","")

Handle1=GetAS("|V","","~","","","","0,1","1,0","","")

Handle2=JoinAS(Handle0,Handle1,"SameLeft")

Handle3=Context(Handle2,50)

$1 indicates an adjective used as an adverbial, *$2* indicates a head predicate (mostly a verb), and *len* means the length. *mid($2)!* = means that the verb does not contain auxiliary verbs such as "起来".

Handle marks different atomic query items with serial numbers. *GetAS* means to qualify an atomic query item, and *$VP-PRD* defines the chunk as a predicate chunk. Handle0 indicates that the atomic query item with the label "$VP-PRD" is obtained.

V means defining the part of speech of the atomic query item as a verb, ~ means any adjective in the adjective list AABB, and *0,1* describes the position of the atomic query item. *Handle1* represents the atomic query item that gets the adjective followed by the verb in the table.

JoinAS represents the order and relationship type of two atomic query items at the time of assembly. *SameLeft* indicates that the relationship between two atomic query items is left aligned. *Handle2* indicates that adjectives and verbs co-exist in a predicate block, and the adjacent adjectives and verbs are right aligned.

Context represents the context of the output retrieval formula, where *50* means 50 words are extracted before and after the output retrieval formula.

References

1. Wang, L.: Modern Chinese Grammar. Zhonghua Book Company, Beijing (1943). (in Chinese)
2. Zhu, D.-X.: Lectures on Grammar. The Commercial Press, Beijing (1982). (in Chinese)

3. Lu, J.-M.: A Course for Chinese Grammar. Peking University Press, Beijing (2003). (in Chinese)
4. Zhang, B.: A Descriptive Grammar of Chinese. The Commercial Press, Beijing (2010). (in Chinese)
5. Mo, P.-L.: A statistical analysis of the syntactic functions of three notional words. J. Nanjing Normal Univ. (Soc. Sci. Edn.) **3**, 55–63 (1985). (in Chinese)
6. Ruriko, Y.: An investigation of disyllabic adjectives as adverbial modifier. Chinese Teach. World. **3**, 27–34 (1995). (in Chinese)
7. Zhang, A.-M.: A comparison between reduplicated adjectives as adverbials and other components. Lang. Teach. Linguist. Stud. **2**, 67–78 (1996). (in Chinese)
8. He, Y.: A study on the use of qualitative adjectives as adverbials. Linguist. Res. **1**, 13–18 (1996). (in Chinese)
9. Liu, Z.-P.: A Cognitive Semantic Study of Adjectives as Adverbials and Complements. The Commercial Press, Beijing (2015). (in Chinese)
10. Xing, F.-Y.: Modern Chinese. Higher Education Press, Beijing (1993). (in Chinese)
11. Liu, Y.-H.: The Practical Grammar of Modern Chinese. The Commercial Press, Beijing (2001).(in Chinese)
12. Li, J.-X.: The New Chinese Grammar. The Commercial Press, Beijing (1924/1998). (in Chinese)
13. Wang, H.: Structure and application of the semantic knowledge-based of modern Chinese. Appl. Linguist. **1**, 134–141 (2006). (in Chinese)
14. Stubbs, M.: Words and Phrases: Corpus Studies of Lexical Semantics. Blackwell Publishers, Hoboken (2001)
15. Lu, L.: A discourse-base Chinese chunkbank. ACTA Autom. Sin. 1–12 (2021). http://kns.cnki.net/kcms/detail/11.2109.TP.20200521.1558.007.html. (in Chinese)
16. Dong, Z.-D., Dong, Q.: Some issues on IT-oriented lexical semantics. Appl. Linguist. **3**, 27–32 (2001). (in Chinese)
17. Dictionary Editorial Office of Institute of Linguistics: CASS: Modern Chinese Dictionary, 7th Edn. The Commercial Press, Beijing (2016). (in Chinese)
18. Lin, X.-G.: Word collocation and related research. Lang. Teach. Linguist. Stud. **4**, 18–25 (1994). (in Chinese)
19. Hu, M.-Y.: A Preliminary Study of Beijing Dialect. The Commercial Press, Beijing (1987). (in Chinese)
20. Yuan, Y.-L.: Classification Manual of Chinese Word Category. Beijing Language and Culture University Press, Beijing (2009). (in Chinese)
21. Wang, Y., Cao, C.-G.: Research on categorization of events based on event attributes. J. Chinese Inf. Process. **34**(10), 39–50 (2020). (in Chinese)
22. Lu, C.: Linguistics for Knowledge Engineering. Tsinghua University Press, Beijing (2010). (in Chinese)
23. Lin, C.-D.: LIN Chongde The Comprehensive Dictionary of Physiologye. Shanghai Educational Publishing Press, Shanghai (2003). (in Chinese)
24. Xu, L.-H., Lin, H.-F., Pan, Y.: Constructing the affective lexicon ontology. J. China Soc. Sci. Techn. Inf. **27**(2), 180–185 (2008). (in Chinese)
25. Shao, T., Wang, C., Rao, G., Xun, E.: The semantic change and distribution of adjoining adverbs in modern Chinese. In: Su, Q., Zhan, W. (eds.) From Minimal Contrast to Meaning Construct. FCL, vol. 9, pp. 149–163. Springer, Singapore (2020). https://doi.org/10.1007/978-981-32-9240-6_11
26. Ding, S.-S., Lv, S.-X., Li, R., Sun, D.-X., Guan, X.-C.: Lectures on the Modern Chinese Grammar. The Commercial Press, Beijing (1961). (in Chinese)

Prepositional Frame Extraction and Semantic Classification Based on Chinese ChunkBank

Liyang Pang[1], Chengwen Wang[2], Guirong Wang[1], Gaoqi Rao[1],
and Endong Xun[1(✉)]

[1] Institute for Language Intelligence, Beijing Language and Culture University, Beijing, China
raogaoqi@blcu.edu.cn, edxun@126.com
[2] The MOE Key Laboratory of Computational Linguistics, Peking University, Beijing, China

Abstract. The "prepositional frame" is a formal marker that can introduce the predicate argument in the form of "A*B", where "A" is a front word, mainly a preposition, and "B" is a back word, mainly orientation words, noun words, conjunctions, verbs, and auxiliaries. The combination of front words and back words in Chinese is relatively fixed. In previous studies, scholars paid more attention to the circumstances where single prepositions are used as the marker of certain semantic components. However, prepositional frames in Chinese also function as markers of semantic components and occur at high frequencies in real life usage of language. The object introduced in the frame is often the argument of the statement verb, and both front and back words can be used as the explicit marker for argument elements. Therefore, based on previous studies, we extracted prepositional frames from the Chinese ChunkBank, semantically classified the extracted data according to the semantic role system of Wang Chengwen and opened the sources of the top 200 high-frequency frames for reference, to provide some knowledge support for both prepositional frame recognition and argument recognition in natural language processing, in this paper.

Keywords: Extraction · Preposition · Prepositional frame · Semantic classification · Semantic role

1 Introduction

Being an important word class in modern Chinese, prepositions have always been an important topic in grammar research. The study on Chinese prepositions was marked by the publication of Ma's Grammar. Li Jinxi's 1986 work A New Grammar of the Chinese National Language began the study of modern Chinese prepositions [1]. Since then, the academic study of prepositions has gradually intensified and notable progress has been made in the development, classification, and application of prepositions. But there is little research on "prepositional frames" and its study began at a later date. Since the beginning of the 21st century, many scholars have explored the cases of

M. Dong et al. (Eds.): CLSW 2021, LNAI 13250, pp. 207–220, 2022.
https://doi.org/10.1007/978-3-031-06547-7_17

prepositional frames, but so far, only a few of them, such as Chen [2–4], Liu [5, 6], and Wang [7], have analyzed the prepositional frame comprehensively and systematically, while even fewer have used corpus or big data to study them. Based on the review of the studies conducted by several scholars, we determined the composition and extension of prepositional frames, and extracted prepositional frames from large corpora. Given that prepositions can be used as the explicit marker of the argument-role relationship between predicate verbs and substantive components [8], this paper semantically classified the extracted prepositional frames according to the type of semantic roles that they represent, which provides certain knowledge support for both prepositional frame recognition and argument recognition in natural language processing.

2   State of the Art

This section discusses the current state of research on prepositional frames and establishes the objectives of this study.

2.1   Research on Prepositional Words and Circumposition

At present, the only comprehensive and systematic studies on the topic have been those by Chen [2–4], Liu [5, 6], and Wang [7], who analyzed prepositional frames in the field of academics. Chen used the term "prepositional frame", while Liu and Wang both called it "circumposition". This subsection briefly summarizes the viewpoints of scholars and provides a comparative summary.

On Prepositional Frame. Chen defines "prepositional frame" from three planes, namely syntax, semantics, and pragmatics [2, 3]. It refers to "a frame formed by a preposition in the front and other words at the back, with the object introduced by the preposition in the middle". The expressive function of this frame is basically the same as that of the prepositional phrase. Prepositions are the front part of prepositional frames, and other words collocated with prepositions, such as nouns of locality, are the back part. Chinese prepositional frames are divided into four categories according to the words following the frame:

(1)   The back word is a noun of locality, such as "从*起/以后/以来(from/after/since), 在*之前/之后 (before/after)".
(2)   The back word is a noun, such as "当*的时候, 在*的时候, 待/等/到*的时候 (when, at, till/until/up to)".
(3)   The back word is a conjunction, a verb, or a preposition, such as "从* 到/往/向, 打/打从*到 (from*to/towards, since/from*until)".
(4)   The back word is a quasi-auxiliary word, such as "按照*来说, 就*来看, 对于*而言 (according to, in regard to, speaking of)".

On Circumposition. Based on the theoretical results of Greenberg [9], Liu [6] defines "circumposition" as a type of adposition composed of a preposition and a postposition with the component dominated by the preposition in the middle [5]. The subordinate concept of "adposition" is formed together with preposition, postposition and circumposition. Liu suggests that prepositions that can form a phrase with NP independently before the NP, are prepositions, while those that can form a phrase with NP independently after the NP, are postpositions [6]; prepositions and postpositions can form circumpositions in sentences, which are usually temporary collocations and are mostly not fixed lexical items. Circumpositions are classified into four categories according to syntactic features, namely:

(1) Dual-component circumpositions, such as "在*上 (on)", "像*一样 (like)", "依* 起见 (for the sake of)".
(2) Verbal circumpositions, such as "对*来说 (for)", "就*而言 (in regard to)".
(3) Intensified circumpositions, such as "为*所 (by)", "跟*一起 (together with)".
(4) Linking circumpositions, such as "用*来 (use*to)", "拿*来 (take*to)", "通过*去 (by)".

Wang [7] referred to the definition by Liu [6] of circumpositions, but the extension is smaller than Liu's "circumpositions" and the definition is "stricter". He argued that circumpositions have at least three important features: firstly, the function of the whole frame is prepositional; secondly, the whole frame is a closed structure such that both the structure and the number of prepositions and postpositions are closed; thirdly, circumpositions are not lexical items but a syntactic phenomenon, with different scopes for prepositions and postpositions. Wang [7] also believed that the combination of circumpositions is temporary, rather than a fixed lexical item. He therefore considered that only the first two categories of the four categories made by Liu [6] are circumpositions in the strict sense and made these two categories the main object of his study. Circumpositions are divided into two categories: time-space category and non-time-space category. The time-space category includes three subcategories: place, time, and the beginning and the end; the non-time-space category includes five subcategories: exclusion, comparison, relevance, basis, and purpose.

Comparative Summary. We carried out a comparative synthesis of the work of these three scholars. Firstly, in terms of naming, Chen called the frame structure of "front component + dominated component + back component" as the "prepositional frame"; Liu named it "circumposition", and Wang continued to use this name. Secondly, Wang listed the categories and examples of front words while the other two illustrated that prepositions can be in the front part of the frame. Finally, the difference among the three on "back words" is the most obvious, which also reflects their different perspectives of study. Chen took three planes of syntax, semantics, and pragmatics as the theoretical basis, and believed that the structure is a frame to accommodate other components in the middle morphologically and a kind of word-word combination, and the back words are independent nouns, nouns of locality, conjunctions, auxiliary words, etc., except that the syntactic function of the frame is equivalent to that of a preposition. From the perspective of typology, Liu believed that "circumposition" is a concept subordinate to "adposition", and that the whole is prepositional. Some back words in Chinese in the prepositional frame that are classified as "auxiliary words" are actually postpositions. Wang made a finer distinction and argued that circumpositions are strictly closed prepositional structures, and that the back items of the 3rd and 4th types of circumposition in Liu's four classifications cannot be regarded as strict postpositions. The back words in the 3rd category, "跟*一起 (together with)" and "为*所 (by)", are not postpositional, and the whole frame cannot be regarded as a closed structure. The back items in the 4th category, "用*来 (use*to)" and "拿*去 (take*to)", are linking element. It is clear that they are closely connected to the predicate elements at the end, and therefore it cannot be regarded as a closed structure [7]. Therefore, only the first two categories are strictly circumpositions.

In addition to the above three scholars, other scholars have also provided a brief classification or description of frame structure. Shao [10] introduced the term of "structure construction" and defined it as "a typical frame formed by two incoherent words that coordinate and rely on each other". Shao [11] further classified them according to the characteristics of their structural forms. However, Shao's study aims at all the frames in Chinese language usage, and the prepositional frame is just one category without independent reference. Wang and Xin [12] pointed out that circumpositions can be classified into place circumposition "在*上 (on)", semantic circumposition "对于*而言 (for)", beginning-end circumposition "从*起 (from)" and "到*为止 (until)", purpose/motivation circumposition "为了*起见 (for the sake of)", passive circumposition "为*所 (by)" and "让*给 (by)", comparative/metaphoric circumposition "像*似的 (like)" and "比*来得 (than)", following circumposition "同*一起 (together with)", and linking circumposition "为*而 (for)" and "用*来 (use*to)". The paper lists the above classifications but does not mention the basis for classifications or the definitions. Zhan [13] mentioned that the attributive structure of "NP + of + VP" can be put into the preposition slot of "在*下 (上/中) (under(on/in))", i.e., he regarded "在*下 (上/中) (under (on/in))" as a slot.

2.2   Prepostional Frame in Our Definition

In this study, "prepositional frame" refers to the structure defined by Chen [2]. The structure consists of a front word, a back word, and an object introduced in the middle, the combination of front word and back word is relatively fixed, and the component between them is often the verb argument. By this time, the front word and back word become the explicit marker of the argument, so they are vividly called the frame. The frame as a whole, is prepositional, and the front words are basically prepositional, so the term "prepositional frame" is adopted. The focus of this paper is the extraction of prepositional frames using big data and the alignment classification of semantic roles based on the function of the introducing argument.

Slightly different from Chen, in this paper, we believe that the back words of the prepositional frame include nouns of locality, noun words, conjunctions, verbs, and quasi-auxiliary words, but not prepositions. In this paper, we used the front and back words as the marker of the frame and restricted front and back words by using rules to extract the frame. If the back word is a preposition, it needs to be followed by an introducing element, such as "从*到* (from*to)". By this time, the frame is not closed and lacks an explicit marker, so this case is not considered, temporarily.

It should also be noted that many scholars (Wang [7], Fang [14], etc.) believe that the "来/去 (to)" in "用*来/去 (use*to)" cannot be used as a back word of the frame as it is not closed and has no dependency. However, this paper starts from the perspective of introducing predicate argument. Any structure that is prepositional, with a collocation of front and back words and an introducing element in the middle is within the scope of this paper. At the same time, compared with the single formal marker "用 (use)", the formal "用*来 (use*to)" is more likely to introduce the argument component of the predicate verb. Therefore, the prepositional framework extracted in this paper includes the case where the back word is "来/去 (to)".

3 Extraction of Prepositional Frame

This section focuses on the resources of structural chunk and the extraction and noise reduction of prepositional frames.

3.1 Resources of the Chinese ChunkBank

The function of prepositions in syntactic structure is to introduce certain syntactic components and to form prepositional phrases together with them as modifiers of predicate verbs [2]. Therefore, the prepositional frame is mostly adjacent to predicate verbs and appears before or after the verb, such as "在餐厅里吃饭 (eat in the restaurant), 放在家里 (put (sth) at home)". Some of them can also be placed at the beginning of sentences, such as "针对法律而言 (for the purpose of law)". Based on this, we used the data from the Chinese ChunkBank in this paper [15]. The chunk has cut sentence components, and prepositional frames are the modifiers in the chunk (described in detail below). The chunk has now built a preliminary quality-assured superficial structure analysis tree to the scale of 10 million Chinese characters, including about 700,000 small sentences, and the corpus involves the texts in Baidu Baike, Sina, Xinhua News, national patents, legal judgments, elementary school students' essays, and other application fields. The annotations of the chunk include manual annotation, machine annotation, and manual proofreading, and the proof test values of data annotation consistency are all greater than 0.8.

With the unit of minor sentence, this chunk classifies sentence components into subject, object, sentence modifier, cohesive item, the "adnex", and auxiliary item, which are labeled with different symbols. The longest phrase block acting as predicate is the "adnex", as defined in the chunk. The adnex consists of a core predicate along with the adverbial modifier block and complement block that modify and complement the core predicate. In addition, some modifying or complementary components are not adjacent to the core predicate but are free before and after the main object. But such components, except for a few adverbial modifiers that appear only at the beginning of the sentence, can be considered as the components modifying and supplementing the core predicate. The adnex is indicated by "()", and the core adnex, adverbial modifier, and complement are distinguished internally by "()". The sentence modifier is indicated by "[]". These words that can modify core predicate are collectively called NULL-MOD (modifier), i.e., the underlined part in Examples 1 to 4.

Example 1: 他 *(狼吞虎咽地* (吃完了)) 饭。 *(He ((ate) his meal hungrily)).*
Example 2: [在他壮年时，] 他(爬上过)珠峰。 *([When he was young,] he (had climbed up) Mount Everest).*
Example 3: 北京 ((坐落) 于中国北部)。 *(Beijing ((is located) in the north of China)).*

Example 4: [别把孩子的教育，](全(寄))希望[于教育机构上]。(*[Don't (put) your child's education] (completely in the hands of) [educational institutions]*).

We extracted all the NULL-MOD from the chunk, a total of 4,000,039 entries, and used them as the original data for the extraction of prepositional frame.

3.2 Extraction of Prepositional Frame and Noise Reduction

This paper adopts an analysis-based method to extract the framework, and the specific process is shown in Fig. 1. The initial data are first subject to word segmentation and part-of-speech tagging, after which the linguistic knowledge is summarized manually by corpus observation and introspection. After that, the code is written to refine the frames and remove the stop words, before the frames with frequency information are extracted. Finally, frequency filtering and manual proofreading are performed. See Appendix 1 for the pseudo-codes of this process.

Word Segmentation and Part-of-Speech Tagging. All modifiers are extracted from the chunk for the frequency statistics. The results are shown in Table 1. Since the prepositional frame consists of at least three words, after word segmentation and part-of-speech tagging, the corpora with less than three words are first eliminated. The remaining corpus forms are shown in Table 2.

Frame Refinement. The extracted modifiers are presented in the form of lines, and each line may have more than one prepositional frame. There may be a case of prepositional frame collocation, in which case, line processing should be performed so that each line is a separate frame to be detected, starting with a preposition. If the first word of each line is not a preposition, it is deleted until the first word is a preposition. If there is no preposition in a line, the whole line will be deleted.

Example 5: "要/v 从/p 根本/n 上/f" → "从/p 根本/n 上/f" *(fundamentally).*
Example 6: "在/p 一定/b 程度/n 上/f通过/p 这种/r 方法/n 来/v" → "在/p 一定/b 程度/n 上/f", "通过/p 这种/r 方法/n 来/v" *(to a certain extent, to*by this method).*

In addition to frame collocation, the case of dual preposition is also taken into consideration, i.e., two prepositions appear at the same time. A total of 11,999 examples of adjacent PP are extracted, with the results shown as follows:

Class 1: The collocation of "对/p 于/p", e.g., "对/p 于/p 女人/n 来说/u" (for women); 6,642 examples in total.
Class 2: The collocation of "在/p X/p", e.g., "在/p 给/p 朋友/n 的/u 信/n 中/f" (in the letter to a friend); 4,271 examples in total.
Class 3: The collocation of "被/p X/p", e.g., "被/p 从/p 死亡线/n 上/f"
(be*from the death line); 122 examples in total.
Class 4: Incorrect frames, e.g., "把/p 对/p 这部/r 法律/n 的/u 修订/vn" (the revision of this law), "从/p 以/p 阶级斗争/l 为/p 纲/n" (with the guidance of class struggle); 1,186 examples in total.

It is found through observation that Class 1 is based upon the incorrect word segmentation of "对于" (for) by the segmentation tool, and is later modified to "对于/p" manually; Class 2 is the case where the preposition "在" is followed by other

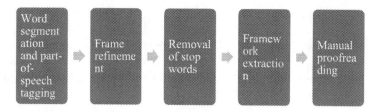

Fig. 1. Processing flow chart.

Table 1. Extracted NULL-MOD and frequency (excerpts).

NULL-MOD (modifier)	Frequency
也 (also)	302,166
已经 (already)	105,008
在研究项目最多的一线城市 (in the first-tier city with the most research projects)	23,948
一定要 (is sure to)	8520

Table 2. NULL-MOD after word segmentation and part-of-speech tagging. (excerpts)

在/p 一定/b 程度/n 上/f (to a certain extent)

很/d 大/a 程度/n 上/f (to a great extent)

在/p 很/d 大/a 程度/n 上/f (to a great extent)

根据/p 规范/n 来说/u (according to the specifications)

在/p 全国/n 范围/n 内/f (on a national scale)

在/p 此/r 基础/n 上/f (on this basis)

prepositions, which is eventually the correct frame in the form of "在*B[1]"; Class 3 only includes 122 examples, all of which are the cases where "被" is placed in front of the prepositional frame, and where the "被" at the beginning of sentences are deleted manually; Class 4 is the case where some nouns act as back words, and which cannot constitute a correct frame at all.

Removal of Stop Words. The components that cannot act as the back items of the frame are removed from every line for increased accuracy and efficiency of the frame. Based on the preliminary literature research and the definition of frame in this paper, by reference to the lexical coding of stuttering participles, it is determined that the part of speech of the back words of the frame in this paper are auxiliary words (u),

---

[1] B refers to a back word.

conjunctions (c), nouns of locality (f), time denoting words (t), verbs (v^2), and nouns (n^3). Thus, the adjectives, adverbs, quantifiers, exclamations, and idioms are deleted, as well as "的, 得, 地" in auxiliary words (u). See Appendix 3 for the details of the part of speech that are deleted. By this time, after checking the number of words, the frames consisting of only one word are also deleted. The frames with adjacent PP after processing are also subject to the above operation.

Frame Extraction and Proofreading. After removing the stop words, the starting and ending words of every line are subject to frame extraction and frequency statistics, producing 18,860 P*B frames, as shown in Table 3. In particular, the highest frequency is 135,166 while the lowest is 1. Based on the ranking from high to low of all the frames, it is found that low-frequency frames are completely dominant in terms of number, and the lower the frequency, the larger the number, however, the accuracy is low. The number of high-frequency frames is relatively small, but the accuracy is high. There are 7,768 frames that have the frequency as 1; 13,698 frames with the frequency less than or equal to 5 cumulatively; and 5,162 frames with the frequency greater than 5. As shown in Fig. 2, frames with the frequency of 1 accounted for 41% of the total number of frames, but only 1.1% of the total frequency; frames with the frequency greater than 5 accounted for 27.4% of the total number of frames, but 96.5% of the total frequency. By reference to the Ziff rate, we deleted the data that has lower frequency and selected the frames with the frequency greater than 5 as the object of further study, for manual proofreading. The incorrect frames were eliminated during the proofreading, and 741 frames were obtained after proofreading. The first 200 are open sourced for readers' reference[4].

4   Semantic Alignment and Classification of Prepositional Frame

In the syntactic-semantic system of modern Chinese, prepositions are not only used to identify the syntactic relation between linguistic components, but also as the explicit marker of semantic role relationship between predicate verbs and substantive components [8]. The optional components of the semantic structure of sentence, such as time, place, instrument, basis, scope, condition, reason, purpose, object of comparison, etc., are usually introduced by prepositions because of their distant relationship with the verb [4]. The required components of sentence, because of the close relationship with the verb, usually do not require prepositions to act as guides. However, they can also be introduced by some prepositions sometimes, such as "把, 被, 给". The syntactic function of prepositional frame is equivalent to that of a preposition and can also be used as a marker to show the role of argument.

---

[2] "从*看/说 (from the aspect of), 按*来/去 (according to)" and other structures, "看, 说, 来, 去", etc. are marked as v.

[3] "在*时候 (at the time of)" and other structures, "时候 (time)" is marked as n.

[4] http://bcc.blcu.edu.cn.

Table 3. Prepositional frame (excerpts).

Prepositional frame	Frequency
在 * 中 (among)	135,166
在 * 上 (on)	129,002
在 * 内 (within)	12,733
在 * 里 (in)	12,323
在 * 中 (from)	11,965
在 * 时 (when)	11,514
在 * 下 (under)	9,478
从 * 上 (on)	8,885

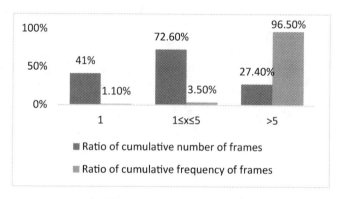

Fig. 2. Cumulative number of frames and frequency ratio.

Based on the analysis of the classification of Chinese semantic role by Yuan [16], Lu and Lin [17] and Zhu [18], Wang et al. [19] followed the "principle of opposites and complementarity", and effectively integrated the system of Yuan [16] Lu and Lin [17], forming a new integrated knowledge system. The system includes a total of 15 semantic roles, which are divided into core and peripheral semantic roles. Core semantic roles include subject, object, and neighbor; peripheral semantic roles include instrument, material, manner, basis, source, end point, scope, time, place, reason, purpose, and quantity. By reference to the semantic role system, a list of semantic role guide words that are often used together is generated. Based on this system and the guide word list, we made a preliminary semantic role alignment classification of prepositional frames and formed a correspondence between frames and semantic roles, in this paper. The specific quantities are shown in Table 4.

Table 4. Semantic classification of prepositional frame.

Semantic role	Quantity	Ratio	Total frequency	Average frequency	Example
Place	459	61.94%	384,095	837	在 * 上 (on)
Time	195	26.32%	34,367	176	于 * 初 (at the beginning of)
Source	8	1.08%	2,110	264	从 * 起 (from)
End point	2	0.27%	70	35	到 * 为止 (until)
Condition	5	0.67%	8,055	1611	通过 * 来 (through)
Purpose	2	0.27%	1,162	581	为 * 起见 (for the sake of)
Reason	4	0.54%	2,095	524	因为 * 而 (because of)
Basis	22	2.97%	5,979	285	按照 * 来 (according to)
Scope	23	3.10%	8,885	386	就 * 来说 (for)
Neighbor	19	2.57%	2,563	135	与 * 一起 (together with)
Object	-	-	-	-	-
Subject	2	2 0.27%	2,161	1080.5	为 * 所 (by)

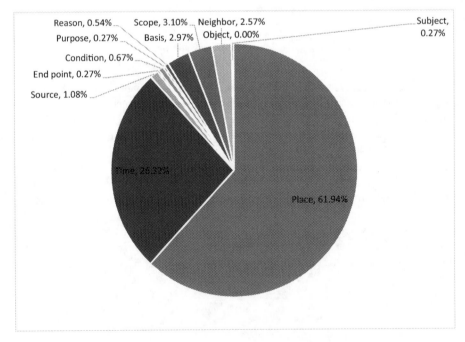

Fig. 3. Quantity ratio of every type of prepositional frame.

The peripheral semantic roles of sentence mostly need to be guided by prepositions, and prepositional frames mostly fall under this category. It can be seen visually in Fig. 3 that the most frequent frames correspond to the role of place, and the back words of the frames are mostly monosyllabic and disyllabic nouns of locality ("上, 下, 前, 南, 之上, 东南 (up, down, front, south, on, southeast)", etc.) as well as "附近, 中部, 中段, 周围 (near, middle part, middle section, around)", etc., which have the sense of place and can be collocated with a preposition to form a frame and then inserted into an argument to signify some nouns of specific place. The frames corresponding to the role of time are the second largest in number, and in this framework, the definition is more broad: anything that is often collocated with a preposition and can mark time is counted as a back word, including partial nouns of locality ("之前, 之内 (before, within), etc."), time denoting words ("中旬, 前期, 初期 (mid, before, early), etc.") and nouns of time ("晚上, 时候, 年, 月 (evening, time, year, month), etc."). The frames corresponding to the role of scope are mostly composed of the prepositions of "对, 对于 (for)" and the back words of "而言, 来说, 说, 来看". The frames corresponding to the role of basis consist of the preposition of "按照 (according to)" and "来, 而, 去". The prepositions such as "因, 因为 (because, as)" and "而" constitute the frames denoting reasons while "为, 为了 (for)" and "而, 起见" constitute the frames denoting purpose. The prepositions such as "在, 从, 自 (since)" and the back words such as "起, 以来" constitute the frames denoting source, and "至, 到 (until, till)" and "为止, 止" constitute the frames denoting end point.

The core semantic roles are generally not introduced by prepositions, but prepositions such as "被, 叫, 把, 将, 与, 和" can sometimes be used to introduce subjects, objects, and neighbors. In the introduction of core argument roles, the most prepositional frames capable of introducing neighboring argument components are "与/跟/同/和/连同* 一起 (with)", "跟/同/和/与* 一样 (the same as)", "除了/除* 外/之外 (in addition to/except for)" and other frames.

The semantics of some frames cannot be determined by the frames themselves. Frames consisting of prepositions such as "通过, 以, 用 (by)" and "来, 去, 而" can represent three roles, namely instrument, manner, and material, depending on the prepositional component. In this paper, they are collectively referred to as the components of condition, by reference to Lu et al. [20], and are specifically determined according to the introducing components. The category of place and orientation is the most basic relational category in human language, and many other relational categories can often be regarded as metaphors or derivations of this category, and are often expressed by borrowing the form or manner of the category of place [6], such as "除了 * 之外 (except for)". Some back words of the category of place can express both time and place, such as "在抽屉里/在七天里 (in the drawer/in the seven days)". In this paper, these multi-semantic frames are temporarily put into the category of place. The prepositional frames in the category of scope can also sometimes indicate the neighboring body, such as "对于法律而言/对于小张而言 (as for the law/for Xiao Zhang)". It is mainly because these two semantic meanings are intrinsically related. Exactly as Lu et al. [20] classified them to the category of 领体 in the classification system of case role, we temporarily classified it to the category of scope, in this paper. The number of each category is also related, to some extent, to the order of prototypical to derived categories in cognitive linguistics.

5 Conclusions and Future Work

By combing previous studies on prepositional frames, we define the composition and extension of prepositional frames and extract prepositional frames from the Chinese ChunkBank to get a total of 18,860 frames, with the highest frequency of 135,166 and the lowest frequency of 1. Due to the huge difference in the number of high and low frequency data, after analyzing the data performance, the first 27% or so of the high frequency frames, which total 5,162, were manually denoised to get 741 frames. Then, the extracted frames were classified from the semantic functions of prepositions by reference to the Chinese semantic roles, and the top 200 frames were open sourced for readers' access. However, there are two areas that still require further study and reflection:

1. The extracted part: (1) Accuracy of word segmentation: As the first step in data processing, word segmentation has a great impact on the accuracy of subsequent processing, and it is important to improve the accuracy of word segmentation; (2) Accuracy of frame: This paper takes part of speech as the entry point to extract prepositional frames from a large-scale corpus based on the markers of front and back words, aiming to go beyond the range of examples given by scholars to obtain as many frames as possible, thus ensuring the universality of frames. Therefore, the accuracy is not ideal. In the future, it is considered that integration on the basis of a sufficient number of frames already obtained should be carried out, and the method of Chinese thesaurus be applied to expand the front and back words of the frames again and test the generalized frames in a larger corpus.
2. The part of semantic classification: (1) In-depth analysis of the semantic classification of frames: This paper fails to make a detailed division of multi-semantic frames such as the category of place, and it is necessary to further refine this aspect in future. (2) The use of prepositional frames also suffers from the omission of front and back words; besides, the identification of the omitted prepositional frames also needs to be a focus of future study. (3) The data used in this paper comes from various fields, such as Baidu Baike, news, and legal judgments, and the semantic performance of prepositional frames in each domain is also worth exploring.

Appendix
Appendix 1

1. Pseudo-codes in the part of frame refinement
foreach every line **in** input file:
    while all the characters in one line:
        if the part of speech of the first character is not 'p':
            remove the first character
    foreach every line **in** input file:
        if the part of speech of this character is 'p':
            put 'p' in a new group, followed by other characters with the part of speech being not 'p'
2. Pseudo-codes in the extraction of PP collocation
foreach every line **in** input file:
    if be able to match the collocation of two characters with the part of speech being 'p' :
        output
3. Pseudo-codes in the processes of removal of stop words and frame extraction
foreach every line **in** input file:
    while all the characters in one line:
        if the part of speech of a character is one of ['d','a','w','m','nr','nt','ns','nz','r','的',
'地','得','了','Ag','ad','an','dg','e','h','i','j','k','l','o','vd','vn','vg','y','z','nx']:
            remove this character
        if the remaining length of this line is smaller than 2 or (the last character is a verb
and not one of ['看','来看','看来','说','来说','说来','讲','来讲','讲来','去','来']) or (the last
character is a noun and not '时候'):
            continue count and output (initial character+'____'+end character) and the
frequency

Appendix 2

See Table 5

Table 5. Table of part of speech deletion.

a adjective	Ag adjective morpheme	ad subsidiary adjective	an noun
d adverb	dg subsidiary morpheme	e exclamation	h front component
i idiom	j aabbreviation	k back component	l learned language
m numeral	nr name	ns name of place	r pronoun
nz other proper nouns	nt institution and organization	o onomatopoeic word	vd subsidiary verb
vg verb morpheme	vn noun-verb	w punctuation	y modal particle
z state word			

References

1. Guo, X.: A review of research on Chinese prepositions. J. Xuzhou Normal Univ. **01**, 136–143 (1986). (in Chinese)
2. Chen, C.-L.: Prepositions and Introducing Function. Anhui Education Publishing House, Hefei (2002).(in Chinese)
3. Chen, C.-L.: Research on Chinese "Prepositional Frame." Commercial Press, Beijing (2014). (in Chinese)
4. Chen, C.-L.: An analysis in pragmatic functions of prepositions in modern Chinese. J. Radio TV Univ. (Philos. Soc. Sci.) **02**, 46–49 & 55 (2005). (in Chinese)
5. Liu, D.-Q.: Circumpositions in Chinese. Contemp. Linguist. **04**, 241–253, 316 (2002). (in Chinese)
6. Liu, D.-Q.: Word Order Typology and Preposition Theory. Commercial Press, Beijing (2003).(in Chinese)
7. Wang, S.-Q.: Research on Circumpositions in Modern Chinese. Nanjing Normal University (2013). (in Chinese)
8. Liu, B.: Omission of Chinese prepositions and substitutions of hidden prepositions. J. Yunnan Normal Univ. **04**, 27–32 (2005). (in Chinese)
9. Greenberg: Circumfixes and typological change. In: Elizabeth, C., et al. (eds.) Papers from the International Conference on Historical Linguistics. John Benjamins, Amsterdam (1980)
10. Shao, J.-M.: The "Lian(连)A ye/dou(也/都)B" discontinous construction and its grammaticalization. Linguist. Sci. **04**, 352–358 (2008). (in Chinese)
11. Shao, J.-M.: On frame constructions in Chinese. Stud. Chinese Lan. **03**, 218–227287 (2011). (in Chinese)
12. Wang, L., Xin, M.: An investigation on the syntactic domain of circumpositions in modern Chinese. J. Liaoning Normal Univ. (Soc. Sci. Edn.) **37**(06), 874–878 (2014). (in Chinese)
13. Zhan, W.-D., Xin, M.: On the attributive structure of "NP+de+VP." Chinese Lang. Learn. **02**, 3–5 (1998). (in Chinese)
14. Fang, Q.-M.: A review of studies on Chinese postposition. Chinese Lang. Learn. **02**, 80–87 (2014). (in Chinese)
15. Lu, L., Jiao, H.-Y., Li, M., Xun, E.-D.: A discourse-base chinese Chunkbank. ACTA Automatic Sinica. 1–12 (2021). http://kns.cnki.net/kcms/detail/11.2109.TP.20200521.1558.007.html. (in Chinese)
16. Yuan, Y.-L.: Hierarchical relationship and semantic characteristics of argument roles. Chinese Teach. World **03**, 10–222 (2002). (in Chinese)
17. Lu, C., Lin, X.-G.: Case relations of modern Chinese grammar. Chinese Lang. Learn. **06**, 11–15 (1989). (in Chinese)
18. Zhu, X.-Y.: Studies on Semantic Structure Patterns of Sentences in Modern Chinese. Peking University Press, Beijing (2001).(in Chinese)
19. Wang, C.-W., Qian, Q.-Q., Xun, E.-D., Xing, D., Li, M., Rao, G.-Q.: Construction of semantic role bank for Chinese verbs from the perspective of ternary collocation. Journal of Chinese Information Processing **34**(09), 19–27 (2020). (in Chinese)
20. Lu, C.-W., Gou, R.-L., Liu, Q.-R.: Tetravalent verbs of trade and classification ofverbal valence in Chinese. Chinese Language Learning **06**, 7–17 (2000). (in Chinese)

From Complex Emotion Words to Insomnia and Mental Health: A Corpus-Based Analysis of the Online Psychological Consultation Discourse About Insomnia Problems in Chinese

Xiaowen Wang[1,2] , Yunfei Long[3,8(✉)] , Panyu Qin[1],
Chunhong Huang[1], Caichan Guo[4], Yong Gao[5],
and Chu-Ren Huang[6,7]

[1] School of English Education, Guangdong University of Foreign Studies,
Guangzhou, China
xiaowen-annie.wang@connect.polyu.hk,
chunhong_huang@yeah.net

[2] Faculty of Humanities, The Hong Kong Polytechnic University, Kowloon,
Hong Kong

[3] School of Computer Science and Electronic Engineering, University of Essex,
Colchester, UK
yl20051@essex.ac.uk

[4] Department of Electronic Business, Guangdong University of Foreign Studies,
Guangzhou, China

[5] Reproductive Medicine Center, The Key Laboratory for Reproductive
Medicine of Guangdong Province, The First Affiliated Hospital of Sun Yat-sen
University, Guangzhou, China
gyong@mail.sysu.edu.cn

[6] Department of Chinese and Bilingual Studies, The Hong Kong Polytechnic
University, Kowloon, Hong Kong
churen.huang@polyu.edu.hk

[7] The Hong Kong Polytechnic University-Peking University Research Centre
on Chinese Linguistics, Kowloon, Hong Kong

[8] Fujian Provincial Key Laboratory of Information Processing and Intelligent
Control, Minjiang University, Fuzhou, China

Abstract. This paper reports the preliminary findings of a cross-disciplinary research on emotions, insomnia and mental health with joint efforts from linguistic, computer science, and medical researchers. We take a computational linguistic approach to analyze a corpus of over 400 posts crawled from online psychological consultation platforms in China that complaint about insomnia problems, with annotations for the psychiatric conditions of post contributors made by professional psychiatrists. Based on results of our automatic analysis of six basic emotions in the posts and their intensity levels, logistic regression and artificial neural network models were successfully performed to predict the mental health conditions of post contributors. Relevance analysis were further run to explore the associations among emotion types and between emotions and

© Springer Nature Switzerland AG 2022
M. Dong et al. (Eds.): CLSW 2021, LNAI 13250, pp. 221–232, 2022.
https://doi.org/10.1007/978-3-031-06547-7_18

the psychiatric disorders of depression and anxiety. Depression and anxiety were found to have divergent association patterns with the basic emotion types. Overall, the findings support the previous hypothesis that emotions modulate insomnia and psychiatric disorders, and have important linguistic and clinical implications.

Keywords: Insomnia · Complex emotions · Depression · Anxiety · Psychiatric disorder

1 Introduction

Insomnia, also called insomnia disorder, refers to the subjective feeling of having difficulties initiating or maintaining sleep or of non-restorative sleep [1]. It is the most common kind of sleep disorder, and also one of the major global burdens of disease (GBD) [1]. In China, 57% of the adults reported insomnia symptoms in a survey conducted by the Sleep Disorders Group of Chinese Society of Neurology in 6 cities in the Chinese Mainland [2], which is much higher than the ratios in the similar epidemiological studies conducted in Europe and North America (20%–35%) [1, 3] and in Hong Kong (39.4%) [1]. The aetiological mechanisms of insomnia are complicated. On the one hand, many studies [4–7] have pointed out that insomnia is associated with emotion dysregulation, showing that emotion dysregulation leads to the maintenance of insomnia [4], and insomnia also has the potential to reinforce emotional problems [5, 6]. In traditional Chinese medicine, excessive emotion disturbance is even emphasized as the most important cause of insomnia [8]. On the other hand, bidirectional association between insomnia and psychiatric disorders of depression and anxiety has also been discovered [5, 9], with insomnia being a risk factor for depression and anxiety, and vice versa. Based on a review of 72 medical publications on emotion and sleep disorder, Baglioni et al. [5] postulates that the relationship between insomnia and psychiatric disorders such as insomnia and depression might be modulated by emotion dysregulation, and highlights that a deeper investigation into the mechanisms of insomnia, mental disorders and emotions is needed for developing effective treatments and preventative interventions. These studies have generally confirmed that poor sleep quality is associated with high negative emotions and low positive emotions [5], yet we find that there are significant gaps to be filled. First, previous studies mostly consider the interaction between sleep and emotional valence in general (i.e., positive vs. negative), but they did not give a comprehensive analysis of the basic emotion types and their associations. Second, most studies rely on subjects' self-identification of insomnia and emotion valence, but the subjects are limited in number and mostly consisted of undergraduate students, which differ from the general population of various age groups and professions. Most importantly, whether and how emotions could be used to predict psychiatric conditions of individuals with insomnia are not clear.

To fill the above gaps, the present paper takes a computational linguistic approach to analyze the associations between emotion, insomnia and mental health based on the naturally occurring big data in Chinese crawled from the web. We conduct an automatic emotion analysis of a corpus composed of over 400 posts in online psychological consultation platforms in China that complaint about insomnia problems, with annotations for the psychiatric conditions of post makers made by professional psychiatrists. Based on that, data mining is performed to answer the following research questions:

1. Can intensity levels of complex emotions detected in the online psychological consultation post about insomnia problems be used to predict whether the post maker has a psychiatric disorder? What are the most significant features among the intensity of six basic emotions that affect the mental health conditions of people with insomnia problems?
2. What is the association among the 6 basic emotion types in the corpus of online psychological consultation about insomnia problems?
3. What is the association between emotion types and the mental diseases of depression and anxiety in the corpus of online psychological consultation about insomnia problems?

To answer the above questions, we raise the following hypotheses: 1) the emotion intensity levels of basic emotion types detected in the posts can be used to predict if a post contributor has psychiatric disorder(s); 2) certain negative emotions might be associated with each other in the corpus; and 3) depression and anxiety might be associated with different types of emotions. By answering the above questions, we hope to better understand the associations among emotion types, insomnia and mental health.

2   Methodology

2.1   Data

In this study, we built a corpus of psychological consultation posts about insomnia problems by filtering the topic of 'insomnia' in the Emotional First Aid dataset [10], which includes crawled chats in online chat rooms or BBS for psychological consultation annotated with categories of topics and psychological conditions by professional psychiatrists or psychology researchers. We cleaned the sub-dataset and only retrieved the first post in each series of conversations in which the post contributor complaints about his or her psychological problems to seek further consultation.

2.2   Emotion Detection

The emotion detection of the corpus is based on dictionaries of emotion words. Following a complex emotion approach [11–14], which holds that emotion words may be an aggregate of two or more types of basic emotions [13], we adapted and merged two emotion lexicons: The emotion lexicon developed by Xu et al. [15] from Dalian University of Technology and the part of Chinese Mainland usage in the database of Chinese emotion words developed by Lin and Yao [14] from the Hong Kong Polytechnic University. The former contains more than 27400 emotion words, classified into 7 major categories (happiness, appreciation, disgust, surprise, fear, anger, sadness) and 21 sub-categories. All words have the primary emotion type and about

14% of the words also have a secondary emotion type, all rated for intensity levels on a scale of 1–9 by the information retrieval research section of Dalian University of Technology. The latter contains 372 words classified into 8 types (happiness, appreciation, disgust, surprise, fear, anger, sadness). Every word in this lexicon was tagged of two emotion types and was annotated for intensity level on a scale of 1–7 by 256 recruited native Chinese speakers through online surveys. We further adjusted the categories of emotions in the two lexicons consulting Chen et al.'s [12] complex emotion taxonomy, which classified disgust emotion words such as 厭惡 *yànwù* 'disgust' as (primarily) anger. As the doctors we consulted believe that the categories of appreciation and disgust do not seem to directly inform clinical considerations and are not regarded as basic emotion types in some of the emotion taxonomies [12], we ignored the appreciation category and replaced the category of disgust in Lin and Yao [14] to anger, while splitting Xu et al.'s [15] major category of disgust into anxiety (comprising the sub-category of anxiety under the major category of disgust in the original lexicon) and anger (comprising the rest of sub-categories under 'disgust'). Since Lin and Yao's [14] version gives a more complex account of emotion types, we refer to this version when the words are repeated in the two lexicons. After standardizing the intensity levels to a range of 0–1 and adjusting a few domain specific words that cannot be rated in a general way (e.g., 精神 *jīngshén* 'spirit' does not show happiness), we finally merged the two types of emotions for each word in the two lexicons into a dictionary, based on which we detected the emotion types and intensity levels of emotion words in our corpus. The intensity level of an emotion word was basically determined by the original intensity level rated in Lin and Yao's [14] taxonomy, or in Xu et al.'s [15] emotion lexicon (if the word is not included in Lin and Yao's [14] list), but a weight is further given based on the degree adverbs that modify the detected emotion word. The intensity level of a post is then an average of the levels of emotion words in the post. We built rule-based modeling to construct a computational emotion analysis engine that 1) works well on social media style but mental health related text, yet readily generalizes to multiple domains, 2) requires no training data, but is constructed from a generalizable, valence-based, human-curated gold standard sentiment lexicon, 3) is fast enough to be used online with streaming data, and 4) does not severely suffer from a speed-performance tradeoff.

In essence, this paper reports on four interrelated efforts in build this dictionary/rule based emotion classifier. First, a gold standard emotion lexicon that is sensitive in both the polarity and the intensity of sentiments expressed in social media microblogs was developed and validated. This lexicon is also generally applicable to sentiment analysis in other domains Second, experimental evaluation of generalizable rules regarding conventional uses of grammatical and syntactical aspects of text for assessing emotion intensity was conducted. Third, considering that negation words and adverbs of degree may impact the valence and intensity of emotion, negation shift was conducted by scanning a list of negation words and intensity levels were adjusted automatically with varied weights assigned to adverbs of degrees. Fourth, the performances of different dictionaries and labelling scales were compared against other established and/or typical emotion analysis baselines. In each of these four efforts, we incorporate an explicit human-centric approach.

After emotion detection, each post was therefore given the intensity levels of six emotion types: happiness (HP), anger (AG), surprise (SP), fear (FR), sadness (SD), and anxiety (AX), and a final manual check of negation shift was conducted by the authors.

2.3   Data Mining Methods

Machine learning models were adopted for data-mining tasks. To answer Research Question 1, logistic regression [16] and artificial neural network (ANN) [17] were used for classification experiments to predict if a post contributor has any of the psychiatric disorder(s) annotated in the corpus with the emotion intensity levels of basic emotion types we detected in the post as features of input. The methods were chosen because they enable a comparison for the contributions of input features to the predictions. To answer Research Questions 2 and 3, relevance analysis was conducted on the binary data of emotion type distribution we detected, and the existence of depression and anxiety symptoms annotated in the First Aid Dataset. For the relevance analysis, the Apriori algorithm [18] that mines frequent item set was used to learn association rules among the emotion types and the psychiatric conditions of depression and anxiety.

3   Results

3.1   Overall Distribution of Emotions and Mental Disease Types

In all, there are 404 posts in the corpus and the average length of a post is 39 Chinese characters. Among them, 62 posts were annotated as indicating a symptom of anxiety, 64 were annotated as indicating depression, 6 indicating bipolar, 7 indicating PTSD, 8 indicating Panic Disorder, and 1 indicating 'others'. The rest of posts (260 cases) were annotated as not meeting the criteria of indicating psychiatric disorders mentioned above. The distribution of detected emotion types for the posts is: 299, 120, 76, 71, 6, and 4 posts show anxiety, anger, sadness, fear, joy, and surprise respectively.

3.2   Prediction of Mental Health Conditions Based on Emotion Intensity Levels

The results of prediction performance by logistic regression and ANN cross-validated each other. For logistic regression, which is used as a baseline, the accuracy of prediction achieved is 70.30%. As shown in Table 1, three attributes of emotion intensity significantly contributed to the prediction results ($p < .01$): sadness ranks first (coefficient = 1.01) while fear (coefficient = 0.57) and anxiety (coefficient = 0.51) show much lower but similar coefficients.

For ANN, we firstly built a simple structure with the intensity levels of 6 emotions as features in the input layer, the binary class of indicating psychiatric disorder or not as output layer, and one hidden layer composed of 1 neutron. The accuracy of prediction at 10000 iterations is 71.29%. The weights of input features that contributed to the prediction are shown in Table 2. All emotion intensity features except surprise have a weight higher than 1. The results corroborate with logistic regression in that sadness, fear and anxiety are the top three most important predictors, but anxiety (weight = 14.6) surpassed fear (weight = 10.9) as the second most important predictor. Afterwards, we also enhanced the ANN model by increasing the hidden layer to 3 layers, each consisting of 10 neurons, which raised the accuracy of prediction to 75.99% and improved the AUC to 75.48% at 10000 iterations. However, the interpretation of feature weights for the complicated ANN model is harder to conduct and hence goes beyond the scope of the current paper.

Table 1. The contribution of input features in the logistic regression model

Class	Coef.	Std. err.	Z	$P > |Z|$
Happiness	−.5683183	.6835945	−0.83	0.406
Surprise	−.3277152	.8537873	−0.38	0.701
Anger	−.4273678	.3320611	−1.29	0.198
Sadness	−1.008237	.2503636	−4.03	0.000
Fear	−.5731584	.1690628	−3.39	0.001
Anxiety	−.5057668	.1165455	−4.34	0.000
Cons	−1.295353	.1624643	−7.97	0.000

For model validation, the comparison of the ROC areas among the logistic regression, the simple ANN and the complicated ANN is shown in Fig. 1, showing that both versions of ANN models have a better performance than the baseline model of logistic regression.

Table 2. The contribution of input features in the simple ANN model

	H1N1W1 (HP)	H1N1W2 (SP)	H1N1W3 (AG)	H1N1W4 (SD)	H1N1W5 (FR)	H1N1W6 (AX)
W	−2.4712818	.20830403	−5.3913534	−14.914221	−10.288345	−14.569564

Note. W = weight; H1N1 = hidden layer 1 neuron 1; HP = happiness; SP = surprise; AG = anger; SD = sadness; FR = fear; AX = anxiety.

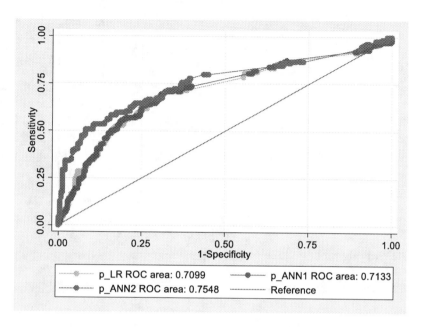

Fig. 1. Comparison of ROC areas for the logistic regression (p_LR), the simple ANN model (p_ANN1) and the complicated ANN model (p_ANN2)

3.3   Relevance Analysis of Emotion Types and Psychiatric Disorders

As shown in Table 3, nine rules have been learnt by the Apriori algorithm. Apriori algorithms learn associate rules based on frequently appearing items in a database. It starts with the most frequent item(s) in the domain and builds larger and larger sets of associations centered around the original 'seeds' based on the frequency of occurrences of the new items in the domain. We can see that each rule describes the association of an item (an emotion type, or a psychological disorder type, either anxiety or depression) with its antecedent(s). Given the high proportion of anxiety emotion words in the corpus, all the rules in the results are about the associations of the anxiety emotion (AX) with other dimensions. Three rules gained support higher than 10: the anxiety emotion (AX) is associated with both psychiatric disorders of depression and anxiety and it is also associated with the sadness emotion. Other rules reported lower support but still gained a lift higher than 1 and reached confidence levels over 80%. Interestingly, although independent dimensions of anger and anxiety are not significantly associated, anger was found to accompany fear and sadness in their associations with anxiety, and to accompany depression and anxiety in their association with anxiety.

Table 3. Rules of relevance learnt by the Apriori algorithm

	Antecedent	Rule id	Instances	Support %	Confidence %	Rule support %	Lift
AX	Depression and SD	6	33	8.17	90.91	7.43	1.23
AX	Anxiety and AG	5	21	5.20	90.48	4.70	1.22
AX	SD and AG	9	26	6.44	88.46	5.69	1.20
AX	Anxiety	1	62	15.35	87.10	13.37	1.18
AX	Depression and AG	7	23	5.69	86.96	4.95	1.17
AX	SD	3	76	18.81	86.84	16.34	1.17
AX	Depression	2	64	15.84	85.94	13.61	1.16
AX	Anxiety and FR	4	24	5.94	83.33	4.95	1.13
AX	FR and AG	8	22	5.45	81.82	4.46	1.11

In accordance with the above rules, we can also tell from the visualized network in Fig. 2 that depression is associated mainly with anxiety, sadness, and anger, whereas anxiety is associated with anxiety, fear and anger, rather than sadness.

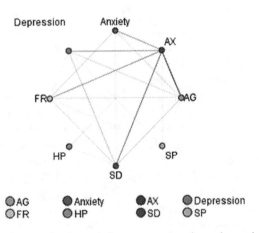

Fig. 2. Visualized network of associations among emotions, depression and anxiety

4   Discussion

1) Can intensity levels of complex emotions detected in the online psychological consultation post about insomnia problems be used to predict whether the post maker has a psychiatric disorder? What are the most significant features among the intensity of six basic emotions that affect the mental health conditions of people with insomnia problems?

Our first hypothesis is supported. Results of our classification experiments with logistic regression and ANN models indicated that intensity levels of complex emotions detected in the online psychological consultation post about insomnia problems be used to predict whether the post maker has a psychiatric disorder, with a prediction accuracy up to 75.99%. Intensity of sadness is the primary predictor, while fear and anxiety are also important contributing features.

2) What is the association among the 6 basic emotion types in the corpus of online psychological consultation about insomnia problems?

The second hypothesis that negative emotions in the corpus are significantly associated is also supported. The emotion of anxiety is most significantly associated with sadness.

3) What is the association between emotion types and the mental diseases of depression and anxiety in the corpus of online psychological consultation about insomnia problems?

The most frequent negative emotion anxiety is significantly associated with both depression and anxiety. Depression and anxiety seem to be associated with different types of emotions: fear is not saliently associated with depression, while sadness is not saliently associated with anxiety. Hence our third hypothesis is also proved true.

In general, the instances of anxiety and depression are quite balanced in our corpus, which contradicts previous medical studies that claimed insomnia as more predictive for subsequent depression than anxiety in UK [9, 19]. Given the higher ratio of reported insomnia in the Chinese Mainland than in Europe [2], it deserves further exploration whether anxiety is more prevalent or whether it has a stronger association with insomnia in China than in the west.

Another surprising result is that sadness rather than the anxiety emotion is the primary predictor of one's mental health, which probably contradicts people's common sense understanding of this issue[1]. Since sadness is more familiar and strongly identified as an emotion of negative polarity, it is possible that it is easier to report with descriptive terms of sadness instead of anxiety. Given the concept that emotions are compositional and complex [12], it might be possible that when one experiences

---

[1] As sadness is found as more highly related with depression than with anxiety in our relevance analysis, the 6th author of this paper, who is an experienced doctor rich in clinical observations of the influence of circadian rhythm disruption on overall bodily health, hypothesizes that people with sleep orders might convey their anxiety through sadness based on his own estimation.

anxiety but feels hard to express, he or she would adopt emotions of sadness. This should be an issue for future studies to confirm.

Some of the associations we identified are in line with previous findings of associations between insomnia and particular negative moods. For example, worry and rumination, which can be understood as a manifestation of anxiety, were reported as relevant with insomnia [20, 21]. Bereavement grief, which is a kind of sadness, was found to be positively associated with sleep disorder [22]. Hostility [23], impulsivity, aggression and anger [24, 25], which are manifestations of anger, were also proved with associations with insomnia [26]. Such associations could be explained by the cognitive models of insomnia. However, fear, which is associated with anxiety in our results, has rarely been discussed before and deserves attentions for future investigation.

5   Linguistic and Clinical Implications and Limitations

Linguistically, the possibility of expressing the anxiety emotion with sadness emotion words that the clinician postulates based on our results deserves further investigation by linguists in collaboration with psychology researchers. A deeper account of the potential discrepancies between reported/expressed emotion and experiential emotion may enrich the current understanding of emotion composition and hence inform emotion detection in natural language processing. In addition, the prediction models we developed have the potential to be applied to other online media texts for detection of psychiatric disorders in comorbidity with insomnia.

From the perspective of medical research, our data mining results in answer to the research questions raised in Sect. 1 seem to support Baglioni et al.'s [5] hypothesis that the relationship between insomnia and psychiatric disorders such as anxiety and depression might be modulated by emotion dysregulation. Baglioni and others [5] have identified "heightened negative emotionality and diminished positive emotionality" might modulate the bidirectional relationship between insomnia and mental disorders and "additional strategies dealing with emotional processes could enhance the efficacy of the treatment". In this study, we add further contribution to position the associations of complex emotion types in relation to insomnia, and mental disorders. As cognitive behavioral therapy is "recommended as the first-line treatment for chronic insomnia in adults of any age (strong recommendation, high-quality evidence)" [27], the associations we found among emotions and the different patterns of their associations with depression and anxiety might have the potential to inform the design of customized interventions to prevent the development of insomnia into depression and anxiety through adjusting insomnia patients' emotion regulation in the cognitive behavior therapies.

Anxiety is prevalent in our corpus, which is understandable. In the modern society, it is very often that pressures from work and family may unavoidably arouse an anxiety emotion. However, we also found that anger accompanies fear and sadness in their associations with the anxiety emotion, and it also accompanies depression and anxiety in their association with anxiety emotion. Hence it seems reasonable for us to postulate that if the anger emotion is controlled, the association of anxiety emotion with the development of anxiety and depression psychiatric disorders may be smaller. It seems plausible that cognitive intervention for insomnia treatment could focus on the management of temper and life attitude to release the patients from continuous or excessive anger, thereby contributing to the prevention of a mutual maintenance between psychiatric disorders and insomnia.

One limitation of this study is that we have not yet take into consideration of user profiles like age and gender, and this will be improved in our future modelling. The performance of classification tasks should also be further enhanced with more advanced computational models in the future.

Acknowledgments. We thank Dr. Sophia Yat Mei Lee and Dr. Yao Yao from Department of Chinese and Bilingual Studies, the Hong Kong Polytechnic University for generously sharing their lists of Chinese emotion taxonomy with us and for recommending useful references. This study was funded by Youth Foundation of Humanities and Social Sciences, Ministry of Education, China (No. 21YJC740058).

Yunfei Long's work was partially funded by the Open Fund Project of the Fujian Provincial Key Laboratory of Information Processing and Intelligent Control (Minjiang University) under Project MJUKF-IPIC201911.

References

1. Li, L., Wu, C., Gan, Y., Qu, X., Lu, Z.: Insomnia and the risk of depression: a meta-analysis of prospective cohort studies. BMC Psychiatry **16** (2016). https://doi.org/10.1186/s12888-016-1075-3
2. Sleep Disorders Group of Chinese Society of Neurology: Guidelines for the diagnosis and treatment of adult insomnia in China. Zhong Hua Shen Jing Ke Za Zhi **51**, 324–335 (2018). (in Chinese)
3. Breslau, N., Roth, T., Rosenthal, L., Andreski, P.: Sleep disturbance and psychiatric disorders: a longitudinal epidemiological study of young adults. Biol. Psychiatry **39**, 411–418 (1996). https://doi.org/10.1016/0006-3223(95)00188-3
4. Gross, J.J.: The emerging field of emotion regulation: an integrative review. Rev. Gen. Psychol. **2**, 271–299 (1997)
5. Baglioni, C., Spiegelhalder, K., Lombardo, C., Riemann, D.: Sleep and emotions: a focus on insomnia. Sleep Med. Rev. **14**, 227–238 (2010). https://doi.org/10.1016/j.smrv.2009.10.007
6. Riemann, D., et al.: The hyperarousal model of insomnia: a review of the concept and its evidence. Sleep Med. Rev. **14**, 19–31 (2010). https://doi.org/10.1016/j.smrv.2009.04.002
7. Harvey, A.G., Murray, G., Chandler, R.A., Soehner, A.: Sleep disturbance as transdiagnostic: consideration of neurobiological mechanisms. Clin. Psychol. Rev. **31**, 225–235 (2011). https://doi.org/10.1016/j.cpr.2010.04.003
8. Chen, Z.-F., Shi Mian De Zhong Yi Zhi Liao: J. China Clin. Tradit. Med. **9**, 1–7 (2003). (in Chinese). https://doi.org/10.6968/TJCCTM.200306.0001
9. Jansson-Fröjmark, M., Lindblom, K.: A bidirectional relationship between anxiety and depression, and insomnia? A prospective study in the general population. J. Psychosom. Res. **64**, 443–449 (2008). https://doi.org/10.1016/j.jpsychores.2007.10.016
10. Wang, H.L., et al.: Emotional First Aid Dataset, Chatopera Inc. (2020)

11. Chen, Y., Lee, S.Y.M., Huang, C.R.: A cognitive-based annotation system for emotion computing. In: The Third Linguistic Annotation Workshop (The LAW III), ACL 2009, Singapore, pp. 1–9 (2009). https://doi.org/10.3115/1698381.1698382
12. Chen, Y., Lee, S.Y.M., Huang, C.R.: Are emotions enumerable or decomposable? And its implications for emotion processing. In: PACLIC 23 - Proceedings of the 23rd Pacific Asia Conference on Language, Information and Computation, vol. 1, pp, 92–100 (2009)
13. Turner, J.: On the Origins of Human Emotions: A Sociological Inquiry into the Evolution of Human Affect. Stanford University Press (2000)
14. Lin, J., Yao, Y.: Encoding emotion in Chinese: a database of Chinese emotion words with information of emotion type, intensity, and valence. Ling. Sin. 2 (2016). https://doi.org/10.1186/s40655-016-0015-y
15. Xu, L., Lin, H., Pan, Y.: Constructing the affective lexical ontology. J. China Soc. Sci. Tech. Inf. 27, 180–185 (2008). (in Chinese)
16. Menard, S.: Applied Logistic Regression Analysis. Sage, Thousand Oaks (2002)
17. Dongare, A.D., Kharde, R.R., Kachare, A.D.: Introduction to artificial neural network (ANN) methods. Int. J. Eng. Innov. Technol. 2, 189–194 (2012)
18. Agrawal, R., Srikant, R.: Fast algorithm for mining association rules. In: Proceedings of the 20th International Conference on Very Large Data Bases, VLDB, Santiago, Chile, pp. 487–499 (1994)
19. Morphy, H., Dunn, K.M., Lewis, M., Boardman, H.F., Croft, P.R.: Epidemiology of insomnia: a longitudinal study in a UK population. Sleep 30, 274–280 (2007). https://doi.org/10.1093/sleep/30.3.274
20. Palagini, L., Moretto, U., Dell'Osso, L., Carney, C.: Sleep-related cognitive processes, arousal, and emotion dysregulation in insomnia disorder: the role of insomnia-specific rumination. Sleep Med. 30, 97–104 (2017). https://doi.org/10.1016/j.sleep.2016.11.004
21. Watts, F.N., Coyle, K., East, M.P.: The contribution of worry to insomnia. Br. J. Clin. Psychol. 33, 211–220 (1994)
22. Hardison, H.G., Neimeyer, R.A., Lichstein, K.L.: Insomnia and complicated grief symptoms in bereaved college students. Behav. Sleep Med. 3, 99–111 (2005). https://doi.org/10.1207/s15402010bsm0302_4
23. Granö, N., Vahtera, J., Virtanen, M., Keltikangas-Järvinen, L., Kivimäki, M.: Association of hostility with sleep duration and sleep disturbances in an employee population. Int. J. Behav. Med. 15(2), 73–80 (2008). https://doi.org/10.1080/10705500801929510
24. Ireland, J.L., Culpin, V.: The relationship between sleeping problems and aggression, anger, and impulsivity in a population of juvenile and young offenders. J. Adolesc. Health 38, 649–655 (2006)
25. Schmidt, R.E., Gay, P., Van der Linden, M.: Facets of impulsivity are differentially linked to insomnia: evidence from an exploratory study. Behav. Sleep Med. 6, 178–192 (2008). https://doi.org/10.1080/15402000802162570
26. Harvey, A.G.: A Cognitive model of insomnia. Behav. Res. Ther. 40, 869–893 (2002)
27. Riemann, D., et al.: European guideline for the diagnosis and treatment of insomnia. J. Sleep Res. 26, 675–700 (2017). https://doi.org/10.1111/jsr.12594

A Quantitative Study on the Measure Index of Syntactic Complexity in Textbooks for Chinese as a Second Language

Caihong Cao, Wenting Cao[2] and Fang Tian[1]

[1] School of Chinese Studies, Beijing Language and Culture University, Beijing, China
[2] School of Mathematics, University of Leeds, Leeds, UK

Abstract. Syntactic complexity is an important index to measure the quality of text. This study identified the quantitative measure indicators of syntactic complexity from the three dimensions of aggregate, length, and relative indexes, and examined the feasibility of these indexes as syntactic complexity measure indicators. The results showed that the aggregate index of the text shows statistical differences; as the basic index to describe syntactic complexity, the aggregate index can be used to assess the suitability of textbook compilation and learners' language output level. Moreover, in the length indexes, only the length of the T-unit and of clauses showed good differences and growth trends in the primary stage. Lastly, in the relative indexes, the number of clauses in the T-unit can be used to examine the syntactic complexity of each grade. The above results contributed to the Chinese as a Second Language teaching or in the compilation of teaching materials.

Keywords: CSL textbooks · Syntactic complexity · Measure indicators · Quantitative research

1 Introduction

Syntactic complexity, an important index to measure the quality of language output, is widely used in the study of English as a first (L1) or second language (L2). In recent years, syntactic complexity has been used to measure learning effectiveness for learners of Chinese. Jiang [1] established the categorizing standard for Chinese T-units—T-unit refers to the shortest segment of a sentence—and analyzed the written language of Chinese learners at the elementary, intermediate, and advanced levels. An [2] added the measure indicator of sentences per T-unit on the basis of Jiang and compared the composition of Chinese learners. Cao and Deng [3] used mean sentence length, T-unit length, and special sentence patterns to compare the syntactic complexity of the written Chinese of Vietnamese senior university students and Chinese elementary school students. Wu [4] conducted an empirical study on the measurements of syntactic complexity of Chinese writing, such as the number of T-units, length of T-units, topic chains, and empty categories, for native English speakers. Wang [5] investigated the measurement method of syntactic complexity for Chinese as a second language (CSL).

© Springer Nature Switzerland AG 2022
M. Dong et al. (Eds.): CLSW 2021, LNAI 13250, pp. 233–245, 2022.
https://doi.org/10.1007/978-3-031-06547-7_19

The commonality of these past studies is their evaluation of the syntactic complexity of CSL learners who are using their language output as corpus. However, given that the quality of a learner's output is highly determined by their learning input, the distribution characteristics of the syntactic complexity of the input material and its quantitative measurements must be determined.

The present study aimed to identify the quantitative measure indicators of syntactic complexity and explore the syntactic complexity of the input materials of CSL learners by using the textbooks as corpus. These textbooks are the main learning materials for CSL learners, and are the early language input materials in which learners immerse. Moreover, being developed according to the language learning and evaluation syllabus by the Ministry of Education of China, these textbooks are standardized learning inputs for L2 Chinese learners. The texts in these textbooks reflect not only the syntactic complexity of Chinese at different learning levels but also the expected level of language output for L2 learners. Therefore, we recognized the necessity of describing the syntactic complexity of the textbook itself in Chinese as a second language teaching resource. Our study focused on evaluating these syntactic complexity measures (SCMs) and identifying the suitable measurements for L2 Chinese learning.

2   Research Methods and Materials

2.1   Data Sources

We used the texts in *ErYa Chinese* as the data source for analysis. *ErYa Chinese* is a series of professional undergraduate-level textbooks for L2 Chinese learners published by Beijing Language and Culture University Press. The textbooks are written with reference to *Syllabus for the Chinese Language Major for Foreign Students in Colleges and Universities, New Chinese Proficiency Test Syllabus (Levels 1–6)*, as well as other syllabuses, standards, and word lists. The comprehensive series of 15 textbooks covers the entire process of Chinese learning from a starting point of absolute beginner to advanced stage. The content of the textbook reflects not only the language learning characteristics but also the language learning objectives that learners should achieve.

Therefore, we described SCMs of Chinese language using the *ErYa* series as research material and examined the effectiveness of different SCMs. This textbook series has 128 texts for learners from beginner level to fourth grade. We selected 103 texts via cluster sampling between grades and random sampling within grades, with a sampling rate of 80.5%. In addition, we sampled each text as a whole to ensure that the corpus would reflect the syntactic characteristics of the complete text, given that an article often shows different stylistic features at the beginning, throughout the narrative process, and the end.

2.2   Selection of Indicators

Syntactic complexity is used to measure the text complexity at the level of sentences. The description of sentences is further divided into concepts, such as sentences (e.g., simple and compound sentences), clauses, and T-units. Therefore, our study established syntactic complexity measure indicators from different dimensions based on these concepts. As the definition for sentences and clauses are clear and need no elaboration, we focused on the concept of the T-unit and its division method.

The concept of the T-unit was first proposed by Hunt to describe the syntactic maturity of native English speakers [6]. A T-unit refers to:

> The shortest segment that can be segmented without leaving any syntactically incomplete residual fragments, [...] is grammatically allowable for any statement containing one main clause, with or without subordinate clauses. Any T-unit can be punctuated as one sentence. [...] Such units must be cut into two or more parts so that each will contain only one main clause [7].

The English T-unit has been proven to be an effective indicator of English syntactic complexity [8, 9]. Jiang and others [1–5] applied the concept of the T-unit to the study of Chinese syntactic complexity. Researchers have defined the Chinese T-unit as "an independent main sentence that contains an independent predicate and other subsidiary clauses or embedded clauses" [1], where the principle of dividing a T-unit is as follows: "if it cannot be converted into an independent simple sentence by simply adding a punctuation at the end of the sentence, it cannot be divided into a T-unit" [5]. Moreover, the T-unit also reflects the ability to temporarily store thoughts and control language in mental processes [10]. Simple and condensed sentences in Chinese can be divided into one T-unit; compound sentences can be divided into different T-units according to whether there are marks in the independent clauses. Embedded clauses in compound sentences are not regarded as independent T-units. Moreover, a run-on sentence is judged for whether it can be divided into T-units according to the type of each clause. The examples below demonstrate the concept:

① 我们并没为你的前信感到什么烦恼或是不安</T>。

(We actually were not troubled or disturbed by your previous letter.)

② 孩子，这些我都懂得</T>，妈妈也懂得</T>。

(Son, I understand all these, and so does mom.)

③尽管将来你我之间离多聚少，但我精神上至少是温暖的，不孤独的</T>。

(Although there will be more separation and fewer meetings between you and me, my spirit is at least warm and not lonely.)

In addition, we defined the division method of compound sentences containing semicolons, colons, and other punctuations according to the definition of the T-unit, with consideration for the independence of the sentences expressed by these punctuations. For instance, if the clauses before and after a semicolon are independent, then they should be divided to two different T-units. The clauses before and after a colon or dash, need to be judged by their independence and completeness of their meanings. If the clauses are complete and their meanings are independent, then they should be divided into two T-units; otherwise, they comprise one T-unit.

2.3   Statistical Index and Calculation Methods

According to the characteristics of basic units and their relations, we established statistical measures with three dimensions. The first is the aggregate index, which includes the average number of sentences, clauses, compound sentences, and T-units; the second is the length index, which includes the mean length of sentences, clauses, compound sentences, and T-units; and the third is the relative index, which includes clause/sentence, clause/T-unit, clause/compound sentence, T-unit/compound sentence, T-unit/sentence, compound sentence/sentence, running sentence/compound sentence, and clause/T-unit.

2.3.1   Aggregate Index

We set this index to examine the quantitative characteristics of the different stage of the text for each index from the aggregate. Each aggregate index is counted according to the above criteria for the division of sentences, clauses, T-units, and compound sentences. The calculation of the average for each grade is to divide the total of the corresponding values by the number of corresponding texts. The specific calculation methods are shown in Table 1.

Table 1. Calculation methods for the aggregate index.

Aggregate index	Abbreviation	Calculation formula
Average number of words in text	AW	$AW = \sum W_i/n$
Average number of sentences in text	AS	$AS = \sum S_i/n$
Average number of clauses in text	AC	$AC = \sum C_i/n$
Average number of compound sentences	AF	$AF = \sum F_i/n$
Average number of T-units in text	AT	$AT = \sum T_i/n$

2.3.2   Length Index

The length index measures the length of the components that make up the whole. It describes the length characteristics of each basic syntactic unit at different learning stages. Regarding the measure unit for each length index, according to Jiang [1] and Deng [11], there is no statistical difference in using characters and words as the unit of measure. As recommended by Jiang [1], our study used the number of words as the unit of measure of each length index. The specific calculation method is shown in Table 2.

Table 2. Length index: abbreviations, definitions, and calculation methods.

Index	Abbreviation	Definition	Calculation method
The mean length of sentences	SL	The mean length of sentences in sampled texts	W/S
The mean length of clauses	CL	The mean length of clauses in sampled texts	W/C
The mean length of compound sentences	FL	The mean length of compound sentences in sampled texts	W/F
The mean length of T-units	TL	The mean length of compound sentences in sampled texts	W/T

2.3.3   Relative Index

This index describes the relative quantitative performance among the syntactic basic units. For example, the relative proportion of clauses in a Chinese sentence can be used to determine whether the number of clauses in a sentence varies with the difficulty of the text. Another example is the T-unit, which It describes the ability to store thoughts temporarily and control language in mental processes [10]: this index indicates whether the number of clauses contained in T-units or the proportion of T-units in a sentence will increase with the progression in language learning stages. Other relative indicators have been established based on similar considerations. The specific calculation methods of each relative index are shown in Table 3.

Table 3. Relative index: abbreviations and calculation methods.

Index	Abbreviation/ Substitution	Definition	Calculation method
The number of clauses in sentence	CS	The number of clauses in the sentence	C/S
The number of compound sentences in a sentence	FS	The number of compound sentences in the sentence	F/S
T-unit/Sentence	TS	The number of T-units in the sentence	T/S
The number of clauses in compound sentence	CdF	The number of clauses in the compound sentence	(C−D)/F
The number of T-units in compound sentence	TdF	The number of T-units in a compound sentence	(T−D)/F
The number of clauses in T-units	CT	The number of clauses in T-unit	C/T
Clause/T-unit	CdTd	The number of clauses contained in the T-unit in compound sentence	(C−D)/(T−D)

3 Results

We conducted statistical tests on the indexes, and the results are as follows.

3.1 Statistical Distribution and Difference Test: Aggregate Index

Table 4 shows the upper and lower limits[1] of the mean value of each aggregate index. Figure 1 shows the mean value of each aggregate index plotted in the grade development trend.

Table 4. Aggregate indexes of each text in each grade.

Language level	Average number of words	Average number of sentences	Average number of clauses	Average number of T-units	Average number of compound sentences
Beginner	61.66	3.64	6.90	5.23	1.74
	99.64	4.74	11.18	8.23	4.34
Grade 1	274.43	11.27	21.71	13.08	4.52
	421.31	15.41	36.65	21.28	13.12
Grade 2	1207.06	35.37	90.96	45.91	23.09
	1449.60	42.29	114.48	60.31	37.13
Grade 3	2638.64	84.21	180.72	92.89	39.26
	3315.12	116.79	279.54	147.99	92.12
Grade 4	4010.26	138.21	327.73	150.84	74.31
	5030.14	182.59	483.47	233.56	165.29

Note. The upper number in each box is the lower limit value of the corresponding index, and the lower one is the corresponding upper limit value.

As shown in Table 4, the upper and lower limits of the aggregate indexes for each grade both increased accordingly. For example, in Grade 1 with HSK level 2, the lower and upper limits of the number of words per lesson increased to 274.43 and 421.31 words, respectively, and the lower and upper limits of the number of sentences per lesson increased to 11.27 and 15.41, respectively. The upper and lower limits of clauses, T-units, and compound sentences in each lesson all increased, as observed in the other grades as well.

Each aggregate index showed a clear trend between grades (see Fig. 1). For example, the number of words of the text increased with the grade, but the change rate between them was different. The rate from absolute beginner to grade 1 was the smallest, followed by those from grade 1 to grade 2 and from grade 2 to 3. The rate increased significantly from grade 3 to 4. Other aggregate indicators also showed a similar change trend.

---

[1] The upper and lower limits of the average value are 95% confidence intervals.

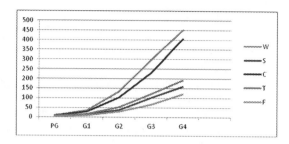

Fig. 1. The development trend of the aggregate indexes in each grade

By conducting multiple non-parametric tests of independent variables for each of the aggregate indicators in Table 4, we obtained the results of the chi-squared test. The chi-squared values of the average number of words in the texts of different grades were 92.947, and the asymptotic significance was 0.000. Therefore, the texts of each grade had different numbers of words. Similarly, other aggregated indicators all passed the difference test. Based on the results of the tests, we concluded that each aggregate index would be different for the text of each grade.

3.2 Statistical Distribution and Difference Test: Length Index

We obtained the statistical distribution of the mean value of each index by analyzing the length indicator, and then calculated the 95% confidence intervals for each indicator based on the standard deviation of the sample (Table 5). Figure 2 graphs the trend of change across grades.

Table 5. Length indexes of texts for each grade (unit: word).

Grade	The mean length of sentences	The mean length of compound sentences	The mean length of clauses	The mean length of T-units
Beginner	15.23	18.06	7.88	10.15
	20.12	23.37	9.11	12.73
Grade 1	23.82	30.45	11.20	18.39
	26.88	34.99	12.74	21.07
Grade 2	31.76	37.50	12.21	22.56
	38.13	45.48	15.03	28.51
Grade 3	29.64	38.12	12.96	24.26
	37.77	46.12	15.64	31.15
Grade 4	24.65	29.30	8.99	21.72
	35.88	42.71	14.55	28.71

Note. The upper number in each box is the lower limit value of the corresponding index, and the lower one is the corresponding upper limit value.

The upper and lower limits of each index showed a gradually increasing trend from the beginner to Grade 2 levels, but the growth trend changed after Grade 3 (Table 5). For example, the upper and lower limits of the mean length of sentences in Grade 3 completely fell within the range of Grade 2. The upper and lower limits of 24.65 and 35.88 for Grade 4 fell within the Grades 1 and 2 ranges, respectively. The mean length of compound sentences for Grade 3 overlapped with that for Grade 2. Similarly, the upper and lower limits of the mean length of clauses and T-units maintained increasing trends before Grade 4, before completely changing in Grade 4. Figure 2 shows the development trend of the mean values of these indexes. Both SL and FL showed increasing trends before Grade 2, whereas CL and TL showed increasing trends before Grade 3.

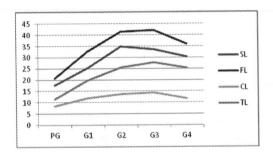

Fig. 2. Trends of length indexes for texts for each grade

All types of the length trend between Grades 2 and 3 and between Grades 3 and 4 were vague or even declining. Therefore, we performed pairwise difference tests for the indexes to determine the grade groups that brought the variability to these indicators (Table 6).

Table 6. Non-parametric independent samples test statistics of length index between grades.

Grade group	Mann-Whitney U asymptotic significance (bilateral)			
	SL	CL	TL	FL
0–1	.000*	.000*	.000*	.000*
1–2	.000*	.013*	.000*	.000*
2–3	.863	.427	.241	.535
3–4	.457	.048*	.620	.137

*Indicates that the grade group does not pass the no-difference test.

As presented in the data in Table 6, there was no significant difference from the beginner level to Grade 1 and from Grade 1 to Grade 2. Moreover, there was no significant difference from Grade 2 to Grade 3. From Grade 3 to Grade 4, except for the length of clauses being slightly less than 0.05, the other indexes were greater than 0.05, indicating no difference. These length indexes showed increasing differences between the lower grades (before Grade 2) but became non-differentiated in the higher grades (after Grade 2), thus losing their instrumental role in evaluating the syntactic complexity of texts.

3.3 Statistical Distribution and Difference Test: Relative Index

The relative indexes in each grade level with 95% confidence intervals are listed in Table 7, and trend graphs of the distribution of grade mean values are shown in Fig. 3.

Table 7. Descriptive statistics of relative indexes of each grade.

F/S	Beginner		Grade 1		Grade 2		Grade 3		Grade 4	
	0.654	0.813	0.613	0.685	0.705	0.801	0.622	0.744	0.730	0.795
C/S	1.976	2.272	2.026	2.280	2.396	2.784	2.158	2.568	2.397	2.747
T/S	1.431	1.773	1.239	1.369	1.301	1.455	1.141	1.312	1.113	1.276
Cd/F	2.219	2.841	2.604	2.927	2.914	3.229	2.801	3.114	2.902	3.215
Td/F	1.603	2.028	1.373	1.565	1.399	1.584	1.215	1.423	1.145	1.368
C/T	1.232	1.486	1.574	1.754	1.844	2.019	1.894	1.976	1.969	2.355
Cd/Td	1.296	1.606	1.807	2.037	1.892	2.213	2.108	2.458	2.226	2.678

Note. The first value in each box is the lower limit value of the corresponding index, and the second one is the corresponding upper limit value.

According to the F/S descriptive statistics in Table 7, the proportion of compound sentences in the sentences of the whole text was 70% on average for all grades. Grades 2 and 4 accounted for the two largest percentages of compound sentences, with confidence interval middle values of 76.6% and 76.22%, respectively. The average proportion of compound sentences in the texts for beginners was not low. The average C/S in the texts of each grade was between 1.976 and 2.784. The T/S value of the beginner level was the largest, with upper and lower limits of 1.431 and 1.773 respectively, followed by Grades 2 and 1; the smallest value was found for Grade 4, with upper and lower limits of 1.113 and 1.276 T units. The T/S value of each grade exceeded 1. The number of clauses contained in compound sentences (Cd/F) at each grade level showed the opposite trend to the number of T-units contained in compound sentences (Td/F). In other words, the higher the grade level, the larger the Cd/F and the smaller the Td/F were. However, we observed a crossover of both indexes in each grade. Grades 2 and 4 had overlapping Cd/F; the Cd/F value of Grade 3 was lower than that of Grade 2. Grades 1 and 2 had overlapping Td/F, and the beginner level had the highest value, which indicated that the beginner level had the highest number of T-units contained in compound sentences. The Td/F number of Grade 4 was the lowest, showing an overall decreasing trend. The number of clauses contained in the T-unit, namely, C/T, followed an overall upward trend. The beginner level had the lowest, followed by Grades 1, 2, 3, and Grade 4; Grades 2 and 3 demonstrated a crossover. The number of clauses contained in a T-unit in a compound sentence is denoted as Cd/Td. The upper and lower limits of the confidence interval increased with grade progression: the beginner level recorded the lowest values, with upper and lower limits of 1.296 and 1.606, and Grade 4 logged the highest values of 2.226 and 2.678, respectively.

As presented in Fig. 3, the proportion of compound sentences in the text, F/S, followed no regular trend. The C/S increased slightly from the beginner level to Grade 1, and increased significantly in Grade 2—the number of clauses contained in the sentence increased substantially. We noted a large fluctuation in Grades 3 and 4, which showed no clear trend in general. The trends for T/S and Td/F were similarly downward. They both started with the largest value in the beginner level and the lowest in the fourth grade; however, fluctuations with a slight increase could be observed in the second grade. The Cd/F trend showed an overall upward trend but fluctuated in the third grade, decreasing slightly instead of rising. Meanwhile, the trends of both C/T and Cd/Td tended downward, with the lowest value for the beginner level and the highest for Grade 4.

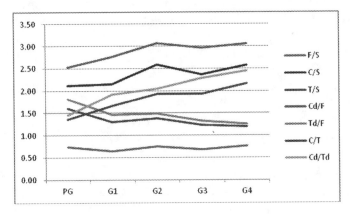

Fig. 3. Development trend of relative indexes of texts for each grade.

Figure 3 demonstrates that in addition to C/T and Cd/Td, the indexes of C/S, T/S, Cd/F, Cs/F and Td/F do not show significantly different trends, and F/S data show no trend feature at all. Therefore, we conducted pair-wise independent samples tests on these indexes to determine which grade group differences contributed to the overall sample differences. The results are listed in Table 8.

Table 8. Non-parametric independent samples test statistics of relative indexes between grades.

Grade group	Mann-Whitney U asymptotic significance (bilateral)							
	C/S	F/S	T/S	Cd/F	Cs/F	Td/F	C/T	Cd/Td
0–1	.440	.106	.002*	.021*	.021*	.002*	.000*	.000*
1–2	.000*	.001*	.048*	.011*	.011*	.261	.003*	.061
2–3	.082	.095	.022*	.153	.153	.054	.850	.278
3–4	.196	.196	.557	.290	.290	.411	.046*	.092

* Indicates that the grade group does not pass the no-difference test.

The asymptotic significance of C/S and F/S between Grades 1 and 2 were less than 0.05, indicating significant difference; that of the other grades was greater than 0.05, indicating no difference between grades. T/S passed the difference test with asymptotic significance less than 0.05 for all grades except Grades 3 and 4, for which no difference was observed (Mann–Whitney U statistic of 35.00 and asymptotic significance of 0.557). Cd/F and Cs/F showed the same difference characteristics. Both passed the difference test from the beginner level to Grade 2, but no difference was found between Grades 2 and 3 and between Grades 3 and 4. Td/F only showed a difference between the beginner level and Grade 1, and failed the test for all other grades. C/T passed the difference test with significance less than 0.05 between the beginner level and Grade 1, Grades 1 and 2, and Grades 3 and 4, but failed the test between Grades 2 and 3. Cd/Td passed the difference test between the beginner level and Grade 1, but the asymptotic significance among other grades was greater than 0.05, indicating failure in the difference test.

4 Discussion and Conclusions

For the aggregate indexes, they all passed the difference test, indicating that syntactic complexity was firstly reflected in the increase of the total quantity. The increase in the total amount of text indicates the increase of the total amount of information to be absorbed. This requires the text's author to have the ability to summarize the points expressed in the text; the stronger their linguistic ability, the stronger the ability to integrate the text. Therefore, the texts at different stages define the total amount index, which increases with the grade level. Correspondingly, the same is true for learners, whose total amount of expression absorbed should increase as the grade level rises. However, the growth rate of these indexes varies by grade level, with the slowest increase occurring from the beginner level to Grade 1, and the fastest increase in total expression from Grades 2 to 3, a trend that continues to Grade 4 and beyond. Given that aggregate indexes are easy to control artificially, text authors can control the difficulty of the text through adjustment in the total amounts when examining the complexity of teaching materials or students' output. It should be noted that the aggregate increase refers to meaningful language output or input, rather than simple meaningless language repetition.

The length indexes showed no difference across several grades. Therefore, these length indexes cannot be used as indicators to distinguish the syntactic complexity of the texts used in different grades. However, the trend graphs of various length indexes all tended to rise rapidly at the primary stage; at the intermediate and advanced levels, each length indicator grows only slightly. This change characteristic decreases or even disappears in the fourth grade. Thus, these indexes are only applicable to the text used in the beginner level. The sentence length trend was particularly noteworthy. Sentence length is distinguishable in English. It is also often used as an important index in the evaluation of the difficulty of Chinese text. However, our results revealed no difference in sentence length in the texts across grade levels. Thus, sentence length may not be used to distinguish the complexity of text. This conclusion is also confirmed by Zhang [12].

The relative indexes did not show differences by grade group. Therefore, they cannot be used as distinguishing indexes. The trend graphs of C/T and Cd/Td did not show statistical differences, despite having obvious growth trends with grade progression. Therefore, these two may be used to examine the syntactic complexity of texts. These two indexes were also highly substitutable. Thus, either can be selected in the assessment of syntactic complexity depending on the situation. In addition, even at the primary stage, the proportion of compound sentences in sentences was extremely large, in contrast to the sensible presumption that the text in the primary stage must be mainly composed of single sentences. At the primary stage, compound sentences are mainly in the form of parallel compound sentences, which are called running sentences by some scholars. This point is worthy of attention in teaching or in the compilation of teaching materials.

Our study empirically examined various indexes of syntactic complexity in CSL textbooks. Therefore, the conclusions in this research are only applicable to CSL textbooks used as learning material for non-native Chinese speakers. Further empirical research is required on whether the learning materials of native speakers are suitable for the methods described here. The sample texts are presented in general Chinese language. Therefore, further studies are needed to determine whether the syntactic complexity of specialized domain languages, such as business Chinese, would also show the same characteristics.

Acknowledgments. The work was supported by the Project of Humanities and Social Sciences of the Ministry of Education: "Research on Graded Reading Standards of Business Chinese for Second Language Teaching" (18YJA740050); Key Project of International Chinese Education Research Topic of Center for Language Education and Cooperation: The Construction of the Evaluation Criterion System of Reading Attainment of International Chinese Education (20YH12B). The authors also gratefully acknowledge the helpful comments and suggestions of the viewers, which have improved the presentation.

References

1. Jiang, W.: Measurements of development in L2 written production: the case of L2 Chinese. Appl. Linguist. **34**(1), 1–24 (2013)
2. An, F.: Analysis of fluency, grammatical complexity and accuracy of CSL writing: a study based on T-unit analysis. Lang. Teach. Linguist. Stud. **03**, 11–20 (2015)
3. Cao, X., Deng, S.: The Contrastive Analysis of the Writing Performance in Chinese as L1 and L2. TCSOL Stud. (02), 39–46 (2012)
4. Wu, J.: The grammatical complexity in English native speakers' Chinese writing. Lang. Teach. Linguist. Stud. (04), 27–35 (2016)
5. Wang, Y.: Research on the Measurement Method of Syntactic Complexity of Chinese as a Second Language. Doctoral Dissertation of Beijing Normal University (2015)
6. Hunt, K.W.: Grammatical Structures Written at Three Grade Levels (report no. 3) Champaign, Il: National Council of Teachers of English (1965)
7. Hunt, K.W.: Do sentences in the second language grow like those in the first? TESOL Q. **4**, 195–202 (1970)

8. Ortega, L.: Syntactic complexity measures and their relationship to L2 proficiency: a research synthesis of college-level L2 writing. Appl. Linguist. **24**(5), 492–518 (2003)
9. Xiaofei, L.: Automatic analysis of syntactic complexity in second language writing. Int. J. Corpus Linguist. **15**(4), 474–496 (2010)
10. Endicott, A.L.: Proposed scale for syntactic complexity. Res. Teach. Engl. **7**(1), 5–12 (1973)
11. Yaochen, D., Zhiwei, F.: A quantitative linguistic study on the relationship between word length and word frequency. J. Foreign Lang. **36**(03), 29–39 (2013)
12. Ningzhi, Z.: Quantitative analysis of the difficulty of Chinese textbook corpus. Chin. Teach. World **3**, 83–88 (2000)

Construction and Quantitative Analysis of Jiangsu Dialect Function Word Knowledgebase

Xiaoru Wu, Yuling Dai, Xuefen Mao, Minxuan Feng[(✉)], and Bin Li

Nanjing Normal University, Nanjing, China
fennel_2006@163.com

Abstract. The traditional studies of Chinese dialects focus on phonetics, phonology and vocabulary, while the studies of grammar such as function words still need to be well conducted. Function words are important means of expressing grammatical meaning in a language, and they are the key features for distinguishing different dialects. In addition, the current application of Chinese information processing, such as dialect conversion, dialect analysis, also needs the information of function words. Therefore, this paper uses the framework of HowNet to describe the features of function words in Jiangsu Dialects, including Yangzhou, Yancheng, Nanjing, Suzhou and Xuzhou. Thus, we build a knowledge base of Jiangsu dialects' function words. Then we make statistics on types of function words and their formal expressions. After the statistics, we find that in some cases, a function word has more than one formal expressions, a formal expression can represent multiple meanings. With the hierarchy of HowNet, we also calculate the similarity of five dialects, finding that the similarity is about 80%.

Keywords: Dialects · Function words · Knowledgebase

1 Introduction

Dialect is the result of the continuous evolution of language. It is a precious "living fossil" for studying a language. Traditional research often pays more attention to the difference in dialect pronunciation, while the systematic research on their vocabulary and grammar is still few. As an important manifestation of grammaticalization, function words are a powerful indicator of language evolution [1]. Meanwhile, they play an important role in expressing grammatical meaning. Therefore, we can study the grammatical differences between dialects through the differences of the function words in different dialects, and try to find the affinity between dialects according to this feature.

This paper was supported by the Project of Social Science Foundation of Jiangsu Province (20JYB004) and the Project of Social Science Foundation of Jiangsu Province (20YYB007), and was supported by the National Social Science Project of China (18BYY127).

M. Dong et al. (Eds.): CLSW 2021, LNAI 13250, pp. 246–257, 2022.
https://doi.org/10.1007/978-3-031-06547-7_20

Some dialects have gradually declined because of the small group of users. At present, some measures have been taken to protect dialects, such as "Dialect Protection Plan" in Iflytek. Participants can input a dialect at will by pronouncing or typing to build a dialect database. However, such measures can't completely cover all types of Chinese dialects; the input information is not standardized, there is often a phenomenon that the voice and text do not correspond; the participants are mainly youth groups, and the dialects they use are mostly nonstandard. In addition, because of the needs of modern communication, the demand for dialect text to speech between dialects is getting stronger. However, due to the variety of dialects and the lack of electronic information of dialects, the accuracy of dialect speech recognition as text is low, only Chinese-Cantonese conversion is put into daily use. Therefore, formal representation of dialect feature information can not only preserve and study dialects but also serve the technical application of dialect speech to text.

The research on dialect function words has gradually developed in recent years, most of them are the description of function words for a certain dialect point or dialect piece, few systematic studies have been made. The resources for formalizing these systematic studies and making use of them by computers are even rarer. From the angle of theory and application, it is necessary to formally express the scattered dialect function words systematically. Taking the function words of five dialect points in Jiangsu as an example, this paper learns from and improves the computable representations of HowNet, from the perspective of Chinese information processing, constructs The Knowledgebase of Function words in Jiangsu Dialects. Based on this knowledge base, we try to calculate the similarity of each dialect and assist computer-oriented dialect research and application.

2 Related Work

2.1 Dialect Research

Phonetic features are often used in the study of distinguishing the differences between dialects abroad. According to accent and syllable-timing, dialects in specific languages such as English and Arabic [2] are classified, while there are few studies on vocabulary and grammar. Westergard predicted the diachronic evolution of two Norwegian dialects by studying their Wh-sentence patterns [3]. According to dialect materials in northeast England, Pichler and Levey verified the grammaticalization [4]. Grieve et al. constructed 139 pairs of vocabulary dialect maps based on the vocabulary data of 1.8 billion geographical locations in Britain on Twitter and BBC traditional dialect survey respectively [5], found the maps are highly consistent, that is, the regional location can be inferred from vocabulary data.

The methods of dialect classification and recognition are gradually developing, calculation methods are more varied, the scale of corpus is further expanded. Shivaprasad constructed a corpus of Telugu dialect and built a model for recognition [6]. Dialect chatbots such as Botta [7] and Nabiha [8] are also emerging.

Zhao Yuanren studied the auxiliary words in Beijing, Suzhou and Changzhou, which initiated the study of dialect grammar [9]. Since then, there have been a series of works on auxiliary words and pronouns, as well as grammatical descriptions of specific dialects or dialects.

The computational characteristics of communication degree and affinity relationship in Chinese dialects are also enriched. Qian Daxiang counted the sharing, uniqueness and distribution of different dialect points in terms of sounds, rhymes, tones, characters, morphemes and vocabulary, and distinguished the affinity between dialect points [10]. Wang Lu used the Levenshtein distance of segments to calculate the degree of communication between dialects [11]; Lin Tiansong learned from the theory of characteristic words and used grammatical features to analyze the similarity of 91 dialect points in Southwest Mandarin [12]. Zhang Yan automatically identified and generated dialect feature vocabularies in different regions according to IP addresses and input words of user input methods, and realized regional visualization of vocabulary through a quantitative comparison of regional distribution of dialect vocabulary from multiple angles [13].

Jiangsu borders Jianghaua (江淮) Mandarin, Wu (吴)Dialect and Zhongyuan (中原) Mandarin, the relationship between dialects is complicated. At present, many monographs have carried out qualitative research on the relationship between dialects in Jiangsu, but there are some inconsistencies in the division of dialects [14]. On the other hand, there is no research on the quantitative characteristics of Jiangsu dialect according to its dialect characteristics.

The above studies show that the perspective of describing dialects tends to be diversified, and we begin to pay attention to other aspects besides pronunciation, but the research results are scattered and still focus on traditional informal resources. There are also innovations in research methods. However, from the perspective of Jiangsu dialect, it is still a long way to go to study the quantitative differences between dialects according to their characteristics.

2.2   Data Resources

Function Words Resources in Chinese Dialects. The existing research and resources of dialect grammar also confirm the view that function words can be regarded as dialect features. Works describing grammatical information about various dialects from the perspective of function words began to appear constantly, such as *Modal Auxiliary Words at the End of Sentences in Guangzhou Dialect* [15], *Research on Auxiliary Words in Guangzhou Dialect* [16]. In addition, dictionaries specializing in dialect function words have also appeared, such as *Modern Chinese Dialect Dictionary* [17] and *Chinese Dialect Dictionary* [18]. In the 21st century, monographs focusing on the grammaticalization of dialect function words began to appear. As you can see, traditional researches on Chinese dialect function words are gradually enriched. But these resources are scattered and cannot be calculated as features without formal processing, so it is difficult to quantitatively apply them to dialect recognition and classification.

Computer-Oriented Dialect Resources. At present, computer-oriented dialect electronic resources mainly include dialect pronunciation, vocabulary, sentences, colloquial words, etc., but no corpus or knowledge base specifically for dialect function words has been found. This paper counts 27 kinds of electronic resources related to Chinese dialects, as shown in Table 1.

Table 1. Collection and distribution of electronic resources of Chinese dialects

Included angle	Pronunciation	Vocabulary	Other
Proportion	70.37%	25.93%	3.70%

It can be seen that the current electronic resources of dialects mainly recorded pronunciation, accounting for about 70% of the statistics in this paper, which is mainly the recording of spoken sentences in specific dialect points or dialect areas, and marked with International Phonetic Alphabet. Only about 1/4 of dialect electronic resources contain vocabulary information, which is mainly the electronization of existing dialect dictionaries and dictionaries.

At present, the electronic resources of Jiangsu dialect mainly include "Jiangsu Language and Culture Resource Library", which contains the recording of 1,000 words, 1,200 words and 50 example sentences from 70 points in Jiangsu, and the recordings of discourses (folk stories, self-selected topics and local Putonghua). The text corpus of all dialect points corresponds to the same Putonghua corpus. A text corpus is few, and it is only a simple preservation of corpus, lacking in-depth research.

3 Construction of the Knowledgebase

In order to convert existing paper dialect function word resources to programmable (that is, recognizable and operable as computers are concerned). This paper refers to *Modern Chinese Function Word Usage Dictionary* [19], improves the semantic tagging system of HowNet [20]. We use the framework of HowNet to construct The Knowledgebase of Function words in Jiangsu Dialects (KFJD). At present, the knowledge base has collected 771 cases of function words in Yangzhou (扬州), Yancheng (盐城), Nanjing (南京), Suzhou (苏州) and Xuzhou (徐州) dialect points in Jiangsu Province.

3.1 Markup Language from HowNet

In this paper, HowNet (2012 edition) is chosen as the basic labeling system, and some sememes are improved according to the *Modern Chinese Usage Dictionary*. In Hownet, the meaning of a word is composed of multiple sememes. Function words are mainly expressed by grammatical or relational sememe. Grammatical sememe is mainly part of speech. The relational sememe indicates the relationship between concepts. The labeling methods of function words in HowNet are as follows (Table 2):

Table 2. Example of description patterns of function words in HowNet

Function word	Descriptive expression
And (和)	DEF = {FuncWord| functional words: and = {?}}

In the descriptive formula of function words, "{" and "}" respectively represent the beginning and end of a conceptual expression, what follows the colon is a detailed description of the concept. "{?}" is a description of the concept "FuncWord| functional word". The equal sign is preceded by the relation sememe, a descendant of an equal sign refers to the value it has. There can be multiple parallel sememes or values in a description. The question mark is a special indicator in KDML. Thus the definition of the concept of "And" means that as long as the word "and" appears, there will be a parallel relationship.

3.2   Corpus and Annotation

At present, KFJD has collected the function words of Yangzhou, Yancheng, Nanjing, Suzhou and Xuzhou dialect points in Jiangsu Province, including prepositions, auxiliary words, conjunctions and modal particles. Yancheng, Yangzhou and Nanjing belong to Jianghuai Mandarin dialect area, while Nanjing, Suzhou and Xuzhou are the representatives of Jianghuai Mandarin, Wu Dialect Area and Zhongyuan Mandarin respectively. These five places can consider the relations and differences within and between dialect areas and this arrangement contributes to a more comprehensive understanding of the dialects. What's more, the research involved in these five dialect function words is more adequate, which can build a knowledge base more conveniently. The source corpus of these five functional words is mainly *Modern Chinese Dialect Dictionary*. It also supplements the words, examples and some literature resources included in the *Dictionary of Chinese Dialects* and Jiangsu Database of Chinese Language Resources. After pre-tagging and perfecting the tagging system of KFJD, we collected the information of function words in the corpus and tagged 437 function words, 711-word examples, and 1,525 example sentences, which were tagged by a graduate student in linguistics. Another graduate student is responsible for proofreading. Table 3 is a labeling example of two prepositional words "Mi Lou" (迷娄) and "Qi" (起) in Xuzhou, Jiangsu Province.

Table 3. Example of KFJD annotation

Function word	Part of speech	Dialect point	Formal description	Paraphrase
Mi Lou (迷娄)	prep	Jiangsu Xuzhou	{FuncWord| functional words: AcccordingTo = {?}}	Follow
Qi (起)	prep	Jiangsu Xuzhou	{FuncWord| functional words: TimeIni = {?}}	Equivalent to Beijing dialect "from"
Qi (起)	prep	Jiangsu Xuzhou	{FuncWord| functional words:LocationIni = {?}}	Equivalent to Beijing dialect "from"
Function word	Usage	Example sentence	Abnormity	Synonymy
Mi Lou (迷娄)		Ni ～ zhe na ge yang zi zuo(你～着那个样子做)<Xf>|～ hu lu hua piao(～葫芦画瓢(<Xf>	Mi Lou(眯娄)	
Qi (起)	Put it in front of the time word, indicating the starting point of time	～ ming tian, zan dou ti qian ban ge xiao shi dao chang(～明天,咱都提前半个小时到厂)<Xf>		
Qi (起)	Put it in front of the place word, indicating the starting point of the place	～che zhan wang bei, zou bu duo yuan, jiu dao an jia l (～车站往北, 走不多远, 就到俺家了)<Xf>		

From Table 3, it can be seen that in addition to the formal expression of dialect function words, KFJD also added dialect point source, interpretation, example sentences, abnormity, synonymy, etc. to describe dialect function words in detail. Among them, "<Xf>" under the example sentence indicates that the example sentence comes from the *Modern Chinese Dialect Dictionary*. Considering the particularity of dialects different word forms may have the same pronunciation. For example, "Mi Lou (迷娄)" has an abnormal word "Mi Lou (眯娄)". For these cases, we added the "synonym" field.

3.3   Statistics and Result Analysis

Table 4 shows the general situation of the collection of dialect function words in KFJD. From Table 4, it can be seen that KFJD has collected a total of 437 cases of dialect function words from five places in Jiangsu. According to the statistics of *Modern Chinese Function Word Usage Dictionary*, there are 559 cases of function words in Mandarin Chinese, far more than the number of function words collected in KFJD. There may be three reasons for analyzing this difference. Firstly, because dialect texts are mostly spoken. While in spoken language, the use frequency of function words is lower than that in written style; Secondly, there are a certain number of function words with the same morphology among different dialects; Thirdly, it is limited by the scale of KFJD and the existing resources of function words in traditional dialects. In addition, the distribution of parts of speech in each dialect point is uneven. For example, Nanjing only contains 2 conjunctions, while Suzhou contains 37 conjunctions. This shows that, there is still a problem of lack of information about function words in specific areas in these resources, and the research on this aspect can be further deepened.

Table 4. Distribution of function words of dialect points in KFJD

Part of speech	Dialect point									
	Nanjing		Suzhou		Xuzhou		Yancheng		Yangzhou	
	Word shape	Word example	Word shape	Word example	Word shape	Word example	Word shape	Word example	Word shape	Word example
Conjunction	2	2	37	41	16	16	16	16	20	20
Preposition	24	47	46	124	29	55	38	56	33	50
Auxiliary word	7	8	29	31	8	12	15	19	3	5
Modal particle	24	47	34	46	13	34	23	43	20	39
Total	57	104	146	242	66	117	92	134	76	114

In order to determine "whether function words can be used as a feature to distinguish different dialect points", this paper makes statistics on the relationship between two variables: function word types and formal expressions between different dialect points in KFJD database.

Table 5. Sharing of function words between dialect points

Dialect points	5	4	3	2	1
Number of shared function words	0	17	27	8	385
Proportion	0.00%	3.89%	6.18%	1.83%	88.10%

Table 5 is the sharing of function words between different dialect points. According to the statistics, it is not found that function words appear among five local languages at the same time. However, a total of 52 function words are shared between at least two local languages, accounting for about 12% of KFJD, which proves that there are a certain number of function words with the same word type among different dialects. However, even though these 52 function words can appear in many local languages at the same time, the usage of them is mostly different in different dialect points. By further counting the formal expressions of these 52 function words, these function words can be roughly divided into three categories. There are 9 examples of function words in the first category. They have the same function in different dialect points.

For example, in Nanjing, Yancheng and Suzhou, Jiangsu Province, "Ask" is used to introduce the substantive words that indicate the source meaning. There are 12 cases of completely inconsistent function words in the second category. Although the word types are the same, the functions and usages expressed in different dialect points are different. For example, "Ganwei" (甘为) appears in Yangzhou dialect and Yancheng dialect. But in the former, "Ganwei" is used to introduce the cause, while in the latter, the purpose is cited. There are 31 cases of function words in the third category, indicating that a certain usage of function words is common between dialects in at least two places.

Besides dialects, there is also a situation that a formal expression corresponds to multiple function words between dialect points. According to statistics, KFJD uses 74 formal labels to describe function words. Among them, there are 9 formal expressions that only appear in one place, accounting for 12.16% of the total number of tags. Limited by the scale of KFJD, about 12% of function words in dialect points express their unique functions. The distinctive features of formal expression between dialect points are obvious. Table 7 lists the concrete function words and dialect point sources marked as such formal expressions. In addition to finding the unique expression of function words in a few dialects, such as "LianDaZai", this statistic can also provide a direction for the subsequent expansion of function words in KFJD (Table 6).

Table 6. Formal expression that appears only in one place

Formal expression	Meaning	Function words	Dialect points
{FuncWord|functional words: accompaniment = {?}}	Accompany	LianDaZai (连搭仔)	Suzhou
{FuncWord|functional words:means = {?}}	Means	Ping (凭)	Yangzhou
{FuncWord|functional words: LocationFin = {?}}	End place	Dao (到)	Nanjing
{FuncWord|functional words:distance = {?}}	Distance	Li (离)	Nanjing
{FuncWord| functional words:concerning = {?}}	About	Dui (对)	Yangzhou
{FuncWord| functional words: aspect = {Vstart|starting}}	Starting	QiLai (起来)	Yancheng
{FuncWord| functional words:aspect = {Vdo-first|in advance}}	In advance	Zhe (着)	Xuzhou
{FuncWord| functional words: approximate = {?}}	approximate number	Tou (头)	Yancheng
{FuncWord| functional words: adjunct = {weak-exclamative|weak sigh}}	Weak sigh	Huo (惑)	Suzhou

In addition, another 60 formal expressions in KFJD can correspond to multiple function words between multiple dialect points, accounting for about 4/5 of the total. In this paper, the corresponding situation of these formal expressions is counted, and it is found that there are 23 kinds of them, which correspond to more than 10 function words, and most of them have the functions of introducing and expressing a mood. There are 32 types of function words that emphasize affirmative tone, such as Table 8. This shows that the use of dialect function words is flexible and rich, especially the function words expressing tone change most, which is also in line with the characteristics of the dialect spoken style.

Table 7. 32 kinds of function words in KFJD that emphasize affirmative tone.

Function word	Function word	Function word	Function word
Le勒	Ai哎	LeHua勒化	LaiLang来浪
口[lia0][a]	Duo哚	Du嘟	LaiLi来里
口[liɤɯ0]	DuoZai哚哉	Ao噢	De的
口[mæ0]	You哟	Sai噻	ZheHuLai着乎来
口[tɛ5]	Li哩	Huo惑	ZheLi着哩
Ne呢	A啊	Kai慨	ZheLai着来
ZaiWan哉畹	Nan喃	Lai来	Du笃
ZaiWei哉喂	Sha嗄	LaiDuo来哚	Ge葛

[a]At present, the words with sounds and no words are represented by the box "口" in dialect library, and only these words are recorded by International Phonetic Alphabet. The international phonetic symbols for phonetic notation are placed in "[]". The Arabic numerals 1, 2, 3, 4 and 5 are used to indicate low, half-low, middle, half-high and high five degrees, and the Arabic numeral 0 is used to indicate soft tone, and the tone value is marked in the upper right corner of syllable.

According to the above statistics, there is a many-to-many relationship between function words and formal expressions among dialect points. To quantify this relationship and examine the degree of affinity between dialect points, according to the tree system of HowNet, this paper calculates the similarity between function words. In the calculation of word similarity in HowNet, the concept similarity is the similarity of relation sememe corresponding to formal expression. The formula for calculating the similarity of sememe is:

$$Sim(p_1, p_2) = \alpha/(d + \alpha)$$

P1 and p2 represent two sememes, "d" is the path length off p1 and p2 in the sememe hierarchy, which is a positive integer, "α" is an adjustable parameter. A function word may have multiple corresponding formal expressions, that is, senses. Therefore, in order to cover every sense of a function word, this paper takes the similarity between functions of a function word as the average of the similar values of each meaning term concept. Then comparing the function words in five local dialects one by one, and take the average value of the similarity of each function word as the similarity between every two dialect points, and get Table 8.

Table 8. Similarity of function words between dialect points (%)

Dialect point	Xuzhou	Nanjing	Yancheng	Yangzhou	Suzhou
Xuzhou	/	/	/	/	
Nanjing	74.44	/	/	/	/
Yancheng	80.62	82.91	/	/	/
Yangzhou	82.27	77.45	82.68	/	/
Suzhou	83.43	81.95	83.86	82.10	/

It can be seen that according to the formal representation characteristics of function words, the similarity of function words in five dialects in Jiangsu is about 80%, and the similarity between Nanjing and Xuzhou is the lowest, 74.44%. Suzhou and Yancheng have the highest similarity of 83.86%. Judging from the feature of function words in KFJD, the degree of dissimilarity between Nanjing and Xuzhou is more prominent. However, there is little difference among other dialect points. According to the further analysis of this paper, firstly, because the five dialect points belong to Jiangsu Province, the geographical position is close. Although there are differences among dialects, there is little difference in general, and there is a strong correlation among dialect points. Secondly, although Suzhou and Yancheng do not belong to the same dialect area, they are geographically closer and have more frequent social exchanges, which makes it more likely that the use of function words between dialects is more similar. Thirdly, although Nanjing and Xuzhou belong to the Jianghuai Mandarin dialect area, the geographical remoteness of the two places may result in the low similarity of function words. Finally, this paper only chooses the formal representation of function words and does not include the investigation of other features such as pronunciation. Therefore, the accuracy of similarity results of function words will be affected to some extent.

4   Conclusion

Function words carry rich grammatical meaning and play an important role in the expression of syntactic and semantic of Chinese sentences, and the existence of function words is also the result of Chinese grammaticalization. Dialects have undergone a long evolution, and there are many differences in pronunciation and grammar between dialects. At present, although most researchers consider the phonetic features of dialect function words, they pay less attention to the function words which have undergone grammatical evolution and do not take the function words as characteristics to study the similarities and differences between dialects. Therefore, this paper uses the framework of HowNet to describe the features of function words and constructs the Knowledge base of Function words in Jiangsu Dialects, taking Yangzhou, Yancheng, Nanjing, Suzhou and Xuzhou as examples. This paper also attempts to investigate the similarity of five dialects in Jiangsu Province, and finds that the similarity is about 80%.

5 Future Work

Since KFJD only involves the function words between five dialect points in Yangzhou, Yancheng, Nanjing, Suzhou and Xuzhou, it still needs to be expanded in scale. In the future, it will further include other dialect points and the function words in Mandarin, and on the basis of a largescale knowledge base, it will weigh the pronunciation and function of the function words, and dig deep into the relationship among dialects. In addition, the link alignment between dialect function words and Mandarin function words will be carried out in the future so that KFJD can better serve various applications of Chinese information processing, such as dialect speech to text.

References

1. Liu, D.-Q.: Grammaticalization theory and dialect. Dialect **31**(02), 106–116 (2009). (刘丹青: 语法化理论与汉语方言语法研究. 方言)
2. Low, E., Grabe, E., Nolan, F.: Quantitative characterizations of speech rhythm: "syllable-timing" in Singapore English. Lang. Speech **43**(4), 3401–3777 (2001)
3. Westergaard, M.R.: Optional word order in, wh-questions in two Norwegian dialects: a diachronic analysis of synchronic variation. Nord. J. Linguist. **28**(02), 269 (2005)
4. Pichler, H., Levey, S.: In search of grammaticalization in synchronic dialect data: general extenders in Northeast England. Engl. Lang. Linguist. **15**(03), 441–471 (2011)
5. Grieve, J., Montgomery, C., Nini, A., Murakami, A., Guo, D.: Mapping lexical dialect variation in British English using Twitter. Front. Artif. Intell. **2**, 1–11 (2019)
6. Shivaprasad, S., Sadanandam, M.: Identification of regional dialects of Telugu language using text independent speech processing models. Int. J. Speech Technol. **23**(2), 251–258 (2020). https://doi.org/10.1007/s10772-020-09678-y
7. Ali, A., Habash, N.: Botta: an Arabic dialect chatbot. In: Computer Science, pp. 208–212 (2016)
8. Al-Ghadhban, D., Al-Twairesh, N.: Nabiha: an Arabic dialect chatbot. Int. J. Adv. Comput. Sci. Appl. **11**(3), 452–459 (2020)
9. Zhao, Y.-R.: The study of Beijing, Suzhou and Changzhou language auxiliary words. J. Tsinghua Univ. (Sci. Technol.) **02**, 865–917 (1926). (赵元任:北京,苏州,常州语助词的研究.清华大学学报(自然科学版))
10. Qian, D.-X.: A metrological study on the relationship between Chinese dialects based on the phonological vocabulary database of modern Chinese dialects. Nanjing Normal University (2009). (钱大香: 基于《现代汉语方言语音词汇库》的汉语方言关系计量研究. 南京师范大学)
11. Wang, L.: Language distance and Wu language intercommunication. East China Normal University (2014). (王璐: 语言距离与吴语互通度. 华东师范大学)
12. Lin, T.-S.: Southwest Mandarin classification based on grammatical features. Stud. Lang. Linguist. **35**(01), 60–66 (2015). (林天送: 基于语法特征的西南官话分类. 语言研究)
13. Zhang, Y.: A quantitative study of Chinese hot words and dialect vocabulary in the Internet environment. Tsinghua University (2014). (张燕: 互联网环境下的中文热词与方言词汇的定量研究. 清华大学)
14. Zhao, Zh.-J.: A survey on the relationship between Jiangsu dialects. Mod. Chin. **03**, 52–57 (2020). (赵志靖: 江苏方言关系研究概况. 现代语文)

15. Fang, X.-Y.: Modal Auxiliary Words at the End of Sentences in Guangzhou Dialect. Jinan University Press, Guangzhou (2003). (方小燕: 广州方言句末语气助词. 暨南大学出版社)
16. Peng, X.-Ch.: Research on Auxiliary Words in Guangzhou Dialect. Jinan University Press, Guangzhou (2010). (彭小川: 广州话助词研究. 暨南大学出版社)
17. Li, R.: Modern Chinese Dialect Dictionary. Phoenix Education Publishing, Ltd., Nanjing (1998). (李荣: 现代汉语方言大词典.江苏教育出版社)
18. Xu, B.-H., Ichiro, M.: Chinese Dialect Dictionary. Zhonghua Book Company, Beijing (1999). (许宝华,宫田一郎: 汉语方言大词典.中华书局)
19. Zan, H.-Y., Zhang, K.-L., Chai, Y.-M., Yu, Sh.-W.: Study on the knowledge base of function words in modern Chinese. J. Chin. Inf. Process. 05, 107–111 (2007). (昝红英, 张坤丽, 柴玉梅, 俞士汶: 现代汉语虚词知识库的研究. 中文信息学报)
20. Dong, Zh.-D., Dong, Q., Hao, Ch.-L.: The theoretical discovery of the HowNet. J. Chin. Inf. Process. 04, 3–9 (2007). (董振东, 董强, 郝长伶: 知网的理论发现. 中文信息学报)

Construction of Event Annotation Corpus for Political News Texts

Ruimin Wang, Yajuan Ye, Kunli Zhang$^{(\boxtimes)}$, Hongying Zan,
and Yingjie Hang

School of Information Engineering, Zhengzhou University, Zhengzhou, China
{iermwang, ieklzhang, iehyzan, ieyjhan}@zzu.edu.cn

Abstract. The extraction of event elements from political news texts can lay the foundation for the construction of knowledge graph of political news events, but the construction of event annotation corpus as the basis of event extraction research is not perfect. In this paper, we discuss the construction of an Event Annotation Corpus for Political News texts (EACPN). The initial corpus used in this paper comes from the 2019 political news text. Based on the investigation of the existing news event annotation corpus, and combined with the characteristics of the political news text, an annotation schema has been established. The schema covers five categories of event elements and sub-categories: visit, conference, investigation, telegram and letter, and foreign affairs activity. Accordingly, we formulated a complete specification for the annotation of political news texts, and then used the distributed annotation platform to carry out multiple rounds of data annotation. EACPN contains more than 20,000 pieces of political news with 128,000 event elements in about 290,000 sentences, and high consistency is achieved in the results.

Keywords: Political news · Annotation specification · Event annotation · Corpus

1 Introduction

With the development of the Internet, a large number of unstructured information resources have been accumulated in the field of news. Especially in the field of political news, it contains a lot of information about political figures, events and activities. Research on how to extract the characters and event relations from the current political news texts can help to grasp the development trend of political events and lay the foundation for the construction of event knowledge graph. Knowledge graph originated from semantic Web [1], which was proposed by Google in May 2012. From the perspective of events, the semantic information of events is structured in the form of knowledge graph to provide theoretical and technical support for event-oriented theory and application research [2]. In 2016, Rospocher et al. [3] proposed an Event Centric Knowledge Graph (ECKG), which extracted the time, place, participants and other event elements from news reports, and established the relationship between events. Event knowledge graph describes events and event relations in the form of structure and has been widely applied in the field of news.

© Springer Nature Switzerland AG 2022
M. Dong et al. (Eds.): CLSW 2021, LNAI 13250, pp. 258–271, 2022.
https://doi.org/10.1007/978-3-031-06547-7_21

Event extraction is the key step for the construction of event knowledge graph, which refers to extracting events and event-related elements from the text [4]. The international assessment conference for the automatic content extraction (ACE) defined two key steps in event extraction: event trigger word extraction and event element extraction [5]. The extraction of event trigger words is to find out the core words that can reflect the occurrence of events and classify them. The extraction of event elements is to extract the event information such as time, place and personnel involved in events. The main information of the text can be obtained according to the result of event extraction, and the text can be classified according to the type of event trigger word or event element.

In the case of instance representation event extraction research in the news field, Zhou et al. [6] used unsupervised model to extract valuable news events from twitter and express them in a structured way. Yuan et al. [7] used entities and entity types in news corpus to establish time slot value pairs to detect events, and generated a structured representation framework of events. Instance representation event extraction can be oriented to events of different field backgrounds and application requirements, and it can also be oriented to event corpus in general domains. However, it is difficult to accurately obtain semantic information for instance representation event extraction due to the complexity of the language structure, which requires a certain artificial method to assist [8]. In terms of frame representation event extraction research, Petroni et al. [9] proposed a framework for extracting emergencies from news reports and social media, defining seven types of emergencies such as "flood", "fire", and "wind". On the basis of 5W1H, the presentation framework (who, what, where, when, why and how) analysis methods of various event elements are designed. Although the annotated corpus of the frame representation events can guarantee the number of each event type, the scale of most annotation corpora is still very small [8].

Event annotation corpus is the basis for event extraction. Many scholars and evaluations have focused on the construction of news event corpora, such as multi-lingual ACE test comment data [5], mainly includes English, Chinese and Arabic. The content of ACE is mainly derived from news corpora, including newswire, broadcast news, etc.

In English, there are two event databases, ICEWS [10] and Gdelt [11], which are based on news corpus. It focuses on defining the type and elements of the event. For Chinese, there is the Chinese Emergency Corpus (CEC) [12], which is constructed by the Semantic Intelligence Laboratory of Shanghai University and contains 332 documents. The news of earthquake, fire, traffic accident, terrorist attack and food poisoning obtained from the Internet is formed by a series of annotation and processing.

The existing open assessment corpus is mostly oriented to the general domain, and a small number of domain-specific event extraction corpus cannot meet the needs of various practical applications. For example, ACE only annotates the common events concerned by the news corpus, CEC only divides the events in detail, but its scale is small. Different types of news have their own peculiarities, and the news corpus in the general field cannot meet the needs of the research in the field of political news. Therefore, it is necessary to construct a corpus according to the characteristics of the political news text. Table 1 shows the comparison between ACE2005 corpus, CEC corpus and the EACPN constructed in this paper. (Where "$\sqrt{}$" means annotated, "$\times$" means unannotated).

Table 1. Corpus comparison

Category	EACPN	ACE2005	CEC
Language	Chinese	Chinese/English/Arabic	Chinese
Article number	21,455	1,635	332
The event type	5	8	5
All events	√	×	√
Event elements	√	√	√
Event relationship	×	×	√
Schema	Event-based	Event-based	Semantic-based

In this paper, we took 2019 political news text as annotation object and carries out fine-grained annotation. Firstly, we established annotation granularity and annotation system through careful analysis and research on the corpus, and then formulated annotation specification. Annotation is mainly divided into event element and event subcategory annotation, and annotation of event participants with different roles. In order to ensure the accuracy and consistency of the annotation results, the event annotation procedure, the control scheme of the annotation consistency and the reasonable evaluation method are established. Finally, the special processing results of typical events and the construction of corpus are analyzed and explained.

2   Annotation System and Standard of Political News Text

2.1   Text Annotation Schema of Political News

According to the event activities in news events, the trigger words of different events are determined, and the political news texts are divided into five categories: visit, conference, investigation, telegram and letter, and foreign affairs activity. Each type of event contains a large number of relationships between political figures and the internal connections of the events. First of all, there will be multiple political figures in the event, and the political figures involved in the same event will have multiple roles. Different types of news events also involve different personas. In order to better distinguish the attributes of multiple people in various events, personas need to be divided. In addition, there are many sub-events in a news event, and there are internal links between sub-events. Especially in a meeting event, there will be organization names nested in the meeting name. Therefore, each type of event needs to be divided into relatively detailed annotation granularity.

Based on the analysis of political news texts, according to the annotation granularity, and referring to the type definitions of ACE2005 and CEC corpus, an annotation system is constructed. As shown in Fig. 1, Event annotation mainly includes four types of event trigger word, event type, event element and element role. For different events, the event trigger words have different modifiers, and each type of event is divided into different sub-events according to the modifiers. The annotation of sub-events is reflected by sub-categories. For example, in visit events, when "国事访问[*guo shi fang wen*](*state visit*)" occurs, the sub-category is "国事访问[*guo shi fang wen*](*state visit*)". If "正式访问 [*zheng shi fang wen*](*official visit*)", "友好访问[*you hao fang wen*](*friendly visit*)", or "友好正式访问[*you hao zheng shi fang wen*](*friendly official visit*)" is displayed, the subcategory is "正式访问[*zheng shi fang wen*](*official visit*)". When there are trigger words such as "访问[*fang wen*](*visit*)" without modifiers, the subcategory is "working visit". When there is "总理会晤 [*zong li hui wu*](*Prime Ministers' conference*)", "领导人非正式会晤[*ling dao ren fei zheng shi hui wu*](*leaders' informal conference*)" and "领导人小型会晤[*ling dao ren xiao xing hui wu*](*leaders' mini-conference*)", the sub-category is "领导人会晤[*ling dao ren hui wu*](*leaders' conference*)".

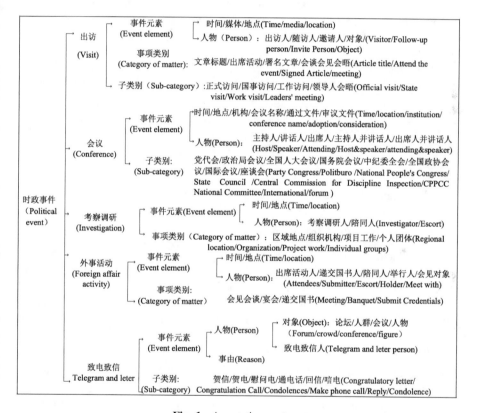

Fig. 1. Annotation system

After analyzing the features of various news events, the following five types of event trigger words are defined:

(1) Visit: 访[*fang*](*visit*), 访问[*fang wen*](*visit*)
(2) Conference: 参加[*can jia*](*attend*), 召开[*zhao kai*](*convene*)
(3) Investigation: 考察[kao cha] (*investigation*), 调研[*diao yan*](*investigation*)
(4) Telegram and letter: 致电[*zhi dian*](*send a telegram*), 致信[*zhi xin*](*send a letter*)
(5) Foreign affairs activity: 会见[*hui jian*](*meet*)

For different event types, nine event element types are defined:

(1) Time: The time when the event occurred.
(2) Location: The location where the incident occurred.
(3) Person: Event participants, according to the relationship between the political figures and the event, different event categories are divided into different roles.
(4) Title of the article: It only exists in the event of the visit, and specifically points out the article published by the visitor on the eve of the visit.
(5) Media: Only exists in the event of a visit, and specifically refers to the media that published articles on the eve of the visit.
(6) Reason: In the case of calling and sending a letter, the reason for calling and sending a letter is usually one sentence, and nesting is allowed.
(7) Conference name: The name of the conference to be held, nesting is allowed.
(8) Organization: The name of the organization that held the meeting, usually nested in the name of the meeting.
(9) Documents: Only exist in meeting events, including deliberation and approval documents.

Three categories are defined for different event types:

(1) Sub-category: Classify the sub-events in the event.
(2) Category of matter: According to a certain event carried out by the person in the event, the category is divided.
(3) Object category: Classify the categories of objects in the event.

2.2 Annotation Syntax Definition

In order to facilitate the data storage of the corpus and subsequent research, the basic form of annotation is defined as "{cited phrases < name: value | name1: value1 | name2: value2 >}". The symbols in the basic form of annotation are all English punctuation characters, elements cannot be missing, and the order is consistent with the definition. The detailed description of the annotation symbols is shown in Table 2.

Table 2. Annotation symbols and meanings

Symbol	Meaning
{}	Rules to identify the range of phrases referenced by annotations and to extract labels and support nesting
<>	The meaning of the marked item must appear at the end of {}; Each {} may occur only once
|	A delimiter for multiple label items in parallel, appearing only within <>; Identification of the referenced phrase produces multiple label items, irrespective of the order of the juxtapositive; The absence of this separator means that the referenced text generates a label
:	The "name: value" separator that identifies a label, which appears only in <>; The label name before the colon is "name", and the label value after the colon is "value". If a label item does not have a colon, it is itself "name" and the referenced phrase is "value"

2.3 Annotation Rules

Based on the characteristics of various political news events, the annotation rules formulated mainly include relevance, not across sentence and nested rules. Among them, the principle of relevance and not across sentence are the constraints on the five types of events. In addition to "subcategory", the annotation of individual event elements can also be nested to ensure the integrity of event information. The following illustrates the three types of annotation rules in combination with annotation examples.

1) Relevance rule

The annotated content should be highly relevant to the attribute to be annotated, and the content should be appropriately short to avoid the introduction of irrelevant content. When there are multiple optional annotated text phrases, the text phrase whose context is more relevant and can fully express the semantics should be annotated as far as possible.

(1) {{市委 < 机构[ji gou](institution) >}召开{常委会扩大会议 < 会议名称[hui yi ming cheng](conference name) >} < 子类别:其他会议[zi lei bie:qi ta hui yi] (Subcategory: Other conferences) >}, 认真学习……精神。(*The Municipal Party Committee held an enlarged meeting of the Standing Committee to study the spirit of...*)

The details of the conferences in this example do not need to be included.

2) The rule of not crossing sentences

"{ }" cannot contain more than one period or paragraph, but can contain multiple clauses separated by commas.

(2) {{{十三届全国政协 < 机构[ji gou](institution) >}第二十一次双周协商座谈会 < 会议名称[hui yi ming chneg](conference name) >}{近日 < 时间[shi jian] (time) >}在{京 < 地点[di sian](location) >}召开 < 子类别:全国政协会议[zi lei bie: quan guo zheng xie hui yi](Subcategory: National Committee of the Chinese People's Political Consultative Conference) >}。中共……主席{汪洋 < 主持人| 讲话人[zhu chi ren | jiang hua ren](host | speaker) >}主持会议并讲话。(*The 21st bi-weekly consultation forum of the 13th National Committee of the Chinese People's Political Consultative Conference was held in Beijing in recent days. CCP... Chairman Wang Yang presided over the meeting and gave a speech.*)

In this example, the person does not appear in the first sentence. The scope of the subcategory can only reach the end of the first sentence, so the figure should not be included within the subcategory.

3) Nested rule

The subcategories in the four types of events of "visit", "conference", "foreign affairs activity", and "telegram and letter" can be nested annotation. If there is no specific subcategory, they will be labeled as "other". The "subcategory" in the event can be nested to include other annotation items, but cannot be contained by other annotation items. The annotation scope of subcategory should follow the principle of minimum and completeness. In addition, the "cause" in a "telegram and letter" event can be nested with other categories, and the "conference name" in the "conference" event can be nested to include "conference institution".

(3) {{中共中央政治局常务委员会 < 机构[ji   gou](institution) >}{3月18日 < 时间 [shi jian](time) >}再次召开会议 < 子类别:政治局会议[zi lei bie: zheng zhi ju hui yi](Subcategory: Politburo conference) >}, 分析......重点工作, {习近平 < 主 持人|讲话人[zhu chi ren | jiang hua ren](host | speaker) >}总书记主持会议并发 表重要讲话。(*The Standing Committee of the Political Bureau of the CPC Central Committee held a conference again on March 18 to analyze... the key tasks. General Secretary Xi Jinping presided over the meeting and delivered an important speech.*)

In this example, "held a conference" is followed by a sentence that has nothing to do with the event category, so the following sentence may not be included when annotating the subcategory.

2.4   Handling of Special Circumstances

The construction of high-quality annotated corpora requires a complete annotation system, annotation procedures, and annotation consistency scheme. In addition, annotators are needed to have the knowledge about the relevant field and gain insight into the annotation specification. In the annotation process, there are several special cases as follows, which are treated differently.

1) Successive locations
   Generally, the location appears singly in the political news event. When the locations appear consecutively, we merge the entire locations and annotate them together. If other words are interspersed in the locations, we annotate them separately.
2) Boundary of event elements
   In the investigation event, it is necessary to pay attention to the difference between "location" and "regional location". If the "location" of the investigation appears continuously with the "regional location" of the item category, the general rule is to split the "location" into the county or city, and the latter part can be marked as "regional location".
3) Range of sub-categories
   In the event of telegram and letter, if there is no word "congratulation" or "congratulation letter" in the text when marking the subcategory, the processing of this paper is to annotate a sentence that reflects the subcategory.

3   Corpus Construction

3.1   Data Preparation and Preprocessing

The data for this annotation comes from the political news of Xinhua net in 2019. There are some garbles, empty texts, and there is also some HTML tag information in the original corpus. These problem corpus will affect the efficiency and quality of annotation, so data cleaning is needed. Due to the differences in annotation of different event categories, in order to improve annotation efficiency, this batch of data needs to be classified into five categories before annotation, including visit, conference, investigation, telegram and letter, and foreign affairs activity. Figure 2 shows the specific data pretreatment process.

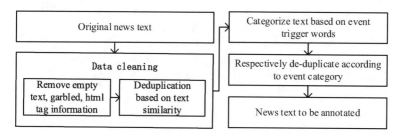

Fig. 2. Data preprocessing process

3.2   Annotation Platform

In order to improve the annotation efficiency, we carried out secondary development and deployment of the existing medical text-oriented entity relationship annotation platform [13], and modified the entity items according to the established annotation system to make it suitable for annotation political news. In addition, on the basis of the instant analysis of annotation data and the generation of annotation comparison report, according to the definition of annotation grammar, a rule-based method is adopted to automatically check the format and content of annotation data. Due to the large number of chapters in the annotated corpus, annotators are allowed to create annotation task that includes multiple files. The name of the completed annotated file is displayed in green to facilitate the annotator to find the files that he has missed. The annotation platform interface is shown in Fig. 3.

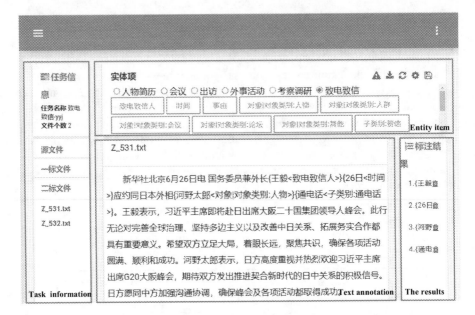

Fig. 3. Annotation platform

3.3 Annotation Consistency Control

According to the established annotation specifications, we adopt a multi-round iterative model to revise and label the specifications, and divide the entire annotation process into two stages: pre-annotation and formal annotation. In the pre-annotation stage, the annotator learns the annotation specification and the operation process of the annotation platform, and allocates a small amount of text for annotation. At this stage, annotators can understand the annotation characteristics of political news text and master the use of the annotation platform, and at the same time, it can detect the stability of the platform. After the pre-annotation process is over, a comparative analysis report will be generated from the results, and the inconsistencies will be discussed and revised. This stage is carried out iteratively until a higher consistency is reached before entering the formal annotation stage.

At the formal annotation stage, two annotators participate in annotating each news text, first by an annotator who annotated it and record the existence question, then by another annotator who recorded the existence question on the basis of annotation, and finally unified by the politics news domain experts to discuss the reasonable solution. In this process, the annotation specification is constantly modified and improved.

As annotators can only perform automatic inspections on the documents they have annotated, there will be a certain number of errors and omissions. Therefore, it is necessary to conduct automated format and content inspections on the entire annotation results, and uniformly modification the inspection results to the annotators for final modification. Figure 4 shows the automatic inspection result style. For example, "WARNING – [一标/时政人物2-考察调研-K_4001-ye/K_4038.txt] 语法错误_括号 未配对[yu fa cuo wu _ kuo hao wei pei dui](Syntax error brackets are not matched)". The inspection results are mainly divided into prompt information (INFO) and warning information (WARNING). The prompt information needs the annotator to confirm whether it needs to be modified, and the warning information must be modified. After annotation, we use the consistency evaluation F1 value [15] as a measure of consistency index.

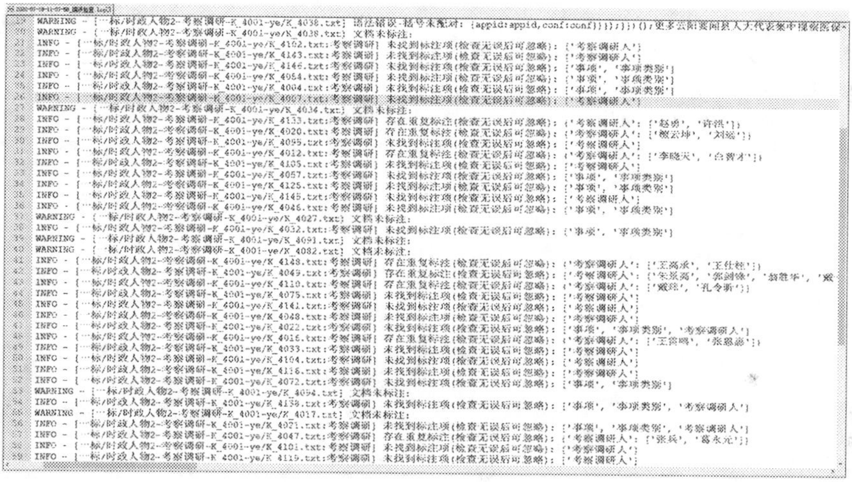

Fig. 4. Automatic inspection result display

4   Analysis of Corpus Annotation Results

4.1   Annotation Result Analysis

The corpus we constructed contains 21,455 annotated texts with a total of approximately 15 million words. The statistics of EACPN are shown in Fig. 5. It can be seen from the figure that compared with other events of the same magnitude, conference events have the largest number of event elements annotated. The reason is that there are multiple sub-conference events in a conference corpus, and some conference events have multiple attendees.

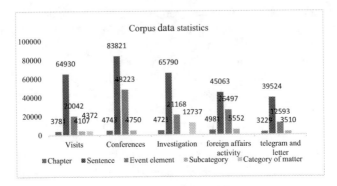

Fig. 5. Corpus data statistics

Figure 6 is the statistics of the number of event elements in the EACPN. The political figures here include specific names and group names. In political news events, except for the telegram and letter events, other categories of events include person, time and location. Therefore, the total number of figures accounted for 57.3% of the total number of event elements. Time and place accounted for 10.8% and 11.8% of the total event elements respectively.

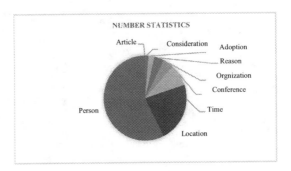

Fig. 6. Number statistics of each event element in corpus

4.2   Annotation Consistency Analysis

Generally, Kappa value [14] and F1 value [15] are used as evaluation indicators for annotation consistency in corpus construction. However, in event element annotation, if unannotated text is taken as counterexamples, it is difficult to count the number of counterexamples. In this case, F1 value is close to Kappa value, so F1 value can be used to evaluate the consistency of annotated corpus [16]. The specific method is to use the annotation result of the first annotator (A1) as the standard answer, and calculate the accuracy (P), recall rate (R) and F1 value of the annotation result of the second annotator (B1).

According to the above methods, the annotation consistency tests were carried out for visit, conference, investigation, telegram and letter, and foreign affairs activity respectively. Table 3 lists the F1 values of these five types of events.

Table 3. Annotation consistency analysis

Category	F1
Visit	0.9072
Conference	0.8153
Investigation	0.7648
Foreign affairs activity	0.8949
Telegram and letter	0.9107
Total	0.8550

It can be seen from Table 3 that the annotation consistency of different event categories is different. The main reason is the complexity of the event itself and different understanding of the event elements by the annotator, but the overall annotation consistency still reached a relatively high level. It is pointed out in literature [17] that the consistency of corpus can be regarded as reliable when the consistency of annotation reaches above 0.8.

4.3   Visual Display of Corpus

The constructed corpus mainly includes five types of events, including visits, conference, investigation, telegram and letter, and foreign affairs activity. Each type of event contains corresponding event elements. Through the analysis of the corpus, the corpus can be divided into event-centered and character-centered or it can be displayed in a time-centric manner. As shown in Fig. 7, each type of event was well visually displayed.

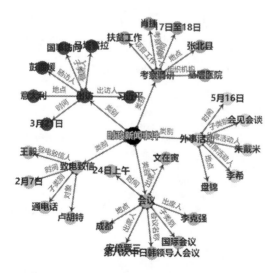

Fig. 7. Shows an example of a visualization

5 Conclusion

Based on the analysis of the characteristics of political news texts, and referring to the type definitions of AEC2005 and CEC corpus, we established the event annotation specification and the annotation consistency control scheme of political news text. After multiple rounds of annotation the news corpus, EACPN completed more than 20,000 political news, and about 290,000 event elements and subcategories of each sentence were labeled. On this basis, a series of data statistics and analysis on the corpus are helpful in discovering some laws of political news texts in different event categories. This fine-grained event annotation corpus of political news text can lay the foundation for future event extraction research and event-based knowledge graphs construction of political figures.

Acknowledgments. We thank the anonymous reviewers for their constructive comments, and gratefully acknowledge the support of National Key Research and Development Program (2017YFB1002101), National Natural Science Foundation of China (62006211), Henan Science and Technology Research Project (192102210260), Henan Medicine Science and Technology Research Plan: Provincial and Ministry Co-construction Project (SB201901021), Ministry of Education Humanities and Social Science Planning Project (20YJA740033), Henan Province Philosophy and Social Science Planning Project (2019BYY016).

References

1. Berners-Lee, T., Hendler, J., Lassila, O.: The semantic web. Sci. Am. **284**(5), 34–43 (2001)
2. Wang, X.-C., Peng, L., Guo, W., et al.: The construction and application of event knowledge graph based on corpus. J. Fuyang Normal Univ. (Nat. Sci. Ed.). **37**(04), 56–60 (2020). (in Chinese)
3. Rospocher, M., Vanerp, M., Vossen, P., et al.: Building event centric knowledge graphs from news. J. Web Semant. **37**, 132451 (2016)
4. Piskorski, J., Tanev, H., Atkinson, M., van der Goot, E., Zavarella, V.: Online news event extraction for global crisis surveillance. In: Nguyen, N.T. (ed.) Transactions on Computational Collective Intelligence V, pp. 182–212. Springer, Heidelberg (2011). https://doi.org/10.1007/978-3-642-24016-4_10
5. Doddingtong, R., Mitchell, A., Przybockim, A., et al.: The automatic content extraction (ACE) program-tasks, data, and evaluation. In: Proceedings of the 2004 International Conference on Language Resources and Evaluation, Lisbon, Portugal, pp. 837–840. European Language Resources Association (2004)
6. Zhou, D., Zhang, X., He, Y.: Event extraction from Twitter using non-parametric Bayesian mixture model with word embeddings. In: Proceedings of the 15th EACL, Valencia, Spain, pp. 808–817. ACL (2017)
7. Yuan, Q., Ren, X., He, W., et al.: Open-schema event profiling for massive news corpora. In: Proceedings of the 27th ACM International Conference on Information and Knowledge Management, Torino, Italy, pp. 587–596. ACM (2018)
8. Xiang, W., Wang, B.: A review of Chinese event extraction. J. Comput. Technol. Dev. **30**(02), 1–6 (2020). (in Chinese)

9. Petroni, F., Raman, N., Nugent, T., et al.: An extensible event extraction system with cross media event resolution. In: Proceedings of the 24th ACM SIGKDD International Conference on Knowledge Discovery & Data Mining, London, United Kingdom, pp. 626–635. ACM (2018)
10. Lautenschlager, J., Shellman, S., Ward, M.: ICEWS events and aggregations. Harvard Dataverse 3 (2015)
11. Leetaru, K., Schrodt, P.A.: GDELT: global data on events, location, and tone, 1979–2012. In: ISA Annual Convention, vol. 2, no. 4, pp. 1–49. Citeseer (2013)
12. Liu, W., Wang, X., Zhang, Y.-J., et al.: An emergency oriented automatic annotation method for text corpus. J. Chin. Inf. Process. **31**(02), 76–85 (2017). (in Chinese)
13. Zhang, K.-L., Zhao, X., Guan, T.-F., et al.: Construction and application of entity and relationship annotation platform for medical text. J. Chin. Inf. Process. **34**(06), 36–44 (2020). (in Chinese)
14. Carletta, J.: Assessing agreement on classification tasks: the kappa statistic. Comput. Linguist. **22**(2), 249–254 (1996)
15. Hripcsak, G., Rothschild, A.S.: Agreement, the f-measure, and reliability in information retrieval. J. Am. Med. Inform. Assoc. JAMIA **12**(3), 296–298 (2005)
16. Ogren, P., Savova, G., Chute, C.: Constructing evaluation corpora for automated clinical named entity recognition. In: Proceedings of the 12th World Congress on Health (Medical) Informatics, Marrakech, Morocco, pp. 2325–2330. European Language Resources Association (ELRA) (2008)
17. Artstein, R., Poesio, M.: Inter-coder agreement for computational linguistics. Comput. Linguist. **34**(4), 555–596 (2008)

Developing a Syntactic and Semantic Annotation Tool for Research on Chinese Vocabulary

Shan Wang[1,2(✉)], Xiaojun Liu[1], and Jie Zhou[1]

[1] Department of Chinese Language and Literature, Faculty of Arts and Humanities, University of Macau, Taipa, Macau, China
shanwang@um.edu.mo
[2] Institute of Collaborative Innovation, University of Macau, Taipa, Macau, China

Abstract. Syntax and semantics are of great importance for vocabulary research. Large-scale corpus-based studies concerning the syntactic and semantic features of Chinese vocabulary are needed. To fill the gap, this study develops a syntactic and semantic annotation tool based on dependency grammar, and delves into the syntax and semantics of the most frequently used disyllabic visual verb *kànjiàn* 'see' as an example. First, this study developed a syntactic and semantic annotation tool of dependency grammar. Second, this study extracted and selected simple sentences with *kànjiàn* from large-scale corpora. Third, the tool was used to conduct syntactic and semantic dependency tagging and manual checking. Results show that *kànjiàn* can appear in six types of syntactic dependencies as a dependent, namely, Head (predicate), Attribute, Coordination, Verb-Object, and Subject-Verb. Moreover, the most frequent syntactic function of *kànjiàn* is being a predicate, which accounts for 85.4%. The semantic roles that *kànjiàn* collocates with fall into five categories, which are CONTENT, EXPERIENCER, PLACE, TIME, and MANNER. The two most frequent ones are CONTENT and EXPERIENCER. Further, this paper compared the results with previous Chinese resources. The outcomes of this study prove the importance of the syntactic and semantic annotation tool in analyzing Chinese vocabulary and help us have a deep understanding of the characteristics of Chinese visual verbs.

Keywords: A syntactic and semantic annotation tool · Dependency grammar · Syntax · Semantics · Visual verbs · *kànjiàn*

1 Introduction

Tesnière's dependency grammar is of great importance for natural language processing (NLP) to analyze the syntax and semantics of language [1, 2], and that's also why it attracts much attention in the field of NLP. For example, large-scale dependency grammar based machine learning studies can be used for classification research [3], which enhances the accuracy with feature extraction based on dependency grammar. However, there are few studies on the syntax and semantics of specific Chinese verbs from the perspective of dependency grammar and tools to annotate their syntactic and semantic dependency are in urgent needed.

© Springer Nature Switzerland AG 2022
M. Dong et al. (Eds.): CLSW 2021, LNAI 13250, pp. 272–294, 2022.
https://doi.org/10.1007/978-3-031-06547-7_22

Eyes are important organs for humans to perceive the world and visual verbs standing for eye activities are the main access for humans to obtain information and knowledge. Previous studies of Chinese visual verbs investigated their semantic features from the qualia structure of Generative Lexicon [4] and Cognitive Construction Grammar [5], while large-scale research on the syntax and semantics of visual verbs are to be explored. Based on dependency grammar, the present study, taking the most frequently used disyllabic visual verb *kànjiàn* 'see' as an example, explores its syntactic and semantic features with the newly self-developed syntactic and semantic annotation tool.

2   Related Research

Dependency grammar originated in France and developed in Germany. Compared with phrase structure grammar, it is more suitable to analyze the syntactic structure of Chinese [6]. Since Feng [7] introduced it to China, dependency grammar has developed a lot and become a widely used analysis method in the field of natural language processing. For example, it was used to improve the accuracy of cluster analysis, and thus to conduct hot topic mining [8]. Some Chinese dependency treebanks were also constructed, such as the multi-view Chinese treebank of Peking University [9] and Chinese Dependency Treebank of Harbin Institute of Technology [10]. These dependency treebanks are helpful to consult the dependency relations of phrases or sentences one by one, but are inconvenient to conduct large-scale analysis and the errors cannot be revised directly. A syntactic and semantic annotation tool based on dependency grammar is strongly in need.

Liu's team has many Chinese studies based on dependency grammar, including probabilistic valence model [11], complex networks [12], second language acquisition [13], and the distribution of part-of-speech [14]. The syntactic network of Chinese is complex [12]. The syntactic function of Chinese verbs with dependency treebank was studied in [15], and the syntactic function of parts of speech in different Chinese genres was explored [16] based on dependency grammar tagged corpus. Li and Liu [17] examined Chinese kids' acquisition of three-word sentences through dependency types, dependency relationship and average dependency distance. Other Chinese studies based on dependency grammar include the comparison of function words [18], the classification of imperative sentences [19], and the valence of verbs [20].

Recently the syntax and semantics of Chinese lexicon have attracted much attention, especially in terms of multiword expressions, collocations, and idioms [15, 21–24]. As for Chinese visual verbs, the research focuses on their semantics, syntax and grammaticalization. Fu [25] considered that diverse visual verbs possess different meaning and key points in the dictionary definitions. Wang and Huang [4] analyzed the compositionality of visual verb *kàn* 'see' based on Generative Lexicon. Xu [26] examined the semantic features and syntactic functions of monosyllabic visual verbs via prototype theory without quantitative analysis. Chen [5] compared result attributes, controllability, semantic domains and conceptual domains of four visual verbs *kàn, kànjiàn, kàndào and kànwán* from Cognitive Construction Grammar. There are also studies concerning the semantic evolution of visual verbs [27] and semantic comparison of visual verbs in different languages [28]. The grammaticalization of visual verbs is reflected in the historical evolution of the meaning of visual verbs [29–32]. However, few studies have conducted in-depth research on the syntax and semantics of the disyllabic visual verb *kànjiàn* using corpus-driven and corpus-based approaches based on large-scale corpora. There is a need to delve into the syntactic and semantic features of *kànjiàn* on the basis of dependency grammar since the latter is convenient and helpful for the syntactic and semantic analysis.

3 Developing a Syntactic and Semantic Annotation Tool

This project developed a syntactic and semantic annotation tool based on dependency grammar. The main modules and functions are: (1) word segmentation and part-of-speech tagging, (2) syntactic dependency analysis, (3) semantic role analysis, (4) semantic dependency analysis, (5) modification and deletion of word segmentation, part-of-speech tagging, wrong sentences, syntactic dependency, and semantic dependency. Modules (1) to (4) use the API interface provided by Harbin Institute of Technology [33]. Specifically, in module (1), word segmentation function uses the CRF model [34], and part-of-speech tagging uses SVMTool3 model. The dependency analysis of module (2) and module (3) adopts high-order graph model [35]. Module (4) is based on a grammar parser and uses the maximum entropy model [35]. This project uses the People's Daily corpus as training data. Module (5) can be used to modify errors in automatic tagging. The interface of the tool is as follows (Fig. 1):

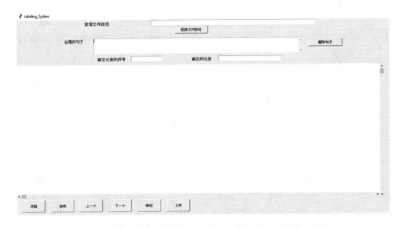

Fig. 1. Syntactic and semantic annotation tool interface

Import sentences through *shùjù wénjiàn lùjìng* "data file path", then the word segmentation result is displayed in *chǔlǐ de jùzi* "processed sentence", followed by the annotation of syntax dependency, semantic roles and semantic dependency.

Take the sentence *nǐ méi kànjiàn dàmā ma?* "Didn't you see the anut?" as an example, the word segmentation result is shown in Fig. 2:

Fig. 2. Word segmentation result of *nǐ méi kànjiàn dàmā ma?* "Didn't you see the aunt?"

If the word segmentation is wrong, modification is done by entering a space in the "processed sentence".

The syntactic dependency parsing and semantic roles labeling are shown in Fig. 3:

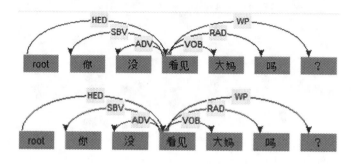

Fig. 3. The syntactic dependency parsing and semantic roles labeling of *nǐ méi kànjiàn dàmā ma?* "Didn't you see the aunt?"

Semantic dependency analysis is shown in Fig. 4:

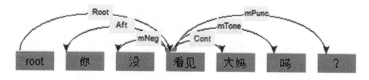

Fig. 4. Semantic dependency analysis of *nǐ méi kànjiàn dàmā ma* "Didn't you see the aunt?"

To modify the syntactic dependency or semantic dependency parsing, first left-click the parent node, and then right-click the child node to delete or change the syntactic dependency or semantic dependency type, as shown in Fig. 5:

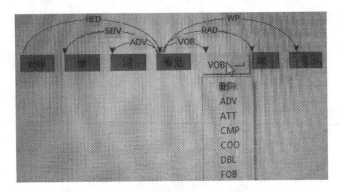

Fig. 5. Modification of syntactic dependency

Sentences can be deleted by clicking *shānchú* "delete the sentence" and an input box will show up to input the reason, shown in Fig. 6.

Fig. 6. Deletion of sentences

4   Dependency Annotation of the Visual Verb *kànjiàn*

4.1   Data Collection

Using the corpora of Sogou Laboratory[1], BCC[2] and CCL[3], single sentences containing *kànjiàn* are extracted according to the following rules: 1) download the paragraphs containing the keyword *kànjiàn* from the corpora; 2) extract sentences containing *kànjiàn* using Chinese periods, exclamation marks, and question marks; 3) exclude

---

[1] https://www.sogou.com/labs/.

[2] http://bcc.blcu.edu.cn/.

[3] http://ccl.pku.edu.cn:8080/ccl_corpus/.

sentences containing commas and semicolons; 4) exclude sentences containing non-Chinese character symbols and non-Chinese punctuation; 5) keep sentences where *kànjiàn* is a verb and the smallest unit of word segmentation after conducting word segmentation and part-of-speech tagging. After collecting single sentences, check them manually to exclude sentences that are complex sentences without punctuations and other sentences that do not conform to modern Chinese norms such as (1), and finally randomly select 1000 *kànjiàn* single sentences out of 9193 sentences. The reason for choosing single sentences is that the syntactic and semantic relationship of the verb can be fully displayed in single sentences. In contrast, complex sentences involve more complicated dependency and their accuracy rate of dependency analysis is much lower than that of single sentences. If only we use a clause containing the target verb in a complex sentence, the clause often has an incomplete meaning. After selecting the 1000 sentences, all of them are first automatically tagged and then manually checked using the annotation tool.

(1) Nàme lèi de chējiān yībānrén chēngbúxiàqù měitiān zǎoshàng kànjiàn shíláiliàng Dàzhòng bānchē xiàbān de gōngrén jǐhū dōu shì shuìzhe de Yīqìdàzhòng shēngyì yījiù zhème hǎo?

such_tiring_DE_workshop_ordinary-people_handle-any-longer_every-day_morning_see_a-dozen-of_Volkswagen_shutttle-bus_get-off-work_DE_worker_almost_all_are_asleep_DE_FAW-Volkswagen_business_still_such_good.

"In such a tiring workshop, most people can't handle it, every morning, almost all the workers who see a dozen Volkswagen shuttle buses are asleep, FAW-Volkswagen business is still so good?"

4.2   An Annotation Norm Different from LTP

The tool adopts API interface of Language Technology Platform (LTP) [33]. There is one annotation norm that is not exactly the same with theirs when we revise the automatic annotation result of *kànjiàn*, which is specifically manifested in the semantic annotation of the two verbs in the DBL (double) structure (i.e. the pivotal construction) ("$V_1 + N + V_2$"). For example, the two verbs *shǐ* 'make' and *nánwàng* "forget hardly" in *shǐwǒ nánwàng* "make me hardly forget" are not directly related in semantics. In the structure "$V_1 + N + V_2$", N is the patient of V1 and the agent of V2 semantically, but there is no semantic relation between V1 and V2. Therefore, unlike LTP which annotates the semantic dependency between the two verbs as "eSUCC" (e-succession), we annotate the semantic dependency between the two verbs of DBL structure as "dCONT" (d-content) (Fig. 7).

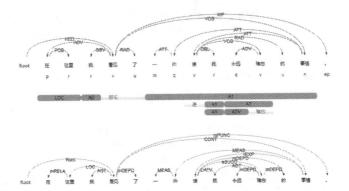

Fig. 7. Difference of annotation norm: DBL structure (Zài zhèlǐ wǒ kànjiàn le yī jiàn shǐ wǒ yǒngyuǎn nánwàng de shìqíng. in_here_I_see_ASP_a_CL_thing_make_I_forever_unforgettable_DE_thing "Here I saw something that makes me forget hardly forever.")

4.3 Annotation Error Analysis

Many errors of automatic annotation occur in the semantic dependency, and the major types are as follows. First, the punctuation is not connected to the head (Fig. 8). The correct annotation is to change the semantic dependency arc "mPUNC" (m-punctuation) (from *méiyǒu* "not" to the punctuation "?") to the semantic dependency arc "mPUNC" (from *kànjiàn* to the punctuation "?").

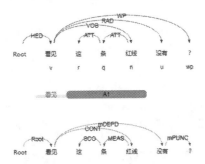

Fig. 8. Error of semantic dependency annotation: punctuation (Kànjiàn zhè tiáo hóngxiàn méiyǒu? see_this_CL_red-line_no "Don't you see this red line?")

Second, when the verb in the object clause of *kànjiàn* is used as an adverbial to modify the main verb of the object clause, the semantic relationship between *kànjiàn* and the verb as an adverbial is tagged incorrectly (Fig. 9). The correct annotation should be that *yǎngtiān* "up to the sky" modifies *píngtǎng* "lie flatly". Therefore, the semantic dependency arc "dCONT" (from *kànjiàn* to *yǎngtiān* "up to the sky") should be deleted and the semantic dependency arc "MANN" (manner) (from *píngtǎng* "lie flatly" to *yǎngtiān* "up to the sky") should be added. Such error frequently occurs when several verbs appear in the same single sentence.

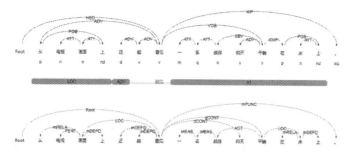

Fig. 9. Error of semantic dependency annotation: verbs as adverbials to modify main verb (Cóng diànshì huàmiàn shàng hái néng <u>kànjiàn</u> yī míng zhànfú yǎngtiān píngtǎng zài chuáng shàng. from_TV_picture_on_still_can_see_a_CL_prison-of-war_up-to-the-sky_lie-flatly_in_bed_on Type="General_Pun">"From the TV screen, a prisoner of war can also be seen lying on the bed up to the sky.")

Third, when prepositional phrases containing the proper noun modify the main verb, the semantic dependency of the proper noun is annotated incorrectly (Fig. 10). Correct annotation is to delete the semantic dependency arc "TIME" (time) (from *kànjiàn* to *shí* "time"), and to add the semantic dependency arc "mDEPD" (m-dependency) (from *shíyuègémìng* "October Revolution" to *shí* "time"); the semantic dependency arc "mRELA" (m-relation) (from *shí* "time" to *zài* "during") is changed to the semantic dependency arc "mRELA" (from *shíyuègémìng* "October Revolution" to *zài* "during").

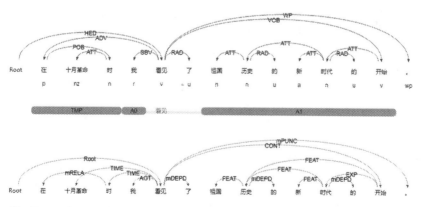

Fig. 10. Error of semantic dependency annotation: proper nouns (Zài Shíyuègémìng shí wǒ <u>kànjiàn</u> le zǔguó lìshǐ de xīn shídài de kāishǐ. in_October-Revolution_time_I_see_ASP_motherland_history_DE_new_era_DE_beginning "During the October Revolution, I saw the beginning of a new era in the history of the Motherland.")

Fourth, the sentence is too long that certain semantic dependency relation is missing (Fig. 11). Comparing Fig. 11(a) and (b), the semantic dependency between *xiāngkè* "pilgrim" and *yóurén* "tourist" is missing in Fig. 11(a). Therefore, Fig. 11(a) should be modified as follows: the semantic dependency arc "eCOO" (e-coordinate)

280   S. Wang et al.

(from *xiāngkè* "pilgrim" to *yóurén* "tourist") is added, and the semantic dependency arc "AGT" (agent) (from *yúnjí* "crowd" to *yóurén* "tourist") is changed to semantic dependency arc "EXP" (experiencer) (from *yúnjí* "crowd" to *yóurén* "tourist").

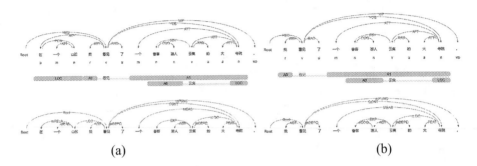

(a)   (b)

Fig. 11. (a) Semantic dependency annotation error: missing (Zài yī gè shān'āo wǒ kànjiàn le yī gè xiāngkè yóurén yúnjí de dà sìyuàn. in_a_CL_cove_I_see_ASP_a_CL_pilgrim_-tourist_crowd_DE_big_temple "In a cove I saw a large temple with pilgrims and tourists."); (b) Semantic dependency annotation (Wǒ kànjiàn le yīgè xiāngkè yóurén yúnjí de dà sìyuàn. I_see_ASP_a_CL_pilgrim_tourist_crowd_DE_big_temple "I saw a large temple with pilgrims and tourists.")

Fifth, errors occur when numeral phrases without nouns function as objects (see Fig. 12). In the sentence *kànjiàn le jǐgè* see_ASP_several_CL "I saw a few.", *jǐgè* "a few" is the CONTENT of *kànjiàn*, and its semantic label should be "CONT", (content) so the semantic dependency arc "MEAS" (measure) (from *kànjiàn* to *jǐgè* "a few") should be changed into "CONT" (from *kànjiàn* to *jǐgè* "a few").

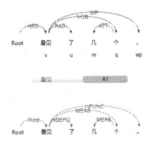

Fig. 12. Error of semantic dependency annotation: numeral phrases without nouns function as objects (Kànjiàn le jǐgè. see_ASP_several_CL "I saw a few.")

There are relatively few annotation errors that occur at the syntactic level. First, errors occur when words like *méiyǒu*, *méi* and *búshì* with negative meaning "not" are behind the object in interrogative sentences (see Fig. 13). Correct annotation is that the syntactic dependency arc "COO" (coordinate) (from *kànjiàn* to *méiyǒu* "not") is changed to the syntactic dependency arc "RAD" (right adjunct) (from *kànjiàn* to *méiyǒu* "not"). Meanwhile, the semantic dependency annotation of this sentence is wrong: the semantic dependency arc "mDEPD" (from *tā* "her" to *méiyǒu* "not") is changed to the semantic dependency arc "mDEPD" (from *kànjiàn* to *méiyǒu* "not"), and the semantic dependency arc "mPUNC" (from *méiyǒu* "not" to the punctuation "?") is changed to the semantic dependency arc "mPUNC" (from *kànjiàn* to the punctuation "?").

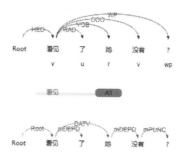

Fig. 13. Error of syntactic dependency annotation: negative words following the main verb (Kànjiàn le tā méiyǒu? see_ASP_she_not "Do (you) see her or not?")

Second, errors occur when several adverbials modify a verb (see Fig. 14). Correct annotation is to change the semantic dependency arc "ADV" (adverbial) (from *kěyǐ* "can" to *jiù* "just") into the semantic dependency arc "ADV" (from *kànjiàn* to *jiù* "just").

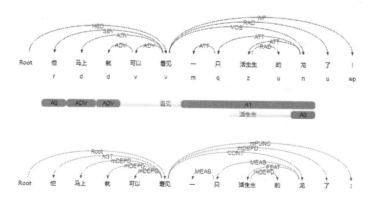

Fig. 14. Error of syntactic dependency annotation: several adverbials modifying a verb (Tā mǎshàng jiù kěyǐ kànjiàn yī zhī huóshēngshēng de long le! he_immediately_just_-can_see_a_CL_living_DE_dragon_ASP "He can just see a living dragon immediately!")

4.4 Arcs of Syntactic and Semantic Dependencies

Functional words do not express meanings but only emphasize functions, leading to the situation that the syntactic dependency arc and the semantic dependency arc of a sentence do not correspond to each other. The typical one is when components like prepositional phrases functioning as adverbials modify the entire sentence: the syntactic dependency arcs are from the main verb to the function word such as preposition, while the semantic dependency arcs are from the main verb to the CONTENT word in the prepositional phrase, as shown in Fig. 15:

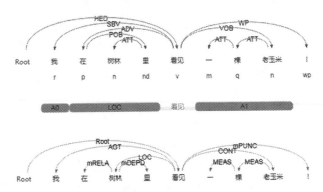

Fig. 15. Differences between arcs of syntactic and semantic dependency: function words (Wǒ zài shùlín lǐ kànjiàn yī kē lǎo yùmǐ. I_in_wood_in_see_a_CL_old_corn "I saw an old corn in the woods.")

5 The Syntax and Semantics of the Visual Verb *kànjiàn*

5.1 Syntactic Dependencies of the Visual Verb *kànjiàn*

1000 single sentences containing *kànjiàn* can be divided into six categories according to the syntactic dependencies of *kànjiàn* as a dependent: HED[4] (head), ATT (attribute), COO (coordination), POB (preposition-object), VOB (verb-object) and SBV (subject-verb), and the distribution is shown in Table 1.

Table 1. Syntactic dependency categories and distributions of *kànjiàn* as a dependent

Category	Number	Percentage	Examples
HED	854	85.4%	Tā kànjiàn yī bǎ hóngsè de yǔsǎn he_see_a_CL_red_DE_umbrella "He saw a red umbrella."
COO	103	10.3%	Xià le lóutī jiù kànjiàn jiēdào down_ASP_stair_just_see_street "(You) see the street when (you) go down the stairs."
ATT	24	2.4%	Nǐ huì yǒu jīhuì shuōshuō nǐ kànjiàn de guòchéng

(continued)

---

[4] The translation of these terms comes from this website: http://ltp.ai/docs/appendix.html. As we confirmed with the developer on April 26, 2022, the translations have some errors which mixed a dependency relation with the dependent in the relation. Since there is no new official translation, we only changed COO (coordinate) into COO (coordination) as it should be a noun not a verb or an adjective.

Table 1. (*continued*)

Category	Number	Percentage	Examples
			you_will_have_opportunity_say_you_see_DE_process "You will have the opportunity to talk about the process you saw."
SBV	14	1.4%	Tāmen kànjiàn de shì běnrén yǐwài de dōngxī they_see_DE_be_self_besides_DE_thing "What they saw was something other than themselves."
POB	4	0.4%	Rén wéile kànjiàn zìjǐ de nèixīn cái huàhuà people_for_see_self_DE_heart_only_draw "People draw pictures in order to see their heart."
VOB	1	0.1%	Nǐ zhè fù chīxiàng rang nǐde gēmí kànjiàn huì bèi xiàsǐ ò you_this_CL_look-of-eating_make_your_fan _see_will_BEI_scare-to-death_oh "Your fans will be scared to death if they see how you eat!"
Total	1000	100%	–

Among them, the sentences with *kànjiàn* as HED accounted for 85.4%, indicating that the visual verb *kànjiàn* is used as the predicate of a single sentence in most cases. As shown in Table 2, there are 830 sentences where *kànjiàn* is HED without a coordinated event, which can be subdivided according to whether there is SBV or VOB. FOB means fronting-object.

Table 2. Distributions of sentences with *kànjiàn* as HED

Type	Number	Percentage	Examples
kànjiàn + COO	24	2.8%	Wǒ yī kànjiàn tā jiù xiangqi Wěipíng. I_once_see_he_at once_think-about_Weiping "As soon as I saw him, I thought of Weiping."
FOB + *kànjiàn*	25	2.9%	Zhěng gè guòchéng tā dōu kànjiàn le. whole_CL_process_he_all_see_ASP "He saw the whole process."
Without SBV & VOB	29	3.4%	Zhēn néng qīngchǔ de kànjiàn. really_can_clearly_DE_see "(I) can see it clearly."
SBV + *kànjiàn*	75	8.8%	Xiànzài nǐ yǐjīng kànjiàn le. now_you_already_see_ASP "Now you have seen it."
kànjiàn + VOB	191	22.4%	Hǎojiǔ méi kànjiàn nǐ le. long-time_no_see_you_ASP "I haven't seen you for a long time."
SBV + *kànjiàn* + VOB	510	59.7%	Lín Dàiyù yòu kànjiàn yī fù duìlián. Daiyu Lin_again_see_one_CL_couplet "Daiyu Lin saw another couplet."
Total	854	100%	–

In single sentences with *kànjiàn* as HED, 24 sentences contain the syntactic dependency COO, therefore, altogether 127 sentences contain the syntactic dependency COO. As shown in Table 3, in the 127 sentences containing COO, 94.5% have two events and 5.5% have three events. Among them, there are 24 sentences with *kànjiàn* being the first event and 103 sentences with *kànjiàn* not being the first event; that is, the probability of the seeing event occurring first (18.9%) is much smaller than the probability of it occurring later (81.1%). In other words, in most cases, seeing happens after another event, such as in (2).

(2) Tā zhuǎnguòshēn kànjiàn Shǐ Dōng wúzhù de guàzài bànkōng zhōng he_turn-around_see_Dong-Shi_helplessly_DE_hang_in-the-air "He turned around and saw Dong Shi hanging helplessly in the air."

Table 3. Distributions of sentences containing COO

Type	Two events		Three events		Total	
	Number	Percentage	Number	Percentage	Number of sentences	Percentage
kànjiàn not being the first event of COO	97	76.4%	6	4.7%	103	81.1%
kànjiàn being the first event of COO	23	18.1%	1	0.8%	24	18.9%
Total	120	94.5%	7	5.5%	127	100%

5.2 Semantic Dependency of *Kànjiàn*

Semantic Dependency Distribution of *Kànjiàn*. The semantic dependencies of *kànjiàn* is shown in Table 4, which can be divided into 5 categories. According to the frequency, they are CONTENT, EXPERIENCER, TIME, LOCATION, and MANNER.

Table 4. Distributions of semantic dependency of *kànjiàn*

Semantic dependency	Number
EXPERIENCER	722
CONTENT	870
TIME	171
LOCTION	108
MANNER	42

Because *kànjiàn* is used as HED in most cases, and EXPERIENCER and CONTENT are the most used semantic dependency types of *kànjiàn*, in one-event sentences with *kànjiàn* as HED, the distribution of EXPERIENCER and CONTENT is as shown in Table 5.

Table 5. Distributions of EXPERIENCER and CONTENT in one-event sentences with *kànjiàn* as HED

Type	Number of EXPERIENCER	Number of CONTENT	Number of sentences
FOB + *kànjiàn*	20	25	25
Without SBV or VOB	0	0	29
SBV + *kànjiàn*	75	0	75
kànjiàn + VOB	0	191	191
SBV + *kànjiàn* + VOB	510	510	510
Total	605	726	830

In the type of "FOB+*kànjiàn*", there are 25 single sentences in which the number of EXPERIENCER and that of CONTENT are 20 and 25 respectively. The referential meanings of EXPERIENCER are all human beings, among which 14 are personal pronouns (e.g. *nǐ* 'you'), four represent relatives or parents (e.g. *bàba* 'father'), and two are nouns denoting persons (e.g. *rén* 'person'). As for CONTENT, only four refer to humans or animals, and the remaining 21 express general things (e.g. *shénme* 'what'), CONTENT (e.g. *tící* 'inscription') or concrete objects (e.g. *fángzi* 'house'). There is no EXPERIENCER or CONTENT in the type of "Without SBV or VOB". In the type of "SBV+*kànjiàn*", there are 75 single sentences with no EXPERIENCER and the number of CONTENT is 75. Seventy-three of them refer to human via personal pronouns, career names or people's names, and the remaining two are zhěnggè_chéngshì 'the whole city' and zìjǐ_de_liángxīn 'one's own self's consciousness.'

In the type of "*kànjiàn*+VOB", there are 191 single sentences with no EXPERIENCER and the number of CONTENT is 191. Among 191 CONTENT roles, 81 are clauses denoting actions (72) or states (9), while 110 are words or phrases referring to animate creatures (e.g. *zánmen* 'we' and *shàngdì* 'God'), concrete things or light (e.g. *jièzhi* 'ring' and *dēngguāng* 'light'), content (e.g. *liúyán* 'message'), locations (e.g. *yùyuāntán* 'Yuyuan Pool'), spirits (e.g. *róngyào* 'glory'), general references (e.g. *dōngxi* 'thing'), whose frequencies are 52, 32, 13, 7, 3, and 2, respectively.

In the type of "SBV+*kànjiàn*+VOB", there are 510 single sentences in which the number of EXPERIENCER and that of CONTENT are both 510. The referential meanings of EXPERIENCER are human beings (507) (e.g. *értóng* 'child' and *zhūxiānshēng* 'Mr. Zhu'), eyes (2) and the sun (1). As for CONTENT, 248 are clauses denoting actions (226) or states (22), while 262 are words or phrases referring to animate creatures or human's body parts (e.g. *yělǘ* 'wild donckey' and *tā_de_liǎn* 'her face'), concrete things or substances (e.g. *yǔsǎn* 'umbrella'), spirits (e.g. *yīngxióng_qìgài* 'herorous spirit'), locations (e.g. *jiǔguǎn* 'tavern'), CONTENT (e.g. *guǎnggào* 'advertisement'), general references (e.g. *shénme* 'what'), actions (e.g. *cháoxiào* 'mockery'), a season (e.g. *qiūtiān* 'autumn'), and an event (e.g. *dàlóu_de_xiūjiàn* 'the construction of buildings'), whose frequencies are 149, 35, 30, 18, 13, 12, 2, 1, and 1, respectively.

Semantic Dependency Collocation of *Kànjiàn*. There are 830 sentences with *kànjiàn* as HED and without COO. Their semantic collocations are analyzed below. Semantic collocations of "FOB+*kànjiàn*" are shown in Table 6. The co-occurrence of EXPERIENCER and CONTENT is 80% (20/25 sentences).

Table 6. Semantic collocations of "FOB + *kànjiàn*"

Type	EXPERIENCER +CONTENT +*kànjiàn*	CONTENT +EXPERIENCER +*kànjiàn*	CONTENT+*kànjiàn*	CONTENT+bèi +EXPERIENCER+*kànjiàn*	FOB +*kànjiàn*
Examples	Wǒ shíme dōu méi kànjiàn I_what_all_no_see "I didn't see anything."	Zhěng gè guòchéng tā dōu kànjiàn le whole_CL_ process_he_ all_see_ASP "He saw the whole process."	Zhè hang tící yuǎnyuǎn de jiù néng kànjiàn this_CL_ inscription_ far-away_DE_ just_can_see "This line of inscription can be seen from a distance."	Xìn bèi nǐ bàbà kànjiàn le letter_BEI_you_father_see_ASP "The letter was seen by your father."	–
Number of sentences	8	8	5	4	25

Semantic collocations of "without SBV & VOB" are shown in Table 7.

Table 7. Semantic collocations of "without SBV or VOB"

Type	*kànjiàn*	TIME +*kànjiàn*	LOCATION+*kànjiàn*	Without SBV or VOB
Examples	Kànjiàn le see_ASP "saw"	Dìyīcì kànjiàn the-first-time_see "see for the first time"	Cóng nà'ér kěyǐ kànjiàn ma? from_there_can_see_MA "Can see from there?"	–
Number of sentences	22	5	2	29

Semantic collocations of "SBV+*kànjiàn*" are shown in Table 8. The most used semantic collocation is "EXPERIENCER+*kànjiàn*", accounting for 73.3% (55/75 sentences).

Table 8. Semantic collocations of "SBV+*kànjiàn*"

Type	EXPERIENCER +*kànjiàn*	EXPERIENCER +LOCATION+*kànjiàn*	EXPERIENCER+TIME +*kànjiàn*	TIME +EXPERIENCER +*kànjiàn*	SBV +*kànjiàn*
Examples	Wáng Lì kànjiàn le Wang-Li_see_ASP "Li Wang saw it!"	Nǐ zài nǎ'ér kànjiàn de? you_in_where_see_ASP "Where did you see (it)?"	Dàn wǒ yǐqián què méi kànjiàn guò but_I_before_yet_no_see_ASP "But I haven't seen (it) before."	Kěshì yǒuyītiān wǒmen kànjiàn le but_one-day_we_see_ASP "But one day we saw (it)."	-
Number of sentences	55	8	6	6	75

Semantic collocations of "*kànjiàn*+VOB" are shown in Table 9. The most used semantic collocation is "*kànjiàn*+CONTENT".

Table 9. Semantic collocations of "*kànjiàn*+VOB"

Type	Number	Examples
kànjiàn+VOB	191	Hǎojiǔ méi <u>kànjiàn</u> nǐ le. long-time_no_see_you_ASP "(I) haven't seen you for a long time."
kànjiàn+CONTENT	62	<u>Kànjiàn</u> wǒde róngyào. see_my_glory "See my glory."
kànjiàn+S$_{CONTENT}$	55	<u>Kànjiàn</u> yī gè lǎoshī shuāidǎo le. see_one_CL_teacher_fall-down_ASP "(I) saw a teacher falling down."
TIME+*kànjiàn* +CONTENT	17	Jīntiān <u>kànjiàn</u> nǐde liúyán. today_see_your_message "Today (I) saw your message."
TIME+*kànjiàn* +S$_{CONTENT}$	16	Jīnzǎo <u>kànjiàn</u> tā shàngbān le. this-morning_see_she_work_ASP "This morning (I) saw her at work."
LOCATION+*kànjiàn* +CONTENT	18	Zài dìtiě lǐ <u>kànjiàn</u> yī gè qínláo de lǎo xiānshēng. in_subway_in_see_one_CL_hardworking_DE_old_man "In the subway (I) saw a hardworking old man."
LOCATION+*kànjiàn* +S$_{CONTENT}$	8	Jiē shàng <u>kànjiàn</u> liǎng zhī duǎntuǐ gǒu pìdiānpìdiān dì zǒu zài wǒ qiánmiàn. street_on_see_two_CL_short-leg_dog_happily_DE_walk_in_I_front "In the street (I) saw two short-legged dogs walking happily in front of me."
TIME+LOCATION +*kànjiàn*+CONTENT	11	Jīntiān zài Kěndéjī <u>kànjiàn</u> le yī gè niángbàole de Wáng Xiǎojiàn. today_in_KFC_see_ASP_one_CL_girlish_DE_Wang-Xiaojian "Today in KFC, (I) saw a girlish Xiaojian Wang."
TIME+LOCATION +*kànjiàn*+S$_{CONTENT}$	1	Nèitiān lùshàng <u>kànjiàn</u> yī gè dàjiě chuān le yī gè hóngdiǎndiǎn de qiūkù. that-day_on-the-road_one_CL_big-sister_wear_ASP_one_CL_red-spotted_DE_trouser "That day on the road, (I) saw a big sister wearing a red-spotted long trouser."
LOCATION+TIME +*kànjiàn*+CONTENT	2	Zài nǎ shenme shíjiān <u>kànjiàn</u> tā de? in_where_what_time_see_she_DE "Where and when did you see her"
LOCATION+TIME +*kànjiàn*+S$_{CONTENT}$	1	Zài yuē yìbǎimǐ chù zhōngyú <u>kànjiàn</u> le pénkǒu cū de qīngquán cóng kēngdǐ liú guò. in_about_100-meters_place_finally_see_ASP_mouth-of-basin_thick_DE_clear-spring_from_the-bottom-of-the-pit_flow_ASP "At about 100 m, (I) finally saw the thick clear spring flowing from the bottom of the pit

Semantic collocations of "SBV+*kànjiàn*+VOB" are shown in Table 10. The most used semantic collocation is "EXPERIENCER+*kànjiàn*+CONTENT".

Table 10. Semantic collocations of "SBV+*kànjiàn*+VOB"

Patterns	Number of sentences	Examples
SBV+*kànjiàn*+VOB	510	Lín Dàiyù yòu <u>kànjiàn</u> yīfù duìlián. Daiyu Lin_again_see_one_CL_couplet "Daiyu Lin saw another couplet."
EXPERIENCER+ *kànjiàn*+CONTENT	201	Lǎolǐ <u>kànjiàn</u> jīngyú. Old-Li_see_whale "Old Li saw the whale."
EXPERIENCER+ *kànjiàn*+S$_{CONTENT}$	185	Lǎoshī <u>kànjiàn</u> xiǎoniǎo zài shù shàng dāwō. teacher_see_bird_in_tree_on_nest "The teacher saw the bird nest in the tree."
EXPERIENCER+TIME+ *kànjiàn*+CONTENT	25	Wǒ jīnwǎn <u>kànjiàn</u> tā le. I_tonight_see_he_ASP "I saw him tonight."
EXPERIENCER+TIME+ *kànjiàn*+S$_{CONTENT}$	25	Wǒ zuótiān <u>kànjiàn</u> nǐ hé yīxiē kǎndérén liáotiān. I_yesterday_see_you_and_some_Kander_chat "I saw you chatting with some Kanders yesterday."
TIME+EXPERIENCER+ *kànjiàn*+CONTENT	11	Dì'èr tiān Pútáo méi <u>kànjiàn</u> Shǎoyǒng. second_day_Putao_no_see_Shaoyong "Putao didn't see Shaoyong the next day."
TIME+EXPERIENCER+ *kànjiàn*+S$_{CONTENT}$	15	Zuótiān wǎnshàng wǒ hái <u>kànjiàn</u> tā hé yī wèi mírén de xiǎojiě tiàowǔ le ne. yesterday_night_I_also_see_he_and_one_ CL_charming_DE_lady_dance_ASP_NE "Last night I saw him dancing with a charming lady."
EXPERIENCER+LOCATION +*kànjiàn*+CONTENT	19	Wǒmen zài zhèlǐ hái <u>kànjiàn</u> le yī zhī huǒjī. we_at_here_also_see_ASP_one_CL_turkey "We also saw a turkey here."
EXPERIENCER+LOCATION +*kànjiàn*+S$_{CONTENT}$	10	Hǎi'ěr tàitai cóng tā lóushàng de chuāngkǒu <u>kànjiàn</u> tā huílái Hai'er_lady_from_she_upstairs_DE_window_see_she_ come-back "Mrs. Haier saw her coming back from her window upstairs."
LOCATION+EXPERIENCER +*kànjiàn*+CONTENT	7	zài_jiē_shàng_tā_méiyǒu_<u>kànjiàn</u>_yī_wèi_shúrén in_sreeet_on_he_no_see_one_CL_acquaintance "In the street he did not see an acquaintance."
LOCATION+ EXPERIENCER+*kànjiàn* +S$_{CONTENT}$	2	Dēngguāng xià tā <u>kànjiàn</u> yī zhī dà tóngguàn shuānzài yī tiáo dà tiěliàn shàng. light_under_he_see_one_CL_big_copper-pot_tie- to_one_CL_ big_iron-chain "Under the light, he saw a large copper pot tied to a large iron chain."
EXPERIENCER+TIME +LOCATION+*kànjiàn* +CONTENT	3	Nín jīntiān cóng wàngyuǎnjìng lǐ <u>kànjiàn</u> le shenme. you_today_from_telescope_in_see_ASP_what "What did you see in the telescope today?"
EXPERIENCER+TIME +LOCATION+*kànjiàn* +S$_{CONTENT}$	1	Wǒ céng zài xiàoyuán fùjìn yuǎnyuǎn <u>kànjiàn</u> tā gēnzhe yī qún xuéshēng zǒu guò. I_once_at_campus_near_far_see_he_follow_one_CL_ student_walk_ASP

(*continued*)

Table 10. (*continued*)

Patterns	Number of sentences	Examples
		"I once saw him walking by with a group of students from a distance near the campus."
EXPERIENCER+LOCATION +TIME+*kànjiàn*+CONTENT	1	Wǒ zài Shànghǎi chángcháng <u>kànjiàn</u> yīxiē dàlóu de xiūjiàn. I_in_Shanghai_often_see_some_building_DE_construction "I often see the construction of some buildings in Shanghai."
TIME+EXPERIENCER +LOCATION+*kànjiàn* +CONTENT	3	Qiánjǐtiān wǒ cóng jìngzi lǐ <u>kànjiàn</u> nǐ le. the-other-day_I_from_mirror_in_see_you_ASP "The other day I saw you in the mirror."
TIME+EXPERIENCER +LOCATION+*kànjiàn* +S$_{\text{CONTENT}}$	2	Zhèshí tā cóng jìngzi lǐ <u>kànjiàn</u> tā lái le. this-moment_she_from_mirror_in_see_he_come_ASP "At this moment she saw him coming in the mirror."

First, there is no structure like "*bǎ*+(CONTENT)+*kànjiàn*", but there exists the structure "*bèi*+(EXPERIENCER)+*kànjiàn*" in "FOB+*kànjiàn*". Action bivalent verbs can generally appear in sentences containing *bǎ* and *bèi* [36], so *kànjiàn* differs from action verbs, which might result from the fact that the subject of *kànjiàn* cannot make changes to CONTENT, but *bǎ* can. Second, in terms of the number of co-occurrence semantic dependencies, in sentences with *kànjiàn* as HED, the number of semantic dependencies co-occurring *kànjiàn* ranges from 0 to 4, 58.4% for collocating with two semantic dependencies, being the highest. Third, in terms of the semantic dependency patterns, the most frequent two patterns are [EXPERIENCER, CONTENT] and [EXPERIENCER, CONTENT, TIME], accounting for 48.9% (406/830 sentences) and 9.2% (76/830 sentences), respectively. According to the usage, *kànjiàn* is usually a divalent verb in grammar.

6   Comparisons with Chinese Dictionaries

There exist some good dictionaries concerning Chinese verbs. Although *Modern Chinese Verb Classification Dictionary* [37] and *The Contemporary Chinese Dictionary* (7th Edition) [38] contain the verb *kànjiàn*, the former only contains its *pinyin*, senses and examples, and the latter only contains the information of *pinyin*, part-of-speech, senses and examples. *Chinese Verb Usage Dictionary* [39] focuses on the functions of verbs with detailed examples, but it lacks an analysis of the whole sentence each verb occurs in. In contrast, this paper provides the frequency information while analyzing the syntactic and semantic dependencies.

Modern Chinese Verb Classification Dictionary [37]:

【看见】kàn jiàn 看到。例①第二天她 ～ 了一群鸽子，一群鸽子围绕着夏日的被弃置的烟囱飞翔。(王蒙《风马牛小说二题·史琴心》) ②一次老效回来，～ 家里的新麦子，逼问媳妇。(铁凝《麦秸垛》)【kànjiàn】kàn jiàn see. Example ① The next day she had seen a group of pigeons, a group of pigeons flying around the abandoned chimney in summer. (Meng Wang's "Fengma Niu Novel Two Topics: Qinxin Shi") ② Once Old Xiao came back, he saw the new wheat at home, and questioned his wife. (Ning Tie "Wheat Straw Stack").

The Contemporary Chinese Dictionary [38]:

【看见】kàn //jiàn 动 看到: 看得见|看不见|从来没 ~ 过这样的怪事。【kàn-jiàn】 kàn //jiàn v. to see: can see | cannot see | have never seen such a weird thing.

Chinese Verb Usage Dictionary [39]:

看见kàn //jiàn 看到。kànjiàn kàn //jiàn to see.

【一般功能】【basic function】

〔名宾〕 ~ 个人 〔nominal object〕 see a person.

〔动宾〕 他 ~ 有人在那儿练太极拳 〔verbal object〕 He saw someone practicing Tai Chi there.

〔小句宾〕 ~ 他在写信|我 ~ 老张出去了 〔clausal object〕 ~ 他在写信|我 ~ 老张出去了 〔小句宾〕 ~ He is writing a letter|I ~ Lao Zhang is out.

〔动时量〕 ~ 一次|~过好儿回 〔classifier for actions〕 see once | see several times.

〔了着过〕 ~ 了一个黑影儿| ~过这本书 〔ASP〕 saw a dark shadow| have read this book.

【名宾类】 [受事] ~ 一张相片|~他的朋友|~了大海 【object$_n$】 [Patient] see a photo| see his friends | saw the sea.

【动结】看//见 【resultative】 kàn 'see'//jiàn 'see'.

The Knowledge-Base of Content Words [40] of Peking University describes the semantic roles, syntactic patterns and grammatical functions of adjectives and verbs commonly used in modern Chinese, as well as the sentiment, qualia role and syntactic patterns. Its analysis of *kànjiàn* is shown in Fig. 16. Both the syntactic and semantic aspects of *kànjiàn* are analyzed. In terms of semantics, the advantage is that the semantic role of the object of the word *kànjiàn* is subdivided, but other semantic roles such as LOCATION/TIME are not included. There are also fewer types of syntactic patterns compared with this study. Firstly, it only shows *kànjiàn* take objects as a predicate, while this study includes six syntactic dependencies that *kànjiàn* can appear in (i.e. HED, ATT, COO, POB, VOB and SBV) (see Table 1). Secondly, the syntactic pattern ① (S: *gǎnshì* 'sentient'+ ~ +*duìxiàng* 'target'/*xìshì* 'relative') is equivalent to "SBV+*kànjiàn*+VOB" in this research, and the syntactic pattern ② (S: *duìxiàng* 'target'/*xìshì* 'relative'+*bèi* (*jīngshì* 'experiencer')+ ~ +le) is equivalent to "FOB +*kànjiàn*" and belongs to "CONTENT+*bèi*+EXPERIENCER+*kànjiàn*" and "EXPERIENCER+*bèi*+*kànjiàn*" in semantic collocations. According to Table 2, this study adds COO (coordinated event structure), "without SBV & VOB", "SBV+*kàn-njiàn*", "*kànjiàn*+VOB", and more sub-types of "FOB+*kànjiàn*" in syntactic patterns. Finally, this research combines the analysis of the semantic dependency of *kànjiàn* to subdivide and summarize each type of syntactic patterns.

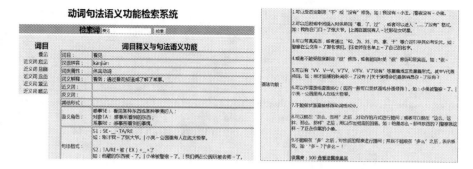

Fig. 16. *kànjiàn* in *The Knowledge-Base of Content Words*

Through the above comparisons, it can be found that this research not only conducts an in-depth analysis of *kànjiàn* from both syntax and semantics, but also provides frequency information, which is more comprehensive and richer than previous studies.

7 Conclusion

Given the importance of syntactic and semantic in vocabulary research and the limited resource for the analysis of syntactic and semantic features in Chinese vocabulary, this paper develops a syntactic and semantic annotation tool based on dependency grammar and applies it to analyze the commonly used visual verb *kànjiàn*. The main work is as follows: (1) Developing a syntactic and semantic annotation tool with the following main modules and functions: ① word segmentation and part-of-speech tagging, ② syntactic dependency analysis, ③ semantic role analysis, ④ semantic dependency analysis, ⑤ modification and deletion. (2) Conducting syntactic and semantic analysis of the visual verb *kànjiàn* and compare with existing dictionaries. This study found that the Chinese visual verb *kànjiàn* shows a variety of syntactic and semantic characteristics, among which the most commonly used syntactic function is being a predicate, and the most commonly used semantic roles are CONTENT and EXPERIENCER. The analysis in this paper is more comprehensive and richer than existing dictionaries, which is helpful for a deeper understanding of the syntactic and semantic features of Chinese visual verbs. It also proves the importance and usefulness of using the syntactic and semantic annotation tool in analyzing Chinese vocabulary.

Acknowledgements. This research is funded by the University of Macau (Project Number: MYRG2019-00013-FAH).

References

1. Liu, H.: Theory and Practice of Dependency Grammar (yīcún yǔfǎ de lǐlùn yǔ shíjiàn). Science Press (kēxué chūbǎnshè), Beijing (2009)
2. De Marneffe, M.-C., Nivre, J.: Dependency grammar. Ann. Rev. Linguist. **5**, 197–218 (2019)

3. Ahmad, F., Rahoman, M.-M.: Named entity classification using dependency grammar. In: 2017 20th International Conference of Computer and Information Technology (ICCIT), Dhaka, pp. 1–7. IEEE (2017)

4. Wang, S., Huang, C.-R.: Compositional operations of Mandarin Chinese perception verb "kàn": a generative lexicon approach. In: Otoguro, R., Ishikawa, K., Umemoto, H., Yoshimoto, K., Harada, Y. (eds.) Proceedings of the 24th Pacific Asia Conference on Language, Information and Computation, pp. 707–714. Tohoku University, Sendai (2010)

5. Chen, C.: An analysis of semantic differentiation of construction of verbs "KAN", "KANJIAN", "KANDAO", and "KANWAN" in Chinese (kàn kànjiàn kàndào yǔ kànwán de yǔyì chàyì tànjiū rènzhī gòushì yǔfǎ shìjiǎo). Foreign Lang. (wàiguó yǔwén) 36, 83–92 (2020)

6. Niu, R., Osborne, T.: Chunks are components: a dependency grammar approach to the syntactic structure of Mandarin. Lingua 224, 60–83 (2019)

7. Feng, Z.: Tessnier's grammaire de dépendance (tèsīníyēěr de cóngshǔ guānxì yǔfǎ). Foreign Linguist. (guówài yǔyánxué) 63–65 (1983)

8. Tang, X., Xiao, L.: Research on micro-blog topics mining model on dependency parsing (jīyú yīcún jùfǎ fènxī de wēibó zhǔtí wājué móxíng yánjiū). Inf. Sci. (qíngbào kēxué) 33, 61–65 (2015)

9. Qiu, L., Zhang, Y., Jin, P., Wang, H.: Multi-view Chinese treebanking. In: Tsujii, J.I., Hajic, J. (eds.) Proceedings of COLING 2014, The 25th International Conference on Computational Linguistics: Technical Papers, pp. 257–268. Dublin City University and Association for Computational Linguistics, Dublin (2014)

10. Liu, T., Ma, J.: Theories and methods of Chinese automatic syntactic parsing: a critical survey (hànyǔ zìdòng jùfǎ fènxī de lǐlùn yǔ fāngfǎ). Contemp. Linguist. (dāngdài yǔyánxué) 11, 100–112 (2009)

11. Liu, H., Feng, Z.: Probabilistic valency pattern theory for natural language processing (zìrán yǔyán chùlǐ de gàilǜ pèijià móshì lǐlùn). Linguist. Sci. (yǔyán kēxué) 32–41 (2007)

12. Liu, H.: The complexity of Chinese syntactic dependency networks. Phys. A Stat. Mech. Appl. 387, 3048–3058 (2008)

13. Jiang, J., Ouyang, J., Liu, H.: Interlanguage: a perspective of quantitative linguistic typology. Lang. Sci. 74, 85–97 (2019)

14. Pan, X., Chen, X., Liu, H.: Harmony in diversity: the language codes in English-Chinese poetry translation. Digit. Scholarsh. Humanit. 33, 128–142 (2018)

15. Gao, S., Yan, W., Liu, H.: A quantitative study on syntactic functions of Chinese verbs based on dependency treebank (jīyú shùkù de xiàndài hànyǔ dòngcí jùfǎ gōngnéng de jìliàng yánjiū). Chin. Lang. Learn. (hànyǔ xuéxí) 5, 105–112 (2010)

16. Liu, B., Niu, Y., Liu, H.: A comparative study on style-related differences in syntactic functions of part of speech (hànyǔ cílèi jùfǎ gōngnéng de yǔtǐ chàyì yánjiū). Lang. Teach. Linguist. Stud. (yǔyán jiāoxué yǔ yánjiū) 5, 97–104 (2013)

17. Li, H., Liu, H.: A study of Chinese children's acquisition of three-word sentences based on an annotated corpus (jīyú jùfǎ biāozhù yǔliàokù de hànyǔ értóng sāncíjù xídé yánjiū). Appl. Linguist. (yǔyán wénzì yīngyòng) 107–116 (2017)

18. Chen, X.: Dependency network syntax: from dependency treebanks to a classification of Chinese function words. In: Hajicova, E., Gerdes, K., Wanner, L. (eds.) Proceedings of the Second International Conference on Dependency Linguistics (DepLing 2013), pp. 41–50. Charles University, Prague (2013)

19. Tu, J., Zhu, M.: Imperative sentences classification based on dependency grammar (jīyú yīcún yǔfǎ de qíshìjù fènlèi yánjiū). Comput. Appl. Softw. (jìsuànjī yīngyòng yǔ ruǎnjiàn) 36, 279–283+322 (2019)

20. Liu, B., Xu, C.: Quantitative analysis on verb valence evolution of Chinese. In: Gerdes, K., Kahane, S. (eds.) Proceedings of the Fifth International Conference on Dependency Linguistics (Depling, SyntaxFest 2019), pp. 175–180. Association for Computational Linguistics (2019)

21. Wang, S.: Chinese Multiword Expressions. Springer, Singapore (2020). https://doi.org/10.1007/978-981-13-8510-0

22. Wang, S., Luo, H.: Exploring the meanings and grammatical functions of idioms in teaching Chinese as a second language. Int. J. Appl. Linguist. **31**, 283–300 (2021). https://doi.org/10.1111/ijal.12334

23. Wang, S., Wu, L., Gong, Q.: The collocations of Chinese tactile adjectives. In: Liu, M., Kit, C., Su, Qi. (eds.) CLSW 2020. LNCS (LNAI), vol. 12278, pp. 711–733. Springer, Cham (2021). https://doi.org/10.1007/978-3-030-81197-6_59

24. Wang, S., Yin, J.: A comparative study of the collocations in legislative Chinese and general Chinese. In: Hong, J.-F., Zhang, Y., Liu, P. (eds.) CLSW 2019. LNCS (LNAI), vol. 11831, pp. 710–724. Springer, Cham (2020). https://doi.org/10.1007/978-3-030-38189-9_72

25. Fu, H.: The similarities, differences and restrictions of the meanings of "kan" and "kanjian" (kàn hé kànjiàn děng cíyì de tóngyì hé zhìyuē). Chin. Lang. Learn. (hànyǔ xuéxí) 1–5 (1993)

26. Xu, S.: The research of the visual Sensory verbs like "kan" in syntactic and semantics (xiàndài hànyǔ kànlèi shìjué gǎnguān dòngcí jùfǎ yǔyì fènxī). Jilin University, Changchun (2015)

27. Yin, D.: The evolution of visual verbs in ancient times (shànggǔ kànshìlèi dòngcí de yǎnbiàn guīlǜ). Seeker (qiúsuǒ) 200–201 (2008)

28. Ma, B., Chen, W.: The sound and meaning association of "kan" and a comparative study of Chinese and English (kàn de yīnyì liánxiǎng jíqí hànyīng bǐjiào yánjiū). Foreign Lang. Res. (wàiyǔ yánjiū) 23–24 (2006)

29. Han, Y.: Semantic projection and grammaticalization of Chinese visual verbs (hànyǔ shìjiào dòngcí de yǔyì tóushè jí yǔfǎhuà gòunǐ). Foreign Lang. Lit. Stud. (wàiguó yǔyán wénxué) 10–13 (2003)

30. Zeng, L.: The subjectivisation of "wo-kan" and "ni-kan" (wǒkàn yǔ nǐkàn de zhǔguānhuà). Chin. Lang. Learn. (hànyǔ xuéxí) 15–22 (2005)

31. Cui, Y.: The grammaticalization path of Chinese visual verb "jian" and its evolutionary motivation and mechanism (hànyǔ shìjiào dòngcí jiàn de yǔfǎhuà lùjìng jíqí yǎnbiàn dòngyīn hé jīzhì). J. Heilongjiang Inst. Educ. (Hēilóngjiāng jiāoyù xuéyuàn xuébào) **33**, 118–119 (2014)

32. Jiang, S., Chi, C.: From visual verbs to disposal prepositions: the grammaticalization and semantic map of "wang" in Wenzhou Dialect (cóng shìjué dòngcí dào chùzhì jiècí wēnzhōu fāngyán wàng de yǔfǎhuà hé yǔyì dìtú). J. Chin. Lang. Hist. (hànyǔshǐ xuébào) 1–11 (2018)

33. Liu, T., Che, W., Li, Z.: Language technology platform (yǔyán jìshù píngtái). J. Chin. Inf. Process. (zhōngwén xìnxī xuébào) **25**, 53–63 (2011)

34. Lafferty, J., McCallum, A., Pereira, F.C.: Conditional random fields: probabilistic models for segmenting and labeling sequence data. In: Brodley, C.E., Danyluk, A.P. (eds.) Proceedings of the 18th International Conference on Machine Learning 2001 (ICML 2001), pp. 282–289. Morgan Kaufmann Publishers Inc., San Francisco (2001)

35. Che, W., Li, Z., Li, Y., Guo, Y., Qin, B., Liu, T.: Multilingual dependency-based syntactic and semantic parsing. In: Stevenson, S., Carreras, X. (eds.) Proceedings of the Thirteenth Conference on Computational Natural Language Learning (CoNLL 2009): Shared Task, pp. 49–54. Association for Computational Linguistics, Boulder (2009)

36. Dai, Y.: Exploration of action bivalent verbs in modern Chinese (xiàndài hànyǔ dòng zuòlèi èrjià dòngcí tànsuǒ). Stud. Chin. Lang. (zhōngguó yǔwén) 3–12 (1998)

37. Guo, D.: Modern Chinese Verb Classification Dictionary (xiàndài hànyǔ dòngcí fènlèi cídiǎn). Jilin Education Press (jílín jiāoyù chūbǎnshè), Changchun (1994)
38. Dictionary Editing Room of Institute of Linguistics, Chinese Academy of Social Sciences: The Contemporary Chinese Dictionary. The Commercial Press (shāngwù yìnshūguǎn), Beijing (2016)
39. Meng, C.: Chinese Verb Usage Dictionary (hànyǔ dòngcí yòngfǎ cídiǎn). The Commercial Press (shāngwù yìnshūguǎn), Beijing (1999)
40. Yuan, Y., Cao, H.: An introduction to the syntactic-semantic knowledge-base of Chinese verbs (dòngcí jùfǎ yǔyì xìnxī cídiǎn zhīshí nèiróng shuōmíngshū). In: Sun, M., Li, S., Zhang, Y., Liu, Y., He, S., Rao, G. (eds.) The Nineteenth China National Conference on Computational Linguistics (CCL 2020), pp. 518–527. The University of Hainan, Hainan (2020)

An Overview of the Construction of Near-Synonyms Discrimination Resources

Juan Li[(✉)]

Department of Chinese Language and Literature,
Peking University, Beijing, China
lijuan@mail.bnu.edu.cn

Abstract. One of the most common lexical misuse problems in the second language context concerns near-synonyms. In addition to traditional discrimination dictionaries of near-synonyms, learners can also use online resources to learn the differences between near-synonyms. This paper investigates the near-synonyms discrimination resources, such as learning dictionaries, corpora, and online learning platforms. The purpose is to discuss the construction status and application value of near-synonyms discrimination resources. We also discuss the shortcomings of the near-synonyms resources in the area of Chinese international education, and put forward suggestions for their further development.

Keywords: Near-synonyms discrimination · Chinese international education · Vocabulary knowledge base

1 Introduction

Near-synonyms refer to two words that are similar in meaning but not exactly equal in meaning and cannot be completely replaced in the context [1]. Although near-synonyms have similar meanings, they can be used differently in different contexts. So, it is very difficult for Chinese second language learners to master the usage of near-synonyms and correctly distinguish the differences between near-synonyms.

We searched word misuses from the "Global Chinese Interlanguage Corpus (V1.0)[1]", and found that most instances of word misuses were errors in the use of near-synonyms, as shown in the following three examples.

（1a）*我也回去沈阳。　（I'm going back to Shenyang, too.）
（1b）　我也回沈阳。　（I'm going back to Shenyang, too.）
（2a）*吃这种东西可以得到病。　（You will get sick if you eat this stuff.）
（2b）　吃这种东西会得病。　（You will get sick if you eat this stuff.）
（3a）*其实中国人太勤劳的。(In fact, Chinese people are very hard-working.)
（3b）　其实中国人很勤劳的。(In fact, Chinese people are very hard-working.)

---

[1] http://qqk.blcu.edu.cn/#/search/searchModuleInde.

© Springer Nature Switzerland AG 2022
M. Dong et al. (Eds.): CLSW 2021, LNAI 13250, pp. 295–305, 2022.
https://doi.org/10.1007/978-3-031-06547-7_23

Li [2] pointed out that when students study a new word named B, they often use the learned word A to associate word B, for example, they will associate "很 (very)" to "非常 (very)", When they fail to grasp the difference between the two near-synonyms, they will think that the meaning and context of the two words learned one after another are exactly the same, so they will use these two near-synonyms incorrectly.

Faced with the difficulty of near-synonyms discrimination, near-synonyms discrimination dictionaries are generally used in the field of Chinese second language teaching to assist students to learn near-synonyms. With the development of the online teaching, Hanban and some scientific research institutions also provide a variety of online learning resources for learners such as corpus, corpus concordance, online textbook resources, online near-synonyms dictionary, etc.

This paper discusses the shortcomings of the near-synonyms resources in the area of Chinese international education, and put forward suggestions for their further development.

2 Chinese Near-Synonyms Discrimination Dictionary

2.1 The Words in the Near-Synonyms Discrimination Dictionary

In the area of Chinese international education, near-synonyms cover a wider range, phrases are sometimes identified as near-synonyms. The main reason is that in the area of Chinese second language teaching, all words with similar meanings that are easy to be confused are included in the scope of attention [3]. Therefore, the near-synonyms included in the export-oriented learning dictionary are not exactly the near-synonyms in Chinese ontology research, and the scope will be expanded.

However, many near-synonyms are not included in the discrimination dictionaries, which will cause the dilemma of no words to look up for learners. He and Zhu [4] made a multi-dimensional investigation of the word selection in the word discriminating column of *The Commercial Press Learner's Dictionary of Contemporary Chinese*. They found that the discriminating objects in the dictionary were insufficient in typification and completeness, and the degree of confusion (confusion rate) of some discriminating words was not high. Therefore, the dictionaries of near-synonyms discrimination published in recent years are not comprehensive. In order to be more targeted to meet the demand of Chinese learners' learning, we need to build a near-synonyms discrimination knowledge base. It should include the frequent term, balance the range of words, and can help learners to grasp the difference of near-synonyms.

The discrimination strategies of Chinese near-synonyms are mainly discussed from the aspects of lexical semantic, semantic attributes, semantic features, and error analysis. *A Dictionary of the English Language* [5] first showed the grammatical information in the learning dictionary, including (1) part of speech; (2) irregular plural forms of nouns; (3) irregular past tense and past participle of verbs; (4) other irregular verb and auxiliary verb forms (5) irregular comparative level; (6) signs of transitive verbs and intransitive verbs. Liu and Espino [6] pointed out that, the illustration configuration of most dictionaries currently follows two basic principles: meaning centered principle and usage centered principle. The meaning-centered principle arranges the examples according to the meaning of the items, and the usage-centered principle arranges the examples according to the lexical or syntactic characteristics when the items are combined with other items. From the perspective of distinguishing confusing words, the usage-centered principle should be the better principle for the construction of a knowledge base.

So how to incorporate usage information into the dictionary?

Wang [7] pointed out that the usage of words includes (1) the syntactic elements and combinatorial restrictions that words can act as in a sentence; (2) the specific vocabulary collocation. The display of grammatical information of words is closely related to vocabulary discrimination. This paper holds that the grammatical information of words includes three aspects: the syntactic function of words, the restrictions in combination relations, the restrictions of common lexical collocation.

The Longman Dictionary of Contemporary English, published in 1978, classifies and encodes the word patterns. The usage and structure of three types of words such as nouns, adjectives, and adverbs are explained by classification coding.

2.2   The Presentation of the Dictionary

What vocabulary knowledge should be presented in the learning dictionary? Which way should it be presented?

Jin [8] summarized the categories of words that should be described by pragmatic information in Chinese learning dictionaries from four perspectives: pragmatic research, Chinese pragmatic features, the features of dictionary, and learners' needs, including appellations, greetings, thank you, apology, farewell, hedges, modal particles, modal verbs, speech act verbs, taboo and taboo words. Pragmatic information is presented through 12 specific information: power information, close relationship information, event intensity information, gender information, occasion information, functional information, polite information, style information, emotional information, attitude information, time information, and geographic information.

The dictionary mainly presents the basic meaning, part of speech, collocation, and example sentences of near-synonyms through table method, rule method, and comprehensive context method.

Jin [9] pointed out the deficiencies of the information presented in the existing learning dictionaries. Existing dictionaries mostly use the method of mutual interpretation of similar meanings to explain the meanings of words, only display example sentences, lack semantic descriptions, and do not dig out the potential information in the example sentences.

There are few studies on the dimension of pragmatic information presented in dictionaries. What kind of pragmatic information should be presented in learning dictionaries? Dictionaries also pay less attention to the way of dictionary information presentation that breaks through the "table method" and "rule method".

2.3   Summary

The export-oriented learning dictionary contains common words that are difficult to distinguish. It provides a reference for learners to distinguish the difference between near-synonyms from the perspective of meaning interpretation, usage analysis, or example sentences.

In terms of the range of words, the principle of discrimination, the selection of example sentences, the language of interpretation, and the methods of discrimination, we think that the sources of near-synonyms should be clearly limited in the syllabus, and can be broader than the existing wordlist. The principle of interpretation based on discrimination and difference should be adopted. Example sentences and interpretation language should be simple to understand. At the same time, there should be specific methods and approaches for near-synonyms discrimination.

It is very difficult for elementary and intermediate Chinese second language learners to master the meaning and usage of words in a specific context. Learners may be influenced by dictionary definitions and deduce the usage context of words incorrectly according to the fragments of paraphrased items [10]. It is difficult for beginners and intermediate learners to obtain the example sentences containing the context in which the near-synonyms are used. When learners search for the example sentences of the near-synonyms through Google, Baidu and other search engines, they cannot effectively obtain the example sentences with different usages from the large-scale internet information.

3 Corpus-Based Resources for Near-Synonyms Discrimination

3.1 Sketch Engine

Sketch Engine is an online corpus concordance tool developed by Adam Kilgarriff [11]. It includes basic functions such as word collocation and indexing. It also has the function of SketchDiff for searching the differences of near-synonyms. Sketch Engine can provide the vocabulary distribution of the corpus and the grammatical relationship between words and other words when searching for content words with similar meanings.

However, the Sketch Engine is somewhat incapable of comparative analysis of the near-synonyms of function words. When searching such function words as "always (经常)" and "always (常常)", the system will return "the data is insufficient to support statistically significant analysis results" [12].

3.2 Chinese Learners Writing Corpus

Errors in the use of near-synonyms are reflected in learners' output materials (oral and composition corpus). Interlanguage corpus collects a large number of real output materials of learners at different levels, which is an important material to investigate learners' vocabulary learning effect.

Chinese Learners writing Corpus was constructed under the leadership of Professor Chen Haoran, director of the Chinese Language Teaching Center at Taiwan Normal University. It contains three million words of writing corpus of more than 40 learners from different native language backgrounds and different learning levels. The errors of the corpus were marked by language professionals. In addition to the errors marked by professionals, the corpus can also select the learner's native language background, corpus source, stylistic selection, article function, category and level, and can also query and display the text before and after keywords.

Users can observe the usage distribution of two words with similar meanings through the analysis of the 1.4 billion words corpus. Based on it, learners can compare the different usage of near-synonyms. For example, in the Chinese learners writing corpus, a search with the keyword "convenience (方便)" found 357 data, and a search with the keyword "convenience (便利)" got 8 data. These data can help us discover which words are more difficult for learners to master.

3.3 Concordance

3.3.1 AntCon

AntConc [13] is a free corpus retrieval tool. It has the functions of making word lists, extracting keywords, highlighting co-occurrence words on the left and right sides of keywords, etc. As is shown in Fig. 1, users can search the co-occurrence words of "wear (穿)" and "wear (戴)", and observe the difference between their collocation (Fig. 2).

Fig. 1. Concordance lines of wear ("穿")

Fig. 2. Concordance lines of wear ("戴")

Concordance can help us find some recurring phenomena in language, but the function of the software is too simple to solve the deeper question. When we need to directly obtain the distinguishing knowledge of near-synonyms, AntConc can't meet our demand.

3.3.2 Tango

TANGO [14] is a bilingual collocate tool that allows users to search for collocates and corpora of near-synonyms. Learners can generalize the using patterns of near-synonyms from the retrieval results. In teaching practices, teachers can present semantically relevant words and corpus index lines in TANGO, and have students compare and contrast near-synonyms in context. If induction is too difficult for most students, teachers can help students find the differences between near-synonyms.

TANGO offers collocations that help students find suitable alternative adjectives among possible collocations, thus facilitating vocabulary learning. TANGO encourages students to check specific collocations of a near-synonyms that they can keep in mind to find the correct word for the context in spoken or written language.

However, the induction tasks and exercises provided by TANGO seem to be insufficient for students' word acquisition, and the units of study in TANGO seem to be less effective for near-synonyms of "hard" and "big" (Chen 2019). So, for "hard" and "big," teachers can use TANGO to provide patterns or hints for word usage, or they can have students practice making sentences out of those words and discuss them in class.

3.4 Online Dictionary of Near-Synonyms

3.4.1 Thesaurus

Thesaurus[2] is an English online near-synonyms dictionary website. It can provide a list of near-synonyms for search terms, and sort them according to the degree of similarity. The darker the color, the more similar the meaning of the word. Click on a word, you can get the dictionary meaning of the word, and at the same time extract sentences grabbed from the internet as example sentences. Learners sometimes use the same word repeatedly in different contexts due to their lack of vocabulary when writing essays. If there are materials of near-synonyms, they can choose the replaceable words themselves to make the expression more authentic.

3.5 Linggle

Linggle[3] can provide the collocation and the collocation frequency of words. Users can view the collocation frequency of near-synonyms and click "example" to view the example sentences. Observing the differences in collocation between different phrases in the examples can help learners to grasp the differences between near-synonyms (Fig. 3).

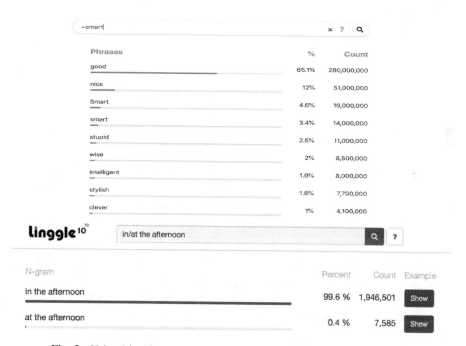

Fig. 3. Using Linggle to distinguish the difference between near-synonyms

---

[2] https://www.thesaurus.com/.

[3] https://www.linggle.com/.

3.6   Summary

Compared with the traditional methods that lack quantitative evidence, the study of near-synonyms based on corpus resources can describe grammatical phenomena more accurately. The corpus resources can effectively maintain the acquisition effect of near-synonyms, mainly in the following aspects: (1) provide a rich and authentic corpus (2) the learner has "deeply processed" the corpus (3) increase the learner's "task input" (4) innovative learning process. In the data-driven learning process, learners are required to act as "researchers". Students independently observe and summarize the usage of Chinese near-synonyms, and discover the usage rules and pragmatic characteristics by themselves. It truly realizes the learning philosophy of "learner-centered" and can cultivate students' analytical and autonomous learning abilities.

4   Challenge and Trend of Chinese Near-Synonyms Resources

4.1   Dimensions of Chinese Near-Synonyms Discrimination

Strategies of near-synonyms discrimination have been divergent from the past to the present, and they are nothing more than discriminating vocabulary semantic usage, semantic attributes, characteristics, and error analysis.

To distinguish the differences between near-synonyms, lexicology mainly starts from the perspectives of literal meaning, implicit meaning, style color, word collocation, upper and lower meaning relations, etc. We usually extract the difference of near-synonyms from the perspectives of grammar, semantics, and pragmatics. However, the method of near-synonyms discrimination is not systematic.

Zhao and Liu [15] proposed a framework for near-synonyms discrimination from the perspectives of semantic comparison, syntactic comparison, and pragmatic comparison. This framework provides a very detailed contrast dimension for near-synonyms discrimination.

Tao [16] analyzed eight near-synonyms (conglai 从来, shizhong 始终, xianglai 向来, yixiang 一向, quanran 全然, genben 根本, benlai 本来, and yizhi 一直) based on the corpus of 500,000 words spoken texts. He pointed out that there are four systematic differences between these adverbs. Firstly, different words have different distribution frequencies in the text. He pointed out that there are four systematic differences between these adverbs. Firstly, different words have different distribution frequencies in the text. Second, these adverbs differ in whether they are preceded by a series of grammatical units or followed by a clause. Thirdly, these adverbs have different semantic connotations when used with the accompanying words. Fourth, these adverbs differ in their text-linking function: whether they are connected forward or backward in context.

In Chinese second language learning, learners do not need to know all the usage of near-synonyms, they just need to grasp the main difference between two words. Grammatical and semantic features are usually easy to grasp.

In my opinion, the differences of near-synonyms in the grammatical information dimension mainly include: (1) the difference of part of speech, such as "often (经常)" and "often (常常)", one is an adjective, the other is an adverb (2) differences in grammatical functions, such as "how (怎样)" and "how (怎么样)", both of which are interrogative pronouns with similar meanings and are used to ask about the state or behavior mode of people or things. "How (怎样)" mostly acts as adverbial, while "how (怎么样)" mostly acts as predicate (3) the collocations of near-synonyms are often different.

In addition to grammatical and semantic features, stylistics, emotional colors, and semantic prosody are also important factors in lexical meaning.

4.2 Construct a Special Knowledge Base for Near-Synonyms Discrimination

Most of the existing online corpus retrieval systems simply provide the example sentences of the target words and lack the linguistic knowledge to show the difference between near-synonyms. The linguistic knowledge can not only provide a reference for teachers to prepare lessons and compile textbooks but also enable learners to improve their language ability more effectively under the data-driven learning model.

The general Chinese corpus lacks the function of word comparison and analysis, so it is necessary to develop a special near-synonyms discrimination knowledge base. Quantitative comparison functions should be developed.

Zhan [12] pointed out that the ideal of the Chinese linguistics research approach should be based on the rational introspection research paradigm of linguistics and the empirical analysis of the real mass language data. The existence of differentiating near-synonyms resources provided only corpora index function and simple measurement data, the linguistic knowledge is very limited. This paper believes that more in-depth linguistic knowledge should be provided, not only the collocation words but also the grammatical, semantic, and pragmatic information of the words, so that users can look up the relevant usage knowledge of the words while observing the corpus. However, it should be clear that the discrimination of near-synonyms should highlight the essential difference between the two words. It is not necessary to list all the usage of a word. We should provide different discrimination methods for different types of near-synonyms.

Visualization of near-synonyms discrimination resources should be considered, and the way of data presentation for words should be more intuitive. The research on the visual representation of language knowledge based on corpus should also be the focus of future research.

Interlanguage corpus provides only errors result, does not provide error analysis. Near-synonyms discrimination resources should provide errors analysis of typical examples. Then learners can query their uncertain whether the content of the typical errors, so as to reduce the occurrence of errors.

In the construction of near-synonyms discrimination resources, we should not only consider how to gather near-synonyms in a better way, but also consider how to increase the "task commitment" of learners and how to increase the "test" function in presenting knowledge resources. Hashemi and Gowdasiaei [17] compared the effectiveness of 60 Iranian college students in learning English in terms of "semantically similar vocabulary sets" and "semantically unrelated vocabulary", the results show that the students who receive the semantically similar word-gathering teaching method can achieve better results in the depth and breadth of vocabulary knowledge. Chen [14] points out that for some less-skilled students, the near-synonyms phrases and related information may seem difficult for them to absorb, and therefore, more test items should be developed to investigate learners' difficulties. Hong [18] believes that the teaching effect of the data-driven method is better than that of the traditional teaching method because the data-driven learning method increases the task commitment and the number of cognitive resources that learners need to invest in completing a specific learning task.

I hope there is a near-synonyms discrimination resource. It can develop the following functions: (1) compared function of near-synonyms: this function shows the differences of two near-synonyms; (2) example sentences: example sentences can display the usage of near-synonyms in the context; (3) provide exercises of near-synonyms for users to test their learning effect.

5   Conclusion

The difficulties of vocabulary teaching lie in: (1) learners should understand the lexical meaning of words; (2) learners should distinguish the difference between near-synonyms; (3) learners should use appropriate words in different contexts. Dictionaries and online thesaurus often overlook the nuances of near-synonyms and make reference to near-synonyms in providing definitions, lack the knowledge of grammar distribution, semantic characteristics, combination restrictions, and using templates. Therefore, it is difficult for second language learners to grasp the semantic differences and implications of near-synonyms. This paper examines the development and application of near-synonyms resources and discusses their possible impact on language learning and the challenges for their further development.

There are still some issues worthy of consideration. Firstly, how to construct high-quality online resources of near-synonyms for learners? Second, how to present the collocational and grammatical knowledge of near-synonyms in a visual way?

Acknowledgments. This paper is supported by Major Project of the "New Generation of Artificial Intelligence" funded by Ministry of Science and Technology of China (Project No. 2020AAA0106701).

References

1. Gries, S.-T., Otani, N.: Behavioral profiles: a corpus-based perspective on near-synonymsy and antonymy. ICAME Journal **34**, 121–150 (2010)
2. Li, S.-L.: The object and principles of discriminating word meanings in teaching Chinese as a second language. Chinese Teach. World. **24**(03), 406–414 (2010). (in Chinese)
3. Huang, C.-R., et al.: Chinese sketch engine and the extraction of grammatical collocations. In Proceedings of the Fourth SIGHAN Workshop on Chinese Language Processing, pp. 48–55 (2005)
4. He, S., Zhu, R.-P.: A study of the word-discrimination columns of The Commercial Press learner's dictionary of contemporary Chinese. J. Yunnan Normal Univ. (Teach. Res. Chinese For. Lang.) **16**(02), 48–55 (2018). (in Chinese)

5. Worcester, J.-E.: A dictionary of the English language. Sampson Low, Son & Company
6. Liu, D., Espino, M.: Actually, genuinely, really, and truly: a corpus-based behavioral Profile study of near-synonymous adverbs. Int. J. Corpus Linguist. **17**(2), 198–228 (2012)
7. Wang, H.: Analysis of noun meaning combination in modern Chinese. Peking University Press, 191 (2004). (in Chinese)
8. Jin, P.-P.: Selection of pragmatic information in Chinese learner's dictionaries based on learners' needs. Lexicogr. Stud. (2019). (in Chinese)
9. Jin, P.-P.: Compilation of the pragmatic information in Chinese learner's dictionaries in the perspective of the learner's feedback. J. Yunnan Normal Univ. (Teach. Stud. Chinese For. Lang. Edn.) (2020). (in Chinese)
10. Ma, Z.: What revelations can wrong cases and error sentences give? A new approach to passive rhetoric. Contemp. Rhetoric. (2019). (in Chinese)
11. Kilgarriff, A., et al.: The Sketch Engine. In: Williams, G., Vessier, S. (eds.) Proceedings of the 11th Euralex International Congress, pp. 105–116. Lorient, Université de Bretagne Sud, France (2004)
12. Zhan, W.-D.: An overview of the advances and applications of online Chinese language resources over three decades. Chinese J. Lang. Policy Plan. (2018). (in Chinese)
13. Anthony, L.: AntConc, version 3.2.2.1. Waseda University, Tokyo, Japan (2011). http://www.antlab.sci.waseda.ac.jp/
14. Chen, M.-H.: Computer-assisted synonymous phrase learning: a feasible approach to lexical development. Int. J. Comput. Assist. Lang. Learn. Teach. (IJCALLT), **9**(2), 1–18 (2019)
15. Zhao, X., Liu, R.-Y.: Some basic problems in compiling foreigner practical near-synonyms dictionary. Lexicogr. Stud. **04**, 57–67 (2005). (in Chinese)
16. Tao, H.-Y.: Adverbs of absolute time and assertiveness in vernacular Chinese: a corpus-based study. J. Chin. Lang. Teach. Assoc. **35**(2), 53–74 (2000)
17. Hashemi, M.-R., Gowdasiaei, F.: An attribute-treatment interaction study: lexical-set versus semantically-unrelated vocabulary instruction. RELC J. **36**(3), 341–361 (2005)
18. Hong, W., Chen, N.: A study on the L2 acquisition of differences in similar sense and dissimilar sense of Chinese near-synonyms. Appl. Linguist. **02**, 99–106 (2013). (in Chinese)

Contemporary Chinese Social Vocative Terms

Xue Zhang[(⊠)]

University International College, Macau University of Science and Technology,
Taipa, Macau
xuzhang@must.edu.mo

Abstract. Regarded as the epitome of culture and society, social appellation terms, and vocatives in particular, always reflect the immediate situation of language use, thus having great value in socio-linguistic research. This paper investigates the contemporary Chinese social vocative terms and analyzes their application principles and distribution patterns. Based on searches in large-scale corpora, questionnaire surveys, and interviews, it is concluded that the contemporary Chinese social vocatives can be grouped into six categories: (1) substitution of greetings; (2) generalization of kinship appellations; (3) the quasi-generalization of the occupational appellations; (4) the generalization of laudatory terms; (5) borrowing cyberspeaks; and (6) conventional terms. The application of these vocatives integrates the four variables of distance, superiority, gender, and age gap. Besides, the tendency of 'intimacy' and 'superior' is observed, which balances the approbation and tact maxim. Meanwhile, the contemporary Chinese social vocatives are changing towards the agreement maxim, and a new tendency of equal respect is emerging.

Keywords: Social appellation · Vocative · Sociolinguistics · Chinese lexicon

1 Introduction

Social Appellation refers to the address people use in social communication (non-kinship) [1]. It is a real-time reflection of the current situation of language use and a microcosm of culture and society [2, 3]. Specifically, social appellation terms are classified into two categories: back-appellation and face-to-face appellation (or vocative term). The back appellation refers to the referents used when talking about someone who is not present. The vocative term refers to the address terms used when facing someone directly.

Since the appellation reflects society and culture in language, it will naturally register the corresponding characteristics of society and culture. This is mainly displayed in two dimensions: diachronically and synchronically. From a diachronic perspective, appellation terms are constantly evolving and changing with the times. From a synchronic point of view, appellation terms are often diversified due to region, community, age, gender, and other personal backgrounds. As an essential part of Chinese

This work was supported by Macau University of Science and Technology General Research Grants (FRG-18-029-UIC).

© Springer Nature Switzerland AG 2022
M. Dong et al. (Eds.): CLSW 2021, LNAI 13250, pp. 306–319, 2022.
https://doi.org/10.1007/978-3-031-06547-7_24

language life, Chinese social appellation terms have received early attention from the academic circle, and the research results have been rich [4–6]. Chinese social appellation terms are consistent with appellation terms in other languages universally, which are used for communicative orientation. They follow standard norms and guidelines such as the Politeness Theory [2, 7]. However, it is noteworthy that the family is the basic unit of Chinese society, and Chinese people attach great importance to the family. Therefore, Chinese people have shown great interest in interpersonal addressing terms from ancient times to the present [4]. The use of Kinship terms has been extended to non-family members. This is a rare phenomenon in languages such as English [8].

Chinese social appellations have also undergone semantic shifts with the development and changes of Chinese society and culture. Many vocatives have undergone the process of 'from nothing to something' and 'from something to nothing' [9–11]. The use and development of appellations such as 'comrade', 'friend', 'sir', 'miss', and 'beauty' all reflect the language life at that moment [12–14]. Based on the current situation, through large-scale corpus collection, questionnaire surveys, language interviews, and other methods, we have outlined the six categories of contemporary Chinese vocative terms and generalized the usage principles and distribution pattern according to their linguistics features and usage constraints.

2 The Six Categories of Social Vocative Terms

2.1 Substitution of Greetings

Among Chinese social vocative, the substitution of greetings is the most common and broad usage. The so-called substitution of greetings is to use greetings such as 'ni hao (hello)' and 'nin hao (honorific hello)' as address terms to achieve the purpose of calling the hearer. The original greeting function of the greeting is still retained, but at the same time, it will play the function of the appellation. This application method does not need to consider the speaking parties' age gap, gender, status, occupation, or occasion. It is a very neutral face-to-face social address, and there is no issue of superiority or inferiority, intimacy or distance. The social vocative function of the greeting term is currently widely used in all groups in Chinese society.

It is worth noting that the phenomenon that Chinese uses greetings for face-to-face social addressing corresponds to the conclusions of the existing language academic circles on the research of address terms. For example, although English social vocative terms are relatively systematic, there is also the phenomenon of substituting with greetings for the appellation, such as 'Hi, Morning, Good morning, Hello, Howdy' [2]. Even the different words (Hi and Good morning) reflect different relationship distances (see Table 1: Brown and Ford [2] p. 381). In Chinese social vocatives, the subtle difference in hierarchy and position between 'ni hao (hello)' and 'nin hao (honorific hello)' also reflects a similar phenomenon.

Table 1. Source: Brown & Ford 1961 p. 381 Table 2.

TABLE 2
Two Forms of Greeting for Four
Classes of Associate

	Equal and Intimate	
	Good Morning	HI
Equal and Distant		
HI	0	4
Good Morning	4	10
	Subordinate	
	Good Morning	HI
Superior		
HI	1	3
Good Morning	13	8

2.2   Generalization of Kinship Terms

The generalization of kinship appellations has a long history in Chinese social appellations, and it has also been noticed by academic circles very early [4]. To this day, this generalized use is still a widespread and mainstream form of social appellation. The generalized use of kinship terms as the vocative purpose is profound and stable.

The most common kinship terms that can be used as social vocatives include '*ye ye (grandpa)*', '*nai nai (grandma)*', '*shu shu (uncle)*', '*a yi (aunt)*', '*da ye (elder uncle)*', '*da ma (elder aunt)*', '*da ge (elder brother)*', '*da jie (eldest sister)*', '*xiao di (younger brother)*', '*xiao mei (younger sister)*', etc. Its selection and use in social conversations follow two rules: (1) gender matching; (2) age gap projection. Regarding 'gender matching', the relative terms used must accurately match the gender of the person being socially addressed. Regarding the 'age gap projection', the speaker needs to judge the age of the hearer and refer to his/her age, project the age gap between the two on the kinship that fits this gap, and then choose the corresponding kinship word the appellation. For example, a 70-year-old man may be called '*ye ye (grandpa)*', '*da ye (elder uncle)*', or '*da ge (elder brother)*', etc. It all depends on to what kind of relative the addresser thinks this 70-year-old man is roughly equivalent. On account of this, there is a phenomenon called 'feedback from the addressee' in kinship generalization as appellation terms. That is, the addressee will evaluate the appellation terms he/she gets. Furthermore, if the appellation terms he/she gets do not match his/her expectation, it may harm the communication. For example, some females do not want to be called '*a yi (aunt)*' but prefer '*jie jie (sister)*'.

In particular, the generalization of kinship terms under the rules of (1) gender matching and (2) age gap projection as social appellation terms has seen a new development in contemporary Chinese, that is, a further generalization. The original generalization of kinship terms is from 'relative' to 'non-relative'; while the further generalization is from 'age gap projection' to 'null age gap'. Examples of related terms are shown in Table 2:

Table 2. Further generalization of kinship terms

Language/Dialect	Vocative terms
Mandarin	xiao ge (little elder brother)
	xiao jie jie (littler elder sister)
Tianjin Dialect	jie jie (elder sister)
Cantonese	ge ge (elder brother)
	jie jie (elder sister)

Take Mandarin as an example. The emerging social vocative terms 'xiao ge (little elder brother)' and 'xiao jie jie (little elder sister)' both ignore the operation of 'age gap projection'. The addressee may be older or younger than the speaker, but as long as it is not too long or too young. Even the Tianjin dialect's 'jie jie (elder sister)' needs only to meet (1) gender matching requirements. This address term can be applied to address unfamiliar women of all ages, even if there is a significant age gap between the speaker and the hearer. This further generalization of kinship appellations is an evolutionary trend in which social vocatives strive to be neutral and avoid subjective judgment.

2.3   Quasi-generalization of the Occupational Terms

Occupational terms are used initially to refer to people with specific occupations or skills. Some of these professional titles can be introduced as social vocative terms in contemporary Chinese, such as 'shi fu (master)' in Mandarin and 'lao shi (teacher)' in Jinan dialect. This 'quasi-generalization' phenomenon occurred in the professional terms used for social vocative addressing rather than 'generalization'. Although the use of some occupational terms as addressing socially is not limited to the people referred to by their original semantics, it is still not fully generalized as broad as 'ni hao (hello)'. The selections follow the principle of 'prototype-like'. We will use the terms 'shi fu (master)' and 'tong xue (classmate)' as examples.

The standard prototype image referred to by the semantics of 'shi fu (master)' is generally (1) non-young and (2) male group. A sentence completion test was conducted to grasp the function of the word 'shi fu (master)' more clearly as a social vocative. Thirty native Chinese speakers were recruited as interview subjects. The interviewees were told that the context situation was 'need to inform the destination to a strange driver' and were asked whether he/she would address the driver as 'shi fu (master)' under the four given scenarios. The results shown in Table 3 below are obtained:

Table 3. Results of sentence completion test

Gender of driver	Age of driver	Number of interviewees who would use 'shi fu'	Percentage of interviewees who would use 'shi fu'
Male	Middle-aged and older	30	100%
Male	Under middle-aged	26	87%
Female	Middle-aged and older	25	83%
Female	Under middle-aged	2	7%

The above results show that: when the driver is middle-aged and older, regardless of male or female, the subjects generally accept 'shi fu' as the appellation. When the driver is young adulthood, if it is a male, 'shi fu' can still be accepted; however, if it is a female, the vast majority of subjects do not accept addressing a young girl 'shi fu'. It can be seen that one of the original two prototype conditions of 'shi fu (master)', which are (1) non-youth AND (2) male, can be and have to be retained as one only when the word as a vocative, i.e., someone is either (1) non-youth OR (2) male. Therefore, this kind of partial retention of the original semantics to seek the prototype-like similarity is called the quasi-generalization phenomenon.

The semantic connotation of the noun 'tong xue (classmate)' is interactive, that is, the conditions of usage are: (1) the speaker is a student, and (2) the hearer is a student. However, in the use of the social vocative term, as long as the age of the hearer meets or is close to the age range of a 'student', there are no strict restrictions on the actual age or occupation of the speaker and hearer. It demonstrates that the original practice conditions of the term 'tong xue (classmate)', which are (1) the speaker is a student AND (2) the hearer is a student, can be and have to be retained as one only when the word as a vocative, i.e. (2) the hearer is/looks like a student. This also conforms to the quasi-generalization pattern of 'prototype-like similarity seeking'.

2.4   Generalization of Laudatory Terms

The laudatory term is the appellation that compliments the hearer for a certain aspect of excellence. In using contemporary Chinese social vocatives, some laudatory terms are borrowed and generalized into general address terms. The most extensively applied ones are 'shuai ge (handsome guy)', 'mei nv (beauty)', 'liang zai (beautiful boy)', 'liang nv (beautiful girl)', 'lao ban (boss)', etc. The initial meaning of these laudatory terms is mostly focused on the outstanding appearance and career of the person being addressed. When it is applied as a social vocative address, the aforementioned factual conditions are no longer required. Regardless of whether the subject is outstanding or not, the laudatory vocative can be implemented as long as it meets the gender matching requirement.

This particular category of social vocatives indicates the approbation maxim in the Politeness Maxims and the principle of 'euphemism courtesy [15]' in Chinese language and culture, which is to communicate in a context that is not entirely authentic, in order to express respect and achieve the purpose of communication. What needs to be pointed out is that the laudatory appellation tends to be diminishing with the development of society gradually. The addressers of the laudatory terms tend to be concentrated in the service industry. Correspondingly, its acceptance also differs due to group characteristics, and not all the addressees are satisfied with the convention of a laudatory term.

2.5 Cyberspeaks Borrowing

The rapid development of e-commerce in China has spawned some social appellations on online platforms, and these appellations have erupted from online to offline and have been borrowed into actual social discourse. Represented by words such as '*qin (short for dear)*' and '*qin ai de (dear)*', these words are often used in the service industry or among young people. The rise and popularity of cyberspeak appellation have certain inevitability and rationality.

Generally, two broad categories of social address terms [2] are reciprocal and non-reciprocal. The so-called 'non-reciprocal' means that the choice of appellation requires consideration of the addressee's actual situation, such as age, gender, occupation, kinship, and power. Therefore, the non-reciprocal appellation used varies from person to person, i.e., 'one person, one term'. The aforementioned terms like '*ye ye (grandfather)*', '*shi fu (master)*', and '*mei nv (beauty)*' are all non-reciprocal appellations. The so-called 'reciprocal' appellation means that the appellation can be used mutually between the two parties in the dialogue. It reflects an equal relationship and does not require individual consideration. For example, '*ni hao (hello)*' in Chinese and '*hello*' in English are reciprocal appellations. When we mentioned the phenomenon of 'substitution of greetings' in the previous Sect. 2.1, It is pointed out that English also has a similar phenomenon. Furthermore, different greetings will reflect subtle differences in intimacy (such as '*good morning*' and '*hey*'). It illustrates that in the 'reciprocal' appellation, although the two parties of the dialogue are equal, this equal relationship can be assorted into three types as neutral, intimate, and distant. In Chinese, the reciprocal appellation term '*ni hao (hello)*' is relatively neutral, while '*nin hao (honorific hello)*' is more respectful and distant. Therefore, in Chinese, if someone wants to use a short-distance appellation that can bring a closer relationship, only non-reciprocal appellation can be applied, which needs to evaluate the addressee's personal information. However, the emerging cyberspeak term represented by '*qin (short for dear)*' provides an intimate and equal entry for the current Chinese social vocative appellation system, makes the system more complete in structure and diverse in functions (see Table 4 below).

Table 4. Reciprocal and non-reciprocal terms in Chinese

Reciprocal		Non-reciprocal
Intimate	Non-intimate	
Cyberspeaks ('*qin*')	Greetings ('*ni hao*', '*nin hao*')	Kinship terms ('*shu shu*')
		Laudatory terms ('*mei nv*')
		Occupational terms ('*shi fu*')

2.6   Conventional Terms

In addition to the above five categories, contemporary Chinese social vocatives still retain some idiomatic expressions that have been practiced for a long time and have a relatively stable linguistic foundation. These words have been inherited in language changes. Although they are gradually declining, they are still part of language life. For example, '*xian sheng (sir)*', '*nv shi (madam)*', '*tong zhi (comrade)*', '*gu niang (young lady)*', '*xiao huo zi (young lad)*', '*xiao peng you (child)*', etc.

3   Principles of Application and Distribution Pattern of Social Vocatives

3.1   Principles of Application

Brown and Ford [2] discussed the principles of using English address terms from the perspectives of reciprocal, status, and intimacy. Ervin-Tripp [3] sketched the address system of American English. On this basis, Wen Qiufang [16] classified the influencing factors of the choice of Chinese address terms into five categories, a total of 16 factors, i.e., (1) the age of the addressed person; (2) the occasion; (3) the relationship between the interlocutors; (4) the distance; and (5) the known name information. Gu Yueguo [6] pointed out that the influencing factors of the choice of Chinese address words include (1) kin or non-kin; (2) politically superior or inferior; (3) professionally prestigious or non-prestigious; (4) interpersonally familiar or unfamiliar, solidary or non-solidary; (5) male or female; (6) old or young; (7) on a formal or informal occasion; (8) family members or non-relatives; and (9) in public or at home. Comprehensively considering the diachronic research results and synchronic conditions, we have summarized the four variables and their application principles based on the six categories mentioned above of contemporary Chinese social vocative terms, as shown in Table 5 below.

The primary variables of selecting social address terms are 'intimate/distant' and 'superior/inferior', which is called the first application principle. 'intimate/distant' refers to the speaker's judgment or expectation of the social distance between the two when addressing the hearer. It has three situations, neutral distance, close distance (intimate) and long distance (distant). All kinship terms are close distance (intimate) terms. Appellations such as '*shuai ge (handsome guy)*' and '*mei nv (beauty)*', which contain subjective evaluation information, are also intimate appellations. Appellations such as '*ni hao (hello)*' and '*nin hao (honorific hello)*' are neutral distance appellations.

Table 5. Variables and application principles of Chinese social vocatives

Priority	Variable	Type		Explanation
1st principle	Intimate or distant	【+distant】		With distance
		【Ø distant】		Neutral
		【−distant】		Intimate
	Superior or inferior	【+superior】		Hearer is superior
		【Ø superior】		Equal
		【−superior】		Hearer is inferior
2nd principle	Gender	Male		
		Female		
		【Ø gender】		Gender irrelevant
	Age gap	【+age gap】	【+2generation】	The hearer is two generations equivalent to older
			【+1generation】	The hearer is one generation equivalent to older
		【Ø age gap】	(1) The age difference is not significant (2) Only need to estimate the age of hearer, no need to judge the age gap between interlocutors (3) Age gap irrelevant	
		【−age gap】	【−1generation】	The hearer is one generation equivalent to younger
			【−2generation】	The hearer is two generations equivalent to younger

Distant appellations are rare because they do not conform to the nature of social appellations implementing, such as conveying politeness and promoting communication [6, 17, 18]. Nevertheless, in the context of negotiation, complaints, and accusations, long-distance appellations will also appear. 'Superior/inferior' refers to the difference in the social status between the two, or the difference in honorability that the speaker hopes to emphasize. For instance, 'ni hao (hello)' and 'nin hao (honorific hello)' are both neutral distant, while the latter is hearer-superior. 'Superior/inferior' status has three situations: neutral status (equal), the addressee's superiority, or the addressee's inferiority. In the generalized employment of kinship terms as vocatives, the superior/inferior criteria will be reflected in the age gap. When the non-relative appellation is practiced, this variable is reflected in information such as occupation, seniority, or hierarchy.

After the 1st principle is established, two variables apply as the 2nd principle, 'gender' and 'age gap'. 'Gender' has three situations, neutral (gender information is irrelevant), male and female. 'Age gap' refers to the judgment result of the age gap between the speaker and the hearer in the speaker's eyes. It has three categories: addressee is significantly older, insignificant age gap and addressee is significantly younger. 'Insignificant age gap' means that the age gap between the addresser and the addressee is equivalent to the same generation, or the age gap can be ignored in the context, or only the age of the addressee is required to be estimated. 'Significantly older' refers that the hearer is at least one generation older than the speaker, and 'significantly younger' means that the hearer is at least one generation younger than the speaker.

According to the combination of the two variables on the first principle, Chinese social vocatives can be classified into nine types, and each type can be further differentiated according to the variables on the second principle. The aforementioned six categories of contemporary Chinese vocatives collected and summarized in Chapter 2 correspond to these nine types, as shown in Table 6 below.

Table 6. Nine types of Chinese social vocatives

Types based on 1ˢᵗ principle	Example	Further marked based on 2ⁿᵈ principle
【+distant, +superior】	*lao ban (boss)*	【Øgender, Øage gap】
【+distant, Øsuperior】	*peng you (friend)*	【Øgender, Øage gap】
【+distant, −superior】	*ai, wei*	【Øgender, Øage gap】
【Ødistant, +superior】	*nin hao (honorific hello)*	【Øgender, Øage gap】
	tong zhi (comrade)	【Øgender, Øage gap】
	shi fu (master)	【+age gap】 OR 【male】
	xian sheng (sir) *nv shi (madam)*	【+gender, Øage gap】
【Ødistant, Øsuperior】	*ni hao (hello)*	【Øgender, Øage gap】
	tong xue (classmate)	【Øgender, −age gap, −1gen】
【Ødistant, −superior】	*gu niang (young lady)* *xiao huo zi (young lad)*	【+gender, −age gap, −1gen】
	xiao peng you (child)	【Øgender, −age gap, −1/2gen】
【−distant, +superior】	*ye ye (grandfather)* *nai nai (grandmother)*	【+gender, + age gap, +2gen】
	da shu (elder uncle) *da ma (elder aunt)*	【+gender, + age gap, +1gen】
	da ge (elder brother) *da jie (elder sister)*	【+gender, Øage gap】
【−distant, Øsuperior】	*qin (short for dear)*	【Øgender, Øage gap】
	shuai ge (handsome man) *mei nv (beauty)*	【 +gender, Øage gap】
	xiao ge (little elder brother) *xiao jie jie (little elder sister)*	【+gender, Øage gap】
【−distant, −superior】	*xiao di (younger brother) xiao mei mei (young sister)*	【+gender, Øage gap】

The complete neutral social address term in Chinese is *'ni hao (hello)'*, which is null in the dimensions of distance, social status, gender, and age. Other neutral-distance terms differ on account of superiority or age gap. For example, *'shi fu (master)'* meets [+superior] and [+male or +age gap]; *'xiao peng you (child)'* meets [−superior] and [−age gap], etc. The intimate types are mainly composed with kinship appellations and laudatory terms. Except '*qin (short for dear)*', intimate terms are generally sensitive to gender and age gaps. The distant terms are not sensitive to gender features or age differences, regardless of social status. The implementation of distant terms often has clear and special social purposes (such as negotiation, complaint, accusation).

3.2 Distribution Pattern

To intuitively explore the distribution of contemporary Chinese social vocatives under the 1st level principle, we have carried out a numerical quadrant transformation: the 'distance' criterion is the horizontal axis x, and the 'superiority' criterion is the vertical axis y. Take '*ni hao (hello)*' as the origin (0, 0). [+distant] is +1 on the x-axis; [−distant] is −1 on the x-axis; [Ø distance] is 0 on the x-axis. The same is true for the vertical axis y 'superiority' criterion. At the same time, the y-axis is also linked with the 'age gap' criterion: the y-axis value is ±0.5 if the age gap is within the same generation; the y-axis value is ±1 if the age gap is one generation; the y-axis value is ±2 if the age gap is two generations. Based on this, each example of the social vocatives in Table 6 has obtained a coordinate value (as shown in Table 7 below).

Table 7. Coordinate value of Chinese social vocatives

Vocative terms	Coordinate value
lao ban (boss)	(1, 0.5)
peng you (friend)	(1, 0)
ai/wei	(1, −0.5)
nin hao (honorific hello)	(0, 0.5)
tong zhi (comrade)	(0, 0.5)
shi fu (master)	(0, 1)
xian sheng (sir)	(0, 0.5)
nv shi (madam)	(0, 0.5)
ni hao (hello)	(0, 0)
tong xue (classmate)	(0, −0.5)
gu niang (young lady)	(0, −0.5)
xiao huo zi (young lad)	(0, −0.5)
xiao peng you (child)	(0, −1)
ye ye (grandfather)	(−1, 2)
nai nai (grandmother)	(−1, 2)
da shu (elder uncle)	(−1, 1)
da ma (elder aunt)	(−1, 1)
da ge (elder brother)	(−1, 0.5)
da jie (elder sister)	(−1, 0.5)
qin (short for dear)	(−1, 0)
shuai ge (handsome guy)	(−1, 0)
me inv (beauty)	(−1, 0)
xiao ge (little elder brother)	(−1, 0)
xiao jie jie (little elder sister)	(−1, 0)
xiao di (younger brother)	(−1, −0.5)
xiao mei mei (younger sister)	(−1, −0.5)

Draw vocative term corresponding to each point into the coordinates according to the coordinate value, and get the distribution diagram as shown in Fig. 1:

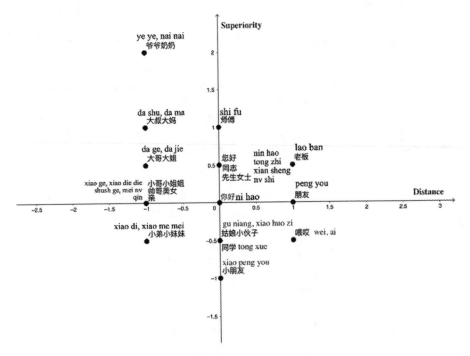

Fig. 1. Distribution diagram of Chinese social vocatives

According to this distribution pattern, contemporary Chinese social vocatives present the following characteristics:

1. Tendency of intimacy: The distribution of vocative terms is dominated by the left quadrant on the y-axis, that is, the principle of [−/Ø distant].
2. Tendency of superiority: the distribution of terms is mainly in the quadrant above the x-axis, that is, the principle of [Ø/ +superior].
3. The coordinate points on the axis are more abundant, especially the y-axis [Ø distant] category.
4. There are cases where different terms correspond to the same coordinate point.

The social vocative terms are still dominated by proximity and respect, which aligns with the politeness principle of language communication [6, 17, 19–21], especially the approbation maxim and the modesty maxim. This has developed into the self-denigration maxim [6] and euphemism courtesy [15] under the Chinese's unique cultural and social environment. The implementations of social vocatives through generalizing kinship appellation and laudatory terms, or borrowing the cyberspeaks, are to express politeness and maintain a positive face while bringing in contact with each other through humility and compliment, and to conduct effective communication. It also meets the requirements of the tact maxim: minimize the expression that implies that others pay; maximize the expression that implies that they benefit. Overall, the maxims of approbation, modesty, and self-denigration should eventually be mutually recognized with tact maxim. This brings about a phenomenon that the choices and diversity of Chinese social address terms decrease with age (as shown in the red box in Fig. 2). Since Chinese vocatives tend to convey the superiority of the addressee, with the increase of addresser's age, the balances between 'tact and generosity', 'approbation and modesty', are broken. For example, it will be highly inappropriate if the elderly still uses the vocative which meets the self-denigration maxim.

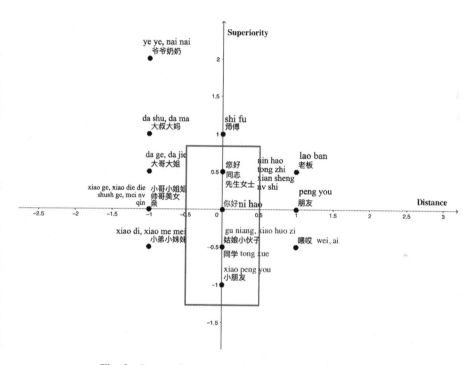

Fig. 2. Range of social vocative terms choices by elderly

The rise and widespread trend of 'neutral distance + superior' terms in Chinese is an increasingly important manifestation of the agreement maxim in contemporary Chinese. This positive polite strategy of seeking solidarity and reducing disagreement [17, 21] is embodied in minimizing inconsistent expressions and maximizing consistent expressions between each other. For example, the sequence of the terms '*shi fu-nin hao-ni hao-xiao peng you (master-honorific hello-hello-child)*', which cover all the age gaps between speaker and hearer, is the product of generalization of vocative terms under both appropriate and solidary strategies, that is, the tendency of 'equal respect'. At the same time, under similar communicative needs, different word choices will appear according to the social factors. For example, the term group '*qin (short for dear)/xiao ge (little elder brother)/shuai ge (handsome guy)*', and the term group '*nin hao (honorific hello)/tong zhi (comrade)/xian sheng (sir)'*. According to the above distribution pattern and coordinate position diagram, the terms in two groups have the same coordinate value correspondingly, and what the different choice revealed is not in the addressing effect but the speaker's characteristics. Under the influence of social identity, personal background, and language habits, speakers will choose different words from the term group for social addressing, leaving a personal discourse label.

4   Conclusion

This article investigates the application of social vocative appellations in contemporary Chinese and summarizes six categories, namely (1) substitution of greetings; (2) generalization of kinship terms; (3) quasi-generalization of occupational terms; (4) generalization of laudatory terms; (5) borrowing cyberspeaks; and (6) conventional terms. The practice of the social vocatives is based on the four variables, i.e., distance, superiority, gender, and age gap. Taking distance and superiority as the two main axes, we outline the distribution pattern of contemporary Chinese social vocatives. Overall, the use of these vocative terms conforms to the basic principles of politeness strategy and conversational principles. As their unique properties, Chinese social vocatives combine the maxims of self-denigration and tact by using kinship terms, laudatory terms, professional terms, and cyberspeaks. In addition, the maxim of agreement is becoming increasingly significant in contemporary Chinese society. Social vocatives that become popular recently show the tendency of being 'equally respectful'. The information such as gender and age of the addressee gradually diminishes in the vocatives, while the speaker's characteristics in the dimensions of language, culture, and society are retained in the addressing choices.

References

1. Parkinson, D.B.: Constructing the Social Context of Communication: Terms of Address in Egyptian Arabic. Walter de Gruyter GmbH & Co KG (2015)
2. Brown, R., Ford, M.: Address in American English. Psychol. Sci. Public Interest **62**(2), 375 (1961)
3. Ervin-Tripp, S.M.: Sociolinguistic rules of address. Lang. Commun. Educ. **162** (1972)
4. Chen, T.S., Shryock, J.K.: Chinese relationship terms. Am. Anthropol. **34**(4), 623–669 (1932)
5. Chao, Y.R.: Chinese terms of address. Language **32**(1), 217–241 (1956)
6. Gu, Y.: Politeness phenomena in modern Chinese. J. Pragmat. **14**(2), 237–257 (1990)
7. Brown, P., Levinson, S.C., Levinson, S.C.: Politeness: Some Universals in Language Usage. Cambridge University Press, Cambridge (1987)
8. Feng, H.Y.: The Chinese Kinship System. Harvard University Press, Cambridge (2014)
9. Scotton, C.M., Wanjin, Z.: The multiple meanings of shī fu, a language change in progress. Anthropol. Linguist. **26**, 326–344 (1984)
10. Lee-Wong, S.M.: Address forms in modern China: changing ideologies and shifting semantics. Linguistics **32**, 299–324 (1994)

11. Qin, X.: Choices in terms of address: a sociolinguistic study of Chinese and American English practices. In: Proceedings of the 20th North American Conference on Chinese Linguistics (NACCL-20), pp. 409–421 (2008)
12. Guo, J.: Common appellation and its characteristics. Zhongguo yuwen **2**, 90–99 (1995). (in Chinese)
13. Shao, J.: A sociolinguistic survey on the controversy over "Meinü" as an address form. Appl. Linguis. **04**, 71–79 (2009). (in Chinese)
14. Zhang, J., Chen, J.: The study of conceptual structures of Chinese address words. Appl. Linguis. **2**, 41–49 (2007). (in Chinese)
15. He, Z.: Socio pragmatics: use language to deal with interpersonal relationship. Foreign Lang. Educ. **39**(06), 1–6 (2018). (In Chinese)
16. Wen, Q.: A sociolinguistic approach to the use rules of Chinese address terms. J. Nanjing Normal Univ. (Social Science Edition) **4**, 73–76 (1987). (in Chinese)
17. Brown, P.: Politeness and language. In: The International Encyclopedia of the Social and Behavioural Sciences (IESBS), 2nd edn., pp. 326–330. Elsevier, Amsterdam (2015)
18. Kádár, D.Z., Haugh, M.: Understanding Politeness. Cambridge University Press, Cambridge (2013)
19. Grice, H.P.: Logic and conversation. In: Cole, p., Morgan, J. (eds.) Speech Acts, pp. 41–58. Brill (1975)
20. Leech, G.: Principles of Pragmatics. Routledge, Abingdon (2016)
21. Brown, P.: Politeness. In: International Encyclopedia of Linguistic Anthropology, pp. 1–8. Wiley-Blackwell, Hoboken (2020)

The Corpus Construction of Basic Noun Compound Phrase in Literature Domain and Its Comparison with News Domain

Yuan Zhong[1], Ying Zhang[1], and Pengyuan Liu[1,2(✉)]

[1] Department of Information Science, Beijing Language and Culture University, 15th Xueyuan Road, Haidian District, Beijing 10083, China
liupengyuan@pku.edu.cn
[2] Center of National Language Recourse and Monitoring Research Print Media Branch, Beijing Language and Culture University, 15th Xueyuan Road, Haidian District, Beijing 100083, China

Abstract. At present, a relatively large number of knowledge bases that contains semantic relation of noun compound has been established, but there is a lack of comparative research on noun phrases between corpora. This paper sets out to review the domestic studies on noun phrases, as well as news language and literary language, and then make a comparative analysis of basic compound noun phrases (BCNP) between linguistically annotated the literature corpus and the news corpus. Subsequently presented are the findings on linguistic characteristics and rules in the two different domains. By extracting BCNP from literature corpus, the semantic relationship is extended and supplemented, and the resources that can be applied to future corpus construction are provided.

Keywords: Basic compound noun phrase · The news corpus · The literature corpus · Comparative analysis

1 Introduction

Noun is the most abundant of all parts of speech. The basic compound noun phrase is a very common combination structure and it is also a concerned field of Chinese and foreign linguistics. This important object of study has also attracted the attention of researchers in the field of natural language processing, and a number of knowledge bases that contain semantic relations of noun phrases has been established.

At present, there is a semantic knowledge base of BCNP in the news field, but there is no such database in the literary field. News is a more formal style of language, while the style of literary works is more personalized. We can discover the characteristics and laws of different fields through the comparison of different styles. By extracting BCNP from literary corpus, the semantic relationship is extended and supplemented. It also provides the resources that can be applied to future corpus construction. The research on BCNP of Chinese is limited. Most of research on BCNP in various corpora are

M. Dong et al. (Eds.): CLSW 2021, LNAI 13250, pp. 320–334, 2022.
https://doi.org/10.1007/978-3-031-06547-7_25

qualitative, lacking of quantitative research and comparative research between different styles. This paper constructs the first corpus of basic noun compound phrases in the literary field. Via Python package jieba, manual screening and confirmation, we gain 11,358 qualified BCNP. On this basis, we propose the following research issues:

1. Comparison of the structural relationship of BCNP between the news corpus and literary corpus.
2. Comparison of nouns forming of BCNP between the news corpus and literary corpus.
3. Comparison of the semantic relations of BCNP between the news corpus and the literature corpus.

Through the comparison of real corpora, which is helpful to more in- depth research on the two styles, this paper can discover the differences between news style and literary style in a more intuitive way. The database can also be applied to tasks such as text classification.

2   Related Works

Noun phrases are phrases whose functions are equivalent to nouns. According to Huang and Liao [1], noun phrases can be divided into 7 categories:

(1)   the endocentric phrases centered on nouns, such as "mù tou fáng zi", which means "wooden house";
(2)   the coordinate phrases composed of nouns, such as "bà ba mā ma" which means "Mom and Dad";
(3)   the classifier phrases composed of nouns and classifiers, such as "yì běn shū" which means "a book";
(4)   the appositive phrase, such as "shǒu dū běi jīng" which means "capital Beijing";
(5)   the phrases with "de", such as "mǎi cài de" which means "the shopper";
(6)   the phrases with "suo", such as "suǒ sī suǒ xiǎng" which means "the thoughts";
(7)   the positional phrases, such as "tiān shang" which means "on the sky".

In word formation, "compound method" refers to the method of combining two different root morphemes to form a word. For example, "Shanshui (mountains and water)" is a combination of the root "shan (mountains)" and the root "shui (water)". The compound noun phrase is derived from the "noun compounds" commonly used by researchers in English study, which is not widely used in Chinese linguistics. We adopt the concept "compound noun phrase" proposed by Wang [2] which is that: A compound noun phrase is a specific type of phrase. It consists of a sequence of adjacent nouns, and its function as a whole is equivalent to a noun, such as "electronic police", "computer company" and "air quality issues". The last noun in the compound noun phrase is usually called the head, and the preceding component is called the modifier. From a grammatical point of view, compound noun phrases are similar to words, and the function of the entire compound noun phrase is equivalent to the function of the head noun. Regarding the structure of compound noun phrases, Wang [2] concluded that there are at least 5 situations in the position of the central word of the Chinese N+N compound structure: (1) the centre of the structure and the semantic focus are both on the right; (2) the centre of the structure is on the right while the semantic focus is on the left; (3) the centre of the structure and the semantic focus are both on the left; (4) the centre of the structure is on the right with two semantic focuses (synonymous or antonymous juxtaposed structure); (5) the centre of the structure is on the right while there is no semantic focus. In the current research on the structure of compound noun phrases, most of the scholars take the last noun as the core of the entire compound noun phrase, and the multiple nouns in the front are used as attributives to modify the core nouns. The combination of "N1+N2" in Chinese usually contains the following structures: (1) attributive structure (traditional culture); (2) apposition phrase (the village head Yu Shi); (3) joint structure (brother and sister); (4) subject-predicate structure (today Monday).

In the comparison of different styles, Chen [3] extracted language data from the Chinese-English comparative corpus LCMC and Frown, and used quantitative linguistic indicators - entropy and topic concentration - to quantitatively analyze and compare the text features of both Chinese and English representative styles and to interpret its causes from the perspective of linguistics. By using "entropy", the author compared the differences among news, governmental documents and novels in the aspect of vocabulary richness. Through the comparison of "relative entropy of part of speech position", it is concluded that different styles have significant differences between narrative and descriptive styles. The comparative researches between the news corpus and literary corpus are mostly qualitative. Ding [4] put forward that the essence and requirement of news is that "the basic requirements of news writing are authenticity, ideology, timeliness, and facts." At the same time, she stated that the essence and requirement of literature is that "the most basic requirement of the language of literary works is to be vivid and delicate, which requires literary works to use a variety of rhetoric methods in the process of writing to complete the artistic needs of literary works." Jiang [5] compared and analyzed the differences between news language and literary language in terms of objectivity and subjectivity, univocality and ambiguity, popularization and individualization, and practicality and aesthetics. Through comparative analysis, it is concluded that "news language is objective and true, with single semantics, and has the characteristics of popularization and practicality, while literary language is a language created on the basis of subjectivity. Its ambiguity, individuality and aesthetics characteristics endow literary works with profound connotation and unique appreciation value." Yang [6] pointed out that the main body of news language is news media, the target is the audience, the behavior is dissemination, and the content is news information. The tool for organizing and disseminating this information is news language. News language is authentic, concise, various and popular, while literary language is a processed, standardized written language, and is also an advanced form of national common language. The characteristics of literary language are: vividness, emotion, and emphasis on the creation of artistic conception and atmosphere. The main difference between news language and literary language lies in the different emphasis and accuracy of expression. News language pays attention to colloquialism, while literary language pays attention to expressing the author's thoughts and emotions.

Most of research on the basic noun compound phrases in the news corpus and literary corpus is qualitative, lacking of quantitative research. Through labeling and statistics of BCNP in the news corpus and literary corpus, we compare and analyze the differences and find out the reasons.

3 Construction of Basic Noun Compound Phrase Database in Literary Domain

3.1 Corpus Selection and Processing

The corpus of this article was selected from works collected by traditional literary corpus, which are mainly modern and contemporary Chinese works, from Qian Liqun's *Thirty Years of Modern Chinese Literature* and Hong Zicheng's *History of Contemporary Chinese Literature*. In the collected corpus, there are more than 140 authors and more than 800 works. The total size of the txt text is 505 MB, with a total of 529,619,066 bytes. We first used a popular word segmentation tool – Jieba to perform word segmentation and part-of-speech tagging processing on the original corpus. After the corpus was preprocessed, the "N+N" sequence pattern was automatically extracted.

3.2 Phrase Extraction and Filtering

Using this simple extraction method, we obtained a total of 826,881 items, of which 41,302 items appeared with a frequency of more than 5. Because it is difficult to identify non-phrase structures by simple structure recognition, there are some illegal and non-compliant structures in the extraction results. We chose phrases with a frequency of more than 5 and manually screened them. Most of the illegal phrases include the following categories:

(1) Wrong segmentation, for example, "women" were mistakenly divided into "female people".
(2) Unrecognized name, for example "Yang Xiaobo", splitting a person's name into two nouns does not meet the definition requirements of BCNP.
(3) Nouns composed of morphemes, for example "Snowfield". In this phrase, N1 and N2 are noun morphemes, and they are a common noun when combined, which does not meet the requirements;
(4) Quantitative phrase + noun structure, for example "The family". In this phrase, N1 is a quantitative phrase composed of a quantifier and a noun, which does not meet the requirement that N1 is a noun;

(5) Part of a multi-level nested noun structure, for example "bourgeois intellectuals". The word segmentation tool divides the "bourgeois intellectuals" into "bourgeois/intellectuals/elements", only part of the phrase is identified when extracting, and there is no direct grammatical relationship between the two.

(6) Inconsistent word segmentation granularity, for example "Beijing Normal University Press", different word segmentation tools divide this phrase into different ways, which is supposed to be a named entity, so it does not meet the requirements.

(7) Part-of-speech tagging errors, for example, in "Suspects", the word segmentation tool incorrectly marks the word "crime" as a noun.

3.3 Corpus Tagging

Firstly, we filtered artificially based on Python Jieba word segmentation and sorted according to word frequency. Secondly, the artificially screened BCNP were labeled with structural relations and named entities, and the top 1000 BCNP in the news corpus and literary corpus were selected according to this word frequency ranking. Through the comparative analysis of basic noun compound phrases between the news corpus and literary corpus, we can find out the differences and analyze the reasons. We referred to Liu [7] for labeling details of the structural relationship and named entity. For the labeling of the structural relations of compound noun phrases, we divided the structure of compound noun phrases into attributive structure, subject-predicate structure, joint structure, and apposition structure, respectively marked as dz (attributive structure), lh (joint structure), tw (appositive structure), zw (subject-predicate structure). The named entities mainly include phrases related to names of persons, phrases related to locations, and phrases related to names of institutions. When labeling, we marked the words in the BCNP that are closely connected to the named entity in terms of position, grammar, as well as morphology and semantically identical to the concept of the name entity. Those words are then labeled with the number label "1". Then, we classified and counted the nouns in BCNP in the news corpus and literary corpus, and compared and analyzed the differences of the top 100 nouns between the two corpora. Lastly, the semantic relations of BCNP in the news corpus and literary corpus were marked, compared, and analyzed.

3.4 Corpus Overview

Finally, through manual screening and confirmation, a total of 11,358 qualified BCNP were obtained (Table 1).

Table 1. The distribution of semantic relations of noun phrases in literary corpus

Semantic relations	Percentage (%)
Of	36.5
Location	8.45
Modify	8.35
Be	8.25
Make	7.35
And	6.85
Content	6.77
Do	4.43
From	4.27
For	4.12
Time	2.57
Use	0.92
Have	0.59
Like	0.51
Cause	0.07

It can be seen from the above table that the semantic relationship that appears most frequently in the literary corpus is the "Of" relationship. Most nouns in the N1 position in the literary corpus are used as attributives to modify and describe the affiliation relationship of things or characters.

Table 2. The distribution of structural relations of noun phrases in literary corpus

Structural relations	Attributive structure	Joint structure	Appositive structure	Subject-predicate structure
Percentage (%)	91.82	6.71	1.08	0.39

In literary corpus, noun phrases with attributive structure account for the vast majority, which is consistent with the advantage of nouns in assuming syntactic components (Table 2).

4 Comparison and Analysis

By labeling the corpus, we have compared and analyzed the following aspects of the corpus. The first is an overview of BCNP. The second is the structural relationship of BCNP. The third is the use of nouns that make up BCNP, including differences in the use of named entities, differences in hapax legomena, differences in the types of nouns that make up phrases.

4.1   Overview of BCNP

Through labeling and statistical analyzing of BCNP in the news corpus and literary corpus, the 10 most frequent phrases and the 10 least frequent phrases in the news corpus and literary corpus are obtained. The average frequency of BCNP in the news corpus and literary corpus is shown in the following Table 3:

Table 3. The phrases in the news corpus and literary corpus

	The news corpus	Literary corpus
The 10 most frequent noun phrases	Leaders and cadres, Chinese people, core value, the masses, the People's Hospital, the local government, press conference, online finance, city center, Xinhua News Agency reporter	Chinese, Japanese, Japanese soldiers, Americans, Qingfeng street, the man in white coats, Mrs. Simon, Aotu Mountain, Shanghai people, Chinese culture
The 10 least frequent noun phrases	Voice call, plant varieties, away results, the total amount of wealth, Shenzhen national tax, the province's temperature, Dongguan Manufacturing Industry, Department of Pediatrics in Health Center, autologous umbilical cord, Jiuzhou Pharmaceutical	Brown hair, governor general secretary, the ancestral home is Shandong, diamond earrings, diamond rose, left calf, the left leg shin, number of works, author's note, the author's life
10 noun phrases with a middle frequency	All the players, industry chaos, farmers, community grid, file material, the nation, civilized city, planning and positioning, the fashion industry, passenger traffic line	Foreign cloth gown, across from the hospital, the hospital's dormitory, artistic point of view, artistic skill, Milan, Italy, silver ring, Milky Way Nebula, Master Yinguang, British girl

Most of the ten most frequent noun phrases in the literary corpus are used to describe characters in a more specific way, while that in the news corpus are used to describe people as well as places and other things, and their references are more abstract and refer to more diversified objects. Among the 10 noun phrases with the middle frequency and the 10 noun phrases with the lowest frequency, the literary corpus is more specific than the news corpus. However, the things referred to by the two corpora are both abundant. The people or things referred to by compound noun phrases in the news corpus are relatively abstract and cover a wide range of concepts, while those in literary corpus mostly refer to more specific people or things. So, it can be seen that news mostly describes abstract events, such as national policies and routes, and the content described in literary works fits real life more closely. We counted the 100 most frequently used nouns in the news corpus and literary corpus, through comparison, we found that there are many multi-category words in the top 100 nouns in the news corpus, for example, "development (vn)", "security (an)", "design (vn)", etc. However, there are no multi-category words in the top 100 nouns of the literary corpus.

Because news works require concise writing and should contain as much content as possible, news language is subject to the requirements of conciseness, authenticity, and objectivity of news works. There is fewer innovative vocabulary and high vocabulary repetition, so a large amount of information will be compressed to nouns or noun phrases. Therefore, the proportion of multi-category words in the news corpus is relatively high. Most of the top 100 nouns in the news corpus represent the subject of the news activity, namely the person or thing in the news event and the time when the news event occurred, for example, "journalist". That verifies the findings of Ma's [8] research on news vocabulary based on a self-built news corpus of hot event. The subject of the news activity "reporter", the personal pronouns "who" related to the news event "he" and "I", and the "day", "month", "time" and "year" related to the news event "when", and other words appear more frequently. The top 100 nouns in literary corpus mostly represent images in real life, such as "dad", "mother", "eyes", etc. This embodies "literature comes from life and is higher than life (Fig. 1)."

4.2   Structural Relations of BCNP

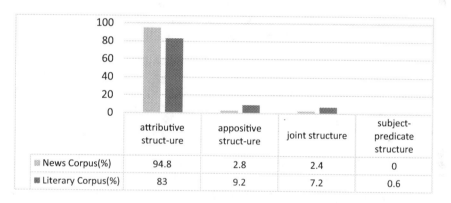

Fig. 1. Comparison of the structure of BCNP in the news corpus and literary corpus

Through labeling and statistical analyzing of the basic compound noun phrase structure types in the news corpus and literary corpus, we can conclude that BCNP with attributive structure composed of nouns as attributives account for the majority in both new corpus and literary corpus. According to Wang [9], 74.4% of nouns can be used as attributives to modify other nouns. Therefore, the overwhelming advantage of attributive structure in BCNP is consistent with the advantage of nouns in assuming syntactic components. In addition to the attributive structure, the appositive structure also account for a relatively large proportion. Appositive structure accounts for 2.8% of the news corpus and 9.2% of literary corpus. Both literary corpus and the news corpus need to refer to some characters or institutions, so the appositive structure is needed to exert its referential function. In the joint structure, the two nouns that make up the joint structure of the literary corpus are mostly collective nouns or individual nouns, which are mostly used to refer to specific people or things, such as "parents and brothers", "sons and daughters", etc. However, the two nouns that make up the joint structure of the news corpus are mostly abstract nouns, which are mostly used to refer to abstract things, such as "institutional mechanism", "cultural art" and so on. In the appositive structure, most of the appositive structure in the literary corpus refers to specific names and geographical names, and the scope of reference is relatively limited. 89.1% of the appositive structures can be marked as named entities. The appositive structure in the news corpus partly refers to more specific names and organizations, and some refer to more abstract things, such as "graduate degree". The appositive structure in the news corpus refers to a relatively large range of concepts. 55.5% of appositive structure can be labeled as named entities. Therefore, it can be seen that literary corpus refers to more specific people or things than the news corpus.

4.3   Usage of Nouns That Make up BCNP

Named Entity. Liu [7] reckons that there are board and narrow definition of name entity. Name entities in a narrow sense include names of persons, places and organizations, whereas name entities in a board sense include some non-conceptual titles. In this article's labeling, we use the broad definition of named entities.

Table 4. Comparison of named entities in the news corpus and literary corpus

	The news corpus	Literary corpus
Named entities (number & percentage)	153 (15.3%)	136 (13.6%)

In terms of quantity, 153 of the first 1000 compound noun phrases in the news corpus are marked as named entities, accounting for about 15.3%. Among the first 1000 compound noun phrases in the literary corpus, 136 are marked as named entities, accounting for about 13.6% (Table 4). It can be seen that there are slightly more named entities in the news corpus than in the literary corpus. In content, the named entities in the news corpus exist objectively in real life, such as "President Xi Jinping" and "Confucius Institute". But some of the named entities in the literary corpus do not exist objectively in real life, however, they refer to images that are created by the author to fit the plot of the story, such as "Bump Mountain" and "Ancient Furnace Village". Such a place may not exist in the real world. This is determined by the essential requirements of news writing and literary writing. The facts of news reports exist objectively. News is supposed to reports fact, and thus its essential requirement is truthfulness, namely let facts speak for themselves. Therefore, news language should be recorded and described truth base on factual information. The difference between literary works and news works is that literary works are derived from life but are higher than life. Literary is highly fictional, and literary language is created by the author based on his subjective initiative. So, it has a strong subjectivity. The differences in the nature and requirements between literary works and news works have caused the difference between named entities in literary corpus and the news corpus.

Differences in the Types of Nouns that Make up Phrases. According to Huang Borong and Liao Xudong's *"Modern Chinese"* (the sixth edition) [1], the nouns in the first 1000 BCNP in the news corpus and literary corpus are classified into Proper nouns (such as China, Lu Xun, etc.), Individual nouns (such as friend, writer, cow, airplane, atom, etc.), Collective nouns (such as people, masses, objects, etc.), Abstract nouns (such as morality, culture, politics, etc.), Material nouns (such as sound, sunlight, etc.), Time nouns (e.g.: autumn, morning, now, etc.), Location nouns (such as river bank, eastern suburbs, surroundings, etc.), Position nouns (such as front, back, above, etc.), in addition, Beijing, Guangdong, Asia, etc. are both proper nouns and location nouns.

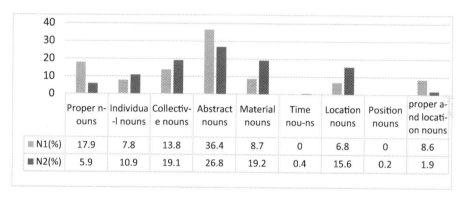

	Proper nouns	Individual nouns	Collective nouns	Abstract nouns	Material nouns	Time nouns	Location nouns	Position nouns	proper and location nouns
▨ N1(%)	17.9	7.8	13.8	36.4	8.7	0	6.8	0	8.6
▨ N2(%)	5.9	10.9	19.1	26.8	19.2	0.4	15.6	0.2	1.9

Fig. 2. Comparison of N1 and N2 noun classifications in the news corpus

In the news corpus, the noun categories that appears most frequently in the N1 position are abstract nouns (about 36.4%), proper nouns (about 17.9%), and collective nouns (about 13.8%); and the noun categories that appears most frequently in the N2 position are abstract nouns (about 26.8%), material nouns (about 19.2%), and collective nouns (about 19.1%) (Fig. 2). In the news corpus, the noun category that appears most frequently is abstract nouns. Because one of the functions of news is to clarify the country's development routes, guidelines, policies, and to introduce work experience, achievements, etc., and the content of such words are mostly abstract. Therefore, abstract nouns appear more frequently in the news corpus. In news, nouns will be used in large quantities to refer to people and things in news events, so the proportion of collective nouns used to represent people and things in the news corpus is relatively high. Since the location and proper nouns in the label refer to places, such as "Beijing" and "Shenzhen", the proportion of location nouns and location and proper nouns used to describe the place where the news occurs is also relatively high.

The proper nouns that appear in the N1 position far exceed the proper nouns that appear in the N2 position. Most of the proper nouns in the N1 position are the names of various countries or institutions, such as "China", "Japan", "Xinhua News Agency", etc., while most of the proper nouns in the N2 position are names of people, such as "Mayor Xu

Qin", "Reporter Yang Liang" and so on. Because news is expected to report on domestic and foreign affairs, proper nouns will appear in the N1 position to modify N2.

The material noun at the N2 position far exceeds the material noun at the N1 position. Because the material nouns appearing in the N2 position are generally used as the core of the noun phrase to indicate the subject referred to by the noun phrase, and one of the elements of news reporting is the subject and object of the news event. Therefore, there will be more material nouns in the N2 position than in the N1 position.

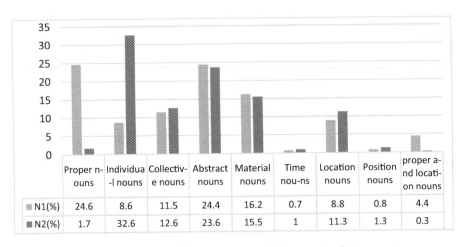

	Proper n-ouns	Individua-l nouns	Collectiv-e nouns	Abstract nouns	Material nouns	Time nou-ns	Location nouns	Position nouns	proper a-nd locati-on nouns
N1(%)	24.6	8.6	11.5	24.4	16.2	0.7	8.8	0.8	4.4
N2(%)	1.7	32.6	12.6	23.6	15.5	1	11.3	1.3	0.3

Fig. 3. Comparison of N1 and N2 noun classifications in literary corpus

In the literary corpus, the nouns categories that appear the most in the N1 position are proper nouns (about 24.6%), abstract nouns (about 24.4%), and material nouns (about 16.2%). The noun categories that appear the most in the N2 position are individual nouns (about 32.6%), abstract nouns (about 23.6%), and material nouns (about 15.5%) (Fig. 3). Literature is an artistic image to reflect social life, so individual nouns and material nouns used to refer to characters in the literary corpus account for a relatively high proportion. Abstract nouns are often used as attributives to modify people or things. So the proportion of abstract nouns in the N1 position is relatively high.

Proper nouns and individual nouns in literary corpus differ from each other greatly. Proper nouns are usually used to modify the attribute or source of something. So they often appear in the N1 position. Individual nouns are usually the subject and object of an event and need to appear in the core position of the noun phrase. So there are more individual nouns in the N2 position.

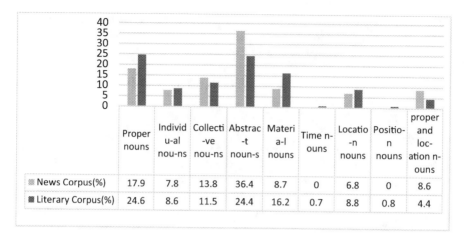

	Proper nouns	Individ u-al nou-ns	Collecti -ve nou-ns	Abstrac -t noun-s	Materi a-l nouns	Time n- ouns	Locatio -n nouns	Positio- n nouns	proper and loc- ation n- ouns
News Corpus(%)	17.9	7.8	13.8	36.4	8.7	0	6.8	0	8.6
Literary Corpus(%)	24.6	8.6	11.5	24.4	16.2	0.7	8.8	0.8	4.4

Fig. 4. Comparison of N1 in the news corpus and literary corpus

In the N1 position, the material nouns in the literary corpus are more than the material nouns in the news corpus, because literary works are good at using metaphors to describe things, or using material terms to modify things so as to illustrate the attributes, sources, and uses of things (Fig. 4).

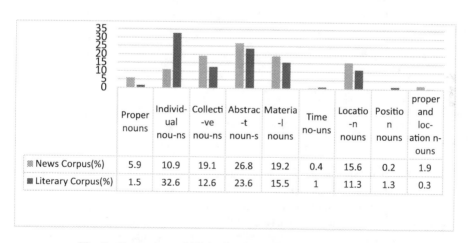

	Proper nouns	Individ- ual nou-ns	Collecti -ve nou-ns	Abstrac -t noun-s	Materia -l nouns	Time no-uns	Locatio -n nouns	Positio n nouns	proper and loc- ation n- ouns
News Corpus(%)	5.9	10.9	19.1	26.8	19.2	0.4	15.6	0.2	1.9
Literary Corpus(%)	1.5	32.6	12.6	23.6	15.5	1	11.3	1.3	0.3

Fig. 5. Comparison of N2 in the news corpus and literary corpus

It can be seen from the figure that in the N2 position, literary corpus only exceeds news corpus in terms of individual nouns because the N2 position is the core of the noun phrase (Fig. 5). It can be seen that the subject and object of the events described in literary works are mostly individuals. In N2 position, the collective nouns in the news corpus are far more than that in the literary corpus. It can be seen that the subject and object of events described in the news corpus are mostly collectives.

The current popular concept in the research of BCNP is that the last noun is the core of the entire compound noun phrase, and multiple nouns in the front are used as attributives to modify the core words. In the structure of Chinese "N1+N2", the core is N2, and N1 is used as a modifier to modify the core word N2. In the literary corpus, the noun category with the most core nouns is individual nouns, accounting for about 32.6%, far exceeding the individual nouns that appear in the N2 position in the news corpus. In the news corpus, the noun category with the most core nouns is abstract nouns, accounting for about 26.8%, slightly higher than the abstract nouns appearing in the N2 position in the literary corpus (about 23.6%).

The core noun reflects the things described in the corpus. News works mostly describe abstract national policies, guidelines, routes, etc., while most of the literary works which are based on real-life, specifically describing people or things in social life. The noun categories that differ most in the position of core words are individual nouns and collective nouns. The collective nouns in the news corpus far exceed the collective nouns in the literary corpus, and the individual nouns in the literary corpus far exceed the individual nouns in the news corpus. It can be seen that the core words also refer to people or things semantically, but literary works focus on the description of individual people or things, while news works focus on the description of collective people or things. In choosing modifier N1, the nouns makes up the highest proportion of the news corpus and literary corpus are both abstract.

Differences in Hapax Legomena. "Single-word" (hapax legomena) refers to "words with a frequency of 1, which supplements the deficiencies of Zipf's law (Table 5)."

Table 5. Comparison of hapax legomena in the news corpus and literary corpus

	The news corpus	Literary corpus
hapax legomena at position N1	329	552
hapax legomena at position N2	335	479
Both N1 and N2 are hapax legomena	164	329

It can be seen from the table that in the basic compound noun phrase, no matter where it is, the hapax legomena in the literary corpus far exceed the hapax legomena in the news corpus. Literature possesses a high level of openness, the vocabulary is "highly innovative and less repetitive". So the vocabulary is relatively rich, while the news corpus is subject to its essential characteristics and requirements. It is not as open as literary corpus. The use of vocabulary is somewhat repetitive and less innovative. So the vocabulary richness is low. The vocabulary of literary works is very rich, and it is usually analyzed from the perspective of "literary style words". Zhang [10] pointed out that literary style words refer to those words that have certain aesthetic characteristics, adapting to the needs of communication field of literary style, and are unique and commonly used, and rarely appear in other styles. The high proportion of hapax legomena reflects that the language vocabulary of literary works is rich and innovative. Authenticity and objectivity require news works to use simple language to convey information and stick to the facts. Therefore, news language vocabulary is not as rich and innovative as a literary language.

4.4   Comparison of Semantic Relations of BCNP

Semantic relationship of BCNP in both the news corpus and literary corpus are labeled based on the classification system of Liu [7], and "modify relationship" is added as complement since the characteristic of literary corpus is taken into consideration. Therefore, fifteen categories are created in total (Fig. 6).

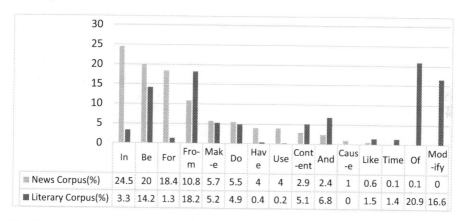

	In	Be	For	Fro-m	Mak-e	Do	Hav e	Use	Cont-ent	And	Caus-e	Like	Time	Of	Mod-ify
News Corpus(%)	24.5	20	18.4	10.8	5.7	5.5	4	4	2.9	2.4	1	0.6	0.1	0.1	0
Literary Corpus(%)	3.3	14.2	1.3	18.2	5.2	4.9	0.4	0.2	5.1	6.8	0	1.5	1.4	20.9	16.6

Fig. 6. Comparison of the semantic relationship between the news corpus and literary corpus

In literary corpus, the semantic relationship that appears most frequently is "Of" (about 20.9%), followed by "From" (about 18.2%), and the third is "Modify" (about 16.6%). Among them, "Modify" is unique in literary corpus, which reflects the individuality and aesthetic characteristics of literary language. Because the characters and things described by different authors have different characteristics, a variety of nouns can be used to describe them in detail. In the news corpus, the semantic relationship that appears the most is "In" (about 24.5%), followed by "Be" (about 20%), and the third is "For" (about 18.4%). Because one of the elements of news reports is to explain the location of the news event, which can be a specific location, such as the "school gate", or a spatial geographic location, such as the "Shenzhen market." Therefore, the proportion of "In" in the news corpus is relatively high.

5   Conclusion

This paper compares the similarities and differences of BCNP in news and literary styles from the following four aspects: the use of BCNP, the structural relations of BCNP, the use of the nouns that compose BCNP and the semantic relations of BCNP. Among them, the use of nouns that make up BCNP includes differences in named entities, differences in noun types that make up phrases, and differences in hapax legomena. Through comparative analysis, it can be found that whether it is news style or literary style, BCNP with attributive structure have an overwhelming advantage, which is also in line with the advantage of nouns assuming syntactic components; the style of news is subjected to its characteristics and requirements of objectively, conciseness, and truthfulness with more repeated word, fewer innovative words and lower lexical richness. The literary style possesses high level of openness and subjectivity, so there are fewer repeated words, more innovative words, and higher lexical richness. In addition, there are more abstract nouns in the news corpus and more individual nouns in the literary corpus due to the influence of descriptive content. In terms of semantic relations, the literary corpus uses a wide variety of nouns to describe characters and things in detail, so there are more modified relations. However, the news corpus, in order to report the location of news events, has more descriptions of site location or spatial position. Therefore, "In" makes up a higher proportion in news corpus.

The drawbacks of this paper is that there is limited data. It only compares the first 1000 phrases in the news corpus and literary corpus. The follow-up research needs more corpus to compare. This paper only provides limited perceptive to compare the BCNP in news style and literary style. In the future, we plan to conduct further research from the perspective of semantic categories and their relations with semantics.

Acknowledgements. This work was funded by the Humanities and Social Science Research Planning Fund of the Ministry of Education (18YJA740030) and Beijing Language and Culture University Chinese and Foreign Postgraduate Innovation Fund Project (21YCX170).

References

1. Borong, H., Xudong, L.: "Modern Chinese" (6th revised edition). Higher Education Press, Beijing (2017)
2. Wang, J.: On the head position in Chinese N+N structure. Lang. Teach. Linguist. Stud. **6**, 33–38 (2005) (in Chinese)
3. Chen, R.-N.: Comparison of Chinese and English Textual Features Based on Quantitative Linguistics Indicators. Zhejiang University, Hangzhou (2017)
4. Ding, X.-W.: On the similarities and differences between literature and news. News Dissemin. **3**,107 (2011). (in Chinese)
5. Jiang, R.: On the Differences between news language and literary language. J. Kaifeng Inst. Educ. **39**(9), 66–67 (2019). (in Chinese)
6. Yang, J.-Q.: The difference between news language and literary language. Theoret. Anal. **3**, 29–30 (2020). (in Chinese)
7. Liu, Y.-J.: Establishment of Knowledge Base of Chinese Noun Compounds and Structural and Semantic Analysis. Beijing Language and Culture University, Beijing (2018)
8. Ma, Z.-E.: Development of the News Corpus of Hot Events and Vocabulary Research. Nanjing Normal University, Nanjing (2012)
9. Wang, H.: Analysis of Noun Meaning Combination in Modern Chinese. Peking University Press, Beijing (2004)
10. Zhang, L: On the choice of word formation of literary genre words. Nanjing J. Soc. Sci. **2**, 129–134 (2007). (in Chinese)

Predicate Annotation for Chinese Intent Detection

Yan Li[1], Likun Qiu[2(✉)], and Zhe Zhao[3]

[1] College of Korean, Chinese, and Literature, Yanbian University, Yanji, China
[2] Department of Chinese Language and Literature, Northwest Minzu University, Lanzhou, China
likun.qiu@foxmail.com
[3] College of Language Intelligence, Sichuan International Studies University, Chongqing, China

Abstract. Intent detection is to automatically classify the intentions expressed by users' language in many scenes, such as human-computer dialogue, question and answer, etc. It is the most critical and basic task in natural language processing tasks. To train a more universal and transferable Chinese intent detection model based on the multi-point semantic representation framework, we focuses on the predicate annotation of users' language in Q&A scenarios. As far as we know, it is the first job to introduce the predicate corpus. Firstly, the predicates are defined under the multi-point semantic framework, and a set of standards of predicate annotation for intent detection is proposed based on the definition. Based on the annotation standards, we select appropriate data. The data annotation and quality control are carried out according to the double annotation method. The constructed corpus includes 14,000 sentences. Finally, through the above data fine-tuning, we use BERT to achieve automatic predicate annotation. The automatic trained annotation model can obtain 89.84% in F-score on the same domain and 81.97% F-score on out-of-domain test sets. The experiment shows the predicate corpus can train the model for processing general domain data with high accuracy, while the accuracy in a specific domain needs to be improved.

1 Introduction

Intelligent products such as smart speakers, mobile phone voice assistants and customer service robots are becoming more and more popular, and the language comprehension ability, which can best embody the intelligence level, has been paid more and more attention by academia. Among these intelligent products, the most critical and basic module of language understanding is called Intent detection. That is, the intention expressed by the user's language is classified into a certain category. For example, smart speakers generally divide user statements into intentions such as playing music, asking about the weather and setting an alarm clock, and the type of intentions is usually within a few dozen; The customer service robot divides the user statements into

M. Dong et al. (Eds.): CLSW 2021, LNAI 13250, pp. 335–352, 2022.
https://doi.org/10.1007/978-3-031-06547-7_26

hundreds of different intentions according to the business scenarios of the customers it serves. Existing language understanding modules usually use a text classification model or semantic matching model to solve the problem of Intent detection. The former is suitable for scenes with few and relatively fixed intention categories, such as smart speakers and mobile phone voice assistants; While the latter is suitable for scenes with many intention categories and frequent changes, such as intelligent customer service robots.

At present, supervised classification models based on CNN, LSTM, Transformer, and other deep neural network structures can achieve high accuracy in supervised Intent detection tasks, but they still face two major challenges. On the one hand, tasks rely heavily on annotation data. For different types of business scenarios or different customer business scenarios, large-scale training data need to be annotated, and the annotated data is difficult to migrate and reuse. On the other hand, it is difficult to sort out the intentional system, which usually requires the joint participation and cooperation of business personnel and technicians. It is mainly carried out manually. The basic reason for the above problems is that there is no internal structure. The very similar intentions cannot share information in the current language understanding system. To solve the above problems, a multi-point semantic representation framework is proposed. It manually is decomposed into four factors: Topic, Predicate, Target, Query type, so that intention has a preliminary internal structure. The effectiveness of the multi-point semantic representation framework in the Intent detection task is verified by the intention classification model based on the attention mechanism. However, this paper does not build an extraterritorial and transferable multi-point semantic representation system, nor does it train the multi-point annotation model to provide matching corpus and knowledge base.

Inspired by [1], this paper attempts to build predicate corpus for Chinese Intent detection based on a multi-point semantic representation framework. Its goal is to provide training data and knowledge base in predicate for Intent detection based on multi-point representation framework so that the predicates annotation has good reusability and migration. The content of this structure is divided into four aspects. Firstly, the predicate is defined and a set of Chinese predicate annotation specifications for intent detection is proposed based on the definition of predicate, and the annotation standards of predicates in various language phenomena are specified and illustrated with examples. Then, based on the annotation specification, the researchers select the data of the "Baidu Zhidao" scene; according to a certain process of annotation and quality control, core predicate corpus is formed. Based on the above data and a variety of deep neural network models, auto annotation of predicates is realized. The automatic trained annotation model can obtain an 89.84% F-score on the same domain and 81.97% F-score on out-of-domain test sets. The experimental results show that the corpus in this paper can train the model for processing general domain data with high accuracy, but the accuracy in specific domains needs to be improved.

2 Multi-point Representation and Core Predicate

2.1 Single-Point Representation and Full Representation in Multi-point Representation

Single-point Representation: In application systems such as human-computer conversation and intelligent Q&A scene, the general practice is to regard the intention in the task-based dialogue scene, the attributes in knowledge graph Q&A and the standard questions in the general Q&A system as category annotates. The intention in the task-based dialogue can be to play music, ask about the weather, set an alarm clock, and so on. In each business scenario, a set of intentional systems containing multiple intentions, attributes, or standard questions can be established, and then a classification algorithm or semantic matching algorithm can be used to realize language understanding. In this type of work, intention, attribute, and standard questions are taken as the basic semantic units respectively, and there is no internal structure. When there is no special description in this paper, we generally use intention to represent intention, attribute, and standard questions. It can be called a single-point representation framework. The advantage of single-point representation is that it is easy to understand and can be quickly implemented and popularized. However, it has two disadvantages: firstly, when the intention system is complex, the problem of knowledge explosion, which is difficult to carry out management effectively, resulting in the deterioration of the system effect; secondly, because the intention has no internal structure, the language understanding is relatively sketchy, which hinders the inheritance of context information and the reuse of training data between different business scenarios.

Full Representation: In the research of basic natural language processing, the common semantic representation method is to regard the word level concept or even smaller sememe as the most basic semantic unit and pursue the complete and deep representation of sentence semantics. It can be called full representation. For example, Combinatory Categorial Grammar (CCG) [2] and Abstract Meaning Representation (AMR) [3] express the deep semantics of sentences in tree or graph structure, respectively. Alexa Meaning Representation Language (AMRL) [4] is also a special full representation. It is similar to AMR in terms of system, but it focuses on Task-based dialogue scenarios such as intelligent speakers. The advantage of full representation is that the representation of sentence semantics is deeper, more comprehensive, and more systematic. In the long run, it must be the ideal goal we want to pursue. In order to achieve complete semantic representation, it is necessary to describe the semantic information from all different levels and involve most words in the sentence and the relationship between words. It leads to the complexity of the representation system and the workload of manually annotation data is too heavy. This directly leads to the high cost of language resources for full representation, so it is difficult to form a large scale and cover more fields, which affects its application in the actual industrial scene.

Multi-point Representation: Multi-point representation is essentially a compromise between full representation and single-point representation, aiming at distinguishing intention, but the goal of full semantic representation is to express intent. When full representation is too complex, and the single-point representation is too sketchy, we can choose an intermediate way that is the intention can be disassembled into multiple key factors to be represented respectively, so as to make the intention have a relatively simple internal structure; It does not require the complete semantics of intention but can distinguish the intentions in the intention system from each other. Because the factors are few, the complexity and workload are within the acceptance range, and large-scale and multi-domain training data can be constructed quickly. Specifically, [1] proposes to express and distinguish different intentions through four types of key factors, namely, Topic, Predicate, Target, Query type. The four factors are combined to form the semantic representation of intention. Among the four types of factors, "Predicate" and "Target" are the main components of propositions in logic and semantics, "Topic" is used to distinguish different small business areas, "Query type" indicates different ways and perspectives of raising questions or requirements. In a domain or scenario, the possible semantic space is limited, so we can distinguish all intentions through a limited number of key concepts.

Multi-point representation has three advantages. Firstly, the annotation cost is relatively small, so it can be applied to various scenes. Secondly, after each intention is decomposed into several key factors, different intentions with the same factor value can share the training data. For example, "set mobile wallpaper" and "set broadband password" have the same predicate factor. Although the intentions are different, the training data in the predicate factor can be shared. Thirdly, multi-point representation strengthens the difference between two similar intentions with only one different factor. For example, two intentional categories of "change mobile phone password" and "change mobile phone ring tone" are similar, but they are different from each other only in object factors.

2.2   Core Predicate

Referring to the working methods of AMR and AMRL, the complete multi-point representation needs to provide the corresponding corpus and hierarchical classification dictionary for the factors of each dimension. This paper focuses on the predicate annotation in multi-point representation and takes the language actively expressed by users in man-machine conversation and Q&A scenes as the description object. Users' languages actively expressing are mainly interrogative sentences, imperative sentences. Declarative sentences, including noun phrase independent sentences, also account for a part of proportion.

In the framework of multi-point representation, the core predicate is the core of the predicate center of a sentence. It is the basis and core of intention, and other factors are directly or indirectly dependent on the core predicate. The predicate is the predicate center. Taking the verb predicate sentence as an example, a sentence is mainly divided into subject and predicate, and the predicate part is further divided into adverbial, complement, and predicate center. For example, in the sentence,

现在深圳龙华富士康招工吗?
[Xiànzài shēnzhèn lónghuá fù shì kāng zhāogōng ma?]
Is Foxconn recruiting in Longhua District, Shenzhen now?

"Recruiting" is the predicate center. In a compound sentence, each clause can have its own predicate center. When we take abstraction as intention, only one predicate may participate in the composition of intention, so it is called core predicate. For example,

淘宝开店现在还要交保证金吗?
[Táobǎo kāidiàn xiànzài hái yào jiāo bǎozhèngjīn ma?]
Do you still have to pay a deposit to run a shop on Taobao?
"Run a shop" and "pay" are predicates, while "pay" is the core predicate.

Generally, simple sentences and subordinative compound sentences have one core predicate, while parallel compound sentences have multiple core predicates. In order to deal with some special phenomena, we introduce the concepts of zero predicate, second-order predicate, and first-order predicate. On the one hand, each sentence has a predicate; on the other hand, the same intention is expressed in different sentence patterns with similar semantic expressions.

Zero Predicate: some sentences are composed of nominals and phrases and do not contain any predicate components. We assume that there is a zero predicate and use it as the core predicate, such as

英飞凌显卡
[Yīng fēi líng xiǎnkǎ].
Infineon graphics boards.

First-Order Predicate: Generally, there is only one predicate in a sentence, which is the first-order predicate. For example,

怎么交话费?银行理财和余额宝哪个划算?
[Zěnme jiāo huàfèi? Yínháng lǐcái hé yú'é bǎo nǎge huásuàn?].
"How to pay the phone bill?" and *"Which is a better deal for bank financial and Yu'e Bao?"* contain a first-order predicate "pay" and "better deal", respectively.

Second-Order Predicate: In some sentences, there are a predicate object verb and a substantive object verb in a sentence at the same time. Both of them can act as the core predicate. At this time, we can think that there are two core predicates in this sentence, one is the second-order predicate, and the other is the first-order predicate. For example,

查一下我还有多少流量?
[Chá yīxià wǒ hái yǒu duōshǎo liúliàng?]
Check how much mobile traffic I still have?

In the sentence, 查*[chá]* "Check" is the second-order predicate, and有*[yǒu]* "have" is the first-order predicate. Dedicate object verbs such as 申请、拒绝、驳回*[Shēnqǐng, jùjué, bóhuí]* "apply, reject and refuse" can also act as second-order predicates. When the predicate structure acts as the subject, 成功、失败*[Chénggōng, shībài]* "succeed, fail", and other words can also act as second-order predicates.

3   Core Predicate Annotation Rules

The core predicate is generally a verb, verb predicate sentence, or an adjective, adjective predicate sentence. However, when the number of verbs and adjectives in a sentence is less than or more than 1, the choice of core predicates will become more complex. For various special language phenomena, we sort them and form a unified annotation standard.

3.1   Simple Sentence

Untypical Predicate Sentence. There is no predicate in the sentence, or the predicate center is not acted by verbs and adjectives,

It includes the following phenomena:

(1) When noun phrases form sentences independently, noun-verbs act as the core predicate. If a sentence consists of a noun phrase and one of the noun-verbs can act as a recessive predicate, it is annotated as the core predicate. For example, in the sentence,

2011闽江学院二本录取结果。

[2011 Mǐn jiāng xuéyuàn èr běn lùqǔ jiéguǒ.]

"Admission results of the second batch of undergraduate students in the unified national examination for enrollment of ordinary colleges and Universities of Minjiang University in 2011," the core predicate is "admission".

充满正能量且具有马克思主义哲学意义的文章。

[Chōngmǎn zhèng néngliàng qiě jùyǒu mǎkèsī zhǔyì zhéxué yìyì de wénzhāng.]

Articles are full of positive energy and have Marxist philosophical significance.

In this sentence, "full" and "with" are annotated.

(2) When a noun phrase forms a sentence independently, the verb in the attributive clause acts as the predicate. If a sentence consists of a noun phrase and the noun phrase contains an attributive clause, the predicate center in the attributive clause is annotated as the core predicate of the whole clause. For example,

正确握拿筷子的方法。

[Zhèngquè wò ná kuàizi de fāngfǎ.]

If *"the correct method of using chopsticks."* is formed into a sentence independently, then "using" is annotated as the core predicate.

(3) When noun phrases form sentences independently, the zero predicate acts as the core predicate. If a sentence is composed of a noun phrase, and the noun phrase is essentially a proper noun such as book name, song name, game name, and an article name, the zero predicate used as the core predicate. For example,

万历十五年。

[Wànlì shíwǔ nián.]

"In Ming Dynasty the 15th year of Wanli." uses the zero predicate as the core predicate. If the predicate of a sentence is a nominal or noun predicate sentence, the zero predicate are annotated as to its core predicate. For example,

小王哪里人?

[Xiǎo wáng nǎlǐ rén?]

Where is Xiao Wang from?

(4) Interrogative pronouns act as core predicates.

XXX怎么样?

[XXX zěnme yang?]

In the "how about ....", if "......" does not contain verbs, we can annotate "how" as the core predicate. Such as these examples all belong to this category.

北京天气怎么样?

东北大学研究生的钢铁冶金专业怎么样?

创意家居饰品店前景怎么样?

[Běijīng tiānqì zěnme yàng?]

[Dōngběi dàxué yánjiūshēng de gāngtiě yějīn zhuānyè zěnme yàng?]

[Chuàngyì jiājū shìpǐn diàn qiánjǐng zěnme yàng?]

How about the weather in Beijing?

How about the major of iron and steel metallurgy of graduate students of Northeast University?

How about the prospect of creative home accessories store?

"Shi" Sentences. "Shi" sentences can be further divided into the following categories. "Shi" is a linking verb in English.

(1) "Shi" + Noun phrase (NP), we can annotate "Shi" as the predicate. For example,
中国第一次参加奥运会是这一年吗?

[Zhōngguó dì yī cì cānjiā àoyùnhuì shì zhè yī nián ma?]

Is this the year when China first participated in the Olympic Games?

(2) "Shi" + Verbal phrase (VP), we can annotate verbs in VP as core predicates. For example,

江西是属于南方吗?

[Jiāngxī shì shǔyú nánfāng ma?]

"Does Jiangxi belong to southern China?" annotate "belongs to" as the core predicate.

超神学院现在是多久一更?

[Chāo shén xuéyuàn xiànzài shì duōjiǔ yī gèng?]

"How often is the super seminary updated now?" annotate "update" as the core predicate.

他人代付费是指什么?

[Tārén dài fùfèi shì zhǐ shénme?]

"What does it mean to pay for another?" annotate "mean" as the core predicate.

"Shi" + VP + "De", removing "Shi" does not affect the meaning of the sentence and defines the core predicate from VP. For example,

电灯是什么时候发明的?

[Diàndēng shì shénme shíhòu fāmíng de?]

When the electric lamp was invented?
In the sentence invention is the core predicate.

"You" Sentences. According to the classification of "Shi" sentences, we can also classify "You" sentences. "You" means "have" in English.

(1)   "You" + NP. Annotate "You" as the predicate, such as this example.

婚纱照活动还有吗?
[Hūnshā zhào huódòng hái yǒu ma?]
Are there any wedding photo discounts?

(2)   "You" + VP. Annotate verbs in VP as core predicates. In the following two sentences,

有显示占用您身份的账户吗?
《家庭教师》中哪几集有出现云雀?
[Yǒu xiǎnshì zhànyòng nín shēnfèn de zhànghù ma?]
["jiātíng jiàoshī" zhōng nǎ jǐ jí yǒu chūxiàn yúnquè?]
Does it show that your account has been occupied?
Which episodes of Tutor have skylarks?
Core predicate is "show" and "have".

(3)   "You" + VP + "De", removing "You" does not affect the meaning of the sentence and define the core predicate from VP. For example,

初一历史书上册有卖的吗?
[Chū yī lìshǐ shū shàngcè yǒu mài de ma?]
Does anyone sell the first volume of the history book of grade one in junior middle school available?
In this sentence, "sell" is the core predicate;
哪里有批发水果的?
[Nǎ li yǒu pīfā shuǐguǒ de?]
"Where can I wholesale fruit?" "wholesale" is the core predicate.

The Semantic Bleaching of the Predicate Center. Light verb structure [5] and some similar structures, the verb meaning is relatively weak, which is not enough to independently express the actions or events involved in the meaning. It is necessary to further expand the scope and bring its complement, object, and even adverbial into the scope of the core predicate. Specifically, it can be divided into the following situations:

(1)   Resultative construction. Consider the complement as part of the core predicate. For example,
如何能把淘宝店铺做好做大做强?
[Rúhé néng bǎ táobǎo diànpù zuò hǎo zuò dà zuò qiáng?]
How to make Taobao stores better, bigger and stronger?
In the sentence "Better, bigger and stronger" are the core predicates respectively;
怎么把手机弄坏?

[Zěnme bǎ shǒujī nòng huài?]

"How did you break your mobile phone?" "break" is the core predicate.

我买黑米手机a5.价格是899是不是买贵了?

[Wǒ mǎi hēi mǐ shǒujī a5 jiàgé shì 899. shì bùshì mǎi guìle?]

I spent 899 yuan on the Hemi mobile phone A5. Is it expensive?

"Expensive" is the core predicate.

刘海剪短了,怎么快速长长?

[Liúhǎi jiǎn duǎnle, zěnme kuàisù zhǎng chǎng?]

Bangs are cut short. How can they grow fast?

In the above sentences, "are cut short" and "grow fast" need to be annotated.

(2) Verb-object structure. The object is served by common nouns. The light verb structure formed by light verbs and common nouns is annotated as the core predicate.

苹果平板电脑怎么打电话?

[Píngguǒ píngbǎn diànnǎo zěnme dǎ diànhuà?]

How to give a call by iPad?

If "give" is the core predicate, it can't fully express the meaning of the sentence. So, "give others a call" needs to be annotated as the core predicate of the sentence. For example,

上海哪里有打耳洞?

银行买理财产品有风险吗?

[Shànghǎi nǎ li yǒu dǎ ěr dòng?].

[Yínháng mǎi lǐcái chǎnpǐn yǒu fēngxiǎn ma?]

Where can I get ears pierced in Shanghai?

Do we need to take risks to buy financial products in banks?

We respectively annotate "get ears pierced" and "take risks" as the core predicates.

吃垃圾食品有什么危害?

初一到十五有哪些讲究?

[Chī lèsè shípǐn yǒu shé me wéihài?]

[Chū yī dào shíwǔ yǒu nǎxiē jiǎngjiù?]

What's the harm of eating junk food?

What customs need to be emphasized from the first to the fifteenth day of the lunar calendar?

We annotate "harm" and "emphasized" as the core predicate. It should be noted that the core predicate here belongs to the discontinuous core predicate.

(3) If the object is acted by the noun-verbs, the noun-verbs are directly annotated as the core predicate. For example,

请您根据这个流程进行操作。

[Qǐng nín gēnjù zhège liúchéng jìnxíng cāozuò.]

Please operate according to this process.

"operate" is annotated as the core predicate.

A Sentence Whose Predicate is Serial Verb Construction or Co-ordinate Structure. If the predicate of a sentence is a verb or adjective serial verb construction or co-ordinate structure, multiple core predicates can be annotated.

(1) Alternative questions. In essence, it also belongs to a coordinated structure, and there may be two parallel predicates. We can annotate both as core predicates. For example,

江西属于南方还是属于北方？

[Jiāngxī shǔyú nánfāng háishì shǔyú běifāng?]

Whether Jiangxi belongs to the South or belongs to the north?

The two "belong" are annotated as the core predicate.

到底是男人累，还是女人累？

[Dàodǐ shì nánrén lèi, háishì nǚrén lèi?]

Whether men are tired or women are tired?

Both "tired" should also be annotated.

秦时明月第五部是周更还是月更？

[Qín shí míngyuè dì wǔ bù shì zhōu gèng háishì yuè gèng?]

Whether season 5 of The Legend of Qin series update weekly or update monthly?

"Update" should also be annotated.

(2) In other cases, you can also annotate multiple core predicates. For example,

请问去国外度蜜月哪里又实惠又好玩？

[Qǐngwèn qù guówài dù mìyuè nǎlǐ yòu shíhuì yòu hǎowán?]

Where is it affordable and fun to spend a honeymoon abroad?

"Affordable" and "Fun" are the core predicates. For another example,

偶尔突然头晕恶心是怎么回事？

[Ǒu'ěr túrán tóuyūn ěxīn shì zěnme huí shì?]

How is it that you suddenly feel dizzy and sick occasionally?

"Dizzy" and "Sick" are annotated as core predicates.

A verbal phrase acts as a subject in a sentence. The predicate of such sentences is usually used by adjectives to evaluate the action or behavior expressed by the subject. We select the verb closest to the interrogative as the core predicate. For example,

话费怎样充最便宜？

染什么颜色的头发好看？

蛋炒饭应该先放蛋还是先放饭比较好？

[Huàfèi zěnyàng chōng zuì piányí?]

[Rǎn shénme yánsè de tóufǎ hǎokàn?]

[Dàn chǎofàn yīnggāi xiān fàng dàn háishì xiān fàng fàn bǐjiào hǎo?]

How to pay the cheapest phone bill?

How to dye hair color more beautiful?

Should eggs or rice be put first for fried rice with eggs?

These three sentences annotate "pay" "dye" and "put" as the core predicates, respectively;

吃垃圾食品有什么危害？

学什么专业比较有前途？

[Chī lèsè shípǐn yǒu shé me wéihài?]

[Xué shénme zhuānyè bǐjiào yǒu qiántú?]
What's the harm of eating junk food?
What major is more promising?

What sounds good after the word "put" In the three sentences, "harm" "promising" and "sounds good" are the core predicates.

A Clause is an Object of a Verb Phrase is the Object. When the predicates are verbs such as

看看, 查查
[Kàn kàn, chá chá]

"Take a look" and *"check"*, we regard the verbs as secondary core predicates and the verbs in the object as primary core predicates. Without special instructions, the mentioned core predicates refer to primary core predicates. For example,

看看我的流量有多少?
[Kàn kàn wǒ de liú liàng yǒu duōshǎo?]
Take a look how much mobile phone traffic I still have?

"Take a look" is a secondary core predicate, and "have" is a primary core predicate. In order to maintain consistency, "check" is also annotated as a secondary core predicate in the sentence.

查查我的流量。
[Chá chá wǒ de liúliàng.]
Check my mobile phone traffic.

The secondary core predicate is a relatively closed set and commonly used verbs such as "query" "consult" "know" and "tell".

Resultative Construction. Different from the light verb structure in resultative construction, if the core predicate is resultative construction and the object is still added after it, at this time, the whole resultative construction is annotated for completeness of meaning. For example,

支付宝充错话费怎么办?
[Zhīfùbǎo chōng cuò huàfèi zěnme bàn?]
What should you do after wrongly paying phone bill by Alipay?

"Wrongly paying" is the core predicate.

怎么让自己变得充满正能量?
[Zěnme ràng zìjǐ biàn dé chōngmǎn zhèng néngliàng?]
How to make yourself full of positive energy?

"Full" is the core predicate.

怎么去掉脸上的痘痘?
[Zěnme qùdiào liǎn shàng de dòu dòu?]
How to remove acne on your face?

"Remove" is the core predicate.

Fixed Format. Some verbs often appear in a sentence in a fixed format; the fixed format is annotated as the core predicate. For example, in the positive and negative questions, the predicate usually appears twice. We annotate the whole verb construction as the core predicate. For example,

这是不是非洲大蜗牛?

[Zhè shì bùshì fēizhōu dà wōniú?].

Is this achatina fulica?

We can annotate "is" as the core predicate. Moreover,

人们把解放军环卫工人和记者比喻成什么?

[Rénmen bǎ jiěfàngjūn huánwèi gōngrén hé jìzhě bǐyù chéng shénme?]

What do people compare people's Liberation Army sanitation workers and journalists?

In this sentence, we annotate "compare" as the core predicate.

哪些购物网站可以货到付款?

[Nǎxiē gòuwù wǎngzhàn kěyǐ huò dào fùkuǎn?]

Which shopping websites can use cash on delivery?

"Cash on delivery" is the core predicate.

什么生意稳赚不赔呢?

[Shénme shēngyì wěn zhuàn bù péi ne?]

What business is sure to make profits without losing?

"Make profits without losing" is the core predicate.

3.2   Complex Sentences

(1) There is the main sentence, and the other sentences are clauses in compound sentences. The core verb of the main sentence is regarded as the core predicate of the whole sentence. For example,

呃, 我还没听到, 请帮我查一下我还剩多少话费?

[È, wǒ hái méi tīng dào, qǐng bāng wǒ chá yīxià wǒ hái shèng duōshǎo huàfèi?].

Well, I haven't heard it yet. Please check how much mobile phone traffic I still have?

The last clause in this sentence is the main sentence, so you only need to annotate "check" and "have" with the second core predicate and the primary core predicate, respectively.

(2) Multiple clauses are juxtaposed, and there is no primary, secondary relationship. If a user's statement contains multiple single sentences, each sentence is annotated with a core predicate. For example,

这是什么字体?哪里可以下载?

上海有哪些区?哪个区最繁华?

网页图片怎么制作?用什么软件?

[Zhè shì shénme zìtǐ? Nǎlǐ kěyǐ xiàzài?].

[Shànghǎi yǒu nǎxiē qū? Nǎge qū zuì fánhuá?].

[Wǎngyè túpiàn zěnme zhìzuò? Yòng shénme ruǎnjiàn?].

What font is this? Where can I download it?

What are the districts in Shanghai? Which district is the most prosperous?

How to make web page pictures? What software is needed to make it?

Each sentence contains two single sentences, which can be annotated with a core verb, respectively.

4   Construction of Core Predicate Corpus

4.1   Data Preparation

The sentences annotated in this paper are from two existing corpora. (1) LCQMC corpus [6], hereinafter referred to as LCQMC dataset, is a Chinese question matching corpus constructed by Shenzhen Research Institute of Harbin Institute of technology, which is presented in the form of sentence pairs. We only use the verification set of the database. After reducing the repetition rate, there are 14657 sentences; The initial source of these sentence is Baidu Zhidao. (2) CCL2018 user intention classification evaluation corpus in the field of Chinese mobile online customer service, hereinafter referred to as CCL dataset, which is an intentional classification dataset with 10859 sentences.

4.2   Annotation Process and Quality Control

When we construct the corpus, we use the double annotation method. The specific process is as follows. (1) The first time annotation: all corpora are manually annotated according to the annotation rules; (2) Automatic annotation based on random sampling: through random sampling, 90% of the data are taken as training data, and 10% of the data are taken as test data each time. The trained model is used to automatically annotate the test data. This process can be repeated several times so that each sentence in the whole dataset can get multiple automatic tagging results. (3) The second time annotation: the second manual annotation shall be carried out for the different parts in cross-validation results and manual annotation results.

5   Experiment

5.1   Datasets and Evaluation Indicators

Dataset. In this experiment, the LCQMC dataset is randomly divided into a training set, development set, and test set in the proportion of 8:1:1. The specific numbers of the three sets are 11727, 1465, and 1465 respectively. For the CCL dataset, we randomly selected 1000 sentences to form the second test set. The two test sets are referred to as the LCQMC test set and CCL test set, respectively.

Evaluation Indicators. Accuracy rate, recall rate, and F1-score were used as evaluation metric.

5.2   Model

We regard the core predicate annotation as a sequence annotation problem. It is words level classification problem. We set up five category labels. "Pred-B, Pred-M, Pred-E, Pred-S, O" are set to represent the beginning, middle, end, and independent words of the predicate, respectively. For example, "Bàofēng yǐngyīn huǎncún de shìpín zěnme kàn bùliǎo a." The correct way to annotate is "Bào/O fēng/O yǐng/O yīn/O huǎn/O cún/O de/O shì/O pín/O zěn/O me/O kàn/O bù/Oliǎo/O a/O." For this annotation task, we try a variety of classical model variants based on BiLSTM to investigate the effects of different types of word vectors on this task; A sequence annotation method based on BERT pre-training language model is also used.

BiLSTM. The BiLSTM model is a common encoder used for sequence annotation tasks. Before the emergence of the BERT model, the best results of many sequence annotation tasks were obtained based on this model. The model takes the word vector as input and encodes it through a bidirectional LSTM layer.

In the process of decoding, we try to use two decoding methods: multilayer perceptron (MLP) and conditional random field.

In the word vector, we try to use two ways: single word vector and single word with twin sub-vectors, which is called N-Gram vector for short.

BERT. Bert (Bidirectional Encoder Representation from Transformers) is a deep neural network model proposed by Google [7]. The encoder layer of the model contains multi-layer transformers, and the core of the transformer is the Multi-Head Self-Attention mechanism. Bert obtains a high-quality pre-training language model by training Masked Language Model and Next Sentence Prediction on a large-scale raw corpus. It can further easily handle language processing tasks such as automatic question answering, machine-reading, and natural language reasoning through fine-tuning. It has achieved state of the art on 11 natural languages processing task, which are greatly improved compared with the previous results. In fine-tuning, the last layer of Bert encoder is used as the input, then a full connection layer is used to project the coding of each word into an MLP hidden layer representation. Finally, the score of each word on each annotate is given through a full connection layer.

5.3   Experiment Setup

Pre-training Word Vector. In the model based on LSTM, the single word[1] vector and twin sub-vectors[2] are from [8], which are trained with standard Word2vec tools and Chinese Wikipedia corpus. Among them, the single word vector contains 9587 single words, and the double word vector contains 883340 double strings, both of which are 100 dimensions.

Pre-training Language Model. The pre-training language model used is Bert-base-Chinese, which is officially provided by Google[3]. The main parameters are: the number

---

[1] http://212.129.155.247/embedding/cn_char_fastnlp_100d.zip.

[2] http://212.129.155.247/embedding/cn_bi_fastnlp_100d.zip.

[3] http://storage.googleapis.com/bert_models/2018_11_03/chinese_L-12_H-768_A-12.zip.

of transformer layers included in the model Encoder is 12, the number of self-attention heads are 12, the hidden layer dimension is 768, and the total quantity of parameter is 110 MB.

Hyper Parameters. The hyper Parameters used by Bert's fine-tuning model are shown in Table 1.

Table 1. Hyper parameters in Bert model

Parameter name	Parameter value
Bert embeds	300
Bert layers	12
embed dropout	.33
mlp hidden size	100
mlp dropout	.33
lr	2e−5
mu	.9
nu	.9
epsilon	1e−12
clip	5.0
batch size	256
epochs	10

Table 2. Main experimental results

Model	LCQMC Test set (%)			CCL Test set (%)		
	Accuracy rate	Recall rate	F-value	Accuracy rate	Recall rate	F-value
char + BiLSTM + MLP	88.23	85.67	86.93	80.41	70.87	75.34
char + BiLSTM + CRF	88.09	86.69	87.38	78.75	70.31	74.29
ngram + BiLSTM + MLP	88.35	88.93	88.64	81.66	74.83	78.09
ngram + BiLSTM + CRF	88.60	88.86	88.73	81.15	78.19	79.64
Bert + MLP	89.11	90.01	89.56	83.55	80.41	81.95
Bert + CRF	89.17	90.52	89.84	82.25	81.70	81.97

5.4 Experimental Results

The main experimental results are shown in Table 2. About coding methods, among the three models of word vector, N-Gram vector and Bert, Bert is the best, N-Gram is the second, and the gap is more obvious in the out-of-domain test set. This shows that the Bert-based model had better domain migration generalization performance. In terms of the decoding method, CRF is better than MLP, but its advantage is relatively small; In the out-of-domain test set, the two are basically the same. Therefore, in practical use, considering the faster speed of MLP, we can consider using the model based on MLP.

5.5   Errors Analysis and Discussion

Through the error analysis of the automatic annotation results of the model, it is found that the automatic annotation errors can be classified into the following categories.

(1) Word segmentation's granularity problem. For example, manual annotation will take "cha-cha" as a word tag, but automatic annotation will only annotate "cha". "cha" is "查". In other words, the granularity will be larger when annotation manually, and the granularity of word segmentation may be smaller when annotation automatically.

(2) Multi verb problem. When a sentence contains more than one verb, the manual annotation is to see that the verb can fully express part of the meaning rather than only half a sentence. For example, *"I want to check the phone, I want to check the phone bill."* the latter "check" is manually annotated. However, in the machine automatically annotates, the "check" in *"I want to check the phone"* will be annotated.

(3) In a sentence, the core predicate of manual tagging is an adjective, while the core predicate of automatic tagging is a verb. For example, *"mobile traffic is used fast."* the core predicate is "fast" in manual annotation, but "use" is the core predicate in automatic annotation.

(4) In some sentences of "You" and "Shi", manual tagging gives priority to whether there is a core verb. If there is a core verb, it will not be annotated with "You" or "Shi", which is also one of the tagging norms. However, the machine will still annotate "You" and "Shi" under the same situation.

(5) The machine recognizes some phrases as words. For example, the "pay the phone bill" machine is annotated as a word. However, in manual annotation, the "charge" "pay" and "check" are consistent, so only "charge" "pay" and "check" are annotated as the core predicate.

6   Related Works

The works related to the core predicate mainly include syntactic annotation corpus, such as Syntax Treebank; And semantic role annotation corpus, such as proposition database.

Syntax Treebank: Representative Chinese syntactic analysis corpora include The Penn treebank [9], Harbin Institute of technology dependency treebank [10], Peking University multi-view treebank [11], Tsinghua University treebank [12], etc. The syntax treebank contains a wealth of syntactic information, including the segmentation of clauses and sentence components such as subject, predicate, object, attribute, adverbial, and complement. When there is only one verb or adjective in a sentence as the predicate center, the predicate center is the core predicate of this paper.

Semantic Role Annotation Corpus: Representative Chinese semantic role annotation corpora include Binzhou Chinese proposition database and Peking University multi-view tree database. Chinese abstract semantic expression corpora can also be classified into this category. In semantic role annotation, the components acting as semantic roles always depend on a predicate in the sentence. From this point of view, semantic role annotation is consistent with multi-point representation in the core predicate annotation. The fundamental difference between the two is that the goal of semantic role annotation is to comprehensively annotate the proposition information of sentences, while the goal of the core predicate annotation in this paper is to annotate the key intention information of sentences, especially questions, so it is different in the choice and granularity of predicates.

The differences between the above syntactic annotation and semantic role annotation corpus and the core predicate annotation in this paper are as follows. First, when the number of verbs or adjectives in a sentence is less than one or more, we makes provisions on the annotation of core predicates, which is different from syntactic and semantic role annotation; Second, the core predicate can be a word, a phrase, or even a discontinuous phrase, and the predicate center in syntactic and semantic color annotation must be a word. Thirdly, the above-mentioned corpus is mainly news articles, while the corpus of this article mainly questions sentences.

7 Conclusion

Based on the multi-point representation framework, this paper proposes the core predicate annotation specification for Q&A dialogue scenes and constructs annotation corpus including 14657 sentences based on this specification. The Bert pre-training in fine-tuning model with CRF is used to accomplish the sequence annotation task. The trained automatic annotate model can obtain an 89.84%, 81.97% F-score on the same domain and out-of-domain test sets, respectively. The experimental results show that the corpus can train the model for processing general domain data with high accuracy, but the accuracy in specific domains needs to be improved.

References

1. Zhang, J., et al.: Multi-point semantic representation for intent classification. In: AAAI (2020)
2. Steedman, M.: Information structure and the syntax-phonology interface. Linguist. Inq. **33**, 649–689 (2000)
3. Banarescu, L.: Abstract meaning representation for Sembanking. In: LAW@ACL (2013)
4. Perera, V., Chung, T., Kollar, T., Strubell, E.: BERT: multi-task learning for parsing the alexa meaning representation language. In: AAAI (2018)
5. Grimshaw, M.: Light verbs and theta-marking. Linguist. Inq. **19**, 205–232 (1988)
6. Liu, X., et al.: LCQMC: a large-scale chinese question matching corpus. In: COLING (2018)
7. Devlin, J., Chang, M.-W., Lee, K., Toutanova, K.: BERT: pretraining of deep bidirectional transformers for language understanding. In: NAACL-HLT (2019)
8. Yan, H., Qiu, X., Huang, X.: Graph-based model for joint Chinese word segmentation and dependency parsing. arXiv: 1904.04697v2 (2019)
9. Marcus, M., et al.: The Penn Treebank: annotating predicate argument structure. In: The ARPA Human Language Technology Workshop (1994)

10. Chen. X.: Active learning for Chinese Dependency Treebank Building. Harbin Institute of Technology. Harbin (2011). (in Chinese)
11. Qiu, L., Jin, P., Wang, H.: A multi-view Chinese treebank based on dependency grammar. J. Chin Inf. Process. **29**, 9–15 (2015).(in Chinese)
12. Li, Y., Sun, J., Zhou, G., Feng, W.: Recognition and classification of relation words in the compound sentences based on Tsinghua Chinese treebank. In: Acta Scinentiarum Naturalium Universitatis Pekinensis (2014). (in Chinese)

The Development of the Chinese Monosyllabic Motion-Directional Constructions: A Diachronic Constructional Approach

Fangqiong Zhan[(⊠)]

Department of Chinese Language and Literature,
Hong Kong Shue Yan University, Braemar Hill Campus,
10 Wai Tsui Crescent, Braemar Hill, North Point, Hong Kong
zhjade2000@gmail.com

Abstract. There are ten monosyllabic motion-directional verbs (MMVs) in Modern Chinese, all of which indicate directional motion and change of location. Syntactically, they can be followed by a locative NP, and a locative phrase introduced by the preposition *dao* 'to' but not by the preposition *zai* 'at'. There have been works focusing on the development of the preposition *zai* and the following locative phrase, but none of them considers the situations where it co-occurs with the MMVs. This paper identifies the trajectory of the development of the micro-construction [MMV zai NPplace]: emergence, strengthening, weakening, and disappear. The data show that this construction emerged in Middle Chinese (220–960), was frequently used in Early Modern Chinese (960–1900), but became obsolete in Modern Chinese (1900-). It is hypothesized that its emergence may have involved double sources, and its disappearance may have been due to the competition with the other extant micro-constructions [MMV (dao) NPplace].

Keywords: Monosyllabic motion-directional constructions · Emergence · Disappearance · Double sources

1 Introduction

There are ten monosyllabic motion-directional verbs (abbreviated as MMVs) in Modern Chinese: *lai* 'come', *qu* 'go', *shang* 'go up', *xia* 'go down', *jin* 'enter', *chu* 'go out', *hui* 'return', *guo* 'cross', *qi* 'go up', *kai* 'go away' (cf. Huang and Liao [1]). Even though these MMVs vary in their aspectual features, all of them indicate directional motion and change of location. Syntactically, all the above MMVs except *qi* and *kai*[1] can be followed by a locative NP (e.g. (1a)), and can be followed by a locative phrase introduced by the preposition *dao* 'to' (e.g. (1b)), but not by the preposition *zai* 'at' (e.g. (1c)).

---

[1] *Qi* and *kai* as MMVs usually occur as the second component of a disyllabic motion verb compound, such as *juqi* 'lift up', *zoukai* 'go away'.

© Springer Nature Switzerland AG 2022
M. Dong et al. (Eds.): CLSW 2021, LNAI 13250, pp. 353–364, 2022.
https://doi.org/10.1007/978-3-031-06547-7_27

(1) a. 我来学校。
       wǒ lái xuéxiào
       I come school
       I come to school.

   b. 我来到学校。
       wǒ lái dào xuéxiào.
       I come to school
       I come to school.

   c. *我来在学校。
       wǒ lái zài xuéxiào.
       I come at school

From a constructional point of view, the monosyllabic motion-directional construction (abbreviated as MMC) in Modern Chinese can be schematized as [MMV (dao) NPplace]*[change of location][2] and examples (1a–b) illustrate respectively its two micro-constructions. However, all the above three syntactic types existed in Classical Chinese. In other words, in Classical Chinese the MMVs could be followed by a locative NP (e.g. (2a)), or by a locative phrase headed by the preposition *dao* (e.g. (2b)) or *zai* (e.g. (2c)). Accordingly, the MMC in Classical Chinese should be schematized as [MDMV (dao/zai) NPplace]*[change of location], and it had three micro-constructions illustrated by (2a–c).

(2) a. 谢家来贵门
       Xiè jiā lái guì mén
       Say goodbye home come to your noble family
       I said goodbye to my home and came to your noble family.
       Kongque dongnan fei (169–220)

   b. 忽然来到娑婆世界耆阇崛山
       Hūrán lái dào suōpó shìjiè qídūjué shān
       Suddenly come to Suopo world Qidujue Mount
       Suddenly I came to the world of Suopo and Mount Qidujue.
       Beiliang Yijing (410–440)

   c. 狗吠何喧喧, 有吏来在门
       Gǒu fèi hé xuānxuān, yǒu lì lái zài mén
       Dog bark very noisy EXIST official come at door
       The dog barked with loud noise, and there are officials who came at the door.
       Huayangguo Zhi (348–354)

As shown in (1) and (2), the MMVs could collocate with *zai* in Classical Chinese but not in Modern Chinese anymore. This paper adopts a diachronic constructional approach focusing on the micro-construction [MMV zai NPplace] (e.g. (2c)) as well as how it came into being and disappeared in the history of Chinese, using extensive data from Classical Chinese.

---

[2] A construction is schematized as [Form]*[Meaning] in this paper.

There have been a few works focusing on the development of the preposition *zai* and the following locative phrase (cf. Yu [2], Feng [3], Li [4]), but none of them considers the situations where it co-occurs with the MMVs. Following Hilpert's [5] four types of change in the constructional network and Van de Velde's et al.'s [6] idea of multiple sources, I identify the trajectory of the development of the micro-construction [MMV zai NPplace]: emergence, strengthening, weakening, and disappear. The data show that this particular construction emerged in Middle Chinese (220–960), was frequently used in Early Modern Chinese (960–1900), but became obsolete in Modern Chinese (1900-). It is hypothesized that its emergence may have involved double sources, specifically that the syntactic properties are inherited from [Vaction zai NPplace], and the meaning from the extant micro-constructions [MMV NPplace], and that its disappearance may have been due to the competition with the other extant micro-constructions [MMV (dao) NPplace].

The paper is structured as follows: the theoretical framework of the paper is outlined in Sect. 2. Section 3 briefly addresses the data and methodology of the study. Section 4 presents key examples of the development of the most frequently used MMC [lai zai NPplace]*[come to the location] with *lai* as the MMV in the construction to illustrate the development of the MMC. Section 5 discusses the mechanisms that enabled the emergence and disappearance of the construction. Section 6 concludes.

2 Some Basic Concepts of the Framework

My approach is historical and constructionalist. Some fundamentals of the framework of diachronic construction grammar and multiple sources are outlined in this section.

2.1 Diachronic Construction Grammar

Diachronic Construction Grammar provides us with a practical theoretical framework to approach the diachronic change of non-compositionality, and provides a new perspective on traditional historical questions in language change. "How do new constructions arise, how should competition in diachronic variation be accounted for, how do constructions weaken and disappear, and how do constructions change in general, formally and/or semantically, and with what implications for the language system as a whole?" (Barðdal et al. [7]:1) Saussure [8] suggests that any linguistic sign is two-sided, as it consists of a sound-image (form) and a concept (meaning). Therefore, various language units/signs such as morphemes, words, phrases, and clauses can be regarded as pairs of form and meaning (a construction). Following Booij [9], I schematize a construction as [F]*[M], and the notion of the constructed pair is the core concept of construction grammar (Croft [10]; Goldberg [11], etc.). The architecture of a constructional network involves both individual substantive constructions and abstract schematic ones (Traugott [12], Zhan and Traugott [13]). In other words, within a given constructional network, the abstract schema is at the superordinate level overarching subschemas (subsets of schemas) and micro-constructions (individual construction types under each subschema) that are less abstract with internal similarity.

Hilpert [5] proposes four types of change in the constructional network: *emergence*, *strengthening*, *weakening*, and *disappearance*. *Emergence* indicates new forms (e.g. *selfie*), new meanings/concepts appear (e.g. 'wireless internet access'), or new connections are formed (e.g. the existing form *gay* forms a new connection with the existing meaning 'homosexual'). *Strengthening* refers to forms gaining in strength of representation (e.g. frequency increase of *like* as a discourse marker), meaning/concepts gaining in strength of representation (e.g. frequency increase of the meaning 'wireless internet access'), or connections gaining in strength (e.g. the form fantastic becomes more strongly associated with the meaning 'wonderful'). *Weakening* indicates forms decreasing in strength of representation (e.g. the frequency decrease of *whom* as a relative pronoun), meanings/concepts decreasing in strength of representation (e.g. frequency decrease of the meaning 'person granted the use of land in exchange for goods and service'), or connection fading in strength (e.g. the verb dislike becomes less strongly associated with the complementation pattern of a following to-infinitive). *Disappearance* refers to forms disappearing (e.g. the form *affuage* is no longer used), meanings/concepts disappearing (e.g. the meaning 'the right to cut firewood in a forest' is no longer expressed with a single word such as *affuage*), or connection disappear (e.g. the English ditransitive construction is no longer associated with the meaning of banishment or exclusion as in *he therefore forbade her the court.*)

2.2 Multiple Sources

Cognitive Construction Grammar posits constructions at various levels of abstraction, from individual, substantive micro-constructions to more abstract schemas. Likewise constructionalization concerns the rise of both individual micro-constructions and of general patterns and schemas. Since construction grammar concerns contentful/lexical as well as procedural/grammatical constructions, constructionalization embraces change in these domains. The range of work on constructionalization is therefore very different from that on grammaticalization, which for the most part has focused on individual changes in the light of unidirectionality, and is exclusively concerned with the development of procedural expressions.

Most researches in grammaticalization generally focus on just one source construction, conceptualizing straight lines between a construction and a single historical ancestor. This linear and unidirectional view has been widely accepted in the grammaticalization tradition (Givón [14], Lehmann [15]). Van de Velde et al. [6] tries to provide a framework for the analysis of the widespread phenomenon of language changes resulting not just from one, but from multiple source constructions. Van de Velde et al. [6] proposes that change often seems to involve multiple source constructions on a macro-level or on a micro-level. On the macro-level, multiple source constructions involve blending of clearly distinct lineages, each of which is an independent source for a linguistic construction. On the micro-level, innovation can take place within what is historically a single lineage, but under the influence of different uses of the same item. (Van de Velde et al. [6]: 473–474) The multiple source constructions are examined with respect to developments at the levels of phonology, semantics and morphosyntax, for example the English *way*-construction in (3), quoted from Van de Velde et al. ([6]: 484):

(3) a. and we were actually kicking our way through rubbish on the stairs (BNC, FY8 633)
    b. a lady who giggled her way through Nightmare on Elm Street (BNC, HGN 134)

Traugott and Trousdale [16] suggest that two different constructions historically contributed to the formation of the Modern English *way*-construction: one was the use of transitive verbs with NPs meaning 'way' as the object indicating creation or acquisition of a path, as in (3a); the other was the use of intransitive motion verbs with 'way' functioning as an adverbial, as in (3b). Therefore, the Modern English *way*-construction is linked to two distinct older constructions.

3 Data and Methodology

This paper makes use of the modern data from the searchable Internet version of the BCC Modern Chinese Corpus created by Beijing Language and Culture University (Xun et al. [17]), and the classical data from the searchable Internet version of the CCL Chinese Classical Corpus created and managed by Peking University (Zhan et al. [18]).

The BCC Modern Chinese corpus was built in 2016 and include data of approximately 12 billion characters including newspapers (2 billion), literature (3 billion), Weibo (3 billion), science and technology (3 billion), and comprehensive data (1 billion). Such a large-scale multi-domain corpus can fully reflect the language life of today's Chinese society. The CCL Classical Chinese corpus was built in 2003 and include data of approximately 201,668,719 characters and contains Chinese texts from the East Zhou Dynasty (Spring and Autumn and Warring states periods) (around 500 BCE) to the middle of the Republic of China (1930 or so) covering 1059 texts. All the classical data selected in the paper were searched from the CCL Classical corpus. The periodization for written Chinese adopted in the paper is as follows (Sun [19]):

Old Chinese: 771 BCE to 220 CE
Middle Chinese: 220 CE to 960
Early Modern Chinese: 960 to 1900
Modern Chinese: 1900 to present

Because of the periodization of the CCL corpus, data for 1900 to 1930 were also searched in CCL Classical Chinese Corpus in addition to data for Old, Middle and Early Modern Chinese. Statistical numbers of extracted forms, together with their values in terms of percentages and frequency in the collected data, are shown in tables, while the qualitative analyses are captured in figures.

From a constructional point of view, the MMC is a subschema of the umbrella schematic directional motion construction. Under the subschema, three micro-constructions are included. Figure 1 illustrates the taxonomy of the schematic directional motion construction.

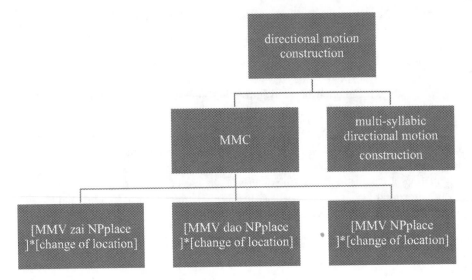

Fig. 1. The taxonomy of the schematic directional motion construction

As mentioned in Sect. 1, there are altogether ten MMVs, and other than *qi* and *kai*, all the other eight verbs can be recruited into the MMC. In this paper, I will focus on the micro-construction [MMV zai NPplace] and consider its emergence, strengthening, weakening and disappearance in the history of Chinese.

A preliminary search of this micro-construction with the eight MMVs was conducted in the CCL Classical Chinese and the attested tokens of [MMV zai NPplace] with different MMVs are summarized in Table 1.

Table 1. Token numbers of [MMV zai NPplace] with different MMVs

	Old Chinese	Middle Chinese	Early Modern Chinese	Modern Chinese
lai zai NPplace	0	71	366	0
qu zai NPplace	0	0	24	0
shang zai NPplace	0	0	15	0
xia zai NPplace	0	0	155	0
jin zai NPplace	0	4	28	0
chu zai NPplace	0	10	107	0
hui zai NPplace	0	2	47	0
guo zai NPplace	0	3	5	0

Table 1 shows that [MMV zai NPplace] emerged in Middle Chinese, was frequently used in Early Modern Chinese, but disappeared in Modern Chinese. It also shows that as an MMV, *lai* is earliest and most frequently used in the construction: it first occurred in ca. 354; in Middle Chinese, there are 71 tokens of [lai zai NPplace], and in Early Modern Chinese, 366 tokens are attested.

4   The Development of the Monosyllabic Directional Construction

As shown in Table 1, *lai* is the most frequently used MMV in the micro-construction [MMV zai NPplace], therefore in this section, I will discuss the development of this particular MMV as in [lai (zai/dao) NPplace]*[come to the location] to illustrate the development of the MMC.

In Old Chinese, *lái* was a motion verb meaning 'come', as in (4).

(4) 有朋自远方来
     Yǒu péng zì yuǎnfāng lái
     have friend from distant place come
     (You) have a friend coming from a distant place.

Lunyu Book 1 (400 BCE)

In most Old Chinese texts, *lai* as a motion-directional verb is frequently found to be the first verb of a verb-verb compound such as 来朝 'come to show respect', 来聘 'come to visit', 来奔 'come to work for', etc. In late Old Chinese, the monosyllabic motion-directional verb *lai* is found to be followed by a place noun, as in (5):

(5) 谢家来贵门
     Xiè jiā lái guì mén
     Say goodbye home come to your noble family
     I said goodbye to my home and come to your noble family.

Kongque dongnan fei (169–220)

In Old Chinese, *zai* was an existential verb denoting the existence (Xu 121). For example:

(6) 父母在, 不远游
     Fùmǔ zài, bù yuǎn yóu
     Parents EXIST not far travel
     When there are parents, sons do not travel far.

Lunyu (400BCE)

Zai was also found followed by a place noun in Old Chinese, as in (7):

(7) 子在齐, 闻韶
     Zi zài qí, wén sháo
     Master be at Qi hear Shao
     Master was at the state of Qi, and heard about Shao.

Lunyu (400BCE)

In (6) and (7) *zai* indicates respectively the location of the subject and the location that the action takes place. Many scholars (cf. Ota [20], Zhang [21]) maintain that *zai* in examples like (7) is also a verb, taking the place noun as its complement and together paralleling with the following VO phrase.

Around the same period of time, [zai + place noun] is found following an action verb, such as:

(8) 禹往见之, 则耕在野
    Yǔ wǎng jiàn zhī, zé gēng zài yě
    Yu go visit him then farm in field
    Yu went to visit him, and then saw him farming in the field.

                                                   Zhuangzi (ca. 400 BCE)

Scholars (cf. Yu [2]) point out that *zai* in (8) should be considered as a proposition rather than a verb, and it together with the following place noun forms the locative adverbial phrase to modify the preceding verb. Accordingly, *zai* in Old Chinese was an existential verb, a stative verb as well as a preposition denoting location.

The first occurrence of [zai + place noun] following the motion-directional verb *lai* appeared in Middle Chinese, as in (9).

(9) 狗吠何喧喧, 有吏来在门
    Gǒu fèi hé xuānxuān, yǒu lì lái zài mén
    Dog bark very noisy EXIST official come at door
    The dog bards with loud noise, and there are officials coming at the door.

                                      Huayangguo Zhi (348–354)

Example (9) is a piece of evidence demonstrating the construction [lai zai NPplace] *[change of location] emerged in Middle Chinese. In Early Modern Chinese the construction became rather frequent (366 tokens attested as shown in Table 1). However, it disappeared in Modern Chinese. About fifty years later, another change of location construction occurred and it is [lai dao NPplace] as in (10).

(10) 一念之顷忽然来到娑婆世界耆阇崛山
    Yī niàn zhī qǐng hūrán lái dào suōpó shìjiè qídūjué shān
    One thought ASSOC time suddenly come arrive Suopo world Qidujue mount
    Just a thought of time, suddenly, (I) came to the Suopo World, Mount Qidujue.

                                          Beiliang Yijing (401–410)

Form constructional point of view, when [lai NPplace] emerged (ex. 5), it demonstrates that the micro-construction [MMV NPplace]*[change of location] came into being and the MMC was established. When [lai zai NPplace] (ex. 9) and [lai dao NPplace] (ex. 10) occurred, the other two micro-constructions [MMV zai/dao NPplace] *[change of location] occurred and were recruited into the MMC. The MMC accordingly expanded to three micro-constructions. Figure 2 illustrates the development of the MMC.

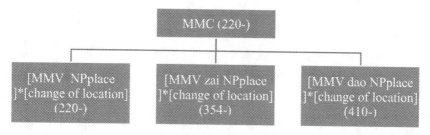

Fig. 2. The development of the MMC

In the following section, I will discuss the mechanisms that enabled the emergence and disappearance of this construction.

5 The Mechanisms of the Emergence and Disappearance of [MMV Zai NPplace]*[Change of Location]

Regarding mechanisms of change, two have been recognized as being crucially important in the field of morphosyntax: reanalysis, also called neoanalysis, and analogy (e.g. Meillet [22], Harris and Campbell [23]). Neoanalysis refers to the hearer (possibly speaker too) analyzing a structure in a different way from the input; it involves change in the status of implicatures associated with lexemes. Analogy, by contrast, refers to the attraction of extant forms to already existing constructions (e.g. Fischer [24]). In the framework of diachronic construction grammar, analogy involves analogical thinking as one of the motivations and analogization as one of the mechanisms that brings about a new fit to an extant pattern (Traugott and Trousdale [16]:37–38). In this section, I examine analogization as the mechanism that enabled the development of the construction [MMV zai NPplace]*[change of location].

5.1 The Emergence of the Construction

As shown in example (8), in Old Chinese the sequence [Vaction zai NPplace] denoting the location of the action became frequent. I argue that this string is the syntactic origin of the construction [MMV zai NPplace]. If we take a closer look at the two constructions:

[Vaction zai NPplace] *[location of the action] (occurred in 400 BCE)
[MMV zai NPplace]*[change of location] (emerged in 354)

We can see that they have partially identical forms (Vaction zai NPplace and MMV zai NPplace), which by hypothesis enabled analogization to take place. I suggest that the pre-existing string [Vaction zai NPplace] is an important syntactic exemplar relevant to the development of the construction [MMV zai NPplace].

As shown in example (5), in late Old Chinese [MMV NPplace]*[change of location] emerged. I argue that this is the other exemplar that influenced the meaning of

[MMV zai NPplace]*[change of location]. Again, if we take a closer look at the two constructions:

[MMV NPplace]*[change of location]
[MMV zai NPplace]*[change of location]

We can see again the partially identical forms (MMV NPplace) which might have enabled analogization and resulted in similar meaning. Based on the above discussion, I suggest that the development of [MMV zai NPplace]*[change of location] involved double origins: structurally, it developed from the combination of an action verb plus preposition phrase denoting the location of the action; semantically it was analogized to the extant MMC [MMV NPplace]*[change of location]. The process of the emergence by hypothesis can be schematized as:

i)   Form: [Vaction zai NPplace] *[location of the action]
ii)   Meaning: [MMV NPplace]*[change of location]

→   [MMV zai NPplace]*[change of location]

As mentioned above, analogization is a mechanism that brings about a new fit to an extant pattern. I hypothesize that in the process of the development of [MMV zai NPplace]*[change of location], it was analogized to [Vaction zai NPplace] as well as the extant MMC [MMV NPplace]*[change of location]. In other words, analogization enabled [MMV zai NPplace]*[change of location] to be a new micro-construction in the construction network of MMC.

5.2   The Disappearance of the Construction

As mentioned above, in Middle Chinese all the three micro-constructions of MMC occurred. Taking [lai (dao/zai) NPplace] as an example, [lai NPplace] occurred before 220 CE, [lai zai NPplace] emerged about 350 CE, and [lai dao NPplace] occurred around 400 CE. Table 2 illustrates the development of the three constructions:

Table 2. Token numbers of [lai (zai/dao) NPplace] in the different period of the history of Chinese

	Late Old Chinese	Middle Chinese	Early Modern Chinese	Modern Chinese
lai NPplace	3	24	5,465	60,307
lai zai NPplace	0	71	366	0
lai dao NPplace	0	46	8,680	23,607

In Middle Chinese, [lai zai NPplace] was the most frequently used, followed by [lai NPplace] and [lai dao NPplace]. All the three constructions were used more frequently in Early Modern Chinese; however, [lai zai NPplace] became the least used construction among the three, following [lai NPplace] and [lai dao NPplace]. In Modern Chinese, [lai NPplace] and [lai dao NPplace] were more and more frequently used, but [lai zai NPplace] became obsolete and disappeared.

It is clear that starting from Early Modern Chinese, among the three alternatives, speakers preferred to use [lai NPplace] and [lai dao NPplace] over [lai zai NPplace], which eventually led to the disappearance of the [lai zai NPplace] and its corresponding MMC micro-construction in Modern Chinese. The reasons for the preference can be hypothesized as follows. First, for the sake of economy, speakers tend to prefer shorter versions if the same meaning can be represented by a variety of forms. Accordingly, [lai NPplace] is preferred than [lai zai NPplace], as the latter is longer than the former. Furthermore, the preposition *dao* in [lai dao NPplace] had been originally a motion verb describing the path towards the destination and referring to the last stage of the trip. When *dao* changed into a preposition in the MMC, even though the motion meaning was bleached, the path towards the destination can still be sensed from its original function. In this case, *dao* is more compatible with *lai* than *zai*, because both *lai* and *dao* entail certain degree of path of a motion, whereas *zai* is more or less existential, and therefore does not denote any sense of path or motion. Therefore, when [lai dao NPplace] and [lai zai NPplace] were in a mode of competition, [lai dao NPplace] naturally stood out.

Based on the above discussion, it is concluded that in terms of the preference among the three micro-constructions by the speakers, because of economy and less of effort, [MMV zai NPplace] lost to [MMV NPplace], and because of the motion direction nature, [MMV zai NPplace] lost to [MMV dao NPplace]. As a result, [MMV zai NPplace] lost its position in the constructional network of MMC and disappeared in Modern Chinese.

6 Conclusion

This paper focuses on the development of a micro-construction of MMC [MMV zai NPplace]. It shows that this particular micro-construction emerged in Middle Chinese (220-960), was frequently used in Early Modern Chinese (960-1900), but became obsolete in Modern Chinese (1900-). It is argued that its emergence may have involved double sources, specifically that the syntactic properties are inherited from [Vaction zai NPplace], and the meaning from the extant micro-constructions [MMV NPplace] *[change of location], and that its disappearance may have been due to the speakers' preference for [MMV (dao) NPplace] over [MMV zai NPplace] starting from Early Modern Chinese.

References

1. Huang, B.R., Liao, X.D.: Xiandai Hanyu 'Modern Chinese'. Gaodeng Jiaoyu Chubanshe, Beijing (1991)
2. Yu, S.S.: The preposition zai in Oracle bones. Res. Ancient Chin. Lang. **4**, 51–53 (2002)

3. Feng, X.D.: The grammaticalization process of the temporal adverb zai. J. Yibin Coll. **1**, 109 (2009)
4. Li, H.: The grammaticalization of zai. Mod. Chin. Res. **2**, 133–134 (2014)
5. Hilpert, M.: Three open questions in Diachronic Construction Grammar. In Coussé, E., Andersson, P., Olofsson, J. (eds.) Grammaticalization Meets Construction Grammar, pp. 21–39. John Benjamins, Amsterdam/Philadelphia (2018)
6. Van de Velde, F., De Smet, H., Ghesquière, L.: On multiple source constructions in language change. Stud. Lang. **37**, 473–488 (2013)
7. Barðdal, J., Smirnova, E., Sommerer, L., Gildea, S. (eds.): Diachronic Construction Grammar. Benjamins, Amsterdam (2015)
8. Saussure, F.D.: Course in General Linguistics. Translated by Harris, R. Open Court, Chicago (1983[1916]) (first published in French in 1916)
9. Booij, G.: Construction Morphology. Oxford University Press, Oxford (2010)
10. Croft, W.: Radical Construction Grammar: Syntactic Theory in Typological Perspective. Oxford University Press, Oxford (2001)
11. Goldberg, A.E.: Constructions at Work: The Nature of Generalization in Language. Oxford University Press, Oxford (2006)
12. Traugott, E.C.: Toward a constructional framework for research on language change. Cogn. Linguist. Stud. **1**, 3–21 (2014). Slightly modified reprint in Hancil, S., König, E. (eds.): Grammaticalization—Theory and Data. Benjamins, Amsterdam 87–105
13. Zhan, F.Q., Traugott, E.C.: A study of the development of the Chinese correlative comparative construction from the perspective of constructionalization. Diachronica **37**, 83–126 (2020)
14. Givón, T.: On Understanding Grammar. Academic Press, New York (1979)
15. Lehmann, C.: New reflections on grammaticalization and lexicalization. In: Wischer, I., Diewald, G. (eds.) New Reflections on Grammaticalization, pp. 1–18. Benjamins, Amsterdam (2002)
16. Traugott, E.C., Trousdale, G.: Constructionalization and Constructional Changes. Oxford University Press, Oxford (2013)
17. Xun, E.D., Rao, G.Q., Xiao, X.Y., Zang, J.J.: The construction of the BCC corpus in the age of big data. Corpus Linguist. **3**, 93–109, 118 (2016)
18. Zhan, W.D., Guo, R., Chen, Y.R.: The CCL Corpus of Chinese Texts: 700 million Chinese Characters, the 11th Century B.C. – present (2003) Available online at the website of Center for Chinese Linguistics (abbreviated as CCL) of Peking University. http://ccl.pku.edu.cn:8080/ccl_corpus
19. Sun, C.F.: Word-Order Change and Grammaticalization in the History of Chinese. Stanford University Press, Stanford (1996)
20. Ota, T.: Zhongguo lishi wenfa. Beijing University Press, Beijing (1987)
21. Zhang, Y.S.: The grammaticalization mechanisms of Chinese adverbs. Stud. Chin. Lang. **1**, 3–15 (2000)
22. Meillet, A.: L'évolution des formes grammaticales. In: Antoine, M. (ed.) Linguistique historique et linguistique générale, pp. 130–148. Champion, Paris (1958 [1912]). (Originally published in Scientia (Rivista di scienza) XXII (1912))
23. Harris, A.C., Campbell, L.: Historical Syntax in Cross-Linguistic Perspective. Cambridge University Press, Cambridge (1995)
24. Fischer, O.: Morphosyntactic Change: Functional and Formal Perspectives. Oxford University Press, Oxford (2007)

A Corpus Study of Anaphora in Chinese Conditionals

Shunting Chen[(⊠)] [ID]

Shanghai International Studies University, Shanghai, China
cst731@gmail.com

Abstract. This corpus research studies different types of anaphoric behaviour in Chinese conditional complex sentences. It investigates 25 conditional subordinators randomly generated from the literature and the newspaper genre of the Center for Chinese Linguistics corpus (CCL). The statistical findings suggest that in terms of anaphora in Chinese conditional complex sentences, other things being equal, 1) pronoun and zero coreference as well as NP and zero coreference are more common than NP and pronoun coreference in both Conjunction-Subject structure (Hereinafter referred to as "Structure A") and Subject-Conjunction structure (Hereinafter referred to as "Structure B"); 2) pronoun and zero coreference are more common than NP and zero coreference in Structure A; 3) NP and zero are more common than pronoun and zero in Structure A; 4) pronoun and zero are more frequently observed in Structure A than in Structure B; 5) NP and zero is more frequently observed in Structure B than in Structure A.

Keywords: Inter-clausal anaphora · Topicality · Discourse information · Corpus study

1 Introduction

Four types of inter-clausal anaphora can be observed: S(ubject)-S anaphora, S-O(bject) anaphora, O-O anaphora, and O-S anaphora. My discussion of anaphora in this study involves S(ubject)-S anaphora, which occurs when bi-clausal sentence subjects co-refer. According to [1], Chinese inter-clausal anaphora carries "a rather striking characteristic" because, in Chinese conditional structures, both the subject-conjunction order where subject is placed before the subordinate conjunction (hereinafter referred to as "structure B") and conjunction-subject order where the subject follows conjunction (hereinafter referred to as "structure A") can be observed. (1a) and (1b) demonstrate the two structures respectively.

(1) a. 小王ᵢ不但∅ᵢ会唱歌，而且∅ᵢ会跳舞。
   Xiaowang not only can sing, but also can dance

'Xiaowang can not only sing but also dance.';

b. 不但小王 $_i$ 会唱歌，他太太 $_j$ 也会。

Not only Xiaowang can sing, his wife also can

'Not only Xiaowang can sing, his wife also can'.

Despite the fact that both structure A and structure B coexists in Chinese conditional complex sentences, they correlate with different references. Structure B most often correlates with coreference while structure A is more often related to disjoint reference as are demonstrated in (1). In (1a), *xiaowang* is a coreference; thus structure B is observed. By contrast in (1b), *xiaowang* and his wife are disjoint reference; thus, Structure A is exhibited.

Different approaches have been adopted to explain structure B: a formal approach by [3, 4], a pragmatic approach by [5], and a combined approach by [6] and [7–9]. Recent studies also include [10], a descriptive approach conforming to the previous conclusion [11, 12], about subject-object anaphora, and [13, 14], a corpus approach on conditional sentences providing incompatible generalization to that of [1] and [8]. So far, [8]'s description and explanation conform to the empirical description by [1] and [2]. [8] adopted a topic-control approach which explains the co-reference pattern with topicality. In his analysis, the subject-conjunction pattern has a topic that controls the subject in the main clause. That's why [1]'s observation exists. However, his data about reference patterns of conditional sentences can not fall into his frequency prediction.

All previous descriptions are different sides of the same coin and have limits in accounting for Chinese inter-clausal anaphora, especially where conditionals are concerned. Names, personal pronouns, and zero are used in their examples as important nominal types. The present study using a larger corpus intends to test 5 hypothesis: 1) Other things being equal, NP[1]-zero[2] and pronoun[3]-zero coreference are more common than NP-pronoun coreference in both structure A and structure B; 2) pronoun and zero coreference are more common than NP and zero coreference in structure A; 3) NP and zero are more common than pronoun and zero in structure B; 4) pronoun and zero are more frequently observed in structure A than in structure B; 5) NP and zero are more frequently observed in structure B than in structure A.

2   Corpus Study: Materials and Methods

2.1   The Selection of Materials

This research adopts a corpus-driven approach, using Center for Chinese Linguistics Corpus [15]. Two genres of materials, literature and newspaper were culled from the corpus. The selection decision is justified by the fact that the materials selected can maximally represent the most current use of the Chinese language. Also, since the selections are from materials written in Chinese, the representiveness is better

---

[1] NP in this study includes names and other nominal phrase.

[2] Zero in this study includes zero pronouns in the second-clausal subject.

[3] Pronoun in this study includes personal pronouns and other pronouns.

guaranteed than if materials are randomly selected from a wider range of genres, which may include the section of materials translated into Chinese from other languages, therefore carrying Europeanized writing style. Besides, the two genres contrast with each other in terms of formality (since the literature materials are inherently more formal than newspaper ones) so that the influence of style factor on reference pattern can also be considered.

2.2 The Selection Procedures

The corpus study is carried out in the following steps:

i. Qualitative Study/ Referential Patterns and Their Coding
   Following Sinclair [16], we identify sentence types by going through one screen of data (about 30 lines) and another screen until there are no novel occurrences. Variables include structure A and structure B; NP; and pronouns.

ii. Quantitative Study/Distribution of the Reference Patterns
   We form an annotation system (description), and then generate sentences from CCL by typing the word into the search box. After that, we put the total number of occurrences in the download box and save these sentences into a text file. Next, we select those newspaper and literature occurrences according to the header if the whole corpus exceeds 2,000 sentences. When this is done, we randomly generate 1,000 sentences if either the newspaper or the literature or both genres exceed 1,000 sentences.[4]

2.3 The Selection Scope

In order to carry out an exhaustive study before time is exhausted, the corpus size has to be carefully adjusted. If the total number of sentences in the corpus is less than 2,000, an exhaustive study is adopted for both genres. Otherwise, 1,000 sentences from newspaper and 1,000 sentences from literature genre are randomly selected as a base to choose structures from. Most often, the newspaper part is many times the size of the literature part, in which the total number of sentences is around 1,000. So the number is reasonable. If there are fewer than 1,000 sentences in one genre, it would be an exhaustive study of either literature or newspaper, or both. In other words, it is to make the corpus smaller but parallel to the original one and then there might be 300 Structure As and 200 Structure Bs in the reduced corpus. Note that some corpus studies also use a subset of a certain corpus (e.g. [17]).

Our research scope is conditional sentences. The most reasonable classification of consideration should be both formal and functional, especially when one would like to

---

[4] The detailed steps are: 1) Number these sentences in Excel; 2) Generate 1,000 random numbers with the random sampling function of poptool; 3) Rank them according to ascending numeral order; 4) Mark those first occurrences of repetitive numbers with * by the following formula = IF (A1 = A2, "*","") typed in another new column; 5) Select the whole working sheet, choose the automatic selection function. Press the button of the new column and selecting *; 6) What appears will be the 1,000 sentences randomlyselected. After that, we annotate and calculate the statistical result for CA, CB, with zero anaphor, NPs, and pronouns.

compare the results across languages, "...mixed functional-formal domain definitions constitute the best strategy for ensuring cross-linguistic comparability" [18]. Comparatively speaking, it is safer to rely on some existent classifications in the grammar books. And according to formal-functional criteria, [19] system will be adopted in this research. Such a system also includes a type of concessive sentences but note such kind of sentences are closely related to conditional sentences because of the relation between "if", "only if", and "even if" [20]. Within each Chinese class of conditionals [19], there could be distinctions between rhetorical conditions, hypothetical conditions, and other conditions. The total numbers of occurrence of conditional subordinators[5] in the present study scope are as follows (Table 1):

Table 1. Conditional subordinators: frequency

Ruguo 如果	104,714	Yidan 一旦	13,804	Wanyi 万一	3,727	Zongran 纵然	1,070
Zhiyou 只有	75,798	Bulun 不论	9,621	Napa 哪怕	3,628	Renping 任凭	935
Zhiyao 只要	37,687	Jiaru 假如	6,883	Zhixu 只需	2,900	Zongshi 纵使	417
Yaoshi 要是	33,904	Jiusuan 就算	6,495	Jiashe 假设	2,789	Tangshi 倘使	327
Wulun 无论	25,575	Chufei 除非	4,374	Weiyou 唯有	2,547		
Jishi 即使	23,367	Ruoshi 若是	4,067	Jiaruo 假若	1,726		
Buguan 不管	20,454	Tangruo 倘若	3,833	Jiashi 假使	1,157		

3   Results and Discussion

3.1   Comparison Within Structure: Hypotheses 1, 2 and 3

Hypothesis 1: Other things being equal, NP-zero and pronoun-zero coreference are more common than NP-pronoun coreference in both structures (Table 2).

---

[5] Note that the single word subordinators *ping* and *ruo* cannot be distinguished from some other subordinators and phrases unless time-consuming work is conducted. These two words were therefore omitted from later analysis.

Table 2. 3 patterns: frequency in total occurrences

Name of coreference pattern	Structure A	Structure B
NP and pronoun	87 62.1%	53 37.9%
Pronoun and zero	756 60.6%	492 39.4%
NP and zero	299 26.6%	827 73.4%

The idea of comparing patterns within a certain structure is not proposed in previous studies. [7] and [14] only focused on the frequency of the combination of reference and structure and zero in all cases and in personal reference cases between structures. The motivation of present comparison is in [21] with the consideration of the length of sentence. If a further annotation is carried out, we will understand how different factors contribute to such differences.

The same trends hold in different genres as stated in Table 3:

Table 3. 3 patterns: frequency in different genres

Name of coreference pattern	Newspaper		Literature	
	Structure A	Structure B	Structure A	Structure B
NP and pronoun	34 60.7%	22 39.3%	53 63%	31 37%
Pronoun and zero	260 66.5%	131 33.5%	496 57.8%	361 42.1%
NP and zero	150 26.7%	411 73.2%	149 26.3%	416 73.6%

Hypothesis 2: Other things being equal, pronoun and zero coreference are more common than NP and zero coreference in Structure A.

We think the data is supportive of our prediction. In structure A, NP and pronoun < Np and zero < Pronoun and zero. The reason why Pronoun and zero would highly exceed NP and zero also supports accumulative accessibility [7] which says a structure where pronoun subject is used is more likely to indicate that there is a salient topic in the previous text.

Since the use of pronoun presupposes the salience of an entity in the previous context, such entity would be salient enough for a zero to access in the subsequent clause. Thus, zero would be more likely to be used in pronoun for NP1 sentences instead of name for NP1 sentences. Our data for separate subordinators are as follows (Table 4):

Table 4. Antecedent of zero anaphor in A

Subor	Str. Pat.	Pronoun	NP	Subor.	Str. Pat.	Pronoun	NP
Zhiyao	CA	71	2	Jiashi	CA	33	2
	%	97.3	2.7		%	94.3	5.7
Zhixu	CA	0	0	Jiaruo	CA	36	10
	%	100	100		%	78.3	21.7
Yidan	CA	13	0	Jiashe	CA	0	1
	%	100	0		%	0	100
Zhiyou	CA	0	0	Tang ruo	CA	63	7
	%	100	100		%	90	10
Weiyou	CA	0	0	Tang shi	CA	17	1
	%	100	100		%	94.4	5.6
Chufei	CA	14	0	Ruoshi	CA	11	3
	%	100	0		%	78.6	21.4
Wulun	CA	82	0	Yaoshi	CA	7	3
	%	100	0		%	70	30
Bulun	CA	18	0	Wanyi	CA	9	3
	%	100	0		%	75	25
Buguan	CA	29	1	Jishi	CA	40	3
	%	96.7	3.3		%	93	7
Renpin	CA	6	1	Jiusuan	CA	66	12
	%	85.7	14.3		%	84.6	15.4
Ruguo	CA	62	4	Zongshi	CA	18	0
	%	93.9	6.1		%	100	0
Jiaru	CA	62	10	Zongran	CA	19	5
	%	86.1	13.9		%	79.1	20.8
Napa	CA	10	0				
	%	100	0				

Note: Subor. = Subordinator;   Str.   Pat. = Structure   Pattern.   This abbreviation is used in the following tables.

In *zhixu, zhiyou, weiyou* sentences, we find no CA patterns. As was mentioned, these subordinate conjunctions have verbal features so they mostly use the B structure. In *jiashe* sentences, only one case of name reference was found. This might result from a certain author style. All other cases support hypothesis 2.

Hypothesis 3: Other things being equal, NP and zero are more common than pronoun and zero in Structure B.

Such prediction has not been made in previous literature. It is interesting to observe that in a subject or topic fronted structure, NP is more often used than pronouns to indicate coreference. Judging from the structure, subject 1 position is highly accessible so a pronoun antecedent should have been preferred. However, it is NP that overrides pronouns both in newspaper and in literature. We propose that NP is often pronounced with more words than pronouns, so it is more used to indicate that two sentences have the same subjects. In oral conversation, such multi-word phrase is easier to enter long-term memory, thus easier to recall across sentences. Or such data distribution suggests that NP is a new topic used in such structures.

By fronting a subject, it is a topic whose salience favors coreference in a bi-clausal sentence [9]. This is called topicality [9]. Here an NP is more likely to serve the topic function than a pronoun. That's why in topicality cases NP overrides the pronoun situation which might suggest a salient topic in the preceding text (Table 5).

Table 5. Antecedent of zero anaphor in B

Subor	Str. Pat.	Pronoun	NP	Subor	Str. Pat.	Pronoun	NP
Zhiyao	CB	34	69	Jiashi	CB	1	44
	%	33	67		%	2.2	97.8
Zhixu	CB	494	66	Jiaruo	CB	3	5
	%	88.2	11.8		%	37.5	62.5
Yidan	CB	29	228	Jiashe	CB	0	0
	%	11.3	88.7		%	0	0
Zhiyou	CB	13	25	Tang ruo	CB	14	107
	%	34.2	65.8		%	11.6	88.4
Weiyou	CB	2	12	Tang shi	CB	0	3
	%	14.3	85.7		%	0	100
Chufei	CB	4	15	Ruoshi	CB	0	3
	%	21	79		%	0	100
Wulun	CB	29	44	Yaoshi	CB	65	8
	%	39.7	60.3		%	89	11
Bulun	CB	15	40	Wanyi	CB	4	2
	%	27.3	72.7		%	66.7	33.3
Buguan	CB	13	19	Jishi	CB	19	35
	%	40.6	59.4		%	35.2	64.8
Renpin	CB	13	19	Jiusuan	CB	53	45
	%	40.6	59.4		%	54.1	45.9
Ruguo	CB	26	37	Zongshi	CB	15	11
	%	41.3	58.7		%	57.7	42.3
Jiaru	CB	7	15	Zongran	CB	53	97
	%	31.8	68.2		%	35.3	64.7
Napa	CB	11	17				
	%	39.3	60.7				

From this table, we can see there are slight variations in data for coreference in structure B. The fact that most of the cases belong to the large group supports hypothesis 3. There are two cases that highly rely on pronouns as their topics/subjects when the second subjects are zeros: *zhixu* and *yaoshi*. This suggests that they retain verb-like features and does not behave like other subordinators which require multi-word phrase to be a topic. What this means is that if it is verb-like, it follows a pronoun easily and does lead the whole sentence as if the two clauses were one sentence. In this sense, such verb-like subordinators form a different group.

Another small violation group include *zongshi, jiusuan*, and *wanyi. Jiusuan* is verb-like too. That is why pronoun uses and NP uses in antecedents are almost equal with pronouns 4 cases more than NP cases. In *zongshi* situation, pronouns are 4 cases more than NP in the antecedent. In *wanyi* situation, pronouns are only 2 cases more. We don't consider this a violation because they don't form a large group.

3.2   Comparisons Between Structures: Hypotheses 4 and 5

Hypothesis 4: Other things being equal, pronoun and zero would be more common in structure A than in structure B.

Table 6. Antecedent of zero anaphor in A and B

Subor	Pronoun in CA	Pronoun in CB	Subor	Pronoun in CA	Pronoun in CB
Zhiyao	71 67.6%	34 32.4%	Jiashi	33 97%	1 3%
Zhixu	0 0%	494 100%	Jiaruo	36 92.3%	3 7.7%
Yidan	13 30.9%	29 69.1%	Jiashe	0 100%	0 100%
Zhiyou	0 0%	13 100%	Tangruo	63 81.8%	14 18.2%
Weiyou	0 0%	2 100%	Tangshi	17 100%	0 0%
Chufei	14 77.8%	4 22.2%	Ruoshi	11 100%	0 0%
Wulun	82 73.8%	29 26.1%	Yaoshi	7 9.7%	65 90.3%
Bulun	18 54.5%	15 45.5%	Wanyi	9 69.2%	4 30.8%
Buguan	29 69%	13 31%	Jishi	40 67.8%	19 32.2%
Renpin	6 31.5%	13 68.4%	Jiusuan	66 55.5%	53 44.5%
Ruguo	62	26	Zongshi	18	15

(*continued*)

Table 6. (*continued*)

Subor	Pronoun in CA	Pronoun in CB	Subor	Pronoun in CA	Pronoun in CB
	70.4%	29.5%		54.5%	45.6%
Jiaru	62	7	Zongran	19	53
	89.9%	10.1%		26.4%	73.6%
Napa	10	11			
	47.6%	52.4%			

As stated in Table 6, 17 subordinators support hypothesis 4. One verb-like subordinator group goes against it with more pronouns used in CB than in CA. The reason is two-folds verb-like subordinators use more B structure than A structure; the factor of being a verb-like subordinator overrides the pronoun preference in CA. This group include *zhixu, zhiyou, weiyou,* and *yaoshi.* Though *jiusuan* is verb-like, it happens that pronouns in A exceed pronouns in B.

Other 4 subordinators that fall into a special group are *zongran, yidan, renpin,* and *napa.* In this group, *zongran* uses about three times more pronouns in structure B than in A. The reason why this group behaves differently requires more study. It is interesting to note that *jiashe* never uses pronouns as antecedents in the first clause.

Hypothesis 5: Other things being equal, NP and zero would be more common in structure B than in Structure A (Table 7).

Table 7. Antecedent of zero anaphor in A

Subor	NP in A	NP in B	Subor	NP in A	NP in B
Zhiyao	2	69	Jiashi	2	44
	2.8%	97.2%		4%	96%
Zhixu	0	66	Jiaruo	10	5
	0%	100%		66.7%	33.3%
Yidan	0	228	Jiashe	1	0
	0%	100%		100%	0%
Zhiyou	0	25	Tangruo	7	107
	0%	100%		6.1%	93.9%
Weiyou	0	12	Tangshi	1	3
	0%	100%		25%	75%
Chufei	0	15	Ruoshi	3	3
	0%	100%		50%	50%
Wulun	0	44	Yaoshi	3	8
	0%	100%		27.3%	72.7%
Bulun	0	40	Wanyi	3	2
	0%	100%		60%	40%
Buguan	1	19	Jishi	3	35

(*continued*)

Table 7. (*continued*)

Subor	NP in A	NP in B	Subor	NP in A	NP in B
	5%	95%		8%	92%
Renpin	1	19	Jiusuan	12	45
	5%	95%		21%	79%
Ruguo	4	37	Zongshi	0	11
	9.8%	90.2%		0%	100%
Jiaru	10	15	Zongran	5	97
	40%	60%		5%	95%
Napa	0	17			
	0%	100%			

Among 25 subordinators we have investigated, 21 supports hypothesis 5 with a significant difference between NP in A and NP in B. Several subordinators never use NP for coreference antecedent in A in the selected part of corpus: *zhixu, yidan, zhiyou, weiyou, chufei, wulun, bulun, napa*, and *zongshi*. Exceptions include *jiaruo, jiashe, wanyi*, and *ruoshi*. For *jiaruo* and *jiashe*, they rely mainly on structure A [13]. For *wanyi*, it is only 1 case more in A and for *ruoshi*, NP in A and B becomes equal with occurrences of 3 in the part of corpus we have built. Considering the larger number of subordinators and the larger occurrences in positive cases, we would like to say that hypothesis 5 holds.

As has been discussed in hypotheses 2 and 3, NP is preferred as a topic in structure B while a pronoun for coreference is more natural in structure A to refer to an already mentioned subject or topic. Hypotheses 4 and 5 further strengthens these statements by comparing across structures. It is a high correlation even in cases where more coreference is indicated in structure B [1, 9, 14].

4   Conclusion

In this study, 5 hypotheses about different anaphoric relations are investigated and are supported in total data. Possible motivations behind such patterns can be attributable to sentence length, accumulative accessibility, topicality, subject length, and structure. If we look into 25 subordinators one by one, hypotheses 1 and 2 are supported while hypotheses 3, 4, and 5 seem to suggest there are different groups of subordinators within the conditional type. Some subordinators heavily rely on structure A such as *jiaru* and *jiaruo*; some subordinators prefer pronouns as antecedents in structure B such as *zhixu, zhiyou*, etc.; other subordinators do not conform to a larger group behavior but are in a small number: *wanyi, zongran*. One can always focus on each in psycholinguistic experiments to reveal the motivation underneath or run a computational model to identify the causal relationship between different factors. Other types of subordinators are also worth a large-scale corpus study and diverse research perspectives to reveal a complete picture of Chinese inter-clausal anaphora.

Acknowledgements. I extend my sincere thanks to Jeroen van de weijer, Xu Yulong, Wu Fuyun, Brendan Gillon, Cheng Wei, Yang Chao, Yuan Chenjie, Liang Yiming, Wang Yixin and reviewers for their advice. This work is supported by the Chinese National Major Social Science Project (17ZDA027); the Chinese National Youth Social Science Project (17CYY017); the Fundamental Research Funds for the Central Universities in China (KY01X0222017095); and Innovative Research Team of Shanghai International Studies University (2020114050).

References

1. Chao, Y.R.: A Grammar of Spoken Chinese. UC Press, Berkeley (1968)
2. Zhu, D.X.: Lecture Notes on Grammar. The Commercial Press, Beijing (1982)
3. Huang, C.T.J.: Logical relations in Chinese and the theory of grammar. Doctoral Dissertation, MIT (1982)
4. Huang, C.T.J.: Logical Relations in Chinese and the Theory of Grammar. Garland, New York (1998)
5. Huang, Y.: A neo-Gricean pragmatic theory of anaphora. J. Linguist. 27(2), 301–335 (1991)
6. Tsao, F.F.: Sentence and Clause Structure in Chinese: A Functional Perspective. Student Book Co., Taipei (1990)
7. Xu, Y.L.: Resolving third-person anaphora in Chinese texts: Towards a functional-pragmatic model. Doctoral Dissertation, The Hong Kong Polytechnic University (1995)
8. Xu, Y.L.: Inter-clausal anaphora in Chinese complex sentences. Contemp. Linguist. (2), 97–107 (2003)
9. Xu, Y.L.: Towards a Functional-pragmatic Model of Discourse Anaphora Resolution: A Study Based on a Data-base Driven Analysis of Chinese Folk Stories and Newspaper Articles. Shanghai Foreign Language Education Press, Shanghai (2004)
10. Wang, C.H.: The marker of Chinese conditional sentences and its order. Linguist. Sci. 9(3), 265–278 (2010)
11. Xu, X.D., Ni, C.B., Chen, L.J.: The influence of topic structure and verb-based implicit causality on pronoun resolution in Mandarin Chinese: Evidence from sentence production and comprehension. Mod. Foreign Lang. (4), 331–339 (2013)
12. Xu, X.D., Chen, L.J., Ni, C.B.: How is pronoun resolution modulated by topic structures and verb-based implicit causality in Mandarin Chinese? An ERP investigation. Foreign Lang. Teach. Res. (5), 323–334 (2017)
13. Chen, S.T.: Inter-clausal Anaphora in Chinese: The Case of Conditionals. Doctoral Dissertation, Shanghai International Studies University (2012)
14. Chen, S.T.: Re-approaching Chinese inter-clausal anaphora: the case of conditional sentences. Foreign Stud. (6), 15–21 (2016)
15. Center for Chinese Linguistics Corpus online. http://ccl.pku.edu.cn:8080/ccl_corpus/. Accessed 01 Mar 2011
16. Sinclair, J.: Reading Concordances: An Introduction. Longman, London (2003)
17. Greenbaum, S., Gerald, N., Michael, W.: Complement clauses in English. In: Thomas, J., Mick, S. (eds.) Using Corpora for Language Research: Studies in Honour of Geoffrey Leech, pp. 76–91. Longman, London (1996)
18. Stassen, L.: The problem of cross-linguistic identification. In: Song, J.J. (ed.) The Oxford Handbook of Linguistic Typology, pp. 90–99. Oxford University Press, Oxford (2011)
19. Huang, B.R., Liao, X.D.: Modern Chinese, Volume II, 3rd edn. High Education Press, Beijing (2002)
20. Dancygier, B.: Conditionals and concessives. In: Fisiak, J. (ed.) Papers and Studies in Contrastive Linguistics 24, pp. 111–121. Adam Mickiewicz University, Poznan (1988)
21. Ariel, M.: Accessing Noun-phrase Antecedents. Routledge, London (1990)

Research on the Distribution and Characteristics of Negative Quasi-Prefixes in Different Registers

Yonghui Xie[1,2,3] (iD) and Erhong Yang[1,2(✉)]

[1] China National Language Monitoring and Research Print Media Center,
Beijing Language and Culture University, Beijing, China
201921198629@stu.blcu.edu.cn, yerhong@blcu.edu.cn
[2] Beijing Advanced Innovation Center for Language Resources, Beijing
Language and Culture University, Beijing, China
[3] School of Information Science, Beijing Language and Culture University,
Beijing, China

Abstract. Morphology refers to the study of words in terms of their inflection and formation; Chinese is an isolating language whose grammatical features mainly include the word order and function words. The study of Chinese affixes is well-established, whilst the study of word-forming quasi-affixes continues to gradually evolve. The current research uses both quantitative and qualitative methods in the form of a literature review and corpus search. The lexical units with the negative quasi-prefixes "非(fēi)-", "不(bù)-" and "无(wú)-" respectively were counted in the literary, scientific and technological, and microblog registers from Beijing Languages and Cultures University (BCC) corpus, and their similarities and differences were analyzed. Finally, the laws of distribution characteristics were identified, for example, "非(fēi)-" is dominant in the scientific and technological register; "不(bù)-" is most frequent in the microblog register, with a strong colloquial style; "无(wú)-" has the highest frequency in the scientific and technological register due to its strong written style.

Keywords: Negative Quasi-prefix · Register · Distribution characteristic

1 Introduction

Chinese is an isolating language, also known as a morphology-free language. The main characteristic of Chinese is its lack of morphological changes, while grammatical means are chiefly reflected by the word order and function words. Although the affix is a major component of morphology, research into this area first emerged when Modern Chinese was initially formed. By the end of the 20th century, some linguists had conducted further in-depth research on quasi-affixes (e.g., [1–3]). These studies revealed that quasi-affixes possess the following characteristics: semantic grammaticalization, multi-layered adhesion units, fixed word-formation positions, and potential abilities of strong analogy. These features can be used as the criteria to judge quasi-affixes.

© Springer Nature Switzerland AG 2022
M. Dong et al. (Eds.): CLSW 2021, LNAI 13250, pp. 376–387, 2022.
https://doi.org/10.1007/978-3-031-06547-7_29

1.1 Negative Quasi-Prefixes in Chinese

Negation is a well-established issue in philosophical research. Words expressing "affirmation" and "negation" are amongst the most basic forms of judging semantics and conveying information; meanwhile they are the first to be exposed during language learning. Therefore, this current research takes negative quasi-prefixes as the research objects. The classification summary of negative quasi-prefixes by some scholars is given in Table 1.

Table 1. Summary of the negative quasi-prefixes.

Negative quasi-prefixes	Quantity
难(nán)-, 不(bù)-, 无(wú)-, 非(fēi)-, 反(fǎn)- [1]	5
非(fēi)-, 无(wú)-, 不(bù)-, 反(fǎn)- [2]	4
反(fǎn)-, 非(fēi)- [4]	2
反(fǎn)-, 非(fēi)-, 伪(wěi)- [5]	3
反(fǎn)-, 非(fēi)-, 伪(wěi)- [6]	3

Evidently, different criteria are employed to judge negative quasi-prefixes. Built on the recognition rate, this current research focused on the negative quasi-prefixes "不(bù)-", "无(wú)-" and "非(fēi) -".

After entering "汉语(hànyǔ)[Chinese]", "否定(fǒudìng)[negation]" and "词缀(cízhuì)[affix]" into the China National Knowledge Infrastructure (CNKI) database, a total of 30 papers were retrieved, most of which were comparative studies of negative quasi-prefixes in two languages. For example, [7] conducted a comparative study on negative prefixes in Chinese and Korean, taking "非(fēi)-", "不(bù)-" and "无(wú)-" for example; [8] compared English-Chinese negative affixes; and [9] studied the expression of the Chinese structure of the quasi-affix "非(fēi)+X" in Uyghur. Moreover, previous studies on the quasi-affix "+X" structure primarily concentrated on a grammatical perspective, including part of speech, syntactic functions, structural relations, and grammaticalization processes. In contrast, the current research exceeds the grammatical level and explores the deeper semantic and pragmatic features of negative quasi-prefixes by comparing different language registers.

1.2 Language Register

The concept of register was first put forward by [10] based on studies of bilingualism. [11] eventually popularized the term register, subsequently introduced to China by [12] in 1977. The language register was further defined by [13], as it was stated that the language we speak and write changes in accordance with the situation. According to [14], by examining the use of language in a particular discourse, the corresponding discourse genre (cultural context) or register that the discourse belongs can be identified. Entering "语域(yǔyù)[register]" as the topic in the CNKI database locates research papers that generally cover the translation register. For example, [15] made use of dialogue from a typical character in The Metro, by Joseph Eugene Stiglitz, to demonstrate the necessity and feasibility of applying register theory to the translation of dialogue in novels.

Currently, there is a lack of research regarding negative quasi-affixes in the Chinese language from the perspective of the register. Therefore, the current research aims to explore the similarities and differences of negative quasi-prefixes in different registers using mixed methods, and research findings can provide references for multidimensional analysis of registers in Chinese.

2   Method and Design

The conclusions stated in previous language features studies were mainly deduced through introspection; however, the current research utilizes a large-scale corpus by combining quantitative and qualitative approaches, which is a more reliable process of establishing conclusions. The BCC corpus [16] was selected as the source corpus as it contains five registers: literature, the press, microblog, science and technology, and ancient Chinese. For the current research, literature (3 billion words), science and technology (3 billion words), and microblog (3 billion words) were chosen. The literary corpus was derived from domestic and foreign literary works, with a lyrical language that emphasizes phonetic harmony, image, and rhythm; the scientific and technological corpus was derived from domestic academic journals, comprising a formal language that is general, abstract, and simple; and finally, the microblog corpus was taken from the Sina microblog in 2013, involving a contemporary, networked, rich and diverse, humorous, and entertaining language. Overall, language registers characteristics of each of these three corpora differ considerably.

The first stage of the research focused on the structures of the negative quasi-prefixes "非(fēi)-", "不(bù)-" and "无(wú)-" combined with grammatical units to form words, which are discussed in the literature review. In regard to the literary, scientific and technological, and microblog sub-corpus of the BCC corpus, the structure of "affixes+grammatical unit" was employed as the input to determine the total frequency of cases and to retrieve the corresponding high-frequency lexical units. Differences of using the above structure were subsequently compared and potential reasons for these differences have been presented. Finally, the three negative quasi-prefixes were compared in the same register to identify the word preference of each register.

3   Statistics and Analysis

3.1   The Negative Quasi-Prefix "非(fēi)-"

In The Eight Hundred Words in Modern Chinese, [17] highlighted that when "非(fēi)" is used as a prefix, it indicates a definition of "not belonging to a certain scope" and can be implemented to construct a noun. [17] also summarized four cases where the prefix "非(fēi)" could be combined with the following grammatical units: "非(fēi) + noun", "非(fēi) + noun + noun", "非(fēi) + verb + noun" and "非(fēi) + adjective + noun".

Thus, it has been determined that "非(fēi)" is generally followed by a nominal component. [18] claimed that this kind of combination feature is influenced by the position of "非(fēi)" as a negative adverb that can modify a noun when it was not previously grammaticalized.

Table 2. The numbers of "非(fēi) + grammatical units" in different registers.

	非(fēi) + n[a]	非(fēi) + n + n	非(fēi) + v + n	非(fēi) + a + n	Total number
Literary register	3,535	602	1,416	333	5,886
Scientific and technological register	255,460	121,258	18,082	18,194	412,994
Microblog register	44,692	12,785	5,655	3,324	66,456
Total number	303,687	134,645	25,153	21,851	485,336

[a]The list of parts of speech used in BCC corpus can be found on http://bcc.blcu.edu.cn/help#pos.

Table 3. High-frequency lexical units with "非(fēi)".

Science and technological register		Microblog register		Literary register	
Lexical units	Tokens	Lexical units	Tokens	Lexical units	Tokens
非公有制 fēigōngyǒuzhì non-public ownership	19,116	非主流 fēizhǔliú non-mainstream	7,020	非理性 fēilǐxìng irrational	88
非理性 fēilǐxìng irrational	10,359	非机动车 fēijīdòngchē non-motorized vehicles	1,263	非正义 fēizhèngyì injustice	66
非政府 fēizhèngfǔ non-government	4,166	非物质 fēiwùzhì intangible	930	非物质 fēiwùzhì intangible	42
非国有企业 fēiguóyǒuqǐyè non-state-owned enterprise	3,851	非专业 fēizhuānyè non-professional	468	非人力 fēirénlì inhuman power	33
非银行 fēiyínháng non-bank	3,792	非人类 fēirénlèi non-human	427	非暴力 fēibàolì non-violent	32
非生产性 fēishēngchǎnxìng nonproductive	2,057	非理性 fēilǐxìng irrational	418	非人类 fēirénlèi non-human	28

Table 2 presents the statistical results of "非(fēi) + grammatical units" in the literary, scientific and technological, and microblog corpus based on the four selected structures. The results show that the quasi-prefix "非(fēi)" appeared most frequently in the scientific and technological register, followed by the microblog register, but was the least frequent in the literary register. The frequency gap of this quasi-prefix between the literary register and the other two registers is large. The high frequency identified in the scientific and technological register implies that "非(fēi)" has an obviously written intensity, which corroborates research viewpoint of [18] that the quasi-prefix "非(fēi)" is mainly used in disciplines being exploration such as science and technology.

The top six high-frequency lexical units with "非(fēi)" from the three registers are shown in Table 3, whereby the most high-frequency lexical unit in the scientific and technological register was found to be "非公有制"; however, example sentences of this lexical unit were not found in the literary register and only 75 example sentences were retrieved from the microblog register. There were also few or no example of other high-frequency lexical units, such as "非国有企业" and "非银行". This suggests that lexical units with "非(fēi)" in the scientific and technological register has a strong uniqueness. Furthermore, in terms of pragmatics, lexical units with "非(fēi)" in the scientific and technological register present a more subtle and euphemistic expression which makes a rhetorical effect than the direct use of their antonyms. For example, "非公有制" and "非国有企业" mean the same as "私有制(sīyǒuzhì)[private ownership]" and "私有企业(sīyǒuqǐyè)[private enterprise]", but in the age of clear consciousness, the use of "非公有制" and "非国有企业" was regarded as more appropriate. In addition, the lexical units with "非(fēi)" emphasize a particular state; examples of this include "非公有制" referring to the state of economy, "非理性" referring to the state of mind, and "非生产性" referring to the activity and economic state in the context of material consumption.

In the microblog register, the most high-frequency lexical unit was "非主流", which subsequently links to other high-frequency lexical units like "非主流发型[non-mainstream hairstyle]", "非主流女生[non-mainstream girl]" and "非主流个性[non-mainstream personality]". In the literary register, only four example sentences of "非主流" were found, and although approximately 1,000 example sentences were identified in the scientific and technological register, this was still considerably fewer than the 7,000 example sentences in the microblog register. No example sentences were found in the literary register of "非机动车", the second high-frequency lexical unit from the microblog register. The most frequent lexical unit in the literary register was "非理性", which also appeared in the scientific and technological and microblog registers. Other high-frequency lexical units, such as "非正义", "非物质" and "非人力", were identified in the other two registers. The results imply that the lexical units with "非(fēi)" in the literary register is not characteristic, which would also explain its low frequency.

In summary, the token frequency of lexical units with "非(fēi)" identified in the scientific and technological register was the largest, in which high-frequency lexical units presented a strong written characteristic; meanwhile, lexical units with "非(fēi)" appeared more often in the microblog register than in the literary register, because high-frequency lexical units such as "非主流" appeared distinctively in the microblog register, while the lexical units found in the literary register were not unique.

3.2   The Negative Quasi-prefix "不(bù)-"

[3] emphasized the inability of the adverb "不(bù)" to be combined with a noun, whilst the affix "不(bù)" can be combined with a noun to form a new word. [19] also highlighted that "不(bù)" is an affix when it serves to form an adjective. Overall, the current research suggests that the negative quasi-prefix "不(bù)" is most commonly combined with nouns or noun morphemes to construct adjectives.

Table 4. The numbers of "不(bù) + grammatical units" in different registers.

	不(bù) + n	不(bù) + Tg[a]	Total number
Literary register	9157	1086	10243
Scientific and technological register	93268	20433	113701
Microblog register	184131	53402	237533
Total number	286556	74921	361477

[a]In the BCC corpus, "Tg" stands for noun morpheme.

Table 5. High-frequency lexical units with "不(bù)".

Microblog register		Scientific and technological register		Literary register	
Lexical units	Tokens	Lexical units	Tokens	Lexical units	Tokens
不规律 bùguīlǜ irregularity	1453	不洁 bùjié uncleanness	1789	不正义 búzhèngyì injustice	318
不确定性 búquèdìngxìng nondeterminacy	1088	不均匀性 bùjūnyúnxìng unevenness	1639	不洁 bùjié uncleanness	165
不专业 bùzhuānyè unprofessional	713	不对称性 búduìchènxìng asymmetry	1505	不雅 bùyǎ indelicacy	152
不仁 bùrén unkind	621	不可逆性 bùkěnìxìng irreversibility	1191	不恭 bùgōng irreverence	86
不人 bùrén no one	389	不合理性 bùhélǐxìng unreasonableness	1139	不人 bùrén no one	66
不淑女 bùshūnǚ unladylike	339	不一致性 bùyīzhìxìng inconsistency	957	不仁 bùrén unkind	53

Table 4 shows the statistical results of lexical units with "不(bù)" retrieved from the literary, scientific and technological, and microblog corpus based on the two structures: "不(bù) + noun", "不(bù) + Nominal morpheme". The greatest number of lexical units deriving from the negative quasi-prefix "不(bù)" was found in the microblog register, followed by the scientific and technological register, whilst the lowest number of these lexical units was identified in the literary register. Consequently, "不(bù)" can be regarded as relatively more colloquial.

Table 5 displays the first six high-frequency lexical units with "不(bù)". From this, the lexical units in the scientific and technological register generally include suffix "-性 (xìng)", such as "不均匀性", "不可逆性" and "不合理性". The five high-frequency cases of "不(bù) + X + 性(xìng)" category in Table 5 were also searched in the microblog register and the literary register, the results of which are shown in Table 6. The findings show that the co-occurrence of the quasi-prefix "不(bù)" and the quasi-suffix "-性(xìng)" in one word is typical of the scientific and technological register, but is less characteristic of the microblog register, and is even rarer in the literary register as no examples were retrieved. [20] stated that the nominal "X + 性(xìng)" structure tends to imply an abstract nature or concept, and should be considered as a marginal member of the noun category. This conclusion is consistent with the feature of linguistic generalization and abstraction in the scientific and technological register.

Table 6. Statistics of the "不(bù) + X + 性(xìng)" structure in different registers.

	不均匀性 bùjūnyúnxìng unevenness	不对称性 búduìchènxìng asymmetry	不可逆性 bùkěnìxìng irreversibility	不合理性 bùhélǐxìng unreasonableness	不一致性 bùyīzhìxìng inconsistency	Total number
Scientific and technological register	1,639	1,505	1,191	1,139	957	6,431
Literary register	0	0	0	0	3	3
Microblog register	0	43	16	21	1	81
Total number	1,639	1,548	1,207	1,160	961	6,515

Within the literary register, the high-frequency lexical units with "不(bù)" express literary colors, such as "不洁", "不雅" and "不恭", which is related to the pursuit of artistic beauty and rhythmic beauty in literary texts, thereby producing more beautiful and readable texts. In contrast to cases of "不(bù)" in the literary and scientific and technological registers, the microblog register possesses more diversified and open lexical units, such as "不仁" with literary color, "不确定性" which is characteristic of the scientific and technological register, and "不淑女" which is absent from the other two registers. Thus, the microblog register was found to have the highest number of words that were combined with the quasi-prefix "不(bù)".

Moreover, a certain commonality was identified in the semantic choice of "不(bù)" cases within the literary and microblog registers. For example, "不(bù) + polar opposites" [20], as "X" and "不(bù) + X" represent two polar opposites, and a mediating concept is usually present in between. For example, "不规律" versus "规律 (guīlǜ)[regular]" in the microblog register serves as two extremes; in addition, there can also be "很规律(hěnguīlǜ) [much regular]", "非常规律(fēichángguīlǜ) [very regular]" and similar intermediary terms. Furthermore, from a syntactic perspective, "不(bù) + X" is modified by adverbs related to degree, also representing a comparative level. Other high-frequency lexical units, such as "不正义", "不雅", "不专业" and "不仁", can be modified by adverbs of degree such as "very", "much", "extremely" and "somewhat".

3.3 The Negative Quasi-Prefix "无(wú)-"

According to *The Eight Hundred Words in Modern Chinese* [17], "无(wú)" emerges in two forms as an affix: "无(wú) + noun + noun", which forms an overall noun; and "无(wú) + noun + verb", which also forms an overall noun.

Table 7. The numbers of "无(wú) + grammatical units" in different registers.

	无(wú) + n + n	无(wú) + n + v	Total number
Literary register	778	2,876	3,654
Scientific and technological register	74,718	42,502	117,220
Microblog register	23,213	30,853	54,066
Total number	98,709	76,231	174,940

Table 8. High-frequency lexical units with "无(wú)".

Scientific and technological register		Microblog register		Literary register	
Lexical units	Tokens	Lexical units	Tokens	Lexical units	Tokens
无纸化 *wúzhǐhuà* paperless	1,362	无头骑士 *wútóuqíshì* dullahan	267	无韵诗 *wúyùnshī* rhyme-free poem	15
无菌条件 *wújūntiáojiàn* aseptic conditions	1,009	无油配方 *wúyóupèifāng* oil-free formula	244	无感情色彩 *wúgǎnqíngsècǎi* emotionless	11
无菌生理盐水 *wújūnshēnglǐyánshuǐ* sterile saline	709	无字幕版 *wúzìmùbǎn* unsubtitled version	212	无血缘关系 *wúxuèyuánguānxì* unrelation	11
无水酒精 *wúshuǐjiǔjīng* alcohol anhydrous	676	无字歌 *wúzìgē* song without words	212	无事人 *wúshìrén* people with nothing to do	10
无菌水 *wújūnshuǐ* sterile water	602	无级变速 *wújíbiànsù* continuously variable transmission	145	无词歌 *wúcígē* song without words	8
无障碍设施 *wúzhàngài shèshī* barrier-free facilities	463	无糖口香糖 *wútángkǒuxiāngtáng* sugar-free chewing gum	123	无利害关系 *wúlìhàiguānxì* disinterested	7

The statistical results of locating "无(wú)" cases in the literary, scientific and technological, and microblog corpus based on the two previously mentioned structures are presented in Table 7. The results show that the quasi-prefix "无(wú)" appears most frequently in the scientific and technological register, followed by the microblog register, and is least common in the literary register. This suggests that the quasi-prefix "无(wú)" depicts a more formal written meaning.

The high-frequency lexical units with quasi-prefix "无(wú)" are shown in Table 8, from each of the different registers. The lexical units have distinct characteristics that are unique to each register, all of which conform to the linguistic style of their respective registers. In the scientific and technological register, the words "无菌条件", "无水酒精" and "无菌水" reflect the biological and natural discipline of the register. However, the frequency of these word types in the microblog and literary registers showed only two examples in the former register and none in the latter register. Overall, the prefix "无(wú)" emerged more frequently in the scientific and technological register than the others. In regard to the microblog register, the words were of a lively, playful, and humorous nature, and would be regarded as highly entertaining. For example, "无头骑士" depicted in Table 8 refers to one of the most famous gods and monsters in Irish folklore, "无字歌" refers to a song that lacks lyrics, and "无油配方" is a description of ingredients found in household products. In addition, the lexical units "无韵诗" "无感情色彩" and "无词歌", found in the literary register, are representative of the characteristics of poetry and literary works; nonetheless, these high-frequency lexical units are relatively frequent in the other two registers, and so, the total frequency in the literary register was lower than in the scientific and technological register and the microblog register.

A commonality was deduced in the semantic choice of "无(wú)" for the lexical units in all three of the registers; for instance, "无(wú) + quality", opposing "有(yǒu) [have] + X" [20], indicates the negation of the existence of a certain quality. For example, "无水酒精" in the scientific and technological register implies that the quality of "酒精" is "无水", whilst "无字歌", "无糖口香糖", "无血缘关系" and "无韵诗" all indicate qualities and characteristics and emphasize attribution.

3.4   Negative Quasi-Prefixes in the Three Registers

Table 9 displays the frequency results of the three negative quasi-prefixes in all three registers, whereby there is a consistent frequency ranking of negative quasi-prefixes in the literary and microblog registers: "不(bù)-" > "非(fēi)-" > "无(wú)-". Moreover, "不(bù)-" was found to be significantly more frequent than the other two affixes. This finding demonstrates that the negative quasi-prefixes in the literary and microblog registers are more inclined to the colloquial "不(bù)-". In regard to the scientific and technological register, the ranking is: "非(fēi)-" > "无(wú)-" > "不(bù)-", where "非(fēi)-" is considerably more frequent than the other two affixes. This indicates that the choice of negative quasi-prefixes in this register is more prone to the formal "非(fēi)-". The balanced register formed by the three registers presents a final ranking of: "非(fēi)-" > "不(bù)-" > "无(wú)-". The difference between "非(fēi)-" and "不(bù)-" is insignificant, which is compatible with the highest-ranked negative quasi-prefixes in each of the three registers.

Overall, the negative quasi-prefixes were found to be most prevalent in the scientific and technological register, followed by the microblog register, and finally, in the literary register, thus showing the considerable difference between the literary register and the other two registers. This is attributed to the expressions of "affirmation" and "negation" in the scientific and technological register being more clear, logical, and precise. Furthermore, the microblog register comprises rich and diverse language, and so the number of lexical units is moderate; in contrast, the language expressions found in the literary register are relatively more subtle, and so the inclusion of "negative" expressions is relatively vague; there is also a tendency to adopt euphemistic words to convey negative meanings.

Table 9. Statistics of three negative quasi-prefixes in the three registers.

	Literary register	Scientific and technological register	Microblog register	Total number
"非(fēi) -"	5,886	412,994	66,456	485,336
"不(bù)-"	10,243	113,701	237,533	361,477
"无(wú)-"	3,654	117,220	54,066	174,940
Total number	19,783	643,915	358,055	1,021,753

4 Conclusion

The distribution characteristics of lexical units with negative quasi-prefixes "非(fēi)-", "不(bù)-", and "无(wú)-" have been explored in the context of literary, scientific and technological, and microblog registers from the BCC corpus. The following conclusions have been drawn based on the current research's findings.

1. The predominance of "非(fēi)-" in the scientific and technological register reveals its own unique area of application and highlights the formal style. Also, lexical units with "非(fēi)-" are deemed more subtle and euphemistic than the direct use of antonyms, which make a rhetorical effect.
2. The most prevalent prefix in the microblog register was "不(bù)-", which has a strong colloquial style. The structure of "不(bù) + X + 性(xìng)" was identified frequently in the scientific and technological register, which aligns with linguistic generalization and abstraction of this type of text. Furthermore, high-frequency lexical units detected in the literary and microblog registers are characterized by the "不(bù) + polarity opposition".
3. "无(wú)-" was most common in the scientific and technological register due to its strong written color. The high-frequency lexical units with "无(wú)-" denote typical aspects of each of the three registers: biology and nature are depicted in the scientific and technological register, living things are depicted in the microblog register, and poetry and literature are depicted in the literary register. These all have the characteristic of "无(wú) + quality".

4. Literary and microblog registers showed a greater preference for "不(bù)-" in regard to negative quasi-prefixes, whilst "非(fēi)-" was preferred in the scientific and technological register.
5. Regarding the overall distribution of negative quasi-prefixes, the scientific and technological register showed the greatest level of distribution, whilst the literary register showed the least. This finding is associated with the linguistic expression habits maintained by each of the registers. The scientific and technological register was found to include strict and precise terms which are clearly defined as right or wrong; alternatively, the literary register used relatively subtle terms and generally implemented euphemisms as a way of conveying negative interpretations.

Overall, this research has demonstrated that there are differences between the negative quasi-prefixes "非(fēi)-", "不(bù)-" and "无(wú)-" in the literary, scientific and technological, and microblog registers. The research findings can contribute to the ongoing analysis of register variation. Currently, this field of study primarily adopts a multidimensional analysis, whereby registers are distinguished by analyzing the usage discrepancy of various sets of co-occurring features, which is regarded as more reliable than differentiating registers based on individual linguistic features. Therefore, a more extensive and absolute pattern of co-occurrence features for multidimensional analysis of the Chinese language can be obtained by verifying whether other linguistic features are discriminative for these three registers, and by ascertaining whether there is co-occurrence between certain distinguishing features.

Acknowledgments. This work is supported by the 2020 Key Project of the 13th Five-Year Plan of the State Language Commission (ZDI135-131), the 2019 Key Project of the 13th Five-Year Plan of the State Language Commission (ZDI135-105), the project of Beijing Advanced Innovation Center for Language Resources (TYZ19005), and the Innovation Fund for Chinese and Foreign Graduate Student (20YCX140).

References

1. Lv, S.-X.: Problems of Chinese grammatical analysis. The Commercial Press, Beijing (1979). (in Chinese)
2. Guo, F.-L.: Prefixes and Suffixes of Modern Chinese. Studies of the Chinese Language, Beijing (1983). (in Chinese)
3. Ren, X.-L.: Chinese Word Formation. China Social Science Press, Beijing (1981). (in Chinese)
4. Tang, Z.-X.: The Synchronic Status of Contemporary Chinese Words and Their Changes Fudan University Press, Shanghai (2000). (in Chinese)
5. Chen, G.-L.: On Chinese Morphology. Xue Lin Press, Shanghai (2001). (in Chinese)
6. Zhang, B.: A New Edition of Modern Chinese. Fudan University Press, Shanghai (2008). (in Chinese)
7. Yan, S.-H.: A comparative study of Chinese-Korean negative prefixes "fei-", "bu-", "wu-" as examples. Nankai J. Linguist. **1**, 116–126 (2016). (in Chinese)
8. Zhang, N.: A study on teaching Chinese noun suffixes to native English learners based on Chinese-English comparison. Liaoning Normal University (2019). (in Chinese)

9. Yao, J.-X.: Expression of Chinese quasi-affix "fei+X" structure in Uyghur. Mod. Lang. J. (2015). (in Chinese)
10. Ure, J., Ellis, J.: Register in descriptive linguistics and linguistic sociology. Issues Sociolinguist. 198 (1977)
11. Halliday, M.A.K.: The linguistic sciences and language teaching. 75 (1964)
12. Fang, L., Hu, Z.-L., Xu, K-R.: Talking about the three systems of modern English grammar and communication grammar. Lang. Teach. Linguist. Stud. 06 (1977). (in Chinese)
13. Hu, Z.-L., Zhu, Y.-S., Zhang, D.-L., et al.: Introduction to Systematic Functional Grammar. Hunan Education Press, Changsha (1989). (in Chinese)
14. Huang, G.-W.: Theory and practice of discourse analysis, 28. Shanghai Foreign Language Education Press, Shanghai (2001). (in Chinese)
15. Chen, Q.-L.: A study on the translation of novel dialogues from the perspective of register theory. Nanjing University (2014). (in Chinese)
16. Xun, E.-D., Rao, G.-Q., Xiao, X.-Y., Zang, J.-J.: The development of BCC corpus in the context of big data. Corpus Linguist. 3(01), 93–109+118 (2016). (in Chinese)
17. Lv, S.-X.: Eight Hundred Words in Modern Chinese. The Commercial Press, Beijing (1999). (in Chinese)
18. Wan, G.-R.: A study of prefix "fei+X." J. Hubei Normal Coll. (Philos. Soc. Sci. Edition) 32 (03), 50–54 (2012). (in Chinese)
19. Ma, Q.-Z.: Ma Qingzhu Volume, Selected Works of a Famous Middle-Aged Linguist. Anhui Education Press, Hefei (2002). (in Chinese)
20. Zhang, W.-R.: The mechanism of producing the Chinese quasi-affixes "sex" and "chemistry." Mod. Lang. 11, 32–37 (2019). (in Chinese)

A Quantitative Study on Mono-Valent Noun and Its Ellipsis

Xiangyu Chi, Gaoqi Rao[✉], and Endong Xun

Beijing Language and Culture University, Bejing, China
{raogaoqi,xunendong}@blcu.edu.cn

Abstract. Based on large scale data of Chinese with syntactic structure annotation, this paper conducts a quantitative study on the ellipsis phenomena of mono-valent nouns and analyzes the reasons for the ellipsis from the cognitive perspective. We firstly developed the word list by looking up the synonyms of the mono-valent nouns that were cited in *The New Compilation of Synonym Cilin (Ci Lin)*. On this basis, millions of annotated data in Beijing Language and Culture University (BLCU) Treebank 1.0 was selected. Sentences in which mono-valent nouns are omitted or redundant in the syntactic level were screened out with the assistant of specific syntactic tags, so as to verify the ellipsis rules of mono-valent nouns. Finally, from the viewpoint of grammatical metonymy, this paper explains the ellipsis of mono-valent nouns and holds that it is related to the salience of the things they refer to.

Keywords: Mono-valent noun · Ellipsis · Metonymic chain

1 Introduction

The study of ellipsis is an important part of natural language processing (NLP). Ellipsis refers to the phenomenon that people leave some language elements in sentences intentionally omitted to make the language concise and brief without altering the meaning in a specific context. However, it is difficult for systems to understand a text containing a large number of omitted words. This paper focuses on the ellipsis of monovalent nouns in valency grammar. It is planned to develop an exhaustive word list of mono-valent nouns, explore the nouns that can be omitted, describe the circumstances for omissions to occur with the assistant of the real large-scale corpus. And at the cognitive level, the causes for ellipsis are explained to contribute to the language resources and format templates for the identification and recovery of ellipsis, which helps to improve the recognition accuracy of ellipsis items and build up the foundation for the performance of other researches in NLP.

2 Related Works

The concept of valence was borrowed from chemistry and it was introduced to linguistics to show how many nominal components belonging to different semantic roles could be controlled by a single verb. The concept of "valence" was firstly introduced to

M. Dong et al. (Eds.): CLSW 2021, LNAI 13250, pp. 388–398, 2022.
https://doi.org/10.1007/978-3-031-06547-7_30

the study of Chinese grammar in Zhu [1]. In 1980, Zhu established the famous formula for calculating the ambiguity index of Chinese "的" structure:

$$P \quad n \quad m$$

In this formula, p represents the ambiguity index of the "的" structure, n represents the valence number of the verb, and m represents the number of nominal components that reflect the valence of the verb in the "的" structure. When p = 0, namely, when all the valences of the verbs appear in "的" structure, the "的" structure cannot refer to anything, but can only form a non-appositives attributive structure (e.g.,他开车的技术→* 他开车的, 他教小王数学的时候→*他教小王数学的).

At present, academia pays more attention to the study of the valency of verbs. The scope of valency research has gradually extended to nouns. Yuan [2, 3] firstly proposed the connotation, denotation, grammatical features, special sentence patterns and elliptical rules of mono-valent nouns and bivalent nouns. Liu [4] pointed out that the dependent noun of mono-valent nouns is presented mainly in the surface structure of sentence in the form of attribute and subject, which forms different sentence patterns. There are some close conversion relations among those sentence patterns. The formal standard for defining bivalent nouns was provided by Geng [5]. Then, Song [6] enriched the theory of spreading activation and provided a more formal explanation for the ellipsis of mono-valent nouns by using the semantic generative mechanism in Generative Lexical Theory. Recently, a new definition of mono-valent nouns was given by Wang [7]. The semantic properties and relevant syntactic issues of mono-valent nouns in valency grammar were revisited. In this chapter, the definition, grammatical characteristics and elliptical rules of mono-valent nouns are provided.

2.1 Definition, Classification and Grammatical Characteristics of Mono-valent Nouns

According to Yuan [3], mono-valent nouns are defined as nouns that indicate a certain object and at the same time imply a certain dependency between one object and another. For example, 爸爸, a person who is someone's male parent. Yuan divided mono-valent nouns into three categories: kinship nouns, such as 妈妈, 丈夫; property nouns, such as 质量, 脾气; and partitive nouns, such as 脚, 尾巴. Meanwhile, it summarized the grammatical characteristics of mono-valent nouns: one is that when a mono-valent noun exists in syntactic combination, another noun is usually used as the governing constituent to co-occur with them. The other is that it can omit in the syntactic surface but leaving the semantics unchanged.

However, it was argued by Yu [8] that when defining mono-valent nouns, not only the static semantic structure but also the noun's semantic orientation should be taken into account. Only when there is a relationship of dependency between the noun and another noun and it is implemented as definiteness in the semantic and syntactic level, the noun could be regarded as a mono-valent noun. Otherwise, it is considered as a zero-valent noun, such as sea, sky and air. It was believed by Wang [7] that monovalent nouns can be defined by two semantic characters: [-alienable] and [+ possessive] from the perspective of the possessive relationship. For instance, 张三的爸爸, the possessive relationship between "Zhang San" and "father" is inalienable. And [+ possessive] means the mono-valent noun 爸爸 presents in the "有" sentence pattern, such as 张三有父亲.

2.2   Ellipsis of Mono-Valent Nouns in Sentences

Yuan [3] emphatically discussed the ellipsis of mono-valent nouns in some sentences and its microcosmic mechanism of semantic activation. In this paper, the mono-valent nouns are always omitted under 3 conditions: 1) the ellipsis of partitive nouns playing the semantic role of a tool (e.g., 用眼睛看了一下→看了一下); 2) the ellipsis of partitive nouns playing the semantic role of a place (e.g., 头上戴着帽子→戴着帽子); and 3) the implication of property nouns in adjective-noun collocations. (e.g., 李伟身材很高大→李伟很高大). According to Yuan [3], the reason for the ellipsis of partitive nouns is that the semantic structure of verbs contains the concept of partitive nouns. And the ellipsis of property nouns in adjective-noun collocations is because the adjective is monosemous and can modify only one attribute.

Liu and Xing [9] explained the implication of property nouns in Chinese "比" sentence. They held that when the adjective can modify multiple attributes, the nouns qualified by basic meaning can be omitted, but the nouns qualified by derived meaning are usually redundant in the surface structure of sentence. Besides, Liu [10] described the ellipsis and redundancy of property nouns and partitive nouns. According to Liu [10], the noun1[subject]+noun2 [attribute]+adjective[predicate] structure implies that the attribute nouns are restricted by subjects and predicates. In terms of the ellipsis of property nouns modified by polysemous adjectives. Liu argues that it has no association with whether the noun is modified by the basic meaning or the derived meaning, but is related to human cognition. When the adjective describes an attribute that people focus on in a specific context, attribute nouns can be omitted. The ellipsis of partitive nouns which are restricted by subject or predicate often occurs in the noun1[subject] +noun2[attribute]+verb[predicate] structure. With collocation frequency of three kinds of color adjectives, Song [6] showed that collocation and its frequency would affect what nouns would be modified by the derived meaning of polysemes. Wang (7) argued that the ellipsis of partitive nouns and property nouns result from the semantic entailment of predicates towards the nouns, rather than grammatical characters of mono-valent nouns.

3   Data Selection and Word List Construction

3.1   BLCU Treebank 1.0

The high-quality annotated data was selected from the BLCU Treebank, a multidomain discourse-based Chinese chunk bank. Four property tags, eight function tags and four sentence tags are designed for the segmentation and identification of chunk boundaries. They describe 3 types and 5 kinds of chunks in sentences. Annotators added notes to the skeleton structure and highlighted the headword of the predicate for each simple sentence.

Ex.1: (随着)专业化生产的发展，工作协作关系(还将日益(扩大))，<因而>{(合理地(制定))工艺价格}(有)重要的意义。

Ex.1 is divided into a sequence of chunks manually with the use of several tags such as "()", "<>", "{}", etc., in which "()" marks the predicate, "<>" marks the conjunction and "{}" marks verbal constructions used as subjects or objects and subject-predicate predicate sentences.

BLCU TreeBank 1.0 sets consistency check (Kappa value ≥ 0.8) as the index to measure the quality of annotation [11]. Better annotation of each group of compared texts was collected, including the discourse of encyclopedia (423), law (228), news (769), patent (636), composition (52), scientific exposition (14). Considering the imbalanced data distribution of discourses, law (500), composition (423) and scientific exposition (14) were added, which leads to annotation quality of 0.8 after modification. Table 1 shows the data distribution in different discourses.

3.2   Word List Construction

Taking Yuan [2, 3] as references, we classified mono-valent nouns into three categories. Firstly, 208 appellations in Zheng [12] were extracted based on the kinship relationship to enrich the word list of kinship nouns. The nouns are divided into consanguineous kinship appellation, affined kinship appellation, nominal kinship appellation, and public relations appellation. Secondly, 1441 component nouns, namely biological components, appliance components, mechanical components and building components searched from Chen and Kang [13] were included in the word list of partitive nouns. Finally, a property noun is a kind of abstract noun. Su [14] looked up the abstract nouns in the *Modern Chinese Content Words Collocation Dictionary* compiled by Zhang Shoukang, in which property nouns are classified into quantity property nouns and fuzzy property nouns. Fuzzy attributes are divided by the grammatical function of reference. After looking up the synonyms of the 253 words summarized by Su [14] in Chen and Kang [13], feedback of 1814 property nouns was obtained.

When redefining mono-valent nouns in this paper, many existing definitions of mono-valent nouns in other related studies were considered. Referring to Yu [8], if some professional appellations share the dependency relationship with another noun in some specific contexts and their semantic orientation can be ensured, they are still identified as mono-valent nouns, for example, 老师, 经理. However, some playful appellations and modest terms, such as 母老虎, 二百五 and 足下, do not meet the semantic standards of [-alienable] and [+possessive], hence they need to be eliminated. At present, the word list of mono-valent nouns is constructed as an open resource for academic research[1]. The semantic classification of mono-valent nouns and the samples of word list are shown in Table 2.

---

[1] Link for Baidu Cloud: https://pan.baidu.com/s/1uX_0PCtuP4aTpASosgOUcg
   Password: yjmc.

Table 1. Data distribution of different discourses in the selected annotation data

Domains of discourse	Number of files	Number of words	Number of sentences	Number of clauses
Encyclopedia	423	421736	10708	24927
Law	728	700870	11761	40961
News	769	1053843	22436	75020
Patent	636	639649	10738	35402
Science expository	28	34359	659	1734
Composition	475	486193	11946	33944

Table 2. Semantic classification of mono-valent nouns and the samples in the word list

Kinship nouns	Consanguineous kinship appellations	爸爸, 妈妈, 女儿, 儿子......(38)
	Affined kinship appellations	丈夫, 妻子......(43)
	Nominal kinship appellations	继父, 继母, 养父, 养母...... (23)
	Fictitious kinship appellations	老爷爷, 老奶奶, 大哥, 小老弟......(42)
	Public relations appellations	老师, 师父, 老板......(3)
	Nickname appellations	阿爹, 阿妈, 老哥, 老姐......(14)
	Social Relationship appellations appellations	教师, 老师, 学生, 同学, 朋友......(24)
	Intimate appellations	囡囡, 宝宝, 哥们儿, 姐们儿......(4)
	Profession appellations	司机, 秘书, 教练, 律师......(18)
Partitive nouns	Biological components	人体, 皮肤...... (1001)
	Appliance components	车轮, 轮胎...... (127)
	Building components	台阶, 地面......(210)
	Mechanical components	齿轮, 弹簧, 转轴, 螺栓, 涡轮, 螺母, 滚筒......(103)
Property nouns	Fuzzy Properties of properties somebody	技术, 能力, 精神, 力量, 思想, 活力, 信心...... (700)
	Properties of something	市场, 方面, 情况, 方向, 中心, 环境, 基础......(596)
	Properties of objects	系统, 结构, 质量, 价格, 体系, 形式, 性能......(266)
	Quantitive properties	高度, 低度, 湿度, 长度, 宽度, 幅度, 难度...... (252)

Table 3 shows the quantitive distribution of mono-valent nouns in terms of word length in BLCU Treebank 1.0. There are 1296 disyllabic nouns, which appear 41,955 times in total. Monosyllabic nouns come next with 157 types and appear 7989 times. There are also a small number of four-syllabic nouns, such as 中枢神经, 自动扶梯.

Table 3. Statistical table of the length of mono-valent nouns

Word length	Monosyllabic	Disyllabic	Three-syllabic	Four-syllabic
Type	157	1296	73	6
Token	7989	41955	532	15

4 Ellipsis Phenomena of Mono-Valent Nouns

4.1 Extract Redundant Sentences and Elliptical Sentences of Mono-Valent Nouns

This paper mainly observes the ellipsis rule of disyllabic partitive and property nouns. *Jieba*, a built-in module in python, was implemented to realize the segmentation and POS tagging of the selected annotation data in BLCU Treebank 1.0. On one hand, when extracting the redundant sentences for mono-valent nouns, the subject-predicate predicate sentences and Chinese "比" sentences were automatically extracted respectively with the assistant of annotation tag "{ }" and POS tag "比/p" in BLCU Treebank 1.0. Then, 156 qualified subject-predicate predicate sentences and 28 qualified Chinese "比" sentences were selected as the redundant sentences of monovalent nouns, that is, the sentences where disyllabic partitive nouns and property nouns are redundant and play the syntactic role of the second subject. After removing the repetitive mono-valent nouns, there are 108 nouns left. The ellipsis phenomena of these 108 nouns were the focus of this paper.

Ex.2 她/r { 个子/n (很/zg (高/a)) } 。

Ex.2 is a redundant sentence of the subject-predicate predicate sentence. "{ }" tags the subject-predicate predicate sentence, "( )" marks the predicate, and property noun 个子 acts as the second subject in this sentence.

Ex.3 其/r { 工程/n 性质/n (比/p 陆地/n (复杂/a)) 。

Ex.3 is a redundant sentence of the Chinese "比" sentence. "比/p" indicates Chinese "比" sentence, "( )" tags the predicate, and the property noun 性质 is the second subject of the sentence.

On the other hand, when extracting elliptical sentences of mono-valent nouns from BLCU Treebank 1.0, firstly, 148 predicates governing the 108 nouns from redundant sentences were extracted with the tag "( )". Then, 393 elliptical sentences were found, in which 148 verbs play the syntactic role of predicate and 108 nouns are omitted but still can be activated by semantic. Since the elliptical sentences were screened out manually, the process mainly relies on people's language intuition and grammar knowledge, rather than specific annotations tags. Ex.4 is an example of the elliptical sentence.

Ex.4: 我/r (看/v) {爸爸/n (高/a) [还是/c] 我/r (高/a)}

Compared to Ex.3, 个子 is omitted in the syntactic surface of Ex.4.

Table 4 shows the frequency of dominant predicates and predicate-noun collocations for 4 property nouns and 4 partitive nouns randomly selected in redundant sentences and elliptical sentences, respectively.

Table 4. Dominant predicate and its predicate-noun collocation frequency of several mono-valent nouns

Mono-valent nouns		Predicates in redundant sentences and their frequency	Predicates in elliptical sentences and their frequency
Property nouns	前景	广阔1 可期1	好3
	个子	高 2 矮小 1	高 3
	能力	强 1 下降 1	强 2 不错 2
	心情	好 2	紧张 16
Partitive nouns	翅膀	舞蹈 1	舞蹈1
	双手	托起 1 举着 2	举着 4
	肚子	饿 1	饿 11
	身体	沉 1 健康 3 不适 1 好 1 受到伤害 1	磕着1 碰着 1 健康 7 挂着 1 受到伤害 2

4.2   Ellipsis Rules of Mono-Valent Nouns

There remain 108 property nouns and partitive nouns in redundant sentences, while the partitive nouns or property nouns activated in the elliptical sentences are beyond the scope of the 108 nouns. That is to say, some mono-valent nouns shown in Table 5 are particularly easy to be omitted. These nouns are attribute nouns whose meanings are generally contained in the semantic structures of predicates, such as (身长) 长, 名次 (排名), (重量) 重, (实力)强大, and (内容)难. Under another circumstance, the nouns are especially susceptible to be activated by their dependent nouns. For instance, in sentence 皙白的脸霎时变得通红, 颜色 can be activated by 脸.

Among the 108 nouns in the redundant sentences, 43 nouns can be omitted, of which 8 nouns are partitive nouns and 35 are property nouns (as shown in Table 5). Partitive nouns are omitted in 38 elliptical sentences and property nouns are omitted in 355 elliptical sentences. It can thus prove that property nouns are easier to be omitted than partitive nouns. In addition, among the predicates that govern the property nouns, there are 25 verbs and 39 adjectives. Meanwhile, among the dominant predicates of partitive nouns, there are 11 verbs and 3 adjectives. Hence, it can be inferred that the omitted partitive nouns are generally dominated by verbs, while the omitted property nouns are more likely to be dominated by adjectives.

If the verb only governs one property noun and the association between them is definite, the property noun can be omid in the sentence 愿天下的老师健康快乐 and 价格 is not needed in 最近海鲜价格都比较便宜. When the adjective is polysemous

Table 5. Table of mono-valent nouns in redundant and elliptical sentences

Mono-valent nouns omitted in elliptical sentences and beyond the scope of the nouns which are redundant in the surface structures of sentences	音量 面积 名次 身长 长度 颜色 身份 深度 盐度 籍贯 面额 质地 性别 票房 形状 重量 经济 浓度 金额 水平 治安 功能 营养 内容 实力 距离 雪量 原理 股价 态度 国力 心肠 (32个)			
The mono-valent nouns which are both able to be omitted in elliptical sentences and exist in redundant sentences	前景 质量 能力 环境 心情 结构 程度 眼球 状态 情况 精神 价格 翅膀 情绪 气氛 力量 双手 感情 种类 脑袋 形势 秩序 姿态 体格 样子 嘴角 神色 气候 肚子 高度 速度 年龄 温度 产量 体积 汇率 数量 强度 容积 个子 个头 力度 身体 (43个)			
Mono-valent nouns in redundant sentences which can't be omitted in elliptical sentences	方向 基础 皮肤 颅脑 门槛 背景	技术 现象 肋骨 思路 局势 智能 外貌 功夫	脾气 舌头	市场 信心 眼神 后门 大门 全身
	心脏 心理 意愿	性能 资质 款式 品种	状况	习惯 风味 走势
	风向 血液 脚腕	地价 心潮 肺脏 胆子	医术	势头 血型 气量
	小肠 流向 期价	形式 语气 文体 性质	头发	行情 口气 单价
	现状 频率 流量 粘度 电量 利率 进程 含量 亮度 处境 (65个)			

and the governing constituent of thetted unconditionally, such as (翅膀)舞蹈, (双手)举着, (脑袋)记住, (肚子)饿, and (身体)受到伤害. When the adjective is monosemous and describes a particular property or partitive noun, then the noun is free to be redundant and omitted. For instance, 健康 and 便宜 specifically modify 身体 and 价格 respectively, so 身体 is omitte property noun it describes has only one matching attribute, it can only choose to modify this attribute. Thus the property noun is omitted.

For instance, the elliptical sentences 桃子林的桃子很大很甜, 胖大海变得越来越大, and 爸爸您要是能小了20岁和我一样大. 个头, 体积 and 年龄 are all omitted in those surface structures of sentences.

The remaining 65 nouns in the redundant sentences are only redundant in the surface structures without ellipsis (as shown in Table 5). When the property noun collocates an adjective, it is necessary to indicate which aspect of the governing constituent the adjective describes, thus the property noun cannot be omitted. For instance, 好 is the predicate of the redundant sentence 我保证他状况好, 徐奶奶人好 and 李涛刹车 时习惯不好. If the ellipsis phenomena exist in the redundant sentences, it can lead to semantic incompleteness or ambiguity. When the verb can collocate with several property nouns, the nouns are generally redundant. For instance, 小猫用舌头碰了下米饭. The verb 碰 can dominate several other property nouns, such as 爪子 and 尾巴.

5   Explanation of the Ellipsis from the Perspective of Grammatical Metonymy

Metonymy is regarded as a concept from rhetoric metonymy in tradition. It can be roughly defined as borrowing the name of the related thing to stand for the thing to be expressed [15]. The linguistic components representing the related things are called vehicles or triggers, and the description is called tenor, targets or topics [16]. For example, in Ex.5, 低眉 should be understood as 低头, and 眉 is used to represent 头. 眉 is the vehicle, while 头 is the tenor.

Ex.5: 低眉信手续续弹, 说尽心中无限事。

This transferred designation is essentially a kind of grammatical metonymy in cognitive linguistics beyond rhetoric metonymy. Taylor, Lackoff and Turner [17] described metonymy as a conceptual mapping in a cognitive domain, that is, the mapping of the source domain provided by the vehicle to the target domain provided by the tenor, thus resulting in the substitution relation of reference. The source domain and the target domain share or belong to the same cognitive domain matrix, which can be abstracted as an Idealized Cognitive Model (ICM). For example, whole and part, container and content, lord and subject, object and property, thing and place, condition and result, predicate and argument, etc. According to the cognitive model of metonymy set up by Shen [18], within a cognitive frame, if A and B are closely related and the salience of A is stronger than B's, the activation of A will lead to B's evoking incidentally. Therefore, A can be transferred to B. Shen [18] also summarized the general law of salience: the whole is more salient than the parts (because the whole is bigger), the container is more salient than content (because the container is visible), aliveness is more salient than dead, near is more salient than far, and concrete is superior to abstract. It is worth noting that salience is also related to some subjective factors. In addition, context can regulate the salience of concepts within the cognitive frame.

The partitive nouns and dependent nouns not only share a possessive relationship but also a whole and part relationship, such as 腹部 and 人体, 零件 and 火箭.

Property nouns are abstract descriptions of some aspects of a person or object, such as 颜色 and 湖水, 身材 and 孩子. According to the law of salience, the whole is more salient than the part, and the concrete is more salient than the abstract. Therefore, under normal circumstances, the dependent noun can be metonymized to stand for its relevant mono-valent noun and collocates with the verb that originally dominates the mono-valent noun, thus resulting in the ellipsis of the nouns with lower salience. For example, in 桃子林的桃子很大又甜. 个头 and 大, 味道 and 甜 share the relationship of object and property respectively, but the salience of 桃子 is superior to these two property nouns, so the nouns are omitted in the surface structure of this sentence.

This paper extracts the predicates that contribute over 70% collocation frequency with the 43 mono-valent nouns that can be omitted in redundant sentences. It also shows the POSes of the dependent nouns to obtain the metonymic chains that can activate the mono-valent nouns semantically (Table 6).

Some special ellipsis phenomena can also be reasonably explained from the perspective of metonymy. With the absence of contextual effect, salience is also influenced by people's attention. For example, the basic meaning of the word 健康, a polysemy, is

Table 6. Metonymic chains with high frequency

Metonymic chain	Verb	Metonymic chain	Verb
r.*[感情]好 n.*[质量]好 ns.*[前景]好 .*比n[质量]好	好	[nr n].*[程度 年龄 身份]为	为
r.*[个子]高 n.*[高度 数量]高 l.*[程度]高	高	n.*[种类 数量]多	多
r*[年龄 个子 个头]小 n.*[个头 容积 体积]小	小	n.*[情绪 样子 体积]变	变
n.*[容积 强度 体积 年龄 力量力度 个头]大	大	r.*[脑袋 眼睛]记住	记住
r.*[肚子]饿	饿	[r n]. + [身体 状态 气氛]健康	健康
[l n].*[数量]达到 n.*[温度]达到	达到	[r n].*[情绪]激动	激动
n.*[质量 重量]	重	[r n].*[形势 神色 心情]紧张	紧张
[s n f ns].*[数量]少	少	[r n].*[价格]便宜	便宜

"having good health and not likely to become ill/sick", so 体格 can be omitted in 让学生在不能户外运动的时候保持健康. However, since 氛围 obtains more attention than 体格 in 整个赛场都非常健康,非常阳光, its salience is improved. Therefore, the noun 氛围 modified by derived meaning is also implied in the sentence.

6 Conclusion

Based on an exhaustive word list of mono-valent nouns and annotated data in BLCU Treebank 1.0, the ellipsis rules of mono-valent nouns verified in this paper are as follows:

Firstly, property nouns are easier to be omitted than partitive nouns. The ellipsis of property nouns is mainly restricted by adjectives and property nouns by verbs.

Secondly, if the verb can only dominate one partitive noun and has a unique relationship with it, the noun can be unconditionally omitted.

Thirdly, if the adjective is monosemous, that is, it specifically describes one certain property or partitive noun, the noun can be freely omitted. If the adjective is polysemous, but when the dependent noun it describes has only one corresponding attribute, it can only choose to modify this attribute, then the property noun can be omitted. Sometimes the attribute noun modified by the derived meaning of polysemous adjectives can also be omitted, because the cognition of people in the metonymy mechanism can adjust the salience of objects.

This paper also introduces some metonymic chains with high frequency, in which mono-valent nouns can be activated. In future studies, the dataset can be expanded and models of machine learning can be trained to enrich the metonymic chains and develop the automatic identification and recovery of ellipsis.

Acknowledgments. This paper is supported by MOE Funds of Humanity and Social Sciences "Quantitative Research on Words Use in Newspaper since late Qing Dynasty" (20YJC740050) and Innovation Fund Project for Chinese and Foreign Postgraduates of BLCU (supported by the Fundamental Research Funds for the Central Universities) (20YCX150).

References

1. Zhu, D.-X.: Study of Modern Chinese Grammar. Commercial Press, Beijing (1980). (in Chinese)
2. Yuan, Y.-L.: Study on the valence of nouns in modern Chinese. Soc. Sci. China **3**, 205–223 (1992). (in Chinese)
3. Yuan, Y.-L: A cognitive study of mono-valent nouns. Stud. Chin. Lang. **4**, 241–253 (1994). (in Chinese)
4. Liu, S.: Mono-valent noun and its dependent-noun eyntactic expression. J. Southern Yangtze Univ. (Humanit. Soc. Sci). **3**(2), 111–115 (2005). (in Chinese)
5. Geng, G.-F.: Two issues about bivalent nouns. J. North Forum. **2**, 54–56 (2008). (in Chinese)
6. Song, Z.-Y.: On the implication of mono-valent noun in adjective-noun collocations. Li Yun Acad. J. (Lang. Vol.) **1**, 150–160 (2013). (in Chinese)
7. Wang, W.-C.: A revisit to properties and relevant syvtactic phenomena of mono-valent nouns. Chin. Teach. World **34**(1), 67–80 (2020). (in Chinese)
8. Yu, L.: A Review on the study about noun's valent in modern Chinese. Mod. Chin. (Edition Lang. Stud.) **6**, 6–8 (2015). (in Chinese)
9. Liu, Y., Xing, H.: A cognitive approach to the comparative-point concealing in Chinese "比" sentence. J. Shanghai Univ. (Soc. Sci.) **11**(3), 107–112 (2004). (in Chinese)
10. Liu, C.-H.: The ellipsis and redundancy of attribute noun and part noun. J. Stud. Lang. Linguist. **30**(2), 93–97 (2010). (in Chinese)
11. Lu, L., Li, M., Xun, E.-D.: A discourse-based Chinese ChunkBank. J. Acta Automarica Sinica (2020). http://kns.cnki.net/kcms/detail/11.2109.TP.20200521.1558.007.html. (in Chinese)
12. Zheng, E.-N.: A study on the sememe of appellation in modern Chinese. Master Dissertation, Nanjing Normal University, Nanjing (2006). (in Chinese)
13. Chen, W.-D., Kang, S.-Y.: The New Compilation of Synonym Cilin. Shanghai Lexico-graphical Publishing House, Shanghai (2015).(in Chinese)
14. Su, N.-N.: Modern Chinese abstract noun and the noun collocation. Master Dissertation, Shandong Normal University, Jinan (2014). (in Chinese)
15. Chen, W.-D.: An Introduction to Rhetoric. Shanghai Educational Publishing House, Shanghai (1997).(in Chinese)
16. Shu, D.-F.: Metaphor and metonymy: similarities and differences. J. Foreign Lang. **3**, 26–34 (2004). (in Chinese)
17. Taylor, R., Lackoff, G., Turner, M.: More than Cool Reason: A Field Guide to Poetic Metaphor. University of Chicago Press, Chicago (1989)
18. Shen, J.-X.: A Metonymic model of transferred designation of de-constructions in Mandarin Chinese. Contemp. Linguist. **1**(1), 3–15 (1999). (in Chinese)

Construction of Chinese Obstetrics Knowledge Graph Based on the Multiple Sources Data

Kunli Zhang[1(✉)], Chenxin Hu[1,2], Yu Song[1], Hongying Zan[1], Yueshu Zhao[1,3], and Wenyan Chu[4]

[1] School of Information Engineering, Zhengzhou University,
Zhengzhou 450001, Henan, China
ieklzhang@zzu.edu.cn
[2] Zhengzhou Zhongye Technology Co., Ltd., Zhengzhou 450001, Henan, China
[3] The Third Affiliated Hospital of Zhengzhou University,
Zhengzhou 450001, Henan, China
[4] School of International Studies, Zhengzhou University,
Zhengzhou 450001, Henan, China

Abstract. With the development of information technology, a large amount of information data has been accumulated in the field of obstetric. The effective ways to manage and apply these data are to construct a professional medical knowledge graph. In this paper, the Chinese Obstetric Knowledge Graph (COKG) based on multiple data sources of the obstetric professional thesauruses, clinical pathways, diagnosis, and treatment norms is constructed by the semi-automated method. The framework of concept classification and the related description are established. Thus COKG conceptual layer is also built. Based on traditional models of BI-LSTM-CRF and PCNN, and the guidance of medical experts, the data layer of COKG was founded by more than 2 million unstructured text words via artificially calibrating. Finally, COKG, which included 2343 diseases and 15249 named entity relationships, is constructed by knowledge fusion of multi-source data. The constructed COKG can provide structured knowledge support for medical question-answering systems, intelligent assisted diagnosis and treatment.

Keywords: Knowledge graph · Knowledge fusion · Named entity recognition · Relation extraction · Obstetrics

1 Introduction

Knowledge Graph (KG) originated from the semantic web in the 1960s. With the development of the World Wide Web and open link data, Google formally proposed the concept of knowledge graph in 2012 to serve its next-generation intelligent search engine [1]. With the advent of the medical big data era, the interconnection of medical knowledge has gradually entered the visual field of people. The medical knowledge graph is the cornerstone of the realization of smart medical care and has gained more and more attention.

© Springer Nature Switzerland AG 2022
M. Dong et al. (Eds.): CLSW 2021, LNAI 13250, pp. 399–410, 2022.
https://doi.org/10.1007/978-3-031-06547-7_31

In the medical field, the international well-known knowledge graphs SNOMED-CT [2, 3] and IBM Watson Health [4] are devoted to building a comprehensive and unified medical terminology system. Domestic scholars have also explored the construction of medical knowledge graphs.

Ruan et al. [5] explored the automatic construction method and standardized flow of Traditional Chinese Medicine Knowledge Graph (TCMKG) by using the techniques of text extraction, relational data conversion and data fusion, TCMKG has integrated a large amount of traditional Chinese medicine data and clinical diagnostic knowledge. Jia et al. [6] began to develop the Chinese medicine language system in 2002, and the constructed knowledge graph was displayed from data collection, content extraction, and graphical interface. The Chinese Medical Knowledge Graph version 2.0 (CMeKG2.0[1]) officially launched in 2019, has a large-scale, high-quality medical knowledge text set, and realized a wide range of knowledge link diseases, symptoms, drugs, clinical diagnosis and treatment technologies. CMeKG2.0 not only expands the coverage of medical knowledge and improves the richness of descriptive information, but also enhances the standardization, normalization and internationalization of medical knowledge.

With the introduction of the Chinese government's multiple birth policy, the health of elderly parturient women and multiples maternal has attracted a lot of attention from medical researchers. It has been shown that their pregnancy complications and the rising incidence of adverse pregnancies pose a greater challenge to obstetric medical institutions. Additionally, with the continuous exploration of obstetric medicine, it is difficult to make effective use of the vast amount of information resources related to obstetrics from a wide range of sources with different structures, therefore, effective methods need to be adopted to organize and integrate this knowledge.

In response to the above problems, we analyzed a multi-source corpus and proposed a description system of knowledge graph for obstetric medicine under expert guidance. Extracting relevant descriptions of obstetric diseases from textbooks, guidelines and catalogs, web resources and other multi-source texts based on the names of obstetric disorders in Obstetrics and Gynaecology, MeSH and ICD10. The extracted text is annotated in a semi-automatic or automatic way and completed with manual checks. The Chinese Obstetrics Knowledge Graph (COKG[2]) has been constructed by knowledge fusion operation of integrating, processing and updating heterogeneous data from multiple sources.

The rest part of this paper is organized as follows. In Sect. 2, we describe the system design. In Sect. 3, we present the construction of the data layer. In Sect. 4, we introduce the data results and display them. Finally, we conclude the paper and list further work.

---

[1] http://cmekg.pcl.ac.cn.

[2] http://www5.zzu.edu.cn/nlp/info/1015/2147.htm.

2 Construction Process of Chinese Obstetrics Knowledge Graph

There are two modes of knowledge graph construction, i.e., top-down and bottom-up [7]. Drawing on the wealth of domestic, international disease classification systems and their related terminology, the COKG is built using a top-down construction model that establishes the schema layer first and then builds the data layer.

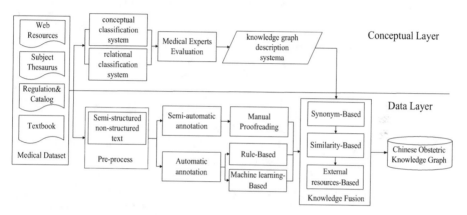

Fig. 1. COKG construction workflow

The construction process of COKG can be divided into two stages. Firstly, designing the conceptual layer, the concept classification system is initially designed according to the international standard medical terminology set (Fig. 1), the relationship classification system is designed through manual annotation and analysis of cases, and the knowledge graph description system is formed after evaluation by medical experts. Secondly, designing the data layer, the multi-source obstetrics-related knowledge, including unstructured and semi-structured text, is annotated with the obtained entity relationships in a semi-automatic or automatic way. In this way, the knowledge ontology of COKG is constructed. Finally, the knowledge fusion of the multi-source data is completed.

3 Conceptual Layers

The COKG, whose descriptive subject is obstetric diseases, establishes hierarchical and associative relationships between entities through triplets and forms a knowledge graph description system containing a conceptual classification system and a relational classification system. Meanwhile, to describe the abundant knowledge, we enlarge the original triplets into sextuplets by adding attributes to each element. where e_1 is entity 1 and e_1_pro is an attribute of entity 1, $r(rel)$ is a relationship and rel_pro is an attribute of the relationship, e_2 is entity 2 and e_2_pro is an attribute of entity 2, in the form of an $<e_1, r, e_2>$ triplet or $<e_1, e_1\_pro, rel, rel\_pro, e_2, e_2\_pro>$ sextuplets.

The 12 categories of medical entities defined in this paper include disease, body part, symptom, drug, examination, other treatment, operation, epidemiology, prognosis, sociology and synonym. The main eleven relationship categories produced by 12 medical entity categories are divided into 44 related sub-categories according to the specific contents. Some of the relationships in the COKG are defined in Table 1. Relational "synonym" contains the English names, aliases, abbreviations, acronyms, colloquialisms of diseases, and is an important basis for knowledge fusion of data from multiple sources. The disease-disease relationship can be subdivided into five sub-relationships: typology, differential diagnosis, complication, cause, transformation.

Table 1. The partial label relationship definition of COKG

Relationship	Relationship type	Relationship definition
Synonym	–	Including English names, aliases, abbreviations, acronyms and colloquialisms, e.g. intrahepatic cholestasis of pregnancy is abbreviated as ICP
Disease - disease	Typology	One disease is a different stage or category of another disease, e.g. Placenta previa is divided into complete placenta previa and partial placenta previa
	Differential diagnosis	One disease is a different stage or category of another disease, e.g. the pathological classification of placenta praevia is complete placenta previa and partial placenta previa
	Complication	The disease causes another disease as it progresses, e.g. a complication of preterm birth is cerebral palsy
	Cause	Meaning that the occurrence of one condition leads to another, e.g. premature rupture of membranes leading to preterm birth, pre-eclampsia transforming into eclampsia
	Transformation	Meaning that one disease is associated with another, or that one disease transforms or is secondary to another, e.g. pre-eclampsia transforms into eclampsia

4   Data Layers

The construction of the data layer mainly includes three parts: obstetric knowledge collection, semi-automatic annotation and knowledge fusion.

4.1   Obstetric Knowledge Acquisition

The COKG focuses on obstetric diseases and the extracted data are shown in Table 2, where "semi" is semi-structured data and "non" is unstructured data. Entities and entity relationships in Obstetrics and Gynaecology, Clinical Pathways, and Clinical Practice texts are annotated Semi-automatically, while extracted automatically in DRUGS DXY and Baidu Encyclopedia.

Table 2. The sources of obstetric data

Name	Description	Structure	Corpus scale
Obstetrics and gynecology	Obstetric diseases and background knowledge	Semi/Non	350,000 words
Clinical Pathways	Standardized treatment models and procedures for diseases	Non	22,000 words
Clinical Practice texts	Disease texts based on evidence-based medicine resources	Non	130,000 words
Drugs DXY	Ingredients, indications and adverse effects of Chinese and Western medicines	Semi	–
Baidu encyclopedia	Medical concepts of disease symptoms, drugs, treatment techniques, herbal medicine	Semi/Non	–

4.2 Semi-automatic Annotating

To improve the annotation efficiency and consistency, entities and entity relations in the corpus are annotated with the help of the developed entity and relation annotation platform for medical texts [8].

As shown in Fig. 2, by a rule-based and machine learning approach, we carried out named entity recognition and relation extraction of semi-structured and unstructured data in drug DXY and Baidu encyclopedia, and then the data processed above is manually proofread, integrated and deduplicated to obtain structured triplets.

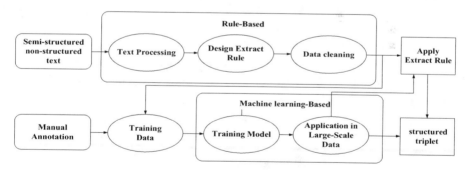

Fig. 2. Entity recognition and automatic relationship extraction workflow

4.2.1 Rule-Based Methods

Firstly, summarizing the semi-automatically annotated corpus, and extracting the relationship mark mode that often appears words and phrases in the same relationship, and then making the mode as a part of the rule description for automatic extraction. Secondly, extracting entities and relationships from semi-structured and structured texts by analyzing different sources texts and designing different rules according to different categories. Finally, the extracted entities and relationships are matched according to the knowledge graph description system.

DRUG DXY describes the medicine's ingredients, indications, contraindications and other attributes. According to MeSH vocabulary and the expanded concept of related diseases, the medicines related to obstetric diseases in the indications can be extracted as <Disease, drug, drug treatment> relationship according to the rules.

4.2.2 Machine Learning Methods

In the machine learning approach, the Bi-LSTM-CRF [9] model in the annotation platform [8] is used directly for entity recognition and the PCNN model [10] for relationship extraction and then manual proofreading. In our experiments, the training set uses manually annotated clinical practice texts based on common diseases with the entity and sub-relationship classification more similar to COKG. The test set uses semi-automated annotated textbooks and clinical practice texts related to obstetric diseases, the objects are the top five frequency entities and their relationships, and the statistics of the number of entities included are shown in Table 3.

Table 3. The experimental data set of entity recognition

Data set	Disease	Symptom	Examination	Drug	Operation	Sum
Training	9,642	3,374	1,944	2,404	436	18,800
Test	1,004	313	144	216	28	1,705
Sum	10,646	3,687	2,088	2,620	464	20,505

(1) The experimental dataset of entity relationships is shown in Table 4. The head entities of these five types of relationships are all diseases, such as "-disease" means "disease-disease". These five types of relationships include a total of 14 sub-relationships, and the subsequent relationship extraction will be classified according to 14 sub-relationships. Bi-LSTM-CRF model

The Bi-LSTM-CRF [9] model is the mainstream deep learning model for entity recognition and it can effectively improve the accuracy rate compared with other models. Therefore this model is chosen for entity identification in this paper.

Table 4. The experimental data set of entity relationship

Data set	Disease	Symptom	Examination	Drug	Operation	Sum
Training	4,503	6, 711	3,829	3,573	720	19,336
Test	502	725	416	402	79	2,124
Sum	5,005	7,436	4,245	3,975	819	21,460

The Bi-LSTM-CRF model is shown in Fig. 3, using BIO as annotation set, the sentence as the unit, the word vector is initialized randomly, and the named entity recognition result is obtained through the Bi-LSTM layer and the CRF layer. In the parameters of our Bi-LSTM-CRF model for entity recognition, Dropout as 0.5, the word vector and hidden layer dimensions as 300, the window size as 7, the learning rate as 0.001, and the Epoch as 32.

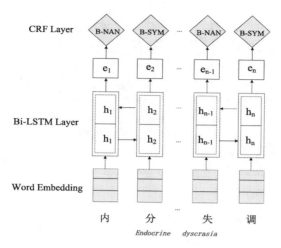

CRF Layer

Bi-LSTM Layer

Word Embedding

内   分   失   调

Endocrine   dyscrasia

Fig. 3. The entity recognition model of Bi-LSTM-CRF

The two types of indicators Strict and Relax are often used to evaluate the entity recognition results. The result of automatic recognition is recorded as $S = \{S_1, S_1, ..., S_m\}$, and the gold standard result as $G = \{g_1, g_1, ..., g_n\}$. The test results are shown in Table 5, the relax index F1r value is 79.05%, and the strict index F1s value is 69.48%. Due to the diverse forms of medical named entities, it is difficult to identify symptom entities, including individual symptoms (such as fever) and body Symptoms of joint parts (such as headache), so the F1 value is the lowest among the five types of entities.

Table 5. The entity recognition results of Bi-LSTM-CRF

Category	P_s (%)	R_s (%)	$F1_s$ (%)	P_r (%)	R_r (%)	$F1_r$ (%)
Disease	72.39	74.70	73.53	78.09	80.57	79.31
Symptom	49.73	59.74	54.28	68.35	82.11	74.60
Examination	69.23	68.75	68.99	79.72	79.17	79.44
Drug	72.65	75.00	73.80	82.06	84.72	83.37
Operation	80.77	75.00	77.78	92.31	85.71	88.89
Sum	67.57	71.50	69.48	76.88	81.35	79.05

(2) PCNN model

The PCNN model [10] can encode the feature distribution and effectively improve the accuracy of relationship extraction. Therefore, the PCNN model is used for relationship extraction in the construction of COKG. The model is shown in Fig. 4.

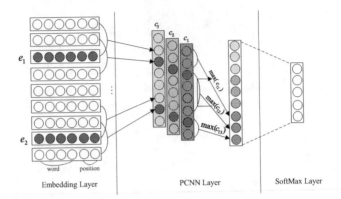

Fig. 4. The entity-relationship recognition model diagram of PCNN

When the entities have been determined, the relationship extraction between entities can be considered as a classification problem. PCNN modifies the traditional CNN maximum pooling method to the segmented pooling, where the input is converted from word and position vectors. In the pooling layer, the output of the convolutional layer is divided into the information c_{i1} before the entity e_1, the information between the entities c_{i2} and the information c_{i3} after the entity e_2, and then the maximum pooling operation is performed on the three parts respectively. Namely $pij = max(c_{ij})$, where $1 \leq i \leq n$, $i \leq j \leq 3$; containing the results of n convolution filters, getting the output of the PCNN layer by tanh function, and transmitting to the softmax layer for relation classification.

The PCNN model is used as relationship extraction experiments, word vector dimension 50, position vector dimension 5, and Dropout 0.33. The test results are shown in Table 6, and most of the F1 are above 80%. Whether semi-automatic pre-annotating or large-scale obstetric-related texts, relatively accurate triplets can be obtained.

Table 6. The entity relation extraction results of PCNN

Type of entity relationship	P (%)	R (%)	F1 (%)
Disease - disease	80.21	84.29	82.20
Disease - symptom	89.07	85.37	87.18
Disease - examination	85.87	87.92	86.88
Disease - drug	94.39	89.69	91.96
Disease - operation	93.67	90.56	92.09

4.3   Knowledge Fusion

The data in this experiment has multiple expression methods of the same entity from different sources, so it is necessary to solve the heterogeneity and redundancy problems between the triplets through knowledge fusion. The noises in the data, such as meaningless punctuation instances, <)输卵管妊娠破裂 (*fallopian tube pregnancy rupture*)>. The extracted triplets will contain some redundant and conflicting information. For example, the strings of uncontrolled domain entities have various expressions but similar meanings, <胎盘植入(*placenta accreta*)>" and <穿透性胎盘植入> (*placenta accreta*) and so on. For the above-mentioned problems, integration, disambiguation, processing and updating of heterogeneous data and other knowledge fusion work are shown in Table 7. This research analyzes manually annotated triplets (5,790 items), automatically annotated triplets (9,459 items), and standardized processing 359 entities. Use controlled entity synonymous relationship triplets to cluster synonymous entities supplemented by manual proofreading to construct 841 standard alias triplets lists. The external resources Chinese Symptom Knowledge Base (CSKB) [11] and Chinese Medicine Knowledge Base (CMKB) [12] were fused, and about 20,000 triplets were extracted after converting their expression format, and 7505 triplets were obtained after deduplication. After knowledge fusion, the quality of knowledge of COKG's obstetric description annotation triplets has been significantly improved.

Table 7. The comparison before and after knowledge fusion

Example	Pre-fusion	Pre-fusion
Entity irregularities	羊水过少@ (*oligohydramnios*)	羊水过少 (*oligohydramnios*)
Multiple synonymous for the same entity	协调性子宫收缩乏力-低张性子宫收缩乏力 协调性子宫收缩乏力-*hypotonic uterine inertia*	协调性子宫收缩乏力-['低张性子宫收缩乏力', '*hypotonic uterine inertia*']
Fusion of entities based on external resources	Symptoms - Related Diseases - Diseases (CSKB) Medicines - Indications – Diseases (CMKB) Obstetric disease - Clinical Symptoms - Symptoms (COKG)	CSKB changes COKG Obstetric disease - Clinical Symptoms - Symptoms CMKB changes COKG Obstetric disease – drug therapy - drug

5   Construction Results and Display

Annotation consistency is used to describe the degree of consistency between two Annotation results, generally expressed by Kappa [13] and F [14] in entity and relationship Annotation, the number of unannotated texts as counterexamples is relatively large, the F is close to Kappa. Therefore, for the results of manual annotation, in addition to the evaluation of the clinicians, the consistency of multiple annotations was also evaluated by F.

In this annotation process, two medical experts and nearly twenty annotators participated. As shown in Table 8, a total of more than 2 million words and 10,674 entity concepts have been marked, of which 4,888 are semi-automatically extracted and 5,786 are automatically extracted. The scale of entity-relationship annotation is shown in

Table 9, which contains 15,249 entity-relationship triplets, of which 5790 are semi-automatically extracted and 9,459 are automatically extracted.

Table 8. Number of annotation entities

Entity type	Number of entities		Sum
	Manual	Automatic	
Disease	1176	1167	2343
Symptoms	1376	1280	2656
Body pare	68	52	120
Examination	359	463	822
Drug	377	2098	2228
Operation	115	2	117
Other treatments	303	0	303
Prognosis	16	0	16
Epidemiology	143	82	225
Sociology	785	336	1121
Others	170	62	232
Sum	4888	5786	10674

Table 9. Number of annotation relationships

Relationship	Semi-automatic	Automatic	Sum
Synonym	262	224	486
Disease - disease	1026	942	1968
Disease - symptoms	1675	3,199	4,874
Disease - body part	78	63	141
Disease - drug	447	612	1,059
Disease - operation	225	2	227
Disease - other treatment	323	0	323
Disease - prognosis	17	0	17
Disease - examination	529	815	1344
Disease - epidemiology	160	84	244
Disease - sociology	878	367	1245
Disease - others	170	2889	3059
Sum	5790	9,459	15,249

To intuitively present the relationship of the concepts in COKG, a visual display platform for knowledge graph has been designed in this paper, the COKG display interface is shown in Fig. 5. The display platform uses the first letter of the disease as a sorting method. At the same time, a search box is set up to make it more convenient for users to query, and the disease is the center and radioactive links to various entities and relationships related to it.

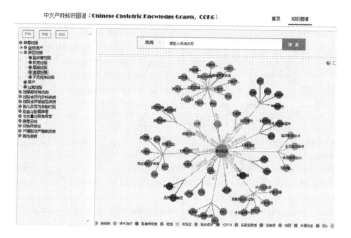

Fig. 5. Displaying interface of obstetrics knowledge graph

6   Conclusion

This article mainly studies the obstetric knowledge graph. In the construction of the conceptual layer, the medical texts from multiple sources are first integrated, and then under the guidance of professionals, the knowledge graph description system is designed; at the data layer, rules and machine learning methods are used. The entities and their relationships are extracted, and then the ontology of the medical knowledge graph is constructed; In the knowledge fusion these manually and automatically annotated triplets are analyzed firstly, and then the data abnormalities are manually checked and summarized. Finally, the Knowledge fusion of multi-source data is completed.

COKG brings health care services to pregnant women and provides data support for the implementation of medical artificial intelligence. In the future, we will continue to improve the Chinese obstetric knowledge graph, expand data sources, and provide services for assisted diagnosis and clinical decision support systems based on the obstetric knowledge graph.

Acknowledgments. We thank the anonymous reviewers for their constructive comments, and gratefully acknowledge the support of National Key Research and Development Program (2017YFB1002101), National Social Science Foundation Major Project (17ZDA138), National Natural Science Foundation of China (62006211), China Postdoctoral Science Foundation Funding Project (2019TQ0286, 2020M682349), Henan Science and Technology Research Project (192102210260), Henan Medicine Science and Technology Research Plan: Provincial and Ministry Co-construction Project (SB201901021), Henan Provincial Key Scientific Research Project of Colleges and Universities (19A520003, 20A520038), Ministry of Education Humanities and Social Science Planning Project (20YJA740033), Henan Province Philosophy and Social Science Planning Project (2019BYY016).

References

1. Singhal, Amit. Introducing the Knowledge Graph: Things, not strings [EB] (2012). http://googleblog.blogspot.ie/2012/05/introducing-knowledge-graph-things-not.html
2. Mu, D.-M., Zhang, Y.-X., Huang, L.-L.: Constructing medical ontology based on SNOMED CT and FCA. J. China Soc. Sci. Tech. Inf. **6**, 653–662 (2013). (in Chinese)
3. Amarilli, A., Galárraga, L., Preda, N., Suchanek, F.M.: Recent topics of research around the YAGO knowledge base. In: Chen, L., Jia, Y., Sellis, T., Liu, G. (eds.) Web Technologies and Applications, pp. 1–12. Springer, Cham (2014). https://doi.org/10.1007/978-3-319-11116-2_1
4. Auer, S., Bizer, C., Kobilarov, G., Lehmann, J., Cyganiak, R., Ives, Z.: DBpedia: a nucleus for a web of open data. In: Aberer, K., et al. (eds.) ASWC/ISWC -2007. LNCS, vol. 4825, pp. 722–735. Springer, Heidelberg (2007). https://doi.org/10.1007/978-3-540-76298-0_52
5. Ruan, T., Sun, C.-L., Wang, H.-F.: Construction of traditional Chinese medicine knowledge graph and its application. J. Med. Inform. **37**(4), 8–13 (2016). (in Chinese)
6. Jia, L.-R., Liu, J., Yu, T.: Construction of traditional Chinese medicine knowledge graph. J. Med. Inform. **36**(8), 51–53 (2015). (in Chinese)
7. Hou, M.-W., Wei, R., Lu, L.: Research review of knowledge graph and its application in medical domain. J. Comput. Res. Dev. **55**(12), 2587–2599 (2018). (in Chinese)
8. Zhang, K.-L., Zhao, X., Guan, T.-F., Shang, B.-Y.: Construction and application of entity and relationship labeling platform for medical texts. J. Chin. Inf. Process. **34**(6), 36–44 (2020). (in Chinese)
9. Kai, X., Zhou, Z., Hao, T., Liu, W.: A bidirectional LSTM and conditional random fields approach to medical named entity recognition. In: Hassanien, A.E., Shaalan, K., Gaber, T., Tolba, M.F. (eds.) AISI 2017. AISC, vol. 639, pp. 355–365. Springer, Cham (2018). https://doi.org/10.1007/978-3-319-64861-3_33
10. Zeng, D.-J., Liu, K., Chen, Y.-B.: Distant supervision for relation extraction via piecewise convolutional neural networks. In: The 2015 Conference on Empirical Methods in Natural Language Processing. ACL: Lisbon, Portugal, pp. 1753–1762 (2015)
11. Zan, H.-Y., Han, Y.-C., Fan, Y.-X.:Construction and analysis of Chinese-symptom knowledge base. J. Chin. Inf. Process. **34**(4), 30–37 (2020). (in Chinese)
12. Zhang, K., Ren, X., Zhuang, L., Zan, H., Zhang, W., Sui, Z.: Construction of Chinese medicine knowledge base. In: Liu, M., Kit, C., Su, Qi. (eds.) CLSW 2020. LNCS (LNAI), vol. 12278, pp. 665–675. Springer, Cham (2021). https://doi.org/10.1007/978-3-030-81197-6_56
13. Carletta, J.: Assessing agreement on classification tasks: the kappa statistic. Comput. Linguist. **22**(2), 249–254 (1996)
14. Hripcsak, G., Rothschild, A.-S.: Agreement, the f-measure, and reliability in information retrieval. J. Am. Med. Inform. Assoc. **12**(3), 296–298 (2005)

Correction to: Social Changes Manifested in the Diachronic Changes of Reform-Related Chinese Near Synonyms

Longxing Li, Vincent Xian Wang, and Chu-Ren Huang

Correction to:
Chapter "Social Changes Manifested in the Diachronic
Changes of Reform-Related Chinese Near Synonyms"
in: M. Dong et al. (Eds.): *Chinese Lexical Semantics*,
LNAI 13250, https://doi.org/10.1007/978-3-031-06547-7_15

In an older version of this paper, there was an error in the affiliation of co-author, Longxing Li. This has now been corrected to: "Faculty of Languages and Translation, Macao Polytechnic University".

The updated version of this chapter can be found at
https://doi.org/10.1007/978-3-031-06547-7_15

© Springer Nature Switzerland AG 2022
M. Dong et al. (Eds.): CLSW 2021, LNAI 13250, p. C1, 2022.
https://doi.org/10.1007/978-3-031-06547-7_32

Author Index

Printed in the United States
by Baker & Taylor Publisher Services